PN
2277
.N5   Broadway   song   &
B64   story
1985

$22•45

DATE		

BROADWAY
SONG & STORY

BROADWAY
SONG & STORY

Playwrights / Lyricists / Composers
Discuss Their Hits

Edited by Otis L. Guernsey Jr.
Introduction by Terrence McNally

DODD, MEAD & COMPANY
NEW YORK

Copyright © 1985 by The Dramatists Guild, Inc.
All rights reserved
No part of this book may be reproduced in any form
without permission in writing from the publisher.
Published by Dodd, Mead & Company, Inc.
79 Madison Avenue, New York, N.Y. 10016
Distributed in Canada by
McClelland and Stewart Limited, Toronto
Manufactured in the United States of America
Designed by Helen Winfield
FIRST EDITION

Library of Congress Cataloging in Publication Data
Main entry under title:

Broadway song and story.

   Includes index.
   1. Theater—New York (N.Y.)—Congresses.   2. Musical
revue, comedy, etc.—New York (N.Y.)—Congresses.
3. Theater—United States—History—20th century—
Sources.   I. Guernsey, Otis L., 1918–
PN2277.N5B64   1985   792'.09747'1   85-15877
ISBN 0-396-08753-1

To MARC CONNELLY *and* DORE SCHARY,
Past Chairmen of the Dramatists Guild Publications Committee,
this book is affectionately dedicated by their colleagues

CONTENTS

PART II—AUTHOR! AUTHOR!

PART III—OUR PROFESSION

INTRODUCTION

It was an evening in early spring, just three years ago. It was a few minutes before curtain time, and the streets in the theater district were nicely teeming with eager theatergoers.

Now I am one of those people who think that the West Forties of Manhattan a little before 8 P.M. are always a special place to be—the vibrancy is palpable—but on this particular evening the temperature was extra perfect, the sky was glowing with the last traces of a special sunset, it wasn't raining, and I had a great pair of aisle seats for a show I was itching to see. If all was not well with the world, at least it seemed okay with our theater.

People had told me it was bad, but I had no idea it would be like this. As I walked down Broadway and turned right onto West Forty-sixth Street, there it was: what they were doing to the Helen Hayes Theater. It was horrible, it was violent, it was obscene. A wrecking ball had half-collapsed the facade, revealing the theater within. The seats were still in place, facing a denuded stage. What had once seemed to be sumptuous interior decorations now fluttered ineffectually in the candid glare of the street lights and neon advertising. A theater is a place of magic; it has never looked too well in the rough light of reality. The Helen Hayes had been raped and brutalized for all the world to see. These 20th century Huns and Visigoths didn't even have the decency to offer the lady a covering to hide her shame. She was bleeding, and I bled with her.

As I stood there in anger and dismay, oblivious to my companion's protests that we would be late for the show I had been so eager to see just a few moments before, I became aware of another person who had stopped to stare at what was left of the Helen Hayes.

I think I knew before I turned to look that it would be her. Something told me it had to be: no one else would do.

She was beautifully dressed and wore a fur. Both she and her escort looked as if they had just alighted from a limousine, but there was none in sight. Together, they contemplated the sorry spectacle spread before us in utter silence.

"Miss Hayes," I wanted to say (yes, of course, it was her; who else? and if you don't believe me you probably won't get very far into this book, which is all about the millions of real miracles that theater is all about), "Miss Hayes, I hate what they've done to your theater, and I wish there were something I could do to show you how much I hate it. We tried protests, we organized committees, and they all failed. But mainly I would like to magically rebuild it in a twinkling. That way you would be standing here smiling in anticipation at the promise of a brightly shining marquee instead of staring at smashed plaster and fallen brick. You know, I think I saw you play in *Mrs. McThing* when I was a child, and this was the Fulton Theater then. It was grand."

Instead, I said nothing and watched Helen Hayes watch what had happened to her theater. She didn't look sad, she didn't look angry, she didn't look particularly anything. Whatever feelings she was experiencing she was keeping to herself. If nothing else, she looked objective: her demeanor was that of a woman whose eyes and mind and heart were recording an event. "So this is what is happening" is all I would presume to read into her expression. The theater is seldom so objective.

Certainly the collection of symposia, monologues, and discussions that follows in this book is more filled with the heat of creation, the joy of accomplishment and the pangs of disappointment than that objective, dispassionate voice that assures us "This is what happened." What follows *is* what happened. It *is* how it was. Reading our symposia on the landmark hits is being as present at the creation as any of us are likely to get who weren't there in the first place. The story is being told in the actual voices of the creators themselves, and sometimes these voices are loud and raucous and contradictory and uncertain of the facts, but they are very clear about the feelings involved. The ladies and gentlemen present in these pages are recalling vital chapters in the history of 20th century American theater. Small wonder that the temperature so often is so high. There's a lot of blood and guts here. There's a lot of laughter and love and genius, too.

It is impossible to duplicate the actual physical excitement of gathering together so many original collaborators on a theatrical landmark, such as *On the Town* or *Death of a Salesman* or *Barefoot in the Park,* in front of a theater full of Dramatists Guild members, to recreate the experience of working together on that original, historic production. It seemed at times that history was being made all over again.

But it *is* possible brilliantly to transcribe the tapes of these proceedings and so make them not only accessible but meaningful to you, the reader; and for his Herculean labors in this department, the Dramatists Guild can only express its profoundest gratitude to Otis L. Guernsey Jr., and his wondrous assistants.

Also, it is impossible to proceed further without registering an "official" and personal thank you to Maggie Grove, the Guild's special projects director for seven years. To Maggie fell the unenviable task of gathering so many busy people together in the same theater at the same time. In return, I hope she received the special satisfaction of knowing that an impossible job had been perfectly performed. We are indebted to her forever.

Some of these discussions may read like scenes from *Rashomon.* Truth in the theater is different from each seat in the house. What makes this collection unique is people who think things happened one way colliding with people (sometimes very old and very dear friends) who remember them happening quite the other. It's not that these people are incapable of telling the truth about what really happened. It's simply that their separate notions of what "really" happened are very often just that: separate and very much their own. That doesn't make them any less true or important. In fact, I think the "truth" about some of these historic productions is more likely to be found amidst the disagreements and confusion of these symposia than in the "official" version that each participant is likely to publish, unchallenged, however good-naturedly, by his collaborators and peers.

I cannot pass through the theater district without mourning the loss of the Helen Hayes, Morosco, and Bijou Theaters. Try as I can to be objective about what has happened on that block between West Forty-fifth and Forty-sixth Streets, all I can come up with is revulsion and despair. No good will come of the destruction of our playhouses. Our theater is not just our culture and our civilization. It is also our humanity. When we touch the Helen Hayes, we destroy a part of ourselves.

I wish I possessed the lady herself's seeming equanimity in the face of such wanton destruction. Maybe she knew that the theater, phoenix that it is, had already decided that another playhouse would be renamed the Helen Hayes. Or maybe all her enigmatic expression meant that spring evening was that this, too, shall pass. After all, theater is more than real estate, as these pages so eloquently testify.

But surely one of the things she must have been thinking about was some of the damn good plays she had seen in that theater that was now in ruins before her. Some of them, no doubt, are in this book. Theaters, playwrights, and players will go, but these productions will live on in the memories of everyone who saw them. What follows is the Dramatists Guild's attempt to preserve and share those memories while the playwrights and players are still with us. The Helen Hayes wasn't so fortunate. It's not a sentimental journey. It's an historic one.

TERRENCE McNALLY
Vice President, the Dramatists Guild
New York City, April 1, 1985

P.S.: "It was 1952, the theater was the ANTA Playhouse and I was thirteen, Miss Hayes."

Part One

LANDMARK HITS

On the Town

Death of a Salesman

Tea and Sympathy

West Side Story

Gypsy

The Fantasticks

Barefoot in the Park

Fiddler on the Roof

Cabaret

Torch Song Trilogy

Who's Afraid of Virginia Woolf?

How does a show become a major hit? What special magic goes into a production on and off Broadway that sets it above all others in instant popularity and lasting entertainment? These and many other questions are answered here in the case of eleven of our theater's biggest hits. It was the idea of Dramatists Guild Vice President Terrence McNally, author of the introduction to this volume, to gather as many of a landmark show's original participants as possible for a free-wheeling discussion of how it was in the very beginning and how success was painstakingly achieved. The eleven sessions in these pages took place over the last few years under the auspices of the Dramatists Guild Projects Committee (Gretchen Cryer, chairman, Maggie Grove, director of special projects), recorded and edited for the information of dramatists in their intercom, the Dramatists Guild Quarterly, and now publicly available in this volume. All the panelists and moderators in these eleven transcripts are identified as they speak. Questioners from the audiences of dramatists are not individually named but are identified by the letter Q.

ON THE TOWN

Arthur Laurents, Moderator
Leonard Bernstein
Betty Comden
Adolph Green
Jerome Robbins
Oliver Smith

ARTHUR LAURENTS: It is time that really tells us which works make an important contribution. Sometimes a work opens and is hailed as daring and striking; then time passes, and it's regarded as having been merely fashionable. Sometimes a work opens and is regarded as crude, or clumsy, or mystifying; and time passes, and it's regarded as having been ahead of its time—something we all fervently pray for.

With a musical, sometimes the elements that are considered important when it opens are not regarded as important elements a long time later. In the case of *On the Town*, probably the most important contribution is that it introduced to the theater Leonard Bernstein, Betty Comden, Adolph Green and Jerome Robbins—now, almost thirty-five years later, it's obvious that the history of the American musical theater couldn't be written without them. Two others made enormous contributions: Oliver Smith, whose scene designs of New York have never been surpassed, and George Abbott, the director, whose contribution to the art of comedy in America is enormous. His influence is still evidenced in the work of Jerry Robbins, Bob Fosse, Hal Prince and many others.

It might be interesting to see how perceptive the critics of 1944 were about these people. At that time there were eight newspapers, and the print didn't come off on your fingers. The names of these critics, by the way, are going to be unfamiliar to most of you, which, I suppose, is a kind of revenge.

We begin, as we still do, with the New York *Times*. The critic was Lewis Nichols, who wrote: "... a perfect example of what a well-knit fusion of the respectable arts can provide for the theater. Taking a literate book by Betty Comden and Adolph Green as a base, Leonard Bernstein has composed all manner of songs which have humor and are unpedantic. Jerome Robbins has

3

supplied perfect dances. Oliver Smith's simple settings are in keeping with the spirit, and George Abbott has done one of his perfect jobs."

John Chapman wrote in the *Daily News:* "Not even the ministrations of George Abbott as director can make *On the Town* anything but a dullish musical comedy." He went on like that and ended, "There are ballets, of course," and I quote, "Cripes what I would give to see a good ole hoof and chorus again."

One more from a man who was probably the best critic: Louis Kronenberger, who wrote for the progressive newspaper *PM.* He said: *"On the Town* is not only much the best musical of the year, it is one of the freshest, gayest, liveliest musicals I have ever seen," which is lovely print. But then he went on to say something I personally think is more important: "It has its faults, but even *they* are engaging, for they are the faults of people trying to do something different, of people willing to take a chance."

So much for the critics. *On the Town* really began the night of April 18, 1944. That was the first night of the first ballet by Jerome Robbins with music by Leonard Bernstein and scenery by Oliver Smith, and the work of all three people was extraordinary. In December, eight months later, *On the Town* opened—and I, for one, would like to know how and what happened. First of all, whose idea was it to expand *Fancy Free* into *On the Town?* And Oliver, since you were the producer, maybe you have the definitive answer.

OLIVER SMITH: Well, I think it was my idea. Lenny and Jerry didn't jump at it, there was a lot of resistance in the beginning. They wanted to do something perhaps more serious. I tried to persuade them as hard as I could, and at a certain point they said, "O.K., let's go." I was introduced to Betty and Adolph, I think by Lenny, and of course I was immediately enchanted with them. They were enthusiastic about the idea and, as I remember, we went at it very rapidly. *Fancy Free* had three sailors, and three sailors need three girls, so we could see the beginning of the story. Betty and Adolph were writers and performers as The Revuers, so we could see a satiric approach. And Jerry was a brilliant choreographer, so we knew there was going to be a lot of dancing.

JEROME ROBBINS: Another thing I'd like to say about *Fancy Free:* it had Lenny's music and Oliver's scenery and my choreography and Betty's Victrola.

BETTY COMDEN: That had a lot to do with that ballet—on stage, my Victrola.

ROBBINS: The ballet was supposed to start with someone singing a song of Lenny's, and at the last minute we found we had no Victrola for the recording.

COMDEN: Adolph and I were sitting out front on opening night. The first ballet was on, and *Fancy Free* was coming up. There was this sudden hysteria—there was nothing to play the song "Big Stuff" to open the ballet. We went to my apartment in a taxi, picked up this table model and rushed it backstage.

LEONARD BERNSTEIN: That was the beginning of our collaboration.

LAURENTS: How was the style set? Did you all work together?

ROBBINS: O.K., on to *On the Town*. To start with, Betty and Adolph did a very rough outline of the show, and then we collaborated. They did the writing, but we all talked about plots, what could happen, where the story should go, whenever we could grab time together, in New York or Hollywood or wherever. Then they would go away and write.

COMDEN: Lenny was in on the book discussions, too. We all planned everything together, but Lenny was away on conducting tours a good deal of the time.

ROBBINS: We spent a lot of time together.

COMDEN: On every step of the story and every idea in it.

ROBBINS: George Abbott wasn't in on it yet.

SMITH: We went right on working and finally took it to the Theater Guild. Lawrence Langner fell asleep during the audition. Elia Kazan turned it down, and we became rather desperate about not having a director. Suddenly we asked ourselves, "Well, if we could have anybody in the world, who would be our first choice?" And so I went to see George Abbott. He was and is a great enthusiast of ballet—he'd seen *Fancy Free*. He said, "I like the smell of this." After about five minutes, he said, "I'd like to do it—let's do it tomorrow." He was taken with Betty and Adolph immediately. He didn't have to be urged to do it, he was immediately enthusiastic.

COMDEN: He'd never heard of Adolph and me, but he admired Jerry and Leonard's work.

LAURENTS: How much of your willingness to take chances, to do something different, was conscious? Were you deliberately trying to achieve a new style?

ROBBINS: I don't believe we were deliberately taking chances. We just went ahead and did what we felt we wanted to do. We weren't asking ourselves, "What would be far out here?" We were just pouring it out the way we wanted to see it, that's all.

LAURENTS: Did you block out the ballets as part of the book?

ROBBINS: Yes, the scenarios were written, and the famous expression "grab and emerge" came out.

COMDEN: We were very aware of the ballets.

SMITH: Even in the scenic outlines. I remember having a meeting with Betty and Adolph at the Russian Tea Room or someplace, and I said, "I want to do a scene in Coney Island."

COMDEN: We said, "All right, we'll get it into the story."

LAURENTS: It was that kind of story.

COMDEN: Actually, at first we all resisted the three-sailor idea; we thought it was too light. We also resisted the title, for the same reason. Maybe we were trying for *Three Bessarabian Ambassadors*, or something. Anyway, we finally settled on the sailors and the title and then made a list of locales with Oliver—if we were going to show a day in New York we could cover all these locales, no matter what the story was going to be.

I think the nature of Leonard's music made it different. It was different from any ever heard before in the musical theater.

ADOLPH GREEN: We resisted the idea of three sailors, not because of *Fancy Free*—which we all agreed was a unique and individual work. I think we were all secretly afraid that once we presented, articulated and moved around these musical comedy sailors we might have what would turn out to be a grade-B movie. But we finally settled on it and went ahead.

LAURENTS: You all seem to have been slightly afraid of doing something you thought was too light for a musical comedy, yet here is a book with characters called "Claire de Lune" and a satiric ballet about Miss Subways, who is esthetic and athletic and sexy and intelligent. Obviously, you knew what you were doing and at one point must have decided, "To hell with whether it's too light," and just gone on with whatever the spirit of the piece was.

ROBBINS: You have to remember the context of the time, the kind of musicals that were being done. And you have to remember that we were all very naive and had no Broadway experience. I had danced in the chorus with some shows—that was it, as far as I was concerned. I had never choreographed. We didn't know what the rules were, but we knew what should and shouldn't be. We all threw our ideas into the pot. In a show about sailors in New York, where would we like to go? What would possibly happen, at what time of day? What events could take place? It was all thrown in.

LAURENTS: Lenny, you haven't said anything about how the show evolved.

COMDEN: Lenny got Adolph and me the job, I know that.

BERNSTEIN: *On the Town* was in no way an expansion of *Fancy Free*, which was a brief, wonderful look at twenty-five minutes in the life of three sailors who had twenty-four hours' shore leave in New York and had some balletic adventures in a bar—indulging in a certain amount of competition culminating in a fight, and then they wound up pals again. Beautiful ballet.

On the Town was not about three sailors competing. It *was* about three sailors with twenty-four hours' shore leave in New York, period. In another important sense it was not an expansion of *Fancy Free:* there was not a note of *Fancy Free* music in *On the Town*. I find there is a prevalent misconception—people keep saying to me, "You didn't have to add much, did you? You already had this whole ballet for the ballet music, and then all you had to do was write a couple of songs." That was not true at all. We started from square one with a totally new series of conceptions, as my colleagues have been pointing out—different plot ideas, different scenarios, which we had great fun bouncing off each other's brains and souls.

I remember the initial spontaneous fun of collaborating. We were all twenty-five years old—at least I was, and they all said they were. I was twenty-six by the time the show got on, I have to confess, but I was twenty-five when we began to write it at the end of June 1944, the ballet having been in April.

It is true that I was conducting a lot. I had just become a conductor, owing to great fortune and strokes of good luck. That's how I was making my living, and therefore I couldn't be at all the story conferences. Once I had persuaded Jerry and Oliver that the ideal people to write this book and these lyrics and if possible *be* in the show were Betty Comden and Adolph Green—my dear friends whom I had known since their first days at the Village Vanguard, the best satirists, the best performers, the most musical, sensitive, the wittiest sharpest, *dearest* people (and I didn't have much trouble selling them)—once we got going it was all sheer fun.

LAURENTS: The show seemed to have been written very quickly.

ROBBINS: As I remember, George Abbott said he would do the show if it could be done within a certain time. He had two weeks free—yes, literally—that we could play out of town.

COMDEN: Ten days.

ROBBINS: When I say we were all naive . . .

COMDEN: We said, "Ten whole days, wow!"

ROBBINS: We just did it. We didn't worry about it. Lenny and I were out on the coast with *Fancy Free*, and so Betty and Adolph came along, and we went right ahead developing it out there.

LAURENTS: Oliver, was there much trouble getting money?

SMITH: In the beginning we raised a small amount—$25,000—of what we would call the initial money, the front money. We couldn't raise a nickel for a long time after that. The minute Abbott came in, the money was oversubscribed the next day. The show only cost about $125,000, which was very little.

BERNSTEIN: I have a memory of our being financially saved at the last minute with a preproduction deal with M-G-M.

SMITH: That was after Abbott agreed to direct it.

LAURENTS: Were there many changes in this brief rehearsal and out-of-town period?

SMITH: No, I wouldn't say there were a great many changes. There was one number about an intermission, with very heavy scenery, that went out.

BERNSTEIN: There were eleven numbers that were *not* in the final show.

SMITH: Not after rehearsal, Lenny.

LAURENTS: When were they cut out?

BERNSTEIN: Well, some of them never got into rehearsal. Some of them did and then were cut.

LAURENTS: Who cut them out?

BERNSTEIN: Some of them were cut by mutual agreement, but we so adored and revered George Abbott, and rightly, that we all looked to him. If we had any doubts or disagreed among ourselves, he was the daddy.

COMDEN: Yes.

BERNSTEIN: We didn't look instantly to the producer. Oliver is an artist, he isn't really an honest-to-God producer, because he was on our side. But we always placed our ultimate faith in George.

ROBBINS: I can't speak for the other collaborators, but it *was* the first show for me, and I was very inexperienced. My only experience had been *Fancy Free,* which I rehearsed and put on, and it was a success, and I thought, "Oh, so that's the way it goes."

I didn't even know you had assistants to help you do a show. I think I staged as much material in *On the Town* as I did in *West Side Story,* finally; it was very dancy, with a lot of musical numbers, and when they went on the stage, a lot of them didn't work. That was a shock to me. It was the first time I learned the lesson that one's work in a musical is not alone on the stage—what comes right before and after it can affect it. A dance may be absolutely wonderful, but it may not go at all because of the way the audience *is* at that point. I also learned that a very poor number sometimes goes very well because of what comes before it.

The master of it all was Mr. Abbott. I myself was floundering when we went to Boston—as with every musical, your labor starts all over again from the beginning when you go out of town. He stepped right in, took my second-act ballet—which I thought was terrific, I still believe in the conception of it—cut it right down the middle and put a scene in between the halves. The ballet was a dream image of what Coney Island was going to be like, and then the reality of it. I wanted to contrast them, but he said, "No, we have to cut this." Fortunately he did this, as I was still staggering, trying to get back on my feet and get into the material again.

COMDEN: We listened to him absolutely on the book. We'd written an almost final version as a flashback. The show opened in a night court where all the characters were gathered, and the judge rapped his gavel and said, "Now tell your stories one at a time," and then you told the story and did *On the Town,* and then you came back to night court where everybody was sitting around and the judge was making his final decisions. We thought it was great. It gave the show form, shape and importance. Then one day Mr. Abbott told us he loved the score, the book, everything—we were so excited. Then he said, "There's just one thing. Cut that prologue, that flashback. You don't need that."

Lenny, Adolph and I retired from that meeting in a rage. We talked about it and decided to go back and tell Mr. Abbott why we needed this flashback as the whole backbone of the show. You say what happened, Adolph.

GREEN: Well, we went back to Mr. Abbott's office and laid down this basic principle of "This is the beginning, the prelude, and that is the ending." And he said, "O.K., I'll tell you what. You can have either me or the prologue."

LAURENTS: Was there a problem for you and Adolph in that you were also performing? Did that help or hurt your view of the material?

GREEN: We were happily ignorant.

COMDEN: Yes, that was partly it. We went out and did the show and had meetings afterwards and made changes. Occasionally Lenny would hold his head saying, "This sick show," and Adolph and I would sort of wonder. We had just come offstage streaming wet, with makeup still on, and we couldn't be quite sure what was really happening. It was difficult, I remember. How many changes did we make?

GREEN: We had to go along with what Mr. Abbott said, just as Jerry did. There was one long sequence in which the boy said to the girl, "Gee, can you go out with me?" And she said, "Oh, no, I am much too busy," and then many scenes went on. He followed her to a theater where an intermission break took place. It was about fifteen minutes' worth of book. Finally he met her again and said, "Can't you see me?" And she said, "How long are you going to be in town?" And he said, "Just tonight." And she said, "O.K., I will."

Well, Mr. Abbott said, "This has got to go—the intermission scene, everything. It's going to be back in the studio, and she says, 'I'm sorry, I'm much too busy, but how long are you going to be in town?' And he says, 'Just tonight.' And she says, 'O.K., I will.' " And that was it. That cut was effected.

COMDEN: The only thing I remember about being both a performer and a writer was on opening night. It was an exciting moment. People were crowding onto the stage, and I guess we sort of realized it had been a great success. But in the museum scene there was one line that always got a laugh. We blew it that night. All Adolph and I were doing was reviewing that one line: "How did we blow that line? Did you move? Did I do this?" That was occupying us much more than our realization that the show was a hit.

LAURENTS: From what you've said, Abbott quickly and very neatly took the scissors and made big cuts which gave the show pace and drive. Is that right?

ROBBINS: I know I had to redo numbers. Sono Osato was extraordinarily helpful and encouraging. I was staggering from having to redo a lot of the work, and she just said, "Come on, let's go to work," and no Equity rules then prevented you from staying around the clock in the bare theater.

COMDEN: Another time we rehearsed late at night in the window of a music store on Boston Common.

SMITH: A passerby came along and wondered whether we were in an advertisement.

BERNSTEIN: What I was very much afraid of was cutting a lot of the so-called symphonic music—which was quite long and complicated and would entail a lot of extra rehearsal time and a slightly larger and more expensive orchestra. I was scared that it might go the way of that intermission sequence, with the easy snipping of Mr. Abbott. He used to make sort of friendly fun of some of my music by calling it "that Prokofieff stuff." I was afraid all "that Prokofieff stuff" would go, but it didn't—not a bar of it. This man George Abbott is such an extraordinary creature, such an absolutely practical man of the theater, that I was amazed to find how deeply esthetic his instincts were.

ROBBINS: Apropos of that, there was a number called "Gabey's Coming" early in the show. Two sailors were trying to teach Gabey how to pick up a date and how to make out with girls. A lot of the show's music was based on that song. That song was cut, and I saw Lenny holding his head and saying "Everything is based on that." In putting on a show, that can happen time and time again: some thematic material upon which a lot of the score is built doesn't work, and it's cut, and the composer wonders, "My God, where do I put my foot down?"

BERNSTEIN: There are two places remaining in the score that are seriously based on that number, including the climax of the second-act ballet.

ROBBINS: I would think we made more changes and cuts than we were conscious of at the time. The show wasn't as simple as we had originally made it.

BERNSTEIN: Jerry, is there anything you regret that was cut?

ROBBINS: Well, I wish I was seeing that whole ballet again.

BERNSTEIN: Except for that.

COMDEN: Well, the intermission scene was great.

GREEN: For only one reason: Jerry's choreography was great, it was brilliant.

COMDEN: The intermission crowd.

GREEN: Somehow, without its ever having been put on, it influenced all the satirical elements that dancers in musical theater have performed ever since.

LAURENTS: It was a light-hearted show filled with satire and nonsense, and yet at the same time it is the *only* show which had these qualities of gaiety and laughter and youth that has had as a base this idiom (Lenny used the word "symphonic") of music and dance. There hasn't been one since. There has been *West Side Story,* but not one which has been light-hearted.

BERNSTEIN: We mustn't ignore *Oklahoma* or *On Your Toes.*

COMDEN: There's no symphonic music in them.

BERNSTEIN: No, but there was a great amount of wonderful dancing in shows which preceded *On the Town.* Also, there have been symphonic arrangements of Dick Rodgers' tunes in *Oklahoma.*

COMDEN: But the texture . . .

BERNSTEIN: And "Slaughter on Tenth Avenue" is not to be sneezed at.

COMDEN: Lenny, don't be so modest.

BERNSTEIN: I don't want to exaggerate our importance.

COMDEN: It isn't a question of importance, it's the quality of the music.

BERNSTEIN: It was revolutionary. All right. It was revolutionary. I'll admit it.

ROBBINS: One of the important things in the show that was not noted was the mixed chorus. It was predominantly white, but there were four black dancers—and for the first time, they danced with the whites, not separately, in social dancing. We had some trouble with that in some of the cities we went to.

LAURENTS: At this point, let's open this session to questions from the audience. Please ask these generous, very gifted people about their work in *On the Town,* not about other things that might be important to you personally.

Q: It seems to me the show was created when this particular group got together. It was in you all, and it came out nicely when George Abbott said, "Now this is the way it goes." It needed that one strong hand, didn't it?

COMDEN: That would be true of any show.

Q: Did you have difficulties in casting?

BERNSTEIN: Well, we turned down Kirk Douglas because he couldn't sing.

COMDEN: We tried to get him to sing, but he couldn't. We started with Sono Osato in mind, and Nancy Walker, didn't we? And then Adolph and I were determined to be in the show.

BERNSTEIN: Our impulse was to have it look realistic, so when we were casting the chorus, instead of the most beautiful people we could find, we picked people who could realistically be identified as music and piano teachers along the Carnegie Hall corridors, people who could really sing and dance well. We had wonderful singers in that chorus, but they weren't necessarily all gorgeous looking. They were real people.

COMDEN: They were New York subway riders, that's all.

Q: In collaborating, do you and Adolph Green offer suggestions to each other at the typewriter?

COMDEN: We meet every day and keep working. We stare at each other across the room.

GREEN: Our collaboration goes back to our days as night club performers.

COMDEN: We don't quite remember at the end of the day who wrote what. We're just glad there's something there.

SMITH: One thing we all shared was the feeling of what the show was really about. It wasn't about three sailors, it was about the enormous love each of us felt for New York City. It was a valentine to New York. We each adored New York in our own way, and that became a unifying theme.

COMDEN: And there was a tremendous emotional base for the story line. The fact there was a war on was working for us all the time; the fact that these boys had just twenty-four hours beginning with their coming off the ship and ending with their saying goodbye and getting on the ship going who knew where. The song "Some Other Time," which comes near the end of the show, is full of emotion. In wartime it had a tremendously poignant feeling.

Q: Mr. Smith, were there any problems negotiating the deal with George Abbott or anybody else in the show?

SMITH: I would say no, there wasn't any great hassle. Everyone wanted to work together, and Bill Fitelson, our lawyer, worked it out so that it would be economically feasible. Of course, we were all very, very close friends, and it was a joyous experience.

COMDEN: Because Adolph and I were in the cast, the kids on the stage would come to us and say, "My wife's having a baby, will you give us a five-dollar raise?" and we would come running to the office to ask for it. We were just mummers, trying to get other actors more money.

Q: Did you have any major disagreements with Mr. Abbott?

COMDEN: I remember that whenever we'd say we didn't like something, he'd say, "What would you suggest? I'll try it." And he did.

GREEN: Thank goodness he was there, or we would never have had a show. He was absolutely objective, while we were totally wrapped up in our material. He was very necessary for us. It wasn't a question of his being in conflict or our opponent in any way.

BERNSTEIN: In no way. Oliver's term "joyous experience" was a very important part of the collaboration. It really was joyous. We loved each other very much, and we loved not only one another's talent, but one another's sensitivity to each other's talent. For example, Jerry's unbelievable musicality: if he would say, "As a practical matter, I've got to have four more bars here or I can't get my dancers from left to right and offstage," and I would say, "I can't do four more bars, that would just drag it out," and I would do four more bars, then it would usually turn out that it was a better piece with the extra material, because Jerry's instincts are incredible, musically.

The same is true of Betty and Adolph. They came to me with a lyric called "Carried Away" that said "I try hard to keep control/But I get carried away/Try to stay aloof and cold/But I get carried away/Carried Away, carried away/ I get just carried away." I wrote this little polka-like cowboy tune. It wasn't like me. It was like "The Surrey With the Fringe on Top." I couldn't bear it, I hated it, but I couldn't think of anything else. After five days of trying I was in despair. Betty and Adolph suggested, "Why don't you try it in the minor?" I said, "Come on, that's so naive, it just makes it sad or agitated. It's an old-fashioned thing to do. I'll try it."

Suddenly we had this operatic feeling which dictated the whole form of the number, the whole duet quality of those two quasi-operatic voices that brought down the house. That was the whole joke of the scene, and I have *them* to thank for it.

COMDEN: Maybe in a sense that illustrates the nature of collaboration. If you're lucky enough to be with people who respond to one another the way we all did, and feel about each other the way we all felt, there is no borderline where one department ends and the other begins. There's never any defensive feeling about that, either. Leonard had book suggestions and character suggestions and lines and lyrics. We talked out everything that was in the show. The overall effect was the important thing, that's what a real collaboration is. I don't think you have a really good show unless you have it, to a big degree.

LAURENTS: Have you ever had it to that extent since?

BERNSTEIN: Not quite the first fine careless rapture, the first love.

Q: If it was going to be revived now, would you do anything to change it?

BERNSTEIN: No, I wouldn't.

COMDEN: It should be done the way it was written. It belongs in its period, with the concepts Jerry and Lenny had that were in the show.

ROBBINS: The time pressure of getting a show on, the pressure of having everybody dependent on its being a hit, all out of a job if it doesn't work, are very limiting. I don't think there's a show I've ever done that I haven't gone to see two or three months later—if I'm lucky, and it's running—that I haven't said to myself, "That was only a fill. I wish we could have had more time on it." I'm sure this happens with plays as well.

BERNSTEIN: There were imperfections, but as the critic said, even the faults are endearing.

GREEN: We're talking about *On the Town* as if there were a gold platter of it somewhere. If we looked at it today, I think we would say, "My, we were naive. I wonder how we dared do some of those things."

BERNSTEIN: That was half the charm of it.

Q: Mr. Bernstein, did you compose the tune for "The Passa Outa"?

COMDEN: Where did you find that, in some museum version of the show? It must have been in an early version of the book, some number in a night club.

BERNSTEIN: When the sailors were touring the night clubs, one of the stops was a sort of Copacabana. They were introducing a great new Latin American bombshell number, "The Passa Outa."

COMDEN: Never got as far as Mr. Abbott. We cut that ourselves.

Q: How do you feel about the show's transition to the movies?

GREEN: Mixed.

BERNSTEIN: The opening is terrific.

COMDEN: It was bought by M-G-M, and they were a little afraid of the Bernstein music. On top of that, Gene Kelly was playing what had to be a romantic lead. He couldn't sing the ballads, so there was a whole shifting over of the story to make it quite different. New songs were written, and Leonard was furious.

BERNSTEIN: Rightly so.

COMDEN: The opening of the show is beautiful, with the original music and feelings. There are only a couple of other moments in the movie that still have that.

BERNSTEIN: I don't think M-G-M was so much afraid of the "Prokofieff music" because almost all of it was used in the movie, all the ballet music, which was a tough nut to crack. What did *not* stay in the film was the songs. An associate producer of the picture arranged to write six songs of his own to replace six of mine. When I finally discovered what happened, I asked them to take my name off the full-frame credit, and credit me only for the songs I wrote—because I really don't want anybody to think I wrote a title song called "On the Town," which I certainly didn't, or songs called "Back Home" or "Mainstreet." But they left my name: "Music by Leonard Bernstein." I wish they would take it off.

Q: At that time, Mr. Bernstein was a symphonic conductor, Mr. Robbins was in ballet, Mr. Smith was in opera and operetta. Were you being criticized for working on Broadway?

ROBBINS: Every time I do a show I'm known as the ballet choreographer, and every time I do a ballet I'm known as the Broadway choreographer.

BERNSTEIN: I can remember Jerry getting some severe slaps from those who said, "You are not being serious." I got some severe slaps from Serge Koussevitsky, for example, who was my great master and could not believe I was going to take all those months off to write a Broadway show. He came to the opening night in Boston, which took some doing because he was very much against the whole project. He came backstage and said, "Good boy, Lenushka, it is a noble jezz." He just decided "a noble, noble jezz," and that sort of excused the whole jazzy thing.

COMDEN: But don't do it again.

GREEN: Betty and I got a few letters asking, "What happened to you? What happened to the *purity* of that act in Greenwich Village? You kids have written a cynical, hard, successful Broadway show."

SMITH: I had no reservations. I was eager to work on Broadway. I also felt that Lenny, Jerry, Betty and Adolph would bring to the show the highest artistic quality. I had no self-consciousness about it at all.

COMDEN: We haven't said enough about the contribution of the scenery itself. Oliver's designs of what the city looked like—the emotions, the garishness, the beauty, that dream Coney Island—are classics, all of them. We did shows then with travelers and drops, and they moved so quickly. It was a great way to do them. Nobody does them that way any more.

BERNSTEIN: When the subway came together . . .

COMDEN: It was extraordinary, a tremendous contribution to the story and the feeling, as the scenery should be.

BERNSTEIN: It was very dramatic and exciting, that moment when the subway came together, it got a two-minute hand from the audience. It was a combination of scenery, dance and music. Another thing about Oliver, apart from his magnificent, very imaginative, inspired scenery, he was and still is an incredible barometer of what we do. When you try something out on Oliver, his reaction is a trustworthy indication of how well you've done. He always expresses it in terms of whether he gets goose pimples.

ROBBINS: Oliver, I don't remember working with you as a collaborator from a scenic point of view as intensely as with the others.

SMITH: That's more or less accurate. We were separated geographically, as I remember, and a lot of the show went into work with very small, undeveloped pencil sketches. There was this great rush to get the show on, and our collaboration wasn't as extensive as it has been on other occasions.

Q: How did the show turn out for you financially?

COMDEN: It was the first time we ever had more than five dollars.

GREEN: Oddly enough, *On the Town* was the last pre-production deal of a musical for many years.

Q: You said that in the initial stages you felt the show might not be serious enough. How do you feel about it now?

BERNSTEIN: It is funny, light-hearted, satirical—but not really terribly satirical. It was a very serious show from a structural point of view and from the point of view of everybody's contribution and the integration of the esthetic elements. The subject matter was light, but the show was serious. I think I can speak for all of us when I say that what we meant about being afraid when Oliver first came to us was that it might get too lightweight. We were very much influenced by our masters, our teachers—people like Koussevitsky, Lucia Chase and others who were trying to goad us into doing more serious things; serious in the sense of being non-Broadway, because as Jerry pointed out, shows on Broadway then were in a very low estate. What we accomplished was a happy and moving show about wartime, in the lightest possible vein but with a most serious esthetic means.

Q: Did you sense that you had a hit?

BERNSTEIN: Heavens, no.

GREEN: I felt very sanguine about it.

ROBBINS: We were too busy working to worry about whether it was going to be a hit until it was on, and then we read the reviews.

BERNSTEIN: I think we would have been terribly surprised if it had *not* been a hit.

COMDEN: That's perfectly true.

Q: How long after the show opened was the album recorded?

BERNSTEIN: We didn't have an album at the time.

COMDEN: There were very few show albums in those days.

BERNSTEIN: Our album was made much later, in the 1960s. We were lucky enough to get together most of the people who were in the show originally— Betty and Adolph, certainly, Nancy Walker.

LAURENTS: I have one final question: Have you all told the truth?

BERNSTEIN: Yes, but not necessarily the whole truth.

DEATH OF A SALESMAN

Garson Kanin, Moderator
Mildred Dunnock
Alan Hewitt
Elia Kazan
Arthur Miller

GARSON KANIN: I am going to ask my colleague Arthur Miller to tell us about the influences, the inspirations, motivations, aspirations, the origin of *Death of a Salesman.* What compelled you to write this particular play when you did, and how old were you when you began to write it?

ARTHUR MILLER: It was 1949, and I was thirty-two. I want to say first of all that apart from being my play, it was the most perfected production I have ever seen when it opened, and Elia Kazan was responsible for that.

The internal material of the play was with me all my life, but what moved me to go ahead and write it as much as anything else was the atmosphere which reigned briefly on Broadway—an atmosphere which I had not known before and was not to know later. For a little moment after World War II, there was a unified audience in the New York theater. To all intents and purposes there was no off-Broadway theater—it hadn't been invented yet. There was a unified audience on Broadway, so that the same people would come to *Death of a Salesman,* manifestly a sad play, as would come to the most trivial comedy or musical; whereas later on, anything serious had to be done off Broadway or in an extremely lucky situation. Perhaps Tennessee Williams could get away with it a little while longer, but the theater was narrowing into a pure entertainment industry.

Nowadays there is almost no place for serious work on Broadway unless it happens to originate someplace else. For example, British National Theater can be brought over, and sometimes one of the regional theaters can be brought in, but the so-called professional Broadway theater is now circuses and what they call "pure entertainment," which is really rather backward from the point of view of most of the history of the theater.

It was quite otherwise when *Death of a Salesman* opened. It was my belief that we were addressing the whole country, that the whole United States was out there in the audience. They weren't, really, but we had the illusion that we were addressing our equals, that the audience was quite as cultured and intelligent as we were, and that we could rely on a sect of partisans who would support a serious work, given a sufficient number of private signals from the stage telling them some of the things that were happening. The playwright in those days had to speak to everyone, not just to the educated or the cultivated.

A lot of this may have been illusionary, but it seemed like that at the time. I believe this had a tremendous effect on the kinds of demands we made on ourselves. Starting with the writer and going right on through with the director and the actors, we would try to deliver our private vision so that it was not mauled or distorted and at the same time could be understood by anybody. That aim I don't think is common any more, the aim of the trivial theater to pursue the audience. But the aim of the serious theater has been "The audience is going to have to understand what I am saying, and if only a small percentage of the audience will understand it, I will seek out and serve that percentage."

There was a crest of the unified American audience in the theater of *Death of a Salesman*, which faded very rapidly and hasn't existed for many years now.

KANIN: How long did it take you to write *Death of a Salesman*?

MILLER: The first half, probably less than a week, but the second part, months. Then too, the job of compression in that play was tremendous and difficult.

KANIN: Aside from the usual rewriting, revising, adjustments, et cetera, how many drafts existed before you gave the play to Molly and Gadge Kazan?

MILLER: It would be difficult to judge now. I suppose a half dozen. I should add that years later, when I moved from one house to another and was clearing out some papers, I found a notebook that I had kept in college. There was *Death of a Salesman*, in an entirely different form. I had completely forgotten about it, but I had obviously written at some time in school about thirty percent of the fundamental things in it. But I didn't really know how to do it until twelve or thirteen years later.

KANIN: Alan, as one of the best and most experienced working actors in our profession, do you have vivid recollections of the first day of rehearsal of *Death of a Salesman*?

ALAN HEWITT: The answer is no, because I wasn't there. I came in five or six days later to replace the actor who started on the first day of rehearsal. I had already read the play several months before in its original form, before Jo Mielziner came up with that remarkable idea for the set, which then resulted in the rearrangement of the text. At that time they offered me the part of Bernard, for which I was absolutely unsuited, and so I rejected it. When they called me again after they went into rehearsal and said they would like me to play Howard, I said, "That's even nuttier than the idea of my playing Bernard."

But they insisted that I come to the producer Kermit Bloomgarden's office and reread the play, which I did. Then I begged to be allowed to read the part for them in order to prove that I could *not* play it. They refused, and somehow or other I ended up in the play.

KANIN: Millie, did they make you read for the part, or did they just engage you?

MILDRED DUNNOCK: Yes, they certainly made me read. I had played the season before in the Kermit Bloomgarden production of *Another Part of the Forest*. When I read in the paper that a play called *Death of a Salesman* (which I thought must be a murder mystery) was going to be directed by Elia Kazan, I asked Kermit, "Isn't there any part in it for me?" He said, "No, there really isn't." I heard that Anne Revere was going to play Linda, and that satisfied me.

Then Kermit called me saying that Anne Revere couldn't take the part and offering me a chance to read for it, but adding, "I might as well tell you, Mr. Kazan doesn't think you're right for it." I asked what was wrong about me, and he said, "The speech is too good, and you aren't earthy enough." I said, "O.K.," took the script home, cut out all the final consonants, told myself, "Be earthy, be earthy," put on a nondescript black dress and came out onto the stage of the Hudson Theater. It was very dark and somber, and the stage manager read the scene with me into absolute blackness out there in the auditorium—I didn't know who was there. I was scared then and for quite a while afterwards. I read the part, and I was dismissed. Three weeks later I'd given it up, when I got a message from Kermit saying, "You're not heavy enough—go and get some padding," so I did. My husband and my daughter poured me into this little robe, and I put a wig on. This time I went to the Coronet Theater and did the reading with the stage manager. Suddenly a voice from the audience said, "Take that stuff off." I had never been so humiliated.

Well, they told me I had the part and had five days to play it—Equity had a trial period of five days in which the production could let you go if they didn't like what you were doing. I was terrified. Kazan was directing with an old broomstick, which he had found backstage and was carrying around. At the end of the fifth day, he came over to me and exclaimed, "When I think I might have had somebody else!" This was the beginning of a very, very small love affair.

KANIN: Gadge, I remember an evening when we met for dinner, and Molly came in absolutely aglow and said, "I've just read Arthur's new play." You said, "Well?" She said, "You're going to do it." What was your immediate reaction to your first reading of *Death of a Salesman*?

ELIA KAZAN: It was the story of my life, about my father, my own family, things I knew. Arthur and I came out of the same experience—the Depression, the same kind of frightened, struggling middle-class people. Arthur caught it perfectly and played it as a classic.

I am a director who has sometimes been accused of meddling with scripts.

When it comes to contemporary plays, the script is central, and I believe that if a script is faulty no director can save it. I also think that if a script is as good as this one was it could have been done by other directors and have been quite as successful. I don't think a director can save a script.

In many plays I've done that finally turned out well, I worked a long time with the author, but that didn't happen on this play. I thought it was perfect, and I had that experience only one other time, with *A Streetcar Named Desire*. I thought that was perfect too, except for a long bit in the last scene which was cut out. *Death of a Salesman* was perfect, and the greatest directorial contribution to it was made, not by myself—although I helped some—but by Jo Mielziner. Arthur wrote the play in a series of scenes, and there was the immediate problem of how to get this bit of scenery off and that bit of scenery on. Jo suggested that there be a vision of a man's life onstage at all times and that all the scenes be played in and around it. When he began to draw it, Arthur and I both agreed. It was a tremendous contribution. I couldn't say it was critical, because nothing could hurt this play, but it was of a creative weight that made everything that followed work.

Also, there was still in New York at this time the remains of the influence of the Group Theater, people who had worked in the Group, or close to the Group. That element of theater, a kind of spiritual realism, still existed. It was alive within the actors I got for this play. They were part of my family, part of all our families. They were people you wouldn't recognize on the street, not stars, but humans who fitted Arthur's play perfectly.

It was an easy rehearsal period once we got going, because everybody was moved by the play. As I said, Arthur had written a play about the families of millions and millions of men. This is the only play I've ever done where I've stood in the back of the audience and heard men sobbing. Night after night I would hear the rather resonant, deep voices of men expressing the pain of their memories, and it was a tremendously moving experience to be part of it.

What Arthur says about the audience in those days is true. There was a confluence of feeling that they were like us, and we were like them and were speaking not only *to* them but also in a sense *for* them—we were their voices.

At the time, I thought nobody could do the part of Willy Loman as well as Lee J. Cobb, but with a really great play there's no such thing as a definitive performance. Different people bring different values, and *Death of a Salesman* is a great play, a masterpiece that could be played in many different ways—not only small, tall, heavy, dark, thin and all that, but many different ways.

Arthur had told me that the play was inspired or motivated a little bit by his uncle, who he thought was all screwed up as far as his ideas about society and politics were concerned. At the same time—perhaps equally or even more so—he loved the man humanly, so there is that ambivalence in the play. You have the sense, "This guy is just a complete fool," but at the same time you say,

"He's me, I can't look down on him, I can't even criticize him. The man is going through what I am going through in life." That's the play's greatness.

KANIN: Arthur, we heard Gadge refer to "this perfect play." Are we then to assume that from the very first day of rehearsal until the curtain went up at the Morosco opening night in New York there was not a single word or line changed?

MILLER: That question has been asked a lot, and I must have some kind of a psychic blank on that subject. I remember adding a few lines to accommodate Uncle Ben coming on and off. The big change that I recall making was in the restaurant scene. I had written a very syncopated scene in which Biff tells his father that he failed, he didn't get the money he wanted, but I had originally written it so that Biff prevaricated to various degrees because he didn't want to destroy his father with his bad news. In one line he lied completely, in the next perhaps he told the truth, and in the third he half lied. In the fourth he lied, sort of—three-quarters of it was true. It was all to try to insinuate to this desperate man that he simply had to accept the fact that his son had failed.

Well, the actors played it as it was written, but of course Gadge directed it with great vitality and rapidity, and they got tangled up. They didn't know when it was half true and half false. You had to be a lawyer to figure it out. So I went home and straightened it out—that was in rehearsal, if I'm not mistaken. I liked the original better, but I broke my heart and rewrote it in order to convey it to the audience.

KAZAN: Can I finish that?

MILLER: Of course.

KAZAN: I think you can say substantially, Arthur, that we didn't make any changes after we went into rehearsal. We had to get this one and that one on and off, moving them around within the unit set. But substantially, we did nothing. This is the only play I remember in which no material changes were made during rehearsals.

KANIN: I once asked Gadge how he differed as a director from the director he was when he began. He said, "When I started directing, the main worry in my mind was, 'Do the actors like me?' Now I don't give a damn whether they like me or not." The great directors don't care how popular they are, because you can't be popular with actors, really, if you are a director.

HEWITT: You can be popular Wednesday and unpopular Thursday.

KAZAN: I had one terrible fight with Lee Cobb, and he went into his dressing room and sulked.

DUNNOCK: I remember that.

KAZAN: I went in there and said, "Look, Lee, I probably overstated and yelled at you a bit. I'm sorry if I did." Lee said, "Even when you apologize you are arrogant."

HEWITT: We were a disparate group of people in that cast. We were not all from the Group Theater or the Actors Studio. We had different backgrounds, and Gadge had an absolute genius for being able to talk to each actor in the language that was right for him.

DUNNOCK: I had a difficult scene, a monologue, and at the end of it was the line most quoted from the play: "Attention must be paid." It was very difficult to find a way to play that lengthy monologue with the conflict it needed. As we rehearsed in Philadelphia that week, Gadge would come over and say, "I have a new attack with it, Millie." He always took upon himself the blame if it didn't work out the way he wanted it. He made you feel you could go whole hog without being humiliated. You felt you could do almost anything with him, and he would take the responsibility for it.

Fundamentally, I am timid, and I think most actresses are insecure. They have to float around between Willy Lomans and Tyrones and many other parts like that. In Philadelphia, Gadge would call me in at two o'clock in the afternoon, saying, "Let's try that monologue again." One afternoon the stage manager said to me, "Mr. Kazan has been given tickets for the symphony, and he wants you to come right over. He's in the top box in the top balcony at the Academy of Music." I went over, got in the back way and went way up. This was a full symphony; it finally went on to the last movement, and *every* instrument was playing full blast. It was very exciting, and when we came downstairs after it was over Gadge said, "That's just what we are going to do tomorrow."

The next day, he had the stick and said, "Now I am going to conduct you." It made the scene work, as he said, "Louder, louder, louder." I was finally screaming the monologue at the top of my voice. I stopped, burst into tears and said, "I can't, I won't do it that way." He said, "That's exactly the way you will do it." I said, "I can't. Where are all the nuances?" And he said, "We'll come to those in a couple of weeks." That's the way he made me play the monologue, and it went down in history: "Attention must be paid."

KAZAN: Can I say something in my own defense? If it had been another actress, I wouldn't have used the stick.

DUNNOCK: You managed me very satisfactorily.

KAZAN: The director is blamed for everything—and he should be. If the script isn't right when you go into rehearsal, the director should have insisted more, earlier. If the scenery isn't what it should be, it's the director's fault—he should have rejected the sets given him and made the scene designer work out other sets. If the costumes are a mess, it's his fault, he never should have allowed them. If the music isn't helpful to the production . . . he heard the damn music, why didn't he get a different composer? The director gets the blame and *should.* Once you say, "I will direct this play," you are saying, "I'm going to stand up for it, it's good, and I am going to make it work." Things that go wrong are your fault.

KANIN: We have just heard that an outstanding American drama was just right, all finished, when it was turned over to the director, who then took charge and chose the designer, the music, the lighting and the cast. He got it straightened out, but the text was there from the start. Arthur, on other occasions you have perhaps done some fixing.

MILLER: Yeah, but I don't think I made anything better. Frankly, I've done some rewriting in early stages of rehearsals, and now when I look back I regret what I did, on the whole. My plays are structured, and when you start jockeying the structure the whole mechanism begins to shudder. If it's a woven, interdependent structure, then I'd advise playwrights to say, "Look, if it's going to fail, let it fail the way I wrote it rather than the way I rewrote it."

KANIN: *Death of a Salesman* was one of the gravest titles any playwright ever put on display. Arthur, was there a lot of pressure on you to change it?

MILLER: The producers took a poll about it on Broadway, asking people if they would go to see a play with that title. Ninety-eight percent said, "Absolutely not." They even made up a list of substitute titles, which mercifully I have forgotten.

KAZAN: I remember one. They got ahold of me one day, told me about the poll and said they wanted to change the title to *Free and Clear*. I told them I was absolutely against it and would bring all my influence to bear on Miller not to change it.

KANIN: Is there anything special that accounts for the popularity of *Death of a Salesman* in England?

MILLER: No, the national element in a play is not really that important unless it's about some local situation, or the vision of the playwright is extraordinarily provincial. There doesn't seem to be any problem with this play or with a number of my others which have played all over the world.

KANIN: How about the film version of *Death of a Salesman*?

KAZAN: It's a very hard play to do on film, and I don't think every successful novel or play should be made into a movie. *Death of a Salesman* is a piece for the theater, and the director of the film had a terrible job. I can't really conceive it—and shouldn't. I'd be interested in Millie's comments, because she was in the movie.

HEWITT: In 1966, seventeen years after the play was first done, she did it again on television with Lee J. Cobb. Lee did a wonderful job of recapturing what he did in 1949. Millie somehow or other seemed to have thought it all over and come up with something that was bigger and more wonderful than the first time.

DUNNOCK: I played with seven different Willy Lomans. I hadn't really liked doing the movie. Fredric March played Willy, and a brilliant actor he was, but he came to the movie from a trip around the world and never looked at the script. I had been indoctrinated by *these* gentlemen and was really nonplussed by March's approach. He knew films. You see, he would walk up to the camera—and I was so unaware of the camera, having been in the play. It was very disconcerting.

Each Willy Loman was different. Thomas Mitchell was a very Irish Willy Loman—remember that? When I got back with Lee again I felt I was coming home, and perhaps that accounts for my TV performance. Then, to eliminate that lovely Jo Mielziner set . . . you cannot reproduce it in films, it just wouldn't work.

But I always liked the play, no matter what.

TEA AND SYMPATHY

Terrence McNally, Moderator
Robert Anderson
Elia Kazan

TERRENCE MCNALLY: Today, as you all know, we are going to be discussing *Tea and Sympathy*. The play opened September 30, 1953. Its history must begin with the playwright, so we will start with Robert Anderson.

ROBERT ANDERSON: This play, like every other play of mine, was turned down by every producer in New York City. My agent, Audrey Wood, took me out for lunch and gave me back the four or five copies, rather dog-eared, that everybody had rejected and said, "There's one out still, and it'll come back soon. Get on to your next play." This was my twelfth full-length play, so I was used to that procedure. Well, that copy did not come back because The Playwrights' Company read it and said they wanted to do it.

Molly Kazan and my first wife, Phyllis, and Elia Kazan all went to Yale Drama School together, and Molly had sort of been watching over my plays for quite a while. When I was in the Navy I used to send plays to her, from the Pacific. Sometimes she was encouraging, but her general feeling was that I was a novelist and not a playwright. Still, when I sent her *Tea and Sympathy* she did write an extraordinary letter to me, saying, "I think that if you play your cards right Gadge (as Kazan was called in those days) might like to do this play." She sent the play to Elia, who was abroad making a picture at that time. When he came back we met with The Playwrights' Company and decided to go ahead with the production.

But I do want to emphasize to all playwrights who think that plays are written and then done, immediately, that this, like all my other plays, had been turned down by almost every producer before it finally was accepted. It was turned down largely on the basis that people thought it would be a *succès de scandale*, that it was a shocking play—hard to believe now—and that was it, period. I think many of them admitted that it was a good play, but most of them were kind of afraid to do it.

The preparation of the play in production was one of the most extraordinary experiences in my life. It was great to be working with Kazan. By the time we went into rehearsal, he knew the play better than I did. No other director since then, and I have had some excellent directors, has *ever* seemed to want to familiarize himself with a play this way. He would even have me read it aloud to him, which was a shocker, and stop me and say, "Why did you read it that way?" We had about eight months of preparation, I believe, before we went into rehearsal, and a great deal of this was casting, which is a very important part of producing (as Kazan used to say, "You get a good play and you get a good cast and what have you got to do?"). Some other directors I have worked with really aren't interested in casting. They have a few people they like to work with, and they have worked with them over and over again, and they don't want to learn about the play through casting.

For example, originally I wanted the roommate to be sort of an Arrow Collar kind of boy. We had no disagreement about this, and we started casting and we saw these Arrow Collar boys, and we suddenly realized that they were very, very wrong for the part. And so we finally cast a wonderfully rugged punk sort of a guy named Dick York.

From the beginning, I wanted Deborah Kerr. Elia did *not* want Deborah Kerr because he wanted this to be *my* play, he wanted this to be the discovery of a new playwright, being my first play on Broadway, and he did not want it to be a discovery of a movie actress who had incidentally been a stage actress in London. I sent the play to Deborah, however—I was not knowledgeable in those days. I didn't realize that you didn't send plays to actresses whom the director didn't want. Actually, I had sent it to her before, during the nine or ten months that the play was being rejected. I had done a radio show with her and thought she was terrific. She didn't want to do the play. She said that when she came to New York she felt that she didn't want to do this kind of play where she would play Lady Bountiful or something of that sort, and she also said she thought it was the boy's play and not the woman's play.

So I had this very interesting problem: I had a director who did not want her and a star who didn't want to do it. I did not tell him, obviously, that she didn't want to do the play, nor did I tell her that he didn't want her. Meanwhile, we saw some marvelous actresses, and I kept saying, "Great, fine, but may we wait for Deborah?" Finally one day I said, "Won't you meet her?" He went to California, and they had tea, and he sent me a telegram saying, "You are absolutely right, and she's going to do the play."

MCNALLY: How long was it from the time you finished the play to this acceptance from The Playwrights' Company?

ANDERSON: The first version I wrote was in 1948. It was a different play, but it was called *Tea and Sympathy.* I went on to other plays that didn't get done, and then I came back to it. I would say that I finished it about 1951.

MCNALLY: Elia Kazan, you were abroad, and this script arrived that your wife recommended to you?

ELIA KAZAN: Why don't you read that letter Molly wrote.

ANDERSON (*reading*): "Dear Bob: That's the best play you ever wrote, by far.

I tried to call you last night, but I guess you are in the country. The scene where the kids practise walks is a heartbreaker. I have a few reservations or suggestions, but they are in the realm of what can be done. Mostly they have to do with Mr. Lee and Bill and the relationship between Bill and Laura. The last isn't there, needs exploring early, needs some dynamics. No relationship is totally absent. Mr. Lee also is sheer frigidity, no room for development because he starts at zero. Your typist or you changed the name on the Betty Lilly character in midstream. But chiefly congratulations. I believe this one will go on and I never said that before." But then she wrote a final sentence which I think is extraordinary. "Two things seem to me way below the level of the play, the title and the tag line."

KAZAN: The two parts of the play that are the most famous.

McNALLY: So your first encounter with the play was in Germany?

KAZAN: Yeah, I liked the play right off the bat. We were making a film in mud and rain, and just to sit in the room and read a nice play was a great experience.

Anyway, I came back and met with Bob. Molly was *extremely* influential with both Bob and me. She always had reservations about everything. If you gave her *Hamlet* she would have some very astute reservations about it.

This play was, from my point of view, the easiest production I've ever been in. Bob has the correct attitude of the playwright to the director—reverential. He is also a very, very detailed and careful workman. He would take many sheets of short notes and type them up very clearly so you could check each note off. Ninety percent of the time I agreed with him—and I would check them off. I was carrying around his checked-off notes with only a few left all the time. It was really a very good experience. We got along very well.

There was only one crisis, the third day of rehearsal. Deborah Kerr wouldn't come out of her dressing room (this happened to me once with Lee Cobb, too). But Deborah was absolutely sweet and didn't call for the help of a psychoanalyst or anything. It was just that I had to go in there and sit quietly and talk to her and tell her how good she was going to be, and we were proud to have her, and she was lovely, and I liked the way she'd had her hair done, and she was going to be damn good in the part. And I took her hand and led her out. She did balk a bit, but that was the only crisis we had.

There was one thing in the play that we *did* work on a lot, as I remember, Bob. Didn't we work on the husband a lot?

ANDERSON: On the husband-wife relationship.

KAZAN: That was the only real revision or alteration I can remember in the course of the preparation. It was a tough part. He had to fulfill certain dramatic requirements; that is, you shouldn't have to mind when she was attracted to the young boy, you shouldn't say, "Oh, she's hurting this fellow." At the same time, she married him, so he's got to be halfway attractive and decent and regular, right? It's one of these things that you are into often with a play. A character has to serve two opposite purposes, and we have to maintain the ambivalence. We have to say, "Well, he's rough, crude, he-mannish, macho in a collegiate way and all that." At the same time you've got to say, "Well, I can see why she liked him. He's regular. He's honest. He's outspoken, and he's healthy looking," and so on, and we were walking this tightrope a lot with the character.

ANDERSON: I'll read a letter that you sent to me because it brings up some of these points, but I want to make one point first about your directing, which I have talked about endlessly in other meetings so I might as well talk about it here. You have a terrific gift of relating to each actor separately. The protocol is that the playwright does not talk to the actors except "Nice work" or "You're beautiful" or "How are you?" or "Isn't it going to rain?" or something like that. The playwright talks to the director, and the director talks to the actor because he develops an absolutely unique way of talking to every actor. One actor would have to be taken out for drinks before he would understand why he should move from point A to point B. Another would have to go into his background of his father or how he loved his mother. Another simply would want to be told, "Get up, take three steps, and sit down." If a playwright walks into the middle of this and gives his version, well, he breaks this very valuable channel.

There's a part of the Deborah Kerr story that you didn't tell. You didn't just go in her dressing room and sit and talk to her. You came up to me that afternoon after rehearsal and said, "Will you go out for drinks with Deborah and me?" and I said, "Sure." We went out with Deborah, and you proceeded to praise the play. I was so embarrassed I couldn't figure out what the hell was going on and you kept saying, "God, we are all lucky to be doing this play, it's a marvelous play"—you've forgotten that?

KAZAN: Yeah.

ANDERSON: And Deborah finally came back with great enthusiasm. Well, that was very skillful. I would never have done that. People have asked me why I don't direct my own plays, and I tell them I would have taken her out and just said, "Deborah, don't you understand the play?" or something like that. But Elia has his ways of going around and around and around and getting exactly what he wants.

After I met with The Playwrights' Company, Elia sent me this letter, which was our first contact about the play: "Dear Bob: I am sending a copy of this to Bob Sherwood and to Roger Stevens. We all agree, I am glad to say, that very little should be done with your play in the way of rewriting, which means that we all think that the basic shape of the piece is right. The most important single thing that has to be done is in relationship to the character of the husband. I think Bob's suggestion of having them married longer may be helpful, but is not nearly enough . . . I think we really need, we really have to prepare the emotions of the audience so that they not only want her to make love to the boy but also think it's right emotionally for her. I think what is needed is a scene between the husband and wife ... which in effect is her last effort to reach him on a common ground of sympathy and spiritual intimacy. . . A scene where she tried and we see her try to keep her marriage together. She fails and without really knowing it gives up. We should feel here that she is right to give up. Unless we see her make this effort . . . we will not have been witness to her effort to save her marriage and therefore will not emotionally and experientially believe it. It is important that in this scene and throughout, in the case of the husband, that he be behaving 'rightly' from his point of view. The scene I suggest that would be best is if we also see *him* making an effort to keep their marriage together; but since his viewpoint is so basically different from hers, the more of an effort he makes, the more we feel that it is hopeless and that the bravest thing is to quit. If some such scene could be found, then the woman would not ever be thought of as 'bad,' but I would like the husband not to be a heavy, either. He just went for wrong ideals and standards and his relationship to women is simply a bad one. If his attitude towards his wife can be dug into just one spadeful deeper, we will both on the one hand understand him better and identify him more clearly and still reject him, for his wife, more surely.

"The other job, it seems to me, is simpler. It has to do with the father. Here again we must be witness to this man's effort to help his son the very best he can . . . what should be added is a short scene where the father and son sit side by side, and the man tries to deal with something that he is totally unequipped by experience and training and taboo to cope with. A feeling of hopelessness for the father, a feeling of pity for him here would make us love the son more too and feel his isolation more deeply. And the rest is bits and tiny pieces for rehearsal. . . . The absolutely crucial thing is the casting. The boy is a search. I will look in Hollywood this trip."

The Playwrights' Company said they would like to produce the play in the fall of 1953. It was now November 1952. But I told them and Elia that it was important to me that we produce the play as soon as possible because Phyllis had terminal cancer. They immediately agreed to get the play on as soon as possible. Elia was involved with *Camino Real*, I think it was, which had been delayed, and we took a chance and postponed the production to the fall of 1953. Phyllis survived until 1956.

I just read over the revisions that I made in February of 1953, and it seems to me pretty close to the version we ended up with. I remember Paul Osborn used to drop by and see us and see the show. He kept saying, "You better explain why she married this man," which was always a problem, but I think finally we did: she married him because he was at that point a different man. He was on sabbatical. He was away from his milieu. He was trying to change.

In the long second scene of the second act—this is the sort of thing a director can do for you and is most helpful—the scene where the Laura character is trying to keep the boy from going to the prostitute, Elia said, "Listen, if you can give me a comic moment in the middle of that scene I can build it better. It's a twenty-minute scene of almost constantly building tension and emotion, and it's very hard to keep that going. If you can give me a break in it, I can then start all over again and build even higher." I came up with the story based on my memory of how much in love I had been with my seventh-grade teacher. It was a very embarrassing and a very funny moment, and we got a nice chuckle from the audience—and then he brings it back to the tension by looking at her and saying, "I'm always falling in love with the wrong people."

Elia is a peripatetic director. He would say, "Let's take a walk." I remember the first scene, the expositional scene, and I remember something he said: "You may never write a scene like this again in your life, but let's try to make this one as good as possible." What we actually did do was to make it a funny scene, because a lot of people coming in to see this play were scared to see it ("I'm not sure I want to see a play about homosexuality"—but it was not a play about homosexuality). And suddenly the first scene is full of laughs, and you could just see this audience sit back and relax.

KAZAN: I know we worked together a long time and in great detail, and he always had an explanation for every line. It was very helpful, actually. Bob helped me direct the play a lot by what he exposed.

I was just going to add one thing. Parts like the husband and the boy's father, no matter what the playwright does to make them work better for the total values in the play, *still* have a problem, and the director can help that problem. I think we *did*, by being lucky with the casting. Leif Erickson, who played the husband, is a . . . just a sweet, good man. He wouldn't hurt anybody. In other words, *he* helped us with our value problem, and the same thing with the father. We cast the most wonderful, wonderful guy for the father, and he was just as cute as a button, and you just watched him with his son, and you were saying, "God, really, raising a son is pretty hard, and if you had to face this problem of someone calling your son a homosexual, why, it would be tough. Look at the poor man."

The whole thing with a play like this is to keep doing this to it, so it doesn't go straight and so it's not predictable, and Bob is very good at that. He'll keep varying the attack, but also we tried to do it with the acting so that it was always going this way, then it was going this way—and you would sort of play with the audience rather than say, "It's going to go from here to there, just watch it go, kid, curtain."

ANDERSON: The casting of Johnny Kerr was inspired. We were lucky to get the entire cast, as a matter of fact.

KAZAN: Well, we worked hard. It wasn't only luck. We had months on casting.

ANDERSON: We had Karl Malden, a very close friend more of Elia's than mine. He spent months seeing the boys.

KAZAN: He wanted to be a director at that time, and I said, "Come on. Be my casting assistant," and he stayed in that damn office up there seeing people. Then he'd show me two or three, and so on. He was wonderful.

ANDERSON: We found Johnny Kerr, and he was so essential. I've seen many productions of this play, and very often they cast it absolutely wrong. They cast to what they consider the type should be, a very willowy person or a very oversensitive person. Johnny Kerr was a very manly man, and that was the essential point of the play, that he was the most manly, boy or man, on stage.

We did have one other disagreement, and you were right. The woman in the beginning—I had visualized and modeled her on a very real woman in a boy's school. I went to Phillips Exeter Academy, and the woman used to drive us crazy in the afternoon. She'd dress up in her high-style clothes and her fox fur stole. She was married to one of the instructors, and she had, obviously, money of her own. She would parade the campus. Well, we cast quite opposite to that, finally. We cast Florida Friebus.

KAZAN: I kept saying to you, as I remember, "Peck & Peck."

ANDERSON: Something else we did, with Jo Mielziner, who did the sets: we went up to Exeter and into this little house where I had lived, which was a small frame house used as a dormitory for about eight boys. Jo did sketches.

I must tell you a story at this point: I thought that Exeter would never want to see me again after this play, but they invited me up to give a talk soon after the play opened. The housemaster and his wife, in whose house I had lived, gave a little party for me. As I walked into the party I put my arm around her and said, "I hope this play hasn't caused you any embarrassment." And she said one of the great lines: "Nobody has been so kind as to suggest that I was the woman."

MCNALLY: I would like to ask Mr. Kazan a question before we get more into the rehearsal. When you read this play, what most struck you about it and made you say, "I want to direct this play?"

KAZAN: Only one thing: humanity, in a word, whatever that word means. These are living human beings, and they are behaving by their own impulses and desires and ends. They are not behaving mechanically. It's an extremely well-structured play, and at the same time no one is being pushed around by the author. If you can get that, you've really got it. The damn play is perfect, but you never feel the author is manipulating the characters. They behave naturally and simply in a modest, decent, believable way.

ANDERSON: I think there's something deeper. There are other things that appealed to you in this play, from your own youth.

KAZAN: I never had a homosexual episode.

ANDERSON: No, but your feelings about yourself at Williams College, and so forth—

KAZAN: Well, I was an outsider through high school and college. I thought I was misunderstood, so that did play a part. But I'll put it the other way: I felt that there were so many *honest* autobiographical revelations in the play. I think that the deepest form of art is some kind of confession. I do believe that, and I think I got to know Bob through the play. You get the same thing with Tennessee Williams. You read *The Glass Menagerie* and you say, "That's Tom." There he is, and it's true. It's a piece of revelation that *only* he could make, and you say, "This man is confessing something" or showing something about himself. Hell, I wouldn't go from here to there to see a well-made play unless there was something like that in it, something new or something that I call "confessional." You read *Anna Karenina*, and you know that there are four characters in there that are part of Tolstoi's life, and he's telling something about himself. And the great thing about *Death of a Salesman* is that the character *is* Arthur Miller's uncle whose view of life he completely disapproved of but whom he adored personally, so there's an ambivalent chord to it.

But you only get that kind of ambivalence through a true memory. You only get it through your own experience, and Bob is all through this play. He's it. He's the boy, and he's had that experience in some way or other—imaginary, true, partially one, partially the other. It is a *true* work of art, small in scale but deep in content, so I liked the play very much. The more I got to know it, the more I directed it, the better I liked it.

ANDERSON: Another very fine director I worked with, Arvin Brown, said in an interview that he wanted to be a writer but didn't dare expose himself the way a writer has to, so he now exposes himself through the writers. I have noticed this in editors. Editors take on books which in a sense they would have liked to have written because it's a part of their life experience.

What was interesting to me to find in *Tea and Sympathy* was how everybody related to it. It reminded me of a phrase of my first wife's—I don't think it was original with her—"Ah, youth, that happy time when I was so sad." I was, excuse the expression, a "big man" at Exeter, and yet I was a lonely, miserable boy. I had never been accused of being a homosexual. This was something I built into it. First of all, I don't think many of us were aware of homosexuality in those days. There might have been certain people we felt uncomfortable with, and we might have felt uncomfortable with them for homosexuality or for any other reason, but this particular master I always was slightly uncomfortable with. And then one day during the spring term, late May or early June, he asked me to go down to the beach. I didn't feel like going, and this gave me the springboard to that part of the story.

The real motivation for the story—this version of the story, not the original *Tea and Sympathy*—was my feelings about my father. My brother was an amateur prizefighter at this point. I was a tennis player, and I wanted to say to my father, "This, too, is a man, you know." My brother was a great golfer, and my father never came over to watch me play tennis, but he played golf with my brother all the time (this is a very limited picture of my father; I have written about him almost endlessly, and I am still going to write him till the end of my life). He was in many ways a remarkable man. At the finals of the golf match I asked, "Who won the club tournament?" He said, "Jimmy won, but Ralph should have won." I said, "Why?" He said, "Well, Ralph's a regular guy, a top guy and a hard hitter" . . . this tremendous feeling he had about what was a man. . .

Another motive was that my first wife was ten years older than I was, and I believe that the younger-older love story is a very important one in many, many boys' and men's lives. The first version of *Tea and Sympathy* had very little to do with that. In the first version the woman was the daughter of the master in the house. It was a puppy love situation with a little boy who lived in the house who later became Tom Lee. The man she went to bed with at the end was a young instructor who had come back from the war with a psychological impotence—and don't ask me how it got from there to here.

Let me give you two examples of how you use autobiography (Picasso said that art is lies that tell the truth). The walking scene where one boy teaches the other boy how to walk: at Harvard a boy knocked on my door one night and said, "You know, these people are razzing me about being feminine and so on and so forth." I said, "Maybe it's the way you walk." He had a little bouncy walk, the walk we gave John Kerr in the play. He came in and I practiced walking with him for the evening.

The scene where he loses his roommate and is crushed by it: at college a roommate that I had been with for three years left me a note one day—"I don't want to room with you anymore because you are all the time with Phyllis." Phyllis was the woman I married, and I was living with her practically three or four days a week, but I was heartbroken because I liked this guy.

So you take these things and switch them and twist them; but when people wonder, "Is this autobiographical?"—and they have been asking me that about my work for thirty years now—I say, "It's autobiographical in spirit if not in fact." Nobody ever slept with me at Exeter, I'm sorry to tell you. When I used to go on book-and-author tours, people would ask, "Is it autobiographical?"—my novels, for example. I have one standard answer: "If I told you it was all made up you would feel cheated, and if I told you it was all real you would be embarrassed."

MCNALLY: You said, I think correctly, that the play is not about homosexuality. What do you think it's about?

ANDERSON: Well, it's about a lot of things. It's about responsibility, that you've got to give a person more than tea and sympathy. I think it's about the mob versus the individual. It's about manliness. I don't think homosexuality excludes manliness at all, but, in this sense, there he was, the most mature, manly person on the stage.

KAZAN: I have a sort of minority report. I've never liked to pin a play's meaning down to a word, responsibility or any other single theme. I think it's good when you don't quite know what a play is about, although you sense many currents running through it, when you have preserved, somewhat, an aura of mystery in a play. I think the emotion of wonder is better in the theater than the emotion of recognition. We should wonder . . . you should wonder who's right. You should wonder what's really happening inside the souls of the people. This play is about everything Bob said, but I think its merit is that we never nailed anything down too clearly.

We used to do this in the Group Theater, where dear Clifford Odets, one of my best friends, felt it necessary in the third act to grab you by the elbow, squeeze it, shake you and say, "Don't you see what this means?" As he got older he wrote letters to people saying, "There are no third acts any more in American life." Well, I think if you tell a story that's rich, complex, true and has the ambivalences that life has, and you go out of the theater saying, "I wonder what's—," well, it's the same experience you have in life. You don't constantly go around saying, "He's a son of a bitch," or, "She's a bore." You say, "I wonder if he's ruining his son?" You say, "I wonder what their relationship is?" You have the sense that you have in life, which is the richest thing in a great novel. You have a sense, that's the way life goes *and* it's still puzzling at the end of it; and you close the book and say, "God Almighty, life is awesome."

ANDERSON: I agree completely, but I think it's important to writers to know what they are writing about, and then obscure or do whatever they want to. There should be what I call a hardened fist within a play that expands into many meanings. People wrote to me that it's a wonderful play about a husband and wife, which is fine. That is what they saw in the play, what they wanted to see in the play. And many people didn't like the play. Many people thought the boy was a whining, puking, muling little boy. Fine. That's what they saw. It was certainly not a didactic play. Still, people come up to me saying, "I saw this play when I was a very young man, and it made an enormous impression on me and changed my views considerably about certain aspects of life," so they got the point.

KAZAN: I think a play and its story should be very firm, but we went through a whole period in the thirties where we were constantly teaching the audience lessons. I made a film, *On the Waterfront,* and at the end I was trying to show that the election was going to get the bad guys out, maybe, and the good guys were going to march in and things were going to be a little better. I went out there last fall and I said, "Do you think things are any better than when we made the picture?" And they said, "Hell, no."

We were constantly, I thought in those days, simplifying life, making life easier, saying "Here's what it means. You better catch on and if you don't, we're going to tell you in so many words." It doesn't do any good; and what Bob didn't tell you in words, he showed you, in an act of humanity from her, a recognition of the boy's *need* for love that he wasn't getting. Bob may not like that formulation of it, but that's a possible formulation. I thought she responded to his need, and I think that's a wonderful thing in ladies, mothers, women, daughters, people, men—it's a beautiful thing in the play as it is in life.

MCNALLY: It's a play a lot of us knew the ending of before we ever read it, the famous last scene, the famous curtain line; but when the play was first performed, how did the audience respond to it?

KAZAN: They were thrilled. They were silent. They were really surprised. It was awesome, really. The silence. There's nothing like silence.

ANDERSON: But, Elia—it's true, as one of the reviewers said, that there never had been such silence in the theater, *but* there were giggles. I remember your saying to Deborah and Jack, who were very upset, "You are talking about things on stage in front of a thousand people which husbands and wives don't talk about in the intimacy of their own bedrooms," and you explained to them that this giggle is a nervous reaction of embarrassment.

KAZAN: But once the play was successful and was running and had good notices, they stopped giggling. Audiences respect success, unfortunately. It is one of the problems in the whole country, that the whole country respects success a lot.

ANDERSON: About theater collaboration: Elia *really* designed the set. My concept of a set had been much larger, much bigger, more or less what they had in France when Ingrid Bergman did it, but Elia said to Jo, "I want a candy box of a set because these are largely scenes between two people, and we must keep it intimate." The last moment was extraordinary theatrically, because the lights were brought down gradually to the point where you didn't know whether you still saw Jack or Deborah or didn't see them, and you felt they were still there—and it was a shock when suddenly the lights came up and the play was over. The electrician (in those days they didn't have the complicated boards and dimmers they have now) was so devoted to the play, and particularly to that magical theatrical moment, I would see him in the afternoon rehearsing that dim-out. It was a perfect combination of script, direction, acting, technicians and design—a marvelous example of collaboration.

KAZAN: About the set: every play, it seems to me, has its own scale. Since I had done quite a few films, this seemed to me a closeup play. In other words, it had to be the scale of her face and his face or the whole figure, but close up— and *if* the set had been too big they would have been rendered small. The play does not live by the actions of the people, but by what they are thinking. You have to watch their faces. It's like mounting a picture. If you have a small picture of, say, your grandmother, you don't put a great big frame around it, you put a small frame around it. The frame embraces it, and it dominates the frame. You look at her face, you don't look at the frame. Jo got the idea right away. I said it should all be pulled together so the set has the warmth that the play has. Jo was an immaculate, truthful, completely responsible, decent man.

ANDERSON: Jo did three or four of my sets though, and I must say that Jo was as good as his director. I did not have that much success with Jo on *I Never Sang for My Father* or *All Summer Long.*

KAZAN: It is the *absolute* responsibility of the director of the play to give the designer a ground plan and to tell him what the scale is, because the designer, especially a good designer, can go twenty different ways. I drew the design of *J. B.*, and then Boris Aronson improved it a million times—but it was never different. There was never something else that would hurt the play.

MCNALLY: Mr. Kazan, one thing you certainly are well known for is casting, and Bob tells us he always wanted Deborah Kerr for the play. Your first response was that she wasn't right.

KAZAN: Bob was right and I was wrong. I am very leery of big movie stars, because when they get in the theater they get a sore throat on the tenth day, and they can't do a hell of a lot, and you have to get in doctors, and they can't come out, and you go visit them at home and have rehearsals in their bed. I mean, they're in bed and you're out of the bed. It's another problem that you don't need. Anyway, as soon as I met her, I was charmed with her and thought she was just right. Bob is *very, very* good on casting and very sensitive.

ANDERSON: He said to me in the beginning, "No matter what happens, let's end up friends."

MCNALLY: Did you go out of town?

ANDERSON: New Haven and Washington. It was very successful. There were very few changes. It was a matter of rehearsing the moments over and over again.

MCNALLY: Is there anything either of you would like to add before we open it up and take some questions?

ANDERSON: Two stories: I got the title of *Tea and Sympathy* from a former student of my first wife. We were walking down the street on a winter's night, and we asked this girl how it was to be an actress in New York. She said, "Well, it's not bad. I live in a rooming house where the woman has us down every once in a while for tea and sympathy." Years later when I used the title I thanked her for it. She said, "I never said it in my life. She didn't have us down for tea, let alone sympathy." But it was in my notebook. Something about me obviously responded to that phrase. There was a great deal of discussion of wanting to change the title right at the last minute. I tried other titles to be pleasant (I always try to be pleasant). None of the others satisfied us, and so we stuck with *Tea and Sympathy*, thank God.

The other story: the last line of the play is "Years from now . . ." and when my first wife read the play it did not have that line. She said, "Do they go on having an affair?" I said, "My God, no. It was just this one time." She said, "Well, the audience is never going to know it." So this line was a response to a practical problem, which is to try to tell the audience in one line that this was just a one-time thing. The line also should show that Laura had a certain sense of rueful humor about it. When Ingrid Bergman did the play in Paris, this is how the line read when it was first sent to me: "Years from now, it may be ten years or fifteen years or possibly as far away as twenty years—when you talk about this—and by talk I don't mean gossip . . ." It went on and on and on. We got it back to where it was, but the French translator was *outraged.*

MCNALLY: Bob, can you quote your own famous line perfectly? I noticed that in some of the reviews the retelling of the line is slightly different.

ANDERSON: *Playboy* did a full-page cartoon on it, and they got it wrong too. The last line is "Years from now . . . when you talk about this . . . and you will . . . be kind." No "please," no "please be kind," just "be kind."

Q: What was the cost, to put the production on Broadway?

ANDERSON: $40,000. Can you imagine?

Q: What was your way of coping with the worst rejections?

ANDERSON: I was very used to rejections by this time. I was thirty-five or thirty-six years old. I was a successful television and radio writer, and I kept writing these plays. One was done in a summer theater. I just went on to write the next play. I have a new play now which everbody loves but nobody wants to do. It's the pattern. Nobody wanted to do *You Know I Can't Hear You When the Water's Running.* Nobody wanted to do *I Never Sang for My Father.*

Q: What was your contact or relationship with an agent who handles your work?

ANDERSON: Audrey Wood has been my agent. Up to the time when she had a stroke, she had been my agent for thirty-five years—a very good relationship. I miss her.

Q: One of the difficult things for playwrights is to get some kind of contact while you are writing. What kind of contact did you have with the professional world?

ANDERSON: None in terms of *Tea and Sympathy.* I happen to be a solitary writer. I believe a play is written in the head, between the playwright and his paper. I know a lot of people like to work with rough drafts with groups and work it out with actors and so on. I can't work that way. So I set it aside when nobody wanted to do it and then came back to it. I remember a note saying, "Let's go back to that story and see if we can handle it a different way."

I always feel that a writer has to have a reservoir of feeling about material before he can write about it. I preach this. To me, the magic phrase is "Art gives form to feeling," and if there is no feeling you are not going to create anything. I still had a reservoir of feeling about this—whether it was a small school or a younger-older love or whatever it was—which brought me back to my material constantly. But I didn't work on it with anybody, and it had no rehearsed readings or anything of that sort. Other people profit from that system. I don't.

MCNALLY: Was the first time you *heard* the play the first day of rehearsal?

ANDERSON: We heard big pieces of it because we had actors read scenes at auditions.

Q: I believe that was the first time The Playwrights' Company did a play other than one by their own group.

ANDERSON: That's not quite correct. They did Sidney Kingsley's *Darkness at Noon* and Jan de Hartog's *The Fourposter* in 1951.

The Playwrights' Company was a great group of men, but at the time I joined the company in 1953 they had stopped writing their best plays, and so it was tough just to keep a company going. They made me a member the night *Tea and Sympathy* opened in New Haven, and I tried to bring in younger members like Paddy Chayefsky but was unsuccessful. Roger Stevens came in to raise money. But Bob Sherwood and Elmer Rice and Max Anderson were simply not writing enough plays to keep the company going, and that was the reason they started to do outside plays.

Q: The story of what happened to *Tea and Sympathy* when it was made into a film seems to me to be worth telling.

ANDERSON: It's an endless story. First of all, Elia and Deborah and I tried to form a company to do it. It bogged down in various ways. Then Sam Goldwyn wanted to do it, but he never wanted to offend women's clubs or mothers' clubs. The censorship office said don't try to make it because we won't let it go by. In 1955 everybody wanted to make it, but they were told "Hands off."

Kay Brown, who was at the agency I was with, came up with the idea of the prologue and the epilogue—I sold myself on this to a certain extent. Had this been written as a novel, I do believe that what took place in the movie was possible. Anyway, it got very complicated, but I am still very glad we made the movie.

I *wish* that we could have made the play as a movie. Redoing it, M-G-M called me and asked me if I would like to bring it up-to-date. I said, "There's no point of bringing it up-to-date. It *is* up-to-date. A boy played Tom Lee in a midwestern college recently, and he was ostracized for the entire rest of the year because he played the part. I asked them to do a cable version of the play but they wouldn't.

McNALLY: Were there changes in the movie, other than this epilogue and prologue?

ANDERSON: Oh, yes, considerable changes. We were not allowed to use the word "homosexuality." The play is infinitely funnier than the movie, and it is infinitely more serious than the movie. The movie seemed to level it all out completely. But I am glad to have the movie as a record of the performances of Deborah and Jack and Leif.

McNALLY: Did you do the screenplay?

ANDERSON: I did the screenplay, but it was a great, great problem to get it by the censors. Finally we were ready to open at Radio City Music Hall, and the Legion of Decency, the Catholic organization, said no, we will give you the equivalent of an X rating, which would then prevent it from playing the Music Hall. So Arthur Loew, who was head of Loew's in those days, sent me over (Daniel in the Lion's Den) to meet with the monsignors and the bishops and others. Going up in the elevator I was introduced to one of the women on this committee. She said, "Oh, Mr. Anderson, I think *Winterset* is a marvelous play." And I said, "Yes, I do too." "And *Anne of the Thousand Days* and *Mary of Scotland*." And I said, "Yes, yes." And she said, "After writing those great plays, how could you write a dirty play like *Tea and Sympathy?*" When I told her it was *Maxwell* Anderson who had written those plays, she kept her mouth shut the rest of the afternoon.

They wanted me to work in the word "sin." I said, "I have gone as far as I can go, and I think the woman did a marvelous thing." I had gone as far as saying they did ruin the husband's life, but I was not going to go as far as to say they had sinned. I said, "Would you rather have the boy commit suicide or her commit adultery?" I think both of them are the top sins. They said, "Oh, no, he wouldn't have committed suicide, he wouldn't have." And I said, "That's for me to say, not for you to say." They let it go, but that was the only battle we won.

Q: What form of writing do you prefer, playwriting, novel writing or television writing?

ANDERSON: Playwriting, by all means, because the playwright has the control, and by that I don't mean authority. I mean you can walk into a rehearsal and find that a scene doesn't work, and you can go back and rewrite it; or if you suddenly decide to cut a scene because it drags, you can take the pieces you need out of that scene, put them in various other places and make a seamless move, whereas in television or the movies the writer is not *there* at the cutting, and they may cut a big scene. This happened with *The Patricia Neal Story.* They cut a big scene out, and the scenes before and after didn't go together. There was no movement from one scene to the other, you cannot perfect (if we may use that term), you cannot perfect the material. In the theater the writer works alongside the director—the director asks him to do things, and he makes suggestions to the director. It doesn't work that way in the movies or television. It moves too fast. You can't possibly see a scene being run through and say, "Oh, I would like to rewrite that scene tonight." They are shooting at $100,000 a minute.

Q: Mr. Anderson, what made you change direction during the course of writing the play?

ANDERSON: You mean change from the earlier version to a later version? I really don't know. I just know the first version didn't work. I kept the whole atmosphere of the school. I kept the loving woman of that age. She became a wife instead of a daughter to the master. I kept the little boy who was in love with her, and I kept her going to bed with somebody to prove something. I really can't remember what happened, how I changed it.

McNALLY: We asked the audience to send in questions in advance. We've covered 99 percent of them, but there's one here that my eye keeps going to: "Would you ever be interested in musicalizing *Tea and Sympathy?*"

ANDERSON: Richard Rodgers wanted to do it and I said, "No, I can't see it." Somebody may do it, God knows they're doing everything.

Q: What American writers are you drawn to?

ANDERSON: I wrote my honors thesis at Harvard on poetic drama. But I can never forget reading the six plays of Clifford Odets in the Modern Library edition in one weekend. I felt that a thunderbolt had hit me—I mean, the vitality of his dialogue, the vitality of his scenes. Also, I admire S. N. Behrman and Philip Barry. The one person who never appealed to me until fairly recently was O'Neill. I think he has had very little influence, actually, on American writers. Until *Long Day's Journey Into Night* his writing was graceless—I couldn't stand to read the dialogue. *Long Day's Journey* obviously is different.

And Noel Coward—at one point, I was known as the Noel Coward of Harvard. I wrote the book, the lyrics and the music of the shows up there.

Q: Mr. Kazan, since you are known so well as a man of the theater, why is it you didn't write for the theater?

KAZAN: I think because I went into film making, and in film making, by selecting images or pictures you tell a story through pictures. Also, I had no impulse to write plays. What I like about writing novels is that you can take excursions. I think the best kind of plays for me are plays that start here and go to there. They may wiggle a bit on the way, and I hope they do, it's better when they do, but they are essentially unilinear. Novels can be diffuse—it's not only permissible but often more lifelike, and also I just enjoy it. It's something new to me. It's a challenge.

ANDERSON: I might say one thing I meant to say earlier. Talking about the genesis of *Tea and Sympathy*, I, as a boy living out in Westchester County, was very often invited with many other boys to a camp by a man and his wife. The man was very much a macho man's man. He married a woman considerably younger who was very beautiful and very sensitive. They would take four or five boys up for the weekend, and I would hang around the kitchen washing dishes with the wife because I was very attracted to her, and I sensed something. We would go in a speedboat to dances across the lake.

KAZAN: How old were you?

ANDERSON: I was about ten or eleven, and I was already almost six feet tall. I was the only one who could dance, and I liked to dance. So she and I danced while the other boys and her husband would just sit there and watch.

Many years later, using a lot of imagination, I wrote a story on this situation which I called *Katherine and Pity and Love and I*, and part of *Tea and Sympathy* came from this story. At the end of the story, as they are leaving the house ready to return to Westchester, the man sends the boy to the bedroom to get his keys. The boy sees the double bed, and he realizes that even though this man might seem to ignore his wife, they do sleep together. And the boy's love for this woman is dashed. I used this same material for part of *Tea and Sympathy*, but this time I changed the character of the husband. In actuality, I knew absolutely nothing about the sexual relations of the couple I had visited.

Faulkner said a writer needs experience, observation and imagination. I used them all in converting this boyhood experience to first the story and then the second version of the play.

MCNALLY: Thank you for sharing these wonderful stories.

WEST SIDE STORY

Terrence McNally, Moderator
Leonard Bernstein
Arthur Laurents
Jerome Robbins
Stephen Sondheim

TERRENCE MCNALLY: It's hard to imagine what the musical theater would be like in 1985 without the efforts of the four gentlemen sitting here with me, the authors of *West Side Story.* In our theater community, they are held in great, great respect and much love. *West Side Story* is the one time these four extraordinary talents came together. I'd like to start with the germ of the idea, the first time somebody said, "Hey, there's a musical there," up through opening night in New York, in this case September 26, 1957, when *West Side Story* opened at the Winter Garden Theater.

JEROME ROBBINS: I don't remember the exact date—it was somewhere around 1949—this friend of mine was offered the role of Romeo. He said to me, "This part seems very passive, would you tell me what you think I should do with it." So I asked myself, "If I were to play this, how would I make it come to life?" I tried to imagine it in terms of today. That clicked in, and I said to myself, "There's a wonderful idea here." So I wrote a very brief outline and started looking for a producer and collaborators who'd be interested. This was not easy. Producers were not at all interested in doing it. Arthur and Lenny were interested, but not in getting together to work on it at that time, so we put it away.

Many years later, they were involved in another musical and asked me to join them. I was not interested in *their* musical, but I did manage to say, "How about *Romeo and Juliet?*" I won them back to the subject, and that started our collaboration.

MCNALLY: Were Arthur and Lenny the first librettist and composer you approached?

ROBBINS: Oh, yes. During the long period we put the project aside, I wasn't actively seeking other collaborators, I thought these were the best people for the material. I stuck to trying to get these guys, and when they came back to me I had the bait to grab them.

MCNALLY: When did Steve come into the picture?

STEPHEN SONDHEIM: 1955. By the time I joined them, Arthur had a three-page outline.

ARTHUR LAURENTS: There should be a preface to all this. Several years ago, Harold Prince wrote his theatrical memoirs—rather prematurely, as it turned out. In them, he talked about producing *West Side Story*. The original producer, the one who stuck all the way, was Roger Stevens. Later, he was joined by Hal Prince and the late Bobby Griffith. I read Hal's recollections, and I phoned Steve and told him, "I don't think that's the way it happened." Steve agreed. My point is not that Hal's account was distorted; he was telling it the way he saw it. Today, each of us is going to tell it the way each of us remembers it. It's a sort of *Rashomon West Side Story*.

ROBBINS: I'm leaving out some details. Leland Heyward was interested in the idea for a while. Cheryl Crawford was interested up to the point where we all four auditioned the show to backers and raised not a cent. We offered it to Richard Rodgers at one point.

LAURENTS: Actually, we were turned down by every producer in the theater except Roger.

ROBBINS: No one should be shocked by that. A *fait accompli* is one thing, but it's not surprising that people said, "I don't understand what that's about" in the case of a work in the embryo stage that was quite radical in its time. They hadn't heard Lenny's score, they hadn't read the script, they certainly hadn't seen what was going to be danced. At that one audition we all got up there and did everything we could to make it happen.

SONDHEIM: We all performed.

LAURENTS: It was in a room in an apartment on the East River, no air conditioning and a lot of tugboats.

SONDHEIM: Windows open, and the sound of tugboats, which we subsequently used in the show.

MCNALLY: Lenny, part of the *West Side Story* lore is that you intended to do the lyrics yourself. Is that true?

LEONARD BERNSTEIN: This will be my contribution to *Rashomon*. All of us recall events slightly differently, and that's as it should be, because we are very subjective people in our objective way. In order to be objective on this occasion, we have to be somewhat subjective, because that's the only way we can tell our truths.

As I recall, the origins of *West Side Story* were indeed in 1949. Jerry called up and gave us this idea and said, "Come over and let me explain it to you." Arthur and I were quite excited by it. I remember that evening in Jerry's apartment as though it were yesterday *because* of the excitement. What was basically different from the way *West Side Story* turned out was that it was conceived as taking place on the *East* Side of New York. It was an East Side version of *Romeo and Juliet*, involving as the feuding parties Catholics and

Jews at the Passover-Easter season with feelings in the streets running very high, with a certain amount of slugging and bloodletting. It seemed to match the Romeo story very well, except that this was not a family feud, but religion-oriented.

As a matter of fact, Arthur and I were so excited about it that Arthur wrote some sketched-out scenes, one of which was pretty complete.

LAURENTS: I remember absolutely none of this.

BERNSTEIN: I can tell you exactly where I was. I was in St. Louis, Missouri, conducting that orchestra when I received the opening scene and an outline of the second scene. I was really excited.

LAURENTS: My reaction was, it was *Abie's Irish Rose*, and that's why we didn't go ahead with it. Lenny and I were involved with James M. Cain's *Serenade*. We brought it to Jerry, who said he wasn't interested. Jerry had come to us a couple of times in the intervening years, but what he did so effectively was knock out *Serenade* and start us thinking about *Romeo and Juliet*. Then, by some coincidence, Lenny and I were at the Beverly Hills pool, and Lenny said, "What about doing it about the chicanos?" In New York we had the Puerto Ricans, and at that time the papers were full of stories about juvenile delinquents and gangs. We got really excited and phoned Jerry, and that started the whole thing.

BERNSTEIN: We were sitting by the pool talking about other things. There was a copy of the Los Angeles *Times* in a nearby deck chair, with a headline which said "Gang Riots on Oliviera Street," about Mexicans and so-called Americans rioting against each other.

What worries me is that all this is really not answering Terrence's question about my originally writing the lyrics. I'm trying to get to it, but it takes a little doing.

Yes, when we began I had—madly—undertaken to do the lyrics as well as the music. In 1955, I was also working on another show, *Candide;* and then the *West Side Story* music turned out to be extraordinarily balletic—which I was very happy about—and turned out to be a tremendously greater amount of music than I had expected, ballet music, symphonic music, developmental music. For those two reasons, I realized that I couldn't do all that music, plus the lyrics, and do them well. Arthur mentioned that he'd heard a young fellow named Stephen Sondheim sing some of his songs at a party. . . .

SONDHEIM: A small correction: Arthur was auditioning people to write the songs for *Serenade*, and that's how he heard my songs, as an audition piece. And then, several months later, I ran into Arthur at a party. . . .

LAURENTS: The opening night of *Isle of Goats* . . .

SONDHEIM: Correct. I asked Arthur what he was doing, and he told me he was beginning to work on this musical. I asked him who was doing the lyrics, and he said, "We don't have anybody because Comden and Green were supposed to do them, but they're in California and may be tied up with a movie

contract. Would you like to come and play your songs for Leonard Bernstein?"
I said, "Sure," and the next day I met Lenny.

BERNSTEIN: I freaked out when Steve came in and sang his songs. From that moment to this, we've been loving colleagues and friends.

SONDHEIM: A week later we learned that the movie would keep Comden and Green in California, so I got the job.

ROBBINS: I'd like to talk a little bit about that period, because it was one of the most exciting I've ever had in the theater; the period of the collaboration, when we were feeding each other all the time. We would meet wherever we could, depending on our schedules. Arthur would come in with a scene, the others would say they could do a song on this material, I'd supply, "How about if we did this as a dance?" There was this wonderful, mutual exchange going on. We can talk here about details, "I did this, I did that," but the essence of it was what we gave to each other, took from each other, yielded to each other, surrendered, reworked, put back together again, all of those things. It was a very important and extraordinary time. The collaboration was most fruitful during that digestive period. I say that because we got turned down so much, and for so many reasons, that we kept going back to the script, or rather our play, saying, "That didn't work, I wonder why not, what didn't they like, let's take a look at it again."

I remember Richard Rodgers's contribution. We had a death scene for Maria—she was going to commit suicide or something, as in Shakespeare. He said, "She's dead already, after this all happens to her." So the walls we hit were helpful to us in a way, sending us back for another look. I'm glad we didn't get *West Side Story* on right away. Between the time we thought of it and finally did it, we did an immense amount of work on it.

BERNSTEIN: Amen to that. This was one of the most extraordinary collaborations of my life, perhaps *the* most, in that very sense of our nourishing one another. There was a generosity on everybody's part that I've rarely seen in the theater. For example, the song "Something's Coming" was a very late comer. We realized we needed a character-introduction kind of song for Tony. There was a marvelous introductory page in the script that Arthur had written, a kind of monologue, the essence of which became the lyric for this song. We raped Arthur's playwriting. I've never seen anyone so encouraging, let alone generous, urging us, "Yes, take it, take it, make it a song." Almost all the "Something's Coming" lyrics had been written as poetic prose by Arthur.

SONDHEIM: Arthur, do you remember it that way? As I remember it, the scene *ended* with the line "Something's coming."

LAURENTS: The main thing is what Jerry said, to an extraordinary degree. If I pushed myself, I could think of a moment when one or two of us were isolated, but in my memory it's the four of us together almost all the time. It's really true, without any·consciousness of it we were all just high on the work and loving it.

BERNSTEIN: This is one of the shortest books of any major Broadway musical, a testimony to Arthur's particular generosity. He never said, "I'm sorry, that's got to be spoken, what's going to happen to my scene, my characters have to be developed"—none of that. He gave whenever he could.

LAURENTS: That's very sweet, but there was one place where I was too careless. We all hold certain set beliefs, and I've always believed that the climax of a musical should be musicalized. Well, the climax of *West Side Story* is *not* musicalized. It's a speech that I wrote as a dummy lyric for an aria for Maria, with flossy words about guns and bullets. It was supposed to be set to music, and it never was.

BERNSTEIN: Yes it was, and discarded, four or five times. It's not that I didn't try.

ROBBINS: We're all four talking about the creative processes because that was the incredibly exciting time, that's what the show came out of. This should be a lesson to future collaborators. At the time, it was a state of creative bliss combined with hard work. Much later, we all went our different ways, and years later we can start to pull it apart with each of us saying, "I did this" or "I did this." But at the time we weren't thinking about that, we were all of us just dedicated to making that show happen. There were pushes and pulls by everybody to get it to where it was.

Arthur had the hardest job of anybody converting a Shakespeare play into musical theater of today. Lenny, Steve and I had nothing to put our work against. Arthur had that text by Mr. William S all the time. We could make our poetry out of the music, the dancing, the song lyrics, but Arthur had the burden of making his text go along with *Romeo and Juliet* and still communicate some of the poetry, the argot, the drives and passions of the 1950s, while trying to match, somehow, the style we were creating as we went along.

SONDHEIM: The book is remarkable not only because it's so brief but because so much happens in it. *Romeo and Juliet* is, after all, a melodrama with something extraordinary happening in every scene, something that has to be set up and then has to pay off. On top of the flavor, there is the compactness of the plot. It's one thing that drives the show even when it isn't well sung or well danced—the plot is still exciting. It was when Shakespeare took it, and it was when Arthur adapted it.

MCNALLY: When you read it, the leanness of it is very impressive; also, a lot of the story is accomplished in the dance sequences.

BERNSTEIN: Another example of how closely we worked together was the prologue. Believe it or not, it originally had words. That extraordinarily instrumental music was sung. It didn't take us long to find out that wouldn't work. That was when Jerry took over and converted all that stuff into this remarkable thing now known as "the prologue to *West Side Story*," all dancing and movement. We all learned something from one another. We learned how to relearn and to teach. It was an extraordinary exchange.

LAURENTS: I remember Jerry asking the most important question asked any time about anything in the theater: "What is it about?" One of the reasons why he is the most brilliant of all choreographers is that he knows a dance has to be *about* something, not just an abstract dance. When it's *about* something, no one knows better how to make it dance and move the story.

MCNALLY: Was this a fast show to write?

LAURENTS: It took us thirteen working months—we counted them up.

SONDHEIM: There was a six-month hiatus in there somewhere after I came aboard, when *Candide* came to life again after being dormant for a while, but it was nice to get away from *West Side Story* for a while and then come back to it fairly coldly.

MCNALLY: Were there big changes after you got to rehearsals?

SONDHEIM: It certainly changed less from the first preview in Washington to the opening in New York than any other show I've ever done, with the exception of *Sweeney Todd*, which also had almost no changes. We fiddled with the opening number in Washington, and Lenny and Jerry fiddled with a second-act ballet.

BERNSTEIN: We also fiddled with a couple of extra numbers that never got in.

SONDHEIM: Yes, but we'd been working on those in New York. On the way to the airport in Washington after a very nice run, I said rather ingenuously to Jerry, "Gee, this is my first show, and I wanted to have the experience of sitting up until three o'clock in the morning in a smoke-filled room rewriting the second act." He looked at me in such anger and said, in effect, "Take that back, don't ever say that out loud. Until you've been through it, you don't know what it's like." I thought it would have been glamorous. I learned that Jerry was right, at two or three o'clock in hotel rooms in subsequent years. But the show was changed very little. It was what it was when it opened.

ROBBINS: We had eight weeks of rehearsals, the first time that was ever done. There was a large amount of dancing, a hell of a book to put on and a lot of song numbers to stage. I got permission from Equity to rehearse four weeks prior to the rest of the rehearsal period.

It also was a wonderfully exceptional cast. I was able to pull them into the reality of that show. As part of our collaboration, we had to sort out whether a specific actor was going to sing, or dance, or just act, and how to put him together with the rest of the show. We were very fortunate in getting the cast that we did, from a great dancer like Chita Rivera to someone like Larry Kert, who had a wonderful voice and could do acrobatic things when we needed it.

BERNSTEIN: It was the hardest show to cast I've ever heard of. Everybody has either to be or seem to be a teenager, to sing a very difficult score, to act a very difficult role and dance very difficult dances. Everybody had to seem to be doing all of these things, so that Larry Kert and Carol Lawrence had to seem to be dancing as much as anybody else. Part of Jerry's magic was to make it seem that way. We were also very lucky to find people like Mickey Calin, who played Riff. He sang "Cool"—not like an operatic star, but the way it should be sung, I felt—and he was a fabulous dancer.

SONDHEIM: The casting went on for a period of six months. Cheryl Crawford held the property for quite a long time but dropped it two months before we were to go into rehearsal. The remaining two months we held auditions in Hal's and Bobby's office.

LAURENTS: Cheryl Crawford didn't like the book; she was on my back from the very beginning about the vocabulary of invented slang. She told me, "No place do they say 'That's how the cookie crumbles.'" She wanted it in very badly. I think maybe if I'd put it in she might have produced the show.

SONDHEIM: She said the essential reason she was withdrawing from the show was, she wanted us to explain why these kids were the way they were. We were making a poetic interpretation of a social situation, but she wanted it to be more realistic.

BERNSTEIN: Do you want to hear a real *Rashomon* comment? I remember her saying, "We have *had* this whole school of ash can realism." I can't have made that up.

LAURENTS: I have a letter from her saying she wanted to see how the neighborhood changes from immigrant Jews to Puerto Ricans and blacks.

ROBBINS: My version of Cheryl's withdrawal is very simple: she couldn't raise the money.

MCNALLY: *West Side Story* seemed to get a mixed reception in a lot of places, including, later on, the critics.

BERNSTEIN: Well, the idea of a musical the first act of which ends with two corpses on the stage was reprehensible. Even the score itself . . . I remember Steve and I, poor bastards that we were, trying by ourselves at a piano to audition this score for Columbia Records, my record company. They said no, there's nothing in it anybody could sing, too depressing, too many tritones, too many words in the lyrics, too rangy—"Ma-ri-a"—nobody could sing notes like that, impossible. They turned it down. Later they changed their minds, but that was an afternoon Steve and I will never forget. I don't think there's any *Rashomon* about it. There was a tremendous animosity to the whole idea.

ROBBINS: Some of the people who helped make that show were the scene, costume and lighting designers who supported us and enhanced what we were doing. Oliver Smith's rumble set for the first-act finale was one of the most beautiful sets, creating the atmosphere for what we were doing before we even started. When Oliver first brought in his designs I became the old-fashioned person asking him, "Where's your close-in in one so we can work in one while you're changing the sets behind?" He said, "Well, we're not going to do that." I thought, "Wait a minute, what's happening, this is going to be a whole new game here." Part of the set was going up and downstage, and I wondered how we were going to get in and out, and how to set the lights. He solved all these problems for us and enhanced us with them. The same goes for Irene Sharaff's costumes and Jean Rosenthal's lighting.

SONDHEIM: About the set, when we got down to Washington there had been a mistake made—somebody hadn't gotten the right dimensions of the stage. When the bedroom set was rolled off in the second act to make room for the dream ballet, which required a totally cleared, empty stage, about a third of it didn't roll off. The space at the National Theater was too small. I was afraid that we couldn't open, but Jerry said that we had fifteen hundred people coming Monday night, so we would just take a saw and saw it in half. He was affected more than anybody because, after all, this was the moment, the ballet, toward which he was building the entire scene and music—and here it just didn't work at all. He was totally cool. They got a saw and sawed the set in half, and on opening night half the bedroom went off one way and half the other.

ROBBINS: As I remember it, the set was supposed to go off, except Oliver designed it not to go off but to leave these arches showing on either side. I was furious inside, and I went to Oliver and said, "That set *has* to go off." I didn't get a saw out, but he solved the problem.

BERNSTEIN: I like the saw version better.

McNALLY: Was *Romeo and Juliet* always a source you kept going back to for parallels?

BERNSTEIN: It was Jerry's source, and Jerry was our source.

ROBBINS: Remarkably, Arthur managed to follow that story as outlined in the Shakespeare play without the audience or critics realizing it. That was a real achievement. These scenes follow each other in a certain way in the long arc of the Shakespearean pattern, but everyone gets so caught up in our story that they don't refer back for similarities.

SONDHEIM: The hardest part—correct me if it was not—was how to find a contemporary, believable substitute for the philter, the potion part of Shakespeare's plot; how somebody takes poison and seems to be dead and then comes alive again. That's what led us eventually to the mad aria Arthur was talking about earlier.

LAURENTS: The thing I'm proudest of in telling the story is why she can't get the message through: because of prejudice. I think it's better than the original story.

BERNSTEIN: It was the point of the Shakespeare plot, if we can call it the Shakespeare plot, where we spent most of the time and had most of the sludge. Arthur was the most faithful, while others of us sometimes wondered, "Why do we have to stick to it at this point?"

While we're toasting absent friends and colleagues, mention should be made of Roger Stevens, because he saved us at the most critical moment, the moment just after Cheryl Crawford told the four of us we'd have to rewrite the whole thing. We all stood up and said goodbye and left gravely, all trusting in one another's fortitude. We walked to the corner of whatever street it was, and as we stood on the corner we all went to jelly: "What are we going to do now?" Arthur went into a phone booth and called Roger Stevens in London, collect, at a number he'd left with us in case we ran into trouble—and God knows, we were in trouble. Arthur came out of that phone booth and told us, "Roger says, whatever happens, keep working. He will guarantee everything somehow. Just don't worry about it." This was the life saver. I can never praise that man enough for that one moment when he gave us the strength to have the courage of our own somewhat shaken convictions.

SONDHEIM: Addenda to that: the Algonquin Hotel played a part. We went in there to have a drink. They wouldn't serve us because Arthur didn't have a tie on. Our entire lives had gone down the drain, and they wouldn't let us have a drink. We went next door to the Iroquois, where we did indeed have a drink. My memory is that Arthur called from a phone booth there—to Germany.

LAURENTS: No, London.

SONDHEIM: Also, I got on the phone that night to Hal Prince and Bobby Griffith in Boston, where they were trying out *New Girl in Town*. I told Hal our problem, and he said, "Why don't you send the material to Bobby and me?" I told him that a few years ago he'd said it wasn't for him. But he knew we'd worked on it, and he was anxious to get onto another show. We sent them what script we had, and within twenty-four hours they called to say they would do it.

It was well for Roger to be the centerpiece, but he had a number of things and couldn't have spent the next two months solely on us. And we had to get the show into rehearsal by a certain date, because Lenny was about to take over the Philharmonic. I think he left October 3, and we opened September 27—we just made it. Those of you who've been through this mill know how hard it is within two months to get the producer to accept the show, raise the money, finish the casting and go ahead and book theaters, particularly a show as unusual and peculiar as this one.

ROBBINS: Does anyone remember what the show cost?

SONDHEIM: $375,000?

LAURENTS: $350,000.

ROBBINS: That was a lot then, mostly caused by the long rehearsal period.

LAURENTS: I remember Bobby and Hal said that Irene's costumes would be too expensive. Jerry said, "How much can you budget?" and they said, "$65,000," and he said, "Irene will do it for that," and she did!

SONDHEIM: When Hal and Bobby came in on it, we all felt we had to make quick decisions and do whatever was required of us. We got very excited. With Cheryl, for all the enthusiasm, there was this feeling that we might not get into rehearsal on time. Suddenly there was this deadline right around the corner, only eight weeks away.

ROBBINS: We started rehearsals in a place called the Chester Hale Studio, which is now gone. It was on Fifty-sixth Street near Carnegie Hall in a loft above a garage. I'd need more space today, but in four weeks we managed to start on the book and stage some of the numbers. I had the assistance of Peter

Gennaro as co-choreographer. He did most of "America" and the Sharks' dances in the dance hall competition, and he was very supportive all the way through.

I remember always being in a state of saying to myself, "Oh, it's moving, it's moving, something's happening, we're going on, not getting stuck." I don't remember getting stuck anywhere. We played around a lot with the marriage scene. It took us a lot of work to try to get that right.

LAURENTS: We made one change in rehearsal that was important. We switched the positions of "One Hand, One Heart" and "Tonight."

ROBBINS: What was wonderful about rehearsals was, we had the chance to try something, to move a number into a spot that turned out to be very exciting, even though in theory it wouldn't be.

SONDHEIM: In one instance we argued that a change didn't make logical sense. Jerry said, "But it makes theatrical sense," and he was absolutely right.

McNALLY: Lenny, were you composing the dance music with Jerry, or were you composing it in advance?

BERNSTEIN: We worked closely together. I remember all my collaborations with Jerry in terms of one tactile bodily feeling: his hands on my shoulders—composing with his hands on my shoulders. This may be metaphorical, but it's the way I remember it. I can feel him standing behind me saying, "Four more beats there," or "No, that's too many," or "Yeah—that's it!"

ROBBINS: Or Lenny would play something and I'd take off right there in the room, telling him, "I can see this kind of movement, or that kind of movement."

I wrote a scenario for the second-act ballet, so that Lenny had that as a premise to start with. He would compose on that, and then we'd get together and he'd play it, and I'd say, "That sounds wonderful, let's have more of this or more of that."

BERNSTEIN: There was only one moment when I was really scared to play something. It was the "Cool" fugue. He liked it so much he freaked out. I was so happy.

McNALLY: Steve, you're very fond of turning against some of the lyrics nowadays. Why didn't you then?

SONDHEIM: I was outvoted. I changed the lyric of "I Feel Pretty" after seeing the run-through in New York because I was ashamed of it. Later the others said they liked it better the way it was before, so I went home. I'm not fond of a lot of the *West Side Story* lyrics. To me, they seem very "written." I like "Something's Coming" and "Jet Song" because they have a kind of energy to them. The more contemplative lyrics I find very self-conscious and a mite pretentious every now and then. I hear a writer at work instead of a character.

McNALLY: How about "Gee, Officer Krupke"?

SONDHEIM: There are some good jokes there. Parenthetically, Jerry staged it in three hours by the clock, three days before we went to Washington. Jerry had been staging everything else, and we kept reminding him that this was a comedy number, and he kept saying, "I'll get to it, I'll get to it." One afternoon he did it in almost no time at all. Maybe the ideas had been cooking, but the staging of "Krupke" is one of the most brilliantly inventive in one number I've ever seen.

ROBBINS: By the end of the rehearsal period you're really into the work, you know the actors, you know the scenes. It isn't like the first days of rehearsals when you're fishing around and going tentatively toward what you want. You're on course. It's like those numbers you write in rehearsal or out of town. By that time, the wheels are rolling, you are into the character, the mood, the energy. Also, I find I do a lot of my best work when I'm tired and have less tension inside of me.

SONDHEIM: One of my objections to "Gee, Officer Krupke" was always that I felt it was out of place in the second act. It should occur in the first act, and "Cool" should occur where "Krupke" is. Here is a group of kids running from a double murder, and for them to stop and do this comic number seemed to me to be out of place. I kept nudging Arthur and Jerry to reverse the two. We didn't, and of course "Krupke" works wonderfully in the second act, on the old Shakespearean drunken-porter principle. In the middle of a melodrama, you cut in with comedy. On the other hand, when Shakespeare does it, it's an irrelevant character. For the movie, the numbers were reversed and weren't nearly as effective, in my opinion. Again, there was theatrical truth in putting "Krupke" there, if not literal truth.

LAURENTS: I was the only one for it, and I sold it with the rather grandiose business about the porter scene in Shakespeare.

MCNALLY: How were the reviews in Washington?

BERNSTEIN: Splendid.

LAURENTS: What I remember about Washington is the first preview. I was sitting in front of Jerry, and at some point we began to get a feeling, and Jerry began pounding me on the back, saying, "They like it, they like it!"

SONDHEIM: The only time "Something's Coming" ever stopped the show was that night. One of the things we did out of town was try to find another ending for "Something's Coming" because it never got that kind of a hand again, though it always worked. We kept writing high loud endings and low trail-off endings, and we finally just gave up. But Arthur's right, there was something about that night.

BERNSTEIN: It was an incredible night. It was August in Washington—horribly hot—and none of us knew whether anyone would listen to the show, or look at it, or stay in the theater. We'd had a lot of insults, a lot of warnings: "You're crazy," "Give it up," and so forth. At intermission I remember Justice Felix Frankfurter, the most distinguished man in Washington, in a wheelchair in tears. And this was only intermission. It was an incredible hello, because we didn't know whether the show was even all right, let alone something special and deeply moving.

ROBBINS: Steve spoke about not being happy with some of the lyrics. I think probably we all look at that work now from this vantage point and think, "Oh, maybe I could have done this, or could have done that." The big point is, the show in its time was quite a radical change. When it's performed now, it doesn't look radical. The techniques, the subject matter, the values seem to be a matter of course in other shows. Sometimes when I see it now it looks a little old-fashioned to me.

MCNALLY: The boldness of the show was very much appreciated by the critics. In rereading the reviews, the one thing that amazed me was the absence of mention of Steve's work. Walter Kerr and Brooks Atkinson talked about the score, the direction, the book, but they did not mention the name "Stephen Sondheim." I don't know who they thought wrote the lyrics.

LAURENTS: There's nothing amazing about that. Reviewers review reputation, not work.

BERNSTEIN: The most recent *West Side Story* I've seen was a couple of months ago in London. The reaction was terrific, and all the reviews mention Steve in the first paragraph, if that's any consolation. To me, Arthur is the one who doesn't get mentioned enough.

MCNALLY: You seem to have resisted making changes in *West Side Story,* though you've had plenty of opportunity to fiddle with it in the revivals and recordings.

BERNSTEIN: There are two big fiddles in the new recording. One is, I'm conducting the score for the first time ever, and the performers are all opera singers. I've always toyed with this idea. It can't be done on the stage, obviously. There is that built-in collision between dance and singing performance in the work. We were very, very lucky with this show, because in every production we've always found people, against all odds, who formed casts and could do all the different things they had to do. But there is an ideal way of hearing "One Hand, One Heart," for example. I've always kept it in the back of my mind, feeling that maybe some day I could hear that song sung the way I've always wanted it to be sung, which is quite slow with real operatic voice control and quality. In some ways it's come true on this record, in which I also have a hand-picked orchestra and a fabulous cast.

That's fiddling, all right, but there are no changes of any sort in the orchestration, in which Sid Ramin and Irwin Kostal assisted me. Actually, they did more than assist, they executed the orchestration. After the others went home at two-thirty in the morning, we had pre-orchestration sessions in which I would indicate exactly what I wanted, note by note, in a shorthand that is intelligible only to orchestrators. They would come back with the score a couple of days later and have a final post-orchestration session at the same time as a pre-session on the next number coming up. So they really executed it in a way without which I couldn't have gotten the score finished.

MCNALLY: Was opening night in New York like opening night in Washington?

SONDHEIM: No, for the first half hour the audience was pretty dead, they'd heard this was a work of art—capital W, capital A—so they sat there like children in church until "America." At that point they realized this was a musical, and they were supposed to be having a good time. From then on it went very well.

BERNSTEIN: What I remember best from opening night was the set change from the quintet, which drew prolonged applause, into the remarkable rumble set that Jerry mentioned. The quintet applause was just beginning to dip as the set changed before your eyes. The whole wave rose again until it doubled the preceding applause. For me, this was one of the most magical moments in the theater. That's where I had the sense that we had a hit.

ROBBINS: We were talking about revivals over the years. As a director I discovered something fascinating. At the time we did the show, the cast understood the material very, very well, deeply and organically. It was part of the times. In the recent revival—and I don't mean to cast any slurs upon it—I found that the cast had rather middle-class attitudes. It was hard for them to understand the street, the turf, the toughness, the necessity to own something, the struggle on the street. I felt I could never get out of them a real understanding of the material from either an acting or a dancing point of view. The original cast knew what it was about and could react to it.

LAURENTS: The day of our first run-through for an audience, they came out on stage in colors they had chosen for Jets and Sharks and their girls. They did it on their own, by themselves, and it was very, very touching.

BERNSTEIN: My impression in London was that they were very understanding of the material, maybe they came to it later.

LAURENTS: They're having a social revolution in England now.

SONDHEIM: It helped that Jerry kept the Jets and the Sharks apart as groups, separate, during rehearsals, even having their meals as separate gangs. I thought it was pretentious, but of course it was perfect, because, without any animosity or hostility, there was a sense of each gang having its own individuality, so that you had two giant personalities onstage. And I believe this is the first show whose chorus had individual characterizations. Maybe one or two people would be characterized, like Agnes de Mille's The Girl Who Falls Down in *Oklahoma,* but in *West Side Story* each of the members of the chorus had a name and a personality and was cast accordingly. Everybody takes that for granted now, but in those days it was a startling notion.

ROBBINS: It was not only cast that way, the collaboration continued, because once we found the people we wanted, Arthur began to write a little for them and even shift lines around. The characters were formed during the rehearsal period, with Arthur being there to see what could happen and what could not happen.

I'd like to add one thing about the scene changes. In Washington, as we were leaving the theater, I happened to turn back as they were flying in the gym set, which had streamers at the corners. By turning my head at the fortunate moment, I saw those streamers come down. I ran to Oliver and asked him, "Can we make a whole curtain of that?" which we did. Without that accident happening, and Oliver being ready to collaborate on it, I don't think that transition going into the gym would have been half as good. You always have to keep your eyes open for the mistakes, because they can be great.

Q: Wasn't there some controversy over the number "America"?

SONDHEIM: I got a letter complaining about the one line "Island of tropic diseases," outraged on behalf of Puerto Rico, claiming that we were making fun of Puerto Rico and being sarcastic about it. But I didn't change it.

BERNSTEIN: Opening night in Washington we had a telephone message from *La Prensa* saying that they'd heard about this song and we would be picketed when we came to New York unless we omitted or changed the song. They made particular reference to "Island of tropic diseases," telling us everybody knows Puerto Rico is free of disease. And it wasn't just that line they objected to. We were insulting not only Puerto Rico but the Puerto Ricans and all immigrants. They didn't hear "Nobody knows in America/Puerto Rico's in America"—it's a little hard to hear at that tempo. We met that threat by doing nothing about it, not changing a syllable, and we were not picketed.

Q: Mr. Laurents, did you plan from the beginning to invent your own slang?

LAURENTS: Yes.

Q: Did you use bebop?

LAURENTS: No . . . now you can see why the book was so short.

Q: Does a difference between logical truth and theatrical truth often occur in shows?

SONDHEIM: It's happened to me a number of times, but never quite as startlingly as in *West Side Story*. That's where I learned that theatrical truth, theatrical time, has nothing to do with real truth, real time. Sometimes it's supplied by the director and sometimes by the writers, saying, "This is theatrical truth, even though . . . " Generally you try to make it true on both levels, because it's richer that way.

Q: It's generally conceded that *West Side Story* was a turning point in the American musical, with a lot of new ideas of form and subject. Does the panel have any additional thoughts about how the show changed the conventions of the musical theater? What did it make possible that had not been possible before?

SONDHEIM: Essentially, it's a blend of all the elements—music, book, lyrics, dance. More than subject matter, its innovation has to do with theatrical style. We were influenced by the movies—there was a fluidity in the staging, which had a cinematic quality. Other shows have done that since. This show demonstrated one way a musical could be done. No show had ever been staged—I'm talking about the larger sense, not just Jerry's work—or conceived this way as a fluid piece which called on the poetic imagination of the audience. This is something that's taken for granted now. Prior to *West Side Story*, shows had been staged fairly stodgily, in the sense that you would do a scene in three, and then the curtain would come down, then there'd be a scene in one, and then a scene in three, and so forth. It's not exactly the first time that convention had been broken down—it was broken down a little in *South Pacific* and *Allegro*. But *West Side Story* has been the major influence.

BERNSTEIN: I agree with what Steve said, its influence went far beyond the subject matter. It had a kind of . . . if you want to be polite, you say bravery, if you want to be impolite, you say chutzpah . . . a kind of bravery in which we all fortified one another, to the point where we could try our utmost; not trying to break rules, not trying to go further—but having the bravery to follow your instincts and follow one another's instincts in order to produce something new, something that has never been envisioned before. It's not so much what it's about, it's how bravely it's done.

ROBBINS: I don't like to theorize about how or if the show changed future musicals. For me what was important about *West Side Story* was in our *aspiration*. I wanted to find out at that time how far we, as "long-haired artists," could go in bringing our crafts and talents to a musical. Why did we have to do it separately and elsewhere? Why did Lenny have to write an opera, Arthur a play, me a ballet? Why couldn't we, in aspiration, try to bring our deepest talents together to the commercial theater in this work? That was the true *gesture* of the show.

LAURENTS: That's the whole point, we all had real respect for each other and, without doing it overtly, challenged each other to do our best. That's all we thought about—doing our best.

GYPSY

Terrence McNally, Moderator
Arthur Laurents
Stephen Sondheim
Jule Styne

TERRENCE MCNALLY: *Gypsy* opened May 21, 1959. It was an enormous success. It ran for 706 performances, and that was only the first time around. It starred Ethel Merman, of course, and Jack Klugman and Sandra Church. Jerome Robbins directed.* It was produced by David Merrick and Leland Hayward. Later it was a movie, and a few seasons ago it was revived very successfully with Angela Lansbury.

What I first want to talk about is how these three men got together and said, "Hey, let's write this show." It started with a book by Gypsy Rose Lee—her memoirs. Now someone had to read that book and decide there was a musical there. Who was that?

ARTHUR LAURENTS: David Merrick.

MCNALLY: Who did Merrick call first with that notion?

LAURENTS: I'm not going to say.

MCNALLY: Hadn't other people tried working on it before you came in?

STEPHEN SONDHEIM: The property had been attacked a number of times before.

LAURENTS: "Attacked" is the word.

SONDHEIM: Ethel Merman had read the book too and had called either Leland or David, so she knew about it before any of the writers did.

LAURENTS: I think she called Jerry Robbins.

MCNALLY: Which of you three gentlemen was the first to get involved with *Gypsy?*

SONDHEIM: Arthur.

* Jerome Robbins, director and choreographer of *Gypsy*, was not included on this panel and has this comment to make about its discussion: "Arthur Laurents, during the *West Side Story* symposium, called our discussion 'a sort of *Rashomon West Side Story*,' and he also said, 'I don't think that's the way it happened.' Those remarks summarize perfectly my own reaction to the *Gypsy* symposium."

LAURENTS: I was asked by Leland Hayward. He told me—true or not, I don't know—that Jerry Robbins would direct the show if I wrote the book. I read Gypsy Rose Lee's memoirs. I thought what she'd written was fun, jazzy. But I wasn't interested in the lady who became the strip-tease queen of America, and I didn't think anyone else would be, so I said no. Leland never took no for an answer. He kept after me. He said, "Oh, you'll find some way."

And then one day a lot of people dropped by my place on the beach for a drink and got very smashed, and I heard one young woman talking about Gypsy Rose Lee's mother. I was fascinated. She apparently was what they used to call a curvaceous, plump blonde. Sort of like Shirley Booth, I gather. Very sweet and an absolute killer.

I had a couple of stipulations for working on this show. One of them was that I wanted to talk to Ethel Merman alone. I had never met her. So we met, and I said, "This woman is a monster. How far are you willing to go?" And Merman said, "I want to act, and I will do anything you want." I think that Steve and Jule will bear me out when I say she was absolutely marvelous during rehearsals.

At any rate, then came the question of the score. They asked Irving Berlin. He read Gypsy's book and said no. They asked Cole Porter. He was very sick, and they thought maybe this project would bring him back to life, but he said no, too. Then . . . Oh well, I might as well just say this. I love Jule and he knows it, but my next thought was to have Steve do the whole score. This was sabotaged by Ethel Merman's agent.

SONDHEIM: Mostly Ethel did not want to take a chance on an unknown composer. At that point, all anybody knew me for was a lyricist. I had written the lyrics for *West Side Story*. Well, Ethel had just done a show called *Happy Hunting* written by two untried writers. It had not been a success. I am now second-guessing, but I suspect her feeling was: once bitten, twice shy.

Jerry Robbins had also hesitated about having me do the whole score. I was working on *A Funny Thing Happened on the Way to the Forum* at about that time, and I played him three of the songs for *Forum*. I guess he was impressed enough because he called Leland and said, "It's O.K. for Sondheim to do the score."

But Ethel said she didn't want to take this chance on me as a composer. Then I think she mentioned Jule by name. So Arthur came to me and asked if I would be willing to do lyrics only.

I was trained as a musician. What I wanted to be was a composer. Lyric writing was a sideline I had slipped into, partly because of the influence of Oscar Hammerstein, and partly because I had to earn a living. I really didn't want to wait another couple of years to write a score myself. But I went to Oscar, and he persuaded me to do *Gypsy*. He said that the chance to work with these people and particularly to write a show for a star (which I had never done before) was invaluable. Also, the show was to have a very short schedule. We were then in the summer, and the show was set to go into rehearsal in February. Oscar persuaded me that, at the worst, it would be six months out of my life. It would involve some frustration, but it was a chance to write in a whole different vein and for a star. Because I liked the piece enough and because I knew and liked Jule's stuff a lot, I said O.K. So instead of doing music and lyrics, I just did lyrics. I haven't regretted it for one second. Not only do I love the score, I love the show.

JULE STYNE: Well, I am glad that Steve conceded. After Steve conceded, Arthur had to be satisfied. He said, "Jule is a great pop song writer, and he's done some shows, but this is a dramatic entity." Well, I was enraged. But I'm going to tell you about it because it all ended up great. That's why we can tell you about everything.

So I did an audition for Arthur. He was a wonderful audience because he loves music. After I played him five or six songs, he decided that I would be able to do it.

It was a most wonderful collaboration. I have done some twenty-five shows but have never had a collaboration like this. Things just happened every day. I mean, it was a song almost every two days.

SONDHEIM: *Gypsy* was written, in essence, in about four and a half months. What Jule is saying is what made that show absolutely unique, at least in my experience (and I suspect in the experiences of most writers of musicals): the show had no trouble in the writing whatsoever.

Arthur worked out an outline. We started to write. We never had a bad week. We never had, I would say, maybe even a bad day. I can't speak for Arthur's own internal problems when he was working the book out, but I don't remember his groaning a lot. It just went right on schedule. It was one of those miracles, and I think it shows. The show has a feeling of spontaneity.

LAURENTS: I would like to point out something here. There was no other person's conception. I did an outline, and the three of us—the three people who *write*—wrote the show. It wasn't even seen by the other people until the writing was over.

SONDHEIM: As a matter of fact, Jerry Robbins was in California most of the time. The first time he heard the score, Jule wasn't even around.

LAURENTS: We were in the last day of rehearsal for the London company of *West Side Story*. I'll never forget, Steve and I went over there, and the feeling was, "We're so tired. Do we have to listen to it now?" I remember Robbins lying down on a wooden bench. Well, it didn't take but Steve singing one or two or three of the songs—

SONDHEIM: I sing loud.

LAURENTS: —and everybody perked up.

MCNALLY: A lot of our members are considering writing shows about famous people. They all wanted to know if you had problems with the estate. Did you have to show the script to Gypsy or June Havoc?

LAURENTS: There was absolutely no problem with Gypsy Rose Lee. She only wanted one thing: the title had to be *Gypsy*. She didn't give a damn about anything else. As a matter of fact, when she saw the script and read the part about Herbie, the mother's boy friend, she said, "God, I wish I had thought of that for my autobiography!" I remember I tried very hard to get her to say how she got the name Gypsy, and she said, "Oh, honey, I've given fourteen or fifteen versions. Yours will be as good as mine."

There was trouble—and big trouble—with June Havoc. These great producers hadn't thought of getting a release from her, so we did not have her approval. Then the script was submitted to her, and she began asking for changes. I kept making them as best I could until finally she wanted me to make it very clear that when, at the end of the first act, she runs away, she was eleven or something. This would really have made the mother beyond horror, at least in the musical theater. I mean, if you don't mention the age, you can get away with it. I refused to make that change. Well, June Havoc hadn't signed the release, and there was talk of taking out an injunction to stop the rehearsals, which were just about to begin.

Then David Merrick came up with an idea. He said, "I am a lawyer myself, and I know something about libel laws. We'll just change the name of the character." Which we did. We called her Claire. When we opened in Philadelphia, they were saying, "Baby Clune," because they didn't know what the hell to call her—Claire or June. Well, June Havoc came to see it and then decided to sign after all.

SONDHEIM: Anyway, you have a lot of trouble with living relatives. That's the answer to that question.

MCNALLY: But changing the name would have made it all right.

SONDHEIM: Apparently.

LAURENTS: One other thing she objected to was the height of the girl playing the role. She said she was tall and it made her look older.

SONDHEIM: One of the reasons they didn't get the rights from her was that they thought they could get away without giving her a percentage of the piece. She ended up getting pieces from both of the producers and from Gypsy. That's what it really came down to—money.

MCNALLY: To get back to the writing of the show, obviously, the original book was called *Gypsy*, and you made it a story about Gypsy's mother. I assume the three of you agreed on that.

SONDHEIM: Correct me if you remember it differently, Arthur. Arthur talked to Gypsy Rose Lee, and he realized from things she said that she had made up most of it. Every time he went back and talked to her, she had a different account of how she got into vaudeville, how she got into burlesque, etc. So he decided he might as well make up his own story. Once he knew that he was free to do that, he was able to think, "What interests me about this? Nothing interests me. I am not interested in backstage musicals." And suddenly he thought, "Wait, if it's about the *mother*, that's an interesting story to tell." So then he was able to write an outline.

Jerry wanted to make it a panorama of vaudeville. We auditioned every vaudeville actor who was still alive in this country, and ended up with none of them.

LAURENTS: No, we hired some on two-week contracts, and they all had to be paid off. There were a lot of jugglers, remember? They were even with us in Philadelphia.

SONDHEIM: It was all worth it for one thing, incidentally. Faith Dane and her trumpet. She was a stripper, and that was part of her act. That went right into the show.

LAURENTS: She, by the way, was the daughter of my high school history teacher.

SONDHEIM: That's the most startling fact of the afternoon.

MCNALLY: Before you sat down to write, though, you knew the show was going to be for a star. The first time any of you had done that.

SONDHEIM: First time I had. I don't know about Jule.

STYNE: I had written for a star.

MCNALLY: And did that impose any problems?

LAURENTS: It gave me one big advantage. I felt that Merman had a quality—with all that brassiness, a quality of naivete, innocence. That helped me to write this woman who *really* didn't know what a monster she was. To help Ethel, I would write stage directions: "slower," "faster," "louder," "softer." You know, that's the way she acted.

SONDHEIM: There's an interesting thing about writing for a star, and I think that's why Oscar wanted me to do it. Most star vehicles today, and certainly in those days, were not what one would call book musicals. They were star vehicles. There's a difference between writing a song for a character named Rose and writing a song for a character named Rose to be played by Ethel Merman. When you know that in advance, you write differently. You write to take advantage of whatever qualities that star has. Arthur might have written Rose differently if he hadn't known that Ethel Merman was going to play the part. I certainly would have written the songs differently.

For example, at the end of the first act I assumed that Ethel Merman would not be able to handle a moment of such emotional complexity because I didn't know whether she could act or not. But what I *did* know was that she had this personality. Arthur had written this speech that was building and building, and how do you top it? Well, if you are not sure she can handle it, the answer is that you can write a song that is the kind of song that she has sung for twenty-five years. "Everything's Coming Up Roses" taken out of context is merely another "Blow, Gabriel, Blow." It's a song about nothing except a certain feeling with some images in it. Essentially it's a performer song. Little did we know that she was a *wonderful* actress, which only made the moment richer. But again, that might not have been the solution if I hadn't known we were writing for Ethel Merman. When you write for a musical comedy star, you write for not just the character but the character played by that personality. This is a lesson that has stood me in very good stead ever since. Is that true for you, Jule?

STYNE: Well, many years ago, I was a vocal coach. Ethel Merman was coached by one of the best vocal coaches of all time. His name was Al Siegel. He got very sick once, so I was sent up to New Haven to work with Ethel on *Red, Hot and Blue.* From that, I knew a lot about Ethel's voice and where it was.

But the most important thing about putting this thing together is that Arthur wrote this wonderful, heavy book, and Steve can write anything and is willing to try anything. I wrote one passage, I remember. It was a double-time piece of music. I played this thing for Steve, and he said, "It's a wonderful rhythmic passage. Save it." And one day he came in, and he said, "I just had a meeting with Arthur, and Arthur would like us to musicalize that second scene." So Steve said, "You know that thing you had? That thing you played for me? Make that be the rhythmic passage, and what I want is to write something to soar on top of this persuasive element—"I had a dream . . ." This became part of the song "Some People."

Arthur has such a great theatrical sense. You know the part where the kids are in the middle of the act and dancing to "The Stars and Stripes Forever," and then, as the lights are flickering, they grow up? That was in Arthur's book. The director staged it, but it was Arthur's idea.

McNALLY: We all want to hear a lot about the writing of the songs. I'll mention the songs, and I would like a sort of free association. Shall we start with "Let Me Entertain You"?

SONDHEIM: We had to find a song—Jule and I—that would act throughout the show. You would see it as a piece of material that the mother would never let go of.

McNALLY: How did you know that in advance? It was a brilliant idea.

LAURENTS: We had an outline.

SONDHEIM: All right, back to basics. Arthur made an outline, and then the three of us sat and talked about where the songs could work. We would toss around ideas. Then he would start writing the scenes. We always wrote into him. I always do as a lyric writer. I like to have the book writer get ahead of me so I can imitate diction and style—let the playwright set the style.

It became apparent that—I don't remember whose idea it was—it would be fun to illustrate the mother's stinginess with material as well as with costumes if she would constantly use the same stuff over and over again. If we could find a song that would act first as a kid's song and then, at the climax of the evening, work as a sultry strip, because we knew obviously we had to get to a moment to reach the strip. So as a lyric writer, I knew I had to find double entendres that could be utilized both in a little kid's voice and in a sultry voice. I remember the idea of "Let Me Entertain You" came to me on the train to Manchester when Arthur and I were going up there to try out *West Side Story.*

LAURENTS: The whole theme of the mother being stingy runs through the book of *Gypsy*.

SONDHEIM: There's a costume thing Arthur put in the book. You don't really notice it, but there are blankets around, and then, two scenes later, you see these wild coats and you say, "Where did these kids get the coats from?" And you suddenly realize they are hotel blankets that the mother stole. It always got the right kind of laugh, because it wasn't a sight gag. It took a while for the audience to catch on. The scene started, and it was "What's wrong with this picture?" And then somebody in the audience would start to laugh, and the other people would whisper, and then soon the whole audience would go. It was *never* pointed out. It was just a subtlety, a through-line. There are a lot of through-lines in *Gypsy* that are interesting, that have to do with costumes.

MCNALLY: One of the questions submitted asked Arthur specifically, "How did you involve the audience in the first five minutes?" All I could think of was Ethel Merman's voice from the back of the theater.

LAURENTS: I wanted to give the star a star entrance. She really had to, practically, start the show. I didn't feel she could sing at that point. So the question was how do you do it theatrically and really knock them on their asses. So I had her come down the aisle.

SONDHEIM: Also, the mother is a disruptive character, and here she's disrupting the show you're at as well as the scene.

MCNALLY: Was this always the first image of the show?

SONDHEIM: The kiddie show and the voice from the back of the theater.

LAURENTS: No, it certainly was not. It was a rehearsal in a vaudeville house, and the first thing you saw was a woman playing a scene. It was supposed to be someone like Ethel Barrymore on tour.

SONDHEIM: There was a painted flat of a fireplace . . .

LAURENTS: . . . with a girl in a sailor middy blouse and some terrible monologue setting the theme of the show. She says, "I must tell you. I am not your sister. I am your mother." And it turned out that she was a whore to put the kid through finishing school.

MCNALLY: That was the theme of the show?

LAURENTS: Mother and daughter.

SONDHEIM: That was the first scene. And you thought, "What is this show we are watching?" Then the blackout would come, and you'd see stagehands come on, and the flat would go out, and there was Uncle Jocko and the kiddie show. And then you realized you were in a vaudeville house and they had just presented, as they did in those days, a dramatic scene before the next musical number. It was just a weird and terribly funny opening, but the show was long. It was cut out, that scene, in Philadelphia.

Regarding "Let Me Entertain You" . . . Originally it was going to show up in each of the vaudeville acts but with different titles. When it showed up later, it was going to be called "Let's Go to the Movies," which we actually wrote. It was a completed song. Each time it was going to be different. Then I decided it would be better just to use the same title all the time, but I thought it might be fun for the audience, "Where have we heard that title before?"

LAURENTS: Rose wouldn't write new lyrics.

SONDHEIM: She wouldn't pay for it.

MCNALLY: Rose first sings in the second number, "Some People."

SONDHEIM: I have the feeling that *Gypsy* may have been—*may* have been—the first show in which there appeared that now familiar device of having the main character, usually in the second song, come right out and say, "I do this," directly to the audience. In those days, we weren't ashamed of what is now a very worn technique, which is to get yourself off the hook by having the main character reveal herself or himself not so much through action as in a monologue. Now in *Gypsy,* this is worked out as a scene, in that she wants that plaque, and that scene and song are about her trying to get it. But essentially, "Some People" is a show-off piece for both the star and the character. That's a little blatant now, and yet we used it again in *Sweeney Todd.*

I remember something that Ethel Merman did during "Some People." No matter how well and how intensely she sang it, she *always* snapped her fingers during the number. In my opinion it was because she wanted the audience to know, "Look, you are going on a trip tonight with a very unpleasant woman. Remember this is Ethel, O.K.?" From that moment on, she played the rest of the show uncompromisingly. Now I don't think she was truly aware of what she was doing, but I gave her that note a couple of times, and she said, "Was I doing that again?" And she did it, and she did it, and she kept doing it all the time.

LAURENTS: Angie always tapped her foot doing it.

SONDHEIM: Well, I wouldn't be surprised if it wasn't for the same reason.

LAURENTS: No, she couldn't stop herself.

SONDHEIM: It's a catchy tune. There is no question about that.

LAURENTS: By the way, on the original cast recording, the line about "88 cents" is done by S. Sondheim.

SONDHEIM: The stage manager forgot to call the guy who played the father to the recording session because he wasn't in any of the singing numbers. So they were stuck without a voice, so they put me in there. I am *not* an actor. I was very fierce to Ethel. I was very annoyed at her at the time because she refused to sing something that I had written. So I put all my annoyance into that line. She was so startled!

MCNALLY: O.K., "Small World." We're in the third scene now.

SONDHEIM: There was a song cut in that scene. Arthur devised a really cute scene—cute and chilling. The two kids are on top of some flat looking down, and what they are watching is the scene between their mother and this man. They are watching their mother con the man and flirt with him so that he will handle her act, the kid. They are watching her. These are wise children. They are only seven and five at the time (or eight and six) but you see how jaded they are already. They know exactly what's going on, and they sing a song called "Mama's Talking Soft." The idea of the song was mama's talking soft, but mama's moving in. Then Rose and Herbie sang "Small World," and then the two songs went together.

It looked charming at the run-through. But the seven-year-old girl who played Louise had severe acrophobia. She was up there twelve or fifteen feet in the air, and she was trying to be a good girl, but she started to cry, and she got hysterical, so we never tried to do the scene again. There was no point. One would have to have been truly cruel and fire her because she couldn't get up there, or else cut the song. So we cut the song. Frankly, we didn't lose that much anyway. But it's something that would probably still be in the show today if that little girl hadn't been afraid of heights.

LAURENTS: I would like to point out something about that, though, which is something that you have to learn in the theater. When a scene doesn't work, for whatever reason, you can't waste time. You have to go home and write a new scene.

The other thing I would like to point out is how subtly funny the lyric of "Small World" is. Part of the thing that makes it so funny is that it's a ballad. It's a very pretty tune, but if you examine the lyric . . . I mean, that woman is *cunning.* There she is saying, "You're a man who likes children. I'm a woman with children. Terrific. We're married." She goes from A to Z in no time at all.

SONDHEIM: You couldn't miss it when the two kids were commenting on it.

MCNALLY: If you had your druthers, would you like to put that song back in?

SONDHEIM: No, it was better as a simpler scene. But I really liked that song that was cut. It was a good lyric and a pretty tune and it was funny. Though we cut it out, the song was still referred to in "Rose's Turn."

The whole idea of "Rose's Turn" was for it to refer to all of the music that had gone before. Now, if we had cut "Mama's Talking Soft" in rehearsals, I would have had time to cut the reference to it in "Rose's Turn." But it was cut in Philly, and we had our hands full with other problems, so it was still in "Rose's Turn" as a sort of dinosaur's appendix of what was there once but no longer existed.

LAURENTS: We changed it later, in London.

SONDHEIM: We did indeed.

MCNALLY: "Mr. Goldstone, I Love You."

SONDHEIM: That originally was in a more complicated form. The idea of the song was that Rose and the kids would be having this party to "Mr. Goldstone, I Love You" in the main room with everybody happy. Then, suddenly, we the audience notice that Louise isn't there. The "Goldstone" song freezes, the lights switch, and there in the other room we see Louise alone with her animals. She sings "Little Lamb," and we see her as a lonely child. Then the lights switch again, and the others go right on with the party. Jerry Robbins was convinced that it wouldn't work. I don't remember how we got to the resolution, but Jerry won his point. They ended up being played as two separate songs, which is probably better because "Mr. Goldstone" got a really nice hand, while "Little Lamb," being the kind of song it is, did not get a big hand and, stuck in the middle of "Goldstone," it probably would have interrupted the rhythm too much. From a show-biz point of view, it was probably better to split them up. Nor do I think we really lost any values. At least that's the way it seems in hindsight.

"Goldstone" is one of those songs—for those of you who are interested in lyric writing—where you are stuck. It's a one-joke idea. Once you get the notion of "Have an eggroll, Mr. Goldstone," that's really all there is to it. That line was Arthur's, incidentally. I saw it, and I said, "Is that the way to begin a song!" Well, of course, it brought the house down. But, once that's been sung, what do you do? Where does the song go?

LAURENTS: Can I interrupt for just one thing: Anybody who writes the book of a musical, no matter what you write, when the lyricist or the composer comes to you and says, "I would like to musicalize this moment," let them do it. It is a musical. It is a musical theater, and you are serving them as well as the show.

SONDHEIM: You see, if it were just a line of dialogue, it would get a huge laugh. But when it became a song, it became a joy, and that joyfulness is exactly what that scene is about. The idea is that they are out of prison at last. If you're in a musical, you express that idea with music. So I needed the line. The problem is, it was just one line. If it were done as dialogue, it would go, "Have an eggroll, Mr. Goldstone. Why don't we sign the contract?" And the scene would go on. But, since the line was the first line of a song, I had to expand it to make a full song. The result is, for those of you who know the lyric, it's the same idea over and over again. It's one of those songs in which you just take one idea and repeat it as cleverly or as interestingly or as wittily as possible and with as much verve as you can and try to give the actors onstage something to do. As I said, it's a one-joke song, and that's not my favorite kind. I like the song fine, but it's what is known as a stage wait.

MCNALLY: Anything you want to tell us about "You'll Never Get Away From Me"?

LAURENTS: Yes, I didn't like it.

MCNALLY: Why not, Arthur?

LAURENTS: I don't think it is as good as the rest of the score. I think Jule's music is some of the best that has ever been written for musical theater, and the same goes for Steve's lyrics. But that song never seemed to be up to the rest of it. I felt that it needed a wildness for the woman that it doesn't really have.

SONDHEIM: I happen to think Arthur is right. I can tell you why it happened. Jule and I had known each other slightly through mutual friends and parties around town. Those of you who have not had the pleasure of hearing Jule play the piano have missed one of the supreme delights. When he was at a party, he would often play. He is, by the way, one of the few composers who are genuinely generous. He plays anybody's music. He doesn't just play his own. So I used to request totally obscure tunes that nobody at the party would know except me. Sometimes even Jule wouldn't remember. But he had one tune that was written for a movie that had never been made. The tune was called "Why Did You Have to Wait So Long?" Sammy Cahn had written the lyrics. He used to play it at parties, and it was always one of my favorite tunes.

The first day we got together to work on *Gypsy*, he handed me thirteen tunes without lyrics, and he said, "Maybe some of these would be useful." I said, "Let's try to write fresh for this show. But," I said, "there is one of your tunes I would really like to get into this show—'Why Did You Have to Wait So Long?' Do you think it would be O.K. with Mr. Cahn?" Jule said, "Sure." So all the time we were writing, I was trying to find a title for that song and a place to put it. So the song came from the wrong impulse. It came from outside instead of from inside the play and inside the characters. I was trying to shoehorn in something that I liked. The result is that Arthur is absolutely right. There's something not of the same weight, tone and texture as the rest of the score. I think it's true of both the music and the lyric.

LAURENTS: May I give the end of the story about this song? After the show opened, one day Steve came running up and said, "I've got the first pressing of the album." I said, "You couldn't have." We'd only recorded it the night before or something. But Steve said, "Here it is." He puts this LP on and the tune of "You'll Never Get Away From Me" starts, played by the orchestra. I thought, "My God, maybe they changed the overture of the record!" Then the singers came in. . . .

SONDHEIM: And what they sang was, "I'm in pursuit of happiness, because the Constitution says I've a right to be. . . . " Same tune. Different words. It was from a musical Jule wrote with Leo Robin based on *Ruggles of Red Gap*. I had found out about it on opening night when a friend of mine gave me a record of *Red Gap* saying, "Here's some of the score you may not have heard."

STYNE: You see, old songs never die.

MCNALLY: "If Mamma Was Married."

SONDHEIM: I don't remember anything particularly about that song, but I like it a lot. It's maybe my favorite song in the show.

STYNE: Steve came back from a meeting with Arthur and said, "I want to write a song—'Mama Gets Married.' " I'd play something. "Something like this, Steve?" "No." "You like this? No? Let's tear it up. Do you like this?"

SONDHEIM: Jule's too modest to tell you, because he probably doesn't know it about himself, but he has one of the most—if not *the* most—fertile musical minds that I have ever met. He can write and make changes like *that*. His mind never stops working musically. He is an ideal collaborator from that point of view, because he is totally flexible and because he can see sixty-four solutions at a time. If anything, the problem is choosing.

"If Mamma Was Married" went through three entirely different kinds of songs before we arrived at it. One song was rather polite, one song was too brassy. We finally found the right approach. Incidentally, for the musicians in the audience, there is a musical device coming out of the release in that song that I don't think has ever been used in another song. You can look at it. I am not going into it now.

STYNE: Steve, no, I would like to elaborate on that. You know, every lyric writer says, "This is funny." But Steve said, "This is a big joke here. You've got to write out two bars. Just fill it in with two bars to give the audience a chance to laugh." So, if you listen to it, you'll notice there's two extra bars there right after one of the biggest laughs in the song. First time in my life I ever had a lyric writer say, "Write two bars extra because that's where we're going to get a laugh."

McNALLY: "All I Need Is the Girl."

SONDHEIM: That was originally the release of a song called "Shut Up and Dance." After having finished "Shut Up and Dance," we decided to take the release and expand it and make it into the song instead.

McNALLY: "Everything's Coming Up Roses."

STYNE: Jerry had directed my first show, *High Button Shoes*. There was a song that was taken out called "I'm Betwixt and Between." Jerry told Steve to ask me to play it for him, so I did, and Steve liked it. That became "Everything's Coming Up Roses." But not the whole tune. Only the opening strain.

SONDHEIM: One of the problems of writing that song was how to top Arthur's speech. Not even top it (in the sense of competing), but to sail off of it. We started with a verse which has no rhythm in it at all, and it leads up to those opening notes of the main section. The most wonderful thing about that tune at that spot is that it starts at the top of its register. "You'll be swell, you'll be great . . ." Now that, as Jule said, was originally the first line of "Betwixt and Between." "I'm betwixt and between . . ." Well, we just used the front part of the melody. I told Jule, "I will find a title, and the title should be at the end of the quatrain, not the beginning. When I get a title, maybe you can set it musically." It took me a week just to find that title.

LAURENTS: Now tell them about going to Manchester.

SONDHEIM: All right. This is a story about directors, right? Jerry is up in Manchester doing *West Side Story*. So we're going to go up there and play him this new song Jule and I have written, which is the end of the first act. Jerry's been waiting for it. So we get up there, and I'm playing the hotel piano in the middle of the night. I am very proud of it, and Arthur is tapping his foot. So I get finished, and Jerry says, "I don't understand that title." And I'm thinking, "Oh, my God, is it too poetic?" Because one of the problems was to come up with a phrase that means "things are going to be better than ever" that isn't flat and yet isn't so poetic that you can't believe that Rose with her street jargon would say it. The point was to find a phrase that sounded as if it had been in the language for years but was, in fact, invented for that show. I was really proud of finding that phrase. And Jerry says, "I just don't understand that title." I say, "Why not, Jerry?" And he says, "Everything's coming up Rose's *what?*" I said, "I'll tell you what, Jerry. If anybody else has that confusion—anybody connected with the production, in the audience, any of your relatives—I will change the title."

MCNALLY: You talked about cutting "Shut Up and Dance." Are there many missing *Gypsy* songs—songs that were cut?

SONDHEIM: No. We wrote one in Philadelphia for Ethel to open the second act. It lasted one performance. I thought it was funny. It was called "Smile, Girls," in which she was coaching the Toreadorables on how to smile. I brought the lyric with me. You remember the situation: the girls have been rehearsing this terrible number, a tango. At any rate, they sit around her in a semicircle and Rose sings:

Smile, girls,
And you'll lay 'em in the aisle, girls.
When you smile, girls,
You don't need a plot.

Smile, girls,
Drive 'em crazy with your youth, girls.
Flash a tooth, girls.
Show 'em everything you've got—
Which ain't an awful lot.

Smile, girls,
Hit 'em right between the eyes, girls.
Otherwise, girls,
It's back to L.A.
Get style, girls,
And the customers will stay.

So smile, Agnes,
Smile, Dolores,
Smile, Thelma,
Smile—whateveryourname is—
Smile, Edna,
Smile, Marjorie May . . .
Smile, girls,   ·
Make 'em think you're very clever.
But whatever
Happens,
Smile.

When the scenery smacks you, smile.
When a stagehand attacks you, smile.

When they boo in the gallery, smile.
When I don't pay your salary, smile
When the comedy's dying, smile.
When Dolores is crying, smile.
When tomatoes are flying—duck.
But smile.

(*The girls attempt to do splits*)

Smile, girls,
It only hurts a little while, girls.
If you smile, girls,
It's sure to go away.

Smile, girls,
Think of getting better billing.
Show a filling.

Get style, girls,
Even if you have to ham it,
But goddammit

Smile, Agnes
Smile, Dolores,
Smile, Thelma,
Smile—whateveryourname is—
Smile, Edna,
Smile, Marjorie May!
Smile, girls,
And when the act begins to sag,
Drag out the flag—
And smile!

MCNALLY: Were there a lot of goodies like that in there?

SONDHEIM: Not a lot.

LAURENTS: We had a whole burlesque show, though.

SONDHEIM: We had a number of burlesque comics, and it really was a lot of fun, but it lasted three and a half hours.

MCNALLY: Actually, the second act had many fewer songs than the first. "Together, Wherever We Go," "You Gotta Get a Gimmick," the reprise of "Let Me Entertain You" and "Rose's Turn."

LAURENTS: I would like to say something about "Let Me Entertain You." I don't think the strip ever worked in New York in the original production. Part of it was that Jerry didn't have much faith in Sandra Church. When it wasn't working, I said, "Let's try having her talk," which is what Gypsy Rose Lee actually did. I think Jerry was very tired then and just sick of the whole thing. But he didn't want to, so we never did.

But when I directed the show in London, I wrote dialogue for the strip, and the number worked infinitely better, which is interesting because, as I say, it went back to the truth. This is what Gypsy really did. She was never much of a stripper. It was her wisecracks that made it work.

MCNALLY: We are getting to "Rose's Turn." Was it always there? Was there one point when the show ended there? Was it the last thing written?

LAURENTS: May I start?

SONDHEIM: Sure. I'm going to make the same point you are.

LAURENTS: When I started working on the outline, I started at the end. I realized that Gypsy was going to have to do her strip, which presumably would be a smash, but the star of the show is Rose, whether she's played by Merman or not. She is the main character, so we had to do something to top the strip theatrically, dramatically, every way you could think of. That's where the notion of "Rose's Turn" came from. I must say that, once I figured that out, the show was comparatively easy to write. In the writing of any show, that is so important—to know what the end is. If you know the end and the beginning, the rest is relatively easy.

SONDHEIM: That was originally going to be a ballet. Jerry thought the climax of the show should be a ballet with Rose seeing her past and sort of nightmare figures. In those days, incidentally, there were three stages of Louise and June. We cut one stage, so you now only see them in two sizes. The ballet was not cut until during the rehearsal. "Rose's Turn" was written during rehearsal and was presented during rehearsal because it became apparent that the whole ballet idea was simply not in keeping with the rest of the show. It was much too pretentious and entirely wrong. So it devolved on us—Jule and me—to try to carry out Arthur's idea of climaxing the show this way, but with no help from anything except the singer herself.

LAURENTS: And the point of the show.

SONDHEIM: Just in terms of performance, to have her come out and sing thirty-two bars at that point, even twice, would simply not have done what was intended. So the idea was to carry out the nightmare quality that Jerry had wanted, only do it entirely through music and lyrics.

Well, how do you do that? You do that with a kind of interrupted consciousness technique. The original idea of the ballet was that it was going to be a visual reprise of her life. When we decided to do it not as a ballet but as a song, we held onto the reprise idea by making the number a nightmare version of the various songs we've already heard in the show. So "Rose's Turn" is essentially a series of variations on songs you've heard before. There are some melodic variations with dissonant accompaniments and some lyrical variations, and they play off all that you've heard and seen all evening, which gives the number a kaleidoscopic feel.

I insisted that the number not reach a hand. A woman having a nervous breakdown should not get applause from an audience. To have a mad scene and then have a bow violated everything that I thought I had learned from Oscar Hammerstein, who taught me to be true to the character and true to the situation. So I forced Jule to not put an ending on it, but to have it fade out with high scratchy violin sounds with those last chords when she's screaming—not singing, but screaming—"For me, for me, for me!" And there would be this chilling quiet moment in the theater, and then, as Arthur wrote it, the daughter would come out of the wings applauding her, and they would go on. It seemed to me to be the honest way to do it. The fact is, in my head there was an arc from the beginning of her breakdown to her capitulation in the three-page scene that followed to the final curtain. It seemed to me one line.

We got to Philadelphia, and Oscar Hammerstein came down to see the show. Arthur and I went tremblingly out to have a drink with him afterward to ask him what he thought, and he said, "I thought there were three major problems. The first one,"—and we were ready to take notes—"the first one is the doorknob in the kitchen set keeps falling off every time anyone comes in." He said, "It's very distracting." So Arthur and I started relaxing and thought we obviously had this terrific show. Then he said, " 'You'll Never Get Away From Me' ought to end that scene." At that point, "You'll Never Get Away From Me" was in the middle of the scene. He said, "Generally it's good to end a scene with a song." Well, as we all know, that's a kind of sophistry that, particularly today, doesn't necessarily apply; but generally, in *that* structure— where you have scene, blackout, scene, blackout—you end each scene with a song. There is a tendency otherwise to piddle away, and the audience doesn't really quite pay attention to the scene.

Then, the most important thing he said: "And you must give Ethel Merman an ending on 'Rose's Turn.' " I started to bristle, and I said, "Why?" And he said, "Because the audience is so anxious to applaud her that they are not listening to the scene that follows. Since the scene that follows is what the entire play is about, if you want them to listen, you must let them release themselves.

And that is what the applause is for. I know it's dishonest, but *please*, fellows, put a big ending on that number if you want the rest of the play to play. Or bring the curtain down there. You have to choose one of those two things."

And, after taking it under advisement, that's exactly what we did. We put an emotionally fake ending on that song. As those of you who've heard it know, she's screaming away and screaming away, and suddenly she hits her big cadence and you just think, "We're in a musical. I forgot." But, as a result of that, the audience bravos and screams and bravos and screams, and then they play the last scene, and the audience listens.

When Arthur directed it for London, he made a slight change. He blended the two things. He did something I wish had struck him or Jerry or us back in 1959. Angela Lansbury bowed to the audience, which, of course, is screaming its lungs out because it's your big eleven o'clock number. The applause started to die. Usually, you know, the action goes on, but not with Angela. The applause died, and she kept bowing. There was dead silence in the house, and she kept bowing. You realized that you were looking at a mad woman, not at a musical. But, in the original, the audience applauded and Ethel Merman sometimes would actually . . . She tried *not* to bow, but she wanted to go on with the play. Then finally Sandra would appear from the wings, and the audience would finally stop applauding because they thought the scene was about to begin, which is the standard way you would recover from a show-stopper. In London, Arthur found that way of recovering from the show-stopper without violating the texture.

LAURENTS: It took a lot of courage on Angie's part. When I asked her to do it, I hoped that the audience would realize this whole number is in her head, so that the applause also was in her head. Well, it's very risky for an actress to keep bowing when there's no applause. You risk the audience thinking that she's trying to milk it. But she did it absolutely brilliantly, and the audience realized she was mad as a hatter when she was finally doing those bows. I must say, the chill in the audience when they realized that was one of the most satisfying things about her performance—for me anyway.

STYNE: Also, above the proscenium, there were lights that went on during the song that spelled out "Rose." It looked like there was a whole show going on called "Rose." And then the lights went out while she was bowing.

SONDHEIM: Yeah, the stage got cold. It was to cue the audience in. But still, the principle is that the audience was able to enjoy both . . .

LAURENTS: And the principle is, if you think hard enough, there is a way to have your cake and eat it too.

SONDHEIM: Not *always*. But it's a mad scene. It's a musical comedy starring a mad scene.

LAURENTS: Terrence, you asked if it ever ended the show. I will tell you that opening night in New York, at the end of the strip, Walter Kerr, who was then the critic for . . . I guess he was on the *Times*.

SONDHEIM: No, he was on the *Trib*.

LAURENTS: Anyway, he was coming up the aisle, and I said to him, "Get back to your seat. It's not over!" And he went back!

SONDHEIM: The reason he went back was that there was no standing room in the theater, so he couldn't stand at the back and watch the rest of the show.

LAURENTS: I was furious with him. I could have killed him.

SONDHEIM: And he loved the show, which just shows that you shouldn't ever think that because a critic leaves your show early he hates it. Not at all. He gave it probably the best review he ever gave any musical, except for *My Fair Lady*. He would have given it the same review if he had left before "Rose's Turn." That's how much he liked it.

STYNE: My early experience of playing in a burlesque house, when I was fourteen years old, served me well in that show. I remembered a lot of things that I needed to remember musically. I made the music different, but it had the same raw feeling and it worked well.

I would like to speak about the overture. I wanted to do something in the overture that would let them know that it was about burlesque, among many things. So I wrote this with Sid Ramin and Robert Ginzler, the orchestrators. We worked it out so that, at the end, the trumpet player stood up and blew the rafters off. It was just the most exciting thing.

Jerry Robbins didn't like it. He said, "All I want is two minutes' worth of music. Just a couple of tunes and then right into the play." I told him I'd make it go three and a half. Well, it went like 4:35. I had lied to him. We tried it out in Philadelphia, and he said, "I don't like it. I don't like it at all." But it went well, and everybody seemed to like it, so we left it in.

He got even with me in New York, however. When we arrived in New York . . . Well, you know, you come in the day the show opens about three o'clock, and everybody sings a song and dances a number. Everybody kind of loosens up. The band plays a little so they won't play cold opening night. Well, anyway, at three o'clock I walked into the pit. This was the Broadway Theater, where the pit is like twenty feet below sea level. They had promised me the pit would be raised. But it was three o'clock in the afternoon, and the pit hadn't been raised. Now, I knew what the overture was going to sound like because we had played it with the pit like that for two previews, and those two previews it hadn't sounded. It hadn't gone like it should. So I'd been promised the pit would be raised.

So I walked up to Leland Hayward and he said, "It sounds fine to me." I said, "Leland, you are a wonderful producer, but you don't know the first thing about music. Besides, Jerry promised me." So then I walked up to Robbins, who was dancing around on the stage. He had no reason to dance around on the stage, because everybody had been dismissed. But I'm trying to talk to him. I remember him with his little cap. And I grabbed him by the throat. I said, "Jerry, I am going to throw you into the pit. Not only that, but when you yell, no one will hear you, just like no one will hear my music!" And he said, "Oh, baby, I'll fix it." But the stagehands were all gone. I was a doomed man. I sat there and actually cried.

Then a friend of mine came over to me and said, "Why are you crying?" I told him I was trying to raise the musicians. He said, "Well, come with me," and we went down to Twenty-fourth Street and Fifth Avenue where his friend owned a wholesale chair store. I got twenty-four bar stools. So the fiddle players were up on these bar stools playing. Jerry walked up to me after the overture—with the audience screaming and cheering—and he said, "See, baby?" And I said, "What do you mean 'See, baby?' They were sitting on twenty-four bar stools!" But that's all fun and games.

SONDHEIM: I just want to add one little footnote about Leland Hayward. He was a terrific fellow. Three times, on three separate occasions in Philadelphia, David Merrick said, "My God, this show is terrible." David said later he was doing it because we were all getting smug. Far from it. We were working very hard in Philly to fix the show. But he said, "I want to get rid of the show" three times, and three times Leland said, "I'll buy you out, David." And each time David shut up.

MCNALLY: But when you talk about fixing in Philadelphia, surely it was minor.

SONDHEIM: Oh no, there was a major structural problem.

LAURENTS: First of all, it was forty-five minutes too long. There was this whole burlesque show which I didn't believe should have been in it, because I felt that if you stayed away from Rose or Gypsy too long—no matter what *divertissement*, as another collaborator was fond of saying—you'd lose the audience. But Jerry wanted a burlesque show. Well, I believe you should try anything if you respect your collaborator. So I wrote it. I wrote it as funny and as dirty as I could, and it was pretty funny and it was very dirty, and I don't know how long it lasted.

SONDHEIM: Ten minutes.

LAURENTS: I mean in the show.

SONDHEIM: Ten minutes.

LAURENTS: Well, the first act was long enough. The second act was too bloody long. In the original second act, there was a marvelous moment that I must say I hated to give up. You saw onstage Louise—this girl who'd only worn pants so you'd never thought of her as attractive or even particularly female. Then, before your eyes, she put on makeup and changed and became Gypsy Rose Lee. You saw it happen onstage. Then she had a scene with Herbie. Then she did the strip, and then Rose was giving her flowers, which, of course, she'd stolen from other people . . .

SONDHEIM: I just want to say one thing. Arthur is not making one point clear. In that version, the strip did not become a montage as it did in the final version. You just saw that night's strip. And you saw her change from a girl into a woman in front of your eyes. You saw her start to get some confidence, and then there was a scene backstage of what happens that night after the show—Rose demanding bigger billing, etc.

LAURENTS: Well, it was too long. Jule came up with the solution, which was to combine the backstage scenes before and after the strip. Now she goes offstage to dress. Rose and Herbie have their scene. He leaves her. Then Gypsy enters, dressed up. This all builds much more dramatically, I think, to the strip.

SONDHEIM: And then the strip, which turns into a montage of strips to cover the passage of time to take us to the final scenes.

LAURENTS: There was one point in Philadelphia when we were still long when Jerry said to me, "Steve says you have ten minutes of cuts marked." I said, "That's right." He said, "When are you going to take them?" I said to him, "When you cut ten minutes of those kiddie numbers." He didn't say anything. He went on with rehearsal. At the end of the rehearsal, he said, "I'll take mine." I said, "I'll take mine." We both cut, and that was that.

MCNALLY: The reason I phrased that question to Steve is that part of the legend of *Gypsy* is that you had a gypsy run-through in New York that was perfect and nothing was ever changed.

SONDHEIM: No, the show wrote very, very easily, but there was this severe problem. Once the solution was arrived at in Philadelphia, it wasn't too hard to write. But, as with all structural problems, it was a very difficult thing to solve. Quite often, that kind of problem has to do with loss of focus. Now, what happened in the second act of this show was that, instead of continuing to be about Rose, it suddenly became about Gypsy. This was a built-in danger, since we knew we had to deal with how the girl becomes a star. That couldn't be relegated to a minor part. What we ended up with was that Gypsy now has a ten-minute passage which is all about her, but everything else in the second act is about Rose, and the focus is still on Rose.

LAURENTS: I would like to talk about one thing I learned accidentally from that show, because I did not do it deliberately. I am terribly conscious of style and tone and consistency, and that show was totally inconsistent. The first scene is vaudeville. Then you have a musical comedy scene. Then an out-and-out farce scene. Then very tough drama. And it keeps going back and forth. It was only afterwards that I realized that I had done that. The reason why it works is that Rose is an outrageous character who's consistent in her attitude. Her attitude carries you through any kind of scene because *she* is consistent.

MCNALLY: Do you want to tell about the fight over "Little Lamb"?

SONDHEIM: Well, I think we should because it involves the Dramatists Guild.

LAURENTS: This was when we were in Philadelphia. I think Jerry was still clinging to some effort to make it more of a dancing show. At the end of "Mr. Goldstone," into this room came all of these characters who also lived in the boarding house, and they began cavorting and juggling and dancing and doing cartwheels, and that was the end of the scene. And he just cut "Little Lamb" without asking anyone.

SONDHEIM: Because "Little Lamb" was not getting a hand.

LAURENTS: It wasn't getting a hand because it came after all this juggling and dancing. Anyway, Jule asked Jerry to put "Little Lamb" back in. Jerry said no. He said, "It doesn't work. It's out." I remember sitting in the theater and Jule coming onstage—very nattily dressed, as he always is—and he came down to the footlights, and he said, "Mr. Robbins, I have spoken to the Dramatists Guild in New York, and I want to tell you I am withdrawing my entire score, as of tonight, unless 'Little Lamb' is put back." It was put back, and that was the end of that. And that's the virtue of the Dramatists Guild, and don't you forget it!

SONDHEIM: One footnote. Jerry said, "All right, Arthur, then *you* direct it." And of course Arthur later did and it was swell.

Q: Is it usual to have so much trouble with a director like Jerome Robbins?

SONDHEIM: Yes. Partially because he's so talented, and partially because directors often like to think they're playwrights.

Q: So maybe he was really wrong for the show.

SONDHEIM: No, he did a lot of terrific things, too. We're just telling the naughty ones because those make for interesting anecdotes. If we told you about a good day, it would be very . . . unusual.

Q: What about "You Gotta Have a Gimmick"?

SONDHEIM: The problem with that was that we wanted a number for the strippers, but to do that we had to justify taking four minutes out to focus on them. The solution, which I suspect was Arthur's, was it should be a lesson for Gypsy, so she would have something to learn from them. I happen to think that idea didn't quite register on the stage, but it didn't matter too much, because it went over well anyway.

In the movie—which I think is a poor movie—there is one really true and terrific moment. It is the only really good moment Natalie Wood has in it. It is a shot of her listening to them. And then you *see* Gypsy Rose Lee born. She's watching and listening as they say "You've got to have a gimmick," and you can see it ringing a bell. You can see that little shine in her eye, and you think "Oh, my God, that girl's going to be a stripper."

Q: How did you coordinate the writing of the songs and the writing of the book?

SONDHEIM: Arthur and I had a minimum of two conversations a day for a period of four months. Minimum. Sometimes we talked about trivial matters, and sometimes it was about trying to form and shape the piece. This is apart from any meetings that the three of us would have or the meetings between Jule and me.

LAURENTS: I'd read him some dialogue over the phone. We'd discuss it, and then Steve would say, "Hey, wait, there's a song there."

SONDHEIM: We'd already done one show together, and we had an obvious rapport.

Q: How can one have the opportunity to hear all the songs you cut?

SONDHEIM: Go to Jule's house for dinner.

THE FANTASTICKS

Richard Maltby Jr., Moderator
Word Baker
Rita Gardner
Tom Jones
Harvey Schmidt

RICHARD MALTBY JR.: The thing that is, to me, hugely significant, other than the fact that *The Fantasticks* is the longest-running show in the history of New York theater, is the impact of the show, how daring or innovative it was in 1960, on May 3, when it opened. Nowadays there are plenty of small musicals; they open ten or fifteen a year. There had never been a show like *The Fantasticks* in 1960. I had just gotten out of college, and I couldn't imagine a show with a cast of nine in a theater that seated 150, no matter how much people told me it was wonderful. I went mostly out of curiosity—and the explosion of that show, and how exciting it was in that small space, were absolutely new! I had never seen anything like it, and neither had anyone else. Most of the reviews said, "warm, pleasant, a little on the fey side, first act is wonderful, lets down a little in the second, you'll have a charming time." The word of mouth was not like that. The word of mouth was: "Go to see it, something special has happened!" Tom, we know you also appeared in the original production under a pseudonym, "Thomas Bruce." What was it like to write this show?

TOM JONES: Well, we were looking to find a subject for a Broadway musical. And I knew of this play by Edmond Rostand called *Les Romanesques* in a version done by a college professor, B. Iden Payne, who had done it in 1902 with Mrs. Patrick Campbell. And his was a translation done in couplets, in the French manner, called *The Fantasticks*. And for some reason that I do not now understand, we thought this would be the subject for a Broadway musical. I don't know—we didn't have any other ideas. So we worked off and on for several years, trying to make a Broadway musical out of this piece. The Rostand was a spoof of *Romeo and Juliet*, so we kept that. . . .

MALTBY: When was this?

JONES: Oh, this was in the mid-1950s. And we worked on it for a long time. And it just wouldn't work. Harvey and I had set it realistically, in the Southwest. We had two adjoining ranches. There was the typical character, an

Apache Indian, if you can believe that. We had a large chorus. And finally it just collapsed under its own weight.

HARVEY SCHMIDT: We used to talk a lot about this Rudolf Friml-type chorus constantly coming in singing and marching in place. . . .

JONES: At the time all that was collapsing, Word Baker came to us and said, "Mildred Dunnock is going to have a summer theater at Barnard College this year, and I've been invited to do three original one-acts. If you can turn that piece into a one-act with a small cast and give it to me in three weeks, I can give you a production three weeks after that." So with that, we threw out all this stuff we had been working on for three or four years—it all came out—and we started over with almost nothing except the Rostand play and lots of ideas that had been in our heads—ideas having to do with commedia dell'arte, with presentational theater, with a wonderful production of Goldoni's *Servant of Two Masters* by the Piccolo Teatro of Milan, and most particularly a book that I had been reading by Harley Granville-Barker called *On Dramatic Method*, which analyzed the techniques of Shakespeare. So with all those influences we sat down and just did a simple little story in a one-act form, and in three weeks there it was on stage.

SCHMIDT: That was in August 1959. We did it at Barnard, and there were two or three people who wanted to move it somewhere to a small off-Broadway theater. Among those people was a man named Lore Noto, who came wearing a white suit and an Italian straw hat. Since he also had his lawyer with him, we decided he was an eccentric millionaire. Having only recently arrived in New York from Texas, we were on the lookout for eccentric millionaires. He loved the show, even though the night he saw it Susan Watson, who was playing the Girl, had lost her voice, and on top of that she had injured her leg.

JONES: She had broken three ribs, I think.

SCHMIDT: So that night we had the choreographer dance alongside Susie, and I sang her songs. Since I was playing the piano onstage, I had my back to the audience, so there I was singing all her songs, and the choreographer dancing beside her, and that's the performance Lore saw! And I have always said that Lore optioned what he thought was a *very* avant garde musical. I think it showed tremendous foresight on his part.

JONES: Our eccentric millionaire—the eccentric half turned out to be true—brought his last savings to the show.

MALTBY: Then what happened?

JONES: There were three offers, and one of them wanted to pay us an option. We decided that it didn't matter how much it was, but somebody had to offer to pay us in some way, since we had been working for years and nobody had ever paid us any money. One other person wanted to do it as a one-act with *New York Scrapbook*, a little revue of our material from Julius Monk days. But the person who wanted to do a full-length and who was willing to pay a $500 option was Lore. And the other thing, a big thing, is that Lore said he would sign a contract in which he agreed that all artistic decisions would be made by Word and Harvey and myself and that he would never voice an opinion on any artistic decision unless we were hopelessly deadlocked. And that was the clincher, as you might well imagine.

MALTBY: Did he honor it?

JONES: He honored it for the first ten years anyway; that's fair enough.

MALTBY: Then you began to extend it from a one-act to a full-length show?

JONES: Well, we had taken the full-length idea from the Rostand play and put it into a one-act. The one-act was just like the full-length thing squeezed together. Except that there are places—it was never intended that the old actors would be in the second act. It became obligatory, in a sense, for form, that they be there.

SCHMIDT: We were very concerned with things like symmetry. If they had a scene in the first act, they had to have one in the second. If you had a song in the first act, you had to have one in the second.

JONES: And we borrowed symmetry from every place; there are lots of stolen lines and stolen images. The moon in the first act, and the sun—again, the symmetrical matching was very much inspired by a production at Stratford of *The Winter's Tale* which John Houseman had done.

MALTBY: So then you took from the summer until the spring to do the second act?

JONES: Well, no, we did that too fast, really. We would work a lot longer and harder if we were doing it today. What we did was get it done and then spend four months doing almost nightly backers' auditions, trying to raise the $15,000 necessary. We couldn't. A lot of people would drop off their aged mothers or their kids. We were like babysitters. We would do our show, and they would say "Thank you" and leave, and so again the next night. . . .

MALTBY: To me, the truly amazing part of that story is that you threw out a previously conceived show and three weeks later had the one-act. Did you then do a great deal of work during three weeks of rehearsal at Barnard?

JONES: No, we didn't rewrite a word, I believe.

WORD BAKER: And there wasn't much rewriting after that, except in additional songs, changing one song from the other. . . .

SCHMIDT: When we expanded it.

MALTBY: And how much of the score was written during that three-week period?

SCHMIDT: I would say about 75 percent of it. It was very exhilarating for us to throw out this huge thing that kept collapsing under its own weight. Once we had the summons from Word, it was like a harmless exercise where we had nothing to lose. And it was suddenly fun, after working on it so big, to do it as tiny as we could. That was the thrilling thing, just to hone away at it.

MALTBY: Do you think part of it was that you didn't have a great deal of time to worry over it, that you went with the idea cleanly from beginning to end?

JONES: I think that can be said to be true. It's funny . . . all those years something built up; there are substrata of perceptions and knowledge that surfaced then, that made themselves known. There had been four years of *something* happening. We had spent years building up to making a statement having to do with a kind of theater that we felt passionately about, and this became the device, after all those years of trying to do a quasi-Rodgers-and-Hammerstein version.

I knew we wanted to have a narrator, for example, because that was part of our vision of the theater. Stanislavsky said a great thing about this method, which is that you may give a great performance without it, but if you don't have the method to fall back on when the great performance isn't happening, then things are very bad. At this point, I would much rather write a piece fifty times. You love it if it comes out perfect the first time, but I am very suspicious of depending upon a thing coming out the first time. I feel better about the ability to go back and work again and work again without losing the shape of the piece.

MALTBY: But one of the things that I found remarkable is that there isn't a wasted moment. Every single instant of the show is moving the action forward. It has exactly the immediacy of someone telling a story. You step sentence by sentence—only this sentence is a song, and by the time you have finished the song you are at the next point. The story is as spare and concentrated as any piece that has ever been written.

JONES: The reason for that—if I may digress for just a second—the influence for me, myself, is more Shakespeare, as the great teacher, than Rodgers and Hammerstein, Cole Porter, the Spewacks or anybody else. That's the kind of theater I like. Not just Shakespeare; it's also the Greeks, Thornton Wilder—a theater that is nonrealistic, presentational. Having a narrator, so you can "cut through" the story; if you want to go some place you can just go there and spend your time on what matters. And the use of language, which is the other big thing: the theater is ultimately a place for language and music, and there is no competition for it in our time. The films do wonderful things, but they do *different* things. And television does a different thing. . . .

MALTBY: But what we are really talking about is a passionate commitment to *a kind* of theater. We're saying a certain kind of event in the theater is concentrated and thrilling.

JONES: Beyond that, the real metaphor underlying *The Fantasticks*, even underlying its romanticism, has to do with seasonal festivals and their relationship to drama and religion. Shaw's introduction to *Androcles and the Lion* knocked me out when I was in college. Then Christopher Fry was an enormous influence on us—the whole linguistic orgy that he reintroduced to the theater, ever so briefly—and I read that he was writing four plays, one for each of the seasons. So I began to get caught up very much in seasonal things, even at Julius Monk's, writing seasonal comedy sketches. And together Word, Harvey and myself were doing a revue called *Portfolio Revue* and, again, doing different things for each of the seasons. So a very conscious choice was made to take a seasonal progression in *The Fantasticks* related to John Barleycorn and the reaping of the wheat.

MALTBY: The other thing that is so stunning is that when you walk into the theater, you cannot imagine that a show could take place there. There's a piano and a harp and about six feet of space, and in this tiny space, once the confetti is thrown, so much magic takes place. How did the style of the show develop?

BAKER: That was stolen. In *Ring Round the Moon* there's a scene where they tear up the money and throw it up in the air. I thought it was the prettiest thing I had ever seen. The space, the stage, is Shakespearean. We used to spend hours talking about "breaking through the proscenium" and getting an "open stage." We didn't know what we were talking about, but we knew what we wanted to get away from.

JONES: That was very much related to our teacher, B. Iden Payne. He directed Shakespearean productions. In addition to influencing us, he gave Helen Hayes her first Broadway show, gave John Barrymore his first serious role in Galsworthy's *Justice.* . . .

MALTBY: There are other startling things. I remember being surprised when I saw that the actors didn't leave the stage.

BAKER: That had simply to do with there being no place they could go off the stage.

SCHMIDT: A lot of what is now considered to be the "style" of *The Fantasticks* had to do with the limitations of that theater. We didn't want that theater. It was the only one we could get, and although the show was already leaning in a certain direction, the restrictions of the space carried it even further. In the Barnard version, that didn't happen; they went offstage.

BAKER: I was just there doing rehearsal the other day, and somebody went off, and I said, "Where are you going?" And he said, "Well, I go off here." And I said, "No, you don't." "But I'm not doing anything." "Well, I don't care. Sit down."

MALTBY: Rita Gardner appeared as The Girl in the original production. Did you see it at Barnard, Rita?

RITA GARDNER: No, I think I was the last one to be cast. As a matter of fact, I was told much later on that they didn't want me.

BAKER: No, that's not right.

GARDNER: I was told that.

SCHMIDT: I wanted you when I heard you sing.

GARDNER: I came to audition because I talked to Lore Noto, and he said, "It's already been cast pretty much, but come anyway, because I like the way you speak on the phone." I thought, "What a nice man." And I went and heard Tom and Harvey singing the songs, because the audition took place in Harvey's apartment on the West Side. I heard Tom banging on a drum, and people were running in and out, and I thought, "I don't think I like this." And I was going to leave. Lore stopped me. "You're Rita Gardner," and I said, "Yes," and he said, "Well, you're next." I was very frightened, because they looked weird to me.

SCHMIDT: You sang "Over the Rainbow."

GARDNER: It was the only song I knew. I was studying to be an opera singer.

SCHMIDT: What I remember loving about your voice, and the way I had always envisioned the part, was that there was no break between chest and head; there's a lot of coloratura in it, and Rita was one of the few girls we saw at the time who had it.

BAKER: We had sworn that we would audition anybody who wanted to be seen. Months we auditioned, and it was a snowy, dreadful day. Harvey's place has this little foyer in it where I found sitting this little bedraggled urchin, and I could have decided, "It's such a terrible day, I should tell her to go home, that we are not going to cast her." But all that went through my mind was, "No, we said we would see anybody, so I can't do that. We have to stick to it." And that was Rita Gardner.

JONES: Another thing that happened to influence all of us: we had three sets of lovers. It was coming down to balancing the lovers, and by coincidence Rita and Kenny Nelson had just done a show together.

SCHMIDT: They had such a warm feeling of rapport.

BAKER: Rita, we called you back three or four times because of these combinations.

GARDNER: When you try so hard to get a role, you work so hard on the scenes and the songs, and you are so tense, you never get the part. I just walked in, really, almost off the street. I came back each time to audition thinking, "Oh, these funny people. Very nice."

MALTBY: When you confronted the material for the first time, did it seem like a foreign country?

GARDNER: When I finally got the script, my husband read it, and he said, "You are doing this? I don't like this. This is a strange piece." And I said, "I think it's wonderful, and it's going to run forever." Then the rehearsal period was so exciting; I would come home so high.

MALTBY: Why?

GARDNER: I knew that the work was wonderful, and the score was beautiful. The people involved were bringing so much to it. We were very free. There was no tension. Most often in a working period there is, of course, but here, we could say, "Let's try this," and it was tried.

MALTBY: What was the nature of the changes after the Barnard production?

BAKER: The production at Barnard was awfully cute.

JONES: The Barnard production had much more of the feeling of a short play called *Aria Da Capo*, by Edna St. Vincent Millay. I happen to like the play, but there was a kind of Pierrot archness; it was verging on being campy. It wasn't as spare at Barnard.

GARDNER: In rehearsals we put in a lot of stuff, and Word would say "Do whatever you want, and I'll pare it down. We'll make it simple." We could never change lines, though.

JONES: The only person who was allowed to do that was "Thomas Bruce."

GARDNER: But even in the musical area, the conductor and Harvey let us try things.

MALTBY: Did you change the score because of the presence of those voices?

SCHMIDT: Not a lot, but we did make some changes. For instance, once Jerry Orbach was cast, we took what had been a rape speech in the Barnard production (because he was so marvelous we wanted to give him more to do musically) and turned it into "The Rape Song." And that was written fairly close to the opening. Then where "They Were You" is now, we had a song called "I Have Acted Like a Fool," which was more dramatic in a sense, but it didn't give you very much emotionally. We felt a simple, touching moment would be nicer.

MALTBY: What was the content of "I Have Acted Like a Fool"?

SCHMIDT: Kind of a conversational song. He would sing, "I have acted like a fool," and she would say, "I know. Me too," and back and forth like that.

MALTBY: It sounds like you replaced a very book-oriented song with an emotional, general song.

JONES: Also, somebody said, "Where's the ballad?" And we thought, "Well, gee, we had better put a ballad in Act Two," so we also wanted something very, very simple and melodic and pretty.

MALTBY: What always struck me about that song was that the story hasn't resolved itself when the song begins—an almost irrelevant emotional song—and then when the song is finished, the story has resolved itself. I would like to think that was calculated right from the beginning.

JONES: Well, we knew that had to happen, so I guess in that way it was calculated. But we didn't set out to do that specifically; it was a music song first. Harvey came out with this ballad, so then I listened and I thought, "What could be the title of that?" and tried different ones, and "They Were You" seemed good. And I worked backward from that.

MALTBY: I'm stunned to hear that "The Rape Song" was written in rehearsal, because it seems like you would construct the first act around that moment. It is the explosion. Everything has been building toward it.

JONES: Yes, if we had been more knowledgeable about things, we probably would have done it in that way for those reasons. We were knowledgeable about some things, but not much about the structure of musicals, actually. A lot of the show was done cerebrally for me, an awful lot of it, but not with a knowledge of the musical form. I was cerebral in experimenting. I had read Harley Granville-Barker, as I mentioned, and he talked about Shakespeare's taking a key image and glueing his plays together by repetition and by working in—as for example he did in *Macbeth*—darkness images. Almost all the images in *Macbeth* are related to darkness, and it's a conscious effort. So having begun with that idea of seasonal change, I was trying to see if I couldn't work in lots of nature images and vegetation images to glue the thing together. When in doubt, put in a vegetation image.

MALTBY: The inside of a leaf.

JONES: The inside of a leaf or the planting of a radish or December snow; the change of seasons. A month goes by; it's a little bit colder. . . . I tried to give the piece a fabric of imagery without being obvious. That was very consciously done. Later on, we did *Celebration*, and we did it so much we pounded it to death. And being a really lousy plot writer—which I really am, you know; I am not a native storyteller. I don't know why I am spending my whole life trying to do original things—anyway, we didn't have a story to lean on. We had interesting characters, interesting metaphors, but we didn't have a simple, clear, clean plot like *The Fantasticks*, like the Rostand play, that we could feel free to do things with as long as we always went back to it or held on to it.

MALTBY: The young lovers in *Fantasticks* could easily have become clichés, and one of the reasons they didn't was that their expression had that peculiar imagery. When he sings, "You are the microscopic inside of a leaf," you know that that's a unique boy.

BAKER: Tom never told us this cerebral part of it. I never heard this before. He never told us to act it or do anything about it. We didn't *act* "seasons."

JONES: No, it was just me and the writing. You know, that great book, *Directors on Directing*—my favorite part in it is Elia Kazan's notes on *Streetcar*, which are simply wonderful. He's coming up with these incredible cerebral images, and he keeps saying, "Don't tell Brando, don't tell Brando." He's stressing that his whole art as a director was *not* to tell them what he knew. I mean, instead of saying to Brando that Stanley still wants a tit to suck on, he said, "Give Marlon a beer bottle. Don't tell him why, just give him a beer bottle." *Instead* of telling him, "You are still in an infantile state, still after immediate gratification." As a playwright, you have your own mysteries to deal with, as a director does. Actors each have their own mysteries. Emotional, intellectual, whatever, I don't think one should give away one's mysteries.

MALTBY: What was the original response, and how did you feel when the show first opened?

JONES: Well, the first response was we thought we were going to die. I thought I was going to die.

MALTBY: Not the show.

JONES: I thought the show was going to die, and I thought it was going to kill me. I had been working in that bookshop so many years. . . .

BAKER: Let's go back to the first preview, the midnight preview. That was wonderful.

JONES: Oh boy, right! At a midnight matinee for actors, and in the week of previews, there was such an electricity! Then, opening night, it was so tense, and *I* was so tense, and one of the critics was there with a date who created a disturbance, who had to be taken across the stage (because there was no exit from that side of the house). She was saying, "What's this thing about?!" and meanwhile, as "Thomas Bruce," I'm playing this part, I'm waiting to go on, my whole life is in the balance, and I'm crouched over in a darkened box along with another actor, and I hear this woman yelling.

Anyway, when the first notices were read to Word or Kenny, I'll never forget somebody crying, and I got into a cab and couldn't make it across Central Park, I just got out of the cab and vomited my way through Central Park. And I went home and thought I was going to die, really. The next day, I managed to get up by noon and eat something, which was very hard to do, I was so sick and hung over. And the afternoon papers were good. The second night, the backers, who had read those not-good notices, were there, and I will never forget that performance. That was hard work.

GARDNER: There was nobody in the house.

JONES: Just a few unhappy backers. Most of them wanted Lore to close the show. It was Thursday night, and the press agent said, "Close it on Sunday." And Lore, eccentric millionaire that he was—he may be a millionaire now, for all I know—he said, "No way," because this had taken the last of his money. In savings, he had $3,000. That was it. He had quit his job, he had burned all his bridges—it committed him, you know. And so we survived.

There were three little girls—remember that?—who lived next door, and *they* would come. We would have audiences of ten, fifteen, twenty people and always these three little sisters. They would wear white gloves and sit in the first row. It was such a comfort to see them, and they knew just when to applaud.

MALTBY: So how long did it take to catch on?

GARDNER: We went to the John Drew Theater and did it there for a week, and a lot of theater people saw it. And somehow the word-of-mouth was so incredible that when we came back, it sold out.

JONES: There were two things: the theater people spread the word, and the *Times* gave us a picture on a Sunday. We ran a big ad. Then we actually started doing some business. There would be twenty theater people at a show, but they would be Richard Rodgers, Jerome Robbins. . . .

SCHMIDT: Cheryl Crawford came down and brought a lot of people into the theater. She called at least a hundred people and sent them down.

JONES: So did Anne Bancroft. Every night, it was somebody like that.

MALTBY: Harvey, was there any kind of philosophical base to the score?

SCHMIDT: For Act One, which is by moonlight, I thought of the music as lush and romantic and made what I consider references to music of earlier periods. I'm not sure that after going through my Texas-German persona they are that obvious, but at least I worked in those terms. There are hints of early Italian street music in the overture, for instance, and operetta clichés in some of the duets.

In Act Two, which is by sunlight and where they are more disillusioned, I wanted a more biting contemporary tone. And that's where most of the strong, dissonant jazz starts up, when the tableau is breaking apart; you hear those dissonant chords right at the top of the act. Most of Act Two is modern and abrasive, until you get to "They Were You" at the end of the reprise of "Try to Remember." Even though the score makes eclectic use of this grab-bag of various musical styles to match the playing around with different theatrical styles onstage, I still wanted it to be sort of a bouncy Broadway score, too.

MALTBY: How did you come up with the instrumentation?

SCHMIDT: For that I have to give credit to Julian Stein. When I was trying to find a musical director, I was just going to use two pianos. I was interviewing, and I had narrowed it down to two people, Julian and one other person, and I really couldn't decide between them. Then Julian said, "You know, I've been thinking, instead of the two pianos, a lot of this would be great on the harp. It's very much like harp music." I thought it was a fabulous idea, because I love harps, and also it seemed basically interesting for a tiny theater. And so the musical director was Julian from then on. It was, I think, a brilliant contribution to the show.

MALTBY: It also seems a simple way of getting a tremendous sound.

SCHMIDT: The harp is very evocative, too, and it often makes you think that you are hearing things you are not. Particularly in combination with the piano, because when you do bass lines on the piano, it no longer sounds like a piano with the harp. There's that feeling sitting in the theater that the sound is just all over the place. It's exploding out of that little space.

JONES: The theater is a little too small for my taste, to tell you the honest truth. I feel a little claustrophobic there. It has worked out O.K., to say the least, but for me, ideally, a bigger house is better.

MALTBY: If you had to say what you are most pleased with, what would you say?

JONES: That's a hard question. It was a lucky combination of elements at the right time. The cross-pollination was good, and it made a fruitful tree, but I can't say that we did it right. It *worked out* right. All the metaphors, all the dissonant chords we were going after—it can all go down the drain if you are not lucky in your group effort. And we were lucky. At all levels, everybody came together and made it happen.

BAKER: I would agree with that and add to it that we didn't think we were doing avant garde or anything with a mission. We just did what we thought of at the time.

SCHMIDT: What we liked, what we wished we could see on the stage.

BAKER: There wasn't any question about its being philosophically this or that. It just worked or it didn't.

GARDNER: And no tremendous egos. Somebody would say, "Let's try this," and nobody said, "Oh, no." Nobody was the star.

JONES: In a way, we had nothing to lose, except our lives.

Q: Did you get any film offers?

JONES: We have had twenty years of negotiating, and we have never made the film deal. But we have certainly met some colorful people.

SCHMIDT: It's a difficult thing to transfer to film. It is so written for the stage; it celebrates stage techniques. We finally have done a screen play ourselves which we think could work, and there is some interest in it at the moment. So we hope that it will happen some time.

JONES: It was done on television in 1963, I believe, a Hallmark version that was about fifty minutes long. It was essentially something quite different, because they had to cut it so much. It had some good people, I must say. John Davidson—it was his first television show—and Susie Watson. And it also had Bert Lahr and Stanley Holloway as the fathers, which is perfect. Except that because of the compression of time and the size of those parts, they made them into old actors, which is a deviate idea, really.

Q: Wasn't there ever the temptation, and if so how did you resist it, to move into a larger theater or produce it on Broadway?

JONES: There were such offers. The Shuberts came in the second or third year and offered us a Broadway house. We just didn't feel—I don't know, it just didn't seem right.

SCHMIDT: It didn't seem like it would work.

Q: How long did most of the cast stay with you?

BAKER: It is incredible how long. They averaged out about one person per part per year. People seem to stay for at least a year, which is great.

JONES: Some of them stayed ten years, off and on.

GARDNER: I was in it about nine months, I think; I got a lot of offers after that. I did a movie, and a musical after that. It started my career.

JONES: One of the reasons people stay with the show, both musicians and actors, is that it is very difficult to do, and therefore it isn't boring. In a sense, it's always just beyond you to do it right. Of course, there are wretched, wretched productions all over the world in which people are so cute that I would hate the show if I only knew it through those productions. The singing is very demanding. Actors, like all creative people, like to be challenged.

BAKER: It is so constituted that you cannot cheat; you have to do it every time. You can't walk through it.

JONES: You can't count on getting your laughs or whatever.

SCHMIDT: The opening twenty minutes are difficult to pull off. Those solo speeches can just go down the drain.

JONES: It's as if the show is always eluding you; an actor knows there are twelve different "colors" that can be hit in one of those speeches. You start getting them, and then one will elude you, and it's challenging.

Q: In the score, why was the accompaniment revised some eight years later?

SCHMIDT: Well, I spent many years collecting a list of sections of the score that people found unneccessarily complicated to play or perform. I am not a trained musician; I never planned to be a musician. I met Tom at school, and we started writing shows together. We put the music down the best way we could, with a transcriber notating it exactly the way I played it, which is the way Julian and the harpist also played it. But it was complicated for most pianists, unneccessarily so. I tried to collect the problem areas and then make it slightly more accessible for people. I put a lot of time into it. I am pleased with the revision; I think it's better and still has the qualities that were innate originally.

MALTBY: How much did the songs contribute to your success? "Try to Remember" was a big hit.

SCHMIDT: "Try to Remember" became a standard, but it hadn't made a big splash initially. Once Harry Belafonte and, particularly, Ed Ames had recorded it, there were a lot of recordings.

JONES: After three or four years, after the television show, we got the first recording, and that did well. And, suddenly, in about the fourth year, we began to sell out our 150 seats. And then we sold out for many, many years, so much so that after a number of years, I went down and saw the "Sorry, this performance is sold out" sign was *not* up, and I thought, "This is the end."

JONES: We never knew that *The Fantasticks* was a hit for about five years, and that's the God's truth. We didn't have any grand expectations.

Eventually, we began to be honored for survival. There was never a thing like a "hit." I have never had a show where I felt after the cast party I could tip the cab driver five dollars with a clear conscience. I've never known what tomorrow was going to bring. Even with Mary Martin and Robert Preston and Gower Champion and David Merrick doing *I Do! I Do!*, when the notices came in, we didn't know. We didn't have the horrible problem of people who have huge hits. But now we are ready to handle that problem. It's been a long preparation and we're ready. I want to have that problem.

WHO'S AFRAID OF VIRGINIA WOOLF?

Terrence McNally, Moderator
Richard Barr
George Grizzard
Uta Hagen
Alan Schneider

TERRENCE MCNALLY: This *Who's Afraid of Virginia Woolf?* panel is unique in a Dramatists Guild symposium because the author is missing—Edward Albee phoned this afternoon to send his great regrets that he is much too ill to attend.* Present, however, are Richard Barr, the play's producer (if I gave you all their credits we'd be here for a very long time, but they have one credit in common, *Virginia Woolf,* and for that alone they all have an important place in the American theater); Alan Schneider, the director; Uta Hagen, who created the role of Martha; and George Grizzard, who created the role of Nick.

RICHARD BARR: I was the co-producer. Clinton Wilder is not here, but he was my partner in this venture.

MCNALLY: Let me read from John McClain's October 13, 1962, review in the New York *Journal-American:* "The opening Saturday night of Edward Albee's *Who's Afraid of Virginia Woolf?* at the Billy Rose Theater was the most enthusiastic outing in several semesters. From almost the first entrance there was the indefinable and infallible aura of success creeping from the stage through the audience. This is a big one."

Let's start with the experience of opening night. There was quite a reaction from the audience. How did you feel, Uta, can you remember what it was like?

UTA HAGEN: I haven't the vaguest recollection. I remember the previews after a very short rehearsal period, by neccessity short. I remember being in a kind of haze and backbreaking work. From the first time I read the first act I felt that it was going to be a huge success. I felt that success all the way through.

* Some of Edward Albee's thoughts about this play and other subjects were expressed later in conversation with Terrence McNally in a Dramatists Guild session recorded and presented in Part Two of this volume.

GEORGE GRIZZARD: I remember it was raining.

MCNALLY: The critics said there was a very palpable sensation in the air that night.

ALAN SCHNEIDER: I remember the first preview, the first audience. We knew that they liked it, that it was exciting. My experience on opening night was exactly the opposite of Uta's—it was the most exciting night I've ever had in the theater, before or since. As I was going to see somebody backstage, a fellow with a worried look was saying to somebody else with a worried look, "I wish I could get rid of my investment." I was wishing I had the money to relieve him of it. I knew from the first preview audience (we had five invitational and five paid previews) that we had something very exciting.

BARR: Absolutely correct. We broke precedent by inviting actors and everyone else in the theater who wished to come, people who usually you don't want anywhere near your show until it's opened and the critics have had their say. We did the opposite, and it helped us find a few necessary changes. Very, very few were made in either the text or the performances, which were pretty damn good from the beginning. It was obvious from the first preview with that marvelous audience of actors that we had something interesting and original. As a matter of fact, it was the first time that I came to rehearsals. We have a solid rule that we stay out of the theater until the director says, "I think maybe you can come in and take a look at the show."

Though we didn't go out of town, we had the set about ten days after we started rehearsing, so while we did change some furniture here and there, the actors were on the stage with the set and the general blocking and the furniture, and to a great extent the lighting, and in some cases the costumes.

SCHNEIDER: And the props.

HAGEN: To me, that was not only precedent-setting, I have never heard of anything like it since. We started rehearsals with a much longer play than we opened with. To start a play of that length and that difficulty *without* the props and scenery, we would have had to rehearse eight weeks longer. To me, this was one of the unique experiences of my entire life in the theater, starting with the things that are food for the play being alive on the stage—every little ice cube, every little clinky glass. I found this the most useful circumstance of any production I've ever been in.

BARR: You know where we learned that, Uta? Off Broadway, where you can move into the theater without paying very much rent for it—so we always began our plays that way, building the set first and then putting the actors on the stage. We thought, "Why not do this when we move uptown?" Uta's evaluation of what happened is absolutely accurate. It was very helpful. And I persuaded Hal Prince to do *Sweeney Todd* that way.

MCNALLY: You opened on a Saturday night—very unusual even then, when there were no TV critics. It's bad enough to wait four or five hours for reviews, but you were waiting thirty-six hours. How did you all survive that long, long period with no response from the critics—even though the audience cheered its head off?

BARR: Part of our off-Broadway policy was never to have opening night parties, and we didn't have one in this case. We felt that when we finally got the reviews we would have to make whatever decision was necessary as quickly as possible, to get into the papers as fast as we could. So we sat at Clinton Wilder's house on Sunday waiting for the notices. The Sunday papers didn't come until late, but we could get through to one or two papers because we had spies.

While we were still waiting for the first word, Billy Rose called up and asked, "Where are you all?" (our play was in his Billy Rose Theater, later the Nederlander) and "Can I come over?" We said yes, and he came by at just about the time our press agent, Howard Atlee, had gotten through to the *Daily News* and was about to have the review read to him over the phone. I said, "Billy, you used to be the champion shorthand taker of the world. Get on the phone and do your job." So Billy sat down and took down in shorthand this John Chapman review, which began with "For dirty-minded females only." That was the first thing we heard about *Virginia Woolf,* and the second from Robert Coleman of the *Mirror* was even worse: "No red-blooded American would bring his wife to this shocking play."

At that time I quit, I left the house, I started walking around the block with Edward. I remember that the expression on Billy Rose's face in repose was not exactly conducive to laughter as he was writing down reviews that were far from positive. For the rest of my life I will thank Edward for remaining calm. He said, "Let's wait for the real reviews." He meant the respectable morning papers, and he really kept us going there for a while. Later on I fell asleep, and Edward woke me up with, "Do you want to hear Walter Kerr?" I said, "Should I?" and he said, "Yes." But Kerr's review, if you remember, was respectful but scarcely a rave.

GRIZZARD: He had really been affected by Edward's language, he used words in his review that were Albee-like words. He called it "a young couple stopping by for a nightmare," taking place in a living room "where they play war games."

HAGEN: Honest to God, I don't read reviews, so all this is new to me. All I want to know is, are we going to run or are we going to close? All I remember about opening night is, I knew we were going to run.

GRIZZARD: I remember an opening night party.

BARR: No. It may be that some of the cast and their friends had a party, but we didn't give one.

HAGEN: We went upstairs at Sardi's and I gave the party.

MCNALLY: All the reviews gave away the secret of the play. Did that bother you? After I saw a preview I thought it was very important not to tell anyone that it was about a couple with an imaginary child. Did you think that giving it away might be a problem?

BARR: No, and I'll tell you why. About a week after we opened and were an enormous success, I was standing in front of the theater while two ladies came out to get into their chauffeur-driven limousine. I overheard them saying, "Well, you know, I like the play very much indeed, but why did they call the wolf Virginia?"

HAGEN: Saul Bellow was in the audience and noticed that two people who were drunk and boisterous at the beginning got quieter and quieter as the play progressed. At the end, as they got up and walked by, Bellow overheard one say to the other, "Whose kid was it?"

SCHNEIDER: So you see, it didn't bother us very much, it didn't matter.

BARR: Reviewers always give something away, usually the best lines. But it didn't bother us about the child, because that is not what the play is about.

MCNALLY: I'd like to ask the actors if they were familiar with Edward's work prior to this, his first full-length play.

HAGEN: I knew *The Zoo Story* and *The American Dream*. I had the reputation of being unbelievably choosy. I don't mean this to be true without exception, but mostly I can tell within ten minutes whether a play is going to interest me. I wonder how many playwrights know that. It's like an actor's audition; when I audition I can tell within thirty seconds whether there's going to be interest in me or not. In the first four pages of the script, I knew I wanted to play *Virginia Woolf*.

MCNALLY: As the critics said, there was that sense of immediacy.

HAGEN: Not in terms of being sensational, but in setting a relationship and a pace. Edward has a tremendous ear for language. His sentences are sometimes two words, incomplete, but you knew where it was going, and it was meat to me. The language itself was spellbinding.

GRIZZARD: I was driving from Hollywood to San Francisco for the weekend, and I stopped by Palo Alto, where Alan was teaching. He asked me, "Do you want to read a play?" and I said, "No." I was on holiday—but I read a little bit, then I would go somewhere, and then I read a little bit more, and I felt about it exactly as I feel today: it's an absolutely brilliant play and not a very good part. I had been cast as Hamlet for the opening of the Guthrie Theater, but I decided I would love to do *Virginia Woolf* if they would let me out after three months to go to Minnesota, and they agreed.

Uta invited Edward and me out to her place at the beach, and we read the play—Edward read George and Honey and we read our parts. It was a wonderful reading. The next morning we took a walk along the beach, and Edward could identify every shell. I was really impressed, and I thought, "I'll stick with him and I'll learn something."

A major problem for me with my role of Nick was staying there in Martha and George's house. I couldn't believe that anyone would stay there and put up with the behavior that was forced upon him. I asked at least three times a day, "Why don't I take my wife and leave?" and Alan would answer, "Why doesn't Hamlet kill the King?"

I knew very little about teaching in a university. I didn't understand tenure; I didn't understand that Nick had better behave himself or he was out on his ear. I thought any man with integrity would just say, "Listen, lady, go shove it," and take his wife and leave. I couldn't believe he would stay and put up with this behavior.

MCNALLY: None of the critics mentioned why Nick and Honey don't leave the house. It's never been an issue.

GRIZZARD: But it was very difficult for me as an actor to rehearse.

MCNALLY: Maybe it had something to do with unity of time and place, because the audience doesn't question it.

SCHNEIDER: The actors make the audience accept it.

MCNALLY: Uta, did you have any problems with Martha?

HAGEN: I always have problems with any part I play, because the difficulty to me as an actress is to find an identification with each psychological move so that it's me up there.

MCNALLY: The reviews refer to Martha in a lot of unpleasant terms like "harridan" and "witch." Were you at all worried about her being too unsympathetic?

HAGEN: Oh, no. I don't know anybody with the most negative and vicious behavior who considers him or herself to be vicious or evil or, in the case of Martha, pardon the expression, ballbreaking. We behave badly, but we justify it when we feel that something has been done to *us*. I found Martha to be a damaged woman who was damaging back. I had no trouble justifying her or worrying whether she was evil.

MCNALLY: The critics in 1962 treated her as though they'd never seen a woman like this on the stage, and they all mention the language—but I think it's accurate to say that if one looks at the play very carefully one will find very few four-letter words in it.

HAGEN: In London, we still had the Lord Chamberlain saying what we could or couldn't say. Out of a number of "Jesus Christs" we were allowed three. I thought it wonderful that we were allowed some and not others. We were allowed to say "hump the hostess" because "hump" is in Shakespeare. We were not allowed to say "screw you" because that was dirty.

MCNALLY: "Screw" is in Shakespeare.

HAGEN: Not in the same way it was used here. And then Arthur Hill's character of George has a line about little slicing operations on the underside of the scrotum. He was not allowed to say "scrotum." The Lord Chamberlain suggested (in his British accent) that Arthur say "on the underside of his privacies" instead. Arthur got that out one night in London, turned pale, started to shake and said, "I am never going to say that again, that's just awful."

SCHNEIDER: The Lord Chamberlain had six or seven pages of deletions from the script. We got him down to a page and a half, but one line he wouldn't budge on was, "She was his right ball." We could say, "She was his right testicle," or "She was his right nut"—which struck me as an interesting improvement—but we couldn't say "right ball." We reached an impasse with the British Empire at that point, and I must give Edward credit for the solution. He remembered an old Southern expression, "right bawl," which means a real good cry. We changed the spelling in the script, and it was then O.K. with the Lord Chamberlain. This shows you the influence of form over content.

HAGEN: The very first entrance line, "Jesus H. Christ," was not allowed. As a joke, Edward changed it to "Mary H. Magdalen," and it was accepted. On opening night in London, after having played it in New York for a year, I rushed on the stage very nervous and said, "Jesus H. Magdalen."

BARR: When Alan and I read the script in my kitchen, there were quite a number of four-letter and even twelve-letter words. Four-letter words had been used on rare occasions off Broadway, but never on. I said to Edward, "I'll tell you what I'll do, I'll bring one 'fuck' uptown." But he got them all out of the script, every one.

MCNALLY: Am I right in remembering a Sunday morning television program with a little excerpt from the play, with an entirely different cast?

SCHNEIDER: Originally, the first scene with George and Martha, a scene of about ten or twelve pages, was written for a program called "Playwright at Work" on Channel Thirteen. Shepperd Strudwick and Peg Feury played George and Martha, and in fact the two other characters named Honey and Dear never got into the scene, they were only talked about. That was a year before the rest of the play was written.

I first read the play, all three acts, in Richard Barr's kitchen, with Richard reading the manuscript and passing it along page by page to me. He would get ahead of me, or behind me, because we didn't read at quite the same rate. We read three acts over a couple of hours. I felt as though I'd been hit over the head with a great big granite boulder—not because of the length of the script, but because of the size of the emotions.

MCNALLY: Were there cuts made in *Virginia Woolf* because of language or taste? Surely in 1962 it was shocking a lot of people.

SCHNEIDER: We made a lot of cuts, but not because of taste, as I remember. There was a whole scene in the third act we took out because it was redundant; and we changed the ending of the second act.

MCNALLY: You cut during rehearsal?

HAGEN: No, after we opened.

SCHNEIDER: We cut during previews.

HAGEN: It was almost a four-hour play when we started.

SCHNEIDER: It was three and a half when we opened, after two and a half weeks' rehearsal. It was like playing summer stock. There was a wonderful speech that was cut out: Arthur Hill's summation of what the evening had been about. I remember Edward saying, "We don't need that."

GRIZZARD: I sent Edward a wire on opening night saying, "Good luck, dot, dot, dot," because I never finished a sentence in the play. My character would say, "Well, I think, uh . . ." and then it would be dot, dot, dot. I had a couple of wonderful speeches, but they didn't end on periods, they ended on dots.

MCNALLY: When you were reading the script for the first time, did the plot device of the child jar you? Did you question it? Or did it seem inevitable and part of the play?

SCHNEIDER: If there's criticism of *Virginia Woolf*, it's always the same: that the characters tend to be "unsympathetic" and that the device of the child is not convincing but seems dragged in, unnecessary.

MCNALLY: Did *you* ever have trouble with the child, or did it seem absolutely as it should be?

SCHNEIDER: I had no trouble with the child that I remember.

HAGEN: Yes, you did. I said to you over and over again, from the first time we met at Sardi's for lunch, that I felt very strongly that it was fabulous. I didn't think of it as a device at all. I asked you, "How do you want to use the child, what do you think it represents?" and you said, "I don't know—I haven't made up my mind." You made up your mind after we opened, but not before. And I asked Edward, "How do you want to use the child?" and he said, "I don't care. However you want."

My questions remained *totally* unanswered, and I made up my own mind. Then after we opened I was given a message that Alan wanted me to know that he had *now* decided what the child means. I totally rejected what I was told, so I won't quote Alan's message.

MCNALLY: Well, how *did* you deal with the child?

HAGEN: That it was a conscious device that my husband and I had planned very early in our marriage; that it had become a reality to us, to the point where I would have liked to see toys on the stage.

SCHNEIDER: The first question I asked Edward was, "Are there toys on the stage?" Edward replied, "Of course not. The characters would be insane." But I don't argue with Uta at all. The child was a conscious, rational decision and became a need, an obsession in their lives, but they are not insane.

HAGEN: Oh, no.

SCHNEIDER: So I don't think a toy would have made any difference. It would not have made them seem any more insane than the way in which they were using the child now.

MCNALLY: Richard, how did you relate to the child?

BARR: The work piece for *Virginia Woolf* was *The Death of Bessie Smith*, whose characters have illusions which give them a reality. For example, the nurse in *Bessie Smith* has an illusion which gives her a reality, but she is conscious of the fact that it is an illusion and she has created it. The child in *Virginia Woolf* never bothered me because we had already discussed the whole problem with *Bessie Smith* (we didn't do that play, at first, because in my opinion it didn't work the way it should). So when I read *Virginia Woolf* I had no problem with it from that point of view.

GRIZZARD: It certainly worked for me. It was absolutely devastating. When my character, Nick, caught on, he had three very big lines of "Jesus Christ, I think I understand." Supposedly, if I did it right, it built (one night I heard somebody say, "I wish I did"). I loved it. I totally disagree with the reviews that said the third act was too minor for the first two acts. The child was a wonderful device, heartbreaking, frightening, electrifying, and I always bought it a hundred percent.

MCNALLY: We're much more familiar now with sexual fantasies, they're so much a part of our culture. Edward was far ahead of his time. People didn't talk about sexual fantasies, but now they do, and there are books. People may not have thought about that aspect of the play as a sexual fantasy, but it was in fact, and perhaps that's why some of them rejected that aspect.

George, your character was branded in some of the reviews as an especially contemptible person. How did you deal with this?

GRIZZARD: Gee, I thought I was cute as hell. I thought I was right.

MCNALLY: We're not talking about your performance, we're talking about the character.

GRIZZARD: It was painful. I've played a lot of heavies, and I always approached them as if I am right and everybody else doesn't seem to understand. I didn't think Nick was a bad guy, but every time Uta or Arthur would stick a knife in they would laugh. They twisted, and then they really fell down and slapped their thighs. It hurt my feelings so badly, I was really delighted to be released from the play. I didn't mind killing six people in *Hamlet* after that.

I remember when I was replaced, there was a difference in the performance. Uta said, "He never went through the pain of finding out where the laughs were." I was a dead setup to be destroyed, and it hurt my feelings badly to be laughed at.

That's one of the problems I had with the play: Nick in many ways is contrived, because he's the kind of person who in Edward's mind should be destroyed. And indeed, I was.

MCNALLY: You didn't anticipate this reaction in the first reading?

GRIZZARD: Not applause when I would get a knife in the heart. I took it very seriously, and it was painful.

HAGEN: I don't agree with you that it's contrived. I personally have met twenty Nicks in life, and in universities.

MCNALLY: Alan, I'd like to have you explain about the rehearsal time of this play.

SCHNEIDER: We had two weeks and two days—fourteen days of rehearsal—and ten previews. The reason we had so little time was that Arthur Hill's movie was delayed and he arrived later than he had expected to.

GRIZZARD: But we started before he got there.

HAGEN: Onstage without him, one or two days, and I distinctly remember praying that he would show up.

GRIZZARD: Also, I was set back because the actress playing my wife, a very good actress and quite tiny, was replaced after about five days by a brilliant actress who was about two inches taller than I. I was supposed to be the stud in the play, and I look around and find I'm the smallest person on the stage. I really felt betrayed because Alan didn't discuss anything, he just brought me in a new wife. I felt betrayed and frightened.

SCHNEIDER: I know. I spent two hours in a phone booth getting you back into the show.

MCNALLY: Do you think Edward was aware of all this?

GRIZZARD: I'm sure he was. He showed up about once a week and would tell us, "You are terrific" and otherwise left us alone. He had great trust in us, it was wonderful of him.

SCHNEIDER: I was in touch with Edward minute by minute. I had done one other show with him, *The American Dream.* He'd been educated by his producer, Richard, not to interfere, but I had spent a lot of time talking about the staging of the show with Edward before we started rehearsals—a long time even before I talked with Uta in Sardi's that time. I read the play every day for six months and talked with Edward at his house, at my house, at restaurants. I finally said, "Let me do an act," and we staged a first act before Edward ever came to rehearsal.

I'd never worked with Uta, and I remember asking her, "Do you want it staged fast or slowly?" and she replied, "Get it on its feet as soon as possible, because then I can really start to work."

HAGEN: I like *not* to be blocked fast, but to start moving fast, and that's what I meant—to me there's a big difference in connotation. Do you follow? Blocking fast panics me.

SCHNEIDER: As I remember, it was on its feet, roughly, in nine days. Edward came in with Richard and Clinton on the third day, when we did the first act. After we ran it through, Edward looked at me sort of seriously and said, "That wasn't the way I had seen it at all." I said, nervously, "What's wrong?" He said, "I'm not sure," and Richard said, thank God, "I loved it. What don't you like?" Edward paced up and down in his tennis shoes and then said, "I think Nick and Honey sit down too soon." I said, "Well, that's a terrifically difficult problem, let me see if I can deal with it," and I suggested that Nick look at the picture a little longer and sit down a line later. When Edward came back to see it again, he said, "Oh yes, you changed the whole thing, didn't you," which is what playwrights tend to do. But every night I talked to Edward about whatever problems I had.

MCNALLY: When you were reading the play before rehearsals, did you ask Edward for changes?

SCHNEIDER: No, I don't think so. Not very many. I just kept asking myself what the play was about, what was happening in each scene, who the people were—really, it was a very difficult play. The script didn't have any stage directions. It was just a conversation. I was trying to find out what was happening to these people, and at that stage the cuts that we later made never occurred to me. It took time to understand, to visualize, to discover. I don't think anybody thought in terms of changes right away. Well, maybe Uta did—she came to Sardi's the first time I met her with a big notebook containing eighty million questions which she had already answered. Her preparation was terrific; she was working the way an actress of great understanding and sensitivity and experience would work. She understood what the problems were much better than Edward or I did at that point, because she had to deal with them.

But I don't think any of us was prepared to say in advance, "Let's cut this or that," though I knew the play was too long. I didn't think it had a chance commercially, anyhow. I always said, "Don't do it on Broadway."

BARR: We almost didn't. Long before Uta or George became involved, Alan and Clinton and I sat around a table discussing our feelings that the play was a serious problem for a commercial Broadway production, whereas we would do very well indeed off Broadway, which was a little more mature than Broadway in those days. I had an idea that we might open on and off Broadway on exactly the same night with two different casts, directors and sets, the point being that one of them might get away with it. Fortunately, Billy Rose put a crimp in it by saying, "You cannot do this to the play. If you're going to pull that kind of a stunt, you cannot have my theater." We thought it over and decided he was right.

MCNALLY: Was the play offered to and rejected by any other theater owners?

BARR: The answer is no, because the Billy Rose was the only theater available for what we wanted to do; move onto an empty stage to put in our set and lights. So we took it to Billy Rose, and he loved it. He wanted to invest in it, but we wouldn't let him touch it because we didn't want any of the control taken out of our hands.

SCHNEIDER: Billy wrote some ads for us.

BARR: Yes, he wrote ads directed to secretaries, saying, "This is a play you all might really like, but don't send the boss, because he will be bored to death." He wrote them himself and signed them, telling the secretaries they would understand the play, but the boss wouldn't. It was intriguing. He didn't have any idea of what the play would be like at that point, but when he came to rehearsals he loved everything except the furniture, which he wanted to make fancier, more ornate, something like the lobby of the Hotel Pierre.

GRIZZARD: After I left the play, I had about two weeks before I went to Minnesota, and I ran into Billy one night at Sardi's. He said, "How come you left my play?" and I said, "Well, I'm going to Minneapolis and play Hamlet."

And he said, "You shouldn't leave the play, that's very dumb of you, it's the biggest hit on Broadway." And I said, "I am going to play Hamlet, Billy." And he said, "I was married to Fanny Brice, and Fanny never left a play until everybody who wanted to see her had seen her in it." And I said, "Billy, I am going to play Hamlet." And he said, "Oh, you actors. Hamlet—it's like Hedy Lamarr blowing hot in your ear. Right?" Wonderful description of Hamlet.

MCNALLY: Today, eighteen years after the fact, do you have any second thoughts about how you would do things differently?

HAGEN: I'm sure I would. I can't remember how I played it, so it would have to be different.

SCHNEIDER: That's the only possible answer, and I'd have to answer in the same way. A play is a discovery. If you're doing it eighteen years later, you're different, and you're going to discover different things. Also, the social context is different.

I remember telling Uta how good she was, and she said, "Wait a minute, I won't be any good until six months after we open." She got better and better and better. Then there was a kind of calm plateau, and I asked her, "What's the matter?" and she said, "Well, you know, a long run." Then we went to London, and suddenly she was twice as terrific.

A play is different every night—that's the hardest thing for people who aren't in the theater to understand. It's organic, so of course it would be different eighteen years later. But I looked at Uta tonight as I came in, and I kept thinking, "My God, she would be terrific as Martha."

Q: You never mentioned why there was a decision to have a different cast for the matinee.

BARR: I didn't read the small print in the theater contract. It said we had to play eight performances a week. We were a smash hit practically from the minute we opened, and Billy Rose pointed out that we had to pay rent for the matinees we weren't playing. I went to Uta and asked her, "Don't you think this is quite a deal to play eight times a week?" She said, "Yes, I think—"

HAGEN: Now, wait a minute! Edward said we would probably rewrite history in this session, and here's the first rewriting of it. I can't believe your memory is so dismal, Mr. Barr. You called me up and announced to me that I was going to be too tired to play the matinees. I said, "I am not." You said, "It's very strenuous." I said, "Listen, I played eight times a week for two years in a row without a vacation in *A Streetcar Named Desire,* and *Virginia Woolf* is not as exhausting as that. This went on, and finally I said, "I don't care, it's the same money." It turned out not to be, but . . . *that's* the real story, and I'm glad it's on the record. The other is baloney, a direct reflection on my ability to work, my energy, my strength. I could have played *Virginia Woolf* twelve times a week.

BARR: I yield to the lady's memory. Anyway, we had to fill those two performances, and we decided to put the understudies in, playing the matinees and serving as understudies in case anything happened to the other actors. We also sent them out to do the play in colleges five or six times. We sold out the matinees as well as the evening performances, so the public obviously accepted this as double casting, though it had never been done before, to my knowledge, on a consistent basis of that kind.

Q: I've never heard a recording of a modern play that works as well as yours. How did you prepare for it?

HAGEN: I'm glad you liked it, but the circumstances were gruesome. The only other album I'd done in those days before tape took six weeks to record, and we were supposed to do this one in one day. They told me, "We'll set up in a studio, it'll be like a performance—just play it." We were told to bring soft shoes so that our feet wouldn't make a tapping noise while we were recording. I vowed to do it well, and not do it at all unless it was going to be wonderful.

When we came in, the set was up, only the proportions were totally different. It was very shallow; and right in front of our noses as we walked across the stage were mikes hanging down, I said, "It's not going to be a performance. It's impossible, but we'll try." After we'd rehearsed about ten minutes, somebody said, "Put your shoes on, it sounds as though the voices are disembodied." Nobody had hard shoes, so they rounded up some secretaries and put them to walking next to us.

Then Edward suddenly wanted ... we actors are very loyal to authors. I would not change a word on purpose, ever, but we'd been playing several months, and in that time period, some of the tiny little words, the "ands" and "ifs" ... tiny little changes had come in. Edward said, "That's not the way it's written." Arthur Hill—a wonderful man and a wonderful actor—got very nervous, he was thrown by all of this. I said to Edward, "We can read it if you want, or we can give our performance, but you can't have it both ways. You can't have us playing it as we would, fully, and still be letter perfect." There was a big to-do, and we finally did play it. Edward turned grumpily at one point and made Arthur do a long speech with a lectern, which was *very* damaging to Arthur's performance.

We started at ten o'clock in the morning, and the day got longer and longer, with the secretaries walking around. It was Sunday, we had been playing all week with colds, and at one point I didn't give a goddamn anymore—none of us had voices left. It was torture, so I'm glad the album works. Anyway, I think it could have been ten times better.

SCHNEIDER: It's a good album. The play comes alive on that recording. Perhaps the exhaustion of the experience fed into the album.

HAGEN: It shouldn't.

GRIZZARD: They used to play what they called the "*Virginia Woolf* game" in Washington. They would put the record on at parties, and every time the characters had a drink they would have a drink. They would get slopped.

Q: The clock underscored and exploited the dramatic intent of the play. Whose idea was that?

SCHNEIDER: It was an actual clock and it kept actual time throughout the play. The chimes rang when the character woke up and said, "I heard chimes."

BARR: That line was the origin of the clock. It was Bill Ritman's idea to have a clock. I don't remember whether it was his or Edward's or mine or a collective decision to have a real clock.

Q: How much of the writing of the play had been done when you decided to direct it, Mr. Schneider?

SCHNEIDER: All of it. Maybe at some point after I directed *American Dream* Edward might have thought of me for this play. But I didn't know about it until after it was written.

Q: Are you comfortable with a lack of stage directions?

GRIZZARD: Yes. Shaw's extraordinary stage directions should be followed to the letter. He was always right, but with any other author, including Edward, the stage directions are pictorial descriptions to help the writer, not the actor. I read them out of respect but invariably change them or suggest changes.

SCHNEIDER: I also begged Edward not to underscore words and speeches, because the actors will always tend to do the exact opposite. If the speech says it right, the actor will read it the right way. If the author underscores or puts in special directions like "sorrowfully" or "with tears in his eyes," the actor will automatically try to do something else.

HAGEN: For an actor, description of behavior is death. Sometimes I'll have the line retyped so that my visual remembrance isn't influenced by it. It's very negative for the creative process of the actor. I once asked Clifford Odets, "What are all those junky, tacky stage descriptions?" He said, "Oh, most of these are for backers, because they don't know how to read."

A piece of stage business where I struggled with the sleeve of a coat that was inside out became a half-page of description of my behavior in print. This makes it more readable for somebody who doesn't know how to read a play, but in the initial stage of the creative process it is very negative.

Q: Underlined words the same?

HAGEN: The same. I hate it.

SCHNEIDER: I begged Edward to stop doing it, but he wouldn't—and still won't.

BARR: Edward's tendency to underline words goes back into the published edition.

SCHNEIDER: Every single word goes back in the published edition, including the cuts.

Q: What was your reaction to and justification for the title of the play?

GRIZZARD: Come on, Richard, where did it come from?

BARR: It came from the wall of a latrine in a Village bar. Edward admits that, but it stimulated him to write the play. He wrote Leonard Woolf a very nice letter, sending him the script and asking, "May I use the title as indicated?" Mr. Woolf wrote back, "For a play this fine, of course you have my permission." It was a very generous and gentle thing to do. The lady who owned the copyright to the song "Who's Afraid of the Big Bad Wolf?" prevented us from using it in the show, as originally planned. So we used "Who's Afraid of Virginia Woolf?" to the tune of the old nursery rhyme "Here We Go Round the Mulberry Bush." What's interesting to me is, none of the critics caught the change in the symbolism because we changed the song.

MCNALLY: One did, one mentioned it.

GRIZZARD: One sidelight we haven't mentioned: originally, the visiting couple were called Honey and Dear, but when I got to my part it was called Nick. Edward told me it was short for Nikita, who at that time was the head of Russia. I was representing the political level of the play: Russian technology vs. the humanity of the West.

BARR: That's not in the text.

GRIZZARD: No. It's now on tape, though.

SCHNEIDER: That's really malarkey. What's the difference whether George and Martha are named for the first President of the United States and his wife? It's a reverberation that has nothing to do with the basic situation. Suppose they had been called Mary and John, would it have changed the play? Would it have a different meaning? No, it's just a kind of in-joke for the author.

Q: During rehearsal, did you use improvisation?

GRIZZARD: We had wonderful words. We didn't need to improvise.

HAGEN: Some members of the matinee company said to us, "We're having a hard time learning these parts because we realize you were allowed to improvise some of these words." I told them, "No, those words were written *exactly* like that, and we learned them faithfully." They couldn't believe it. They thought we had improvised those lines to make them sound so real.

Q: Was the play written originally about two homosexual couples?

SCHNEIDER: No, that was just somebody trying to manufacture controversy and sensationalism.

Q: So there's nothing to it?

SCHNEIDER: I know there's nothing to it.

BARR: I can speak for Edward. He said, "If I wanted to write a play about two homosexual couples, I know how to write a play about two homosexual couples." There's no question about it. They tried it that way once in a San Francisco production, but we enjoined them after one performance and stopped it.

Q: Did you have backers' auditions? Was it difficult to raise money?

BARR: No, we did not have backers' auditions; and no, it was *not* difficult to raise money because Edward was fairly well known for *Zoo Story, American Dream* and *Bessie Smith.* And after we got Uta Hagen and George Grizzard and Arthur Hill and put it all together, we didn't have any trouble raising money—but remember, it only cost $75,000 including the bonds. We opened for $45,000.

SCHNEIDER: $47,000.

BARR: $47,000 including the matinee company.

SCHNEIDER: And it paid off.

BARR: In three weeks.

MCNALLY: I think you have all been wonderfully frank and generous.

BARR: We rewrote history very well.

GRIZZARD: I still remember a party.

BAREFOOT IN THE PARK

Terrence McNally, Moderator
Mildred Natwick
Mike Nichols
Neil Simon

TERRENCE MCNALLY: *Barefoot in the Park* hasn't dated, it's warm, funny, accurate. We want you to recreate your experience with the play—obviously, each of you had a different one. Neil, at some point you had some blank pages and a typewriter and got this notion.

NEIL SIMON: The play was going to be autobiographical, the way *Come Blow Your Horn* was about my brother and myself. This was going to be about my first wife, Joan, and myself living in an apartment on Tenth Street and University Place, a five-floor walkup almost identical to the Oliver Smith set. It had the living room with the skylight that had a hole in it so the snow fell in. We did have a little dressing room we used as a bedroom, and you did have to climb over the bed to get to the closet.

I wrote about half the play and then quit on it. I said to myself, "No one's going to be interested in these two kids having fights about whether their marriage will continue after a week." It seemed so innocuous. I showed it to Saint Subber, and he begged me just to finish it. I was going on to *Little Me*, but I finished *Barefoot in the Park* and Saint loved it. When I asked him who we'd get to direct it, he said, "I have a wonderful idea: Mike Nichols. He's never directed before, but I think he's brilliant." We showed the play to Mike, who, I assume, loved it and said, "Let's do it in Bucks County."

My experience prior to this had been working for many years in television doing the Bilko show and *Your Show of Shows*. When you sat around the table, everyone was used to laughing at the jokes—that was how you'd tell if the script was good or not. We had a reading of *Barefoot in the Park* prior to going to Bucks County with Mike and some of the cast members at Saint Subber's house, and there wasn't a single laugh around the table. Maybe a giggle from Mike once in a while, but otherwise everyone just sat. I was saying to myself, "We will never do this play, I will not permit this embarrassment anywhere."

After the actors left, I just sat very silently and then said to Mike, "Forget it, I'm not going to do the play." Mike explained that the actors were all paying attention to their own parts, "They're worried about their own work, they're too involved to laugh at the play." We went on from there, and at rehearsals I thought it was the unfunniest play I'd ever see. Mike said, "Please be patient, it will be all right. Go outside and have an ice cream."

We got down to Bucks County Playhouse, and there were kids in the theater who would come in to clean up and would watch the rehearsals without laughing. At the dress rehearsal, I asked the man who ran the Bucks County Playhouse, Mike Ellis, "Is it the worst thing you've ever seen in your life?" He said, "Well, not the worst."

Then came the opening night. The curtain went up, and as soon as Elizabeth Ashley as Corie came onstage and opened up the valise with the logs and Herb Edelman as the telephone man came up and breathed, the audience started to laugh, and they haven't stopped laughing in twenty years—and I still don't understand it.

McNALLY: When your producer suggested Mike Nichols, did you have any trepidations about giving your play, your second, to an untried director?

SIMON: No, I admired Nichols and May so much, my instincts told me anyone that funny had to be brilliant. If he wasn't, we'd leave him in Bucks County, that's all there was to it.

McNALLY: When you became discouraged with the play, was it because of any particular scene, or the end of an act?

SIMON: You won't believe this, but the play originally took place in Switzerland. The original inspiration for the play was that Joan and I had gone to Switzerland. It was practically our honeymoon, and I don't know if it was a sexual fantasy or something that really happened. The play was going to open with this attractive girl sitting in the bar. This guy comes into the place from the cold and takes off his coat and sits down, and then he starts to talk to her, trying to pick her up. She is paying no attention to him, and he is trying harder and harder. Then he starts to walk away, and she says, "Oh, come back, we'll try again."

The characters were acting out this fantasy. And then we met a middle-aged couple there who used to go to Saint Moritz every year. Joan and I were with them, and we decided to take a walk into the mountains. I found that the woman and I were unable to make the whole trip, while Joan and the guy were gallivanting to the top of the mountain. I was furious at her. They were sort of the prototypes of what I eventually wrote, but where do you go in Switzerland with the rest of this play? It is not very identifiable. And so I came back to this area.

McNALLY: You showed this much to Saint Subber, who said, "Finish it?"

SIMON: I don't know if I ever showed him the Tyrolean thing. But eventually, after I came back, I bogged down, thinking altogether no one would be interested in the play. Then Saint pushed me into it, and then I got very involved with it and went through easily to the end.

McNALLY: And then this cast started appearing once you and Mike were working together.

SIMON: Yeah, I don't recall where it came from, but I remember first seeing

Elizabeth Ashley in *Take Her, She's Mine* and seeing Robert Redford in *Sunday in New York* and seeing Mildred Natwick in everything I ever saw that was wonderful, including *Waltz of the Toreadors*. That was pretty much the cast.

MCNALLY: The casting was done quickly, then?

MIKE NICHOLS: Well, no. My memory is entirely different. When Saint sent me the play, Elizabeth had been, as it were, already "found." I met her, and I told Saint, "Yeah, she's great. I don't know if I can do this at all, but if you have Elizabeth and if we can have that guy I saw on television last night—he played a Nazi in a Playhouse 90, but I understand he's not German—and he's real good.... That was Robert Redford. Do you remember that?

SIMON: No.

NICHOLS: There's going to be a lot of this. You and Saint and I sat for weeks saying actresses' names for the mother. Every name that came up, there were always two that wanted her and one that didn't. Then somebody said "Mildred Natwick," and everybody said "Yeah!" and that was the end of it.

MCNALLY: And George Voskovec was in the play in Bucks County?

SIMON: Yes, everybody else stayed the same except for that part, later cast with Kurt Kasznar.

MCNALLY: What happened in Bucks County? Did you make a lot of changes?

SIMON: As I recall, Herb Edelman was only in the first act, but he worked so well that we decided to use him again as a catalyst for their getting together again. And the symmetry of having him come back seemed so right. It would have been pointless for a character who worked so well to come in only for that appearance.

NICHOLS: Do any of you remember that we did the whole rehearsal period in one week? It's inconceivable now. We rehearsed for six days in some New York hall, and then we went to Bucks County and had our dress rehearsal at which Mike Ellis made his famous remark. Neil, you took me outside and said, "This play was never a play. Saint insisted that I finish it, but it's just not a play. We're taking it off." And I said, "Why don't you look at it tomorrow with the audience?"

What was great about the short rehearsal time, there was no time to discuss anything. We had to just do it. We blocked it and then we opened. That's pretty much it. Incredible.

SIMON: I remember standing in the middle of the stage with Mike and pointing to somebody, saying, "You say this," and Mike saying, "You say that."

MILDRED NATWICK: That's right!

MIKE: I remember the ending before the ultimate ending. It was that Millie was going to Europe. When we did the play in Bucks County, the night spent together by Millie's character and the upstairs neighbor never took place. Millie had a new wardrobe, and then she went to Europe. That was pretty much it, don't you remember?

NATWICK: Oh, my dear.

NICHOLS: And the idea for them to have spent the night together came a *long* time later in New York.

SIMON: Also, I might add, at that time the play was not called *Barefoot in the Park.* It was called *Nobody Loves Me,* and there was a reason for that. I knew I wanted to use the title *Barefoot in the Park,* but I was afraid that the play might not really work at first, and I didn't want the word to get out that *Barefoot in the Park* would be a bomb. I thought, let *Nobody Loves Me* be a bomb, we'll fix *Barefoot in the Park.*

MCNALLY: How long was it between Bucks County and the New York production?

SIMON: I would guess about six months.

NICHOLS: I thought less, somewhere between three and six months.

MCNALLY: Can Millie tell us something about her reaction when the script called *Nobody Loves Me* arrived?

NATWICK: I remember reading it in summer, in warm weather. Isn't it funny, I remember I was sort of hot. Saint had called me—it's unusual for a producer to call—and was very tentative, asking me to read it. I did, and I found myself laughing out loud all alone, which never happens. I thought, it's a divine play and a divine part. I quickly called back and said I'd love to do it.

MCNALLY: The reviews talk about the young couple's first big fight scene as a classic of staging. They hailed Mike for the virtuosity of it. When you read the script now, a lot of the stage directions are there. How much was already there and how much came out of improvisation, collaboration?

SIMON: I never knew. It was such a perfect collaboration between the two of us that I never knew what Mike suggested and what I suggested. I knew the fight scene was really sensational, though, when one night into about the third week Liz and Redford were really going at it, and I said to Mike, "I think we should leave, because this is too private a moment." It was *so* private I didn't think we should intrude on it, and I knew then it was spectacular.

MCNALLY: My impression of that scene was, the audience kept changing sides. First they'd agree with Corie, then "No, no, Paul's right." Did you improvise much in rehearsal?

NICHOLS: I don't remember. What I remember is, Redford's first replacement after years in the part was Richard Benjamin. He came in and did a wonderful reading, we cast him, and I started to rehearse him. On the third day, he said, "Nobody can do all this business and say the lines, too. Do you realize that in three lines you have me taking off all my clothes, pressing my tie in the dictionary, standing on the bed in the bedroom, and I have to be back by the time I say *this* line. Nobody can do it." We weren't aware of how much we had added, one line or piece of business at a time.

A specific I *do* remember is Redford asking, "Can I try something?" I said sure, and he said, "Could I carry Millie in this scene?"

MCNALLY: In every review they talk about Robert Redford coming in carrying Mildred Natwick. That was his idea?

NICHOLS: Yes, that was his idea, although Doc and I didn't really keep track of what came from where. To go back, I didn't like the play that much when I read it—

NATWICK: At last it's out!

SIMON: You had to get one shot in. Well, you were our third choice.

NICHOLS: —because I had gone to the University of Chicago, and we had been trained to dislike Broadway. I read the play, and I thought, "This is very nice but, you know, Broadway—but I need a job." I decided to see whether I could do it and whether it would work. What I didn't know before this experience, and what I learned *from* this experience is, what people *do* is crucial to a play, more than what they *say*—what is the situation? Doc and I didn't have the knowledge at the time to realize that everything in the play (and this is what I came to love so much about the play and still do) is heightened, both figuratively and literally. They lived way up on the top floor, so everyone who comes in has to go up all those stairs, so immediately there is a physical reality.

NATWICK: I remember you making us run up and down those damn stairs, practicing.

MCNALLY: When you read the script, did it occur to you that the playwright's asking them all to play out of breath for the whole play, and that you'd have to keep the joke from becoming stale?

NICHOLS: No.

MCNALLY: It never occurred to you? Every review says it's genius, astonishing, that we're still laughing at this same joke in Act Three.

SIMON: What joke? When you climb five flights of stairs, you're out of breath.

MCNALLY: They gave credit to Mike and the actors for this.

NICHOLS: The credit belongs in the conception of the circumstances. That was the *spine* of what happened to all of us. We had a week, and we just did the play. But in the circumstances, everything was heightened. It was the beginning of their marriage. They had just left the Plaza Hotel. What higher time in anybody's life?

MCNALLY: Were these elements always in the script? The five flights, just moving in after a wild honeymoon, just gotten out of the cab from the Plaza?

NICHOLS: Absolutely. And the mother had been widowed not that long ago. She was dealing with a new situation. They were all in a new and heightened state.

SIMON: And the apartment was bare, completely empty. With that image in my mind, I felt, "What a terrific place to go!" Walter Kerr pointed out in his review what occurred to me in my mind: what they fill it up with is a play. That was the intention.

MCNALLY: The audience must have been astonished to find a comedy in which there was no place for the actors to sit or stand when the curtain went up, except paint buckets and briefcases. It's an incredibly concrete play. You can feel the lack of heat, the stairs, the absence of furniture, the leak in the closet. . . .

SIMON: What I love about working with Mike, he's such a taskmaster. He would call me at three o'clock in the morning and ask, "Are you sleeping?" and I'd say "No, no, I was waiting for your call, Mike," and he'd say, "Do we really need that line?" and I'd say, "No, I'll take it out if you won't call me any more at three in the morning."

NICHOLS: I decided on the first day of rehearsal that I loved the play and that we were all going to be very happy going through the events that Neil had conceived: a bare apartment, five flights up, the beginning of a marriage, the beginning of a widowhood, the heightened situation. We were very lucky that the lines were wonderful, but they came after that skeleton.

I remember that we were in Boston or Washington hanging around waiting for the performance, and Neil told me, "I've had an idea for another play: two guys, separated from their wives, share an apartment and begin to treat each other as they did their wives. What do you think of it?" I said, "I want to do it." I wasn't looking for anything to do in those days, but I wanted to do *that* because . . . I mean, from Doc's point of view, it wasn't *done* when he said that, but from my point of view it was done when he said that, because . . .

MCNALLY: You could see something.

NICHOLS: I could see that tension. I could see something happening. When you have an idea that permits, that forces, that makes it necessary for something to *happen*, then you have an idea for a play. You can have the greatest lines, the greatest gags, the most beautiful language in the world—it makes no difference if it isn't set up, if there isn't a kind of *tripod* in the situation that holds (I'm stuck with the image) the camera that is the play.

MCNALLY: I've been teaching playwriting and saying exactly that. It's not lines or dialogue, it's what people *do* that makes a play, not what they say. But it's very difficult to convince playwrights of that. Actors are quicker to grasp it.

NATWICK: Doc, you would go home one evening and come back the next day with a scene better than the one we had done.

SIMON: The improvisations were so stimulating they opened me up to new ideas. Mike is wonderful at it. Many times with some of the plays we've done I would get stuck trying to fix something and Mike would say, "Why don't you just not do that idea at all, throw it out completely?" The concept of having that option—that you should throw something out after spending all that time working on it—never occurred to me. It's like poker playing. Forget that bad hand and go on to a new one. It always helped clear things. I felt fresh when I was able to do that.

MCNALLY: You have the reputation of being an author who is absolutely willing to say, "It doesn't work, here's something new, something better."

NICHOLS: When you're working on a show in trouble, it begins with the producer saying you haven't done so-and-so, and the writer and actors and director saying to the producer you haven't publicized it, and the director saying to the writer nobody could stage this scene, and the writer saying to the director you screwed it up. We were blessed because we were the opposite. I remember *begging* Doc not to rewrite scenes, to give me another hour to figure out how to do it, but not to blame his script. Of all the writers I've worked with, he is the only one—I'm sure the only one in the history of the theater—who has never said, "The line would work if the actor said it right!" He never has the thought. He thinks if the line works it works no matter how you say it, and if it doesn't work it's not the actor's fault. Who ever heard a writer say such a thing? Nobody in the theater.

SIMON: My feeling is, if the actor has been good all along and suddenly it's not working, the actor didn't suddenly get bad, the script got bad, so I've got to change it. I would give Mike the pages, and I would sit there waiting to hear this giggle, and he'd say, "You're going to hate me, but I like the old pages better." He was invariably right. He'd realize something was not working, so I'd go back and make an adjustment by doing something that was worse, which made him see what was better about the old version and a new way to do it.

MCNALLY: I assume what you're talking about took place while you were out of town, not in that one frantic week.

SIMON: No, not in the first week.

NATWICK: You were also willing to take all sorts of ideas, as I remember. Wasn't it Lillian Hellman who thought of my coming down in the bathrobe?

SIMON: Yes, Lillian Hellman and I collaborated.

NATWICK: It showed where the character had been and what she'd been doing.

NICHOLS: I remember that Neil and I had talked about dozens of possible third acts, and one night Lillian Hellman was at my house talking about the play, which she loved. I told her Neil was still trying different things in the third act because we still weren't happy with it at the time we were starting rehearsals for Broadway. Being about the same age as the character, Lillian Hellman said, "When I saw the play I thought the mother was going to end up staying over with the neighbor." I immediately went to tell Doc, and the impression Miss Hellman had formed of this situation led Doc to filter it through his sensibilities. It turned out very Neil Simon: the mother had slipped on the ice, lost her shoes down the sewer and stayed over, and then Corie was shocked in the morning to discover her in the neighbor's bathrobe.

It took a week to figure out how to do the scene when you comfort each other, remember? I was getting worried, and Kurt Kazsnar reminded me, "Listen, we open soon." The next day, after a week, it occurred to me that they would break up laughing.

NATWICK: Absolutely. It was in Washington, awfully late for the tryout.

NICHOLS: Maybe to me the most interesting thing is that when you have a problem the solution almost always lies back earlier. The solution to the problem with the third act took place at the end of the second act. You can never solve the problem in the place in which it occurs. It's too late.

SIMON: I can give you an example of that from another play Mike and I did, *The Prisoner of Second Avenue*. We went through the final dress rehearsals, and Mike came over and said the end of the play was not going to work. I said, "Well, we'll know tomorrow night," and he said, "But I know *now*." And I said, "Well, you may know now, but it's one o'clock in the morning and it's not going to help us." He suggested we sit and talk, and we tried to figure out what would happen that would give us the conclusion to this play. We went on and on, and finally we both fell silent, sitting there in the hotel lobby in New Haven. For about an hour we kept sitting there, and they mopped up all around us. Finally I said, "What if the snow came down and he got his shovel?" Mike said, "I'll see you in the morning, and I'll get the snow," and we went to bed. I love that kind of collaboration. Any playwright who gets a director like that, who pushes you, is very, very fortunate.

NICHOLS: It's always there earlier in the play.

SIMON: That's where it came from, yes.

NICHOLS: You set it up without knowing it. Over and over again, circumstances are established in a play that have their effect on the audience; but you're so used to them that, to begin with, you don't necessarily follow them through to their logical conclusion.

McNALLY: The changes you made in *Barefoot* don't seem major. I sense that it went smoothly, and you were always improving the play, but the play was there.

SIMON: The major changes occurred between Bucks County and the New York rehearsal. After that, we didn't make major changes.

Mike hates little laughs. He says, "Get them out, they are the ones that do you in."

NICHOLS: Remember that strange laugh in *Plaza Suite*? I think of it often. The first play was serious, very touching, but had funny things in it. There was this moment when George C. Scott was leaving Maureen Stapleton, and the audience was very moved. But Scott would say, "See you later," and there was this huge laugh. None of us wanted a laugh there, so I said, "George, try saying it before you go to the door." It still got a huge laugh. So finally in desperation Neil said, "Take it out, just go to the door, look at her and then leave." Scott got to the door and turned and got a huge laugh.

Laughter is energy. You can interrupt the flow, the arc, of a large laugh by getting these little piddly ones on the way. The energy builds up if you take out the little ones.

McNALLY: Did you ever get rid of this offending laugh?

NICHOLS: I don't think we did. Have you ever noticed that if somebody coughs on your favorite laugh line, the laugh comes on the next line?

McNALLY: It's true.

NICHOLS: If something is building up, and you stop it here, it comes out there.

MCNALLY: We asked Guild members to send in questions, and there's a theme running through several of them. People asked if you would make any changes in the character of Corie if you were writing the play today—so there's some element in her character that some people think maybe hasn't kept up with women's consciousness. Do you think that's true?

SIMON: Yes, probably. Specifically, the speech Millie makes when she talks about taking care of her husband: "Give up a little of you for him." That would not go down well today, but I didn't think I was sexist at all, I was making a relationship work. And I think she evened it out in the rest of the sentence. I don't recall her exact words, but she was saying, "Don't fight so hard for everything you want. Give a little, he'll give back." But I don't think I put it in quite the right way.

NICHOLS: I would fight for that line if we were doing the play now.

SIMON: You would?

NICHOLS: Because he gives up a little of himself for her at the end in a highly entertaining way. He makes an enormous step in his character, prodded by her. I'd like to keep that.

MCNALLY: Here's another submitted question for all of you. "What percentage of your success do you attribute to luck, what percentage to hard work and what percentage to talent?"

NICHOLS: They're all the same thing. I worked on a picture once with a great actor named Marcel Dalio who played the Jew in *Grand Illusion*. He was old and quite worried, but after he did a long, long scene the crew applauded, and I told him he was wonderful and thanked him. He said, "If you're an actor you have to pray every day for a small miracle, because you can't make it come. You have to pray that it will come."

That's true. To be talented is to be lucky, and that's all there is to it. And then the hard work comes because you love what you are doing and don't experience it as work. The thing into which you are pulled, without even knowing you've been up all night on it, is the thing for which you are gifted. Then comes the point where you have to pray that it will keep coming because no effort of will will make it so. That's the luck.

NATWICK: That was a great answer. Luck has a lot to do with it—think of being lucky enough to be sent this play, and then lucky enough to have Mike Nichols directing it. I would be able to go to Mike and ask, "What shall I do with this line? How shall I bring out what's funny in it?" He would always come up with the perfect answer. The comedy came from the situation and the character. You never had to *try* to be funny. That was lucky and wonderful, too.

SIMON: There is a certain amount of luck involved in writing, but you have to seize the opportunity—I guess you have to have some talent to be able to recognize the luck when it comes along and grab it. A case in point would be when Oscar was reading a letter Felix left on his pillow in *The Odd Couple*, in the third act when Oscar was furious at Felix and wanted to throw him out. I started to write the letter, which I wanted to be annoying to Oscar. Oscar picks it up saying, "You leave me little notes on the pillow," and then he reads, "We're all out of cornflakes." That was the letter. I said to myself, that's not funny. He would sign it. So I said, sign it "Felix." Sign it "Felix Unger." I said, that's not funny. So I put his initials down: "F.U." I didn't think of it, I stumbled on it. I guess there's a certain amount of gift in recognizing it when you stumble on it. People thought I had that joke in mind and made his name Felix Unger so that two acts later I could get to that moment.

NICHOLS: That was a rewrite, that speech. It came in Boston. Walter Matthau said, "We're all out of cornflakes. F.U." and then sat down and read a newspaper during the laugh, which went on so long that he had time to read most of it.

SIMON: Sometimes the comedy would escape both Mike and myself. Suddenly, standing in the back, we'd hear this big laugh, and we'd look at each other and say, "Let's keep it."

NICHOLS: What I miss most about having worked on five Simon plays is, the audience always liked them better than we did. We always thought we had more to do—Neil thought he had more to do, I *knew* I had more to do, the actors felt they had more to do, but the audience was perfectly happy. You get so spoiled when you've had that happen.

SIMON: You kept saying to the cast, "Remember, this is the first time they are seeing it."

Q: What new discoveries have you made with new casts? Did the play change from New York to Chicago, where I saw it with Richard Benjamin and Joan Van Ark?

NICHOLS: Sure, you free actors to find their own way. Benjamin was *wonderful*, funny and true, and so were the people who played afterward. But Neil and I and Elizabeth and Redford—certainly not you, Millie, but the rest of us—were in a state of *becoming*. There were things, for instance, that Millie did that others turned themselves inside out to try to do because they had become an important part of the play. Like juggling that meatball. They simply were unable to do it. The first time was *it*.

McNALLY: The stage directions in the printed copy of the play now make all these things sound so easy.

NICHOLS: There was a lot of discovery that went into finding those moments.

Q: Mr. Simon, you said the play started out being autobiographical. When did imagination take over?

SIMON: Right in the beginning. The inspiration is what's autobiographical. I had the set in mind—the apartment that Joan and I had lived in—and the essence of the play—moving into the apartment. I wanted to express the love affair that was going on. It's remarkable to me that they are nice to each other only for the first five minutes of the play and never nice to each other again until the very last moment. Once you start to write, you mix up what is real and what isn't. I don't try to remember incidents that happened.

Q: Mr. Nichols, is there a reason why you yourself do not write full-length plays?

NICHOLS: It's pretty hard. I can't. I would if I could.

Q: Mr. Nichols, what is the difference between a George S. Kaufman comedy and a Neil Simon comedy?

NICHOLS: They are almost the reverse of each other. You envy George Kaufman not only because of what he wrote but because he chose so early a character that allowed him to get through life. Dammit, why didn't I think of being a curmudgeon? You get away with so much. You tell somebody to go to hell, and everybody says, "Isn't he wonderful, isn't he funny?" Kaufman was, quite brilliantly, a very angry man.

Well, with Neil it's this great generosity, this thing that none of us has said about *Barefoot,* this thing that killed you when you saw it, the sweetness, the inordinate decency of the characters, in spite of the violence of the fights and the newlywed bride's Joan of Arc despair. It's true of everything Neil writes. Simon and Kaufman are opposites.

Q: How are you able to eliminate the big laugh when you find it is spoiling the theme of the play?

SIMON: I don't know what you mean by "How." You just take it out. Mike would point out, wisely, "This play should work if we don't get a single laugh all night. They should still be interested in the characters. If they laugh, fine." So he never treats the play as a comedy. The first day we were sitting around, and he said, "We have to treat this play as though we were doing *King Lear.* You *must* have that kind of conviction. This is life and death to you people."

It's not hard to take out the laughs when you know you have lots of other laughs. You never want cheap laughs if you can avoid them, you want important laughs.

Q: Mr. Simon, did you ever want to direct a play yourself?

SIMON: I did until I worked with Mike. I answer the same way Mike just did about writing a play. I feel I could direct a play, but I get so intimidated after having watched him. I once decided I would watch Mike very closely so that I would be able to direct my own play some day. But I never saw what he did. It was so mysterious.

Q: Mr. Simon, how many rewrites of *Barefoot* did you do before the first rehearsal?

SIMON: Well, there was the Tyrolean version, and then I think I did just one version that Mike read and we worked on. You can never tell how many versions, there's always fixing to do. At that time, neither one of us was *that* experienced to know *exactly* what was going to work and what wasn't. We learned so much at Bucks County, and then during the four weeks of rehearsal there were countless rewrites, and countless rewrites out of town.

Q: Mr. Simon, some comedy writers work as a team and get feedback from each other. Have you ever worked with anyone else, and how do you feel about comedy writers working as a team?

SIMON: I don't even like to think of playwriting in terms of comedy writing. I think of it as writing, sometimes funny and sometimes not. All those days in television I worked with other people and couldn't wait to become a playwright so I could write by myself, because I think you have to have an *absolutely* personal point of view. I don't think two people can have the *exact* same point of view. For example, *The Odd Couple* was about my brother's life, but had he written the play it would have been completely different. Had we collaborated, we would have had different points of view. For some people it works—Lindsay and Crouse were able to do it—but for me writing is an expression of myself and my own attitudes, and I don't want to share that in the process.

Q: Mr. Simon, did you ever consider making Paul anything other than a lawyer, so that a lot of people would be able to identify with him?

SIMON: I don't know why I picked a lawyer. I don't know that he had that much going for him, he was just out of law school, with his very first case coming up. I thought of him as a young kid just starting out, he couldn't even afford that apartment. That's why he was so worried that she was spending so much time showing him her black negligée when he wanted to get to work on the case.

Q: What would you suggest to a beginning writer about playwriting versus film writing?

SIMON: Stay with playwriting. You learn more about writing character. From my point of view, film writing is more of a craft, playwriting more of an art. I don't know why. I love being restricted to that one set when writing a one-set play, which you invariably do. It *forces* you to deal with the characters rather than write, "The car will drive along, and you will see this magnificent view," and all the other things you can bring in to help you.

Also, when you write a film, it ultimately is going to come out through the vision of the director, who sees it much differently than you do. I don't think the director's job in film—Mike may disagree with me—is to make your screenplay work. The writer has to function for the director, because he has the control. On the stage, maybe it's historically true that the director tries to service the playwright.

NICHOLS: I agree, but I would add that the screenplay is the movie, the movie is its screenplay. There is no good movie with a bad screenplay. Your example of driving along and seeing the scenery gives the larger portion of the audience's experience to the director. But the structure, the premise, the events, the circumstances, the characters are the screenplay, and without them there is no movie.

MCNALLY: Millie, did your performance in the movie version of *Barefoot* seem different to you?

NATWICK: No, I thought there was maybe a spot or two where I would have liked the director to have done what he did in the play. But not a lot. It seemed pretty much the same to me. Having played it on the stage, it was much easier to do the movie without having to think up a character.

MCNALLY: How long did you play it?

NATWICK: Two years on Broadway, then a season in London, then in the movies. It was a lifetime thing. I thought I was always going to be carried into the bedroom.

SIMON: Millie was always such a perfectionist.

Q: Mr. Simon, some of your work was reinterpreted into books. Did these novelizations tell you anything about your work?

SIMON: I never read any of them. All the studios do it, and they were paying the money, and I guess it was very mercenary of me, but I said fine, let them do it. It has nothing to do with what I have written.

Q: You said earlier you'd change a line in *Barefoot* to come to terms with the way we regard women today. Do you feel that every time a character says something you are being sociologically judgmental?

SIMON: I don't try to think like me when I'm writing the characters. I try to think like each character I write. I try to take their point of view and see where they are, in their time of life, in this situation. I try by osmosis to get into their psyche and write what I think they would say at the time. I don't try to propagandize or try to make points for myself about social issues. I don't really think I'm a social writer.

MCNALLY: I don't think there is any appropriate way to thank the three of you enough. I've learned a lot. I can't thank you enough.

FIDDLER ON THE ROOF

Peter Stone, Moderator
Jerry Bock
Sheldon Harnick
Joseph Stein

PETER STONE: *Fiddler on the Roof* certainly has to be counted among the five or ten greatest shows ever to appear on Broadway. There would be no disputing that. I guess we will have to say it was the second longest-running musical—3,242 performances. After eight years it ran out of people. Everybody in the world had seen it, so it closed. It opened on September 22, 1964, to *mostly* nice reviews. Not entirely nice. Walter Kerr, writing for a newspaper that did not survive *Fiddler on the Roof,* said, "It takes place in Anatevka in Russia, and I think it might be an altogether charming musical if only the people of Anatevka did not pause every now and again to give their regards to Broadway with remembrances to Herald Square." He ended the review: "*Fiddler on the Roof* dips below its own best possible level by touching on character too casually and sometimes soiling it with the lesser energies of easy quips, lyrics that stray too far from the land and occasional high-pressure outbursts. The result is a very near miss."

I read that not to embarrass my fellow panelists but to show that critics are not only fallible, they can be monumentally wrong.

Now, I think the best way to begin this is historically: Where and how did it start? Who called whom? On what occasion? Who liked the idea and who didn't, and who had to be persuaded? In other words, what was the very first time any of you heard about it?

SHELDON HARNICK: The very beginning was that a friend told me I should read a novel by Sholom Aleichem called *Wandering Star.* He said there was a musical in it. So I read the book, which is a big sprawling novel about a Yiddish theatrical group touring Russia, and I loved it. I gave it to Jerry Bock, who then read it and loved it. We then gave it to Joe Stein. Joe said, "It's too sprawling. You cannot put this on the stage. There's just too much of it. It covers too much time." But—and I don't know whether it was Joe or Jerry—one of them said, "Let's look at some more of Sholom Aleichem."

JOSEPH STEIN: I think it was me because I remember I had heard the Tevye stories when I was very young. We tried to pick up a copy of that book. As a matter of fact, it was out of print at the time. I got a copy from a very unlikely source: O'Malley's Bookstore. That was an out-of-print shop. All three of us read the stories, and we felt that within those stories, and within the character of Tevye, there was the basis of an intriguing musical. For those of you who are not familiar with them, the stories are isolated tales connected only in the sense that they are told through the author as monologues by Tevye. They can be read in any order, because each tale tells a single story. There are seven stories about his daughters; Tevye originally had seven daughters. For financial and other reasons, in *Fiddler* we cut the number down to five. In addition to the stories about him and his daughters, there were also a number of other stories about Tevye. Out of all of this material, we selected three (and some of a fourth) story around which we felt a total overall story could be written. That was the genesis of it.

HARNICK: According to my notes, that must have been in 1961.

STONE: When it was decided to do the show, when you agreed that there was something here, did you, Joe, go away and write a book and come back to Jerry and Sheldon with it, or did all three of you sit down and lay it out together?

HARNICK: Before he answers that, there's another matter to discuss. This was a new experience for Jerry and me. This was the first show that we had ever done that *we* had decided to do. Everything else that we had done had been an assignment or a commission from a producer. This one *we* decided to do. A lot of people, including us, weren't sure whether the material was in the public domain, so we had to inaugurate a copyright search. It turned out that it was still copyrighted, so we had to secure the rights to do it.

STEIN: As a matter of fact, one of the reasons that we did it ourselves was that I couldn't conceive of going to a producer and saying, "We have this idea of a show about a lot of Jews in Russia. You know, they have a pogrom and get thrown out of their village." A producer would have just stared at us. So we decided to go ahead on our own. Meeting with Jerry and Sheldon, I roughed out an outline of the total story. The original stories, of course, were written in a different form for a different audience in a different language. In order to make the material into a stage piece, we decided to make it the story of this community—the story of the breakdown of this community with the stories of the three daughters illustrating that breakdown. So I worked out an outline, and then I think Jerry and Sheldon started to work on the score.

HARNICK: This is one of the first moments when we have different memories. My memory is that the revelation that these stories added up to the changing of a way of life came later. My memory is that when we started to work, we concentrated more on the romances of the various daughters and Tevye's relation to them and not so much on the dissolution of the culture. Incidentally, not too long before we did ours, there had been a play version of the Tevye stories by Arnold Perl, which was not successful. It ran for about two or three months in the basement of what was then the Carnegie Theater.

STEIN: I never saw that play. I read it after we had finished the draft of *Fiddler* because I didn't want to be influenced by it. But as I remember it, it was made up of three isolated one-act plays built around the same characters.

HARNICK: I think that was the first important decision that we had to arrive at—how much we wanted to mesh those stories.

JERRY BOCK: The hardest task was organization. What to select from this vast amount of unbelievably exciting and emotional material? How to organize it? What disciplines to use to extrapolate what we wanted? How to get it onto the stage? That was a continuous problem, by the way, from the beginning through Jerry Robbins's vision, if you will.

STONE: O.K., so basically there was an outline, and the outline was worked out among the three of you.

BOCK: Yes, we had some conferences. Joe went back to the outline, and eventually we agreed how to follow a course.

HARNICK: Jerry and I had evolved a method: we would both read the source material, then Jerry would go off to his studio to work on musical ideas which he then put onto tape.

STONE: Let's clear something up. Do you write lyrics to music or do you write music to lyrics?

HARNICK: Both, but I found that to break the ice, to get the momentum going, it was much simpler to have music first. Then I didn't have to search for the form. The form was inherent in the music.

BOCK: I found it was much simpler to have lyrics first.

HARNICK: So I would be studying the source material, looking for the easiest numbers to start with. Jerry would give me a tape. The tape might have anything from a dozen to two dozen musical ideas worked out. I must say that on the tape Jerry would say "Well, I see this number for the butcher" or "I think this number is for somebody else." My reaction was almost always, "Wrong. That's not the butcher." The most exciting numbers were always the ones where I would hear his voice saying, "I don't know what this is." For some reason, those were always the best. Also, I was looking for the moments which I thought would be obligatory moments, moments which would have to remain no matter what changes were made in the book along the way.

One such moment I thought had to stay comes late in the first act. Tevye has given his oldest daughter permission to marry the tailor, even though he's already made a match for her with the butcher, and to persuade his wife, he invents a dream. I thought, "That's a moment that's always going to stay." As it happened, Jerry had done a rather complex piece of music. I no longer remember whether it was from beginning to end all of a piece, but I do know that that was the first lyric that I started on—that dream which was written in September of 1961 and I don't think was ever changed.

STONE: How many songs were written that did not appear in the show?

BOCK: I can answer that because I went through the files today. I must preface this by saying that when we opened a show, my favorite gift always came after opening night: Sheldon's loose-leaf notebook of lyrics for that particular show. The notebook is organized approximately this way: First, songs that made the final version. Then, songs that were rehearsed or performed but did not reach opening night. Then, songs that never reached rehearsal. In *Fiddler* he had fourth and fifth categories: "Bête Noir No. 1" and "Bête Noir No. 2." Originally, we wrote fourteen songs. Approximately seven more were put into rehearsal or saw out-of-town performance. Approximately seven more never reached rehearsal. So that's twenty-eight. We wrote two for every one we ended up with.

HARNICK: My list was close to forty-eight.

BOCK: Wait, I am getting to that! In the section of the notebook marked "Bête Noir No. 1" was the material we had written for Perchik. We wrote something like fourteen songs till we finally got to "Now I Have Everything." The section he labelled "Bête Noir No. 2" contained second-act production numbers. There were five versions of "Anatevka" aside from the one that we ended up with. So we wrote close to forty. That doesn't count individual changes of lines, replacement of verses, cuts, editing, etc. So we ended up with about a three-to-one ratio.

STONE: How does this ratio compare to your other shows?

BOCK: I know that *Fiorello* was very close to three to one. *She Loves Me* had about twenty-one or twenty-three songs in its final version, and I think we wrote at least twice that many.

HARNICK: *The Rothschilds* also went well into the forties. I never mastered the knack of getting the right idea the first time around. In fact, what I found about myself was that each draft acquainted me with another level of a character's personality, so successive drafts made the character more real to me, more three-dimensional, which in turn affected the show as a whole. I always took to heart the truism "Shows are not written, they are rewritten." At least that's been our experience.

STONE: There's an apocryphal story that in *The Rothschilds* there was once a song called "Now That I'm a Rich Man." Ever hear that?

HARNICK: No, but I'll tell you a true story. One of the songs that we had written for *Fiddler* was a number early in the show called "The Richest Man in Town." It was a very pretty song in which Motel the tailor tells Tzeitel that he has nothing—but, because she loves him, he is the richest man in town. Well, for one reason or another it was not used in *Fiddler*. When we did *The Rothschilds* I thought that it was an even more appropriate song for Meyer Rothschild. We didn't tell our director and producer that this was something that had come from *Fiddler on the Roof* when we played it for them. When we were finished, they said "That's a pretty song, but you know something, the *texture* doesn't seem right for this show." That's our blessing and our curse. Songs that we write and don't use do not wind up being trunk songs that can be used elsewhere. They seem to be locked into the shows for which they were written.

STEIN: I remember I finished the draft of the first act of *Fiddler* sometime around October 1961. The total draft was finished, oh, I guess sometime around the end of that year. As a matter of fact, I reread it today in preparation for this meeting. It's curious how very similar it is to the final version, and yet how very different; similar because the basic line of the show always remained the same. Aside from the introduction of "Tradition" (which was written a good deal later), it always started with the house scene, and it always went pretty much the way it ended up through the wedding and the pogrom. Sheldon said earlier that we came to the idea of the community thing later, but I always had in mind that the line of the show was the community. The first act always ended with the pogrom. The second act always ended with the exodus to America. For me, the community was always central to the story.

STONE: Were entire scenes dropped in the rehearsal or out-of-town processes?

STEIN: They were dropped in the rewriting. The first-act draft originally had scenes like—well, there was a scene with Tevye and Perchik in which they played chess while Perchik outlined his attitude towards society and why he was a revolutionist. That was dropped because we found that we could say it much more simply and quickly in his very first appearance. There were a number of similar scenes that were dropped later. We had a scene which lasted up to the opening in Detroit in which Tevye read a letter from his brother-in-law in America. It was an amusing scene, and it led to a song called "Letters From America" or "Anatevka" in which the people sang of how very happy they were being in Anatevka. "America may sound fine but we are very, very happy in Anatevka." After that scene and that song were dropped, a piece of that happy song became the basis for the song now known as "Anatevka." It was just slowed down and became almost what might be called a dirge.

BOCK: Well, hardly that, but sort of poignant, you know. A totally changed mood.

HARNICK: There was one other very difficult decision that had to be made. Sholom Aleichem addressed an audience of Yiddish-speaking and reading people with whom he had certain values in common. Knowing that, we were never sure, in the story about the daughter who marries the gentile, if what Sholom Aleichem was trying to do was to open up his audience's mind to the possibility that somebody could marry out of the faith and still be accepted, which I gather was not something that was done, really. As Joe said, Sholom Aleichem wrote the stories as Tevye's monologues. In that particular story, Tevye tells about how his daughter married the Russian, but at the end of it he doesn't tell you what happened. Instead, he lays it in the readers' laps by saying, "What would you have done?" It was unresolved. So we had to make a choice. It seemed fairly clear to us that even here Tevye would have found some way of bending; some way to accept the daughter he adored, even though she had done something that was unconscionable to him. That was our choice, but we had a lot of talks about how we should end that scene. I think it was Joe who came up with that extraordinary solution of having Tevye say, "God be with you!" to the air. He says the words but not to his daughter.

BOCK: Joe started the book in August 1961. We started the score in September 1961, working both together and separately. The first notation I have is 7/25/62.

STEIN: I have that, too.

BOCK: We played it for Fred Coe, and he wanted to produce it.

STONE: Did you play it for him first?

BOCK: No. It was turned down endlessly.

STONE: How many times would you estimate that it was turned down? Who turned it down?

STEIN: Hal Prince turned it down. He was the first person. He said he liked it but was unsure of its commercial possibilities. Which was very understandable.

HARNICK: We played it for Saint Subber. It turned out that when he was very young, Saint Subber's father had been killed in an automobile accident and he had been turned over to a Jewish grandmother to be raised. So he grew up knowing these stories in the original Yiddish. We had one act when we went to him, as I recall. We played the score. He was dissolved to tears, and he wanted to do it. But we were told that at the time he was having trouble raising money for shows.

STEIN: Well, he had trouble on this one, anyway.

HARNICK: But we never gave it to him to raise the money. As I recall, we decided not to take the chance.

STONE: You say you played it for Hal Prince first and he turned it down?

BOCK: Hal originally felt that it was not his material.

STEIN: We showed it to one producer, who shall remain anonymous, who said, "I love it, but what will we do when we run out of the Hadassah benefits?"

STONE: So you kept going, and you finally showed it to Fred Coe?

BOCK: An unlikely prospect, by the way. A Southern gentleman of, I think, impeccable taste. He loved it and wanted to do it.

HARNICK: We took it to him because we were so impressed by the kind of shows he had produced. He seemed to like serious material and, God knows, we thought what we had was serious.

BOCK: And he in turn asked Arthur Penn to hear the score. According to my notes, we played it for Arthur. He wrote us a letter of both admiration and consolation, saying that he couldn't do it because of other commitments, but he thought it was a very important show. In the middle of all this, by the way, there was a long hiatus when we put this show aside to do other shows. This was around 1962 or 1963.

HARNICK: What happened was that producers came along with an offer for Jerry and me to do *She Loves Me*. The idea was so appealing that we decided to give *Fiddler* a vacation while we did that.

STEIN: While they did *She Loves Me*, I did *Enter Laughing*. After those shows were open, we came back to *Fiddler*.

BOCK: There was never any question of not going back. We had the extra motivation of this project being *our* idea.

HARNICK: And of course we had invested some money for the rights.

STONE: Who was the next person to get involved?

BOCK: Jerome Robbins.

HARNICK: How did we get to him?

BOCK: Joe and you and I had a session one night about directors, and we landed on Robbins. So we asked Fred to speak to him, and we auditioned it for him.

STONE: And his reaction was—?

HARNICK: He wanted to do it, but he found there was much wanting in what he heard. He loved the source material. Somewhere along the line he told us that when he was six he had been taken to Poland. He said he never forgot the experience because his forebears came from there. Robbins said what he wanted to do was put the stetl life onstage to give another twenty-five years of life to that stetl culture which had been devastated during World War II. That was his vision.

BOCK: We talked to Robbins two or three times in long, extended diggings that were in the end enormously helpful.

HARNICK: The first thing, he asked what I thought was a surprising question. And he kept asking and hammering at us for months: "What is this show about?" If we gave him an answer like, "Well, it's about this dairy man, and he has three daughters," he would reply, "No. If that's what the show is about, then it's the previous adventures of the Goldberg family, and it's not enough." He said, "We have to find out what it is that gives these stories their power." And he kept asking that same question: "What's it about? What's it about?" I don't know which one of us finally said it. Maybe it was Jerry in one of those endless pre-production meetings. But *somebody* said, "Do you know what this play is about? It's about the dissolution of a way of life." Robbins got very excited. "If that's what it's about," he said, "then we have to show our audience more of the way of life that is about to dissolve. We have to have an opening number about the traditions that are going to change. This number has to be like a tapestry against which the entire show will play." And that was the beginning of "Tradition."

STONE: Did you have a title for the show yet?

BOCK: I think we had more titles than we had songs. We started with *The Old Country* and then went to *Tevye*, which we stayed with until we heard someone pronounce it "TV."

STONE: The title came from where? Not from a Chagall.

STEIN: In a sense, it did come from Chagall. Actually, when Jerry was working out the form of the show—I mean the physical structure—he was going to use a fiddler to move us from one scene to the next. So the sense of a fiddler being a part of the show was very much in our minds. Then one of us saw the Chagall painting, and the title came from that. Oddly enough, in rehearsal the fiddler kept getting dropped more and more so that, although originally he was supposed to be on the stage continually, I think now he is on the stage only briefly—possibly three or four times.

HARNICK: When Hal Prince rejoined us and became our co-producer along with Fred Coe, he looked at the list of titles, and what appealed to him about *Fiddler on the Roof* was that the word "fiddler" connected the show with music.

STONE: How did Hal get back into the picture as producer?

BOCK: Fred was having difficulty raising money, and either Jerry suggested or we all suggested he take on a co-producer.

HARNICK: Jerry Robbins was beginning to get very edgy. He wanted to do as much work as possible before the rehearsal period started, which was one of the reasons why we had those endless pre-production meetings. As you all know, or will know, once the rehearsal period starts, it seems like there's never any time. It goes too quickly. So he wanted to do all of that work. He was trying to make up his mind—driving himself and all of us crazy—over who would be the proper orchestrator and the proper set designer. He finally made up his mind. A month later, Boris Aronson called and said, "I thought you wanted me. Where's the contract?" Fred Coe, either because he wasn't able to raise the money or whatever, was not sending out contracts, and Robbins was getting very edgy about that.

BOCK: So Hal was invited to join Fred. I think Hal was persuaded, quite frankly, because Robbins was on the show.

STONE: Why did you think of Hal Prince at this point after he had rejected you at the start?

STEIN: Well, we had always wanted Hal to be in the picture if possible. Apparently Hal kind of warmed up to the material more, and, because he was intrigued by the fact that Jerry liked it, we thought there was no harm in asking him.

HARNICK: I think Hal's wife also liked the material a lot.

STONE: So Hal comes in and Fred Coe drops out.

STEIN: Fred dropped out because he became involved in another project. He was going to direct the film version of *A Thousand Clowns*, so he dropped out as the active producer after making some kind of arrangement with Hal. And Hal became the sole producer.

STONE: Immediately one thinks that there is a lead part and that part has to be cast. How long was the list of potential Tevyes?

BOCK: There were many people who auditioned and whom we considered.

HARNICK: And there were people whose agents let it be known that they wanted the role, among whom was Frank Sinatra.

BOCK: Danny Kaye ultimately decided that he was too young to have five daughters. He didn't want to play that image.

STEIN: But Zero was someone we always very seriously considered. It wasn't as though he was the last resort. He was one of the people we were very interested in from the beginning. But there were quite a number of others who were auditioned.

STONE: How far toward the head of the list was Zero Mostel?

STEIN: Pretty high up. I think with Robbins he was the first choice, and with others of us.

STONE: Was that an easy sell? To Zero?

BOCK: Well, it happened as it always does with a star. We went up to Zero and played him the score, and he read the book and wanted to do it. He loved it. It reminded him of much of his own background. I think one of the influences was his wife, Kate, who is not Jewish but was very moved by the show. I had the feeling that she was going to hit him if he didn't accept the role.

We went on and on with the pre-production meetings. Once Robbins got the handle that the show was about the dissolution of traditions, then, in his mind, in some way every scene had to deal with that. The score we had written suddenly was no longer appropriate. If I remember right, we had to rewrite nine songs because, as his idea of what the book was changed, we were carried along with it.

STEIN: In the meantime, of course, I was on the fourth or fifth draft of the book.

BOCK: I have about five drafts in my files, Joe. I assume you have twice as many.

STEIN: I don't know where they are, because I moved a lot. I have a few drafts, but there were at least five drafts written. Although we stayed with the essence and the feeling of the original material, very little of the scenes and the dialogue came directly from the original material. All of the family scenes and all of the community scenes had to be created in order to make the story work. So we were continually rewriting the book to make it of a piece.

HARNICK: I think Joe accomplished something rather remarkable. We all thought that there was a lot of dialogue from the stories which would work onstage. What we all discovered was that, when spoken aloud, it lost its quality. It was literary. Joe had to invent material—particularly the malaprops and the whole style of speech for Tevye—out of his own imagination. His reward for that was that many of the critics said, "Well, you know, how could he go wrong with that wonderful Sholom Aleichem material?"

STEIN: At the beginning, I had Tevye talking to his horse. We originally had the horse onstage. So he was talking to it and complaining about his life. Well,

Jerry didn't want a horse onstage, which was how Tevye started talking to God.

BOCK: He didn't want a horse onstage for a reason which was not the reason I thought of. He said that the scenery was going to be quite stylized, and to have a real horse that size would just throw everything out. I remember saying to him, "Well, Jerry, we *are* going to have real people." It didn't influence him at all.

STONE: Now we get to May or June 1964. The show is ready to go into rehearsal.

BOCK: We have been auditioning since September 1963 for our company.

STONE: So by the time rehearsal started, you'd put in about three weeks of work.

HARNICK: Jerry, did we have the opening number when we went into rehearsal?

BOCK: No. "Tradition" accumulated. It was not written. It just kept rolling to a bigger moment. Nobody knew what was going to happen with that thing.

STEIN: I remember I kept writing bits and pieces of dialogue for "Tradition." It was put together like a tapestry. I mean, a piece of dialogue here to introduce the rabbi, another to introduce Yente, others to introduce various other characters. They were just bits and pieces of dialogue, and somehow it was put together with the song so that it worked.

HARNICK: We had a real problem casting. We wanted people who would look as though they could conceivably be linked with this community at that time. When it came to the three daughters, we really had two different sets of needs. Jerry and I were hoping we would get some people who could sing, and Joe Stein and Jerry Robbins were looking for people who could act.

For instance, there was no question that, when she auditioned, Joanna Merlin was the best actress for the role, both physically and in what she brought in acting experience. But—and this was odd—she chose to audition in a soprano voice, and it was not good. We looked at other people. I think Joanna was brought back about five or six times. It was maddening for her, but we couldn't decide. Finally, she came back, and somebody told her to sing in a chest voice, and I think that Jerry Bock and I were so relieved that time to hear something that sounded rather pleasant that we just said, "O.K., O.K., hire her." That was the end of it.

But it was the same problem with each daughter. By the time we got into rehearsal, we had only one daughter who could really sing, and that was Julia Migenes as the second daughter. The third daughter, Tanya Everett, was a dancer essentially, and, as I say, Joanna was an actress. We had written a song—I don't remember the title—and we got into rehearsal and found they couldn't sing it. It was just too difficult for them. So we had to write a new song for them quickly. The song that we had originally written to open the show was called "We've Never Missed a Sabbath Yet." It introduced the family as it tried to get ready for the Sabbath before sunset. Jerry took part of the melody of that song and converted it into "Matchmaker, Matchmaker." It was done very quickly—in about two days. We knew the problems we had to face with these three girls, so it was written to be something they could handle.

BOCK: Case in point of writing it after you've cast it and having it work out better.

STONE: Now, all of these people come together—actors, writers, director and all the other disparate elements. Was it a fairly tranquil family from the beginning?

BOCK: Of course not!

STEIN: No, actually, I don't think we had as many problems as other shows had, because we all had the same vision of the show. Sure, there was a tremendous amount of work to be done during the rehearsal period and out of town, but I don't feel that there was any difficulty.

STONE: Did the alliance between the three of you and the director remain strong throughout?

BOCK: The alliance between ourselves—the writers—was strong. As a result, I think in relating to this *very* strong director, we were able to make an even stronger alliance.

HARNICK: Robbins is the kind of director who takes total charge, because he has a total vision, a vision which encompasses every element of the show.

For instance, I remember the first orchestra reading in Detroit. I always look forward to that moment, wondering what the score is going to sound like with all the orchestral colors. Well, I was delighted with what I heard. But Robbins kept saying no to Don Walker. "No, this is not right. This is not right. Change this. Change that." Ripping things apart. I remember Jerry Bock and myself feeling, "Oh, my God, this poor man! He's done such brilliant work, and he's being treated like an amateur." At the end of the rehearsal, we went up to Don and said, "Gee, we're sorry he was that rough on you." Don said, "I worked with him before. This was easy. He loved it."

STONE: How right was Robbins?

BOCK: As I remember, his main response was that it was over-orchestrated. Don, who is a genius, orchestrates on three or four levels so that if you say, "Cut the brass down, cut the wind section down," he has enough remaining to give you pleasure. It's not that he had to go back and re-orchestrate. It was really a matter of judicious editing and thinning out. Jerry didn't want to be overpowered by the sound he heard for the score. Predictably, Don had done his homework, and he was prepared for this kind of day.

STONE: At the same time, you had a producer who was just about at the end of his nondirecting life. Shortly thereafter, he emerged as a director, never to submerge again. How deeply was he involved creatively at this point?

STEIN: I don't think Hal was very deeply involved in the creative elements at all except as a critic. In other words, he would say, "Don't you think this scene is too long?" But basically he left it in Robbins's hands.

BOCK: He trusted Robbins so implicitly, he really felt no need to intervene.

STONE: All right, you're rehearsing and approaching the opening. At what point did your star start to become a star?

BOCK: The night after we opened. Up until that point, he was a pussycat. Out of town. No, it was when he was justly celebrated in New York that it happened. Up until then he was fantastic. He added so much.

STONE: There were stories about a certain amount of ad-libbing that had gone on even on the road.

STEIN: There wasn't any real ad-libbing on the road.

HARNICK: The only ad-libbing I can remember . . . We had a house. Part of it was on a turntable, and the wings of the house would fold out. Well, once, when Zero came on, something happened to one of the wings, and it got torn away from the side of the house and fell flat onto the stage. Zero just looked at it and said, "They're not building them like they used to."

Parenthetically, we were very careful not to have any Yiddish words either in the book or in the score, except for *l'chaim* and *mazel tov*, which everybody knows. Our theory was that we were doing the English version of what they were speaking. We had no Yiddish at all. Later on, in the New York run, Zero found that he could get some extra laughs by throwing in a couple of Yiddish words, which infuriated us.

BOCK: Zero's improvisations pre–New York were very constructive, very creative and often gave us a new insight into the character. Post-opening, they became rather destructive as far as we were concerned. I suppose it was natural. After all, he was so celebrated.

HARNICK: I must say I was running scared most of the time because here we had a show that seemed to be long, that was Jewish and was very serious. I thought, "Will an audience accept this?" In light of what happened to the show, it seems that we should have known they would. But our thought was that we hoped we would realize this gorgeous Sholom Aleichem material well enough so that maybe we would last a year.

When Zero joined us, we knew we had to do a new number for him. We had thrown out a number that Tevye did to his horse called "What a Life." So we did "If I Were a Rich Man." Along the way, I got scared. The end of it is very serious, and I wondered if it were too serious. I suggested that we cut it and end on a funnier note. Zero screamed. He said, "No! These lines—they *are* this man. You must leave them, you must!" He was so forceful about it that we decided to go with his instincts. He was absolutely right. So he did a number of things for us.

STONE: You opened first in Detroit. How long were you in Detroit, and what kind of notice did you get?

STEIN: We were roughly half an hour longer than we should have been. We knew we had to cut it by that much.

The notices? Well, they were nonexistent, except one. As it happened, there was a newspaper strike in Detroit, so the only notice we got was from *Variety*.

It was devastating. I don't remember the exact words, but it said something like, "An ordinary, run-of-the-mill show, looks like all of the other shows, amateur time, etc." We were very depressed.

BOCK: We were thrown by it.

STEIN: Except, from the very opening preview there was something in this show that the audience responded to. We did have problems. Not only were we long, but at that point the second act was clumsy. Most of the work done out of town was on the second act. But I remember the very first preview audience. I was in the back of the theater during the intermission when the people came out. I was standing next to Hal Prince when some lady ran for the telephone. She called her husband and said, "Harry, you should have given up your card game tonight. This is a very wonderful show. You won't believe it. In the middle of everything, they have a pogrom!" Except she said it in Yiddish, so I had to translate it for Hal.

HARNICK: I have never been as nervous on opening night in my life. I expected people to be walking out in droves. But it got near midnight and they didn't. A few people left, but most of the people stayed, which was an immense relief. The reception was quite warm, in spite of all the problems with the show.

STEIN: As a matter of fact, it turned out that first night was a benefit for some Jewish organization. I heard a number of people in the lobby saying, "Well, we like it, but I don't know if *they* will like it." The next night "they" came because it was a benefit, I think, for the Red Cross, and "they" did like it! So we felt we had something rather special.

STONE: How many weeks did you have out of town?

HARNICK: I guess Robbins was anxious about the amount of work that had to be done, so we spent the entire summer in Detroit and Washington. In retrospect, that may have been too long. You see, in addition to the time in Detroit and Washington, we had an extra-long rehearsal period which Robbins had demanded. We had an eight-week rehearsal.

BOCK: Yes, that's double long.

HARNICK: So we were at the show a long time.

STONE: How much of your work was done during the four weeks in Detroit?

STEIN: Quite a bit. As I said, most of the work out of town was done during the second act. The first act ended up substantially the way that we started.

STONE: But your cutting was going on?

STEIN: Well, we tightened. But in the second act we had several major problems. One of them was a very long ballet. Jerry had fashioned it at the point where Tevye learns that his daughter has married out of the faith. The ballet involved his reeling around the town, and how distraught he was, and how he was going mad, and so on. It went on for a long time—ten or twelve minutes. We found that the show died after that. We were all worried about it. We urged Robbins to cut it. And he did. He kept cutting it and cutting it. Finally, it was down to that tiny little crossover called "Chavaleh." That helped the show.

STONE: And how long is that?

STEIN: Oh, maybe a minute or two.

HARNICK: With the dancing, it runs between two and three minutes.

STEIN: So at least ten minutes were cut out of that ballet. Then, of course, when we opened in Detroit we had that scene I referred to earlier—"The Letter From America." We found it was mildly amusing, but it wasn't worth it.

HARNICK: Knowing that we were coming here, I got out the Detroit program. Musically, the first act ended up pretty much as it was. But the second act . . . the opening was a song for the revolutionary Perchik called "As Much as That." That was dropped. Next I see a number in the program called "A New World," which I don't recall having written. My guess is that they were preparing the program, and they knew we were going to have a number there, so they asked what it was going to be, and I said, "Oh, call it 'A New World,' and we'll write something." The third number was "A Letter From America," which, as we said, was changed. The next was the only song that remained— "Far From the Home I Love."

The next was a song for the tailor called "Dear, Sweet Sewing Machine." It had been one of the *most* successful songs in all the auditions that we did. People loved it. I remember during rehearsal, one day as he was staging it Robbins said, "There's something wrong with this song. I don't know what it is." Then he said, "Well, maybe it's my imagination." He kept on working on it. Well, we got to the first preview, and Austin Pendleton and Joanna Merlin got to that song. When they finished, there was no applause. They did the number O.K., but, as Jerry Bock said, there was one applaud. We couldn't believe it. In a situation like that, the first thing you say is the orchestra is too loud. So, the next preview, they took down the orchestra so you could hear the words. Still—one applaud. We never did find out why the number didn't work, although I think it was someone's theory that the show went forward all the time. You met new people, and you got involved with new relationships, and you couldn't go back to an old relationship and explore it in depth any more.

BOCK: We also saved five minutes by cutting it.

HARNICK: Then there were two songs—"Get Thee Out" and a song called "When Messiah Comes." Then there was the epilogue, "The Circle," which remained the same.

"When Messiah Comes" was originally for the rabbi. It was a conception of the Messiah having a guilty conscience; it's a funny number. This is a number which works wonderfully at parties, but when it came along onstage, the audience was very uncomfortable. As a lyricist, I was asking them to laugh at the same time the situation onstage said not to. So we had to cut it. Zero protested because he loved the number, but it just wasn't working.

STEIN: We tried it first with the rabbi, and it didn't work. Then we tried it with Zero, and it didn't work twice. As Sheldon says, the audience didn't want that kind of number. It was replaced by what is now "Anatevka."

There were a couple of other changes made in the second act. For one thing, once that large ballet was cut, Jerry was very eager to have some more dancing in the show. We struggled with where and for what purpose and finally came up with the notion of someone from another town stopping in Anatevka. Do you remember that?

HARNICK: Oh, yes.

STEIN: He had been thrown out of his own town. A peddler. I wrote a little scene between him and Tevye. Tevye is bargaining with him for the sewing machine for his son-in-law. It was kind of an amusing little scene, ending with the peddler saying, "I'm leaving here." The people of Anatevka say, "Why don't you stay? This is a nice little town." And the peddler says, "It's nothing." And the townspeople say, "Why, it's a lovely place!" And they start describing how wonderful Anatevka is, and they go into a dance.

Well, I think we spent a week and a half or two weeks trying to put that dance on the stage; but we felt that, too, was in the way of the story. It was just holding us back. We had a certain kind of movement which was being interrupted by that scene and dance. We cut it, so there's practically no dancing in that second act.

HARNICK: We were working on a song for that moment called "A Little Bit of This." Robbins had very inventively created a band out of items that these people who had been forced out of their homes carried onstage—their pots, their pans. Suddenly, all these sound effects made a percussive and a rhythmic beat. He did some absolutely beautiful things for the girl dancers. But he wasn't sure about the number. He showed it to Hal—as much as there was to show—and Hal very objectively said, "You can't do that. It's not that kind of show. This is, in effect, the villagers gamboling on the green, and they wouldn't do that." He said, "Let's be brave and do what the moment *really* is. It's a serious moment." At that point, Robbins agreed and decided we should take that piece of music we were talking about before—which originally was a Russian dance—and slow it down and put a new lyric to it. That, introduced by some of the music from "A Little Bit of This," became "Anatevka." Out of these pieces was developed a moment that was right for the show and which the audience accepted.

STONE: You've told us about Detroit. How were you received in Washington?

STEIN: As I remember, we were received very well. I think we just about sold out in Washington.

HARNICK: The reviews were very good. Plus there were long lines before we opened, which pleased us because it meant, obviously, some good word had come out of Detroit.

BOCK: Incidentally, toward the end of the run in Detroit, we were building an audience. So, even though the only review we got in Detroit—the one from *Variety*—was bad, there was good word-of-mouth.

STONE: You close in Washington, and you come to New York. By whatever mysterious jungle drum system that operates, the word has filtered into New York that there's a good show in Washington. You previewed in New York for how long?

STEIN: Not long. I think there were three or four previews at most. The show in New York was substantially the same as the one in Washington. We didn't make that many changes in Washington.

HARNICK: Of course, there was some cleaning up, but according to the program, by the time we got to Washington, the second act was in the shape it was when we opened in New York. Except we still had "When Messiah Comes," and "Anatevka" wasn't listed in the program until we came to New York.

STEIN: "Anatevka" did play in Washington, though.

STONE: O.K., it's now the morning of the opening. You wake up not having slept all night. What do you each say to yourself?

HARNICK: I said, "It doesn't matter what the critics say." By this time we knew what the audience response was. For maybe the only time in my life I thought it really didn't matter what the critics were going to say. I hated what they said anyway.

STONE: Had you built an advance?

STEIN: Oh yes, by that time there were long lines at the box office.

HARNICK: The newspaper reviews were not that good.

STONE: They were very strong for the star, as is often the case.

HARNICK: As I remember it, John McClain said, "It would have been a nice show if they hadn't put that damn pogrom in."

STONE: The *Post* headline read: "The Brilliance of Zero Mostel." And the *Journal-American* said, "Mostel Makes Musical Tick." As though it wouldn't have ticked without Mostel.

BOCK: To that point for a moment: out of town, I think it was Washington, Zero became ill.

HARNICK: Yes, it was Washington.

BOCK: He was out of the show suddenly for four performances. Paul Lipson, his understudy, went on. It was the first time he had played it. No tickets were returned.

STEIN: The thing that astonished us about that performance was that Paul had never had a rehearsal in the role. All he knew about the part was watching it. He was in the chorus, and he was Zero's understudy, but he had never played the role and never sung any of the numbers. I remember we were scared to death to put him on. I was standing in the wings feeding him lines between scenes—just two or three key lines—and the other actors were mumbling lines to him and pushing him around. The astonishing thing was, as the audience was going out I heard one woman say, "Well, Zero couldn't be better than *that!*" It was at that point I felt we had something rather special.

HARNICK: I had a friend in the audience. I spoke to him afterwards. I don't think Paul had gotten two lines of dialogue right, so I started saying to my friend, "Listen, you really didn't hear any of the dialogue." My friend didn't even hear me. He said, "Oh, the show is just wonderful! But you have got to do something about Tevye's dialogue."

STONE: Did you at any time do any work on the show for subsequent productions?

HARNICK: When the film was being made, the director, Norman Jewison, did not feel "Now I Have Everything" was revolutionary enough. I agreed with him. As part of my research, I read *A Diary of a Revolutionary.* I read all sorts of things, but, being hopelessly middle class, I couldn't write a revolutionary song. But Norman asked us if we would try to write another song for Perchik, and we did. Jerry came up with a wonderful piece of music that has the same quality as that Russian folk tune, "Meadowland." I tried my best to do a number that had some revolutionary fervor in it, and Norman accepted it. They even got as far as recording it. But then, when they realized the film was too long, something had to go. Well, that was an expendable number, and it was cut.

STONE: I was disappointed in one aspect of the film. I think that, in a sense, Norman (who is gentile in all things except his name) was so nervous about the responsibility of doing this very Jewish piece and took it so seriously that a great deal of the humor that had been in the stage version was missing from the film. I knew that Topol had been a brilliant Tevye onstage in London, but none of his fun was in the picture. The seriousness was there, but it was as if the director were too self-conscious, too nervous about it . . .

STEIN: I agree with you, Peter. He did cut a lot of the humor.

STONE: Topol played a leading man and not a comic.

STEIN: Also, he didn't play a peasant.

STONE: But he had in London. I saw his performance onstage there, and he was really wonderful.

HARNICK: To go back to your previous question about other productions . . . I didn't go to many of them—three or four, when I was asked. The only one I had any real problem with was the one in Israel. Usually, although I don't know the language in any of these countries, I can follow what's happening because I know the text well. But at the run-through in Israel, there were things happening on the stage that I didn't recognize at all. I found that the adaptor had decided to improve it! So there were scenes that went on forever, and there were scenes where he put in little jokes—*joke*-jokes. So what we had to do was go through the whole bloody thing and re-translate back to the original to clean this up. But, as far as I know, that was the only time in which we had any real problem with a foreign production.

BOCK: In the beginning, I think we dedicated this show to something personal in our lives—our fathers, our grandmothers, whatever. Having said that, I am forever astonished by what has happened to that show—the size it's taken and the geography it's taken on. I know none of us ever predicted it.

STEIN: It seems to touch people in a very special way. I don't know exactly why. Sheldon and I were in Japan for that opening. We thought that culture was as remote as we could get from the material of the show. Then, at the run-through, the Japanese producer turned to us and said, "Tell me, do they understand this show in America?" I said, "What do you mean?" He said, "It's so Japanese!"

HARNICK: We all put more into the show than we knew. I know of one particular moment . . . on the road, we thought we needed a song for Tevye and Golde in the second act. Well, I had an idea for a song. All I had was: "Do you love me?" "What?" That was the beginning of a song which took a long time to write. It took about a week of just wandering around every day trying to get another two lines and another two lines . . . I finally gave Jerry a lyric which I thought was not a lyric. It was like a dialogue scene. I gave it to him saying, "Do the best you can with it. I'll change anything if you come up with a tune." To my surprise, Jerry found a way to set the lyric and have it musically coherent. I was delighted about that. But it was an assignment. It was something that had to be done, so we did it. We put it into rehearsal, and it worked, so that was a relief. And we went on to solve whatever the next problem was.

I was watching the show about three nights after the number went in. At the end of that song, to my surprise, I suddenly burst into tears. I thought, "Why am I crying? Why am I crying?" And it was because the relationship between Tevye and Golde came out of a deep fantasy I had about my own parents, out of wanting my own parents to have related that way, which they didn't. There was a lot there that I had no idea was there until my emotions told me.

There have been so many interviews over the years, at one point I realized that we tended to forget that as good as our work was—and I do think it was good—the whole thing came from those stories, those Sholom Aleichem stories. Sholom Aleichem was so at one with those people, had such a depth of understanding, was so emotionally moved himself to say what he said, that the stories proved to be intensely universal. There would be no show if it weren't for those stories.

STONE: A question was sent in I thought I'd ask you: "I am currently reading about musicals and would like to know the difference between old-fashioned and up-to-date." I think that's an interesting question, because it addresses itself to musical comedy then, today and the day after tomorrow. Let me restate it in three parts: If *Fiddler* opened today in the exact same form as seventeen years ago, would it have the same effect? If not, what would it have to be? And where are we going?

HARNICK: The answer to all of those questions is "Yes" or "I don't know." To ask whether it would have the same impact if it opened today in the same form

... I don't think it would have opened in the same form. From my viewpoint, *Fiddler* is old-fashioned in the sense that it's a musical with a rather even balance between music and dialogue. What's happened in the last ten years is that the musical element has entered more and more into the musical so that the musical element is really becoming paramount. There is less and less spoken dialogue.

STONE: As artists, if you were doing it for today's audience, knowing the fifty-odd shows you've seen between the opening of your show then and now, is there a trend you think you would have fallen into? Is there any particular development you think would have moved you in a direction that, writing *Fiddler* today, would have resulted in any significant differences? Jerry, would you be composing the same sound? Joe, would you write the book in the same form? Sheldon, would your lyrics be much different if you were to face Tevye today?

BOCK: We *believed* in the book as nourishment for the score, so I think we would have arrived at approximately the same form. We also would go into the ethnic resource for our score and be as true to Sholom Aleichem as the ultimate source. So I can't imagine our approaching it differently, because of our fundamental belief in the book as the motivating source for the art.

STEIN: I can't conceive of writing it any differently today. I think it's the right way to tell this particular story. Old-fashioned or not, this is the way to tell this story.

HARNICK: I personally would change not the show but my attitude. I think over the years I keep learning the same lesson over and over again, which is that it always pays to be brave and to be true to the material. So if I were to start working on the show again with what I know now, I would hope that the songs would come out the same, but I think a lot of time would have been saved by not looking for things which I regarded as necessary then—like a second-act production number and comedy moments where the material should be serious. I would have been braver, and we would have saved a lot of time by not going down faulty avenues, and we would have arrived pretty much at the same show we have.

STONE: Joe, the libretto is a slowly vanishing breed. You will find that some shows don't have them at all. *Evita* won the Tony for best book, and there isn't even a credit in the program for a book. *Ain't Misbehavin'* won for best musical, and it doesn't have a libretto. So we are facing a situation in which the libretto is disappearing from the stage.

STEIN: You wrote one for *Woman of the Year.*

STONE: Well, it took its lumps. I wonder whether you feel you took your lumps. I wonder whether you feel that maybe that's partly responsible for the sickly condition of the musical theater? It seems to be very discouraging to anyone coming up.

STEIN: Certain musicals have to have librettos, and others don't. I can't conceive of *Fiddler* being done without one. I can't conceive of *She Loves Me* being done without one. It depends on the nature of the story you want to tell. I don't think the libretto is going to disappear.

STONE: Of course, a lot of the director-choreographers who have so much power in the theater today get very nervous with words. Gower Champion did not like words very much. Jerry Robbins is slightly more prone to understand them. Fosse hates them. With *Dancin'*, he went so far as to create a libretto-less musical. Jerry, Sheldon—are you conceiving shows, separately or together, that don't have any?

HARNICK: No, but a friend made a very interesting observation: Because of television, we are so deluged with stories that little by little we have absorbed all this material, making us much quicker to comprehend a situation in a theatrical setting. Because of this, we grow impatient very quickly, and that means there have to be fewer and stronger words to get the point across. I don't know whether that's true, but it sounds reasonable to me. Between television and movies, we are bombarded with visual images. I would say that the word is less important—then a show comes along like *Sweeney Todd* in which all the words are important, whether spoken or sung.

STEIN: I think you have to take advantage of a disadvantage. If this is in fact a trend—a trend to little or no book—it seems to me to demand that those who feel very strongly about the importance of character relationships, story development, etc. in musicals express this in their work. I personally believe in the libretto.

STONE: On that happy note, I want to thank the three of you for coming here and sharing with us *Fiddler on the Roof.*

CABARET

Sheldon Harnick, Moderator
Fred Ebb
Ronald Field
John Kander
Joe Masteroff

SHELDON HARNICK: One of the reasons this panel is especially interesting to me is that, years ago, someone said to me, "You know what would make a wonderful musical? *The Berlin Stories* by Christopher Isherwood." I read it and I thought, "It can't be done. Maybe you could make a play out of it, but not a musical." So I am particularly interested in how *Cabaret* came about. Whose idea was it?

JOE MASTEROFF: It came from Hal Prince, as everything seems to. I had just done *She Loves Me* with Hal, the lyrics of which were written by Sheldon Harnick, whom you may know. Hal and I were together one day, and he talked about the possibility of doing *I Am a Camera*, the John van Druten play based on the Isherwood stories, as a musical. We both agreed that if we were going to do *I Am a Camera*, what was interesting to us basically was the sound of Germany in that period. Obviously we had heard all the Kurt Weill music, all of the Lotte Lenya records, and somehow in the back of our heads that is how we wanted it to sound.

HARNICK: At that time, was Hal contemplating doing it as both producer and director?

MASTEROFF: Absolutely. He had just directed *She Loves Me*, as you know, and he was all gung-ho to do another one.

HARNICK: Fred and John, were you called by Hal then?

FRED EBB: We were doing *Flora, the Red Menace*, which we all know and hum. Hal was not directing. George Abbott directed that, and Hal produced it. Anyway, sometime during the Boston run Hal said, "Would you like to do *I Am a Camera*?" He said, "No matter what happens to *Flora*, the day after it opens we'll go to work." That seemed like a good deal to me. So we agreed to do it. I didn't have a clue how to do it, I must say. The fact is, *Flora* was not a success; and the fact is, at four o'clock the next afternoon we did meet.

MASTEROFF: I want to add a little postscript to that, just to show how incredibly wonderful my taste is. Hal asked me what I thought of having Fred and John do *I Am a Camera,* and I told him I thought it was a terrific idea because I thought, and still think, that the score of *Flora, the Red Menace* was sensational. One of the best scores ever written.

JOHN KANDER: Thank you.

HARNICK: It *is.*

EBB: I am very glad I came here!

HARNICK: I think everybody here is aware of what a far cry *Cabaret* is from *I Am a Camera.* How did the concept of the show develop? Were there meetings, discussions? How was the book approached?

MASTEROFF: There were thousands of meetings. I went back and looked at my notes today to refresh my mind, and I see that my first outline for this projected musical was done in the summer of 1963. The show eventually opened in November of 1966. Along the way there are outline after outline, notes from Hal to me, notes from me to Hal. Lyrics of songs that have long since been forgotten by everybody but Fred and John and me. The show had a very, very gradual metamorphosis. Not a painful one, I think. But it certainly did change as we went along.

HARNICK: How many of these meetings were group meetings with you and John and Fred and Hal as opposed to meetings with just you and Hal?

MASTEROFF: I think we almost always all met together. Once we started on this show, it was very much a cooperative effort. Don't you recall it that way?

EBB: Yes, I do.

KANDER: One of the best things about Hal as a leader of a collaboration is, as you said, you have thousands of meetings, and by the time you get finished with those thousands of meetings you are all doing the same show. It rarely happens with a Hal Prince show that you get out of town and the choreographer is doing one piece and the song writers are doing another and the playwright is doing another. It all happened in a very close, collaborative way.

HARNICK: Ron, when did you become associated with the production?

RONALD FIELD: I remember I was in Beirut doing my fifth night club show when *Flora* opened. I was doing a lot of night club work all over the world at the time. I had done two flop shows on Broadway, so I was out doing my nightclub work. One day I got back from Beirut, and my agent said that Liza Minnelli needed an act. She had won the Tony Award for *Flora,* which had closed, and she was very hot. My agent asked if I would think about doing her act. I said, "For *nothing* I would do that act!"

So I met her, and she took a chance on me. Based on that act, which turned out to be an enormous success for us all, Fred and John then used their powers of persuasion on Hal to convince him that I should do the dances and nightclub numbers for *Cabaret.* He finally was convinced and signed me. Then he saw a terrible production of *Show Boat* I did at Lincoln Center, and I was told he was having great trouble with the decision he had made and that he was very nervous about me. So it was under that cloud I went into rehearsal for *Cabaret.*

HARNICK: You had not been part of the meetings?

FIELD: No. I spent a summer with Hal, off and on, discussing the show. Let me say that in the mature age I have gotten to, I now realize I paid no attention to the things I should have paid attention to working with that man.

HARNICK: When did the idea of the cabaret as the central metaphor of the show arise? How did that evolve?

MASTEROFF: It was again a very gradual thing. John and Fred had written a number of songs that we called cabaret songs. They didn't seem to relate to anything in particular, except that they sounded vaguely Germanic—like what you might have heard in a night club in Germany in 1930.

EBB: These were not book songs. Hal thought that the show should open atmospherically and that we should do a mélange of songs taking place all over Berlin to set up where we were, what was going on at the time. So we wrote five of them. They were very short, and they were supposed to be like a prologue to the piece. One was about Herman the German. One took place in a radio station.

KANDER: One was a Chinese song.

EBB: Sung by a Chinese girl, yes. You see, we were going for what was exotic and—

KANDER: —decadent—

EBB: —about that period. One of these five songs was called "Wilkommen," and it was sung by a little man in a night club. At the end of these five songs, the story was going to begin. The prologue was the first creative writing we did on the show. Then we had the idea of using this little man as a thread for the entire musical. It was quite by accident that we stumbled onto him. We may have even been in the sixth month of our meetings by that time.

KANDER: "Wilkommen" was literally the first song we wrote for the show.

HARNICK: Let me ask the basic question: Which comes first, the music or the lyrics?

KANDER: With Fred and me?

HARNICK: Yes. Or *does* either come first?

KANDER: No. We work in the same room at the same time, and Fred usually has an idea for something. Or we talk over the theatrical moment, and then we begin to improvise together. Most of the time this is the way it works. We are always in the same room at the same time. We once wrote a song for this show on the telephone, but it was like being in the same room. That was "Meeskite."

HARNICK: So it was your thought that following the prologue what would most likely develop would be a traditional libretto of scenes and songs?

EBB: Exactly.

HARNICK: Joe, were you hearing these songs as they were written?

MASTEROFF: Yes. As I said, originally it was thought these five songs would be put at the beginning of the show. Along the way, we decided to insert them in between the book scenes. I looked at the early scripts today—of which I have lots—and I see that they were put between the book scenes in a rather random fashion and eventually, as we all know, somehow they each seemed to reflect on the book scene that had gone before. I don't know whether we artfully put them there. I guess we did. But somehow in the early scripts they were just sort of higgledy-piggledy. There was a book scene, and then there was one of these five songs, and then there was another book scene.

The show evolved in a very lucky way. Even the accidents that happened were fortunate ones. A lot of the things we have been most congratulated on over the years were things that really happened sort of accidentally. We made the best of what had gone wrong and somehow it turned out great.

HARNICK: Well, but as they say, chance favors the prepared mind, right?

EBB: Is that what they say?

HARNICK: In other words, with these ideas being discussed and played over the months, suddenly a light went on in somebody's mind with the thought, "Hey, there's a cabaret here!"

EBB: I think it was the use of this little character. We probably used the five original songs at random throughout, but what kept them unified was the use of this little man. This little MC. Then we decided to relate these numbers to the book. So most of the five songs went. The character stayed and only "Wilkommen" remained of the five.

HARNICK: Aside from the cabaret, what were the other differences between *Cabaret* and *I Am a Camera*?

MASTEROFF: Well. *I Am a Camera* is a very thin play, unfortunately. I'm one of the few people old enough to have seen it when Julie Harris first did it on Broadway. She was incredible. She made the play work. But I don't think it would have been very much without her.

HARNICK: Was she a cabaret singer in it?

MASTEROFF: Well, yes, but obviously she didn't sing because it wasn't a musical.

HARNICK: Was that from the original story in *The Berlin Stories*?

MASTEROFF: Yes. As far as the guy was concerned, there really was no character there either in *The Berlin Stories* or in *I Am a Camera*. He was, as Isherwood said in the book, a camera. Sort of a cypher. When writing the musical, we felt we had to create some sort of a guy. I was more comfortable writing an American than an Englishman, so Christopher Isherwood was turned into an American named Clifford Bradshaw. I wrote Sally pretty much as she had been written in *I Am a Camera*, but I think her character was never very successful in *Cabaret*. This worried me a lot until it was pointed out to me that there just isn't time in a musical to develop characters very thoroughly. If I'd had more stage time, I think Sally could have been a much more interesting character.

I don't think any of the actresses who have ever played the part has ever been too successful with it. I have always said, "It's really my fault. The part just isn't there." Though I must say that, as I was going through the old scripts today, I saw a lot of terrific stuff I wrote for her that we had to cut out along the way. But that always happens.

HARNICK: This is a slight digression, but was there a real Sally Bowles; and, if so, do you know anything about her?

MASTEROFF: There was a real Sally Bowles.° Isherwood said he knew her in Berlin and that she was very much as he pictured her in his book.

HARNICK: You fellows were writing songs that suggested the period and color of Germany at the time. But traditionally, before you start to write the book songs, you have an idea of what the book is going to be. Joe, did you give them an outline at some point?

MASTEROFF: As I said, my first outline was in the summer of 1963, and I outlined and wrote and outlined and wrote and re-outlined constantly from then on. So I think there was always material around for John and Fred to work from.

EBB: It seems to me, at one point we counted up and found we had written about forty-seven songs out of which we eventually used fifteen. The narrative kept shifting, and there were many more scenes that were seriously considered that never were done. Also, characters were being added. The whole Lenya-Gilford relationship came later, I think. So we were never working from a completed libretto. But I don't know of any time we ever have.

HARNICK: Joe, I remember when we did *She Loves Me*, you just gave us an outline with no moments for songs marked in. You left it up to Jerry Bock and myself to pick those spots. Did you follow the same procedure with *Cabaret*?

MASTEROFF: Yeah. I think it is a terrific way to work. I mean, I wrote scenes and Fred and John plucked the songs out of them in every case. I'm talking about the book songs, of course. We never talked about it in advance. They just took the scenes and found what turned them on.

HARNICK: I am a redoubtable dialogue thief. I tend to take the best jokes of the book I am working with and put them into the songs so I get the credit and the book writer doesn't. I was wondering, Fred, do you work with dialogue that way?

EBB: Oh, sure.

HARNICK: I don't mean necessarily as a thief, which I am. But to reshape what may be given to you as a dialogue scene so that it comes out as song.

EBB: Yes. Particularly in *Cabaret* it seems to me we did that. I think Joe wrote the whole pineapple exchange. That was a dialogue scene.

KANDER: And we stole it.

° Editor's Note: In his book, *Christopher and His Kind*, Isherwood wrote that her real name was Jean Ross and that she died in 1973.

EBB: I lifted it and said, "Can I write a song?" I turned out to be very clever for having thought of this wonderful idea of a gift when in fact it was Joe's. That happens any number of times—the librettist hits on something you can use like that. Some librettists won't give them to you, but most will.

MASTEROFF: But the interesting thing I have noticed is, with these gentlemen, the really terrific songs in the show are always the ones in which they have gone beyond what I have written—beyond the book scene—and into their own imaginations. When they play a song for me, it is so exciting because it really is so much better. In other words, I have gone up to seventy-five, and they start at seventy-six and take it to a hundred. I think that is terrific.

HARNICK: I played the record this morning to remind myself of the score and found myself marvelling at it even more than the previous times I have heard it. There was one song—"Meeskite"—which I listened to, I guess as a lyricist. I thought, "That's a perfect lyric! That is an absolutely perfect lyric!" The development of it from the beginning, the idea, the expression of the idea, and that *totally* satisfying ending! Was this suggested by anything in the material, or was this just a God-given . . . ?

KANDER: It all came from Fred. All of it.

EBB: It was a story my mother told me, in fact.

MASTEROFF: You steal from your mother?

EBB: Oh, I steal from my mother, yeah! My mother told me that exact story. It was about two very unattractive people that she had known and they had this fabulous-looking child. The purpose of the song in the show was to expose, at his own engagement party, that Gilford's character was in fact Jewish; to create the inherent drama there. I was asked by Hal if possibly it could be comic. Now I knew by this time that Gilford was cast, or at least being seriously thought of, so I had an image of a guy. Jack is a very specific personality to me. The rest came from that. So I called my mother . . .

I think we are all a little bit like that. People who write tend to remember things. You store them away, and then you never know when you are going to use them or when they are going to just jump to the front of your head for some reason. But that's how that happened. It wasn't a story I really invented. It's a story I heard.

HARNICK: The way you expressed it, the way you put it into verse, is just absolutely superb.

MASTEROFF: It is such a beautiful and loving song, too. I mean, when you hear it, you think what a nice person must have written that. And then you meet Fred.

EBB: *Now* it starts!

HARNICK: As I recall, there was a problem with one song, "If You Could See Her."

EBB: Oh, that was so awful.

HARNICK: In writing this show, you must have been walking a fine line as to how much you really should go into the anti-Semitism of the period and the country.

EBB: I dreamed it. I had a dream. It was on the set of *Hello, Dolly!* that this was happening, so I clearly was having a success dream. What happened on this runway was that Joel Grey came out, and there was a gorilla in a tutu. That's the truth. No words, no music, but that was the image. And then I told Hal I had dreamed it. I said that I dreamed about a number in which Joel would come out with a gorilla in a tutu, and he thought that was kind of baroque. Which it was. And then I tried to get a song—I know it is silly—to fit that image. It was so clear to me that it would look wonderful. Eventually this song came. It was him, of course, loving this gorilla. And at the end he said, "And if you could see her through my eyes, she wouldn't look Jewish at all." So the song could serve to show how anti-Semitism was creeping in. I thought it had a dramatic validity. This memory is very clear to me: Johnny lived in the Village, and we were working down there, and we called Hal on the phone. I sang it to him over the phone, and he really loved it. He wanted very much to go with it. And, in fact, we did go with it.

HARNICK: With that ending in it?

EBB: Yes, indeed. We opened with it. It got an amazing reaction from the audience, because they did laugh, and then they kind of realized what they were laughing at, and they would stop laughing. There was sort of a polite hand. It made them very nervous, which is exactly what Hal wanted. I must say that it was exciting me to put the audience into that frame of mind, because we were building, after all, to a climax there. I mean, everybody knew the ending of this story. So everything that happened had a lot of weight because we all knew that the Nazis were going to come to power and all those things would happen. So it was successful in that way, and nobody criticized it.

But towards the end of the Boston run, we started to get letters. One was from a rabbi who said that the graves of six million Jews were pleading for us not to do this. It was a very upsetting letter. And then we got to New York, and, about the second night of previews, some lady literally accosted me in the back of the theater. I am now told that lady never existed, but she *did* exist. She had a clipboard and a sweater, and she asked me if I was, in fact, the lyric writer? I said yes, I was. And she said that the line at the end of the gorilla song had to be changed, and that, if it were not changed, pressure groups would be after us. This line was totally unacceptable to her. She created this enormous commotion.

Hal was worried. Deeply worried. And deeply pressured. There was a visit to his office where there was a real threat of cancelling theater parties over *one* lyric line. There was a meeting at the bottom of the Broadhurst Theater, which I remember vividly, where I was asked to take that line out. Hal (who of course is noted for his courage and his daring) could not at that moment in his life—with as much as *Cabaret* meant to him and to all of us—take the chance of bucking an enormous group. All I ever saw was this skinny lady in a sweater, but apparently there were a lot of her. I had a lot of hysterics about that. And I *did* change it. The line we changed it to was, "She isn't a *meeskite* at all." Everybody was made very unhappy about that.

The original line was sometimes thrown in. I remember I asked if I could have the line when Walter Kerr came. I remember I asked if I could have the line for the Actors Fund performance. And Joel would literally go out and say it as if he had just forgotten that he was forbidden to say it.

And we had it, "She isn't a *meeskite* at all" for the three years we ran in New York. In the movie, Bob Fosse was willing to put the original line back. But if you listen very carefully, it is totally tacit in the movie. Joel turns to the camera and says, whispering: "She wouldn't look Jewish at all." There is no music. And that is because, had *he* had any flak, he could have gone in and re-recorded it.

KANDER: The curious thing about that, not to labor this too much, is that we *all* seemed to have made some theatrical miscalculation which to this day I can't understand. The song was to end that way, to have you laughing and then catch your breath, to make you, the audience, realize how easily you could fall into a trap of prejudice. And the Jewish members of the audience, my family included, all insisted that the song was really saying that Jews looked like gorillas. It's a puzzle that has never been solved.

HARNICK: I would imagine—and this is just a guess on my part—that you must have reached a certain point in the development of the show where things began to snowball, where the show's concept solidified and everything fell into place. Am I right?

MASTEROFF: I guess it was a small snowball. It just seemed to evolve very gradually. I don't recall that we ever were seriously going in the wrong direction or were ever terribly concerned about the possibility that what we were doing was bad. We all were rather turned on by the material. I know I was. I know Fred and John were. Hal certainly was. Ron was. We were all quite happy to be doing what we were doing, and it just evolved in the way most shows evolve.

HARNICK: It also sounds as though there was no pressure on you. There was no deadline. I know too often in the past I have committed to certain deadlines and then regretted it bitterly when the show seemed to suffer because of lack of time to think and write. From what you say, it sounds like Hal just really let this develop.

MASTEROFF: As a matter of fact, at one point we were about to go into production, I don't remember the exact date, but Hal decided to postpone it for six months. He felt that the show wasn't ready. I think he was and that he was right to postpone it. None of us felt bad about that. I'm sure I didn't. So, at that time, he did *Superman* instead.

EBB: Well, we had made a big structural error in *Cabaret*. Didn't we open in three acts?

MASTEROFF: Oh yeah, but that was easy to change. We thought it would be fun to open in three acts because musicals were always in two. At one time, musicals used to be in three, and somehow this seemed to fall into a three-act shape. We liked the idea of doing it in three acts, because it was sort of different. We thought there were a lot of different things about this show. But when we opened, it didn't work very well in three. It was quite easy to put it into two. It was immediately better in two, I thought, though some people consistently said three acts were better.

EBB: Me.

KANDER: The night it went into two acts, Fred took to his bed. Shortly afterwards I can remember him in the Bradford Hotel with Joel Grey on one side with one hand and me on the other side with the other hand saying, "It's not a disaster."

EBB: Well, we lost two terrific songs, I'll tell you that. There was one song called "The End of the Party" that ended—was it the first act or the second?

KANDER: It must have been the second. The first act had an ending I always loved, which was "Tomorrow Belongs to Me" done very sweetly.

EBB: I think I was really missing the musical moments. See, we got good reviews in three acts. I guess every time there was changing, I was afraid they were taking a hit away from me. It would have been my first, and it was.

KANDER: You should know that if anybody in an audience doesn't like the show, they will find Fred. It can be a very successful night, and all the rest of the collaborators can be feeling quite cheery, and Fred will come along and be extremely unhappy because he sat in back of a man who picked up and went home in high dudgeon. Or say Fred went to the men's room, somebody would attack him saying, "Are you connected with this show?"

I remember once we were all sitting in the back of a theater having a meeting while the show was going on. About forty-five minutes into the show, this man sort of assaulted us. He said, "I have been sitting there for an hour waiting for you to grab me. When are you going to grab me?" And Hal furiously said, "Well, we certainly can't grab you when you are out here!"

MASTEROFF: It's interesting that I never thought the show would be a hit. When you talk about sitting in the back of the theater, it seems to me that when we were in Boston, people just kept streaming out of the theater. Ten minutes after the curtain went up, people started departing.

EBB: That's right.

KANDER: Yeah, we lost a lot of people.

MASTEROFF: The reason was that audiences really didn't know what to expect at that point. The name of the show was *Cabaret*, and they expected it to be a normal kind of Broadway musical. Within ten minutes, they had seen these not-so-great-looking chorus girls, and the show seemed to be a little on the grim side, and people began trooping up the aisles. Believe me, we were all very depressed about it! It wasn't a cheerful time at all, at least not for me.

HARNICK: You probably didn't have to do backers' auditions for this show, did you?

EBB: Not with Hal Prince's track record.

HARNICK: Did you have to play for the theater party ladies?

KANDER: Yeah.

HARNICK: And how did they react?

KANDER: Well, there was this one very grim theater party lady who was a man.

EBB: It was at my apartment. All these people came. I had never done it before, and of course I was very nervous.

HARNICK: Just for any of you who don't know what we are talking about, this is when you play for a group of women who sell theater parties. They are very important to the advance sale of the show.

EBB: *Really* important. There was this really grim type there, you know, with his hair sticking out. He kept frowning at me, and I got a fix on him. I did the whole show, and I didn't think I did it very well. And I thought this particular person really hated it. It turned out it was Boris Aronson, our set designer. He had just showed up to hear the material. I thought he was a theater party lady, and he threw me into a real panic. I don't remember if the theater party ladies loved it or not. If they love it, they are not supposed to tell you they love it. It's all very polite. I think that was the only time we ever had to play it for anybody.

HARNICK: Was there anything particularly odd about the casting of this show? Or was this a standard show to be cast, with the exception of the little man?

EBB: I remember Joe or Hal had very specific actors in mind for everything. One of the miracles of *Cabaret* was that we got them. I mean, the people we had in mind were the people we got.

KANDER: We really were writing for Lenya and Gilford by the time we started writing those parts.

EBB: And the MC was written for Joel. That was an enormous advantage, I remember.

MASTEROFF: But, of course, we did have a lot of trouble with our other two leads. Sally Bowles and Christopher. I don't think we ever found exactly what we wanted for those parts.

HARNICK: I thought Jill Haworth was a very attractive performer, and, reading the reviews again, I was stunned to find that Walter Kerr, who loved the show, hated her and thought she was such a tremendous drawback.

KANDER: That was a very unfortunate situation. If I remember correctly, he had raved about practically every female star that season. He was getting some rather bad letters about the fact he had gone overboard for women stars. I think Barbara Harris had opened just before that in *The Apple Tree*. Maybe it's oversimplifying to say that, because poor Jill was next up at bat, Kerr tried to compensate by slaughtering her. She didn't deserve that sort of review. She really did not.

EBB: I remember, one of Hal's ideas was to put her in a black wig.

KANDER: Before that it was to put her in three wigs. One color for each act. Sally Bowles was supposed to be so bizarre and crazy and baroque that she was going to be a blonde, a redhead and a brunette. And I rememeber just thinking, "This sounds weird!" Jill was a gorgeous blonde girl. Gorgeous. What the black wig did was to soften that sort of American prettiness and put her into a more bizarre mode. Her green fingernails worked with the black hair.

MASTEROFF: It is very interesting that *I Am a Camera* was totally about Sally Bowles, and she was what made the show work. And yet, with *Cabaret*, one of the points Hal made while we were in Boston was that the show was not going to live or die on how well her character registered. If, God forbid, she didn't work, the show would still succeed. In many ways, he turned out to be right.

KANDER: One of the people all three of us were considering for the role, by the way, was Liza Minnelli. Hal felt that she was absolutely wrong for it.

MASTEROFF: I must say, I felt that way, too. I must take equal blame.

EBB: There's no blame there. In the stage version she was supposed to be British.

MASTEROFF: Liza is phenomenally talented and was the same then. But she was extremely young at the time, and somehow she could not be a British girl. The movie's solution, which was to make her American, did not occur to us. Had it occurred to us, I think it would have been rather late to make that shift. It would have been a major overhaul.

HARNICK: Let me ask John and Fred, did you do much research? It came to mind when you mentioned Lenya. I was listening to the album this morning, and the songs for her are very characteristic of that period. They do have a Brecht-Weill flavor, and at the same time they are very much your own. I was curious as to what kind of research you had done.

KANDER: What I did musically was to get records of German jazz and German cabaret songs of the Twenties. There was an incredible collection that came out on LP—I don't know if it's still available—about six records of all kinds of people. I listened and listened and listened and then put them away and forgot about them. So when we came to writing the songs, I didn't think in terms of writing pastiche or imitations. Somehow or other, the flavor had soaked in just enough.

In some of the reviews that were bad for me, I was told that I had written watered-down Kurt Weill. I sort of anticipated that criticism. I remember telling Lenya that I suspected that it might happen in some of the reviews, and telling her that I never intended to imitate Mr. Weill at all. She took my face in her hands and said, "No, no, darling. It is not Weill. It is not Kurt. When I walk out on stage and sing those songs, it is *Berlin*." And I thought if she felt that way, to hell with everybody else.

HARNICK: Fred, what kind of research did you do?

EBB: It was harder for me because, you know, those records didn't come with a text. So I never knew what the jokes were. But there was a *sound.* I think you just do what you think is right.

HARNICK: You didn't bother reading histories of the period, or did you?

EBB: Not really. I looked at some, just quickly. Mostly I was interested in musical theater there and, of course, cabaret. There wasn't a lot of literature available to me in that particular area. So I heard all the records that Johnny brought over. That gave me sort of a feeling. I remember one of them was during a live performance of something and it was getting *screams!* It was the most frustrating record you could possibly have. Clearly, the songs were impudent and irreverent and were often sexual. I knew I should probably go for some good sex jokes.

HARNICK: Ron, for you research must have been more neccessary. How did you go about it?

FIELD: I just imagined myself a choreographer in Berlin in 1930.

HARNICK: As simple as that?

FIELD: It almost was. I thought about what I would do if I were a choreographer in Berlin working in a second-rate nightclub. I thought that my reference probably would be American movies.

HARNICK: Not German?

FIELD: No, American. I had worked so much in Europe, and I understood the European choreographers. They were always ten years behind us. "Le jazz hot" and all that. The genesis was always on this side of the ocean. So I imagined that I was a German choreographer. So everything became harder and more Germanic. The time-steps weren't Fred Astaire-like. They were Brunnhilde-like. Fred would sing the song to me, and, with that orientation in mind, I'd go ahead. And I hired girls with sort of heavy thighs and had the costumes cut in sort of the wrong places.

HARNICK: Was there an overlap of directing and choreography, or were your two functions essentially separate?

FIELD: They were totally separate. In fact, we worked about twelve blocks away from where Hal was rehearsing. He was at the George Abbott Theater, and I was down at the Diplomat Hotel in some funny ballroom with Joel and all the dancers. I can remember one time Joel just being so depressed and unhappy because he had nothing to do with the book. He never even saw Hal Prince. He said, "I don't like this at all. I feel I have no connection with the show." I can remember saying to him, "I have this sneaky suspicion that this is the part people would dream to have. The part of the decade."

So I just went on. I would only meet Hal at run-throughs, when he would see my work. It was a very alienating kind of feeling, and yet—because I had spent time with him during the summer and had really spent time with Fred and John and the music—it worked.

HARNICK: When you became associated with the production, were you given a script and score which you then had to stage? Or were you asked to contribute your own notions for songs at all?

FIELD: I wouldn't have even presumed. It never occurred to anyone to turn to me and ask, "What do you think?" I just sat there listening and soaking it in. I was amazed at the way Fred and John would just come in and sing song after song, and Hal would just turn and say, "For *this* production?!" And the next day they would be back with another song, and I would go, "Oh, wait a minute, this is so much better than what they did yesterday." I was amazed that in one day they had written an entirely new song.

I remember saying to John and Fred, "I don't believe how good-natured you are. You sell a song to Hal, and he says, 'What high school production would you like that to be in?'" I was so admiring of their being able to go through that. I was sitting in Fred's living room when I said that. Fred turned to John and said, "Well, let's show him." And they showed me this stack of music that had been turned down by Hal. They played me three of the songs. One of them began, "What good is sitting alone in your room?" I stuttered, "But that's wonderful! Why isn't that in the show?" And Fred said, "Hal says he doesn't want two title songs." I asked, "What's the other one?" And it was "Wilkommen," because it had the stuff about welcome to the cabaret in it. So Hal figured that that was the title song, and he didn't want another song with the word "cabaret" in it in the second act. "Oh, my Lord," I said, "that is *so* wonderful." So they said, "Well, tomorrow at the meeting would you . . . ?"

I remember I was so nervous. We were sitting in George Abbott's office, and I said, "Hal, I heard a song yesterday that I think is just wonderful." And he said, "Well, play it again." And John and Fred got up and played it, and it went into the show.

HARNICK: Was there much thrown out on the road? Was there much rewriting on the road? Or was it pretty well set?

EBB: When we went from three acts into two, we lost a couple, and there was a song we had called "Roommates" that turned into "Perfectly Marvelous."

KANDER: We did write another song called "Song of Love." It was for Joel. It was absolutely filthy and I loved it, but it never made it.

HARNICK: I think I'll ask now some of the questions that were submitted. When you went into rehearsal, did you make lead sheets to give to the cast, or did you distribute a piano arrangement?

KANDER: What you give the singer depends on whether the singer can read music or not. My process is to write out a piano-vocal version of the song. It gets printed and distributed to those who can use it. We did *Cabaret* before cassettes were used so extensively, so most of the time, if somebody could not read music, I or the rehearsal pianist would simply play it over and over again for the person.

HARNICK: Have you ever considered rewriting the stage version to include songs written for the film version that are now hits? Such as "Maybe This Time" and "The Money Song"? Has that occurred to you?

EBB: It's not that it occurs to you. People license *Cabaret* and you find them doing it anyway. Every production I've seen since the movie has included "Maybe This Time." Somehow or other they've always managed to squeeze it in. And they also tend to do the new "Money Song" as opposed to the one we used in the stage production. What they are doing is beefing up Sally's part. You know, it's not a very good part. She has two and a half songs. If you get what would be considered a star on the summer circuit, for example, she would no doubt consider that unsatisfactory. Adding those two numbers gives her another solo and a duet. She was not in the original "Money Song."

HARNICK: Somebody wanted to know the story of "I Don't Care Much," how it was written for *Cabaret*, why it was dropped, and why it appeared in an early version of the vocal selections from *Cabaret*.

KANDER: "I Don't Care Much" was written for *Cabaret*. It was written when Fred and I were having dinner together with a couple of friends. This was early in our collaboration, and we were showing off about how fast we could write a song. We bragged about it, so the other two people cleared the table. We said we would write it between dessert and coffee. So they said fine, and we went to the piano. Fred said, "What will we write about?" I just responded with, "I don't care much." So that's what we did. I started playing some sort of waltz rhythm, and Fred started singing "I Don't Care Much," and in fifteen minutes we had this song. That's the truth. It was a song Hal liked particularly. For a time, we considered making it one of the Berlin songs because we always saw it being done by somebody in a trench coat up against a lamp post. But it was never seriously considered.

Then, when we were previewing in New York, Goddard Lieberson, who was producing the original cast album, felt that "Cabaret"—which was by that time a hit song—should be in the first act. He thought it would be stronger there. He thought that we could put another song, perhaps "I Don't Care Much," where "Cabaret" had been. For some reason which I will never understand, Hal agreed to that. And for two performances that is the way it played. And never again. It was a disaster.

HARNICK: I would love you to comment on the "Telephone Song." Where did that come from? Was that called for in the script?

MASTEROFF: The idea always was that the night club had telephones on the tables over which people could talk to each other.

EBB: I think this is an interesting example of musical theater working in the best way it can, given that we are so collaborative. In this case, the librettist gives the composer and lyric writer this wonderful idea, and we write a song, and then we give it to Ron. I don't know how many of you saw *Cabaret* onstage, but the "Telephone Song" became, in my opinion, one of the best musical comedy dance moments I have ever seen. Ron went one step further. These people who met by phone connected. He had one couple who met and kissed and never stopped kissing. They never broke their embrace from the beginning of the number to the end. I remember they were called "the kiss couple."

HARNICK: On the record, what is fascinating is the development of the idea, the way it goes another chorus, another chorus, and then it goes somewhere else.

KANDER: There's a curious thing about that song on the record. Ron's staging was absolutely brilliant, but when we came to record it, there was no way, by just listening to it, you got the excitement that he brought to it. Now this is an example of Goddard Lieberson having a good idea: He suggested, to my horror, that we double the tempo on the recording. We tried it reluctantly. And all of a sudden there was some semblance of the excitement that Ron had brought to it.

FIELD: The scary moment in my life was when Jerome Robbins came to see the run-through that we gave before we went to Boston. I was nervous about him seeing my work. Naturally, Hal has a great deal of respect and affection for Jerry. Jerry thought the show was wonderful, but his strong suggestion was that any dancing that didn't take place as part of the performance at the Kit Kat Klub be cut from the show. In other words, his suggestion was that we cut that telephone number and cut the engagement party dance that Lenya did with the sailors.

EBB: Oh, I remember that.

FIELD: Scary! Hal really just overruled it, a decision I will always be grateful for.

HARNICK: Just one last question. Though your contracts give you all approval of your own collaboration, what happens if your director doesn't want to stage a song or a scene or wants the play restructured? This would possibly take you away from discussing *Cabaret* because I know that this doesn't come up much working with Hal, but how would you answer that?

KANDER: For me every situation defines itself differently. Certainly in *Cabaret,* if Hal felt very strongly about something, I'm sure we would have— often did—give in. There are other situations where you know that you are in less-than-adequate hands, and you had better stand up. And then you don't. And then you are very sorry.

EBB: A wise man once said, "Show business contracts with writers are basically unenforceable." I think that's true, because you can't really get anybody to do anything. No matter what you have got on the paper about approval or about how you have to have this or that, your option eventually becomes, "I either leave this project and don't have any more to do with it, or I go along with the majority opinion." You can't just stand there and refuse to do something, even though it is written in there that you are allowed to refuse. I mean, what good is that? Eventually you are talking about getting a show on and succeeding. The best that we all can do is collaborate, and maybe eight out of ten times things aren't going to come in exactly the way you had in mind. *Cabaret* is one of the happiest memories I have because that was *mostly* what I had in mind, and I think mostly is the best you can do.

TORCH SONG TRILOGY

Peter Stone, Moderator
Harvey Fierstein
Estelle Getty
John Glines
Ada Janik
Lawrence Lane
Ned Levy

PETER STONE: We are here to celebrate and examine and inquire after and bisect, and we are fortunate in having a very large representation of the show. Let's start at the beginning with the author. When did you first set a pencil to paper?

HARVEY FIERSTEIN: In high school I took creative writing, but I didn't do well at it. Later on, at La Mama, a lot of people were writing plays for me to perform, and I thought it would be fun to create a play for them all to act in. Its original title was *Who's Afraid of Ellen Stewart?*, later changed to *In Search of the Cobra Jewels.* I put all the playwrights in it, and we did it. I don't think I would ever have written again, except that the *Village Voice* sent a critic who called me the devil come to earth for writing this horrible thing. So I figured this is a talent I should work on.

STONE: *Torch Song Trilogy* existed off off and off Broadway, in its several parts and as a whole, before it came to Broadway. What was the very first second that something of it occurred to you that you wanted to put on paper?

FIERSTEIN: In 1976, Theater for the New City wanted several short plays for a bicentennial festival program to be called "Village Writers on the Village." I wrote the back room scene of *International Stud* for that. Then I had the idea of doing a sort of floor show, for which I wrote *Drag Monologue*—so there were two of the four scenes of *International Stud.* I knew I needed something more, so I went out, fell in love, got him to leave me and—ah hah—I had the rest of the show.

Ellen Stewart was finally wheeled into putting on *International Stud* at La Mama, though she didn't want to at first, because some of it takes place in the back room, and she didn't want any of that action in her theater. . . .

151

STONE: After all these years of that action in her theater?

FIERSTEIN: Yea . . . I then got ahold of Ned Levy, who had been my musical director from *Flatbush Tosca* on, and we put *International Stud* together. It was a hit at La Mama, and Eric Concklin, who was its director then, immediately said, "Go to Ellen and tell her it's a trilogy—that way we don't have to fight for space next year, she's already committed." So I did, and I was then stuck with writing the rest of *Torch Song Trilogy*.

Diane Tarleton played Lady Blues originally. She didn't realize when she auditioned that the part had no lines, otherwise she would never have taken it. So I promised her, "I'm stuck with writing a trilogy, I'll write a part for you." I wrote Laurel for her, and she was still playing it when we moved to Broadway.

Estelle Getty over here was driving me nuts: "Why don't you have a mother in this show?" So I sat down and wrote a mother for her, and *she* was still playing it on Broadway.

Anyhow, to get back to Part Two, the *Fugue in a Nursery* segment, there was a CETA program at La Mama (everything happens so much by accident). In Part One, *International Stud*, we had a piano, and Ellen said, "In Part Two you've got to have more instruments. I've got these CETA musicians . . ." Ada Janik was in the CETA program, so I asked her to write a score for *Fugue*.

Meanwhile, Ellen found this turntable from another production she had to get out of a theater because they needed more room, and she told me, "Honey, put a turntable in there." I said, "I don't need a turntable." She said, "Put the bed on a turntable, you'll have the bed on one side, the musicians on the other." That was the birth of the turntable in *Torch Song Trilogy*.

STONE: You see how calculated writing for the theater is? Accident itself is a very important creative force—the coincidence of the chance encounter, one telephone call coming before another instead of the other way around, one suggestion arriving before the other. What keeps it an art is, your talent selects from the accidents: "Hey, that's a terrific idea." It's not just attrition at work, it's a series of accidents from which you select. If you are talented, creative, receptive, you order these accidents so that they contribute. Always the accidents come up at these symposia, and people think, "Well, I guess I just haven't had the right accident happen to me." The right accident can happen to a bad play forever, and nothing will be accomplished. It's a question of what Harvey selected from his accidents. I mean, he accepted the turntable. It happened to have been there, but he took it. He hasn't mentioned the eight things that were wrong for his play that he did *not* take.

FIERSTEIN: I found in writing *Torch Song Trilogy*—going from the solitude of *Stud* to the realistic side of *Widows and Children First*, the third and final segment—that the story dictates the form; and that is an accident too. It all depends on how your characters decide their story wants to be told.

STONE: How did you two producers first hear of this project?

JOHN GLINES: Larry Lane and I were running a gay arts organization called

The Glines. We produced the first gay American arts festival. I had heard of Harvey's work but had never seen any of it, and we invited him to do a reading one night because we thought he should be included in the festival. He chose to do selected scenes from the complete trilogy. I was stunned. I introduced myself and told him, "If you ever want to put those plays together, will you please talk to us." At that time *Widows* was optioned for Broadway, so he didn't want to talk.

FIERSTEIN: Once *Widows* was written I wanted to do the whole trilogy together, but I'd made one of those dumb mistakes of signing away something before I wrote it. I had given an option on whatever I wrote next, so I was stuck.

GLINES: We didn't talk again for another year, when the option had lapsed.

FIERSTEIN: This other producer had promised me that if I let him do each play separately off Broadway, he would then put them together for me. He couldn't. La Mama wanted to do one play on each of three floors. They didn't have the money. For a year and a half I went to every theater in America with the good reviews the show had received. No one would do it.

STONE: How much of that did you attribute to subject matter as opposed to dramaturgy?

FIERSTEIN: A hundred percent.

STONE: So you felt confident of its quality?

FIERSTEIN: Every letter we got back said, "Really respect the material, love the plays, think they are fabulous. Our audience would not go for this kind of stuff. Does he have anything about straight people?"

GLINES: We began talking with Harvey about doing the plays in repertory. But Harvey wanted the audience to be able to see all three plays in proper sequence, at least on Saturday. *Stud* and *Fugue* had already been done off Broadway, and we thought that in repertory we'd probably get an enormous audience for *Widows*, but what would we do the other two nights? And then I picked up the paper and saw an ad for *Nicholas Nickleby*, and I thought, "Let's make it the *Nicholas Nickleby* of off off Broadway." And that's the way we did sell it.

STONE: You're speaking about length. If people were going to sit for nine hours of Dickens, they'd sit for four hours of Fierstein.

GLINES: Right. We'd catch the wave.

LAWRENCE LANE: I remember we talked to Harvey about doing two of them on one night and one on the next night. We went around and around with that.

GLINES: We couldn't figure out how to do it, whether to do *Studs* and *Fugue* one night and *Fugue* and *Widows* the next—and if somebody already saw one program, could they get a discount ticket to the second one? When we opened at the Richard Allen Center, how long did the play run, Larry?

LANE: I think it was five hours.

STONE: How much of the play itself did you actually have at that time?

LANE: Oh, four and a half.

STONE: And now?

LANE: Three forty.

FIERSTEIN: And we'd already cut. When we decided to put them all together, the first thing I did was cut an hour.

STONE: Ned, where were you when this play came into your life as its musical director and arranger?

NED LEVY: You brought up the subject of fortuitous circumstances—when I left Chicago to come back here, I caught my thumb in a cab door so I couldn't play the piano. When it got better, I went to see about the Christmas show at La Mama, and Harvey was in it. We did some things in the show together, then I did another show, and then suddenly he called up about *Flatbush Tosca*. I stage-managed for two years, and did some editing—one does a lot of things in New York to keep alive—and then Harvey called up out of the blue about this play.

FIERSTEIN: He was the only man I knew with a piano who was home at that time.

STONE: And Ada, you were where?

ADA JANIK: I was in the CETA program. Harvey was running it.

FIERSTEIN: It was a government training program—different theaters got grants to hire people for a year. At La Mama we had, I believe, twenty musicians, twenty-five actors and twenty technicians, being paid by the government every week, which made the actors who were working free at La Mama very angry.

JANIK: There were consequently a lot of shows to be done by these CETA people. I had just written a musical theater piece, *Poems of e.e. cummings*, which Harvey heard and thereupon presented me with his script and commanded, "Write!" I very much appreciated the fact that he didn't specifically tell me, "I want a music cue here, a music cue there." He left it inherent in the writing, where the music responds to certain emotional places and the counterpoint really gets going.

FIERSTEIN: I cut only one piece of music from what Ada originally presented, one thing that sounded like a theme from *Jaws*.

JANIK: That was a very strident section, Harvey.

FIERSTEIN: It was during one of my speeches. I didn't want people saying to themselves, "That's from *Jaws*," during one of my speeches.

STONE: What else involving the music was cut?

FIERSTEIN: One of the things that has been cut from the original La Mama production is the telephone call of Laurel inviting Arnold for the weekend. The bed was on one side of the turntable, the music stand on the other. As the phone call played, four musicians climbed up onto the podium with Ada, who conducted from the middle of the circle. The bed turned around, and the headboard was formed by the four live musicians—so you had a live musician playing the character of the person sitting below, playing the music of the person sitting below. You could afford to do that with a government grant; you can't afford it otherwise, off off, off or on Broadway.

STONE: Estelle, what were you doing all this time?

ESTELLE GETTY: I was an actress from the time I was a little girl. I married, went out of the business, then back into the business some fifteen years ago. Again fortuitously, we had mutual friends, Harvey and I. They took me to see *International Stud,* and I was wiped out by his·talent. Then I went to see *Fugue* and was even more wiped out. By this time we had grown to be friends, though he had never seen me work. I did indeed dare him to write a part for me—demanded, cajoled, beat him up.

STONE: It's an extraordinary characterization.

GETTY: Thank you. It's an extraordinary part.

STONE: Thank you for saying that. I find that is usually the case. It's very hard for an actor to be wonderful without a wonderful part.

Harvey, the people who see *Torch Song Trilogy* as a whole and who aren't aware of its history—which takes in 99.9 percent of the audience—see it not as a trilogy at all, but as a three-act play. It has an entirety to it. There is a definite continuing story. It's three acts that found one another through a constant period of simmering on the stove. What would the time frame be from the beginning of the first play to the end of the last?

FIERSTEIN: The first play is a year long; the second is four days long; the third is five years later. Six years over all. That's the hardest part for the actors, playing the two characters that go all the way through. It's such a subtle process, playing the aging of six years, and yet very necessary for the audience to see.

STONE: Having established *Torch Song Trilogy* as a full evening, clearly a lot had to be cut for time. What did everybody lose?

FIERSTEIN: First, obviously, the exposition, the information at the beginning of each act to tell what happened in the act before. Also, any joke you could live without. One song went, because the music had to take its cuts too. The first act survived, but you miss some great little moments. The third act survived, but you also miss some of my favorite moments. The second act suffered the most, and I don't believe it's what it should be—but because of time, it can't be.

LANE: It became the most static act, because of where it took place.

FIERSTEIN: It had a texture of tiny little scenes, switching back and forth. Ed would say something to Arnold on Monday, and when Arnold would answer him it would be Thursday. Laurel would say something to Arnold, though we were in two different rooms—there was a lot of that sort of switching. When I started cutting, I put scenes together to make bigger scenes, taking the flavor scenes out. It became a matter of why that act was there within the trilogy as a whole. We needed it to establish that gay relationships were exactly the same as straight relationships, and we needed to introduce Alan so that his death would affect us in the third act; also, to show that Arnold had a complete turnaround. In the first act, Arnold is slightly virginal. In the last act, he is celibate. There is a step missing, his whore period, so we had to leave the whore period in the middle.

LANE: It had to function as a second act instead of its own play.

STONE: Well, it is the proper second act. We've talked on other occasions about the dramatic pattern referred to in Francis Fergusson's book *The Idea of a Theater:* "purpose, passion, perception." *Fugue* is the passionate act and there's no question that it's in the proper place. You couldn't get from the first act to the third without it.

FIERSTEIN: That's what's hard for a writer to see. I came in to The Glines that day with three plays, and I left with one. When people would ask me, "How many plays have you written?" I used to say "Ten," and now I'm down to seven. That's why I'm glad the scripts of all three plays have been printed in full.

STONE: The three acts have such totally different dramatic styles. There is a linear, more conventional dramatic style to one and three, but the second is quite different, and yet it does have a continuity. The middle act plays with time even in the version that remains. It plays with space. Each act has properties that are different from the other two. Would you have constructed it this way if it had been conceived as one play?

FIERSTEIN: Yeah.

STONE: Changing the style from act to act?

FIERSTEIN: If you're going to have acts dramatizing whole different sections of somebody's life, it's like writing separate plays anyway. No, I didn't sit down to write a play that took place in bed in the second act. I had my four characters, I started writing their dialogue. They began talking to me, telling me what they wanted to say, arguing with each other. You write it and you write it and you write it, and all of a sudden you realize that most of this is going on in a bed. The playwright comes in as a referee later on, after the characters have done their thing and said O.K., there's your material, go edit it.

The conversations of the two pairs of *Fugue* characters, straight and gay, were exactly the same, so I said to myself, I'm going to put them together and have them taking place at the same time. They are arguing about the same thing. And then I realized that most of this was taking place in bed, so why not a big bed? And then I went back and decorated the set, as it were. But the characters told me how to do that play.

The same with *Widows*, but there the choice is more conscious, because I knew I was going to write a play that was going to convince an audience that a fifteen-year-old should be brought up to be gay. I knew I was going to have trouble with some people, so I started it out as normal as I could, as *safe* as I could. The opening of that play is written with a sort of pseudo Neil Simon mix-matched roommates, *Odd Couple*-style—and the mother when she first enters is written as the typical Jewish mother—so that the audience sits back, says to itself, "We're going to have a lot of laughs here, I know who all these people are," and then gets kicked in the face. I started the play knowing I wanted to do that.

Stylistically, as a whole, the trilogy works on an emotional level of maturing Arnold and Ed. In the first play they are very immature, seeing themselves, as we all do, as the center of their own universe. Ed exists only in Arnold's mind, Arnold exists only in Ed's mind. They always appear alone onstage until the final scene of *International Stud,* when they have been apart for six months. They aren't really having a relationship with each other, they are doing it by themselves. In the second act they're a bit more mature. We take in our tight little group of friends, and it becomes us against the world. That's *Fugue.* That's why it's in a nursery, and I wanted nothing seen on the sides of the bed, as though you'd fall into an abyss if you stepped off that little world. In the third act, because of events, Alan being murdered, the father dying, adopting this son, they've accepted the world, or the world's forced its way into Arnold's life, so it can have the most realistic style.

LEVY: There's a musical aspect to this, a wonderful musical adjunct to the play as a totality. The rather phony, romantic ideal of love in the first play is reflected realistically in the music. When you get to the second play with relationships and attitudes intertwining, the music is abstracted to an instrumental fugue, a *phenomenal* piece of fugal writing—interesting, jazzy, modern tonal, atonal, a lot of things all at once. Then when the world intrudes into the third play, as Harvey said, the music is simply coming out of the radio. We've gone from live singing to live abstracted instrumental to the same kinds of tunes coming out of the radio. There was no musical director for all three plays at once who said, "Let's do this, Harvey," this was one of those fortuitous circumstances that developed. I have no idea whether this affects anybody besides me when I see the play, but I am aware that there is a distancing going on, and I think it must have a subtle psychological effect.

STONE: Ada, in writing the score, did you have to blend these styles?

JANIK: No, I wrote only for the second play, *Fugue,* when it was a complete play by itself.

FIERSTEIN: When the first play was done as one play, it wanted to be a longer play, so we did more songs. When we put the plays together as a three-act piece, the problem was that each song in its position had to take you from some place to somewhere else emotionally, commenting on what was happening but not giving away what was going to happen. It was an interesting problem, choosing those songs. They aren't just *there,* they don't happen to be some old song you sing at that point.

STONE: What kind of a job did you have when the time came for you to replace your leading actor on Broadway in a play that was clearly and completely identified with Harvey?

GLINES: Replacement was never the hardest thing. The role is so demanding that somebody else has always played Arnold at matinees. No actor can play either Arnold or Ed at all eight performances. So it's murder casting the role at all, even without Harvey's shadow on it. Many an actor is a stand-up comedian who does the first and second acts beautifully but can't handle the drama in the third act—or the other way around. Both companies, here and in San Francisco, are double-cast.

LANE: We thought it was important for Harvey to relinquish the role eventually, sit back as a playwright and let the play live on its own.

FIERSTEIN: I'd already played Arnold from 1978 to 1981, and when we first discussed the trilogy I didn't want to play it any more. But John insisted.

GLINES: The deal was, he had to play Arnold.

LANE: That was part of the interest for us—Harvey as a total person, actor and playwright. But it was important, too, that the play develop a life of its own with other people.

GLINES: The early reviewers said they couldn't imagine the play without Harvey. We knew we had to face this one day, so we picked San Francisco to show that the play could survive without him.

STONE: Or they would review the playwright when they were really reviewing the actor.

GLINES: Yes.

STONE: Or they would review the actor when they were really reviewing the playwright.

FIERSTEIN: That happens anywhere. The actor gets great reviews and says "Yes, thank you, it was my performance and not the writing."

STONE: What has been the impact of the play, post-Harvey?

GLINES: We never sought reviewers after we had to. We never reopened the show after Richard Allen Center. When we went from off off Broadway to off, we simply moved it and did the same when we went to Broadway. We didn't dare put it up for new reviews.

LANE: We couldn't get better reviews than we already had.

GLINES: Right. We suffered at the box office because we didn't make a big fuss reopening on Broadway. We also believed that had we opened originally on Broadway, we would never have made it.

GETTY: I thought that Harvey would be my age by the time he got out of *Torch Song Trilogy.* The way I figured it, he'd be in his sixties and I'd be playing his mother at a hundred and ten. I couldn't imagine doing the play with anybody but Harvey. But the wonderful thing about the piece he wrote is, the role of Arnold is so good that no actor could do anything wrong with it. It's like sex—even when it's bad, it's good. Obviously I loved playing the role with Harvey, because that's the way we started it, but it's been very exciting doing it with other people. We found that each actor *can* make it his own, and not be Harvey, and it works, each time it works.

STONE: Was the understudy—the one doing the matinees—giving Harvey's performance?

GETTY: Nobody gives Harvey's performance.

GLINES: Yes, he had to, to a degree, because if he went on for Harvey he had to be in Harvey's rhythms. When Donald Corren, who had been a matinee Arnold and Harvey's understudy, went out to San Francisco, he started over again in rehearsal to make Arnold much more his own.

As far as business impact post-Harvey is concerned, once we won the Tony, the box office took off, both here and in San Francisco.

FIERSTEIN: In other words, since I left the show we're making a fortune.

GLINES: Our hardest job was talking you into going to Broadway. That took two months, at least.

LANE: He didn't want to go.

GLINES: Absolutely refused. Finally got mad as hell and said, "How dare you call my mother to have her call me and tell me I should go to Broadway?"

STONE: Did the times make the subject matter of *Torch Song Trilogy* a success, or did the subject matter make the times ripe for it?

FIERSTEIN: John said it before. If we'd opened *Torch Song Trilogy* off or on Broadway, it would have gotten bombed. But the circumstances of the Richard Allen Center worked out perfectly. Here we were in this horrible third-floor theater where the rain poured in, the cold poured in, and these people went to this hell hole and discovered this *thing*. It was one of those accidents that worked just right.

STONE: Do you think the world of stock and amateur production is ready for *Torch Song Trilogy*?

FIERSTEIN: Yes, I get lots of requests.

GLINES: I'd be very careful, it's still a long play on a tough subject.

STONE: Has there been a film interest of any kind?

FIERSTEIN: Yes, there have been offers.

LANE: Harvey is concerned with having it done properly.

GLINES: He faces the same thing he faced with producers who wouldn't do it in the first place. Cut the back room scene, do this, do that, to make it viable and commercial. He's refusing.

STONE: Then there's the casting of the very heavy star part. The movies have a tendency to hedge bets. Often the audience comes in to see a film and finds itself patently deceived by the casting. I mean, it would be tough to put Burt Reynolds in the part, whether he could play it or not.

FIERSTEIN: Henry Winkler almost did it.

GLINES: I can't imagine anyone but Harvey playing Arnold in the movie.

FIERSTEIN: We're going to do it as an independent film, because I cannot, until the script is written, tell a movie producer that this is going to be a two-hour or a four-hour movie. The play has always taken very good care of itself and has done everything I wanted it to do. I didn't care if the show moved to Broadway, and I don't care if the movie never gets made. And I'm not scared that my genius performance would be lost, because we filmed it for the Lincoln Center Library when it was off Broadway—it's locked up in a vault, and they will let it out in sixty years. And I don't care if it gets sold to television. I don't care if *Torch Song Trilogy* never makes another cent, as long as I don't sell out *Torch Song*. So we're putting together our own production company and are going to make the film ourselves. I would love Richard Chamberlain to play Ed. I never had an Ed in mind when I first wrote it, so why not Richard Chamberlain?

STONE: Estelle wants to know who's playing the mother in the movie. Thelma Ritter's dead, right?

FIERSTEIN: But she said she'd come back.

GETTY: So would I.

FIERSTEIN: Also, we've had offers to make it into a TV sitcom, you know, Arnold and his mother fighting weekly over the child he's adopted that month, each half hour ending with them going to the cemetery to see whose grave looks better.

STONE: One aspect of the theme we mentioned but haven't discussed is the proselytizing of the fifteen-year-old boy.

FIERSTEIN: I intended to turn the audience to accept the fact that this boy was gay and was going to be raised as a gay person.

STONE: But there was no doubt that he was going to be gay, whether he was encouraged or not.

FIERSTEIN: Right. As the characters say in the bench scene, "No matter how many petitions they sign, you can't get God to raise the age of puberty to eighteen. Kids have sex." I mean, the fifteen-year-old is already a practising homosexual.

STONE: One of the questions submitted in advance that we haven't already answered in the course of this conversation is: "Will the parts that have been cut from the original ever see the light of day again?"

FIERSTEIN: There are two published versions of the play, one by Gay Presses of New York in softcover and one by Villard Press in hardcover. All the cuts are restored in both versions.

STONE: Here's another: "Did you make any changes in the text because of the change from off Broadway to Broadway?"

FIERSTEIN: Absolutely and utterly *not*. It's amazing to watch an audience that everyone, but everyone, told us would not sit through the back room scene, sit through it nightly and laugh.

STONE: Because it's funny and goes beyond outrage. You know, it hasn't been so long since their entire experience was Milton Berle in a dress.

FIERSTEIN: They read that the play is about a drag queen, and when the lights come up on this singer at the very opening, you hear, "It's a man," "That's not," "I'm telling you, I read about this, that's a man." And then the light would come on me: "Now, *that's* a man," "Does he think he's pretty?"

STONE: Here's a question about the use of that torch singer: "Is the desperation in the lyrics of these songs exclusively related to Arnold, or are they implemented to suggest something about the gay lifestyle in general?"

FIERSTEIN: No, they're those love songs we all grew up on: "Oh, the pain of unrequited love is wonderful, I'm so unhappy!" People make a living off being miserable. When I would have a fight with a particular gentleman, I'd put my Billie Holiday on and suffer. That's what these songs say—how wonderful it is. I grew up thinking that's what love was going to be like, because I listened to all these love songs. That's what I'm doing with the audience, playing a song about "It's all over" and then telling them it's not as romantic as they say it's supposed to be. It's your life, it's not a song. That's what torch songs are for in the first place, the romantic ideal of how this scene should turn out. And then we play the scene, and it doesn't turn out that way.

Stage-wise, the torch songs are to conjure the scenes. The singer is there, not to comment on the scene that just happened, but to conjure the next one, to make the lights come up and bring that scene out of the song, out of the romantic ideal into the real light of what it's really like. And then, as Ned said before, in the last act you've got songs on the radio that do just the opposite. The first song the radio announcer introduces is "I Was Born That Way, What's Your Excuse?" which is going to be the theme of the boy; and then at the very end the boy dedicates "I'll Never Turn My Back on You" to his parents.

STONE: Was there originally any other title for the show?

FIERSTEIN: No, and I wish there were, because *Torch Song Trilogy* is very hard to say.

STONE: Any particular writer or group of writers have an influence on you?

FIERSTEIN: Among my contemporaries, the whole theater of the ridiculous. In the more commercial field, James Goldman—this is a man I respect a great deal. Beckett, Genet. Plays I read once a year are *The Lion in Winter* and *Happy Days.* They're my favorite works.

STONE: Did you commit any part of your royalty anywhere along the way?

FIERSTEIN: You don't want to ask that question.

STONE: Well, I do, a little bit.

FIERSTEIN: La Mama takes a small percentage for having produced the plays. *International Stud* was moved off Broadway, done poorly and didn't do well, but the producer earned some subsidiary rights. *Fugue* was bought for off Broadway, was worse than the first one, and the producer did not earn subsidiary rights (I bought him out for a very small amount). . . What you have to remember is, no matter how much you love your play and want to get it on, it is a piece of property that you own. You give away little pieces of the property, and it gets smaller and smaller until, even though you love the play, it isn't worth it for you to have it put on.

STONE: It used to be that you submitted a play, and producers were versatile, experienced and adventurous enough to read it and say, "This is what I want to do." In this new world, Broadway producers are less and less adventurous and therefore travel around looking at plays rather than reading them.

GLINES: I take exception. I think the economics are such that it is very difficult to produce an unknown play, and there are certain plays like *Torch Song* that should *not* start on Broadway. It's not a matter of a lack of adventure.

STONE: There's no such thing as an unknown play, because an unknown writer can have the same impact on Broadway as a known writer these days. : . .

Another question: It isn't often that an author plays in his own play. Were there parts of it you found especially difficult to do?

FIERSTEIN: When I first wrote the parts of the play and would walk into La Mama with hands waving to put them on, they were very close to my heart, and it was hard. By the time we did the trilogy, I was returning to the role, and it wasn't so difficult to refine it. It was physically difficult—we opened five performances a week and then moved up to six, and I really didn't think I'd live through it a few times. I've even had days when my understudy was sick. He never went on for me.

GLINES: You used to get headaches a lot.

FIERSTEIN: Yeah, I took an average of six aspirin a performance for the year and a half that *Trilogy* ran. Some nights, by the time *Widows* came around I was completely blind from the pain. Dumb thing to do to yourself.

STONE: *Torch Song Trilogy* is obviously a critical and financial hit, but even a hit can be a horrendous experience. Has this been a happy experience?

GLINES: Yes, pretty much. It was miraculous. We planned only an eight-week run in an off-off Broadway situation, and every step up we'd say, "Isn't it fabulous that we've gotten this far?"

GETTY: I know it's a Broadway cliché to say "We're a very close company," but *our* company really is: wonderful actors, wonderful people, a loving family. I'm in such a good play, and so visible in it, it's a joy.

JANIK: It was a lovely challenge to write the music, with the choice of instruments being the characters. Not only is it contrapuntal, but each character has his or her own theme.

LANE: The producer of a play I just saw was telling me horror stories about the playwright getting in the way of everything. In our case, Harvey made it happen. We couldn't have done it without him, as playwright and as actor.

FIERSTEIN: I've never before had a producer say to me, "What do you want to do with your script, what is your dream?" It was easy to get involved and stay involved, with Larry Lane out on the roof of the Richard Allen Center in a snowstorm, tarring the roof in the middle of a performance so it wouldn't drip onto the stage. It's a whole different thing when you have producers who care in that way.

STONE: I want to thank all of you for coming here to share the experience of *Torch Song Trilogy* with us.

Part Two

AUTHOR! AUTHOR!

Robert Anderson	Stephen Sondheim
Neil Simon	Edward Albee
Marsha Norman	Leonard Melfi
Jerry Herman	Garson Kanin
Arthur Miller	Terrence McNally
Sidney Kingsley	Marc Connelly

Dramatists are noted for their generosity of spirit toward each other. This has made their intercom, the Dramatists Guild Quarterly (edited by Otis L. Guernsey Jr.) so freely and intimately informative. Again and again, "established" dramatists have given their all in experience, expertise and intuition to audiences of aspiring playwrights and to the whole Dramatists Guild membership in the transcripts of these sessions in their magazine. Most of the contributions in this anthology (collected with the editing assistance of Jeffrey Sweet, Sally Dixon Wiener and Dale Ramsey) originated from the spoken word, in which dramatists, of course, are particularly at home. We begin these dozen examples of their open-heartedness with Robert Anderson, present chairman of the committee that oversees the Dramatists Guild Quarterly. (Its other members are Lee Adams, Ruth Goetz, Garson Kanin and Terrence McNally.)

ROBERT ANDERSON

A Multi-Media Dramatist's Inner Space

ROBERT ANDERSON: I want to give you some wall mottoes. The first, which I put up over my desk on a shirt cardboard about twenty-eight years ago (when I was very self-pitying) says simply, "Nobody asked you to be a playwright." Every once in a while I look up at that damn thing and think, "That's true, but the situation is still awful."

The second is by the painter Auguste Renoir: "First learn to be a good craftsman. This will not keep you from being a genius." So many writers I've worked with don't want to know anything about craft, don't want to study.

The third is by the statesman Edmund Burke: "Never despair, but if you do, work on in despair." It's good not only for playwriting but for the rest of life, too.

The fourth is by Georges Simenon, the French novelist: "Writing is not a profession but a vocation of unhappiness."

I've been told that it might be helpful if I gave you a quick run-down on myself. I was working at Harvard for my Ph.D. and at the same time acting in plays, and, to show you my chutzpah, writing the book, the music, the lyrics and directing musicals. The night before I went away to war, I took my orals for my Ph.D. They passed me, I think on the assumption that I would not come back to embarrass them.

When we had time off after Iwo Jima and Okinawa and places like that, instead of going on the beach every afternoon and drinking that terrible green beer, I sometimes stayed on board ship and wrote plays. I was worried about two things: that I might be killed and leave the world no immortal play, and that I might not be killed and would have to go back and finish my Ph.D. Anyway, I won an Army-Navy prize for the best play written by a serviceman overseas. I wrote two more plays, and when I came back I had a $2,000 Rockefeller fellowship, which in those days was a great deal. So I didn't have to go back and finish my Ph.D. I settled in New York, where my wife had become associated with the Theater Guild.

My "prizewinning" play was done off Broadway, and the American Theater Wing asked me to teach playwriting in their Professional Training Program. I told them I had never taught playwriting. They said I had written plays, and I had done some teaching. "Put them together." So I taught the class, and incidentally taught myself. If you want to learn something, teach it.

Then I wanted to write for radio, but they told me, "You're a promising playwright, but radio is quite a different medium." For about two months I sat in front of my radio set and listened, with pencil and paper, trying to figure out the mysteries of radio. I finally got a chance to write for *The Theater Guild on the Air.* It was an extraordinary learning experience for a young writer. I finally ended up writing more than thirty shows for them for such actors as Rex Harrison, Humphrey Bogart, the Lunts, Deborah Kerr, Helen Hayes, Montgomery Clift.

Then television came in, and we went through the same dreary nonsense about it being a "different" medium, until I finally became a television writer. Then *Tea and Sympathy* was produced on the stage and bought for films by M-G-M. They told me, "Of course you can't write the screen play because movies are a totally different medium." But they let me write a first draft to try to lick censorship problems. They decided it was all right, and so I became a film writer.

Nobody told me I couldn't write a novel. I told myself that. But I had some subject matter that I couldn't handle as a play, so I took a deep plunge, and it came out all right. I happened to live in a community where I saw Bill Styron and Philip Roth and Robert Penn Warren from time to time at parties. During the time when I was trying these novels, and they would ask me what I was up to, I would never dare to say I was working on a novel. I would just say, "I'm working on something."

If all this has any point, I think it is that the most difficult form of writing is playwriting. Once you know how to write a play, the chances are you can move ahead and write in any other dramatic medium just by studying the particular requirements of that medium. The novel is something else. I would never call myself a novelist, but by adhering to certain principles of drama, I managed to tell two stories in the novel form.

When a writer sits down to work, he is faced each time with at least two challenges: the challenge of his material and the challenge of the form. As I said, I don't know enough about the novel to do anything but tell a story, but in the theater, I do have to think about what I am going to do about the form . . . to have some idea what other writers over the centuries have done with the form, to decide if I want to adhere to one of the many accepted forms or to modify them to my use. In *Double Solitaire,* for instance, I said, "I'm sick of the theater of activity." I had thought for a long while that the matter with the theater is: the manner is the matter. It's another way of saying the medium is the message, or that the way a thing was being done was more important than what was being done. I was not coming out of the theater moved. I was not coming out laughing. I was coming out aware of trapezes and revolving stages and theatrical effects.

So I set out to write a play of emotional action, to strip the play down to what was basic for the emotional relationship between the people. I put a table and chair there, and a table and chair there, and a husband there and a wife there. Except for people coming in and out and sitting at those tables, nobody moved. I drained the dialogue of such lines as "Will you have a cigarette?" or "Is the tea boiling?" Now, I knew what a play should be. I knew what I was doing *without*. I knew that I would have to compensate for it with something else. I felt that I had really wrestled with the form and come up with something creatively interesting. The only critic to notice anything was Clive Barnes, who said something to the effect that "It's a strange form, but it works."

As I read plays and teach, I find it isn't that people can't write plays, it's that they have nothing to write about. At the American Theater Wing in 1947, I had a student who was an extremely talented and skillful playwright, but his plays were mild. I wasn't going to take him on for a second semester. He came to talk to me about this. After a few minutes, we somehow got into the subject of family, and he held me spellbound talking about his father. At the end of the afternoon, he asked me, "Are you going to let me stay in the course?" I said, "Yes, if you write a play about your father." He wrote a play about his father, which led into another play about his father, *A Hole in the Head,* which was enormously successful and was made into a movie with Frank Sinatra, then into a musical. Its author was Arnold Schulman, a very successful screenwriter.

Which brings me to another wall motto I don't need to hang over my desk because it is so central to my belief: "Art gives form to feeling." If there is no feeling behind what a person writes, no matter how skillful he is it's going to be lifeless. Someone once wrote this about the work of an aging French painter: "The skill of his hands could not make up for the emptiness in his heart." There's a frightening truth in this. Writers don't lose their skill, but as they grow older they are in danger of losing the intensity of their feelings.

When I read as a judge in playwriting contests I don't necessarily read for the skill. The skill can be learned. I read for the heart in it, the urgency in it. A few years ago I taught fiction at the University of Iowa Writers Workshop, and I was constantly asking my students, "Why did you write this story?" Years ago, I sent a young writer and his story to the editor of the *Atlantic Monthly.* The editor read the story, then said, "You wanted to write a story, but you didn't want to write *this* story." You should write only when you have some feeling about your material, a feeling of delight or joy or humor or sadness or tragedy or excitement. I used to say there are no dull subjects, just dull playwrights. If a playwright feels strongly enough about almost any subject, he can write a good play about it.

Howard Lindsay once said that a play must "pay off" in one of three coinages: humor or excitement or emotion. If you pay off a little in each, people are going to say, "Well, it's all right but . . ." Mildness is a curse in the theater. Usually a play pays off principally in one of these coinages. "Enough" is a key word here. Is it funny enough, or moving enough, or exciting enough? I want to go to the theater to be "shattered" either by emotion or laughter or excitement.

There is really not much any of us can do about our subject matter except to discover it in ourselves. Our life experiences condition each of us to feel and respond to different stimuli. Each of us has a kind of built-in Geiger counter that reacts to material. The first and last lines of *I Never Sang for My Father* are "Death ends a life but it does not end a relationship, which struggles on in the survivor's mind towards some resolution which it may never find." In retrospect I find that a great deal of my work has been written in an effort to resolve some relationship that obviously "bugged" me. My novel *After* was about the relationship between a surviving husband and a dead wife. My last novel, *Getting Up and Going Home*, is about a separation. Now, my first wife died, and then I went through a divorce, but these novels are not factually autobiographical. Autobiography is not fiction. I was not writing about my wives or myself, but I was writing in an area of experience I had some feeling for. A writer may have a reservoir of feeling about something because of events in his life. Then he comes upon or slowly develops a story, quite different possibly from his own life, which releases all those feelings. When I am asked to do an adaptation for the films, I look for stories which may have no bearing on my own actual life, but which engage my very deep feelings.

Tea and Sympathy was about many things: responsibility, the mob and the individual, false charges, manliness (it was *not* about homosexuality!!!). But principally it was about my father and myself, I think. My father had a certain concept of what a man was, a tough guy and a hard hitter. In my adolescence, my brother (now a doctor) was an amateur prize fighter, and I was a tennis player with a mean chopping game. I think I wanted to say to my father (and, I suppose to everyone else preaching macho-ism) "This also can be a man."

Picasso wrote, "Art is lies that tell the truth." *I Never Sang for My Father*, the most autobiographical play I've ever written, didn't end originally as it does now with father and son tearing each other to bits. It ended as it had in life. My wife-to-be and I were giving my father a birthday party. She gave him a gift and kissed him on the cheek. He held her and said, "On the lips, my dear." That was originally the break-up scene between father and son, the son finally realizing the father's subconscious impulse to castrate him.

Just before we left for Philadelphia, the actors and my director, Alan Schneider, kept saying, "Bob, this play doesn't end right." I told him, "That's the way I want it to end." And since the playwright doesn't have to change a semicolon if he doesn't want to, that's the way they rehearsed it until finally it dawned on me that they were right. I went back to my desk (my father was long since dead) and I said, "Okay, Dad. Let's have a scene we never had." This scene, along with the scene between the brother and sister, is the only non-factual scene in the play, but it is the most truthful. It was the imaginative leap that saved the play.

People relate to this play. They care. They say to me, "How did you know my father?" As a matter of fact, they interchange the sexes: "How did you know my mother?" It seems with a play like this, all you have to do is state the subject matter and the audience writes the play for you. Their own play is going on in their heads while my play is going on on the stage. (That is, if they are willing to open up and relate. With some people the subject is so threatening, they clam up, shut off their feelings, won't even listen to a play.)

You have to be lucky to tie into one of these universal subjects. You cannot do it intentionally. I wrote out of my personal feelings about the sadness and indignity of old age, and specifically about what you do with an old man for whom you've had ambivalent feelings when he's left in your hands. Robert Morley once said (when he was writing plays), "We are like weavers. We all know how to weave, but we never know when we're weaving in gold."

I found the same thing was true of my novel *After*. It was written from very personal feelings, but now I find it is being used in hospitals and medical schools by those people dealing with terminal patients and survivors. I hope the same thing will prove true of my later book, *Getting Up and Going Home*, which is about separation and divorce. I guess I have led a fairly conventional life of people falling in love, dying, divorcing, and the things I write become more or less "letters from the front" of this kind of life. I do know that when I have pushed away from my desk after a day's work with the thought that what I had written was so personal that nobody would understand it . . . what I had written those days turned out to be my best work.

I repeat that autobiography is not fiction, and when I say "personal," I do not mean revealing personal facts of my life. But . . . one woman, who I have known for a long time, said to me after seeing *Double Solitaire*, "If I were your wife, I'd divorce you." Of course this made me angry. Though she was an actress, she did not understand "the imaginative leap," "the lies that tell the truth," etc. She went on to say, "Well, even if I believe you that this play had nothing to do with your marriage, I could not live with the intimacy of your writing."

Sometimes I feel that a writer should wear a sign around his neck. "Leper! Don't get involved with me because I write plays." When I wrote *I Never Sang for My Father*, I was afraid that I was writing a harsh picture of my father. One day in Boston, a woman who had been a very old friend of his came to see the play. I didn't see her after, but she left a note in my box: "You *have* sung for your father. . ." So you move on, writing the only way you know how to write.

I have a friend who is writing a novel, a very honest and beautiful and sad picture of a marriage. His wife came across some pages and insisted on reading it all. He let her read it on the condition that she wouldn't comment because he was still in the middle of it. She handed the manuscript back without comment, but with her wedding ring on top of it.

I'll tell you one rule I follow: I don't show anything to anybody until it's finished. My first wife was a producer and agent, a brilliant judge of plays, and she kept asking me to tell her something about the play I was writing, *Tea and Sympathy.* For months I wouldn't tell her anything, but finally I said, "All right, I'll tell you one thing. It's a play about a boy's school." She said, "Oh, God, not another play about a boy's school!" That's why I don't talk any more. And I don't read a word I've written until it's finished. I think I must have such a weak ego that if I knew how poorly I was writing day by day, how far short I was falling of what I thought I was writing, I'd never go on. But once I have a hundred pages of play, or five hundred pages of novel . . . then I risk reading it. It's always a disappointment, but there it is, and I can sit down and say, "All right, what are we going to do about it?"

How you *conceive* dramatically is really the point. You learn that plays are usually about desperate people in crucial situations. The story starts, moves on and ends; the all-important "progression." There must be the feeling of "no exit." Arthur Miller likes to say that nobody in a play can pick up his hat and walk out. It's a struggle to the death. Even in farce, there must be this intensity.

A crisis implies someone wanting or having to do something. Hamlet wanting to avenge the murder of his father; Oedipus wanting to rid his land of the plague; Amanda in *The Glass Menagerie* having to find a way to support the family. Something is at stake in every play. My brother once commented about the characters in one of my plays, "I don't care for them." I asked why. "They stand to lose nothing."

Never forget the work *progression.* A play has to move. If you have only a short distance to go, slice every scene thin. You can never let an audience say to itself, "I've been here before." There must be progression in the relationships between the characters or in the plot or both.

Sometimes you have a favorite scene you feel you can't get rid of. Well, it's no good if it doesn't take the play any place. In tragedy you can move at a snail's pace because you are more involved with depth of character than you are in farce. Howard Lindsay used to compare progression to passing telegraph poles. In tragedy you pass them slowly. In farce, all you have is story, and you have to get to each new story point fast and move on.

In writing for the screen the ABCs of dramatic story telling are much the same. Of course, it's obvious to all of us that the screen is a visual medium. One director calls movie dialogue "foreground noise." But the concept of a dramatic story and its need to progress are very much the same as in the theater.

In screenwriting schools they'll sometimes teach you about closeups, dolly shots, medium long shots, etc. This has nothing to do with screenwriting. Do not put them into your scripts. They are an insult to the director who will decide how he wants to shoot each shot. Just indicate the setting, interior or exterior, day or night. If there is some special way you see the scene, write it in, in plain English: "We follow Mary as she comes up the walk." But don't fill your script so full of technical directions that nobody can read it and tell whether or not there's a picture there in the first place.

In a novel, very often the dialogue is used simply to give you the sounds of the character's voice, a flavor. Then the story is carried in the narrative paragraphs. The first novel I wrote years ago (never published) was sent around with a fake name on it. It came back again and again with the comment, "This was written by a playwright, wasn't it?"

Much of the dialogue in a novel is unusable when the book is adapted to dramatic form. Dialogue in a play moves things along in some way. I did a radio adaptation of *A Farewell to Arms* for Humphrey Bogart, and I found I couldn't use a single line of the famous Hemingway dialogue. It didn't take the story or the characters any place. I had to invent Hemingway dialogue and, of course, all the reviews said the Hemingway dialogue carried the show. Well, that was my job.

An exception to this is John Steinbeck's *Of Mice and Men.* The novel and the play are almost identical. He told me he did this as an exercise to see how close he could come to play form in a novel.

Which reminds me that at one point in my life Steinbeck was very helpful to me. After my wife died, I was stopped. I couldn't write for a very long time. Steinbeck told me that whenever he was stuck, he started writing poetry. He never published this poetry or showed it to anybody because he did not consider himself a poet. But he felt poetry was the most direct line to his feelings. This was very valuable to me. I was on my way to London to more or less hide out with my depression. But I started to write poetry, and within two weeks I knew I wanted to write the play *Silent Night, Lonely Night.*

Scott Fitzgerald once said something to the effect that "We all have two or three things happen to us, and we keep writing about them in one way or another until nobody wants to listen any more." In the last years of his life, the great photographer Steichen was trying to take the perfect picture of a bush outside his window. Someone once suggested that I go some place new to experience something new to write about. I told her, "It's better for me to go to my desk and discover what I didn't know I knew about what I've experienced already." In the Middle Ages, the map makers drew in the world as far as they knew it, and around the edges of that known world they wrote in big letters, BEYOND HERE ARE MONSTERS. Well, playwrights are always venturing into that world of monsters . . . personal monsters, to find out what they didn't know they knew, and often what they didn't know they felt. That can be frightening, and healthy for playwrights.

NEIL SIMON

In Conversation With Terrence McNally

MCNALLY: You were born on the Fourth of July, which is very fitting for America's most popular playwright.

SIMON: Did you know that George M. Cohan was not born on July Fourth? He was born on the fifth, and he changed it to be the Yankee Doodle Dandy.

MCNALLY: There are two volumes of your plays, and in one of them you talk about the writer as a split personality: as a monster that goes around observing people and writing about them, skewering their faults, *and* as a human being whom the monster observes and skewers. Today I want to talk to the human being about what the monster has wrought. For example, when you were growing up in New York City, did you go to the theater a lot? Who were your influences?

SIMON: The theater did not become a part of my life until I was fifteen or sixteen years old. My family was not very much interested in the theater, so I was a movie buff. Also quite an avid reader. I never really thought much about becoming a playwright. It was much too lofty an aspiration for me, to write something that had all those plot twists and developments. It was far beyond what I imagined I could do. I would settle just for writing jokes for Earl Wilson's column. Gradually, my brother Danny and I started to work writing sketches—monologues, at first—for the comics who at that time were playing Broadway, which was filled with theaters like the Strand, the Roxy, the Capitol, Loew's State, Paramount. They all had the big bands, like Glenn Miller's, and the singers, like Frank Sinatra, and the comics, who always needed new material. And my brother and I, for many years when I was a teenager, wrote material for these comics. I remember the night of my high school prom, we went to a night club where the comic was performing material that I wrote— and none of the kids at my table would believe me. When I tried to get backstage later, and they didn't let me, they still wouldn't believe me.

Then Danny and I started writing sketches. I think the first job we may have gotten was for the original show in the Johnny Carson time slot, which was *Broadway Open House*, with Jerry Lester. My brother and I wrote for two nights a week, and another writer wrote the other nights.

MCNALLY: When you were that young boy going to the movies, when did it occur to you that someone was writing the funny lines, situations and characters? Was there a moment you realized the power of writing it?

SIMON: The inspiration came from the books I read. My heroes then were Robert Benchley, Stephen Leacock and Mark Twain. When I would do any writing, it was to emulate them. So before I began writing with my brother, I would do comic, Robert Benchley–type essays. I didn't think at that time about movies being *written.* Nobody knew screenwriters—they still don't know screenwriters.

MCNALLY: When you started writing jokes for the comics, how did you get a joke to these people? You were very young.

SIMON: Fortunately, my brother was eight years older, and he did that. I couldn't; I was scared stiff. The first radio show that we ever worked on, I would sit next to him and whisper things. The head writer, Goodman Ace, was an awesome character; I would whisper, "What if the fellow said such-and-such?" and he would say, *"What?"* and I would say, "Nothing." I did that for weeks, and finally he said, "Why do we need this kid here? He's not contributing anything." I was doing that as late as 1954. I was in my twenties, and I was whispering to Carl Reiner, working on *Your Show of Shows.* It's kind of rough sitting in a room with Mel Brooks and Larry Gelbart and Sid Caesar, and being shy. But I'm still shy.

They were such a boisterous group, extroverts all of them; it was like a cocktail party where you had to scream your line out. I was so happy when my career turned and I became a playwright. I could sit alone in a room and work without the shouting. But I type lightly.

MCNALLY: As an adolescent, were you a funny person?

SIMON: It's hard to think I was funny at that time, but I guess so. My brother was encouraging me when I was fourteen and fifteen years old. He would say, "God, that's funny," he would laugh, and he would say, "I'm telling you, someday you're going to be a top comedy writer." I never dreamed that would be possible. I can't remember a single thing that I said that was funny—or that I wrote. I remember showing him certain pieces that he liked. And I was always able to do that.

MCNALLY: There must have been a period when you made a real decision to write for the theater.

SIMON: I think it started germinating in my mind in the late 1950s. I had been writing for television and making a very good living, but I saw no future to it. I was still waiting for calls from agents saying, "Do you want to work on such-and-such a show next year?" Or I was calling them and saying, "Can you get me a movie?" and they were saying, "No, can't get you a movie until you've written a movie," you know, catch-22. So the only way was to write a play. I thought I would do it as an experiment, to see if I could put together a hundred and twenty pages that made sense. And that I started around 1958.

MCNALLY: This is *Come Blow Your Horn?*

SIMON: Yes. And the hundred and twenty pages came, without exaggeration, to about twelve hundred pages. I don't mean one version of it. I wrote it ten times, maybe twenty times, from beginning to end. It had five different titles. I took it to maybe fifteen of the top Broadway producers of the day—Joshua Logan, George Abbott, David Merrick. They all liked it; all told me to fix this scene, fix that scene. The three years I spent were equivalent to a first-rate college course in playwriting, which I got from all of them. But there were then all these plays that had to be assembled into one.

I did what was sort of suicidal in those days, doing the play in summer stock. Most plays that originated in summer stock ended in summer stock. Regional theater had not yet surfaced. But I couldn't get the play on. So I had an agent—it was the last time I had an agent, in 1961—and we tried the play at the Bucks County Playhouse in New Hope, Pennsylvania. I think, in a sense, it saved my career. If we had gone to Philadelphia with it, it would have died, and I would have been decimated and had to make a living writing *My Three Sons* for the next ten years. But the play had enough promise for me to work on rewriting it. And by the time we did the pre-Broadway production in Philadelphia, it was a much better play. I look back on it as pretty primitive now, but it was entertaining, it had a good story, good characters, and it was, in a farcical sense, very truthful. It was about my family, about myself and my brother.

MCNALLY: You said television seemed to have no future. Did you feel that the quality of television was so low that no one could change it?

SIMON: It wasn't that television wasn't good enough. At that time, which is called "The Golden Age of Television," when *Sergeant Bilko* and *Your Show of Shows* were on, there were a lot of good shows. I'm talking specifically about the light comedy shows. But that was also when Paddy Chayefsky, Tad Mosel, Horton Foote, Robert Alan Aurthur—all those terrific writers—were writing wonderful plays.

But television meant doing the same thing for the rest of my life, writing what other people wanted me to write. And I had a lot of things that I wanted to say for myself, about myself. I wanted freedom of expression, and you're never going to get it in television. I had to deal not only with the comedian I was working for, but the sponsor; and the sponsor had to deal with the network. We all had someone to answer to. Writing for the theater you have no one but the public and the critics to answer to.

MCNALLY: Did you find all the years of writing sketches and half-hour shows for television a good training for the theater?

SIMON: It was great, because it taught us to work under pressure. When I worked on the Bilko show, we did thirty-nine shows a season—now it's twenty-six—and it was like writing a half-hour movie every single week. The pressure was enormous, so that later on when I got out of town to work on a play, and the first act wasn't working, I didn't panic; it was thirty or forty pages, and I felt in four weeks I could certainly do the work. Had I not had the experience turning out material week after week, it would have frightened me.

The other advantage it had was that, in those days, the quality of the material was far superior to today's shows. Today's shows are, I think, subnormal, most of them—the situation comedy shows. There are exceptions, of course, but not an awful lot of them. The experience you'd get now would not be first-rate. Sid Caesar, who I thought was a genius, and the writers I mentioned—and Woody Allen came on eventually—all were tops in their field. And all went on to do terrific things. I don't think situation comedy writing today is going to prepare you for a life in the theater.

In a way, I suffered the first years in the theater. I had to shake that training for getting jokes into the material instead of character. When you write a twenty-six-minute show, in which they want a lot of laughs, it's hard to create character. The Bilko show was character comedy, and situation, but it's hard to find that today.

MCNALLY: It's interesting, what you got out of it, because so many playwrights today think that writing for television is the absolute worst thing for anyone who aspires to the theater—it teaches you a million bad habits.

SIMON: I think it applies to actors and directors as well. I've seen some first-rate actors lose their abilities by working in television for so many years. They start shouting everything, they start becoming one-dimensional. And when they go back to the theater, it's tough for them to make the jump.

MCNALLY: I worked on thirteen episodes of a show, and they say to you, "We want a joke by every third line." The laughs are nice to get, so I know how it could happen.

SIMON: It's not only that so much; when you write for television, and you sit down at the typewriter and try to imagine the quintessential audience that you will be writing for on any given night, there's a possibility that it'll be forty million people. Well, it's impossible to write for forty million people—to try to reach that audience—because they have too many demands and come from too many different strata of life. Whereas, in my mind, I pick out those nine hundred or a thousand people coming to the theater, spending a fair amount of money, who want the best kind of entertainment. I find them the toughest, most critical, and also the most open audience. But you can't give them *Hee-Haw*.

MCNALLY: The director I worked with in television was Paul Bogart, and he said, "Just remember, it's an actor's medium." That made me feel better. "They remember Lucille Ball, not who wrote or directed her shows," he said.

When you got to your first play at Bucks County, you had cast approval, no words could be changed—or maybe the producers *did* tell you to change this, change that—

SIMON: The theater owners, everybody. Michael Ellis and William Hammerstein produced it.

MCNALLY: And what wasn't working about it?

SIMON: Oh, tons.

MCNALLY: And you knew it—you didn't want to blame the director, the audience or the cast.

SIMON: I had people coming up to me: "It was a bad night, it was hot in the theater," and I knew the difference—the play wasn't working. I had a man on the telephone for twenty minutes at the beginning explaining what was going on. I learned, okay, that is not the way to do the exposition. You've got to dramatize it. And I had some opportunity to fix it a little during that run, but it was in the six months afterwards, mostly, that I started to dramatize it.

MCNALLY: This was work you did with the director?

SIMON: No, I did it on my own. And we opened the revised play in Philadelphia at the Walnut. On the opening night in the middle of the first act, a man died in the balcony. I heard a woman scream, "Oh, my God, Harry!" and I said, "Oh, my God, my career." It stopped everything cold that night. But the play became a big hit in Philadelphia; we sold out for the three weeks. And we came to New York. I assumed that all New York was waiting at Grand Central Station for me. I found out that we had $175 in advance sales.

We opened, and this is how your fate can change because of the whim or ingenuity of one person. There were seven daily newspapers in 1961, and very little television coverage. There was word-of-mouth, eventually, but you lived or died by those critics. We got mixed reviews, some were good, some not good. I went down to the box office the next day—there was one woman there buying a ticket, and she found out it was the wrong play. So we didn't sell anything, and Mike Ellis and Bill Hammerstein posted the closing notice. I was heartbroken. The general manager, Wally Fried, said, "You can't close this play! The audiences love it!" He said, "Go out on the corners and give the tickets away—anybody who walks by. Get them into the theater!" And for the first week, that's what we did. We had a quarter of the house all sitting there for free—and enjoying it. They started to tell people about it, and gradually people started to buy tickets. Then we started giving out tickets for half the house. Irving Lazar, the agent, came and laughed his head off and told Groucho Marx. Groucho saw it, came backstage—I had my picture taken with him—and said: "It's one of the funniest plays I've ever seen," and the play caught on. It ran two years. Had Wally Fried not told them he believed in this play, it would have been over, and I'd be back on *My Three Sons*.

MCNALLY: Do you wonder if you would have written another play if it had closed that first week?

SIMON: Yes, because I was working in television during this, and to write I had to find weekends, nights; I had a wife and a baby to support. If those three years had gone down the drain, it would have kept me, possibly, from doing the second play. What *Come Blow Your Horn* did was subsidize my next play. When Paramount offered me the chance to do the screen play for something like $75,000, more money than I'd ever dreamed of, I turned it down. I said, "No, I know what happens. If I go out there and write the screen play, and it works, they'll offer me another one, and I'll end up in Hollywood." Which is not what I wanted to do. I wanted to be a playwright. So I started to work on *Barefoot in the Park*. And digressed to *Little Me*.

MCNALLY: Was there any tone in the reviews of *Come Blow Your Horn* that this was a comedy by a television writer and therefore not a *real* playwright?

SIMON: Not much. A lot of my friends in television would be quoted in the reviews as saying this was a television comedy, written by a television writer. I don't remember that as being in the reviews as a penalty to pay.

MCNALLY: *Little Me* brought you back with Sid Caesar?

SIMON: Yes, I wrote it for Sid Caesar. It was a part that required the portrayal of seven different roles, and I didn't know anyone as good as Sid. After *Your Show of Shows* went off the air, I'd stayed with Max Liebman, the producer, who was doing a series of specials—two a month. The first would be a revue, with people like Maurice Chevalier and Marcel Marceau, international stars. The other part of the month we would adapt a Broadway book show: *Best Foot Forward, A Connecticut Yankee, Dearest Enemy*—all Rodgers and Hart shows. Some Gershwin shows. The books were dated, so we got permission from the estates of these properties to update them. It was another learning experience for the theater: I learned to write books for musicals.

MCNALLY: You interrupted *Barefoot in the Park* to write *Little Me*?

SIMON: Yes, and then went back to *Barefoot*. I was lucky to have *Come Blow Your Horn* as the first show, because it was not such an awesome hit that you say, "God, what do I do now?" *Barefoot* was a huge hit; it ran four years. I had never read reviews like that. "Funniest play I've ever seen; funniest play in the last fifty years." I would sure hate that to be my first play; there's no way that you could live up to that. It would have scared the life out of me. But having done two shows before, *Barefoot* just became my third show. It was kind of scary, but I was lucky, because I had a good idea for the next show while that was happening, which was *The Odd Couple*. So, I didn't let that success intimidate me.

MCNALLY: With *Barefoot*, you started working with Mike Nichols, which was one of the most successful collaborations in recent history.

SIMON: Mike is the most helpful director, to a writer, that I've ever worked with. And I've worked with wonderful directors—Gene Saks, Herbert Ross, Bob Fosse. They all have their individual talents, but Mike, working with a writer, is incomparable.

MCNALLY: In what way is he most helpful?

SIMON: He just makes you think differently. The first day of *The Odd Couple* we sat around a table and read the play, the first act was terrific, and the second was even better. And the producer, Saint Subber, went home; he said, "You don't need me here. I'm going out to sell theater parties, because this play is a smash." Saint didn't hear the third act, and it was a bomb. And I really panicked about that, because it had taken me three or four months to write the third act. Mike said, "I'll rehearse the first and second acts, and you go home and write a new third act." So in about four days I wrote a new third act that I told myself was brilliant. And I brought it in and Mike read it, hysterically laughing; and we sat down and read it, and it was worse than the first third act.

So for the second time I had to go back, and I didn't feel so brilliant any more. I was getting real scared then. I came in with another version a week later, after missing the rehearsals and the rewrites needed for the first and second acts. Mike said, "No, it's not so good, but we'll have to open in Wilmington with this third act. But we'll talk on the train." Which we did. And as the train pulled in, we had pretty much evolved what the third act should be about. So I went to my hotel and spent a day and a night writing this new third act. Mike and I had breakfast, and he sat and read it—he has this wonderful giggle that makes you feel wonderful—and he said, "This is not it in its entirety, but you're on the right track. I think in here eventually will be the third act that we want."

We still had three days before we opened in Wilmington. I kept working on it. And what I had was infinitely better than what we were rehearsing, so Mike called the cast together and he said, "There is no point in performing a third act we will never perform after leaving this theater. We have a third act which is not right yet, but it will eventually be the final third act. So I want you to learn it for opening night." Some of the actors thought he was crazy; they said, "Go out there with something we learned in three days? We still don't even know the first two acts." Mike said, "You'll just have to do it." So we did it.

The first two acts went great, and the third act—we just threw it at them—survived. And I kept improving it as we went; fortunately, we had six weeks on the road with the play.

MCNALLY: Out of town, have you ever felt panic?

SIMON: Oh, yeah, I go crazy. It's happened to me on many, many shows. When you know a show is really working, when you get out of town, you prune it, you edit, you do some work. But the ones that don't seem to be working at all, you say, "What do I do? Should I just leave it?" What I do is hit rock bottom emotionally. I say, "This is a disaster, my career is over, I'll never write again, I never *want* to write again." And having hit rock bottom, there's no further place to go except to start up again. And then I get charged, I get angry that I goofed up. I say, "Maybe I can save it, maybe I can do something with it."

That's what happened with *The Gingerbread Lady* out of town. That play was a departure for me. Although *Plaza Suite* had been leaning towards a departure, *The Gingerbread Lady* really was; it was about an alcoholic trying to get herself on her feet again. So when we opened in New Haven, the audience didn't quite know how to accept the play; they were thrown by it. They were receptive, but this was not going to be a smash. When we went to Boston, it was much scarier. They were expecting another kind of play, and the reviews were not good at all. And Saint Subber called me at the restaurant where we were on opening night and said, "I think we ought to close the play." And I said, "Are the reviews so bad that we can't save it?" He said, "Well, I think so." And when I told the cast, Maureen Stapleton was furious with me; she said, "If you close this play, I'll never speak to you again. It is a good play. It needs some work, but we'll do it. We'll learn whatever pages you give us."

But I was down at rock bottom. It was going to be my first flop, and I was devastated by it. We decided to post the closing notice, and I went to the airport to fly back to New York. But I picked up the *Christian Science Monitor*, just to see if another review had come in. And there I found an out-and-out rave for the play. It said that the author does need to make some changes, to orient audiences towards accepting the play, but it said, "Don't close this play!" I felt spurred on by this review. I decided to take the train back to New York because the ride would take four hours; I could start working and then be able to start typing something when I arrived. And typing something meant that I was in it, in the flow.

I worked on the play, and then we came to New York with it. We weren't a hit, but we got respectful notices, and Maureen won the Tony. We had a season's run out of it. And the play has survived over the years. I made it into a film, *Only When I Laugh*, that I like. So a lot of things happened from reading that one review and being spurred on by it.

MCNALLY: I think I read that it is one of the film adaptations of yours that you think is superior to the play.

SIMON: Yes. There are two. I think *The Sunshine Boys*, which I really like as a play, is even better as a film. I had the opportunity to open up the story in a couple of key scenes: specifically, when Richard Benjamin goes to New Jersey to visit George Burns; and when they are doing the show, when we see them in the dressing room and see Walter Matthau having a heart attack and falling down the stairs. All those were visual ways of showing what was happening and worked better on the screen than they did on the stage. And I think *Only When I Laugh* was a big improvement on *The Gingerbread Lady*. Many of the other films were not nearly as good as the plays. They were written as plays and just didn't open up as films; the action was contained in an apartment or whatever.

MCNALLY: You said with *The Gingerbread Lady* the audience's expectations made them unprepared. Have you made a conscious effort since then to solve that? I think now audiences come to your work prepared for a depth that they didn't expect in the earlier plays.

SIMON: Yes. Well, in *Gingerbread Lady*, wherever there was a chance to get humor into the play, I put it there. And I don't think that was invalid, because the character was based on women I'd met, in theater and films, who had drinking problems and who were also enormously witty people. They were funnier than most of the dialogue I could write.

I remember Lillian Hellman saying, "Never try to mix comedy with drama. The critics will never buy it." And for the most part, it's true, and it really bothers me; it's been a great gripe of mine for years. Since life is neither all comedy nor all tragedy, why can't it be that way in plays? But audiences do get thrown if you start off very funny. If the play suddenly switches to something else, they say, "I'm not comfortable with this. I don't want to see this drama; get back to where it's funny."

In all our lives, we're feeling our very best, life is wonderful, and we suddenly get a phone call that's filled with tragedy. Life shifts. And I've wanted to do that on the stage: to *feel* that shift from the audience, to pull them into another area. You hear them gasp—when you do it right. When it seems organic, when it's the right thing to happen at the moment, they believe it.

MCNALLY: Do you think you're taken less seriously as a writer because of your reputation for humor?

SIMON: I'm taken less seriously by the so-called serious critics. They would, ironically, rather have me write funny. I remember when Robert Brustein saw *Plaza Suite*. The first play is a fairly serious play about a couple breaking up. The play he liked best of the three was the out-and-out farce, in which the bride is locked in the bathroom. It doesn't *really* bother me, though, because I'm going to keep doing what I'm doing as long as I can do it. And I'll let *them* deal with it.

MCNALLY: Well, certainly your work has gotten deeper, richer, over the past few years.

SIMON: There was sort of a breakthrough for me in *Brighton Beach Memoirs*. I had never tried to write a tapestry play before. Most of my plays were a confrontation between two people, and the other people around them were peripheral. I never went into much depth about the other characters. In doing *Brighton Beach Memoirs*, despite my telling it through the eyes of Eugene Jerome, the fifteen-year-old boy, I said, "This play is about every character, and I will tell each of their stories." And it's what I tried to do in the sequel, *Biloxi Blues*. I tried to treat each character as a three-dimensional character that one could possibly write a full play about.

MCNALLY: I first felt I was seeing a new side of Neil Simon when I saw the character Linda Lavin played in *Last of the Red Hot Lovers*.

SIMON: I was changing. The times were changing, society was changing, I was getting older, and I had different viewpoints. It was the middle of the sexual revolution, and people in their early forties then were saying, "I missed it! It went right by me!" So I wrote about a man who had missed it. And that play is tragicomic to me.

MCNALLY: Did you write it with James Coco in mind?

SIMON: I don't remember, really. I know I did that with Walter Matthau. I was writing *The Odd Couple* when I met Walter, and I said, "Please don't accept a job for the next year." I think I may have done the same with Jimmy

Coco. Some of the producers who read the play thought it was an offbeat way of casting it, but they all missed the idea of the play. I thought Jimmy was the quintessential guy who missed the sexual revolution.

MCNALLY: *The Good Doctor*—I felt you were present in it, as the writer speaks to the audience. That was an unusual play for you, too.

SIMON: You never know where a play will come from, and that's why I do not like it when critics talk about a "typical Neil Simon play." I really don't know what it is. I think they look at your biggest hits and say they're typical. But *The Good Doctor* came out of my reading short stories by Chekhov. I read *Death of a Civil Servant,* and I had never known Chekhov was that funny. So I did some research into Chekhov and found out that when he was a young man he did comic articles every day for the newspapers.

My first idea was to find as many funny Russian short stories as I could and make an evening of them. I couldn't find enough of them, so I stuck with Chekhov's funny ones—and some other ones—till I had about fifteen pieces that I liked. We went into rehearsal, and four of them didn't work. And we were about to go to New Haven, so I had to write my own Chekhov short stories. One of them was a monologue for Marsha Mason, in which she auditions for Chekhov; one was when Chekhov takes his young son to a brothel for the first time; another was about an elderly couple, which I wrote as a lyric called "Too Late for Happiness"; and my favorite one in the play, based on a terrific piece by Chekhov, was *How to Seduce Another Man's Wife.* I had a real good time doing that, and I think I did good work with it.

MCNALLY: The speeches of the writer to the audience are nowhere in Chekhov? That's all yours?

SIMON: Bits and pieces are from Chekhov. There are lines from Trigorin, in *The Seagull,* where he says that he cannot stop writing. I identified so strongly with him, saying that when he sees a cloud and thinks it looks like a piano, it starts to turn into an idea for a story.

MCNALLY: Do you start first with a theme, a character, a situation? All three?

SIMON: All three. The theme less so. The character and the story—what it's about—come first, and I sort of discover the theme. Sometimes I discover it when I read the reviews and they tell me what it is.

Doing *Brighton Beach Memoirs,* I hadn't the slightest idea where I was going. I wanted to write about that period, write about those people, but from page to page I did not know where the story was going to go. I didn't know the father was going to have a heart attack until I got to it. And then everything seemed organic. And it was not a memory play; some of those things did not happen specifically to me.

MCNALLY: Not knowing where it was going was atypical for you, then? Do you ever work from an outline?

SIMON: No, I tried that in the beginning, and found it did not work for me. It took the fun out of the writing. I prefer to take the chance of saying, "I like this character, I like the situation, I'm just going to go with it." And I discover the play the same way the audience does. It makes me laugh sometimes: I'll write a play that way and a critic says the ending was predictable, and I'd never known the ending.

MCNALLY: When you finish the first draft, is there anyone you show it to?

SIMON: Generally my family. I show it to my wife, my two daughters—I respect their opinions greatly. And generally the producer that I'm working with, Saint Subber or Emanuel Azenberg. On occasion I've shown a play to Mike Nichols for his opinion, even though he was too busy to direct it.

I learned a lesson from *The Odd Couple*, which is to have a preliminary reading. I don't want to find out on the first day of rehearsal that I'm in trouble. I liked what I heard in the *Biloxi* reading, but I saw spots that needed rewriting in the six weeks before rehearsals started.

MCNALLY: You've made that message very clear to other writers. Every interview you ever gave, you said, "Fix it now—not in rehearsals!"

One crazy question: I've heard that you did some work on *A Chorus Line*. Would you like to lay that one to rest?

SIMON: I did. Michael Bennett was a friend of mine; we had worked on *Promises, Promises*. And he asked me to come down to the Public Theater to see *A Chorus Line* there. Well, it was a knockout; you knew it was going to be a smash. And Michael said, "Come talk to me." We went out to a Chinese restaurant, and he said, "You know, it just needs some funny things here and there. Will you do it?" And I said, "Well, it's against the Dramatists Guild rules to do that." And he said, "What if I got permission?" So I wanted to do it. I was thrilled with the show, and it would make me feel good to make a contribution to it, as long as it didn't create trouble. I wrote not an enormous number of lines, and many more lines than he actually used. But I never took credit and I never got money for it.

I read about Moss Hart, when I was growing up, going out of town to help with someone else's play. Friends would help friends. It doesn't happen very often any more, but I would like to do it a lot if the shows are worth saving. Mike Nichols did that with me; he came to help out with *Fools*, purely out of friendship.

MCNALLY: I want to ask you about analysis. Did it affect you as a writer?

SIMON: I've been in analysis only three or four times, always during critical times in my life. I find it invaluable, not only in getting me through those tough periods: it taught me a way to think about plays. Plays are a reflection of life, and you must think of them that way. If you think of them as artificial things, then that's what they will come out to be. So the lessons that I learned in analysis—questions I learned to ask myself—I apply to my plays when I get into trouble. I ask the characters those same questions, and I find answers for them. I'm a very analytical person, and analysis, for me, is very logical (if you can get someone to explain it to you logically). And I've applied it successfully, for the most part, in my life and in my work.

Q: I'm curious about what plays you may have given up on, and why.

SIMON: I have about forty plays that I've given up on. The only way for me to know if I feel like writing a play is to start to write it. I do think about it—it'll be in my head for some time—but I'll get into it, and suddenly it will hit a dead end for me. Sometimes I put it aside for a long, long time and go back and see that it's really good. That happened with *The Sunshine Boys*. After I'd put it aside, I was having dinner with Mike Nichols, and he asked what I was doing. I said I was working on a play, but it didn't seem like much. I told him the story, and he said, "You're crazy. That's wonderful." So I went home and finished the play. But the others, they just sit there, and they may sit there forever. If the play is good enough, it *demands* to be written.

Q: I saw *Fools*, and I loved it. Why do you think it closed so quickly?

SIMON: We never should have done *Fools* on Broadway. I never meant for it to be done on Broadway. It was a diversion, the kind of play I write when I don't feel like writing a play that deals with my own life. I always meant it as a children's fable, and I always wanted to do it in a regional theater. It's hard for me to do plays there, because the press comes down hard on me: "Those theaters are subsidized and exist to encourage young and experimental writers, and you're an establishment writer." So I've been sort of kicked out of that field and have to stay in the commercial field. The Goodman Theater has asked me to do plays there a number of times, so I guess if I really looked . . . But I really didn't listen to my instincts with *Fools*. I should have done it off Broadway somewhere. It has been done at the Mark Taper Forum in Los Angeles.

Q: Do you have a daily discipline?

SIMON: I'm very disciplined. I work five days a week, if I can. There are so many distractions. I try to keep at it all the time, and when I'm on a new play that I really like, I don't like to get off it, especially when it really captures me. Then I will sacrifice most of my personal life to complete it. With *Brighton Beach*, I was at it night and day.

Q: Have you ever thought of directing your own material, as many writers do?

SIMON: No, I have no desire to do it. I'd rather have a director that I really respect putting his input into the play. Also, I have no patience for it.

I like to walk away from a play sometimes. I won't go to a rehearsal after they've reached the point where they don't need me. I have to give the actors the chance to learn, to catch up to me. And I don't want to spend that time going over it with them; it's not what I enjoy best. I really like being alone in a room, writing.

MARSHA NORMAN

In Conversation With Robert Brustein

ROBERT BRUSTEIN: Marsha, you have in a relatively brief period of time emerged as one of America's leading dramatists. What accounts for your development as a theater artist?

MARSHA NORMAN: Why *me,* as opposed to a number of other people? There are a number of things in my life that seemed curses at the time that turned out to be great blessings in terms of making a writer. I was driven—I had a very isolated childhood, read a lot, played a lot and wasn't allowed to frown. It was a very cheerful household. I spent a lot of time imagining what I would like to say at a given moment, say, while I was having to smile and eat my dinner. I think that is what you see in my work: a sense of what you would like to say, of the conversations you would like to hear, of how it goes when people actually *do* say those things.

Some of what is interesting in *'night, Mother* is the terror that someone would actually come to you and say, "I'm going to kill myself." What on earth do you say back? There are things that need to be said between people that ultimately approach the unsayable. Things we most want to tell somebody are so secret and private that we don't ever hear them. I feel that my responsibility in writing is to say the unsaid; to listen for things that I might need to say one day.

I lived in a very secret world, and I still do. Most writers do. I'm often told, "You look so different from your work. Shave your head, smoke cigars, wear strange clothes, and then we'll believe you actually have done this writing." What happens inside us is very private, but it is my responsibility to speak out as clearly as possible. Not that I have the answers—I am just beginning to realize that all I want to do is make confusion clear. I want to say, "This is the exact thing I do not understand, right here." I don't want to pretend to understand. Maybe I will in forty years, but by then I won't be able to write any more or tell anybody. It's that permanent sense of isolation that was always with me from my earliest memories.

BRUSTEIN: What is there about this highly public and exposed art called the theater that attracts you as the medium for making the confused clear?

NORMAN: It's simple, the only thing I do very well is listen. I don't see very well, I don't notice things painters would notice, but I can listen to the way people use talk to try to tell another person who they are. They may not do it very well, or they may do it brilliantly, or they may do it to mislead—but listening is what I do, I am an eavesdropper. You can go out to lunch with me, and I can tell you what is happening at tables all around the restaurant while pretending I'm talking to you. It's one of those odd little skills, and fortunately mine seems to be paying off right now.

It may be that in a while this listening will turn against me. Quite often, you hear things you don't want to hear. That's one of the curses, but that is what I do. I couldn't, at this point, write a novel—I don't watch how people move. I have a theory that what we do in theater is say, "This is how this person talks, and this person is going to talk about some things you know about. You will be able to tell the difference between them and you by comparing what they say with what you would say." For example, in *Getting Out*, Arlene says, "I ain't never eatin' no more scrambled eggs." We all have a sentence we would say about scrambled eggs, but suddenly when you hear Arlene talk you know the difference between Arlene and you, and then you know who she is.

You will see references to ordinary things again and again in my work. That is no accident. We all need common reference points. The caramel candy in *'night, Mother* somehow lets you know that that could be you there. The audience looks around the stage and says, "Oh, yeah, I know that candy. I know that chair. I wouldn't have bought that chair," and suddenly you have the audience transported up onto the stage and involved, with something at stake. There are helpful objects in the world that connect the audience to the people in the play, and I use them.

BRUSTEIN: You've had five plays produced now. Which is your favorite, and why?

NORMAN: I have a problem about that—I go through my work very quickly. The last time I went to see *'night, Mother* I felt that I could do better than that now. I also felt that the last line of *'night, Mother* belonged to the new play rather than to that one, which was interesting because that last line was actually written in the time frame of the new play, rather than a few years ago when I wrote *'night, Mother.* I come very quickly through a time of being attached to the play, and I begin to turn around and ask myself, "Did I really write that line?" I begin to think that the jokes are terrible. I have to say that the play I have just written is the one I like best and the only one in which I am still *actively* involved.

I'm fortunate in that I don't really fall in love with the plays, or rather, stay in love with the plays. There is always a terrible moment when I realize the play and I are going to separate. It's a moment you look forward to, but it's always awful. You've been waiting to hear whether this important director wants to do it, or that this theater has a place for it. "Ah," you think, "two more days and you'll know. As soon as you get the decision you'll be on your way." The two days pass, and you know the answer—you've got the theater, the director, you have it all, and you go into this crashing depression. It's the first moment of knowing the play is not yours, that it belongs to the world now, that it is going on without you, that it may turn around and murder you, it may leave you in its wake.

But if the play doesn't leave your control it will never have a life. I have a friend who's carrying around a score in his briefcase—nobody can hear it in there. That moment of separation is very important, and I think I meet it pretty well, saying, "Well, all right, there it goes. God bless it, and I hope I can get out of the way if it falls."

Some people wonder why I'm there following it around. I told somebody the other day that being a writer is like designing a skyscraper; what you *can't* do after the building is built is spend the day riding in the elevators. If you do that, you will never design any more buildings—you will never even see what the building you've made looks like. There is a real need to pull away from it, look at it from the outside, read other plays, find out what in fact your work *is* so you can make a decision about where it needs to go *now*. So my favorite play is the last one.

BRUSTEIN: You speak about your plays in a metaphor of children who reach a certain age when they gain independence, and make you let them go. Some of the children you've created are not quite as loved as *'night, Mother* and *Getting Out*. What kind of position do they have in your heart?

NORMAN: Two plays of mine were failures in production. One is *Circus Valentine*, about a small family circus that plays parking lots. An aging trapeze artist goes up to try a triple somersault in order to save this small circus, falls and dies. Isn't that a cheery plot? I wasn't equipped emotionally to write it—I tried it ahead of time. I got too much help in the process, and it never really had a chance. There are some incredible speeches in it, but fortunately it was stopped. All the critics in the world came down to Louisville to see this play, and all of them wrote that it was anywhere from a disaster to a disappointment. They said perfectly clearly that this play will go further (when you do a play in a big festival like that it has one chance, so there are pros and cons to festivals; you can lose a play completely). Yet for me that was real good. I needed to put that play away and go on, I didn't need to spend another two years following it around trying to convince other people that it was good. As my husband, who used to be in the retail business, says, "You need to take your markdowns right away."

I had the opposite experience with a play called *The Hold Up*. It has some funny speeches and nice things in it, and I've spent three years listening to people tell me it's wonderful and just needs *their* production. But I have felt all along that there's something wrong with it at the conception level that I could not fix, so that it doesn't really have a chance. Two summers ago, I finally got the will to say, "This play will not be done, I don't care who wants to do it. I don't want anybody to walk into a theater and have that play be their first experience with my work."

Learning to put plays away is a tough lesson, but absolutely critical. Some plays are exercises. They needed to be written to explore points of craft, but they don't have ultimately to be presented onstage to have great meaning, great significance for you as a writer. *The Hold Up,* for example, was the first time I ever tried to close the set. That is to say, as soon as everybody gets onstage nobody can leave, and what happens has to happen because of who these people are. What I learned in *The Hold Up* paid off in *'night, Mother* when Jessie and Mama are onstage together for those ninety minutes and you know nobody is coming. That's something I had to learn to do, to keep two people talking for ninety minutes and not have six hundred people go to sleep, without needing the intervention of the third character, that funny person who comes in to stir up the situation so that you can get the resolution you couldn't get with just these two people talking. That's the sort of thing a failed play helps you learn.

It's also very important for us all to keep writing, more important than to see pieces produced. There are lessons to be learned from production, but I see too many people spending too much time waiting for the phone to ring to hear yet another juror call in about their play. That can be very dangerous.

BRUSTEIN: How much do you feel your plays owe to your collaborators in production? Once you've done this silent and solitary business of writing the play, it enters the community of people known as theater—the director, the actors, the designer. How much have they contributed to your awareness and your extension of your play?

NORMAN: Enormously. The great joy is to find someone who speaks English the way you do, who understands the territory that you are investigating. There's an incredible sign language, a wonderful shorthand. It's the classic whole being greater than the sum of its parts—what you can do together is much more than you can do separately.

What is dangerous, I think, is premature collaboration. The script must have singleness of vision and purpose, one mind saying, "I saw this and it hurt me," or "I lost this, did you lose it too?" Often when collaborators get close they start to talk about the play too soon and begin to suggest changes of direction and character. Collaborators need to know where the boundaries are. They need to practice that sentence, "I don't want to talk about that right now." You as a writer need to know how to protect yourself from good advice until you know what it is you are trying to do—and then you have to write that down so you won't forget it or get swayed.

We must work with the best possible actors, because they can tell us so much. Watch them, and they can tell you when they're uncomfortable. They can tell you when you don't make sense, when they are making it up, when they are performing instead of living what you have written. You have to learn to watch for those signs of uneasiness or great joy. They won't be able to remember a line, say, and you know it isn't because they aren't ready, there is something actually the matter with the line.

In an important collaboration, you can learn to listen for symptoms of a problem rather than for the problem itself. There is a moment in *'night, Mother* when Jessie is saying no to all of the people in her life and problems she can't fix. The director felt that this "no" speech was too long. We talked about it, and I asked him why he was feeling uncomfortable, what it was he didn't like. Ultimately, I realized that it wasn't too long, it wasn't long *enough.*

To listen is a key skill for a playwright, but don't let anybody tell you exactly what to do, to cut or drop a character. Don't listen for the solution, listen for the correct description of the problem, and then *you* as a writer will know what to do. It's a little like what doctors do—you say, "My fingers are numb, and there's this tingling," and he doesn't put your fingers in splints, he knows you have a disc problem. You have a nerve problem, but the implications run all the way down your arm. As a playwright, you know how your play works, where the fuses are that will turn the lights on in the hall. Good collaborations encourage you to look at the fuse box, while dangerous ones simply advise, "This has to be cut."

BRUSTEIN: That's very similar to what Chekhov said about his function as a dramatist—not to offer the solution to a problem but the correct presentation of it. How much do you involve yourself in the production process? Do you do much rewriting, and what form do these revisions usually take?

NORMAN: Generally they're mechanical, having to do with transportation on the stage. If you want to get somebody out of a door, you have to have something that gets them there, a sentence that becomes like a little corridor crossing the stage. This is what you need to make the thing work mechanically, and you don't know until you begin to work with the director.

I knew when I finished the new play it didn't quite have the last three scenes. I had a sketch, but I knew I had to go and live some more before I'd really know how to write them. Yesterday I got two of those three. Sometime between now and when this new play opens I will get the last one, I hope, and that may come about as a result of what I see in rehearsal—or it may be something I get walking on the street.

BRUSTEIN: Here's a question submitted in advance by a member of the Dramatists Guild: "Why did you decide to do *'night, Mother* in a resident theater outside New York?"

NORMAN: First of all, American Repertory Theater is a wonderful theater. The playwright needs a chance to live the work, to work on a play in an environment that's supportive and friendly and feels like life, not like the march to the guillotine. One of the joys of being a playwright is coming out of the solitude, the isolation, for the rehearsal period. It's about as much as I can take of communication with other people, but it's a wonderful time, a time of focus and energy. The world goes away. It's harder for people to get you on the phone. You don't have your regular lunch dates or anything else you normally do.

During the rehearsals for *'night, Mother,* ART was a place where I felt supported and secure and encouraged and loved and challenged. Working in resident theaters provides an opportunity to enjoy the production process and *be* with the people you are working with. You know how New York is—you never see them. People sort of vanish once they get onto the street, so you don't have that closeness, you don't have those talks when people say those things they probably shouldn't. There are dangers, of course. You can learn things about them that you didn't want to know. You might find out you don't like the people you are working with.

ART is human in scale. With *'night, Mother* I would never watch the play. I would sit back in the green room and listen—as I said, listening is what I do. I would come out at the end, and there would be those clumps of people still sitting in the theater talking to each other. I really loved that. In New York, we can't let people sit in the theater and talk, we have to send them out into the streets.

BRUSTEIN: That was a most remarkable reaction we had—people just sitting there thirty, forty, fifty minutes after the play was over, not wanting to leave the theater, preferring to remain in their seats and talk about it.

Here's a real zinger: Sigmund Freud said that when a man and woman make love, there are usually at least four more people in the bedroom, assuming that the parents are there as well. When you write a play, are there other people in the room—for example, characters remembered from your past or perhaps even playwrights hovering over your shoulder?

NORMAN: I almost always write about the spirit of some person I have known—not ever really the person, but certainly the bravery, the nobility, some act of great courage of which I have been in awe.

And then there are people that I read. It's fairly clear, I'm sure, that Kierkegaard was around when I was writing *'night, Mother.* Those that have been by me all along are not always as much help as I think they should be, but they are there in a guiding way. Plato's allegory of the cave is for me a really central principle. I can't tell you how it affects my work—all I know is, that's the pain I'm talking about, and I talk about it all the time.

Sometimes I don't understand what specific lines mean until years later. It's good to preserve a kind of innocence about the work you are currently doing. It's not a good idea to ask yourself, "What does this mean? Does it mean I really hate my mother?" That's not a thought you want to have cluttering up your desk as you are trying to work. You want to work out of a kind of innocence that allows you to speak freely. That's why it's dangerous to base plays on people that you know, because suddenly you are afraid of offending them. None of us wants to hurt people with what we do.

It's very dangerous even to have the audience in the room. I remember when I was still living in Louisville there was a man I knew fairly well who represented the Louisville audience in my mind. I would ask myself, "Is he going along with that? Is he going to nod his head and say, 'That's the truth'?" I realized I was writing toward him, and ultimately I decided that was very dangerous. When you begin to understand the audience too well, you begin to give them exactly what you think it is they want. The *last* thing a playwright needs to do is second-guess the audience.

And the playwright absolutely must not have critics or advisors drumming their fingers on the table waiting for the play. The playwright needs to walk into the study absolutely free of obligations except to honor those spirits who are celebrated in the play, to tell the truth as you know it, or to present the problem as clearly as you can. Your obligation at your typewriter is to that central premise, those characters. Suddenly you begin to have real relationships with imaginary people, much stronger in that moment than any of your relationships with real people. At that point everybody else needs to become sort of imaginary. Suddenly, real confusion exists in an exciting way about who's real and who's imaginary.

In the time of writing, you owe your loyalty to those people you are writing about, and *not* to anybody else. One of the many ways to lose your way as a writer is to begin to think about anything other than that work. The moment you say, "Does anybody else care about this?" you're in trouble. One of the great things we can do is examine ourselves and trust that we have something in common with the rest of the world, that we're not here in vain, that we've seen what is going on, that we've felt something of what everybody feels. The moment you come onstage as a playwright trying to say, "I am special, I am not like you," you are in trouble. As a writer, you come into the theater to *search*, and if you do your work you find something. Or at least you identify the path.

BRUSTEIN: Whom do you admire most among playwrights past and present?

NORMAN: You can look at my work and know that it's *Oedipus*, *Medea* and *King Lear*, that particular real old tragic sense. Aristotle is very important to me. A while back, I learned that the rules really *are* the rules, and now I am not interested in breaking them or seeing how they could be stretched or changed.

I am really interested in knowing why the rules have been working for so long and in watching them work. In *Traveler in the Dark*, for example, we are watching a terrible tragedy brought on by the central character. And I've really just understood over the last six months the rule about tragedy being written only about great people. I feel as though I'm fighting a battle that's been going on for thousands and thousands of years in the theater, struggling with what seem to be unbreakable laws. I like the feeling that somehow what I do establishes them all over again.

Other people write incredible plays which break all those rules. But for me, the path is an ancient one.

As for others I admire, it's a bizarre list. Sam Shepard is incredible. I love *Our Town* and I think *The Importance of Being Earnest* is a terrific piece. The play that has probably had the most influence on me in the last couple of years is Brian Friel's *The Faith Healer,* a spectacular piece. Christopher Hampton is an incredible writer. Lanford Wilson writes the best dialogue, wonderful silky smooth conversation that is always such a joy to hear. You know that if you were in a Lanford Wilson play you'd never say anything, you'd just listen. We had three late Samuel Beckett plays in New York recently; the questions haven't changed, but he's further into them now. He understands them better—that's exciting.

This is a fascinating time in the American theater, because we have a fierce fight with the influence of television. I get so concerned and angry when I see that a person has not been reading but has been sitting in front of the television. And there are so many plays published, and so few of them are actually read. I am concerned about that, particularly with student writers. I don't know who is *not* putting plays in people's hands, but somebody.

BRUSTEIN: That's true. People are not reading plays anymore.

NORMAN: I have a philosophy background, and those are the guides for me, more so than the theatrical people.

BRUSTEIN: Who besides Kierkegaard and Aristotle?

NORMAN: Jaspers.

BRUSTEIN: Nietzsche?

NORMAN: I don't know if I've been guided by him, but you certainly have to read him. I have the sense of taking part in a continuing conversation that stretches way back, I can't imagine how far or where it goes in the future.

BRUSTEIN: Here's another submitted question: "Do you feel any political responsibilities as a writer, apart from your private activities? For example, do you feel a responsibility to the women's movement?"

NORMAN: I feel that my responsibility to my work *is* a political responsibility. When I do my work well, that's how I can help. I have a strong commitment to students. It's very important to me that no eighth-grade girl in Kentucky is going to have the problem I did, growing up in Kentucky and thinking writers never come from there. It's not going to take anybody as long as it took me. I am going to say in whatever way I can, "Come on. We need you." Some day I'm going to be sixty-five years old, and they are going to come to the nursing home and take me to the theater on the bus, and I want to see something nice.

About my work being a political act: *'night, Mother* came along at the exact moment when a play about two women, written by a woman, could be seen as "a human play." You don't go to see it because you're a woman. You don't stay away because you're a man. But it proves that what happens to women is important, that the mother-daughter relationship is as deserving of attention as father-son.

I'm a member of some political action groups, but I find that inevitably on the afternoon I'm supposed to go to the meeting I want to stay home and work. The loyalty is there, but someone else does the organization work better. I may arrive at a time in my life when I'm more available, but right now this is my writing time. I have maybe ten or fifteen more years to write, and I have to conserve energy so that I can do it. That requires my saying no to some things I'd like to be involved in.

BRUSTEIN: What, if anything, do you learn from critics? Do you feel they are necessary; and in that unlikely event, what functions do they serve?

NORMAN: You learn suffering from critics. It's an interesting time for critics, particularly in New York. There aren't many plays around, so the critics are all sort of looking for something to write about. We desperately need writing about the *world* of the theater, not just the kind of consumer journalism we've suffered from for so long, like a checklist, buy or don't buy. We don't need critics stamping out plays as though they were forest fires or dangerous diseases. Word of mouth is good at stamping out plays, it will take care of the bad ones—the audience knows whether to come see a show or not.

We need more *writing* like the kind of work Benedict Nightingale was doing in the Sunday New York *Times,* not just a review but great long pages talking about everything he happens to think about a particular production. It's a sort of musing about how else this might have been done—what are the historical effects here?—what tradition does this piece come from?—how have all these people gathered to make this play?

The kind of criticism we've had lately, at least in the newspapers, hasn't done its part to educate and engage the audience. All you know from most recent criticism is, "You have to be careful about plays. You can get a bad one, you know." We've known that all along, we know it about apples, we know it about cars, but there is *more* to be known about the world of the theater. Somebody needs to write a stunning piece about realism—we need to explain to people that it is not necessarily real because there is a stove in the set. There are a lot of issues like that that need to be addressed by critics. There are a few good ones, and I do learn interesting things from them, but I don't read people who hate me, I don't need to carry that around.

If there is anybody listening right now who thinks she or he has what it takes for really fine writing about the world of the theater, I am here to say that we need you. Work, read, study, practice, write, do your homework and come and help us. There is probably something you know that we have not sufficiently developed. I mean, we train everybody else. We need to train critics with the same care we do playwrights, actors and directors.

BRUSTEIN: Here's another submitted question: "How has fame affected your life? Considering the roller-coaster ride our media put playwrights and other American artists on, are you worried about this in regard to your own career and how your next play will be received?"

NORMAN: Of course I worry about it. After the great promise of an enormous success, you next have a failure because that makes a wonderful narrative line. That's how it's supposed to go—you build to this peak, and then you collapse—so that in fact it's a lot of what happens. A failure gets to be almost predictable because of the size of the previous success. It fits the needs of good storytelling among the people who cover plays.

I did a lot of press in order to sell tickets to *'night, Mother*. It worked, and people came, and I still do a good deal of publicity about it, but I don't enjoy it. I get the feeling that some people would rather go have lunch with a reporter than work. That never happens to me, I am happiest when I am alone, when it is totally quiet and nobody is asking me anything. Talking is very difficult for me; I am actually a hermit.

As for the new play, it follows directly from *'night, Mother*, though other people may not see that. It's quite a risk, I think. There are things in it I've never tried before but was curious about. It will be interesting to see how people feel about it, whether it will in any way suffer from comparison with *'night, Mother.*

BRUSTEIN: Any questions from the floor?

Q: Do you consider yourself a realistic writer?

NORMAN: We have a problem with the word "realistic." This is where we could use some really fine criticism to help us quit throwing this word around. It's very confusing—we need somebody to say once and for all what is "naturalism" and what is "realism." I know that *'night, Mother* is not real, but it is true—O.K.? There is a difference. The writing is exaggerated, but you don't notice it. Those aren't the exact words people say, they were very carefully chosen. If a conversation like *'night, Mother* actually started in real life, it would wander off into nowhere, it would be a disaster.

What is *not* real about *'night, Mother* is the agenda. I'm back there collapsing lots of real-life experiences to create a theatrical one that is perhaps a useful model, one that seems real, that seems to work in the way that real situations work, but is not real in the sense that it is exactly what they would say. It's a hypothetical act of someone saying, "I'm going to kill myself, Mother."

All my work is like that, and on this level of shoptalk I'd like to mention exactly how I think the illusion is created. I always want to give you the sense very quickly that you are in very good hands. There is somebody driving this car. It is going somewhere. You are going to get in, I am going to tell you where we are going, it will be a nice safe ride, and you will get there. We won't stop along the way or get into a traffic jam. We won't have that ski-lift feeling I used to have listening to a play, thinking it was going up this ascent, but then the gears crank and it just hangs there, and at that point you begin to look down and say, "Oh my God, what am I doing here?" That's the question you don't want the audience ever to ask, you don't want them to know they're eighty thousand feet off the ground until they arrive at the top where they can see it. It's an illusion, it's a journey, a map, it moves, it doesn't just amble along, we're not just going for a Sunday afternoon drive.

Q: What do you mean when you say a tragic hero has to be great? I thought the mother and daughter in *'night, Mother* were great people. Do you mean godlike, or normal people who are great?

NORMAN: I might give you a different answer on this next year, but right now I feel that the most tragic of tragedies is brought on by the person him or herself. In *'night, Mother*, Mama has contributed to the tragedy that unfolds on the stage, but she didn't actually set it in motion directly. Right now, in my writing life I'm interested in the person who is ultimately going to suffer setting the tragedy in motion.

I'm just saying that there is about the classic tragic heroes a kind of power that enables them to destroy themselves. King Lear can say, "I have a kingdom and I am going to divide it up" and thereby set his tragedy in motion. People who have no power to bring on their own tragedy must suffer it at the hands of someone else, and that makes them victims. I'm not sure I know the answer to this just yet, but I really do think a person having the power to destroy himself is critical in tragedy as we have known it.

Q: Will you comment on the development of characters who are *not* on the stage, like the father and brother in *'night, Mother*?

NORMAN: I've been working on that a long time, and I'm very careful about it. I'm absolutely determined that you never hear the exposition, you come in and learn all you need to know without knowing you are learning it. It's very tricky, and I love the process of working on it. It's always the detail that convinces, the fact that the father in the play is described as a big old faded blue man in a chair, with his pipe cleaners—all kinds of things that let you know he is a specific individual, things about him that you can feel and smell. You know who he is because you know the stuff that is in his pockets and how he felt about it. Ultimately what convinces you about characters is what they care about, what they would *not* do without.

Q: In the initial stages of playwriting, do you ever discuss your ideas with your husband or a close friend?

NORMAN: I never talk about what I'm thinking about writing. I never want to get myself committed to something unless I'm absolutely sure—you don't want to put the rocket on the pad unless you have the fuel to get where you want to go. You need to wait a long time to make the commitment to a piece. You need to have stamina and to fight it off as hard as you can. As a matter of course I reject out of hand every idea I have for a play as soon as I think of it. I force that idea to fight for its own survival, to come after me and say, "You must write this. You are the only person who can write this."

The moment comes when suddenly I understand that it is inevitable that I am going to write this play. I am in its possession. I don't talk about it, but I say as much as I need to say to make the people around me comfortable. When it happens, it's as though somebody moved in with my husband and me.

There's a kind of pressure that has to build, that you write from, that comes from *not* talking it out, *not* hearing what anybody else says. You have to impose a silence on the subject so that suddenly, when you get ready to write it, you let the top off and it goes. You have the energy to propel you through it.

There are moments when you will be in such pain, you will sit there at dinner and you won't be able to say a word, or you will do something that is bizarre. You need to say to someone you trust, "I'm having trouble with this writing," but you just can't say too much. My husband and I have a sort of a mystery talk—he has seventy-five wonderful, vague lines like "Well, honey, I'm sure it will be just fine. You've been this miserable before and you'll be this miserable again, and I really understand how you feel. It must be hard to do it." This means, "It's O.K. You figure it out. I can't help you." The danger of talking to someone in too great detail is that you'll get their solution, not yours. You'll get what seems to them to be a good answer when in fact they have the problem defined in a whole different way than you do, so the answer is likely to be wrong.

When I get to the place where the first draft is written I ask a few people to read it and respond. Then I generally have actors, wonderful actors, over to my house to read it for me, so I can listen to how it fits. Does it feel good? You are trying it on real people both as listeners and actors. Their conversation is valuable if you go into those readings knowing what you want to know. You must have your own agenda when you go into a reading. You can't just ask, "Well, what do you think?" because you can get hurt and misled. You have to have specific objectives, in which case readings can be helpful.

Q: Have you reached an impasse at times in production, and if so, is the solution the playwright's? You mentioned that there's sometimes a line you don't understand until later in the rereading process. What do you do at those moments when the director, or someone, hears that line and says, "No, I need something else?"

NORMAN: A useful thing to say at that point is "Let me think about it." Sometimes what you need to do in those situations is get away. Directors are human, they like to have problems solved, and sometimes they don't yet understand what to do and hope to make their work easier by simply eliminating the source of confusion. As a writer, you have ultimately to decide who is right, you or the director, and that is hard. Trust comes into play, and it's so difficult working with someone you don't know. It takes you all that time of rehearsal to develop the relationship you know you needed to start the process on the very first day of rehearsal. If you do your preparatory work with the director carefully, you can know early which are problem lines, which gives you more time. You need to use as much time as you possibly can to think before you make changes. You don't *have* to make any changes with the Dramatists Guild behind you, but complex questions arise: "Are you really dealing with a higher intelligence in this director, and should you go along with him or her?" There's no easy way to answer that. Make friends with somebody close to the production so they'll be there in that moment when you're confused. But always take time before you make changes. Go back to that piece of paper on which you've written what it was you were trying to do, and use it as the arbitrator.

BRUSTEIN: I must call this session to an end, and of course I would like to thank Marsha Norman for giving us the privilege of her presence and the honesty and absolute truthfulness of her responses.

JERRY HERMAN

In Conversation With Sheldon Harnick

SHELDON HARNICK: Jerry Herman is certainly one of the most successful writers for the musical theater in our generation. What always fascinates me is how people wind up where they are from where they started. How did you get into the field of music? Did you study piano, did your mother think you were going to be the next Paderewski? Where were you born?

JERRY HERMAN: I was born on Fiftieth Street at the old Polyclinic overlooking the Winter Garden (my mother was no fool). At a very impressionable age I was taken to see *Annie Get Your Gun,* and I came home starry-eyed. I knew I had to have something to do with writing for the musical theater. The combination of the Irving Berlin songs and Ethel Merman was overpowering.

I started writing at a tender age. Nobody would trust me with a book musical, so I gathered a large amount of material and finally found someone to do a first revue of mine at a little cabaret called The Showplace on West Fourth Street. It was called *Nightcap* and starred Jane Romano and Charles Nelson Reilly, his first job in New York City. A gentleman came up to the piano one night and said, "I'm doing a musical set in Israel. We're going to try to do it on Broadway, and I'd like to talk to you." I thought, "This just really doesn't happen except in Judy Garland-Mickey Rooney films," but that's how *Milk and Honey* was born. I found myself at a *very* tender age with a Broadway show.

HARNICK: Not only a Broadway show, but a *successful* Broadway show. But had you studied piano earlier?

HERMAN: When I was about five we were living in a two-story home in Jersey City. My mother called out, "Who's there with you, Jerry?" and came downstairs to find this little kid playing the Marines Hymn with all the right chords—she had been worried that somebody else was in the house with me. She encouraged my playing for fun and training my ear, and at the proper time she hired a piano teacher who gave me "The Happy Farmer." I heard her play it once and then sat down and played it with all of the flourishes. She was kind of horrified, she ran out of the house, and that was the end of my piano lessons.

I took a little excursion into design and architecture for a year or so at the Parsons School of Design, then switched to the University of Miami, where I graduated with a B.A. in the drama department. I did their variety shows, a wonderful experience *doing* theater rather than sitting in a classroom learning concept.

At the university they made you write shows, act in shows, do costumes, sets and lights. At the time I didn't understand why I had to know what an amber gel would do. Out of town with *Mame*, Tharon Musser was having trouble lighting "If You Walked Into My Life," and I said, "Try an amber gel." She was impressed, so the university really did teach me something.

HARNICK: What were your academic subjects relating to theater?

HERMAN: Elizabethan playwrights, etc., but mostly I am grateful to Miami for the *doing* of theater. I saw a musical of mine performed in front of an audience and saw what was wrong with it, what was right with it, a learning experience whose value cannot be measured. A knowledge of theater literature doesn't hurt, but I don't think I've ever used it.

HARNICK: Were you at all interested in formal poetry?

HERMAN: No, I'm one of those people who think that lyric writing and poetry are two totally different things. I have no aspiration to be a poet. Is it fair to ask *you* a question?

HARNICK: Sure, if it reveals anything about you.

HERMAN: Your lyrics are poetry, but do you write poetry as such?

HARNICK: I came to poetry very late. Because of unfortunate experiences early in my life, I was convinced that poetry and opera were beyond me intellectually. Later on, I thought about writing a poem and wrote three lines and thought, "Gee, this would make a good song"—so I don't write poetry.

HERMAN: I write both music and lyrics, and I don't think of lyrics as an independent art form. I think of them as being connected to the melody. That's part of the reason I would have to say, I don't write poetry. I write lyrics.

HARNICK: As you were growing up, which lyricists did you particularly admire, besides Irving Berlin?

HERMAN: Sheldon Harnick, but I grew up *with* you.

HARNICK: Were you a W.S. Gilbert fan?

HERMAN: Absolutely. I loved Oscar Hammerstein for the warmth and sweetness. I loved Frank Loesser for the bite and strength. I loved Alan Jay Lerner. I could go on down the list, I am simply a fan of musical theater. They have all entertained me, and I have gotten something from all of them. Irving Berlin's simplicity has had the greatest influence on me, I think. He hit the whole nation in the heart, and that's quite an accomplishment.

HARNICK: Were you impressed, influenced, inspired, whatever, by movie musicals when you were growing up?

HERMAN: Anything Judy Garland ever did inspired me. I was a big fan of movie musicals. I got from them my love of glamor. Glamor plays a very important part in my concept of Broadway, and I learned that at Loew's Jersey City seeing M-G-M musicals. But I have very little intention of writing a Hollywood musical. I'm in love with live theater. There's something about an overture and the curtain going up that just does it for me.

HARNICK: Here's one of the questions submitted by Dramatists Guild members in advance: "It has often been said that the best songs come quickly. What is your opinion?"

HERMAN: That's been very true in my life. I wrote "Before the Parade Passes By" in about twenty minutes in a hotel room in Detroit under the most awful conditions, with everyone screaming at me because the first act finale wasn't working. I love that song. I love what it says, the way it says it, the simplicity, and it really just poured out. I wrote the title song of *Mame* in an hour or so.

I must add, though, I had worked on the musical and the Mixmaster had been going for about a year, I had been thinking about those people and what they would say and how they would sing for a year of my life, so I don't honestly know whether I wrote "Before the Parade Passes By" in twenty minutes or a year and twenty minutes.

HARNICK: Have you ever poured out a song in twenty minutes at the beginning of a project when you knew the source of the material but the libretto hadn't been written yet?

HERMAN: Yes, *La Cage aux Folles* is an example. I wrote "A Little More Mascara" before there was a book, even before I had my first meeting with Harvey Fierstein. I got the idea of the audience seeing the transformation from a middle-aged man in a tatty bathrobe into a glamorous creature named Zaza. Neither the play nor the film gave the audience that. I was so enchanted with the idea that I sat down and wrote the song, and not a word or note was changed. Harvey wrote up to it, collaborated in that way with me. Songs happen quickly for me if I'm in love with the general concept of the song and the character. If I have to struggle over a song, I invariably throw it out.

HARNICK: But I assume there have been songs that have worked in shows that took you a while to write.

HERMAN: Yes, I didn't know how to finish "Open a New Window" for almost a year. I had three-quarters of it, and I kept on putting it aside. The day arrived when I decided I'd better throw it out because it just wasn't working—if I can't finish a song there's something wrong with it—and then I got out the last lines. But that's rare for me. Usually it comes quickly.

HARNICK: Somebody asked the question, "Which comes first, the book, the lyrics or the music?" Usually the standard question is, "Which comes first, the lyrics or the music?" but it's good to add in the book, an important element in our particular field.

HERMAN: For me, music and lyrics happen simultaneously. I don't write a complete lyric and then musicalize it or write a piece of music and then write a lyric for it. Obviously, once in a while that has happened when I have used something from the trunk, but generally I construct my songs like a jigsaw puzzle. For example, I'll get a title idea and musicalize the opening phrase, then skip to the end, knowing I am going to end the song "I Won't Send Roses" with the phrase "And roses suit you so." I musicalized that, then I went back and filled in the middle, like doing an enormous jigsaw puzzle—that's my way. I don't write either first.

When you add the book, I've done it all different ways. *The Matchmaker* was written as a book for *Hello, Dolly!* before I was involved. I filled in the blanks, and we adjusted and adapted, but the book was written first. With *La Cage*, book and score were written simultaneously.

HARNICK: Have you ever done just songs without a book?

HERMAN: I'm turned on by musicalizing characters, and if I don't have a character I don't go to the piano.

HARNICK: You wrote some of the best songs in *A Day in Hollywood/A Night in the Ukraine*. A couple of those songs knocked me out. I knew they'd been interpolated, and I checked to see who wrote them and found it was you. In essence that was a revue, and with a revue you don't have the luxury of a developed character. You are writing special material. How did you approach that?

HERMAN: With revue material—I began with revue material—I make up a character. I become the book writer for that day of my life. For example, we needed a number for Priscilla Lopez, and all I was told was that she was playing an usherette. Priscilla Lopez, usherette, go do something. I imagined a whole situation—without writing a line—in which this girl's father kept telling her she was the best performer in the world, so she went to Hollywood. The scene became a little playlet, a little musical vignette all on its own. I tried to be the book writer thinking of a situation for the girl, rather than just picking music and lyrics out of thin air. My other songs in that show were the Jeanette MacDonald-Nelson Eddy parody and my favorite, the opening "Just Go to the Movies." I took the whole subject of Hollywood movies and did a song about it.

HARNICK: Here's another question submitted in advance. "In what ways should aspiring lyricists go about learning their craft?"

HERMAN: That's not an easy question to answer today. When I began, I had an outlet at the University of Miami. I believe in doing theater, writing, seeing audience reaction to your work. There is nothing that teaches you more than that, and I was lucky to be working at a time when there were the Julius Monk kind of revues all over New York. I see some of that happening again. They are a marvelous outlet for aspiring lyricists and composers, because you can sit back and hear people laugh at your work or remain in stony silence when you think you've written something funny. You will never learn anything more succinctly than by watching people respond.

HARNICK: "Can you give examples of songs that didn't work in a show, or that originally didn't work but were rewritten so they *did* work—and if so, how did you change them?"

HERMAN: There was a song for Mabel in *Mack and Mabel* I loved very much, called "Today I Am Gonna Think About Me." When we got into serious rehearsal and I saw the whole show together I realized that the approach I'd taken was too sophisticated. The girl who had just sung "I'm plain little Nellie, the kid from the deli" suddenly had become a woman of the world with this song, which was her next one. I told Gower Champion, "This is wrong, it's not going to work. Let me fix it, let me decide what to do with it." He said, "Fine," and I changed it to "Wherever He Ain't." The very title kept her the kid from the deli, and the song worked beautifully.

I threw a song out of *La Cage* that everybody thought was the best in the show. You have to be crazy or brave to do that. It was called "Have a Nice Day," and at the backers' audition in my home in New York it was the big comedy number, a laundry list of every racial and ethnic slur you can possibly think of. It was sung by the girl's father, and everybody just fell apart. In the middle of Act One I have this big comedy gem, I am really in terrific shape. We went into rehearsal, and something kept bothering me every time I got to that number. The cast would laugh—that's always death. I realized that what we had in *La Cage* was a very wholesome show. It is, you know; Harvey says it's about "Honor thy father and thy mother." The costume sketches were crisp and pastel, very lovely, very wholesome. The set designs were blue sky. And then all of a sudden I had this ugly song—funny, but ugly. I told Arthur Laurents, "You are going to throw me out of this theater, but I would like to cut 'Have a Nice Day.'" He said, "Don't you want to try it in Boston and see what an audience thinks of it?" I said, "Even if an audience loves it, for me it's out of kilter with what we've done." So it went.

HARNICK: "How much do you involve yourself in elements of a show not having to do with music and lyrics?"

HERMAN: Tremendously. I have a dangerous amount of design knowledge. I am very interested in the look of a show, and in the book of a show, so I get involved in everything. I try to do it very gently, so as not to be resented by anyone. With my first two shows I just sat back and let everybody do what they wanted, but with my third show, *Mame*, I started exercising influence on other departments. It's very satisfying to be part of the design element of a show—and in between shows, I design houses.

HARNICK: "Before you begin to write a song, you must have some kind of process by which you extract what you consider to be the book's potentially most musical moments. Will you describe this process and how it applies to you?"

HERMAN: What we are talking about is choices, and to me the most important choice is what to musicalize and what not to. In a show like *Mame* the choices were endless because it's such a lyrical piece. I could have written three scores for the character of Auntie Mame, so that choosing the exact moment for her to burst into song was a really important decision. How you make it is impossible to describe, simply because you do it from nothing but instinct. My instinct tells me that a certain moment in a scene would be better sung, and that "Life is a banquet and most sons of bitches are starving to death" should never be sung. Something has to tell you that. I can only call it instinct.

HARNICK: Ultimately, it's your talent, and talent is indefinable.

HERMAN: I don't know why I picked that moment of "If He Walked Into My Life," except that something told me the whole play was going toward the point where a woman looks back and asks herself, "Would I make the same mistake if I had to do it over again?" There are other moments in that very scene that could have been musicalized, but I chose that one. I don't know why.

HARNICK: "How do you conceptualize a big production number?"

HERMAN: By using all the M-G-M musical tricks I lived through, that I stored in my head visually. I'm a very visual person. I *see* a number. I *saw* Albin physically change into Zaza. I saw the makeup table and the color of the bathrobe. I described the scene in detail to Theoni Aldredge and Arthur Laurents, I said, "I see steps coming out at this moment in the lyric, and at the end I see Albin descending a step at a time." Everything I visualized was on the stage. I was fortunate enough, this time, to be working with a team that respected and did *exactly* what I visualized. It's thrilling for me to see my dream actually on the stage, not just in music and lyrics but the whole picture I had in my head.

HARNICK: You'll never be caught short writing a number that can't be staged, as Jerry Bock and I once were with a number we wrote for *Fiorello*. They couldn't find a way to stage it, so it was dropped. Are you writing even when you're not working on a show?

HERMAN: No, I doodle. I love to sit and play the piano for hours, but I don't really write when I'm not working on a show.

HARNICK: Do you ever come up with a melody that you write down?

HERMAN: I have a trunkful of that sort of thing. I look at them every once in a while and say to myself, "That's pretty, I might use it some day," but I usually don't. That system of mine comes into play, and I usually start from scratch with a character in mind.

HARNICK: A number written in the abstract may not have any character.

HERMAN: Exactly.

HARNICK: Is there an element that draws you to a show, something that you might consistently find in all of your shows?

HERMAN: Yes, definitely. Positivism. Mame and Dolly and Zaza are positive thinkers. They are people who say, "The best of times is now." I like "up" themes and "up" characters, and I will inevitably turn down a show that has a negative hero or heroine.

HARNICK: Here's a technical query: "How do you work on rhymes for your lyrics? Do you use a rhyming dictionary, or do they just come to you? Do you keep notes on random rhymes you think of on a day-to-day basis?"

HERMAN: No, to the last question. I use a thesaurus occasionally, a rhyming dictionary occasionally and a dictionary a lot. Most of the time rhymes come to me. I don't sit and pore over those books, but once in a while I will use them.

HARNICK: When you start a song the music and lyrics occur at the same time, but it strikes me that you may in that process actually finish the music before you finish the lyrics.

HERMAN: Yes, especially in patter or comedy numbers like "Gooch's Song." That melody was finished with the first verse, and then I went on and wrote lyrics to my existing notes.

HARNICK: Someone once asked Marshall Barer, "Don't you find that writing lyrics is a lot like carpentry and crossword puzzles?" He hit the ceiling. He refused to acknowledge it, because it took away all the passion and poetry.

HERMAN: For me, the passion has to come first. I have to be excited about the discovery of the terminology and where I am going, but *then* it becomes work. It becomes labor to find that third verse of a comedy song, pulling rhymes and words out of the air. I agree with both points of view, but I don't agree with one without the other.

HARNICK: In working with book writers, have you ever found a scene which struck you as the basis for a song, so that with the permission of the book writer you have taken some of his lines or his jokes and converted them into a song?

HERMAN: Absolutely. The lines "I put my hand in here, I put my hand in there," for example, are Thornton Wilder's which Michael Stewart kept in his scene. The lovely thing about all book writers I have worked with is, they totally understand the word "collaboration." I asked Mike whether I could have those lines, and he said, "Of course, if it makes a better song, what difference does it make?" I've never worked with one who said no. The line "Ribbons down my back" is also Thornton Wilder. The line "Somewhere between forty and death" describing Vera was a stage direction in Jerome Lawrence and Robert E. Lee's play *Auntie Mame.* I said, "I've got to have it. I know how to use it," and they said, "You can do anything you want with it," and I used it as a lyric.

HARNICK: Book writers have to be generous and understanding when the lyricist approaches and says, "I am going to use your joke as a capper for my song." And sometimes the lyricist is able to contribute a line to the book writer.

HERMAN: Yes, it's give and take.

HARNICK: Have you done shows where the book is pretty much complete and the book writer has a good idea of what and where the songs should be?

HERMAN: Forgive me, book writers, but I find that the worst possible way to work. I've done it several times, but I hate putting songs into a finished book. For me, the truly creative and successful method is starting from scratch with a book writer, a lyricist and a composer—whether they are three, two or one doesn't matter—in the same room at the same time. The reason *Hello, Dolly!* had so much trouble on the road was that we had to change a lot because the songs were in the wrong places.

HARNICK: "Have you ever worked with another lyricist or composer?"

HERMAN: No, never.

HARNICK: "How many songs did you write before your first major success?"

HERMAN: Probably more than a hundred before *Milk and Honey:* fifty in college and fifty or sixty pieces of revue material, fifteen of which I used in *Parade* and *Nightcap.* Each song teaches you something. For five or six years after college I was playing in night clubs, knocking on producers' doors trying to peddle revue material. One afternoon Kermit Bloomgarden listened to my stuff and said, "I am really impressed, but can you picture me hiring you to write the score for a million-dollar musical?" or whatever it cost in those days. I couldn't get anybody to pay serious attention to me for years.

HARNICK: "Do you compose at the keyboard, or do melodies first occur in your head? Which has proved most successful, artistically and commercially?"

HERMAN: I've worked both ways, about fifty-fifty. I'm most comfortable at the keyboard, but I wrote "It's Today" walking along Eighth Avenue. That whole melodic structure was driving me crazy, and I couldn't wait until I got home to see if I liked it. I've written a great deal walking on the streets of New York City, but invariably when I get to the piano I feel I'm on safe ground in comfortable territory. I guess I'd have to answer that I feel more comfortable and successful at the keyboard.

HARNICK: I never believe in a song until I've heard it sung, either by myself or someone else. When you're working on a song, do you sing it?

HERMAN: I sing it, but I don't hear myself. I hear Garland, I hear Merman. If I like the way they sound coming out of me, I think it's terrific.

HARNICK: "Did you have formal courses in harmony and counterpoint?"

HERMAN: No, no, no.

HARNICK: At one of our Dramatists Guild seminars, Jule Styne and everybody else on the panel kept saying, "This is no longer a day when one should worry about getting recordable songs out of a show. You worry about characters, plot, the demands of the show and forget about the commercial success of individual songs." I argue with that to a certain extent. But do you deliberately look for moments which you think will both serve the show and can be taken out of the show?

HERMAN: Absolutely yes. I believe in the show song that you can carry home, that you can dance to, that can be recorded by Perry Como. Obviously, an entire score cannot and should not come under that heading. But if a man can stand on a stage and sing "I Am What I Am," and if he can make his point so effectively that he stops the show, and then if somebody can make a disco record out of it, isn't that terrific, isn't that what it's really about? There's no question that first and foremost it has to work in the show. "If He Walked Into My Life" could easily have been a song never heard outside the show, it was specifically about Mame and a little boy, but the fact that Eydie Gormé recorded it and it was able to work both ways is what I am all about. Dolly Levi's opening number "I Put My Hand In" cannot be done any other way, but when I can I try to write what I call a "liftable" song.

HARNICK: Dick Rodgers called them "take home" songs.

HERMAN: I like that.

HARNICK: Have you ever been presented with an idea for a show which was positive but which you turned down because you couldn't see yourself writing songs for it, particularly "liftable" ones?

HERMAN: Constantly. Ninety percent of the things that pass over my desk are perfectly valid ideas for musicals, but I don't see songs coming out of them, and I say no.

HARNICK: Have you ever found yourself writing a song which you had to revise musically—or would you just write a new song if that happened?

HERMAN: I revised several *Dolly* numbers for Carol Channing because I wanted her to be comfortable. I believe in the comfort of a star above anything else, I would throw out the best song in a score if it did not sound comfortable in the star's mouth.

HARNICK: Dick Rodgers was extremely finicky about how his songs were performed onstage, every eighth note and dot had to be observed. How do you feel about that?

HERMAN: I oversee every bar of what happens onstage, but I am not finicky about what happens to the songs that go out into the commercial field. The "I Am What I Am" disco recording doesn't even use all of my notes, and I couldn't care less.

HARNICK: Do you have a director working with you while the book, lyrics and music are being created?

HERMAN: I've worked all different ways. In *Mame*, Gene Saks came in late but was very helpful. In *Dolly*, Gower Champion came in after we had done all of our work. In *La Cage*, Arthur Laurents worked with us from the very first day. That's my favorite way of working.

HARNICK: How did you get the *Dolly* job?

HERMAN: *Milk and Honey* was running at the Martin Beck, and after seeing it David Merrick told me about his project but said, "I think you're talented, but I don't know whether you're American enough to write Thornton Wilder." I assured him that up until that one Israeli operetta everything I'd done was as American as apple pie. He looked at me skeptically, but he gave me a copy of the script. So, without telling my agent, who would not have allowed me to do this (and I would never have gotten the job if I hadn't done this), I locked myself in my apartment and wrote four songs over one long weekend, based on a Michael Stewart script with the title *Matchmaker, Draft*

Number One, I wrote "Put on Your Sunday Clothes," "Dancing," "I Put My Hand In" and a song for Mrs. Malloy that I later cut and replaced with "Ribbons Down My Back." Monday afternoon, with a singer, I did these four songs for Mr. Merrick. He was bowled over by my chutzpah, and the speed at which I wrote—and he liked the songs and said, "Kid, the show is yours."

HARNICK: You did it on "spec."

HERMAN: Yes, sometimes it doesn't pay to ask advice from an agent or anybody else. You must do what your heart tells you. I knew the material was right for me, I loved the characters, I had to prove myself. I just went and did what I had to do to get that show.

Of course, you have to know your own limitations. I cannot write contemporary music. I would be a total failure if I tried to write a rock musical. As I indicated before, the word "glamor" turns me on. Give me a musical about a lady who's going to put on feathers and beads, and I am in heaven. I am interested in theatrical subjects, in positive uplifting statements that make the audience feel a little better when they leave.

HARNICK: "At what point and to whom do you open up your work to criticism?"

HERMAN: When I've finished four or five songs, I feel I have a mini score, and I take it to a dear friend I went to college with, Carol Dorian, the lady who sings for my backers' auditions. She's a tough critic. I play my songs for her, and she tells me exactly what she thinks.

HARNICK: Are you anxious at that point?

HERMAN: Oh yes, I'm as insecure as anybody can possibly be. But you obviously have to believe in your own work, and I do, until the audience tells me I'm wrong. I go to Carol Dorian and then to my collaborators—the acid test. If I pass them, I feel secure. But I wrote one song for *La Cage* that passed Carol Dorian with flying colors. It was called "Where Did We Go Wrong," when the two men find out the son is marrying a woman. I thought, "Oh boy, I've got a good one here," and I still think it's funny. Well, I played it for Arthur Laurents. Absolute stoneface, and he said, "You are going to offend every homosexual in the audience." I didn't see it, but it scared me, and I threw the song out. I have never discussed it since.

HARNICK: Have you been in a position where you had to fight for a song?

HERMAN: Oh yes, if I believe in a song I will do everything to give that song its proper due. An orchestration can kill a song; I've made songs work by changing orchestrations. After trying everything, if the song still makes people take their programs out . . . That's one of my barometers, by the way. I will sit in a box and watch the audience during an entire performance, never looking at the stage. If they're sitting still, you know you are doing something right. If they open their programs or start talking to each other, and if it happens at the same place every night, you know you are doing something wrong.

HARNICK: "Did working with Angela Lansbury in *Mame* help you to write for her as a specific performer in *Dear World*?"

HERMAN: No, I don't write for stars, I think that's destructive. I wrote *Dear World* the way I write everything, for the character. I wrote what I thought the character should sing, and I was thrilled when Angela then wanted to do it, but I didn't write for her.

HARNICK: Here are related questions submitted by different people: "My understanding is that *Mack and Mabel*, one of my all-time favorite musicals, was not a huge success. Have you any thoughts as to why?" And "Many think that *Mack and Mabel* was one of your best scores. Will the book be rewritten so that a new version of this glorious show will come back to Broadway?"

HERMAN: *Mack and Mabel* is my favorite work, and it was the only true disappointment I've ever had, even though I've had other musicals that did not work. It was a heartbreaker because I loved it so much. It didn't work, I think, because ultimately we exhausted the audience with the tragedy of the piece. Basically it's a very "up" story, a very American upbeat, go-get-'em story, about young people leaving Brooklyn and creating silent movies in Hollywood. It was done as a tragic musical in a dark brown set. A murder was going on during the number "Tap Your Troubles Away." Mike Stewart and I feel the same way about it. We are in love with it and have rewritten it, not drastically, but taking a lot of the *Sturm und Drang* out of it. We are going to redo it one of these days.

HARNICK: How many more songs did you write for *La Cage* before you finished the final score as we know it now?

HERMAN: Just the two that I've already mentioned.

HARNICK: Do you feel that a show like *La Cage* with a homosexual theme has any moral or political responsibility to speak for homosexuals?

HERMAN: If responsible people are writing about any minority or specific group, they have an obligation to speak positively for that group. I'm very pleased with the way *La Cage* treats the subject. It treats Albin and George just as people in love, which is one of the underlying reasons for its success. The Boston audience that I was most afraid of accepted them as people they ended up truly caring about. That has done more for the homosexual image than if we had written a militant piece.

Several critics slapped us a little bit. Even giving us lovely notices, one or two of them said, "But they should have gone further." Had we gone further, we wouldn't have had an identifiable statement that all audiences are enjoying. We would have had a militant piece.

HARNICK: "How has the writing of musicals changed from *Hello, Dolly!* to *La Cage aux Folles?*"

HERMAN: It hasn't changed at all. The thing that has changed more than the writing is the visuals of a show. The director's role has changed.

HARNICK: To me, one of the differences between today and fifteen years ago is that today there seems to be much more music written, more areas covered by music. Does *La Cage* have the same balance between music and book that your previous shows had?

HERMAN: It has half again as many bars of music.

HARNICK: "Does *La Cage* indicate a return to tunefulness in musicals?"

HERMAN: I pray to God that it does. I believe passionately in song and melody, simple—yes—old-fashioned song. When I think about great musical theater, I think about songs like "I Got Rhythm" and "Some Enchanted Evening." I think audiences have been missing that—I have been missing it as an audience. I want to take six songs home, and I hope we see more of the same.

HARNICK: "In addition to chemistry, what should a playwright and composer look for in each other?"

HERMAN: Nothing. Gilbert and Sullivan hated each other. It doesn't matter. As long as your vision of the show is the same and you believe in each other's talent, nothing else is important.

HARNICK: "How elaborate a musical demo tape should be produced by unknown lyricists and composers submitting a musical score for consideration by producers? Does it justify the cost of having a number orchestrated and recorded in a professional studio?"

HERMAN: No. If a producer can't tell whether a score has value by listening to a good pianist and a good singer (I don't say it has to be done by the composer), then he has no business being a producer of musicals. To spend a fortune on those orchestrations is ludicrous, because they won't be what ultimately will be done. Just present your work with all the love and care you possibly can, and hope that your producer doesn't have a tin ear.

HARNICK: "For non-established writers, is an agent the best avenue to pursue to get a musical on the boards?"

HERMAN: If you can find one who will go with you. I couldn't, before I put work on the stage. I had to go knock on doors.

HARNICK: "What is the best advice you can give to a songwriter trying to sell or write his first show?"

HERMAN: You need guts.

HARNICK: I think I would add "belief" to that.

Q: Have you ever abandoned any properties, and if so do you know why you abandoned them?

HERMAN: I abandoned *Some Like It Hot* before it was done as *Sugar* because the vision Mike Stewart and I had wasn't the vision that the producer had. I saw nothing ahead but heartache if we continued on divergent courses. I thought it had great potential and was quite in love with it, but if you are not on the same beam as the people you are working with I don't think it would be a happy or a successful experience.

Q: How do you deal in your heart with bad reviews?

HERMAN: It absolutely knocks me out. It is one of the most difficult things to come to terms with, even where I sit right now, because most of the people reviewing don't have the credentials. If someone like Walter Kerr, whom I respect and have admired during his career, tells me I have done something wrong, it hurts a little bit, but I say to myself, "It came from Walter Kerr, and he knows what he is talking about." I can live with that, but when some of these people without background or credentials tell you you've written a terrible score, and you know you haven't, it's very painful. You need guts, and you need to believe in your heart that you know more about what you are doing than the person who has told you you don't. That's when inner strength becomes a necessity in this business. If your head is in the right place, the day arrives when you push that far enough into the background to be able to go back to the piano or the typewriter and start again.

Q: Do you aim for a certain overall style?

HERMAN: Definitely. The French Riviera and music hall quality of *La Cage* is obvious in the first bars of music. In *Dolly*, the central character is very garrulous, and so is her music. The material guides me, and after two or three songs I usually feel that a flavor has come into the work. I will try to carry that through the whole score.

Q: For an established writer, is it best to try to sell a musical by means of a live audition?

HERMAN: Absolutely, and if you have got the choice, go there in person. Hearing a disc doesn't have half the value of sitting there talking and smiling live, live, live. You are working in a live medium, keep everything live.

HARNICK: Thank you, Jerry, for sharing your vitality, your optimism, your positiveness.

ARTHUR MILLER

Purposes

ARTHUR MILLER: The idea of art having a purpose is a subject that could fill a library. And has. I don't propose to try to come to any conclusions about it today, but it is a subject that leads to certain issues that can be discussed with some profit.

In the broadest sense I believe that a theater's purpose springs directly out of the kind of society it finds itself in at the time.

I was talking about the Chinese theater to some people who came from China recently. One of them was an American who had lived there for twenty-six years and only came out about two and a half years ago. He had been an actor for many years. He played European villains in their movies. He told me about the plots of the plays that the Chinese produce, which are all government-controlled, as in many other places. The plots may vary in detail, but in general terms they're very similar. At the beginning, the protagonist is struggling with some problems he doesn't know how to resolve. By one means or another, a representative of the Party enters the story. This representative is conscious, as the protagonist is not, of the whole social scene, the system under which the protagonist is living. Through the guidance of the "correct line" the protagonist, in effect, is saved. This actor told me that they were up against a problem because of the boredom that was setting in as a result of the fundamental repetitiousness of this plot scheme.

This theme of the lost being saved reminds me of medieval drama, such as *Everyman,* which also was involved with salvation. As medieval theater was effectively under the control of the church, the plays of that time all involved the lost being saved by the discovery of the love of God or Jesus or both and the renouncing of evil as a result.

Lay Renaissance drama, which sprang out of medieval drama, was no longer bound to the single dramatic purpose of portraying the road to redemption. A great variety of experience entered into these plays, as we see preeminently in Shakespeare. So, in effect, when the theater left the church, it lost its purpose, in the old ideological sense.

In the Greek plays—which along with the Elizabethan plays, I believe, are probably the highest developed of the drama—one again encounters purpose. That is, at least some of the fundamental questions that the dramatists dealt with seemed to be agreed upon in advance. As I read it, the Greek drama is always involved with man facing the mystery of God in one respect or another, in one aspect or another—in the tragedies anyway.

In contrast to the Greek, medieval and contemporary Chinese plays, our theater has nothing but the variety of life. In the West, drama is certainly not advised or ordered to obey or work under any particular ideology. Therefore, to face this completely unreligious theater and to ask of it that it have a purpose (at least as purpose was conceived of in the past) seems vain.

But I think a play always has a purpose, even though it may not be announced or conscious. When people assemble in an auditorium and see human beings behaving in a certain way on the stage, they are searching for something, whether they are conscious of it or not. They want an image of life, of what they are. They do or don't connect with a play on the basis of whether or not it seems to reflect some recognizable stage of being for them. The theater throws back at the audience an image of themselves. It can be an elevated image, or an idealistic one, a depraved one, a skeptical one, or what you will. But it always has a content, no matter how trivial it appears or even wants to be.

We may not be conscious of this unless it crosses some tender spot. If we are facing something that the consensus tells us is perfectly safe and inoffensive, it seems inevitable, and we are not aware of it having any attitude towards reality; but as soon as it sets us in conflict with custom, we are suddenly aware that there is a viewpoint and, hence, a purpose implicit in what we are seeing, one with which we either agree or disagree. But purpose need not be dissident, it is only more obvious when it is.

Thirty or forty years ago it was common for races and ethnic groups to be the butt of comedy because of certain qualities. There were Jewish comics who made fun of themselves being Jewish, there were German comics who used their Germanness as the butt of humor. The same with blacks and Chinese and so on. This offended nobody in particular back then, probably because most minorities were still trying to assimilate and leave all identities behind.

Then suddenly, because society was in conflict over racial and ethnic questions, these stock-in-trade ethnic and racial jokes, which had not previously been thought of as being even related to reality, ceased to be jokes. Society became conscious that these images coming off the stage—comically as they may have been intended—were serious. They had to do with life, they were sublimations of dangerous resentments.

So, as I say, any play has a purpose and a meaning, even when it announces that it's meaningless, because then it's telling people that life is meaningless, which is a statement that has meaning. There's no escape from this. The only escape is silence. Besides, somebody who really believes that life is meaningless will usually not have anything to say. As soon as he speaks, life at least means that he expects to get a royalty.

When I am writing a play, I don't feel I have a purpose in any programmatic sense, but surely there's the hope of illuminating some otherwise concealed process in life which, if the audience (and first of all myself) could see and understand it, would somehow give order to what otherwise would be chaotic in the so-to-speak real world. In the theater, you have the great possibility of confronting people where they are most troubled, most confused and most desirous of some kind of patterns for the chaos. I believe that the theater is most suited to deal with this hidden, interior world, if only because anybody who can hear and understand a language is conceivably a member of the audience. You don't even have to know how to read to attend.

All I'm saying is that the nature of the theater is practically a direct reflection of the preoccupation of society and hence reveals something of its real nature. It is far more closely bounded and propelled by social than temperamental imperatives. But it is impossible at any given moment to know what the direction is in society, one can only write as one citizen groping for his own sense of what is real.

You only really learn after the fact how relevant your gropings are for others. For instance, I didn't understand any of this when I wrote *Death of a Salesman*. It was only later that I could think about it and come to some conclusions about why it had the impact it did.

Salesman opened at a time when the hopefulness of the 1930s and 1940s had been spent. I know it sounds odd to use the word "hope" in relation to the Depression period, but there *was* hope in this country then in the sense that there was the belief that, if one had the right idea, one could save the country. That's different than what we have now. Today we think probably no idea is going to save anything; that something will either happen or it won't. But the concept of the rationality of existence was very powerful in the 1930s, and, to a degree, in the 1940s. In the 1940s, we had the war. Now the war caught us fundamentally unprepared, but our leadership said, "If you do this, this and this, we will win the war," and we did. We did not go under. This rational sense I speak of—the idea that if you do *this* then *that* will happen—was all over by 1949 when *Death of a Salesman* opened. At least, I sensed this. I felt a certain falling apart of what had been a kind of unity in the country. So there was a crossing of the national purpose with my purpose at that instant. Perhaps if *Salesman* had come a little later, nobody would have listened to me at all. Four or five years later, we were into the McCarthy period, and I don't know how well the play would have done then.

I don't know whether I believe that plays change society as such. I would rather lean towards saying that when a play has a really strong effect, it brings to consciousness what is lying in the dark dustbin of the society's unconsciousness. In effect, what happens when you see such a work is that you are delighted by the surprise of recognition. You see something in it which seems to make perfectly clear and obvious something that was, before, right at the tip of your consciousness. Such works are few and far between, but I think they are the ones you remember. So, in that sense you change society because you sharpen its consciousness. You make it aware of what it had repressed. So there's a change there. But by and large, plays are obviously not that directly tangent to actual political developments.

Of course, it's hard to make a living as a serious playwright. But whoever said that a serious playwright would ever be able to make his living in the theater? Think about Ibsen. When he was writing *A Doll's House* or *Ghosts*, he could run maybe a month, because that's all the audience there was in Oslo for the theater. Give him another three weeks in Dresden. Three days in Leipzig. They ran in Germany a little bit longer, but not much. He was always in debt until quite late in his life, when publishers would advance him a little money from time to time.

The emphasis may change from year to year, but, on the whole, most of what people pay to see is entertainment that does not particularly irritate them, but rather makes them feel comfortable, or at least not uncomfortable.

There is a tiny minority of works, the kind of which I spoke a few minutes ago, that lift society's consciousness—maybe one in seventy-five—which everybody talks about for years and years as being the significant works of their times. They're generally what might be called dissident works which somehow confront the audience's or the critics' presumptions about life and society and imply that something might be terribly hollow or tragically wrong about them. There's some alarming center within these few works, for whatever reason. These are the works that the professors write books about forever and ever; the kind that make other playwrights feel that the theater is a place where the spirit can be addressed.

The rest of it, as I say, is entertainment. That's why they built the theaters and why people go to them. That's what people enjoy seeing. I think that's fundamentally the way it's always been. That's why it's always a problem to do significant work. Because you are contradicting the main reason why people in the West—meaning Europe, England, the United States, etc.—come to the theater.

When I started, they used to have a slogan: "If you have a message, send it by Western Union." This was a big witticism. You were supposed to roll around on the floor laughing. It was never an easy thing to try to penetrate this world of entertainment.

When I came around, most of the producers were hard-headed bookers of vaudeville acts. When they heard that a play had speeches longer than three sentences, they wouldn't be inclined to do it.

I think maybe today it's easier. Serious plays have more prestige commercially. There are a lot of producers now who didn't exist when I first came around. These producers are maybe college graduates, actors, cultivated people, former rabbis . . . not the sort of people who were producers in the old days.

Today you've got I-don't-know-how-many off- and off-off-Broadway theaters that are reputable, where people go and pay money to see all kinds of serious stuff. This was unheard of when I arrived. Back then, you ended up on these four or five blocks that are Broadway, or nothing. There was nothing else.

I think that one has to come to grips with what one wants to do, apart from how acceptable one imagines the damn thing is going to be. But nobody writing plays should disdain whatever legitimate means there are to attract an audience, to grab an audience, to fascinate an audience into making them feel that they are beholding wonder. The theater is not—and I do not want anybody to think that I feel otherwise in any part of my mind—the theater is *not* a church. The theater is *theater,* where people have a perfect right to come and expect works of the imagination to fire them up. There is nothing wrong with that.

The challenge is to come up with works of value. And, of course, there's no set procedure for doing that, and it is futile to waste effort trying to find it.

Q: I understand you're writing a musical version of your play, *The Creation of the World and Other Business.* What made you decide to write a musical, and could you tell us about how you find the experience?

MILLER: I had written one short lyric in the original play which was sung by Eve. The music was written by Stanley Silverman, who is an extraordinarily inventive composer, both serious and hip. He writes stuff that the Philharmonic plays and also writes musicals that will never get to Broadway, perhaps because they're too parodistic. He's a serious musician with a flair for the American language of music that I think is extraordinary.

Anyway, Stanley had done incidental music for the original play, and when its run was over—such as it was—he got an offer from the Whitney Museum to run his music one night, including that little song for Eve. He came to me and said, "You know, if we had one other little lyric, for a male voice, I could get two musical actors and we would do it."

I said, "Well, I never wrote lyrics, but I'll do something." And I did, and he wrote this perfectly lovely song. Then I made that song a little longer, because it was a little too short. Then I made the initial song a little longer. And then Stanley said, "Now look, if we had just one quartet . . ." So I knocked that off, and he came back with a piece of music. By this time, I was hooked.

Then he gave up the idea of doing it in the Whitney Museum. But now there were just enough songs to make a concert unlikely. So we needed more songs. So I wrote more songs.

By this time, I was really enjoying it. I was finding that there were esthetic problems in it that were interesting. I had never attributed an esthetic problem to a musical in my life. I found out that you could tell a whole story in four lines, and that you didn't need all the surrounding material because the music itself was dramatic.

Then I got an offer from the University of Michigan, my alma mater, to come out there and do something, and they would pay the bills. So we got together a cast of young people and wrote some more songs and worked on it there. I was directing, if you want to call it that. And we got sort of the first half of it pretty good. But the rest we never got to, so it was half a musical, and the rest was really dramatic.

Since that time, we've been filling up the sausage. As time would go by, I'd think up an idea for another song, or he would. The nice thing was, we did it when we felt like it. For periods I would concentrate on it, then he would run off and take a year to write four songs.

Well, now it's all done. It seems like thirty years have gone by. I think it's quite lovely now. What it is I don't know—a musical or a kind of an opera or just a failure. I have no idea. But there are certainly some beautiful things in it. Maybe it's too beautiful for now. It should be uglier. It would be a bigger hit.

It's far more intricate than meets the eye. Nobody will know how serious a work it is. Certainly no critic will. It's a quite serious work of music. The hip people who know something about music know that. The audience will just come in and enjoy it, and that's fine. It's very lyrical.

Q: Do you feel that being a success when you were relatively young put a special pressure on you as a writer?

MILLER: Well, I wasn't really all that young. I was thirty-one or so when I started to get produced, and I had been working since I was nineteen or twenty-one. So I had been working ten or twelve years before I got anything onstage. I had written maybe thirty radio plays and seven or eight original plays that nobody wanted to do.

I wrote a long, tragic play about Montezuma and Cortez, the story of which I told a few years ago to a very fine Mexican novelist who promptly wrote it as a novel. He never told me he was writing it, but on the frontispiece I get his compliments. But I'm glad he wrote it. I never would have gone back to work on that play anyway.

I wrote one that was fundamentally about my own family. I got that out of my way.

I wrote another one about a prison in Michigan where I'd worked for a while.

I wrote another very adventurous one about the crew of a ship.

Q: Do you have a sense of what you learned from writing those early plays—a sense of the progression of your craft?

MILLER: On the whole, I suppose that one learns how to condense everything. Those plays simply made too much out of too little. They tended to take too long to say what, later on, I would have wanted to say very (I hope) deftly and quickly. There were just too many words used, on the whole. That's why I like to read poetry. Usually—when it's good—it's very dense. Its effects are made through condensation. If you take two lines of Shakespeare and try to write them in prose—to summarize them and give the color and feeling of them—you'll find you'll have to write much more.

Q: Did success influence your choices of what you wanted to write?

MILLER: I don't think so. You don't change that way. I don't know anybody who has. I suppose if your success is the result of a formula of some sort, which does exist in some of the lighter entertainment, it might.

But I don't fundamentally believe that writers would write differently if the conditions were different. In other words, you don't adopt a style because the public likes it. I think you adopt a style because that's how you are.

Q: You said a few minutes ago that perhaps your musical should be uglier to have more of a chance to be a hit. Is that a reflection of the theater or of our times or both?

MILLER: Well, this particular musical is not about the mode of life today. It is not perverse. I find a kind of despairing perversity in a lot of work today—and rightly so, because civilization is that way. But it isn't in this musical, so maybe nobody will be able to connect with it.

Q: You've recently taken to directing your own plays, as have several other playwrights. Could you talk about that?

MILLER: I haven't taken to it, I've been driven to it. I don't want to direct anything or anybody. Well, I might want to do it if I had developed differently and if I'd had a permanent theater, which, for a number of reasons, I didn't, and I regret it. But if there were a number of actors that I worked with regularly and that I loved, then it would be different.

But the prospect of meeting strange people and of having three and a half weeks in which to indoctrinate them in a play they'd never read before is . . . Well, I'd have too much to say, so it would take me longer. I don't really like to talk that much, I don't like to *see* people that often. I mean, the idea of having to come in every day and see these people again is just . . . terrible. I'm extroverted, but not in that way.

I don't like to direct, but I have had to do it because I've found that something wasn't getting over that I was sure *could* come over. Even when that happens, I avoid directing as long as possible. In some cases, I've avoided it too long. But I can do it. I don't think it's a tremendously mysterious art. It *is* an art, but it can be managed.

Q: There's long been a myth in the theater that a playwright doesn't understand his own play.

MILLER: Well, he doesn't, and neither, usually, does the director. I worked best with Elia Kazan. He really thought it was his job to put the playwright's play on the stage. This is a heresy these days. But he thought that was the hardest thing to do. Now, many directors think that that isn't even the task. They think the idea is to show the director off.

Q: Do you have a continuous work pattern, or is it spontaneous?

MILLER: The only thing spontaneous is the sun. It comes up every day and goes down. Otherwise, you have to do it.

SIDNEY KINGSLEY

In Conversation With Ruth Goetz and John Guare

SIDNEY KINGSLEY: Many years ago when *Men in White* was playing in London, I was taken to a theater where George Bernard Shaw was directing his play *On the Rocks*. I watched him direct and was fascinated. Afterwards, in the intermission, I was introduced to him. The great man asked me, "Whatever made you choose this godless profession?" It is a hard question to answer, particularly coming from George Bernard Shaw. I stammered, "The gods chose it for me, and you, foremost amongst them," or something idiotic like that. On second thought, not so idiotic perhaps. The plays we have witnessed and read as youngsters drew us into this historic and possibly god-like profession with some mighty gravitational force.

A few years ago, an occasion arose on which I had to really examine that question a little deeper. The American Academy of Psychoanalysts held their annual meeting, and their subject was "Creativity." They invited a dozen or so artists in various fields to speak. I thought, "Well, since they are psychoanalysts, I ought to talk to them in their own terms." I examined my own dream life and hit on something significant. When I was a little boy, I had a recurrent nightmare. I'd be standing in a long, dark hallway, similar to the one in our railroad flat, when suddenly in the dimness the figure of a woman appeared, some eight feet tall, clad in gray. She swept me up in her arms and carried me as she glided silently through the hallway. I never forgot that dream. It haunted me.

Years later, when I was a student at Cornell, I wrote a play based upon this dream. It won the first Drummond Prize. Now, a poor boy in those days in my circumstances did not say, "I want to be a playwright." He became a lawyer or a doctor. Winning the prize for that play based on a dream, however, convinced me to become a playwright—a foolhardy thing to do, as you all know. More important, that prize convinced my mother, who supported me against a hostile family.

Many years later, I was standing at my mother's deathbed. As she died, her body, which had crumpled, slowly straightened up more and more, and she smiled and died.

After the terrible business arrangements of death, as I walked home along the park, I suddenly had the strangest illusion that somebody was walking alongside me. I turned and there was the figure of my mother, and she grew and grew and grew, taller and taller. And suddenly it was the figure that had appeared in my dream thirty years before. I told this story to the psychoanalysts. I expressed my conviction that this might very well be the creative source of my work. Writing that play at Cornell, I discovered the most important source for a play is within yourself—something deep in your soul, even if you don't understand it, even though it is a mystery, as it was and still is in this case.

JOHN GUARE: I reread your plays in preparation for this event, and I assumed—because of your work with the Group Theater in the Thirties—that they would be very much about people trapped by the Depression, victims of society. What's odd is that they aren't—there's some other force. There's a line in *The Patriots* that says there is a tide that sweeps men to the fashioning of some strange destiny, even against their will. I think it's that dream-like quality which is present even in *Detective Story*. You feel that the people are trapped in a dream that they're about to wake up from. That's what's very surprising about the plays.

To get to the submitted questions: A number of people said they wanted to hear what you had to say about the Group Theater.

KINGSLEY: I came to it as a friend and left it as a friend. In fact, Lee Strasberg, who was the heart and soul of the Group, and I were friends for fifty years, until his death. There's no question that my mind and heart were turned more to the problems of the Thirties by exposure to the ideas of the Group Theater.

When I wrote *Men in White*, however, I was not exposed to those ideas. I was exposed to an environment. My best friend was a young intern, and I would socialize with him and the young nurses, and hang around the hospital, fascinated by its color and the often cynical contrast between the daily matter-of-fact routine of the interns and the life and death values of their world. When it became, in a sense, my world, inevitably I had to fashion it into a play.

You're quite right: In all of my plays I search for those elements of reality which have a poetic or a dream quality. But then I find in all reality a strong dream quality.

The experience of watching the preparations for a major operation was so surreal and ritualistic, so like a strange ballet, it inevitably found its way into the climactic scene of *Men in White* as, in fact, a balletic scene.

Three producers purchased an option on the play and couldn't raise the money. The fourth, the team of Sidney Harmon and James Ullman, two very bright young men, bought the option, then informed me they wanted to produce it very much but couldn't raise more than half the money. I knew a press agent who knew the press agent for the Shuberts. He read the play, liked it and passed it on to Lee Shubert. Lee summoned me to the Shubert sanctum sanctorum and advised me that, while he thought the play had great merit, it wasn't his dish of tea, and did I object if he showed it to the Theater Guild? Of course I was happy about that. He did show it to the Theater Guild, and they passed it on to a wild, fanatical young bunch who called themselves the Group Theater. The Group had a lot of doubts about the play because it wasn't left enough for their purposes; nevertheless, summer came and they had nothing else to rehearse, so they went into rehearsal.

Still no money. Cheryl Crawford, one of the directors, scouted around and came up with an angel, albeit an angel with clipped wings—Doris Warner, a lovely young lady who liked the play and wanted to get into show business. She went to her father, one of the Warner movie moguls who hated "show biz"—and thereby hung a new theater legend in the making. Papa Warner wanted to teach his daughter a lesson not to fool around with the theater. To do this, he gave her the money, confident that she would lose it—all $10,000 of it. He was certain she would burn her fingers and never fiddle around with the theater again. As it turned out, Papa Warner was, perhaps for the first time in his life, wrong. And after many, many, many vicissitudes, the play saw daylight. Much to everybody's amazement—except mine—it was a big hit—a big, big hit, and later won the Pulitzer Prize. If you need any further evidence of a dream quality guiding our destiny, there it is.

GUARE: Harold Clurman in *The Fervent Years*, his book about the Group Theater, says that *Men in White* was the crowning achievement of Strasberg's career.

KINGSLEY: Lee did a marvelous job. Because not all of the actors were that good, you know. Some of them were mediocre and some were damn bad. Lee made them look good.

GUARE: There's a script of yours I couldn't find, I wish you'd tell us something about. It's called *Ten Million Ghosts*. The description sounds quite remarkable. It used film, music . . .

KINGSLEY: Well, at that time, I was interested in multi-media—the use of projections, and so on.

GUARE: This was back in 1936.

KINGSLEY: I think it was the first time this sort of thing was done. But I didn't really spend enough time working with the scene designer. I was placing too great a burden on the scene designer to do something new and complex. It had sensational moments, but on the whole it didn't work out too well.

The play was about the munition makers and about the great conspiracy between the French and the German munition makers to prolong World War I. They were two branches of the same family—German and French—and they arranged it so that neither side could bomb the factories of the other.

GUARE: What was the film you used? Footage of the war?

KINGSLEY: I used some stock footage, but I used the negative instead of the positive so that the figures had the appearance of ghosts. Hence, the title. We had some startling shots of people being blown to bits and cities crumbling.

RUTH GOETZ: Who produced that, Sidney?

KINGSLEY: I did. I had a good cast. Martin Gabel, Barbara O'Neil and a fine young actor named Orson Welles. It almost worked.

GUARE: The story of our lives.

GOETZ: You directed *Dead End*, didn't you?

KINGSLEY: Yes.

GOETZ: The scene in *Dead End* with the mother . . .

GUARE: A gangster, public enemy number one, has had his face rebuilt—

GOETZ: In order to escape the police. One of the filthiest, slimiest men in the city . . .

GUARE: —and he comes back to his neighborhood because he wants to see his mother before he goes away.

GOETZ: So you expect a rather touching scene. Here he is on the lam, and nevertheless he wants to pay his respect to his mother.

GUARE: And the mother just refuses . . . has such contempt and venom and hatred for this man she has brought into the world . . .

GOETZ: And yet it is such a poetic scene! There is poetry in that scene of her loathing of what has come out of her that is devastating.

KINGSLEY: We used a technical device to heighten that scene. We had enormously powerful lights all coming from one source on the stage. You had to be careful where you placed the people so that one didn't throw the other into dark shadows, but kept that hot, white light hitting both their faces. To achieve that in the dialogue, the actors had to be placed so that the actor further away from the source of the light was always downstage.

Marjorie Main, who played the mother, and she was marvelous, only got the part through a fluke. When she came into my office for the audition, she was in a dirty house dress, her hair disheveled and dropping over the face . . . and she literally smelled. She didn't know what the part was; she just came in on a lost, forlorn hope. She never normally would have been cast. My stage manager made a face and shook his head in disapproval, but I thought she was just wonderful, smell and all. She had a kind of dry, monotonous quality, almost a dead quality that chilled me.

Many years later I learned the story behind that audition. Her husband had died several months before, and she was down to her last few dollars. She decided to go out this one last time for casting, and then she planned to go back home, kill herself and join her husband. But she got the part . . . talk of the fragile and dream-like quality of our profession. I didn't learn until a week after we were in rehearsals that Norman Bel Geddes didn't have the money and was about to call off rehearsals. If you need any further proof of the tenuous and dream-like quality of my life in art!

GOETZ: And of course she had a considerable career after that. She was a film star.

There was a profound societal sense in the play. These were the early Roosevelt years. A period of desperation. The image of children jumping off of piers into filthy water to amuse themselves.

GUARE: But the main event is the stealing of a wristwatch from a little boy.

GOETZ: It's a wonderful play. A wonderful American play.

GUARE: Tell us a little about the set for *Dead End.*

KINGSLEY: Norman Bel Geddes was going to produce the play. His specialty as a designer was stylized, abstract sets, and he desperately wanted to design this production in a series of levels. I said, "No, it's a realistic play, and we must make as real a dead end street as possible." He said, "Well, I can't do it that way." He phoned Jo Mielziner and said, "Will you design the set? I can't please this young author-director." Mielziner said, "No, I'm too busy." Finally, Bel Geddes shook his head and gritted his teeth and said, "All right. I'll do it your way, but I go on record as saying it won't work."

Then he went to look over the theater—the Belasco. As soon as I saw the musicians' pit, the set reversed itself in my mind. I said, "Wait a minute. If we put the East River upstage, that means we'll have to use a cyclorama, and it will throw our actors in shadow; also, they're going to be sitting way upstage, looking the wrong way with their backs to the audience. But here is this deep orchestra pit, practically asking us to build the wharf downstage." The boys and the people seated there would be downstage, where I wanted them, peering out front. The river would be in the audience. The kids would be jumping into the pit. Great! It was actually at that point that Bel Geddes said he couldn't design the set. But finally, he did design it that way, though under protest. It worked, and it was his most successful set.

GUARE: The orchestra pit was flooded with water?

KINGSLEY: No, no, no. That would have been disastrous. The theater was drafty, the kids would inevitably come down with pneumonia. The kids leaped into a net in the pit. Once they jumped, the assistant stage manager threw a geyser of water up in the air, representing the splash. During one show, someone sitting in the front row couldn't resist his curiosity, leaned over and got a scoop of water in his face, much to the audience's delight.

Even the nakedness of the kids presented us with a problem. In preparing for the production, I sent my secretary out to buy every kind of body oil he could find. Finally, one oil gleamed like water on their bodies. The minute they jumped in, the assistant stage manager rubbed them down with oil, and they came out glistening as if they were wet, but actually the oil protected them from the chill. We also fed them daily with vitamins.

During rehearsal, Bel Geddes had provided us with a sciopticon, a lighting device which projected a repeated pattern against the side of the wharf. I didn't like it because it repeated the same pattern over and over again. It became an obvious mechanical device. I suggested, "Why can't we do what nature does? In nature, the agitation of the water throws unending different patterns against the wharf." That's what we did. We used a bowl of water with a mirror in the bottom, set up a small fan to agitate it, and then placed a spotlight to hit the mirror and bounce the reflection through the water onto the wharf. The result was that unending variety of beautiful patterns that nature creates.

When they made the film, Sam Goldwyn, the producer, wanted to use some Hollywood kids. I said, "You're crazy. These kids are the real thing." William Wyler, the director, agreed, and they used my kids. Then the kids' mothers called me and asked me if I would manage them. I said, "No, thanks." I could have made a lot of money. But I really didn't want to make this my life's work. I wanted to get on to the next play.

With *Detective Story,* I owned a percentage of the film. I owned seventeen and one-half percent of the distributor's gross. To this day I receive checks. And my backers have been receiving money from it every Christmas.

GUARE: I was told that Harold Clurman once said, "All artists dream, and when they dream they dream of money."

KINGSLEY: Do you know that marvelous story about Bernard Shaw and Sam Goldwyn? Goldwyn was trying to persuade Shaw to do a film, and finally Shaw said, "We'll never get together, Mr. Goldwyn. You're only interested in art, and I'm only interested in money."

GUARE: *Men in White,* your first play, revolves around the case of a young woman who dies in an abortion. A number of years later, in *Detective Story,* you wrote again about abortion.

KINGSLEY: When I was researching *Men in White,* I spent some time at the morgue, and I saw an autopsy of a young woman who died of a septic abortion. It made a searing imprint on me. In *Men in White* I proselytized for legalized abortion. That was probably the first time anyone expressed that opinion out loud on a stage. I had known some wise and good physicians who felt that I was right. At that time, there were millions of illegal abortions in the United States, and God knows how many women died because, being operated on illegally, they weren't operated on with proper medical care. In *Detective Story,* I was dealing with another side of the coin. The man was not a doctor, he was a truck farmer. At one point the protagonist said he saw the dirty kitchen, the filthy table on which these delicate operations were performed. So this was a kind of murder, really. I had arrived at this element in the play, not because I wanted to repeat this obsessive interest of mine, but because a number of detectives I spoke to—who were rather sensitive, educated men—felt that the criminal they hated most was this kind of murderer—the illegal abortionist. So things keep repeating themselves.

GUARE: How did you do the research for *Detective Story?*

KINGSLEY: I made arrangements with the district attorney's office. I spent a year and a half going every night to the detectives' squad room.

GOETZ: Sidney, that means you had made up your mind before then that this was your next play's area of concern.

KINGSLEY: Yes.

GOETZ: You were looking for the background material. But had you already a story?

KINGSLEY: No. My stories evolve very slowly out of a circumstance, an environment. From the beginning, my philosophy has been that people are shaped by their environments. Man is the only animal who can create his own environment and thereby create himself. I always looked for this environment and imprint.

The Patriots is about men creating their own environment politically—constructing a new government, a new world. I wrote that play at a time when it looked as though this nation, this democracy, might very well be destroyed. Hitler was marching. Nothing was stopping him. Mussolini had thrown in with him. And then the Soviet Union signed a pact with him. The three of them looked as if they were unbeatable. I thought to myself, "I am just going into the army. What is this country which I might be called upon to die for? What is its essential nature?"

I didn't start out to write a play about Jefferson. I didn't know exactly *what* I was going to write about, except that I was going to address myself to that problem—a problem of that moment and of this world. As I researched it, I discovered that the answer I was searching for lay, perhaps, in the founding of this government. Eventually, it became a play about Jefferson and Washington and Hamilton struggling to make a new world.

GOETZ: Isn't it true, Sidney, that the play also reflected something of the stress that was around Roosevelt at the time? Roosevelt was, as I recall, facing a very reactionary segment of this country.

KINGSLEY: Yes, that's part of the play. Many people resented Roosevelt and his feeling for the people. But also there was another feeling that democracy could not survive against the single-mindedness and the centralized power of the fascist countries. Well, we did survive, and we did win. One thing that the research made clear to me is that this is a continuing and unending struggle. The nature of our country is precisely that—that each generation has to make the country over again. A democracy must always be working out its destiny. You can't just set it in place and let it go. Jefferson made that quite clear.

GUARE: Jefferson also said, "It's not the people who have failed us, it's we who have failed the people." Do you still feel the people are that magical, that great, force that somehow will heal itself, right itself?

KINGSLEY: Well, Jefferson said something else which I think is very true. He said the people know when they're being given a harsh time.

GOETZ: And the people know when they are in an audience. The people in the audience are unbelievably wise, I think.

KINGSLEY: Yes, always true. Even Aristotle observed that. An audience knows if a play is right. An audience knows this instinctively. They don't have to have been in a police station to know if the color and the details of *Detective Story* are true. That is really the basis of my own philosophy as a playwright—

reality. Reality, as I said before, always has an element of fantasy in it. There is something very unreal about absolute reality. Only a few years ago in Paris the artists were talking about something called "magic realism." That's close to what I look for.

GUARE: What drew you in 1951 to adapt Arthur Koestler's *Darkness at Noon* into a play?

KINGSLEY: Well, I had been to the Soviet Union.

GUARE: In what capacity?

KINGSLEY: I had gone with Lee Strasberg as an observer.

GOETZ: To the theater conference . . .

KINGSLEY: The festival, yes. Lee went straight to Moscow. I went to Budapest first to see the production there of *Men in White*, which I'd heard was a big hit.

I had no idea how big a hit it was. I was received like royalty. It was really quite wonderful and exciting to be guided in through a little door in the theater and to walk down a long aisle and open another door and come out into the director's box, which was filled with flowers. I asked, "What are these for?" The director said, "You." The lights in the theater went on. There were about four tiers of balconies. The people stood up and cheered and applauded. And I asked, "What's all this about?" The producer said, "It's for you. Stand up. Take a bow." I was twenty-six or twenty-seven at the time and looked about nineteen. It was unbelievable. I felt I was in a dream. Then they brought me up on the stage to take more bows. At a big party afterwards, I was presented with a book of the notices. The notices in the two most important newspapers were printed on the front page, and there were headlines two inches high. The play was obviously an enormous and very special event in Budapest, which was a city that was theater-crazy, anyway. Apparently the play inspired a lot of young people there to study medicine.

GUARE: Medicine? Not the theater?

KINGSLEY: That's right. Medicine. The statistics were staggering. Then off I went to join Lee Strasberg in Moscow, and I had a hassle with my passport in Poland. As a result, I arrived a day late, on May Day. My bus stopped on the outside of Red Square. The parade in Red Square was in full swing. I was going to miss everything because my hotel was on the other side of Red Square. Well, a group was forming to march in the parade. I could tell by their armbands and white clothes that they were doctors and nurses. I'd written *Men in White*, so I thought, "What the hell! I'll join them." I got out of the bus and asked them if I could march in the parade with them—not for any political reason, but because I wanted to get to the other side of the Square. They argued amongst themselves a bit, and then they decided, sure, they'd let me. So I marched in the parade. I was as close to Stalin and Voroshilov as I am to you. I marched and waved at Stalin, and he laughed and waved back at me.

At the other side of the Square, I said goodbye to my new marching companions, and went to my hotel . . . up to the roof where Lee was watching the parade. When he saw me, his mouth dropped open. He said, "Was that you down there?" I said, "That's nothing! Look here." I plucked the Hungarian notices of *Men in White* out of my pocket and waved them at him. "That's nothing," he said. "Look what we have here." And he handed me a cablegram from New York. It said, "Congratulations, you've just won the Pulitzer Prize." You may be sure it was an occasion I'll long remember. Talk about dream quality of our world!

GUARE: If only Stalin had given you the prize!

KINGSLEY: He gave me a prize, but of quite a different nature. The Russians asked Lee and myself if there was anyone we wanted to see in the Soviet Union. And I said, "There's one man I *must* see, and that's Gorky." The officials I was talking to turned pale and shook. And they said, "No, you can't see him." I said, "Why not?" They said, "He's very ill." I said, "Well, if I could just go into his anteroom and leave some flowers . . ." "No," they said. They reacted so strangely that I was very curious. That curiosity wasn't satisfied until many years later when I learned that in Moscow it was common knowledge at the time that Stalin was murdering Gorky. Everybody in Moscow knew it. I didn't learn about this until after I did *Darkness at Noon,* or I would have used it. But, at any rate, the prize Stalin gave me and the world was *Darkness at Noon.*

GUARE: At the end of Koestler's novel, Rubashov is asked if he has any last wish. In the novel, there is silence. In your play, when they ask him if he has any last wish, you have him say, "To die."

KINGSLEY: The point I wanted to make with the play was: This was a man who'd had a great faith, and this faith was totally destroyed.

GUARE: Mirroring, perhaps, your own loss of faith?

KINGSLEY: No, I didn't have that kind of faith. I had been open-minded and had flirted with it a little, but then some members of the Communist Party came to me and asked me to make a speech for some occasion. I didn't agree with what they wanted me to say. And they said, "Well, that's the party line." And I replied, "I don't agree with it." They said, "It doesn't matter. That's the party line." I said, "Then to hell with it and you. All I have is my judgment, my own integrity. That's all I have to offer." That was the end of the flirtation.

Q: Did you ever reach a period in your life when you felt that the whole thing—the battle to be a playwright—just might not be worth it?

KINGSLEY: No, I didn't. But my wife did. On many occasions. There were times when I was working on a play that I couldn't solve, and she thought I was giving myself too much of a beating. But that's par for the course, as we all know.

Q: Do you think that television, which has done so many variations on your type of play—*Hill Street Blues, St. Elsewhere* and so on—has killed off the so-called realistic play on Broadway, or is it the economics?

KINGSLEY: No, I don't think what I called "magic realism" has been killed off. Look at *Glengarry Glen Ross*. It's a wonderful play.

GUARE: Someone else asked the question, "How do you know when you've finished revising a script?"

KINGSLEY: When the curtain goes down on opening night.

Q: Can you talk a little about being a playwright who directs his own work—the problems and pluses of that?

KINGSLEY: I was trained, even as a boy, in directing and scene designing and acting, and I found it enormously helpful. I could never have gotten *Dead End* or *Detective Story* on the stage if I hadn't had the ability and the power to change lines instantly. For instance, I decided to direct *Detective Story* in a very special way. I wanted to direct it so that the heads of the audience would be like the heads of the audience at a tennis match, moving rhythmically from side to side. In order to do that, I had to constantly attract the audience's attention in one direction, then the other. That often meant changing lines or improvising them on the spot in rehearsal. Very often there was a line written for "over here" when I wanted the audience looking "over there," so I'd take that line out. Or I'd give somebody walking across the stage a line so that we'd watch him and shift our attention with him and follow him. I remember standing at the back of the house with Max Anderson. He asked, "Do you think it's working?" I said, "Look at the audience." And sure enough, looking at the audience—their heads moved back and forth rhythmically, together.

GUARE: Were you ever tempted to direct a film?

KINGSLEY: Twice, but the project was not to my liking.

Q: I'm always interested in the projects writers abandon. Could you tell us of any you began and put aside and why?

KINGSLEY: I have one I'm still hoping one day to work on. Only last week I was thinking I really ought to finish that play. I started it more than thirty years ago. I started doing research the minute the atom bomb was announced. I began my research with an interview with Albert Einstein—a very important interview for me because we got along very well together. I visited Cal Tech, Columbia, Cornell and Princeton. I have enough material on the subject so that the Society of Physicists in fact asked me to leave my research notes to them in my will.

A couple of years ago, I gave a talk at Rockefeller University on the subject. Rockefeller University has more Nobel Prize winners on its faculty than any other university, so I was addressing myself to a group that knew that subject much better than I did. I brought with me a letter I had received from Einstein. In my meeting with Einstein, he said unfortunately revolutions were spinal, not cerebral. I told him that the American Revolution, or rather the American reformation, was a cerebral revolution. He was interested, and I sent him a copy of *The Patriots*. He sent me a letter which was the best review I ever received. I brought that letter with me to Rockefeller University. I was addressing some of the foremost physicists in the world, and I wanted a little support, so I read them the letter from Albert Einstein.

I told them about my research on the play and how finally I had thought I would focus on Oppenheimer. I mean, here was the great hero, and there was the villain—Uncle Sam—who treated him badly. I'd had the play all set in my mind. I went to interview Oppenheimer, and it went out the window. After I was through with the interview, I couldn't accept the premise that this man was an abused hero. I told this to them at Rockefeller University. Somebody asked me, "Well, wouldn't *that* have been a good play?" And I said, "Maybe, but I'm not ready to write it yet."

At the end of the evening, the president of the university approached me and said, "You know, an awful lot of young people believe in Oppenheimer; wouldn't you be doing them a great disservice if you wrote an expose of him?" And I said, "You may be right. That may be the reason why I've hesitated to write it."

But then going home in the cab, I looked at the letter from Einstein, and I thought, "I've had this letter for twenty-five years hanging on my wall, and I've never understood it. I thought he was praising me, but he wasn't. He was praising the contents of the play—not me—basically praising Jefferson and Washington and the people who founded this country. Therefore, my obligation is to Einstein and the men who founded this country and not to Oppenheimer.

GUARE: That brings up an interesting point. Do you think the role of the theater is to uphold audience illusions, to bind us together?

KINGSLEY: No. We know that Molière went in the face of some of the strongest prejudices of the time.

GUARE: I'm talking about Kingsley, though.

KINGSLEY: No, I'm perfectly willing to challenge current beliefs. In *Men in White* I challenged the law on abortion. Lord knows half a century later that is still flying in the face of a powerful collective prejudice. In *Detective Story* I dealt with the paradox that on the one hand we need the police, and on the other they have to be controlled and watched. No, I'm not afraid. In fact, I welcome a good struggle. A good battle in a good cause. What can be better stuff for a playwright?

Q: I remember years ago you came and talked at New Dramatists . . .

KINGSLEY: I'm going to impress you with my memory. They said to me that Josh Logan had been there the week before, and his advice had been, "Write what you know about."

Q: And you said . . .

KINGSLEY: "Know what you write about."

STEPHEN SONDHEIM

The Musical Theater

STEPHEN SONDHEIM: Since we're here to talk shop, let's talk, without false modesty. I've been the object of a cult admiration because of shows like *Anyone Can Whistle*—those nine-performance wonders that make people think, "It's so gorgeous!" because it lasted only nine performances. They wouldn't like that show as much if it had run a year, but because the lucky few, the lucky three hundred, saw the show, they give it a cachet.

Also, I write generally experimental, unexpected work. The critical fraternity doesn't like not knowing exactly what they are going to see. It really upsets them. In some of the notices that were hostile toward *Pacific Overtures* I could detect that they thought it was going to be a kind of sophisticated treatment of East-West relationships like *A Little Night Music*, "Oh, how witty, oh, how trenchant," and all that. They didn't understand that it was going to be a *real* attempt to translate one kind of theatrical culture into another. Part of the basic metaphor is that if you are going to talk about the Westernization of the East, then you've got to show it in terms of the style of the piece. But that wasn't the style that people expected or, indeed, wanted.

I think I'm getting more and more accepted, but I'm still essentially a cult figure. My kind of work is caviar to the general. It's not that it's too good for people, it's just that it's too unexpected to sustain itself very firmly in the commercial theater. You may all be surprised to learn that *West Side Story* was not a smash hit. It ran for a year and nine months on Broadway before it went on the road, then came back for six months on twofers. In fact, the last six months of its first run were on twofers. It got excellent critical press, and people left in droves. It was just a little too unexpected.

When the movie appeared, it became a big hit. In the four years between 1957, when it opened on Broadway, and 1961, when the movie came out, there were exactly two singles made of the score of *West Side Story*. Dinah Shore made a recording of one and Johnny Mathis of another, and they sold to my family and friends. But the movie spent a lot on the advertising campaign. Disc jockeys all over the country were pushed to plug the songs. All the critics had said, "Ah, what an interesting and exciting score. Too bad you can't hum any of the tunes"; and then suddenly four years later they could hum the tunes—because they were played often enough. And like *any* art that baffles you, the more you see it or listen or whatever, the more chance you have of understanding and, indeed, liking it.

The only *really* popular show I've ever had is *A Funny Thing Happened on the Way to the Forum,* for obvious reasons. The audience could ignore anything that was experimental about it and just go along with the farce. People don't recognize that *Forum* was just as experimental in its own way. It was the first one-set Broadway musical, as far as I know; certainly, one-set *popular* Broadway musical; just one set, and nobody changed costume.

The other shows have either been gigantic disasters or just made their money back. They've gotten for the most part excellent critical press, but there's something about the shows that makes people a little uncomfortable in the theater—which is, incidentally, not my intention. But that's the way they come out, because what's interesting to write is something you haven't done before.

I don't understand the kind of writer who keeps writing the same stuff over and over again, although there are many *great* writers who have mined one vein all their professional lives. I'm not that kind of writer. I have to go for something I haven't done before, because if it's territory revisited it bores me to write. I don't feel I'm using myself. The result is, people don't know what to expect from show to show, and there's a certain resistance—and, of course, there's also a certain fanaticism. The people who like my stuff like it a lot, and the people who don't don't like it a lot.

The form that Rodgers and Hammerstein developed tells a story through character and song; it expands the characters, and the characters therefore cause the things to happen in the story, and it goes song-scene, song-scene, song-scene, song-scene. I'm very proud of *Gypsy*, but when it was all over I thought, "That's the last one of those I want to do. Now let's try different things." In *Night Music* I was trying to do a *Gypsy* as an operetta; that is to say, individual character-drawing in individual situations in which there is nothing experimental with the form but something experimental with the texture of the piece. In *Company* we were up against one of the oldest dramatic problems in the world: how do you write about a cypher without making him a cypher? In *Follies* we deliberately decided *not* to create characters with warts and all. Everybody would be, not a type, but an essence of whatever they were about, which is why James Goldman's book got so heavily criticized. People didn't understand what he was trying to do. I kept hearing people say, "Those people seem so bloodless." Yes. That's the idea of the piece. Now that may be a wrong notion, but it was a very conscious choice, to create poetic essences, and by poetic I mean the reduction of a human character in a situation to its most succinct form. They never spoke a normal English sentence. Everything was written. Jim was drawing essences. That's his style of writing.

Pacific Overtures was an attempt to tell a story that has no character in it at all, that is entirely about ideas. *Sweeney Todd, the Demon Barber of Fleet*

Street gets back to very specific characters, except that they are melodramatic characters—large, dark people skulking around the stage and killing people.

I'm a lazy writer. My idea of heaven is not writing. On the other hand, I'm obviously compulsive about it. And I don't really look for properties. I'm usually dragged in kicking and screaming by somebody. Occasionally, as in the case of *Follies*, I've gone to a writer and said "Let's do a musical"; I went to James Goldman because I'd read a play of his called *They Might Be Giants* that bowled me over. And I said, "Have you any ideas?" In the case of *Forum*, the same thing; I wanted to work with Burt Shevelove because I admired his work.

Generally, however, people ask me to do shows. I have a reputation for being intimidating and for writing rather arty work, and so I don't get an awful lot of offers—which is all right by me, because it's hard for me to say no. I'm afraid of offending people. I also take a long time to write.

The case of *Pacific Overtures* is, I suppose, typical. Harold Prince handed me the script. It was a straight play by John Weidman, his first play. Hal had been trying to do it as a straight play for two years and had decided that it needed a kind of epic theater expansion, which meant music. And so he asked me. I couldn't have been less interested in politics or in this particular kind of theater, Japanese theater, which I'd always found just silly and screaming and endless and slow and boring. As usually happens—I'm sure it's true of most of you—the more you get into something, the more in love with it you become, and by the time I was three months into it I thought it was just the best idea in the world. But the first three months I thought, why am I doing this? What usually happens is, I resist everything and then try to work on it because I know that the only way to give a notion a chance is to plow into it. By the time you're inside of it you then know whether it's a feasible piece or not, whether it can really work or not as a piece of writing. Obviously, you can't tell whether it's going to work on the stage.

When I found the musical style for *Pacific Overtures*, I was hooked. When I started it the obvious worry was, how do you find a style of both lyrics and music that doesn't violate the whole spirit of Japanese theater and at the same time is neither pretentious nor coy (because that's what that kind of ritualized theater tends to promulgate)? I decided I would attack the musical aspect of it first, and I thought, now what kind of sound is going to work here? For a month I just kind of fiddled and did some research into Japanese music. And I made the, for me, remarkable discovery that the Japanese pentatonic scale (which is unlike the Chinese pentatonic scale) has a minor modal feeling and kept reminding me of the composer De Falla, whose work I admire a lot. A Spanish guitar principle or modality that underlies his music was precisely the Japanese modality. I know De Falla's music, so I just started to imitate him. I took the pentatonic scale and bunched the chords together until they resembled that terrific Spanish guitar sound. And then I was able to relate to it, because suddenly it had a Western feeling and at the same time an Eastern feeling. I became excited. I had seldom written in minor keys; it seldom occurs to me to write in the minor, but because I had to have the feeling of Japanese tonality, this afforded me the opportunity to do it.

Finding the lyric style was much less difficult than I thought it would be: a kind of translator-ese, parable sentences, very simple language with very simple subject-predicate structures, and very little in the way of rhyme. The only heavily rhymed song in the show is the admirals' song, which is all about foreign powers.

The show starts in the middle of the nineteenth century, when the Americans came in, and then it's about the Americanization of Japan. I decided that as the score went on it would get a little closer to Broadway, until finally it would become an industrial show. We were very heavily criticized for this. In fact, *Variety*, which didn't like it, said, "The last number looks like nothing so much as an industrial show." I took it as a high compliment.

This gave me a progression, both musically and lyrically, particularly musically. Once you discover a kind of framework for a piece, it helps a lot. You get into terrible trouble if you don't know what your end is going to be. What made *Pacific Overtures* easy—and in fact it's true of all shows—was knowing the beginning and the end and then finding the style of diction and the style of music. You either fall in love with the material or you don't, and I've seldom abandoned a show in the middle. I find that generally the love affair lasts.

Follies started out as a kind of murder mystery—a who'll-do-it rather than a whodunit. The four come together for the party, and all the old emotions start to recur. Until Hal Prince came in on it near the end of our series of drafts, we never had the four characters as young people. It was always the older people, and when they had their slip into the past the actors themselves remained the same, they just behaved and spoke like twenty-one-year-olds reliving the traumatic incidents, including a key semi-rape scene played up in the old office that used to look down on the stage. At the end of the first act they each had a reason to hate and be murderous towards each other, so it was who-will-do-it-to-whom in the second act. It turns out that Sally tries to kill Ben, although he can't even see that she has a gun because he doesn't have his glasses on. It was all done as sort of black comedy. She missed, and then they all went home unhappy.

We found as we wrote the first draft that for the first ten minutes when people were collecting for the party it seemed terrific. As soon as incidents started to happen, it all seemed a little in the wrong way melodramatic. We thought, "Maybe we won't have anything happen until half way through the first act," so we wrote a draft—and the first half of the first act was terrific. It took us four drafts to learn the lesson that in this particular piece, *nothing* must happen. We finally ended up taking all the incidents out.

Finally, Hal suggested that we were being foolishly scrupulous keeping the four characters' young selves off the stage. He said, "I think there's a way to do it—not flashbacks but a cinematic simultaneity of action." So at about the eighteenth draft, Jim started to write two scripts, on the right-hand page everything that was going on among the middle-aged people, on the left-hand page, passages of dialogue among the young characters. And Hal said, "Don't worry about where everything occurs. I will figure out how to make it work on the stage." We didn't have to worry about the staging of those particular scenes because Hal wanted the challenge. It became a schizophrenic script, even in print. I think this was the right choice, but I'm not sure. I'd like to see it the way we wrote it at about the ninth draft, just for fun, with all the incidents out but all being done by the middle-aged characters.

The so-called integrated musical in which the story could be told *through* its songs, not just *with* its songs, was the contribution of Rodgers and Hammerstein in 1943. Before that, integrated shows were not musicals, they were operas or operettas. The development of the so-called integrated piece over the last thirty years has come from close collaborations.

The musical, more than any other kind of theatrical piece, is a collaborative effort; and what is required is that everybody sit down together from the first day of the inception and talk about what the show should be. The hardest aspect of writing a musical is to be sure that you and your collaborators are writing the same show. Now, that sounds like sophistry but it is *very* difficult.

I'll give you an example. We worked for four years on *Forum*, which was based on some Plautus comedies all mashed together. Burt Shevelove got me the usual academic dreadful translations, but the plays are still funny. I couldn't figure out why I was laughing, because the language was so terrible. But the plays are that good, and so we determined that we would make a musical out of them. He got a collaborator to work with him on the book, Larry Gelbart. Larry and Burt started working on a sort of general outline, and then Burt and I would make lists of songs that were actually used in the Plautus plays.

Over a period of four years, we worked on *Forum* three of the years because farce is, I think, the most difficult form of playwriting. I've stated it before and I don't see any reason not to state it now: I think that *Forum* is the best farce ever written. I think it makes Feydeau look like a piker. *Forum* is much more elegant than anything Feydeau ever wrote and much, much more tightly plotted. There's not a wasted moment in *Forum*, and the truth and the test of it is that the play is just as funny when performed by a group of high school students as it is when performed on Broadway. It is never *not* funny. The reason is, it is based on situations so solid that you cannot *not* laugh.

We were about to go into production when I got a funny feeling in the pit of my stomach that something was dreadfully wrong with the score. I thought maybe it was just the usual writer's neurosis, you know, everything I write is terrible, everything everybody else writes is wonderful. I had James Goldman come down to the house and first I had him read the script. He said, "It's delightful and it's brilliantly put together and it's very elegant." And then I had him listen to the score, and he said, "It's a terrific score." I said, "Why do I feel peculiar? Am I just getting nervous?" This was about two months before rehearsal. And he said, "No, it's just that the score and the book have nothing to do with each other. The book is written on a kind of low comedy vaudeville level with elegant language, and you have written a witty score, a salon score. Either the score should be lower or the book should be more of a salon piece."

Well, of course it was too late to do anything about it. The test of it was, when we opened out of town the score didn't work at all. There was only one number that the audience enjoyed at all, "Everybody Ought to Have a Maid." It was a throwaway song—I had this whole intellectual notion that all the songs would be. I thought that would be the right thing for a farce. One of the problems with writing a score for a farce (and I kept complaining to Burt about this all the time) is that it interrupts the action instead of carrying it on. It interrupts because it's not about character, those are not songs that develop people and story. Burt said, "You must use songs in a different way than you have used them before." He said, "There are other ways to write songs besides the Rodgers and Hammerstein school," which is what I was trained in by Hammerstein himself. He said, "There are songs that just act as respites. That is the way they were used when the Romans used them, and that's the way you should use them."

It was very hard for me to do. It was like a series of night club numbers. It was precisely in trying to do it that I made the error, and the result was that the numbers didn't hold up on their own because they were written in a different style. There was a big difference between what was going on on the stage and what was going on in the songs. And that's really why the audience only enjoyed that one number, because it was the only number written in the right style. I then resuscitated a number that had been thrown out in the four years that we were writing *Forum*, called "Impossible," and that's also in the right style. But everything else in that show—and I'm proud of some of those songs—is really wrong for that show. "Pretty Little Picture" is a perfect example of what's wrong. In fact, we dropped it in the revival. It's a very elegant, rather witty song, very verbal, and has nothing to do with the way the play is written.

Burt Shevelove used to say about *Forum*, "It's a scenario for vaudevillians. I want to give five terrific vaudevillians a chance to cavort on that stage. I want to give them a structure that is so rigid that the plot will keep them going; but within that, if somebody wants to take a page and just smell mare's sweat, he can do it." Zero Mostel could do that for fifteen seconds or thirty seconds or a minute and a half, smelling the mare's sweat on Davey Burns. And Davey Burns could do it. So they had a routine worked out. Now, you know, in the East Keokuk High School they don't do a routine. They just do the lines, but . . . maybe if they have an inventive young man there, he will do a routine on smelling mare's sweat. That's the idea of it. Burt wanted every performance and every production to be different.

You have to be careful about what demands you make on an audience. How much do you want them to listen? How much do you want them to just look and receive? In a show like *Forum*, it's very important that they *don't* have to listen a lot. In a show like *Company* it's very important they *do* have to listen a lot, because you're making points. *Forum* is not about making points. It's a situation comedy, you know, it's the basis of everything from *Sergeant Bilko* to *I Love Lucy*. Plautus invented it all.

To make a score sound like a score when it's interrupted by great chunks of dialogue is difficult. In a sense, opera is easier to write because it's through-composed. The libretto and the spoken text take much less precedence. I have used arbitrary methods, although not as arbitrary as they seem, to hold scores together. Certainly leitmotifs are useful (but a very bald device, when every time a character comes on you get the Jet whistle and you know he's a Jet). In *Night Music* I put everything in some form of triple time so that the whole score would feel vaguely like a long waltz with scherzi in between so that no song would seem to have come from another texture. In the case of *Pacific Overtures* I kept a very limited harmonic language, with very little harmonic motion in the songs. *Pacific Overtures* had static songs, harmonically. They don't go anywhere. "Someone in a Tree" is an example of a song that's built almost entirely on two chords and an endless rhythmic vamp that bored the audience to death in some cases. But I found that since Japanese music is relentless, you've got to have some relentless songs. The score of *Pacific Overtures* holds together because it all has the same harmonic texture and the same lack of variety within the songs, as opposed to a score like *Follies* which is *built* on variety. Nothing whatsoever holds the *Follies* score together. All I tried to do was keep the so-called book songs and the so-called pastiche numbers entirely separate in style so that you would have the sense of seeing two shows at once. I'm a firm believer in content dictating form, and when you're faced with a play in which you have two casts, one of older people, one of younger people, then you've got to have two kinds of music going. And there were two kinds of music going in *Follies*. I was splitting the attention, but that was the *idea*. It's a schizophrenic piece, and it's supposed to be.

I tried to hold the score of *Company* together through subject matter. I thought, O.K., I'm going to write thirteen songs, all about marriage, and the only thing to avoid is monotony. What will hold it together will be that everything is dealing with one-to-one relationships (with one exception: we cast a girl named Pam Myers, and we wanted to write something in for her).

Incidentally, in every show there should be a secret metaphor that nobody knows except the authors. As in Elgar's *Enigma Variations*, you only hear the overstructure, but something is holding together underneath that's inaudible or invisible. In *Company*, we were making a comparison between a contemporary marriage and the island of Manhattan—in fact it was even spoken about at one point. We made a vaudeville joke about it in the middle of "Side by Side by Side," and then we took it out because we decided never to let anybody know that that was what we were about. But it justified my writing a song about Manhattan, "Another Hundred People," which is the *only* song that doesn't deal with one-to-one relationships.

Anyone Can Whistle is sort of a music student's score. That whole score is based on the opening four notes of the overture, which is a second going to a fourth. All the songs are based on seconds and fourths and the relationship between a D and an E and a C and an F. The fallacy is that the music isn't continuous, so that it doesn't mean anything to the audience's ear *really*—except to some musicians who could possibly hear it. But the seed doesn't germinate the way it does in a symphony with a continuous spread. It germinates, and then there is dialogue, and then I remind everybody that it's based on the second or fourth . . . it's all too late. But it helped *me* to make the score.

Sweeney Todd is almost continuously underscored. You can't really underscore—unless you're writing an opera—until you have staged it. You see, for underscoring in an opera, the director has to fill in those moments where the composer is making tiny little intermezzi, but in a musical you do a lot of underscoring during rehearsal because it would be foolish, when there are so many cuts and changes to be made, to try to write everything in advance. You can't. That's also why composers can't orchestrate their own work unless it's a very small band—because you don't know what the keys are going to be until you are in rehearsal. You can say, "We will have underscoring and bridge from there to there," but until you put it on the stage you can't outline it or write it. You make so many changes out of town, it would become prohibitively expensive to keep changing all the underscoring, because you can't just keep underscoring with single instruments. If you design it carefully enough, however, I think you can get a lot in.

There is some danger that total underscoring would be distracting to an audience. The difference between sung and spoken is a *huge* difference. It's one of the reasons why there is such trouble making rock work on the stage—the contrast between that kind of singing, which is, you know, highly sung, so to speak, and the dialogue—the drop is so much. The same thing is true of underscoring. You might think, "Oh, oh, here comes a song," and then you'd be unconsciously waiting for the song, whereas it's just going to go on underscoring.

In collaboration, we talk about the material until we eventually get down to that terrific moment, after a number of weeks, when the secret metaphor becomes clear. I work with Hal Prince because he's so creative and so stimulating. I sit with him and the librettist and sometimes the set designer because Hal always goes to the set designer first. Like most directors, he gets a visual concept before he even gets an oral one. But Hal also has an impeccable sense of what a *whole* evening should be, what the totality is supposed to be. And there comes that moment, usually somewhere between the second and fourth week—meeting twice a week or three times a week—where you all look at each other and somebody says, "You know what this show is *really* about? It's really about X." And everybody says, "Yes!"

Once you know that, you can start writing. Now, that X is never stated baldly. I want a certain mystery for an audience, something that they can sense and even discuss and have to discover for themselves. Or they don't. If they don't, that's O.K., too. It's something . . . something that holds the evening together, gives it a reason but isn't stated because as soon as you state it, it's like bursting a balloon.

There are certain things that, the minute you talk about them, lose their charm. Certainly in a sustained piece of any weight or seriousness, there should be a mystery. Sometimes you have to deliberately create that mystery, but usually it's there anyway. The thing that makes you write the piece is quite often something unspoken that you only discover *as* you're writing it. Why does this piece appeal to me? Why do I want to tell this story? And then one day you say to yourself "Oh, I see, it's about blank blank blank, and that's something I relate to" (but I think it's important *not* to state it). It grows on you, and if it doesn't the work is probably too shallow. I want to know what's going on underneath, but I don't have to know in a sentence. It doesn't have to be like English II where you reduce *Macbeth* to one sentence. It's not exactly subtext, I understand that to be something else, although I suppose you could call it a subtextual matter.

If you find the underlying metaphor and then *don't* state it, it helps shape the whole work. But it's your secret, yours and your collaborators'. You may find that you all think the show, on certain levels, means something different. If you asked Hal Prince to state what *Company* is about in one sentence, and asked George Furth, and asked me, we would probably come up with different sentences. But we all know about this underlying metaphor of Manhattan, which is after all the handiest locale for the inhumanity of contemporary living and the difficulties in making relationships.

That comparison, incidentally, wasn't in George's mind when he wrote the plays, which were about California couples. They were the first plays he'd ever written, a series of seven one-act plays, each of which had either two or three people in it, all variations on marriage. Hal read them and said, "I think they could be a musical." And I said, "They are so unmusical. They are so unsinging." George writes non-singing people. And Hal said, "That's what's interesting about it." And I said, "You've got me hooked." I was so stimulated, it sparked something in my head. Hal wanted to change the locale to New York, and George kept asking why, or saying, "Maybe the pot scene could be in Westchester," and Hal said, "No, I think everything ought to be in Manhattan." In discussing why, we discovered, the three of us, that there was a metaphor that was pertinent; not just laid on, not arbitrary, but something inherent in the material.

In the case of *Sweeney Todd, the Demon Barber of Fleet Street*, I dealt with a play written in 1847 and rewritten constantly over the last one hundred and fifty years. It's one of the most popular plays in the history of British theater, almost never done in London but often done in the provinces—like *The Drunkard* or *The Face on the Barroom Floor* in this country. It's about a barber who slits the throats of people who come to him, beginning with good reason and ending up very nasty. The guy who wrote the original was the king of melodrama in 1847. He was the most popular playwright of his time. His name was George Dibdin Pitt. During the nineteenth century, actor-managers toured this play all over the country and of course would beef up their own parts or parts for their wives or whatever. There are six or seven different published versions. The original is still in the British Museum, a perfectly awful play. But in 1973, a thirty-two-year-old Liverpool playwright named Christopher Bond wrote a version of it that was done at Joan Littlewood's theater in London. I saw it, and it just knocked me out. This new version is a tiny play, still a melodrama, but also a legend, elegantly written, part in blank verse which I didn't even recognize till I read the script. It had a weight to it, and I couldn't figure out how the language was so rich and thick without being fruity; it was because he wrote certain characters in blank verse. He also infused into it plot elements from Jacobean tragedy and *The Count of Monte Cristo*. He was able to take all these disparate elements that had been in existence rather dully for a hundred and some-odd years and make them into a first-rate play. It's the other side of farce. It's as cleverly plotted as *Forum* but not as intricate, and it does have a couple of surprises that are terrific.

I'm not going to tell you my underlying metaphor for *Sweeney Todd*. I discovered it somewhere between the third and fourth song I was playing for the first person that had heard them, namely my agent. Something she said suddenly made me understand *why* I was interested in this piece, and had been for four years. I understood what it was about.

Sweeney Todd is so tight, all I wanted to do was sing it. I thought I could do the snipping and trimming necessary without a collaborator, but then I started to look into it and realized that though it's a short play it's so tightly packed with plot and so economically written that I was afraid to tamper with the structure. At the same time, if I sang everything it would be nine hours long. It's just a melodrama, it's simply not the Ring cycle, not worth nine hours. It's a tiny little ten-twenty-thirty melodrama about blood, so I asked Hugh Wheeler to do some cutting for me because I trust his sense of structure. It's still mostly Chris Bond's play, but I did not want to take on the responsibility of adapting the script by myself.

I feel very shaky about tampering with a good libretto, a good book, a good play. Very shaky, probably shakier than I should feel. It's hard enough, as you all know, to write a good play. To write a good libretto, you have to accomplish everything a play accomplishes in half the time. Of course, songs—if they are sympathetic to the piece—can give you an enormous amount of substance and richness. Nevertheless, the amount of words that Arthur Laurents used in *West Side Story*, which is one of the most highly plotted musicals ever, I think is the second fewest on record, for a real book show. I think *Follies* is the shortest book. *Follies* is a mood piece. Jim Goldman had to establish characters, but Arthur had to tell this very melodramatic plot in which a great deal happens just in terms of story; yet it's a very, very short book. That kind of economy is something learned only through years of experience.

If I wrote a libretto it would probably be endlessly long and moderately clumsy. I can write dialogue, and I can plot, but I don't know that I can write a libretto. It's so hard. Also, I enjoy the abrasion of collaboration. Writing is lonely, and it's nice to have somebody to try ideas out on, to argue with, and indeed to supply you with something when you're stuck. How nice to have Arthur Laurents or Hal Prince to call up and get you over those little blocks.

It's also useful to work with a director, because he has a sense of the way things look, and I think it's useful when you're writing songs to know *exactly* what the stage looks like. I didn't start one note of *Company* (I was just doing my usual procrastination number) until the entire set had been designed, a model built and a picture of the model shown to me. The opening number of *Company* is about the set. I wrote it to present the cast and the set to the audience and also to tell them what the evening's about. I could never have written it without actually seeing the set and knowing there were five distinct playing areas where the couples could be.

I learned this from Jerome Robbins: those of us who write songs should stage each number within an inch of its life in our own heads when we write. We should be able to tell the director and the choreographer, "All right, now when he starts to sing the song he's sitting down in a chair. Now around the second quatrain he gets up and crosses to the fireplace and throws her note in the fireplace. Then he sings the third quatrain directly to the audience, then he goes back and shoots himself and sings the fourth quatrain." I mean, *really* plot everything in detail, because directors and choreographers hate nothing so much (and I can't blame them) as being presented with a song and a notation, "And then, during the song, the seasons change." Well, that's what the song's supposed to accomplish—the season change. But you should plot it out for them: "Now at this point he's looking at the tree and the leaves are red. Then when it gets to the line about the grass, he turns around, the leaves are green."

Now, your plot may be impossible to put on the stage; that isn't the point. The point is, you have it choreographed in your own head, then they take off from it. They may not use anything in your blueprint at all, but they have something to work on, something to build from. And so you're collaborating with them. Just the way I call Hal and he gives me ideas, I give him ideas, and he can say, "That won't work, but I know exactly what to do with it." He knows that in the song there's supposed to be a change of tone, motion, lighting, costume, action, whatever. Maybe my staging is clumsy, because I'm not a stager, but it gives him something to work from.

In the opening number of *Company*, I wanted to pick a moment when the elevator would work. It had an elaborate set of glass and chrome, and there was a workable elevator on the stage. That's a moment you don't want to throw away, you want to stun an audience with that. So I had to figure: where in the opening number am I going to use that elevator, and what justifies it being used? I built the number to the moment where the elevator goes, and I thought, now, wait a minute. It's going to take quite a while to get those people off those levels, some of them down in the elevator, some down on the stairs; to get them down to the central level for the last chorus. I called Boris Aronson and asked, "How long do you think it will take somebody to get from the top level to the floor, down the stairs, the longest way?" He said, "Oh, about fifteen seconds." I thought, all right, I've got to have something going on for fifteen seconds. I ended up with just having a sustained note on the word "love," the key word of the song. That is not just a held note, it was timed to fit Boris's set so that when Michael Bennett got to working on the musical numbers he wouldn't be stuck for another eight bars to get the performers down off the set.

If you don't do that, suddenly not only is the choreographer stuck, but also your structure has to be changed. Supposing you didn't allow for that, and he says, "I need eight bars." Suddenly there's this hole in the middle of the song where everybody just holds a chord or a note, or there's some dance music or something like that. If you want your piece to be closely structured, allow for every single thing that should happen on the stage—a *very* important lesson and I think not a widely known one. The way I learned it was the first time we played the *West Side Story* score for Jerry Robbins, of whom I was very frightened, being very young at the time. When we got to "Maria," he said, "Now what happens there?"

I said, "Well, you know, he is standing outside her house and, you know, he senses that she's going to appear on the balcony."

He said, "Yeah, but what is he doing?"

I said, "Oh, he's standing there and singing a song."

He said, *"What is he doing?"*

I said, "Well, he sings, 'Maria, Maria, I just met a girl named Maria and suddenly that name will never be the same to me'."

He said, "And then what happens?"

I said, "Then he sings . . . "

"You mean," he said, "he just stands looking at the audience?"

I said, "Well, yes."

He said, *"You* stage it."

I know exactly what he meant. He was being grumpy, but what he was saying was, "Give me something to play so the audience will be *interested*." After all, it's not an art song, it's part of a dramatic action. There are certain kinds of shows which are presentational. You just get out there and sing the song. But that's not *West Side Story*. It's supposed to be an integrated musical. It's supposed to be full of action. It's supposed to carry you forward in the story, which means that every second should carry you forward in some way. Well, it's up to the songwriter to think those things up before you put the show in the director's lap. If you don't, you get clumsy staging or static songs and you end up throwing lots of things out on the road because they don't work. They work wonderfully in a living room, but they don't work on the stage because nobody thought about what should be happening. And in fact you sometimes find that you've written a song where nothing *can* happen. To avoid that static moment, plot and plan within an inch of its life every bar that you can.

It's very useful, therefore, to have a collaborator like Hal who is the director and also has an ear as well as an eye. You can talk about what can happen on the stage. Often I will call him and ask, "What do you see on the stage at this moment? I mean, tell me what it looks like," and he will say, "Well, there's a tree over there, and there's the Treaty House there, and I want space in between." And you start to stage the song, and then you make people come in and go out, and you plot it, and you write your scene—because a song is a scene, after all, in this context.

When music and lyrics are done by different people, the best way for the lyricist to collaborate with the composer is in the same room whenever possible. Very close collaboration is the best. First, you must talk very clearly about what the number is to accomplish emotionally, in terms of the plot, in terms of the character. I mean, *overtalk* it so you are sure that you are both writing the same song. Then there's more chance that you'll be able to work together, to give each other enough kind of supple space to invent and not be restricted.

Obviously, the hardest kind of lyric in the world to set is often the best kind to read. Iambic pentameter is wonderful to read and terrible to set. I learned from Oscar and Cole Porter: as you're writing a lyric, get a rhythm even if you don't have a tune in your head. Maybe make up a tune. Hammerstein, as you may or may not know, almost always wrote to well-known tunes. He just wouldn't tell Rodgers what they were. He would take operatic arias or whatever. He was not a composer, he couldn't think up melodies, so he used other people's.

Porter, who was able to think up melodies, said he always wrote knowing exactly what the rhythmic structure of the melody was, even if he didn't know the notes. That's generally what I do when I'm working on a lyric, whether it's with somebody else or when I'm doing the music myself. If I have a musical atmosphere, I don't worry so much about the melodic line until I start to get the melodic rhythm of a lyric, so that the two will go together. *Then* you start filling in the actual vocal line and let the vocal line expand, because you don't want it to be lagging behind the lyric. It's very useful to have an absolute rhythm in your head. Sometimes when I'm sketching out lyrics, just making free-association phrases here and there, I put in little notations, little dotted halves and things like that just to know where the accents fall; little arrows saying the line's got to rise there, to sketch it before I start working on the music per se. If you do that, you won't get anything singsong or boring or repetitious, because you'll be bored on the third line. You'll say, "Wait a minute, I've heard enough of di da di da di da di da." In a couple of instances, with Jule Styne and Dick Rodgers, I gave them a lyric written on music paper, with the exact rhythms marked so they would have something to follow. They may make some variations on it, but they know exactly what I have in mind.

I find the notion that the same lyric can apply in the first act and the second act *very* suspect. In writing a play, if a character is undergoing the same emotion late in the evening that he went through before, you can reprise a line, can't you? Or, in a musical, reprise a song? Well, most of the time it doesn't happen. Most of the time the character has moved beyond, particularly if you are telling a story of any weight or density. *Company* was a show where we could have used reprises, because it is about a fellow who stays exactly the same; but I didn't want him to be the essential singing character, so I decided not to. In the case of *Forum,* we did a reprise for comic intent. That is to say, you heard the song again, but in an entirely different context, and in fact with a different lyric.

Maybe there are instances where it *does* happen, but even if you are using the same musical material it seems to me something has progressed, and the lyric can't be the same. Also, satisfying as it is for an audience to hear a tune that they've heard before, I think it is more satisfying that they follow and be excited by and be intrigued by the story and the characters. It's nice to be able to combine the two if you can find an instance. I have found places where the music could be reprised, but I've never found one where the lyric could be reprised.

I'm not downgrading reprises, I'm saying it's very difficult to find a way that is honest for the evening and therefore doesn't break the audience's concentration and doesn't remind them that they are in a Broadway theater listening to a reprise of a song that still maintains the mood and yet is a reprise. I just think it's very hard. I remember when we were writing *Do I Hear a Waltz?* Dick Rodgers wanted a reprise of "Take the Moment." I asked why. He said, "I want them to hear the tune again." For me, that isn't enough reason.

I never worry about intermissions. If it feels like there's a natural break at some point, a natural pause, like a comma in a sentence, then that might be a place for an intermission. Quite often you write something that doesn't seem to have a break, as with *Follies.* When we opened *Follies* out of town, it was two hours and five minutes long, with no intermission. We *knew* it was wrong.

The audience, though absorbed, was slightly exhausted. We tried desperately to find an act break, tried desperately, but couldn't. I think an intermission would have lost many people in *Follies*, because it wasn't a plot piece. It was a mood piece. Once you've broken the mood, people go out onto the street and see the neon lights and are smoking their cigarettes, and you hear chatter about "Well, are we going to get home in time for the baby sitter?" It's very hard to get back in the mood. If it's a plotted piece, you go back to see what happens next. But in a mood piece, an intermission can be dangerous.

Anyway, I think there are a number of shows that would not have been as successful as they were if they had been done in two acts. I think an audience would have left. There are a number of shows, however, where the act break is needed. I don't think there's any general principle.

Music writing and lyric writing are very different skills. Music writing is a technique on which you have to spend a number of years of training in order to know what you're doing; otherwise you're at the mercy of insufficient tools. Many composers write with no tools at their disposal, and their music is dull.

I give the arranger very complete piano copy, which is why Jonathan Tunick likes to work with me. He doesn't have to invent anything. I was trained as a pianist, and I don't know much about orchestration. I mean, I know what the instruments are, but I don't really know anything about the techniques of blending them. I wouldn't have the time to do it even if I did. But virtually every note that is in the score is there in the piano copy when I write it. Jonathan will sometimes add lines—I won't say fills, because I always do those fills that occur between the vocal lines myself—but, for example, he will put a high string line on because he'll feel that something has to hold it together.

When we discuss orchestration and the makeup of the orchestra, which we do right from the beginning—sometimes even before I write any music—Jonathan doesn't want to be told, "I want a cello," he wants general ideas. I will say to him as I did, for example (and this may sound pretentious), on *Night Music*, "I want the whole show to have a perfume quality, not just to bubble like champagne. It is about sex, and I'll take care of the bubble, but I want some sense of musk on the stage all the time." That's exactly what Jonathan wants. He doesn't want to hear, "I want it all to be a string sound." *He'll* do that.

When it gets down to the individual pieces, I will occasionally turn to him and say, "Is this accompaniment too pianistic?" and he will say yes or no. If he says yes, I will then say, "Is there something I should try to do about it? Should I try to simplify?" He will say, "No, I know how to take care of it, but I'm going to have to change your figure so that instead of three notes up and one down, it's going to be two notes up and a breath and one down. I think it will sound all right."

I must say, every time he's changed any figuration, he makes the orchestra sound exactly the way I do it on the piano. When I play "Another Hundred

People," it's a very pianistic accompaniment. When you look at the orchestration, some of the notes are left out, and yet it *sounds* like all the notes are in there, because what he's done is voice the instruments so that they jigsaw with each other. It's very complete.

I've never used lead sheets, and neither has any self-respecting composer with any training. Give me a melodic line and I'll harmonize it one way, you may harmonize it another way. It's an entirely different song, even though it's got the same melodic line. Music is made up of a number of elements, and it is the putting together of all those elements that gives the song its flavor, character, quality, weight, texture, everything else. Lead sheets have nothing to do with anything as far as I'm concerned. If you leave it up to the orchestrator to fill in the textural details in the orchestra, it becomes essentially an arranger's score. That's what the word "arranger" really means: somebody who takes lead sheet and chords and makes an arrangement of a tune. Now, for my money that's the composer's job, otherwise he's not composing. A lot of people aren't trained to do that and need arrangers, but not any of the composers whose work I respect.

An arrangement is not clothing (I don't even like the word "arrangement"). There *is* the song or there is *not* the song, and a song doesn't consist of a sketch, which is what a lead sheet is, any more than a scene consists of what is going to happen in the scene. No, give me the dialogue. I don't care what a brilliant idea for a scene it is, I've got to see the scene. In the same way, I don't care what the sketch of a song is, I've got to see the song, or hear what's going on in the music. It's more than chords, more than rhythm. Music consists of many elements blended together, making much more than the sum of the elements. It's a geometrical progression.

I try to work away from the piano as much as possible, because if you work at the piano you get limited by your own technique. I have a fairly decent technique, but fingers tend to fall into favorite patterns, you know, and so maybe there's that thirteenth chord again. I didn't want any thirteenth chord in *Pacific Overtures*. That's what I like to play, so I wrote as much as I could away from the piano. I wish I could say it was seventy percent, but it was more like forty percent.

Very few people know anything about writing lyrics. It's a tiny little craft. It's like making pewter ash trays when I was in camp. You get your piece of pewter, and for day after day you work on it, and then eventually you have an ash tray with a lot of holes, and you give it to your parents, and they say it's terrific. I don't think there's that much to learn about the techniques. I've often said, probably extravagantly, that I think you can learn everything there is to know about the principles of lyric writing in a couple of afternoons, six hours maybe. But it's the carrying-out of those principles that counts, and it seems to me, as in playwriting or any form of writing, the best kind of instruction is criticism. That is to say, do it and then have somebody who knows something about it tell you, "No, you see, you're missing the point here. This won't work because the ear can't take that in."

If you have a feeling for language you can try writing lyrics, but I can't imagine anybody writing lyrics without a composer. It's never a waste of time to put something down on paper and say "Here's the play. This is the idea of the evening. Here's what it's about," but I wouldn't work on any details, if I were you. I wouldn't sweat blood over a lyric, because it may be for naught, it may not stimulate the composer. I wouldn't even sweat blood over individual lines of dialogue, because the composer may come in and say, "You know, you've musicalized the wrong part of the scene. It's this part of the scene, the part that you spent three days trying to get the lines right, that should be sung. Let's throw that out and write a song about it."

It's barely possible that a lyric could influence a producer to put a show on, but I'm skeptical about that. I don't think producers can read lyrics any better than they can read plays. Until they hear the rhythmic structure with music, they don't know what they're reading. Remember that most producers and most agents and most directors are illiterate. Some of them are talented and/or intelligent, but most of them are illiterate. They're not writers, and it's very, very hard for them to judge. They are also afraid. I mean, who wants to be turning down George Bernard Shaw? So, they are fence-sitters because they don't want to be caught with their pants down. But if you bring them a whole project, they at least have a grasp of what's intended.

I myself find it difficult to read a lyric and get any sense of whether I like it until I hear it set musically. If it's set wrong, it's not a brilliant line. If you read the lyric of "Oh, What a Beautiful Morning," you really would be asleep by the time the song was over. Who would know that it's the best opening number in the world? A script with songs outlined as to what they should accomplish might be more effective and easier for a producer to read. An outline says, "At this point she sings of her need to be the president of IBM." The lyric reads, "I'm going to be president of IBM. I'm going to be president of IBM. I'm going to be president of IBM. Hoorah!" This is maybe the kind of song you want, a kind of repetitious march, but on paper it's going to look ridiculous.

In *West Side Story* I wrote one dry lyric. One evening I got the notion for "A Boy Like That," and I just wrote it out and handed it to Leonard Bernstein. I had a rhythm in mind. He set it entirely differently. He heard a rhythm himself when he saw the lyric and was able to set it with almost no changes. In a couple of instances he handed me some music. He had been writing *Candide* and had thrown some tunes out that he thought would be useful in *West Side Story* (*Candide* was done while we were writing *West Side*). "Officer Krupke" was one that I set to a tune called "Where Does It Get You in the End" from *Candide*. "One Hand, One Heart" was a tune called "One" from *Candide*.

Otherwise, *West Side* was all collaborative, and you don't make it too rigid for the other person. And when you are wearing two hats writing to your own music, you're the other person. You don't want to hamstring yourself as a composer. That's the easy part of working with yourself, you can make the adjustments as you go along without having to have phone calls or meetings.

Once the lyric starts to take shape, I don't want it to get too far ahead of the music, and vice versa. Then it's a matter of developing both simultaneously. I generally do it section by section, and I generally make a kind of long line reduction in the music, because I was trained in a sort of conservative school of composition about the long line. I generally make a reduction of the long line and know what the key relationships are going to be in the various sections of the song and how the general long line is going to go down or up or cover the third or fifth or whatever it is. But it is just a matter of shaping a little bit at a time, like doing a jigsaw puzzle. It gradually closes in until it's all there.

The length of time it takes to write an individual lyric has to do with its structural problems. If it's a short lyric that's making one point and developing it just a little bit and then over with quickly, except for fussing around with the words it shouldn't take too long. But structuring a lyric obviously takes a very long time, and I find it useful to write a general outline of the lyric before doing it. When I did the admirals' number in *Pacific Overtures*, I wrote down on a separate piece of paper for each admiral what had to be accomplished with that admiral. I knew what the order had to be because I wanted to give a history lesson as well as write a funny number. Then I thought, all right, now how do I make these all into one song instead of five separate songs? That took a long time to do, but because I knew what each one had to accomplish, it made it a little easier.

I think it is useful to write the last line first—not necessarily the last line, but the thought at the end. We know we're starting at point A, that's built in. Where do I want point B to be? At what point does the song end? I think you should probably *not* try to structure a lyric until you know that. Again, you don't have to know the exact line, but you should know exactly where you are going, not vaguely, because vaguely where you are going generally gets you in trouble and usually makes for very verbose lyrics. It sounds like a small point, but I also believe in writing with soft pencils, because you want to *not* impede the process. A soft pencil writes just that much faster.

It is very important to keep all sections of the song separate. I use an entirely separate yellow pad for the A section, the B section, the C section, the A Prime section, the B Prime section, the C Prime section, to keep the structures separate but together. You have a quatrain, you've got a *whole* yellow pad just to work on that quatrain. Once I have that, I copy it onto a clean pad and start to work on the second one; and then I transfer the second one. Now I have two quatrains to look at and I can say, "Yes, it seems to be progressing right," or "No, I'd better go back to the original outline, because something is very wrong here." If you don't keep them separate, all the thoughts jumble together, and you'll find yourself taking thoughts that should be in the third quatrain and putting them into the first because you've got a hole in the first. But if you know that the third quatrain has to include the word "red," you don't want to put it in the first quatrain, and so you want to keep "red" on a pad over here. That's the red section. Don't touch that until you get the blue and the green done or it becomes all jumbled. Obviously, the most difficult and the most important part of any lyric is clarity for the audience, to let them follow with their ear what's going on. This is the principle most often violated by lyric writers.

The dividing line between verse and chorus is no longer what it used to be. Songs are much freer in form. The verse is a form of bridging dialogue into song and, if it's a fairly free-form verse, has a feeling to it of a kind of heightened speech. It's a way of leading them in gently by the hand. I'd say keep it going as long as it's interesting, as long as you've got something to say. You can have a five-minute verse, fine, it will keep my attention. You want it not to overwhelm the chorus, however, if you really want a chorus feeling. If you want the sense of a refrain, then you don't want a top-heavy poem, but I wouldn't make any rule about that. It's like writing anything, it's good insofar as it holds your interest and no longer.

The placement of songs is always a problem, and it's like a writing problem—how do you decide who speaks next? Arthur Laurents is the most sensitive collaborator I've ever had in knowing where a song should occur. He has an instinct for it, and I realized after a long period of time it was his playwright's instinct for knowing when a speech should rise, when a speech should fall; when somebody should not talk, when they should talk; when somebody should talk in an elliptical sentence and when they should talk in a complete sentence. He has a true dramatist's talent, that's why he writes plays instead of novels.

I like to be able to justify verbally everything I do, because I think by being forced to justify it you discover what might be the danger in it. But there are times when you are reduced to saying, "I don't know. It just . . . it just feels right to me. Let me do it and see if you don't think I'm right." Usually I am, because sometimes your instinct takes over and it's not immediately analyzable. Most of the time, though, I think you can say, "That's the moment. That's the moment for a song."

There is very little consideration of budget at the writing stage. As we are writing, Hal is making up a budget with his office, and only very occasionally come those moments when he will say, "Look, we . . ." For example, there was to be a pavilion in *Night Music*, lower left hand corner of the stage. It was to sit there all evening and was to be the scene of the duel at the end, which is from the original movie. Hal said, "I think we're going to have to cut down on the scenery because it's going to be fairly elaborate, and I would like to consider letting the pavilion be played offstage." That's indeed what we did. Now, there was another reason for eliminating it: a feeling that it would visually distract the audience all evening. Nothing else was to happen there except the duel at the end of the show, and it had to be a structure large enough to open up and have two men sit at a table and have a wine-drinking duel. And Hal said, "I have a feeling we need space"; but at any rate, it was also a budgetary consideration. Budget seldom gets in the way until the final stage when everything is written and Hal may say, "Look, I would like somehow to cut down on some of the scenery," or "I would like fewer costume changes. Here are some suggestions I have." But it certainly never gets in the way of the writing as you are writing. Never.

The closer a show gets to rehearsal, the more I'm writing. I end up working seventeen hours a day, because I'm a procrastinator. It's my own fault. I don't write nine-to-five. I'm disciplined in the work but not disciplined in work habits. Once in rehearsal it becomes very hectic, because you spend half your time coaching (I'm going to have a lot of halves in this sentence), half your time attending rehearsals and giving advice, half your time rewriting and half your time writing new songs. I don't happen to like rehearsals a lot, so I try to keep as far behind as possible so I have to stay home.

Arthur Laurents once dragged me to two sessions of the Actors Studio while we were writing *Gypsy,* telling me, "You must know what an actor's problems are if you're going to be a playwright or a writer for the theater. You must know the way they think, because you are writing for them." And I must say, I learned a lot. It helps me when I'm dealing with performers, as I'm coaching them on the songs, to know that they are not writers. They are not looking at the song the way I do, and I can't expect them to. They are looking at what they can do *with* it, not necessarily *for* it; how they are going to score. Either I should stay away and let somebody else coach them or I must put up with an actor's ego and understand where he or she is coming from. I can do that now. I could never do that, as easily, before I saw those two horrifying Actors Studio sessions which were nothing but group therapy. I once acted in *June Moon* on TV as a favor to Burt Shevelove, but I learned nothing and was embarrassed by the whole experience. There was only one part I ever wanted to play, and I played it in college: Danny in *Night Must Fall,* an insane murderer.

I let the musical director teach the performers the notes because that's just a matter of rote and time, and I can't be any more useful than he can—less useful, in fact, because he knows more about how you teach notes to people who can't read music. Once that is done, I have a thorough session on each song with each singer to tell them what the song is about or listen to them and see what points they are missing. I usually have other sessions later on in rehearsals where we get down to the refined details. But the important thing is to let the singer know exactly how the song is supposed to function, both for himself as an actor and for the scene and, therefore, for the entire show. Generally they have a pretty good idea, but people who have never sung before are skittish. With people who have sung too much, you have to reduce the vocal production. An awful lot of trained singers tend to drop their acting style the minute they hit the song.

When we were doing *Forum*, Jerry Robbins was going to direct it at one point, and he was being very skittish about committing himself to the project. He wasn't sure how it was going to come out, although he liked the idea, the script and the songs. He asked to have a reading with professional actors. Hal Prince got a number of actors, including some who ended up in the cast. We read through the show and played the songs and learned a lot about what was right and what was wrong. It was so valuable that Hal has done it on every musical since.

About four months before rehearsal date, no matter how much is written—even if it's just one act and five songs—we get a professional group together, and I play the songs and the actors read the script. It costs very little. The actors get something like fifteen or twenty-five dollars because it's just a reading, they don't rehearse. Afterwards, we discuss what is good and bad, and then we do the same thing about six weeks later. Sometimes we get the same actors, sometimes we deliberately get others. Now there are eight songs written and an act and a half. And we do it a third time—sometimes Hal will read it all by himself and I'll play the songs. We keep doing it anywhere from two to four times before the rehearsals begin, and as a result we are always in much better shape when we open in Boston than most shows are.

Ideally, shows should be put together the way Brecht put his plays together: you work on it for six months and then you throw everything out and start over again. He worked with the actors, wrote the play, saw it, designed it, sets were built. He performed it and said, "O.K., I see what's wrong. We'll start all over again. I'll see you in January. And I know exactly what to do." You can't do that now because of costs, but that's the way to do it. Who can put a complicated piece like a musical together in five weeks? So we take every precaution we can by auditioning for ourselves in advance.

Out of town, my replacement average is very low. I've never had to write more than two songs out of town because the show has been so thoroughly and carefully worked. The whole show may be in error, but in terms of what's going on it's really pretty much what we want to see. *Forum*'s the only time when it was all in turmoil. As I said, the score and the book didn't go together, and it was too late to do anything about it.

There is a kind of legend in the theater that many of the best songs get written out of town because of pressure on the writer. No, pressure is not what it's about. It's about the fact that when you've seen the play on its feet with those actors playing those parts that used to exist just on paper, you know exactly what to write for it. When I wrote "Send in the Clowns" it wasn't for Desiree, it was for Glynis Johns *playing* Desiree. That's a whole other thing and *much* easier to write. Therefore, good songs quite often get written out of town because you know the exigencies of the script, the production, the cast. Although it takes just as much hard work to write a song, you aren't doing it in a void. You know exactly what is required, not only in terms of the individual performing the scene, but where it fits into the whole texture of the show. You know so much about what's needed because it's right there on the stage.

You want some examples? In *Company*, "Being Alive" was written out of town; in *Follies*, it was "I'm Still Here" and "Lucy and Jessie"; in *Night Music*, the men's duet, "It Would Have Been Wonderful," was written out of town (I knew there was going to be a song in that spot and I hadn't finished it, that wasn't a replacement); and in *Pacific Overtures*, I fiddled with the opening and wrote "Chrysanthemum Tea" out of town. That was a very complicated number, and it took a long time to write.

Only one of my songs has been a hit on records, "Send in the Clowns," though I thought somebody might pick up "Losing My Mind"—an easy song—but nobody ever did. My own favorite among my songs is "Someone in a Tree." My second favorite is the original version of "Waiting for the Girls Upstairs," as it is now performed in *Side by Side by Sondheim*, as a duet, which is the way it was originally written. As for favorite show, I really like all but one very much. I'm not very fond of *Do I Hear a Waltz?*, a perfectly fine show but not a very interesting one. There was no need to write it, and I think that's what's wrong with it—it is a well-formed dead baby. If I were stuck on a desert island I *think* what I would want is *Company* if I could have the original cast. If I can't, then I'll take something else. Maybe *Forum* would last the best over a period of time if I had to see it every night.

What's coming up? I can't predict the future, but I do know that what's happened is, obviously, a split between popular and theatrical music. It has widened over the last twenty years because the notion of popular music, which has to do with relentlessness, electric amplification and a kind of insistence, is, I think, anti-theatrical; anti-dramatic, to be a little more accurate. I don't think that kind of music can ever define character, because it's essentially always the same, and it must be the same, because that's its quality. It's also a performer's medium; it's the singer, not the song. It's everything that the kind of theater *we're* talking about isn't. Pop music is swell for rock concerts. Whether they are rock concerts called *Hair* or *Jesus Christ Superstar* or rock concerts called "Rock Concerts" doesn't matter. But when it comes to defining character and telling a story through character, which is after all what playwriting is about, then I think it's useless and can never work.

Since so much of pop music depends on electronic amplification, the minute the people start to speak, after they have just screamed at you through a microphone, you're going to have an anticlimax. That's why, when they try to make rock versions of stories like *Billy Budd* or *Georgy Girl*, it can't work out. And, well, let's not talk about the quality of the writing; it can't work because it's not what drama is about.

Pop music has as strong a hold as ever, and it weakens the theater audience.

I mean, so many young people miss in the musical theater what they can get on a record. How can I tell them the musical theater is just a different way of looking at things? They haven't been exposed to it, so it seems wishy-washy and unsatisfying to them because it is not what they require from music.

I have no idea what is going to happen, but writing for the musical theater is the only thing I know how to do. I don't know how to do anything else now, and I'll do it as long as someone will put on the shows.

EDWARD ALBEE

In Conversation With Terrence McNally

TERRENCE MCNALLY: Do you remember the first play you saw?

EDWARD ALBEE: *Jumbo.* I was tiny. I remember the elephants, and I remember Jimmy Durante, and that's it.

My grandfather had a whole vaudeville chain, the Keith-Albee circuit. Out of some lack of wisdom, he sold it in the depths of the beginning of the Depression, so I didn't really have much contact with the theater when I was growing up—though I do remember that Ed Wynn and Sophie Tucker and other strange people who used to be in vaudeville would come by the house from time to time. I don't know whether this generated my interest in the theater or not.

My grandfather used to send me to see plays. Some of them had a powerful impact on me. Whether they were any good I don't know. I remember seeing *The Iceman Cometh* when it was first done. And I remember being enormously moved by one of Tennessee Williams's plays, *Suddenly Last Summer.* That was an extraordinary theatrical experience for me.

MCNALLY: You were much older when you saw that.

ALBEE: Yes.

MCNALLY: But you were not a child who went to the theater a lot?

ALBEE: We didn't have regional theater in Larchmont.

MCNALLY: I thought you grew up in the city.

ALBEE: No. We lived in Larchmont, which is about twenty miles outside of New York City. After I left—indeed, got thrown out of—college, I moved to New York. I lived in the Village then, of course. I started going to the theater twice a day. This was back in the middle 1950s, in the beginning of off Broadway, when you could see things like *The Dog Beneath the Skin* or *Who Was Francis?* and Picasso's *Desire Trapped by the Tail.* I was exposed to Beckett, Ionesco, Genet and Williams and a number of other provocative playwrights. What I didn't see, I read. So I knew what a play looked like, basically, but I didn't know what the experience of writing one would be like until *The Zoo Story.*

But I'm trying to think of the first play that was not a musical that had a profound effect on me. It was probably the O'Neill play. Either that or my first experience with Chekhov, down in lower Manhattan at the Folksbiene Playhouse, which was probably in 1950 or '51.

MCNALLY: Did you participate in theater when you went to Choate? Did you ever act?

ALBEE: At that point, they only did Gilbert and Sullivan and minor Shaw. I think I played something not very interesting in *Androcles and the Lion* once. I concluded my acting career just before I got thrown out of Trinity College (not for my acting, though that might have had something to do with it). I played the Emperor Franz Josef of Austria in Maxwell Anderson's awful, awful, verse play, *The Masque of Kings.*

MCNALLY: When did you start writing plays? One of the myths about you is that *The Zoo Story* was your very first play.

ALBEE: Let's perpetuate that.

MCNALLY: I know you would like to, but I don't think it inspires people. I think they find it depressing to think that it's your very first play.

ALBEE: Well, it isn't. I wrote a very brief three-act play when I was twelve. Then, having lost my mind when I was nineteen, I wrote something in rhymed couplets. It was either a very, very long poem or a very foolish play, called *The Making of a Saint*, which I sent to Virgil Thomson asking him if he would like to make it into an opera. Virgil generously declined. He said, "I have already done my 'Saint' opera."

If we are to believe a scholarly paper that has been written by Andy Harris at Columbia University, I made several false starts on other plays. There are fragments of plays. There's even a rumor that he has a complete play by me. I deny it, but he has it.

It wasn't until I wrote *The Zoo Story* that it all clicked into place. I was twenty-nine, and maybe I had gotten my head together just a little bit. That was the first time in my entire life I felt that I had written something that was at least halfway worthwhile.

MCNALLY: When did the notion of being a playwright occur to you, as opposed to being a poet or a novelist?

ALBEE: After I wrote *The Zoo Story.*

MCNALLY: But when you wrote *The Zoo Story* you weren't a playwright.

ALBEE: No. Well, I mean, I was, but I didn't know it. Once I wrote it, it all fell into place. I said, "Ah ha, you silly person, you've been a playwright all these years! Why haven't you been writing a lot of plays?" I had started writing poems when I was very, very young—six or something like that. I wrote thousands of poems, and I wasn't a very good poet. I wrote two novels in my teens—enormously long and enormously bad novels. And I wrote essays and short stories. Anything except plays. And then, finally, when I was twenty-nine, I wrote a play.

MCNALLY: With *The Zoo Story*, you had what seemed to be an overnight, meteoric triumph.

ALBEE: I have never anticipated anything in my life. I am astonished by many things, but I have never been surprised by anything, if you understand the distinction. I didn't know what it was like to be a playwright until I wrote

The Zoo Story. I had absolutely no expectation of whether the play would be well or badly received. Does it sound immodest if I say that, since it was received the way it was, that suggested to me that it was a rather good play? I had not yet come to understand that so much of commercial success has absolutely nothing to do with artistic merit. I equated the two. But remember one other thing: There were very few younger American playwrights functioning at the time. There was Jack Gelber, who had done *The Connection* the year before. Then I did *The Zoo Story,* and then Jack Richardson did *The Prodigal,* and a year or so later Arthur Kopit did *Oh Dad, Poor Dad.* There was just a handful of us. Lanford Wilson hadn't even begun yet, I don't think. People were sort of waiting for this new generation of American theater, so it was an ideal time for us to come along. We probably got pushed at least as much as we deserved, certainly no less.

MCNALLY: Pushed?

ALBEE: By critics, by the popular press which said how wonderful it was to have a whole new generation of American playwrights.

MCNALLY: There really wasn't an off Broadway until almost precisely that time.

ALBEE: Oh, in the middle 1950s there were maybe eight or ten productions a year in small experimental theaters. Then, by 1964, there were three hundred. The whole thing exploded.

MCNALLY: An incredible explosion of new plays and playwrights.

ALBEE: Nothing compared to the quality and quantity of new playwrights we have now.

MCNALLY: *The Zoo Story* was done first in Germany.

ALBEE: Yes. The point is, I didn't know what you did with plays when you wrote them. I knew no theater people when I started, but I did know some composers. I knew Aaron Copland, so I sent the play to Aaron. Aaron sent it to William Inge, who wrote me a very nice letter saying, "This is a very interesting play." He didn't do anything else, but you know that was nice. David Diamond was living in Italy at the time he read *The Zoo Story,* and he gave it to a Swiss-German actor friend of his. This actor made a translation of it and recorded it into German, playing both roles. He sent it to a friend who ran the S. Fischer Publishing House in Frankfurt and who arranged for its production in West Berlin in German. It had its world premiere in 1959.

At the same time that was happening, the play was floating around New York. I believe it even had a reading at the Actors Studio. I think it was picked up by Richard Barr, who decided to produce it off Broadway with the same play it had been produced with in Berlin—Beckett's *Krapp's Last Tape.* So the New York production wasn't the result of the Berlin production. While I was in Berlin in September 1959, Dick Barr acquired the worldwide rights from my agent. I came back to discover that I had a New York production planned for January.

MCNALLY: How did it go in Berlin?

ALBEE: Well, that was rather exciting. I had never seen a play of mine, of course, and I didn't know how it was supposed to be. And, of course, it was being played in German. I knew the play fairly well, not as well as I know it now, since I have directed it so often since, but I could sort of follow it.

I didn't know, though, quite how an audience was supposed to respond. I remember watching the audience during the premiere performance, being fascinated by the way it was responding to something *I* had written. It was my first experience of seeing and sensing and smelling an audience's response to something I had done.

The end of the play came. Jerry was dying on the bench, and Peter said, "Oh, my God!" offstage. The lights went down, and then there was absolute silence in the theater for what struck me as being minutes. It was probably only eight seconds. However long it was, I was a bit put off by the silence. And then thunderous applause started. That was a very exciting moment.

As I think back on it and some of the productions I have seen since—it was pretty good. It was a damn good production. Much better than the production of *The American Dream* that was done the next year in Berlin. It's supposed to play about fifty-two minutes, and that version ran just under two hours. It's true that things *do* take a little longer in German, but ...

MCNALLY: Milton Katselas directed *The Zoo Story* in New York, didn't he?

ALBEE: He directed the first three weeks.

MCNALLY: Alan Schneider directed *Krapp's Last Tape*, the other part of the bill. Did he have any involvement with *The Zoo Story?*

ALBEE: Not to my knowledge. But that's when I met Alan. I guess I had seen some of his work before.

MCNALLY: I'd like to ask you a little bit about working with Alan. Certainly anyone who writes was very saddened by his death.

ALBEE: Within a short time, I had a double family loss—Alan getting killed in London and then William Ritman dying. Alan directed thirteen or fourteen of my plays, and Bill designed the sets for certainly an equal number. To lose both of them in such a short period of time was awful.

Alan was an extraordinary director. He set a kind of standard for respect of text. He only directed plays he had some respect for. Since he did respect them, his interest was getting the author's intention, whatever it was, whether it was right or wrong. He would try to help the author a little bit here and there. Not to impose, but to get the author's intention onstage as accurately and as clearly as possible. Some people found him difficult to work with, but he and I never had a serious problem. He was the kind of director who would want to have conversations six months before rehearsals began. He would keep coming with lists of twenty, thirty, forty questions to ask me about the play. Rather nice to work that way, rather than how you sometimes do—walking into rehearsal the first day and meeting your director for the first time and discovering he's planning to direct a play somewhat other than the one you think you wrote. Alan was an intelligent and dedicated man.

MCNALLY: You told me you thought this would be a good opportunity to set the record straight on *Who's Afraid of Virginia Woolf?* What sort of things would you like to set straight?

ALBEE: Well, I remember when I read the transcript of the Dramatists Guild session on *Virginia Woolf* I had a couple of quarrels with people's memories. Everybody remembers what they want. Everybody corrects fact, you know. But facts aren't interesting. Truth is.

One thing I did want to get said was that Uta Hagen was not the first person who was asked to play the role of Martha. I am damn glad she *did* play it, because she played it extraordinarily well. But I asked Gerry Page to play Martha first. She read the play, liked it a lot and said that she had to ask Lee Strasberg. Why she had to ask Lee is her own business. I got a message back saying that Gerry would be very happy to do the play, but Lee had to be at all the rehearsals as a kind supervising eminence. That indeed was the situation. She wanted Lee to be there. Alan was already set to direct it, and it didn't strike us that you could have two directors. Besides, I had seen Strasberg's work as a director, and I wasn't terribly happy with it. I had also seen his work as a supervising eminence on a Chekhov production, and that made me even unhappier. So Gerry Page did not play Martha and Uta Hagen did, and wasn't that wonderful?

Around that time, though, we did try to start a playwrights theater at the Actors Studio: Geraldine Page, Arthur Penn, Rip Torn, Jack Richardson and I—and I think Paul Newman was involved. There was a playwrights unit at the Actors Studio at that time, so we all got together and thought, "How wonderful. We have got a marvelous pool of acting talent, some wonderful directors, all these writers." But it didn't work out.

MCNALLY: But you and Dick Barr and Clinton Wilder started the Playwrights Unit at the Cherry Lane Theater.

ALBEE: Well, you know, we were making an awful lot of money on *Virginia Woolf,* and it was going to go to taxes if we didn't figure out something else, so we put it into doing this experimental theater. Over a period of—what?—ten or eleven years, I guess we did a hundred and twenty workshop productions of almost everybody's first play. Sam Shepard, Lanford Wilson, John Guare and just about everybody had their first work done there. And you, too.

MCNALLY: A lot of famous plays were first done at the Playwrights Unit—*The Boys in the Band*—

ALBEE: That was one play I didn't want done. I thought it was a lousy play. Dick wanted me to co-produce it when he transferred it to off Broadway. I put principle above principal, I guess. Anyhow, too bad.

But we did an awful lot of interesting work at the Playwrights Unit. That was a nice time to be working off Broadway, off off Broadway. Everybody worked terribly hard and for nothing. The audiences were interested and enthusiastic. It hadn't become riddled with commerce the way the off-Broadway theater has now.

MCNALLY: The Playwrights Unit was really the founding spirit for so many other organizations.

ALBEE: The Living Theater had begun it all, of course. They were doing Paul Goodman and Jack Gelber. And the Judson Poets Theater was doing some good work.

MCNALLY: But because of your name, and I think, Alan's involvement, the Playwrights Unit had a promise of new American plays in a way the others didn't. The New Dramatists always seemed more traditionally Broadway-oriented. The Actors Studio, for all the good work that was done there, was always Lee's building somehow. Even though there was a playwrights unit there, you felt that you were talking about acting as much as the play. It was so hard to escape Lee's presence. It was your Playwrights Unit that really was so important.

ALBEE: We had a good time doing it. Then other people started doing similar things, and the other people seemed to be able to get the foundation grants and government support. At the same time, it began to be enormously expensive for us, so we had to stop.

MCNALLY: At that time, after *Virginia Woolf,* when everyone was saying, "What's he going to do next?" you did your first adaptation.

ALBEE: Carson McCullers's *The Ballad of the Sad Cafe.* I seem to lose my mind about every fifth play and do an adaptation. I was quite happy with *Ballad,* and so was Carson. It didn't run more than eight months. I got a very nice compliment from one of the critics on it. He said, "Albee didn't do very much with this adaptation. All he did was take the dialogue from the book and put it on the stage." That's one of the nicest reviews I ever got because there is not one line of dialogue in Carson McCullers's book.

I have done four adaptations, and none of them has contributed very much to the luster of my career. My adaptation of James Purdy's *Malcolm* sank the Lusitania. *Everything in the Garden,* which I adapted from the play by Giles Cooper, had a respectable run, but nothing great. And my adaptation of Nabokov's *Lolita,* of course, was never done on Broadway. Something called *Lolita* with my name attached to it was produced on Broadway, but it was not my adaptation of Nabokov's *Lolita.* The one really truly ugly theater experience I have had in a long and reasonably happy career was the experience of losing control of the production of that play. It never happened to me before and I will never let it happen again. The script has been published by Dramatists Play Service, so maybe it will be done somewhere as written.

MCNALLY: Did you think of closing the play, of saying, "I am a member of the Dramatists Guild, and you can't change the script without my approval?"

ALBEE: I kept wanting to do it. I should have had the wisdom to pull out and make them close it. But you know, you get involved in something like a losing musical, and you keep thinking that if you go on with it, maybe it will turn out right in the end—and you get deeper and deeper into the quicksand. So the damn thing opened finally, not my text, not acted or directed or produced the way I wanted—and guess who got the bad reviews?

The Dramatists Guild does protect its members by a contract which permits no tampering with the text and gives the author certain controls over casting and choice of director. What often happens is, our beginning authors, out of— what?—insecurity, or, occasionally, greed, give up all their protections. They tell themselves somebody else knows better, so they rewrite that marvelous role written for a twenty-six-year-old man because a thirty-five-year-old star is available. If a writer gives in to that situation, there's nothing we at the Guild can do to protect him. You really have to be on your guard at all times and as tough as you can possibly be. I'm still puzzled as to how all this happened with *Lolita.* If anybody is supposed to know better than to allow this sort of thing to happen, it is me.

MCNALLY: You wrote the libretto for *Breakfast at Tiffany's,* and it closed in previews. As you can see, I am trying to bring up your famous flops.

ALBEE: I was sitting at home one day, minding my own business, when I got a telephone call from David Merrick, who, until that moment, I did not know had a sense of humor. David said, in effect, "Edward, I have a musical in trouble in Boston." I said, "That's nice, David." And he said, "I would like you to go up and take a look at it and maybe take over the writing of the book."

This struck me as such a bizarre idea that, well, I went to Boston and saw this musical which, at that time, was entitled *Holly Golightly.* A very creative move—to change the title from *Breakfast at Tiffany's* to *Holly Golightly.* But it wasn't bad. Abe Burrows had done a perfectly workmanlike job of translating it into a musical. It wasn't much like the original book. Truman Capote had written a rather tough little book, and the movie that they made out of it with Audrey Hepburn turned out to be about a hooker who was also a virgin. But that was what was on the stage in Boston—a musical of the movie, and it was all right. It probably would have limped along for about six months on Broadway. It had a couple of youngish people in it whose careers have not suffered too terribly by being involved with it, Richard Chamberlain and Mary Tyler Moore.

But I looked at it and I said, "Gee, maybe it would be interesting to take this over and bring it back to Truman's book, make it a real tough musical." I guess I thought I was going to be Brecht and Weill all over again, so I signed on. Never having done a musical, I thought it was nice to earn while I learned. So I rewrote it, taking out all the dancing boys and girls, reducing the size of the cast, taking out almost all of the songs that were in and putting back in all the songs that had been taken out because I thought they were a lot better.

The only trouble working on a musical is that you, the book writer, have to work with the lyricist, the composer, the director, the choreographer, the producer and the various stars. Trying to get everybody together for a meeting to make intelligent decisions was impossible because we couldn't coordinate.

Anyway, I did indeed take the show over and managed, in only two weeks, to turn something which would have been a six-month mediocrity into an instant disaster.

MCNALLY: You wrote the book in two weeks. And how many previews did you give in New York?

ALBEE: Five.

MCNALLY: So you only saw your version performed those five times?

ALBEE: Well, we put a few of my scenes in during the last week in Boston. That was very interesting. The show would be going along on its own merry way, and all of a sudden one of my scenes—having nothing to do with anything else in the show—would appear, and then it would be over, and then it would go right back to doing what it had done before.

My version played in New York. I remember, during the previews at the Broadhurst Theater, after we had put in some of my changes, people were milling around the lobby at intermission looking for David Merrick: "Where is Merrick? How dare he do this to us?" I think, had we had another two or three weeks, we could have pulled it off. I think it could have been a tough and interesting musical.

MCNALLY: Counting that script, then, you have done five adaptations. Do you think you're going to lose your mind again and do another one?

ALBEE: I always announce that I'm never going to do another one again. I wonder when the next one will occur.

MCNALLY: Your last few plays have not been treated kindly by the critics. You don't let it stop you.

ALBEE: No, I don't stop. I go right on. *The Man Who Had Three Arms* was commissioned by the Miami Arts Festival, where it opened and did rather nicely. It was picked up by the Goodman Theater in Chicago, where it ran for six filled weeks to very good press. Robert Drivas starred in it and did an extraordinary job. So it occurred to some people, since the play was receiving some very good audience response and good critical response, perhaps it could survive on Broadway. So we brought it into New York, where it opened, after playing, I think, ten previews to an enormously enthusiastic and friendly audience. It opened to an almost unanimously hostile press, an extraordinarily hostile reaction. Well of course, given the fact that the play was, in part, about critics and about the bitch goddess success, and about a number of other misinformations that the public receives about itself through our press, I am not terribly surprised.

But what interested me most was that this play, of all my plays, is the one for which I received the most enthusiastic and favorable response from people in the arts—my peers. Writers, composers, painters, sculptors, poets—they seemed to like this play more than many others I have written. Isn't it interesting that the critical response was so hostile and negative?

MCNALLY: In New York. This was not true in Chicago.

ALBEE: Only in New York. Very interesting.

McNALLY: What do you think accounts for the difference?

ALBEE: I don't know quite how to explain it. I am puzzled and interested by the fact that the New York critics did not review the play that I wrote but the play they *wished* I had written.

McNALLY: Do you feel you are a little provocative in that play?

ALBEE: Whatever do you mean, Terrence?

McNALLY: Well, the character kept referring to a lady of the press in the audience very unflatteringly. Surely, people must have said to you, "Edward, the critics are going to perceive this as an attack on them."

ALBEE: If they were bright enough to figure out it was an attack on them . . . you take your chances. The play was about an advertising man, somebody with absolutely no talent whatsoever, who grew a third arm. A literal third arm. Not a metaphorical third arm, as a number of people decided, but a literal and real third arm, through no fault of his own. And so he becomes the most famous person in the world, rich and famous, through no fault of his own. He is asked to run for public office, his opinion is solicited on everything, he becomes powerful and is probably corrupted by this a bit. And then, all of a sudden, the arm starts going away. Now he has only two arms, and he's reduced to being on the lecture circuit talking about what it was like when he had his famous third arm.

What bothered me about the critical response to the play was that the press said that this play was a metaphor for my own career. They said, "Isn't it a pity that he doesn't write as brilliantly as he used to." But the play was very carefully contrived to be about somebody who never had any talent to begin with. If I was going to write an autobiographical play, I would have written it about someone who had at least *some* talent.

McNALLY: When I read the script, I thought it was a brilliant play. But I remember saying to you that I thought there was a danger that the play might be perceived that way. I thought you were terribly exposed in the play. The critics went for the most vulnerable spots.

ALBEE: But, you know, you shrug and go about your business.

McNALLY: What do you say to people who come up and say, "If you had done that play off Broadway, it would still be running"? Do you think that's true?

ALBEE: It's possible that the critical response might have been mitigated if the critics thought that the play would not reach a large audience by its being done in a small theater. That's quite possible, yes, because, after all, the safety and middlebrowism of Broadway should not be tampered with.

McNALLY: And equally, I have heard people say that if the play had been done by a Dustin Hoffman or an Al Pacino, they wouldn't have dared . . . A star makes the playwright less vulnerable.

ALBEE: That's quite possible. But I can't imagine anyone doing a better job with that role than Bobby Drivas did. There was a producer who wanted to do the play on Broadway who did ask me to do that, to take him out of the play and offer it to a star—

MCNALLY: After he had done it out of town.

ALBEE: Yes, and I wouldn't do it.

MCNALLY: You directed that play.

ALBEE: I've directed quite a few of my plays. I am one of those playwrights who, I think, can be sufficiently objective about his own works to be trusted with them.

MCNALLY: How did you learn to direct?

ALBEE: I learned an awful lot from observing Alan direct, and I started observing other directors direct my work around the world—Zeffirelli, Ingmar Bergman, Jean-Louis Barrault, Peter Hall—people like that.

MCNALLY: Do you feel confident directing your own work now?

ALBEE: Yes, I do. Every once in a while I run into an actor who will not permit me to direct my own work. If I want that actor . . . I'm thinking about *The Lady From Dubuque.* Irene Worth did not wish me to direct her, and I couldn't imagine a better actress for the role, so Alan directed it, and he did a very good job. But I like directing my own work. I do have kind of an access into what I intended, and I think, since I know the craft of directing reasonably well, I can probably give people as accurate a picture of what I had in my mind when I wrote the play as anybody can.

MCNALLY: But directing a new play requires a lot of concentration. How would it be possible for you to do that and to handle extensive revisions, should you be in that situation?

ALBEE: I usually think about plays for quite a while before I write them down. I have kept some plays in my head—in one fashion or another—for several years. I have never written a play that I haven't thought about for at least six months. So I probably do less revision than most people do. I tend to do the revision in my head while I am thinking about the play.

MCNALLY: Would you like to direct somebody else's play?

ALBEE: I would love to direct other people's work. There's only one problem—I would have to direct work that I respected without reservation. I have a fairly strong author's personality, and, while I will not permit another director to mess with my work, I am terribly afraid that if I came upon a play I thought needed some work, I probably would want to do to it that which I as an author would not allow.

Sometimes, you know, I get better reviews as a director than I do as an author. One critic—John Simon, a provocative mind, sick with spleen—wrote in his review of *Seascape* on Broadway that my direction was so clear, so precise, so splendid, so right on the mark that one could see, without any quarrel, how terrible the play was. Something seems to happen to Simon's mind in the middle of sentences. How could he be so right in the first part of that sentence and so wrong in the second? This leads to the conclusion that one should read only the first half of John Simon's sentences.

I was, in fact, invited to direct a revival of Tennessee Williams's *Sweet Bird of Youth.* Later I was uninvited, but while I was still invited, I said, "I think I have got to reread the play. I remember something I have a problem with." And so I went and read it again and remembered what the problem was. Tennessee wrote two plays there. He wrote a wonderful two-character play set in the bedroom, and then he added this whole second act with lots of other characters, which didn't strike me as being anywhere near as interesting. I realized I couldn't direct that second act. I was going to have to go to Tennessee and say, "Look, what are we going to do about this?" Well, you couldn't go to a man who was the dean of American playwrights and tell him to do something about his second act.

I like working with young playwrights who have works-in-progress and are interested in a few suggestions—but I don't believe in this business of "developing works." I don't think any play should go into rehearsal unless it is ready to be performed. I hate this notion of working through a play with the aid of actors and directors and audiences and critics. I think that's nonsense.

There are a number of classics I would like to get my hands on. There are a couple of things to be said about *Uncle Vanya* that are not said very often, and I'd like to do *Edward II.* But nothing fascinates me as much as writing. I don't get the sense of exhilaration from directing that I do from writing.

McNALLY: One of the questions writers are often asked is how much their characters are taken from life.

ALBEE: I have never written a character that is either autobiographical or biographical. I have never written about myself consciously, and I have never limited a character to a real individual. I find that if you do that, you are limited. At the same time, every character I have written has doubtless been shaped by the limits of my own perception, by that which I have experienced. But a good deal of it is simply made up. It was interesting to me, of course, that within the first five or six years after I wrote *Virginia Woolf,* whenever I appeared at a university to lecture, almost invariably someone would come up and say, "You have obviously been here before. You must have known Dr. So-and-so." A simple matter of life imitating art, as it is supposed to do.

McNALLY: What about writing for a specific actor?

ALBEE: I think that would be very dangerous, because then you would be writing for the personality of a performer rather than the personality of the character. And what if the actor you've written for decides not to do the role?

McNALLY: When you wrote *Virginia Woolf,* who did you hear in your head as Martha?

ALBEE: Martha. I will grant that when I am three-quarters of the way through writing a play, and I know pretty much how it's going to go and that I won't be influenced by hearing other voices, I will permit myself to start hearing the voice of this actor or the actress as I am writing, but never when I am at the beginning of a play.

MCNALLY: When you see *Virginia Woolf* now, do you sometimes hear the original cast still?

ALBEE: I hear Uta Hagen and Arthur Hill, but I was deeply involved with the second production on Broadway with Colleen Dewhurst and Ben Gazzara, so I hear them just as much. I don't hear Burton and Taylor as much.

MCNALLY: Is it true, as I heard somewhere, that there was once a third act of *Seascape*?

ALBEE: *Seascape* was originally a three-act play longer than *Parsifal.* There was a second act which took place at the bottom of the sea, which presented a number of design problems, among others. When I had the first reading of the play in New York, I realized that I had written my own *Don Juan in Hell* and that second act was extraneous. At the end of rehearsal I said, "I'll see you guys tomorrow," and I went home and removed it. The first day of rehearsal it was a three-act play, the second day it was a two-act play. The fact that I could take out an entire act of the play so quickly and without any great loss does suggest that perhaps it was not absolutely necessary. When it was done in Holland, however, by mischance they got hold of the three-act version and had it translated. I tried to get them to do the two-act version, but no, they liked the three-act version, and so the second act was performed there.

MCNALLY: Which of your plays would you most like to see revived?

ALBEE: I dislike the term "revival" so much. It suggests bringing back from the dead. I tend to have a protective affection for those which have been most profoundly misunderstood, and those are the ones I think should be done. *Who's Afraid of Virginia Woolf?* and *A Delicate Balance* can take care of themselves. But there are some plays which may be a bit better, a bit more provocative, that didn't do particularly well, that I think might be nice to have back again.

Q: Can you define the one-act form?

ALBEE: Fairly simple: a one-act play is a play that is in one act. It started out rather well. One of the first one-act plays was *Oedipus Rex,* and after that things sort of went downhill for a while. The one-act form was considered a curtain-raiser, a frivolous piece, a throwaway, to be done by amateurs on purpose rather than by the usual accident in which we suddenly discover our plays done by amateurs when we thought they were being done by professionals.

Now the one-act form has begun a kind of resurgence. In the middle 1950s I discovered some rather wonderful things about one-act plays, simply because they were being written by people like Beckett and Ionesco and Genet. All of a sudden it occurred to me that this canard about the one-act being a frivolous, empty curtain-raiser was absolute nonsense. It was merely a play that stopped when it was over; and it stopped when it was over because it was written by good writers who knew when there was nothing more to say.

Maybe that's the definition of a good writer: he stops when he has finished what he has to say, he doesn't go on.

The fact that what a writer has to say can be contained within the one-act form does not diminish the quality of what he has to say. Indeed, it probably makes what he has to say a good deal more concise, more intense. I think the public has begun to realize that the one-act is a serious art form—especially with the fortunate birth of off Broadway and off off Broadway, which have permitted those of us who choose to write one-acts to have them done without having to give them to commercial Broadway managements.

Why write a one-act play? You stop when you are done; and if you don't have to change scenes a lot, and there is no great time passing, and the action of the play happens not to want to be interrupted by people smoking cigarettes and going to the bathroom and talking to each other, then I suggest you have a one-act play.

My one-acts vary in length from *The Sandbox*, about twelve minutes, to *The Ballad of the Sad Cafe*, which is two hours but also happens to be a one-act play. I don't think there are any definitions of length, subject matter or structure to describe what a one-act play *is*. Thornton Wilder wrote a set of very brief one-act plays, two or three or four minutes long. I remember seeing them at Circle in the Square. I thought one of them was a trifle long, but the others were of quite proper length.

Q: Why do you choose to work in the one-act form?

ALBEE: I guess the form is a way of being able to say something you can't say in two-acts or three-acts dealing with a more panoramic universe (but you can't be more panoramic than the one-act *Waiting for Godot*). I still feel the need to express myself in that way—it's closer to the feeling of poetry, perhaps.

It's true that the one-act play is more difficult to market in the commercial theater than what they out there refer to as the "full evening" play which may be one of the reasons why so much first-rate, experimental, slightly hermetic work has been done in one-act form. One is not trying for the brass ring but is making a personal, intense and sometimes (if you are lucky) more profound statement with the one-act.

Before the existence of off Broadway it was almost impossible for one-acts to be done in New York City. Commercial managements were not going to do them. The last time before the birth of off Broadway a commercial management did some one-acts was Eugene O'Neill's short sea plays, which I believe were transferred from Provincetown, Mass. to the Provincetown Theater, New York, and then were eventually done in a revival on Broadway. With the birth of off Broadway, audiences were ready for experiment and were more interested in it than the usual commercial audience. Once Beckett and Ionesco and Genet began showing us the way, a whole generation of American play-wrights sprang up. Since there was at last a healthy, comfortable home where the one-act play could be done, we all began writing one-acts, not because we didn't know how to write two- and three-acts.

Q: When does one know the play one is writing is a one-act?

ALBEE: When you've finished writing it and you haven't had an intermission. I suppose it's possible to start a play you think is going to be in more than one act and discover it is in one act. I remember a reverse example where I decided I was going to write two one-act plays called *Life* and *Death.* The play about life turned into *Seascape,* which ran in two acts, and the play about death turned into *All Over,* which also ran in two acts. I can't remember ever starting a play I thought was going to be in more than one act that turned out to be only in one, but then I can't remember that I asked myself a question about length when I started writing.

Q: Since you find a one-act where you find it, you are going to find things in it that don't fit any definition. Is that why we all jump on the intermission, or lack of it, the one thing we can be sure of and hold on to in defining a one-act?

ALBEE: Can we perhaps say that the one-act play must run less than an hour to be a one-act play? Must its action be continuous, or may it have scenes within that action? It's very hard to come up with a definition. Some longer pieces are done without intermission for fear that the audience might leave and not come back for the second act. I had the opposite thought in mind with *The Ballad of the Sad Cafe,* I just got so interested in what was going on that I didn't want to break the spell. Maybe a two-hour play that could conceivably have had an intermission is not a one-act play. Maybe there *is* a definition of what a one-act play is that wouldn't diminish the nature of the one-act play. Maybe we could find it in the distinctions between the novel and novella and short story. A novella is really a kind of concise short novel without intermission. The short story is a different way of looking at a subject, and a number of short stories that I've read strike me as being every bit as inclusive and complete experiences as the majority of novels.

When Richard Barr, Clinton Wilder and I were producing off Broadway, we came upon an extraordinary play, *Funnyhouse of a Negro* by Adrienne Kennedy, an amazing play. It ran about an hour and five minutes. I suggested, "This is so complete an experience, let's not put anything with it, let's perform it twice an evening and charge one dollar" (the off-Broadway ticket price was two dollars in those days). They could come and see it at eight o'clock before dinner or nine-thirty after dinner. I thought that would work marvelously for Adrienne's play; but even though people were only paying half price they felt cheated. They felt they weren't getting a complete evening in the theater.

Maybe there's a parallel with the symphony and the string quartet. The audience for the flashy symphony is a great deal larger than the audience for the string quartet, which is a more naked and ultimately more difficult form. You can't cover up with sound and tympani and crashing about; each note must be precise and count. Most one-act plays tend to be chamber plays, but that is hardly a demeaning definition.

Nobody should ever try to stretch a one-act play into a two-act play because they think it is going to be more marketable. The stretch marks will show, and we all know what stretch marks look like. Also, plays have their ideal audience and their ideal size of the theater they belong in. Putting them before the wrong audience in the wrong place is an error.

Sometimes the ideas that occupy us are going to demand to be in one-act form. The most important thing to remember about one-acts if you discover that you are in the middle of committing one is: don't fight it. Don't try to stretch it, and don't try to cut a longer play down to one act. If your mind has created a one-act play, there is absolutely nothing to be done about it. It may not get the brass ring, it will probably not be done on Broadway, but chances are pretty good that you are trying something a little more complex, a little more daring, that you would not try if you were consciously trying something commercial. It's an *important* form; and the more we can persuade people that it is not frivolous or unimportant, or a lesser form of theater, the better off we would all be—authors, audiences, the entire theater.

LEONARD MELFI

Tales of a New York Playwright

I love this day!

But first I must go back because it's very important. I was living in an apartment, subleasing it, in the belief that the landlord was aware of this. But he wasn't. When he met me in the hallway and found out that I was subleasing, well, he was furious. He didn't want me there.

At the same time there was some sort of screw-up with Con Edison: all these reminders of turn-off notices, for no reason at all, except dumb computer problems.

During this time I had also bought a marvelous hat for thirty dollars down on Orchard Street. I had always wanted a hat like the one I bought and now I finally had it. I loved wearing it. It was a Barcelona, made of imported furs: genuine velour. It was sort of a smooth tan with a dark-brown-light-brown-red-striped band around it and a few autumn feathers coming out of it.

Also during this time all of my own furniture was in storage including two very good and very large dictionaries, which I had had for years. And so, when I subleased the apartment, I was without a dictionary. I kept putting off buying one, because I thought it was an extravagant thing for me to do at the moment.

And now let's get back to this day that I love so much: a day of days that could only happen in New York.

I woke up early in the morning. There was a knock on my door. I knew it was the landlord. I had been avoiding him for weeks. I believed he wanted to tell me that I must give up the apartment. After not having answered the door for a couple of weeks because I figured it was him (I really wanted to stay in the apartment), I decided that I had to face reality. I opened the door. It was the landlord. He smiled at me and told me he was glad that I was in the building, and that was it. I couldn't believe it.

I then turned on my radio. Harold Melvin and the Blue Notes were doing "The Love I Lost." I couldn't believe that, either, because it's hardly ever heard on the radio any more, and because it's one of my favorite, happily sentimental, recordings.

I felt pretty good. But that day was also the day that Con Ed was going to turn off my services if I didn't come to their offices in the morning. And so I had to face that hassle. Suddenly the telephone rings. It's Con Ed. Everything's okay. They say they're sorry, etc.

Not bad. Not bad at all. I decide to stay in and write. I really go on a writing splurge. It's also the first time that I really think I'm going to have to splurge on a new dictionary since I really could have used one during that writing session.

Now I realize that I'm out of cigarettes. I also realize that I only have 45 cents on me. I decide I'm going to have to get to my bank before three o'clock. The bank is midtown and I'm uptown in the Eighties. I've got to take the subway in order to get there in time. But I've only got 45 cents. I need 5 cents more. I'm also freaking out now because I don't have a single cigarette left. I decide to see if I can run or jog all the way to the bank. I've got a half hour to do it in.

I put on my beautiful hat and leave my place. On the way out of my building I check my mail. There's a letter of apology from Con Ed. "Right on," I say to myself. Then I run to the corner of Columbus Avenue, thinking I might meet a friend who will loan me a couple of bucks so that I can buy a pack of cigarettes and a token in order to get to my bank by three o'clock.

A well-dressed, Indian-looking man comes up to me, from out of nowhere, so it seems to me. He has a huge sack-like thing slung over his shoulder.

"Do you smoke?" he asks me with a bright smile.

"Yes," I answer. I don't quite believe it already.

"Regular or menthol?" he asks me.

"Regular . . ." I mumble.

The man reaches into his sack and pulls out a free sample pack of cigarettes. He hands them to me (I don't believe it). It's a red pack, Eagle 20's, twenty Class A Cigarettes, with a white and golden eagle on it.

"Every time you buy a pack of Eagle 20's you save a nickel," the Indian-looking man told me. And then he handed me a card from a whole pack of cards that he took from his pocket. It was a laminated advertisement card and it said: "New Eagle 20's. Every time you buy a pack you save a nickel." And there was a picture of a red pack (regular) and a green pack (menthol) on it. And in the middle of the card there was a nickel, *a real nickel*, held so that it would not fall off the card (it was hard for me to believe).

I thanked the man a whole lot and then I turned back towards my block and began to walk very fast up towards the subway station. But about halfway in the middle of my block I see a big thick book. It's all by itself on the concrete ledge of a little garden in front of a nice brownstone type of building. At the same time a man is getting out of a plumber's truck. He goes to the book and picks it up. I can tell that he's not going to take it. "Who wants a dictionary?" he asks out loud, placing it back down where it was, and then going into the building.

Yes, I went to the book, waiting the way it was there, and yes: *it was a dictionary!*—as though someone did not really want to throw it in the garbage, and so they left it out very nicely for someone to see, for someone to take it who really needed it. There it was. I picked it up as though it were some sacred thing, some miracle-like object. It was in very good shape: Funk & Wag-nalls New Desk Standard Dictionary, with almost a thousand pages and a thumb index besides!

I was in some sort of ecstatic state by this time. I began to run towards the subway again, along Central Park West, clutching my dictionary, my cigarettes, my nickel, and my soul, which was feeling awfully religious all of a sudden.

I began to run past a hot-dog vendor and his vending cart. But suddenly there was a wind that I didn't count on. It blew my beautiful hat off my head! The hat went flying and then it blew down and went rolling across the street. I thought to myself, "Well, that's it."

My hat began to roll on the traffic-ridden street, and I just stood there and watched, along with the hot-dog vendor. Well, my beautiful hat missed every passing car. It was hard to even imagine. And then, without any warning at all, it stopped just perfectly on its bottom right smack in the center of the street where no car could hit it. It just stood as though it were waiting on a shelf in some hat shop. I went out and picked it up and put it on my head again.

"It's a miracle," the vendor remarked to me.

I agreed with him and then went down into the subway and got to my bank just in time.

C'mon, everybody: there is harmony, after all. Especially in the Big Apple: there's harmony, and it's there when you least expect it, but when you really want it.

Ah! Big Apple! Delicious big red ripe shiny apple!

Ah! Big Apple playwright . . . !

☆

It's a good morning, this morning. I've just finished reading a piece in the New York *Times*, the opening sentence of which goes like this: "The years ahead will see rebirth in this city." The closing sentence goes like this: "We are still brave enough to re-create New York." It's made my day for me. Immediately afterward I begin to work on my latest play. The setting? New York, of course. I've written almost twenty full-length plays, you see, and I've also written almost thirty one-act plays, you see, and every single one of them, with two exceptions (but Woodstock and Niagara Falls are still in the Empire State, at least), takes place in New York City.

I was in California about three summers ago as a guest playwright conducting a playwrights' seminar. Almost all of the aspiring young (and old) playwrights were dedicated Californians. When they would ask me for suggestions which related to their playwriting careers I would always tell them to move to New York, but they wouldn't hear of it. Not only are there eight million dramas here, but it's also the marketplace. Ironically, almost all of their plays were set in New York, and the two playwrights whom I personally considered the most promising were not Californians. They were from New York and Boston and their plays were also set in New York City.

☆

Once upon a time, I was invited to attend a small dinner party up in the Mayfair Towers on the West Side. The hostess, Elaine Dundy, was also a dear friend to Tennessee Williams, who also lived in the Mayfair Towers. Elaine had invited the two of us to her very special dinner party, mainly because I wanted her to, having expressed many times to her that Tennessee Williams was my favorite American playwright. I was really excited, already in a state of awe, nervous, overjoyed, and I could hardly wait for the event to take place.

When I left the elevator I began to walk slowly towards Elaine's apartment. All of a sudden I stopped in my tracks. I could hear Elaine's voice. She was greeting Tennessee Williams at her door. And then I heard his voice. A definite lump began to form in my throat. I knew his voice fairly well because when I was in high school up in Binghamton, New York, I used to play a record over and over again from the public library which had Tennessee Williams reading from his plays and also reading some of his poetry.

I peeked very carefully around the corner of the hallway. I could see him standing there with his arm around Elaine. I turned around real fast and went tiptoeing back to the elevator doors. I remained there until I felt that I was in control again, you know: extra-cool and everything else like that.

When I finally met him that night it was really and truly a wonderful and inspiring experience for me. He asked a number of questions, most of them pertaining to Cafe LaMama and Ellen Stewart, LaMama Herself.

"By the way, Tom," Elaine eventually said. "Len just received his first Rockefeller Grant for playwriting."

"Congratulations, Leonard," Tennessee responded. "How much was your grant for?"

I told him it was for about $6,500 for a whole year.

"Well, now," he said. "That's a lot of money: $6,500. Back in 1939 I only received $1,500 from the same people, those Rockefellers and their foundations, for a whole year too. But, of course, during that time, well, you could go to Schrafft's and order chicken à la king with all of the fresh biscuits and butter you wanted, plus coffee, for only 35 cents. So you see, Leonard: when you really think about it, we both actually got the same amount of money."

☆

A few years ago I was conducting a workshop for playwrights at Circle in the Square. It was the first day. I was a little nervous before I went into the classroom. There were twelve budding playwrights waiting for me, and once I closed the door after me, well, I knew that everything was going to be all right.

In order to make the workshop as relaxed as possible I asked the group to stand up one after the other and give their names and say three things about themselves (I myself also did the same thing afterwards). Eventually, one of my fellow-playwrights realized that it was his turn. He stood up and gave his name. Then he told all of us: "I'm married. I work in an advertising agency on Madison Avenue. I'm a playwright, also."

I told him that he should have said he was a playwright first, that the order was all wrong as far as I was concerned. I really believed I was right in saying that to him, I really did. I felt that, being in the serious situation that I was in, it was my honest responsibility.

The following week at the time for my second playwrights' workshop session he wasn't there. And he never showed up again after that.

I *know* I was right in what I said to him, now.

☆

The biggest heart-warming treat in town right now, the greatest super bargain in the city at the moment, is also totally *free*, and it takes place on one special New York City block, the same certain block, in fact, where the Dramatists Guild is located, in the happy heart of the midtown theater district. It's all for no charge and it's also "pure"—in the true sense of the word—meaning that it is not actually planned or advertised: a lovely, fascinating, unrehearsed "happening," which one simply encounters by sheer accident, if one is lucky enough.

It takes place every early night in Manhattan, while it's still light outdoors—so that you can see everything easier—and it takes about an hour, beginning at around seven o'clock, and ending at just about curtain time, at eight o'clock. (Extra treat: if you come back when it's dark, when the curtains are beginning to fall, well, you get to see the tiger too: a real live tiger on a leash, being led back to his very private, separate place in a gigantic, parked van. I mean, man: a real live tiger from out of the jungles right smack in the human heart of the Big Apple.)

The happy, harmonious block, is, of course, West Forty-fourth Street, going merrily west from restless, reckless Times Square over to equally restless, reckless Eighth Avenue: where things are *really* getting ready to happen.

The whole block is filled with a very special sort of air: the air of the circus, the carnival, the theater, all wrapped up into one bazaar-like pathway, on the sidewalks, in the street. Circus music is heard, and you can hear a carnival barker too, as well as spectators clapping their hands every so often in curious and grateful applause. The front of the St. James Theater is like being at a street circus, and, of course, why not? *Barnum* is being performed there. A brightly costumed juggler is entertaining the public out front as the nostalgic circus music comes piping out of the St. James Theater over low-keyed loudspeakers. The crowd applauds again. And now a man dressed in a red-and-white-striped shirt stands on a soap box, replacing the juggler, and he begins to do magic tricks. More applause.

Eventually, you can begin to smell the circus atmosphere, not just because of the horses that the policemen are riding, but also because directly across the street from *Barnum* we suddenly turn to see a real-live elephant: a three-and-a-half ton jungle beast in the middle of the jungle of cities! He is led out of the long, huge, parked van in front of the Majestic Theater where *Blackstone! The Magnificent Musical Magic Show* is being performed. The great, gigantic elephant is now on the sidewalk near the stage door to the Majestic Theater, along with his young trainer who proudly carries a cane-like stick in his hands. And, lo and behold! We now look into the wide-opened back door of the parked van, and the smells of the circus and of the jungle become even more real, because there is a real-live camel looking out at all of us. It's really beautiful, because the elephant and the camel both begin to dance to the organ-grinding music that is coming from the *Barnum* theater. Everybody is delighted; everybody claps their hands. The elephant does tricks for us on the sidewalk under the guidance of his trainer/master. He lies down, rolls over, gets up, stands on just his two hind feet and then lifts way up, stands on his two front feet and also lifts way up. The crowd is happily amazed. He picks his trainer/master up in his trunk and does a dizzying spin. The crowd moves back a bit; there are gasps and laughs and giggles.

A couple of hookers from nearby Eighth Avenue appear on the scene. One of them exclaims to the other: "Oh, honey, look! An elephant! I've never seen an elephant before, I mean except on television!" The two grown-up hookers begin to laugh hysterically, like two little girls. Their eyes go back and forth, from the performing elephant to the dancing, swaying camel. The other hooker says: "I never thought an elephant could be so cute, especially when he's dancing like that, but I wouldn't wanna mess around with that camel, he looks real mean to me!"

And then a man lies down on the sidewalk on his back, and with the guidance of the trainer/master the gigantic elephant slowly steps over the brave man lying down. More gasps, giggles, and, finally, loud applause when the act is over with.

The block is jammed now; the traffic is snail-like as people in taxis and cars gape out their windows, hearing the music of the circus organ grinder, the sound of the circus barker, looking in slight disbelief at a real elephant and a real camel.

It's eight o'clock now. Everybody is entering all of the theaters on the joyous block. Finally, the elephant and the camel are led into the Majestic Theater, where they both have a show to do.

The block is more or less back to "normal" again. You take a quiet, curious, satisfying look around. High above the street, as I mentioned before, there's the Dramatists Guild—and rightly, appropriately so. No other location in the world could be more perfect, more fitting, for "the home of the playwrights."

☆

First, I heard it over my telephone, when it was about midnight. It was the voice of a distressed friend who was calling from California and who had just seen it flashed over a television screen out there. It was the depressing news, so sudden, so unexpected, that John Lennon had been shot to death in cold crazy blood, right at the entrance to the place where he lived, not too far from where I live. I hung up my telephone, hoping and praying that it just wasn't true. I turned on my radio and my television set, both at the same time, wishing that I wouldn't hear anything about it, because I was struggling to believe that there was nothing to report.

It was very cold outside that night, and my radio and my television set both let me know that this was no false alarm. I decided that I would get dressed up, go out and walk over to the Dakota because now I knew that it wasn't a false alarm, and I realized how it was getting to me, and the Dakota was in such close walking distance, and, finally, because I was thinking about the first and the only time that I had met John Lennon . . . and what a very special meeting it was! He arrived alone, very briefly, at a small party, and instead of talking about his music he talked about playwriting. I never even got the chance to stop him in order to tell him how much I loved his songs. (I have always thought that his songs were all certain kinds of plays in themselves.) It was one of the warmest encounters I have ever experienced.

When I got near the Dakota I saw many people gathering around: all ages, all types. Actually, that's about all I remember: the people arriving there, the media, the policemen . . . everything else seems sort of in dreamy, unreal fog-land right now. I hung around for about a half hour, and then I walked back home. I thought that was the best thing to do, at least for me.

The following afternoon I went down to the Theater for the New City to begin casting a new play of mine. As I approached the theater I saw black banners flying in the cold breezes from the awning poles. Inside, nobody said a word about it, but everybody had copies of all three New York newspapers with them. The same thing on the subways . . . the same thing on the buses . . . all over the quiet town now. Silent souls of New York City with copies of all of their newspapers with blaring headlines, newspapers with blood-curdling, cold-blood paragraphs inside.

Another day went by. I walked by the Dakota again. It was very difficult not to, especially if you lived in the neighborhood. I was in awe of the temporary shrine that covered the fancy gates at the entrance. It was filled with all kinds of fresh flowers, photographs of John, and there was even a multicolored display of bright balloons floating above it all.

I saw a woman who was about thirty-five, maybe forty, in a nice fur coat, looking pretty elegant, go up to one of the policemen in front of the gates—the temporary shrine—and hand him a flower, a single, long-stemmed, white rose, asking him to add it to the temporary shrine, which he immediately did, very gladly indeed. I also saw a man who was about thirty-five who handed another policeman-guard an envelope which was sealed. "This is for Yoko," the man said. "Is there a chance that she'll get it?"

"She'll definitely get it," the policeman-guard replied, looking very satisfied that he was able to say it back to the man.

There were street hucksters now suddenly, all over the place, selling John Lennon buttons, Beatle T-shirts, and even single fresh flowers for the temporary shrine. Some people chanted for us not to buy anything that exploited the killing of John Lennon. I thought to myself: "Well, the guys are trying to make a few extra bucks for Christmas, what the hell. John Lennon could buy that." I almost *did* buy a flower, but then I changed my mind. Maybe I thought that the people chanting were really right . . . I don't know.

☆

Whenever I'm walking in the Times Square area (and in a few other areas around town these days too) I always know that I'll be offered a number of paper advertisements—pink, light blue, white: with bold black lettering—and sometimes there'll even be a picture or a photograph of some beautiful, sexy-looking woman in some gorgeous, provocative, really tempting-looking pose. I never refuse the pieces of paper advertisement. Over the past two or three years or more, if I had kept every one of those handout fliers, I would have a large enough collection of scrap paper in my apartment to write a whole brand-new play on, and not a short one-acter, either. It would be more like *Strange Interlude.*

I really don't like refusing all those guys on all of those street corners and in front of those doorways, when they extend their invitation. As you walk towards them and they see you coming, they usually know that you're going to accept their handout, let alone that you're also accepting their way of making a living. As you approach them they flip-and-flap their paper proclamation in a very affirmative way, definitely special, as though they were getting ready to hand you a sudden gift of a crisp, brand-new five- or ten-dollar bill. When you accept "the gift," they never really smile, but they say "Check it out!" in a way that is more friendly—like "you're one of the guys like me."

I always half-smile when I take the flier and I say "Thanks, man." If you do that they get carried away and they usually say something back to you, like: "Hey, man, you'll get a reduced rate if you check it out right now!"

No matter what you think, they've really got their hearts into what they're doing, like hustling people to buy tickets to a play they wrote. There's nothing wrong with that.

Last week I was walking along West Forty-third Street, heading toward Times Square. I'm halfway in the middle of the block when I spot one of the guys. I get ready for the "common event." He's getting ready too. He hands me a flier that is larger than most, and it is on white paper folded in half. He seems a little different than most of the other guys, and, as I said before, the flier is extra large. But I really don't think anything of it, that is, not until I accept the flier from him, and he doesn't tell me to "Check it out." And then I say, "Thanks, man." He says back to me, "Don't miss it, man! And you can bring your lunch too!"

Bring my lunch too? I say to myself, as I go on walking, maybe a little confused now, I say to myself: I wonder what kind of place this one is . . . it sounds pretty interesting to me . . . real different . . . a real class act, maybe . . . maybe I should "check it out," even though he never told me to do it.

By the time I get to the corner of the block in front of Nathan's, I've unfolded the large white paper advertisement, and what I see I don't quite believe. You wouldn't, either. It's a flier advertising an early one-act play of mine! It's part of the Quaigh Theater's Lunchtime Series in the Hotel Diplomat, which I've just passed on the block. Ironically, my play is called *Lunchtime,* and at the bottom of the flier it says "Bring your lunch!" And there's a cartoon-like picture of a naked couple having lunch in bed. It's a better come-on than most of the massage parlors could ever dream up. I laugh to myself, and I almost want to go back to the guy who handed the flier to me. But I don't. I keep on going my way. I say to myself: "Why not?!" It makes me secretly happy. I'm only concerned about one thing: I hope that the guys who come to see my play—thinking they're going into something quite the opposite—aren't too disappointed, that's all.

A favorite time:

My collection of plays had just been published. I was invited to a tiny dinner party in a penthouse overlooking Fifth Avenue in the Village. When I arrived, Clare Boothe Luce was already there, sitting on a small sofa in a cozy library, inspecting my new book of plays. We shook hands, and then I sat down in a chair opposite her.

"You must be very pleased," Mrs. Luce said to me, holding my book up.

"I really am," I replied.

"It's quite miraculous," Mrs. Luce went on. "This off-off-Broadway movement that's taking place. It would have been unheard-of when I was writing plays to have them published unless, of course, they had been produced on Broadway and were established successes. And published by Random House, no less."

Mrs. Luce then began to flip lightly through the pages of my book.

"You love it, don't you?" she said. "You love writing plays."

"Yes, I really do, Mrs. Luce," I answered.

"I can tell by the feeling I get from the book itself," Mrs. Luce continued. "Congratulations. And good luck. And don't let any of this spoil you. You must keep on loving what you love to do most. That's all that matters, Leonard."

☆

On the opening night of *42nd Street* at the Winter Garden Theater, there were crowds all over the area behind police barricades, huge spotlights panning the sky and thronging first-nighters walking along a gloriously bright red carpet that felt like soft velvet and was surely brand-new for the occasion, and which covered every part of the sidewalk in front of the theater.

The inside of the Winter Garden was slowly filling up, and you could just sense it, smell it in the wonderful air: a special sort of feeling—vibrations, or whatever—of anticipated excitement slowly surging up inside every single member of the opening night audience, like thousands of grown-up little kids, all dressed up, all looking marvelous, heading towards their seats, waiting for the magical explosion of their own individual Emerald City in each and every one of their minds of theatrical fantasy.

I have hardly ever gone to Broadway openings, and so I was really extra-impressed, to put it mildly. Being a playwright made it all twice as exciting for me, particularly proud and overwhelmed to be a part of it all.

I was sitting next to my agent, Helen Harvey, and just before the curtain went up I whispered in her ear: "Thanks very much for inviting me to be your guest tonight, I'll always remember it, and the show hasn't even begun yet!" And then we squeezed each other's hand, smiling with good luck glances coming from our eyes, as the overture finally began. The music starting, the curtain rising, the opening number—the whole audience themselves!—well, there was no way, *no way* any of us could ever be disappointed that night, or ever let down that night; for me, it seemed impossible, and I was perfectly right—it proved to be totally impossible. From the very beginning to the very end, the show was all pure and powerful joy. The whole audience rose to its feet, applauding and cheering wildly: twelve standing ovation curtain calls! It could have gone on and on.

But the producer of the show suddenly appeared onstage. The audience, recognizing that it was David Merrick, began to applaud him now, along with flashes of laughter everywhere. But Mr. Merrick looked very sad. He tried to get us to stop our applause. I heard someone remark wryly: "Oh, what's he got up his sleeve now?!"

Finally, Mr. Merrick got us all to quiet down.

And we all waited.

DAVID MERRICK (*barely audible*): This is a very tragic moment for me.

AUDIENCE (*lots of sudden laughter again, and lots of sudden applauding again*).

CAST (*most of them in the same mood as the audience*).

DAVID MERRICK (*raising his hands for us to be quiet again*).

AUDIENCE (*dead silence this time*).

CAST (*dead silence too*).

DAVID MERRICK (*looks pale and deeply troubled. Then, quickly, clearly*): This is tragic. Gower Champion died this afternoon.

AUDIENCE (*one long, gigantic, moaning gasp, all together at once, like a sudden, mammoth, blowing, sighing wind, created without rehearsal by a great throng of human beings, coming automatically, uniformly from every seat in the house, the likes of which will always remain haunting and unforgettable, and especially when thought of in terms of the contrast just a few short moments before*).

CAST (*crying, shocked, infinitely saddened, some of them reaching out to one another. Tammy Grimes holding one hand to her mouth, the other hand grabbing Jerry Orbach's hand. Orbach folds his arms with a look of utter disbelief on his shocked-looking face; Wanda Richert's face, first pained, then sobbing. Merrick immediately turns and goes to Wanda Richert, his arms outstretched, tears filling his eyes*).

AUDIENCE (*mostly silence now, sounds of crying here and there, no words, staring at the stage. I get to feeling numb all over, like everybody else: not knowing what to do. I put my hand on Helen's shoulder. She is staring straight ahead, in deep, numb thought, her lips quivering*).

JERRY ORBACH (*suddenly*): Bring it down! (*He looks out in the direction of offstage right.*) BRING IT DOWN! (*The curtain begins to fall slowly. Respectfully, to the audience*) Good night . . . !

The audience does not respond, but I remember automatically saying "Good night" back to him out loud. The curtain is down. The audience doesn't seem to know how to leave the Winter Garden. We had all been standing up during the last few minutes. Many were now falling back down into their seats. Many were just standing there at their seats.

Slowly, they move out; very little talk; Mr. and Mrs. Joshua Logan, nearby, not knowing what to do, looking very sad; Anne Baxter, in front of me, dropping back into her seat and crying; Helen finally just letting the tears take over now too.

I hear my name called; an actress friend of mine is standing behind me; we reach out and hold hands over a row or two of seats. She was a very close friend of Gower Champion's, and she tells me, "I was with him when he died. I was with him all morning. He wanted it this way. He was very happy about the show. He was very proud of it. He told us, right before he died, that we had to be here in the audience tonight, no matter what. It was his opening, and he wanted us to be here, even though he couldn't be here. He told us to be here and go to the parties afterwards, too." A pause. "Oh, yes, Leonard, he was really happy about the show. And he really didn't suffer, either." A pause. "As I said to you just before: *he wanted it this way.*"

The Winter Garden is almost empty now. The curtain is up again. The stage is dark and bare, stripped of everything. There are only two other people left in the orchestra now: Ruth Gordon and Garson Kanin. Mr. Kanin is simply standing, not looking anywhere in particular, dazed I believe, standing at his seat. Miss Gordon is sitting; sometimes her head is bowed; sometimes she gazes at the empty and silent stage.

A stagehand comes out. He is carrying the familiar arc light, used when a show is over for the night; that naked, burning bulb attached very simply, plainly, to the top of a thin, long, skeleton-like standard. The stagehand places the burning arc light in the middle of the stage and then exits.

I get a strange feeling at first, standing there in the back of the theater staring at the wide-open stage; full of hope and happiness. The burning arc light makes me think of the single burning vigil light on the altars of churches when I was growing up (and I was an altar boy once), and how the vigil light always seemed comforting to me. I feel better now, because I am thinking of lasting things . . . eternity, I guess . . . the supreme endlessness of the theater, I suppose. And as I leave the theater I think of Gower Champion and feel comforted.

☆

Here in the city I usually come back to my apartment at five o'clock in the morning, after all of the bars are closed. At five o'clock in the morning during the hot, humid, perspiring, *human,* big-city-summertime, I can hear a siren; I can hear sprinkling water too: the sanitation truck cleaning up the street; I can hear soft Bach coming from a window; I can hear the door of a taxicab slamming shut, and a person's footsteps right afterwards, and the sound of the taxicab taking off again, after hearing pleasant exchanges of lazy "good nights"; I hear a telephone ringing vaguely; I hear some glass break, followed by hazy laughter. In other words, I hear the sounds of *people,* and sounds made because of people, all at five o'clock on a morning in New York City, amid the "sweet summer symphony" of the humming of cooling electric fans and the whirring of countless air conditioners.

I begin to think of something, however . . . something very special . . . very precious and very beautiful, an incident that took place during the four days when I was visiting in the country.

I got all dressed up in the guest house because I was going to a very fancy dinner party. It was about eight-thirty and I decided, with a nice drink of Wild Turkey on the rocks in my hand, to take a little walk around the place where I was staying, just to see what was there, actually, and what it all looked like. I walked past a cluster of trees and tiny bushes, where everything was lush and green and peaceful. The grass looked like smooth, rich green velvet. It was really quiet. It was strange, yet particularly comforting. I didn't know why, but I liked it a whole lot, and it made me feel nicely delicate. I walked down a couple of old gray stone steps, which took me to a lower level. I had to duck underneath and then around a tree that looked like some wild piece of ancient sculpture. When I did this, my drink still in my hand, I found myself in an area that was also a very tiny clearing, with the green grass below me and a low ceiling of green leaves with streams of light above me. The silence seemed unreal.

Had someone been watching me enter this lovely little space of nature? I turned to my right, and there he was, looking like the perfect statue of a simply beautiful animal; gleaming eyes, like the eyes of a kind but possibly frightened human being; like the warmest, softest color of lush light brown, with cotton-like spots, standing there, in the unreal atmosphere of still green light and still green shadows, as erect and as beautiful as one of the great trees around me.

He was a baby deer, and he was cautiously alarmed, and so was I, and I was frozen too. Funny, though, the baby deer almost made me want to offer him a sip of my drink. He had been watching me unexpectedly cross over into this private little path of his, and now he made me feel as though he knew everything about me and that he knew everything that I was thinking, right there on that beautiful spot and ecstatic occasion, which I will never forget, and always cherish for the rest of my life.

I moved just a split inch towards him, my drink extended high up in his direction. But he turned around in the fastest second possible, and then, in the swiftest second of all time, he disappeared in a vast maze of darkening greenness somewhere in the oncoming night, like sheer authentic magic.

I stood there alone, quiet and still, no motion, a little nervous, perhaps, but with great joy and immense satisfaction. He had made me think that if I had asked him something, he would probably have given me an answer. I would have asked him if he had finished his latest play yet; and he would have replied, "Yes, about five minutes ago."

☆

(*Curtain up. Lights up. The stage is empty. No sets. No people. No sounds. Finally The Dramatist enters. He is alone. Now, in the background, we can hear faint sounds: traffic and music and general noise coming from the theater district in the heart of Times Square, New York City.*)

THE DRAMATIST (*to himself, out loud, sometimes to the audience*): I just met this friend of mine, a terrific actress, at a table in Barrymore's. She wasn't feeling too good. She said there were broken glass window cases in front of the Helen Hayes Theater, and they hadn't even begun to tear it down yet. I told her I really believed they wouldn't tear it down and not the Morosco either. But she believed otherwise. I went by the Helen Hayes, and my good friend was right. It was being torn down before it was even official, or whatever. I thought about the inside of that beautiful theater. I crossed the street and looked at the beautiful outside of it. I really got mad. A playwright thinks of a place first. No matter where it be, big or small, but just simply a place "for the kid to have a home for a little while," that's all . . . the kid, of course, not being the dramatist/playwright but the baby: the play itself. I remember coming to New York when I was a kid myself and seeing a play in that same theater, then called the Fulton Theater. The play I saw was called *The Seven Year Itch*, and later on I saw another play called *A Touch of the Poet*. Man, I was getting mad this afternoon! I ran over to Forty-fifth Street. I used to dream that I would have a play of mine done some day at the Morosco, because it became my favorite playhouse of them all, I don't know why. I guess it had to do with the fact that my mother and father always stayed at the Piccadilly Hotel when they took me to New York, and the Morosco was right next door to the hotel. I was also aware of the fact that it was an historic theater because of Eugene O'Neill, and in those days I must have read that bronze plaque a million times, outside the Morosco, honoring O'Neill. And I saw Kim Stanley there in *Cheri,* and I'll never forget her. And I saw *Cat on a Hot Tin Roof* there, and I'll always remember it. But now, this afternoon, the paint is peeling away on the Morosco. And next door? The little Bijou! I was really young when I saw a play by William Saroyan called *The Cave Dwellers* in that little theater, and it left a beautiful impression upon me. Now the little Bijou Theater has been torn apart.

> *A pause.*

The last few weeks or so I've been going around looking at the exterior designs of all our legit theaters, never being more fully aware of how great-looking they all are; and I'm deeply more aware of the insides of them too, now. I guess it's never too late to appreciate what should always be appreciated, right?

> *A pause.*

When I was younger, and when I first came here to live, I used to know the names of every theater on Broadway. I still do. I even knew the streets they were on. I still do. I've watched some go for good, I've watched some new ones being built. I've watched some become discos, and I've watched some being turned back from skin-flick houses to crowning little jewels again.

> *A pause.*

Aw, well: I guess it ain't all that bad then, is it now? Except, of course, to me it still is that bad! You see, everyone has his own way of trying to get to sleep whenever one is having a hard time with restlessness and just plain pure insomnia. I never counted sheep. I never counted backward from one hundred. I used to count the Broadway theaters, naming each one of them out loud as I did. And no matter what, I always began with the Morosco.

> *A pause.*

Now you know why I'm really mad, why I feel attacked and violated.

> *A pause.*

I'd better get off this stage right now. I mean: there's nothing worse than a self-pitying character in a play, especially since that character's self-pity comes from buildings rather than human beings, right?

> *A pause.*

But wait a minute now—I'm not self-pitying. I just feel cheated, that's all . . . and I'm thinking of all the other human beings out there—all of you—who are being cheated, too.

A pause.

It'll be O.K.

A pause.

It is O.K., no matter what.

A pause.

See you around.

(*The Dramatist exits. We can hear the sudden sounds of drilling and falling bricks smashing as the curtain falls.*)

GARSON KANIN

The Magic Bubble

GARSON KANIN: I frequently advise young playwrights who ask me about re-writing—that out-of-town rewriting to which we have all been subjected. To what degree should they be stubborn and stick by their guns? (The Dramatists Guild contract puts the dramatist in total control of the words.) To what de-gree should they give in to the whims of the star, the director, the producer, the producer's wife? They may be working under a good deal of pressure and persuasion—in some instances the director might have a viable, valuable idea. It could happen, but it's up to the dramatist to decide whether or not he wants that idea. So I give them a standard response: "Of course don't be inflexible, of course don't be intransigent. Rewrite, of course, maybe you will make it bet-ter. Rewrite anything and everything—except the play. Rewrite a curtain line, a character, a scene, but *don't* rewrite the play, the thing that was the magic bubble that burst and compelled you to sit down and write 'Act One, Scene One.' "

The first play I ever wrote ran on Broadway four years. The second one I wrote ran four nights. I'm not sure the first one deserved to run for four years, and sometimes I think the second one deserved to run longer than four nights. But so it goes.

The French playwright Marcel Achard once told me, "I could never work in New York theater. Everything that is new has to be a hit, a smash." I asked him, "How is it in France?" He replied, "You know what we consider to be a great playwright? One who has not *only* flops."

Thornton Wilder once stood before a group like this, in which I was sitting, and he began his remarks, "We should all agree that playwriting is not an in-tellectual pursuit. In many instances, successful plays have been written by dunderheads." He went on to say that playwriting is a knack, a gift, a trick—something akin to being able to wiggle one's ears. He pointed out that authors without any other literary aspirations or achievements have written enor-mously successful plays over and over again.

Consider this: practically every eminent playwright of the last fifty years has attempted to write novels. Robert Sherwood, Elmer Rice, Tennessee Williams, Arthur Miller, Philip Barry, Sidney Howard wrote novels, not one of them a successful novel. Conversely, Ernest Hemingway tried to write a play, John

Steinbeck wanted to write plays. Saul Bellow, winner of the Nobel Prize, has attempted plays without success. The point is that writing and playwriting are indeed two different disciplines, different crafts, different magics. I'm not going to try to explain the trick to you, because I don't know what it is, I can't wiggle my ears.

Thornton Wilder is an outstanding exception, having won prizes for his novels and written *Our Town, The Skin of Our Teeth* and the glorious one-acts, one of them, *The Long Christmas Dinner,* arguably one of the best plays ever written in any language. In England, W. Somerset Maugham seemed to straddle the curious creative river, and the same might be said of John Galsworthy. But by and large I think it is true that playwriting is a special trick which includes sensing the presence of an audience. All plays take place in the present. Even if they are laid in 1860, the audience sees them at this moment. It is happening now, he's kissing her now, he's killing him now, now, now. That's why plays, as a rule, are written in the present tense—and very few novels are written in the present tense.

You've all heard people who can tell stories. You listen because you know there's going to be a development, a climax, an end. It's going to be a story, a function with an end to it, and the sense of climax is vitally important in the construction of a play. I liken the performance of a play in a theater to a sexual experience. There is the titillation of the partner with foreplay, in this case the partner being the audience and the foreplay being the first fifteen or twenty minutes of the first act, the excitation of imagination. Then the parties need to be conjoined, as it were, and come to grips, and so on until the inevitable, greatly desired, agonizing wish for a climax. The performance of a play without a climax is akin to a sexual involvement without orgasm. There has to be the complete experience. It has to be satisfying, meaning it comes out the way the audience wanted it to come out, be it the suicide of Willy Loman or finding the wearer of the glass slipper.

Wilder also used to say that writing is a coy game you play with your own consciousness. We sit at our typewriters, we write a line, and we laugh. That happens to me daily, and I'm sure it happens to most of you. Hey, wait a minute, how is that possible? I have discussed it through the night with Chaplin, Buster Keaton, Harold Lloyd, Jack Benny, Bob Hope, Danny Kaye, Ed Wynn, Bert Lahr, Bobby Clark—and all are in agreement that what produces a laugh in the theater is surprise. There are at least three hundred thousand kinds of surprises, and variations on them, but surprise is the element. If the audience anticipates the comeback after the straight line is spoken, it is not going to laugh when the comedy line comes. If you know what is going to be said as a result of the plant line, you might appreciate it, you might say to yourself, "Wow, he thought of a good comedy line there," but you are not going to laugh, physically laugh, unless you are taken by surprise.

If that's true, how is it possible for us to laugh at something we have just written down ourselves? The answer is, we didn't know what was going to run down our sleeve at that moment. Wilder is right, you tap the unconscious when you write, you let go and it flows, and if you are really a writer you will surprise yourself every day of your life. You will be astonished to find out you know what you know. This appears to me to be the important contribution of Gertrude Stein to literature and the craft of writing. Through early medical training at Johns Hopkins, as a student of William James and as an experimenter in what was called "automatic writing," she began to discover the wonders that lay between the hidden folds of her unconscious. Wilder once asked her, "Gertrude, why do you write," and she replied, "For praise, for praise, for praise!" I don't think that's a feckless ambition. Why not? Why not some acceptance, some credit?

Q: I know that you studied at the American Academy of Dramatic Arts; did you study all aspects of theater there?

KANIN: No, no, when I went there it was strictly a school of acting. Please remember that I am a person with very, very little formal education, I went to high school for only about four months and then dropped out and never went back. But I am a disciple of Thornton Wilder's. His coming into my life was an extremely important matter, he turned out to be my school and my university, my major and my minor.

Q: When you get a play idea, how do you get it going? Do you block it out or start stream of consciousness?

KANIN: I don't think anyone *knows* how to write a play. Each subject presents its own problems: Does the form affect the content? Does the content dictate the form? In some instances I've begun to write just scenes without quite knowing where they were going to go or whether they were going to be in the play at all. But I had a rough idea of who the characters were and what their relationship was to each other. So I'd write a scene between mother and daughter, between daughter and her beau. In just writing scene after scene, I began to know the characters better. In playwriting, what it comes down to in the end is characters.

I once told Wilder I was writing a complicated play and would have to spend a year researching it. He told me, "No, no, no, no, you've got it the wrong way around. First write the play and *then* do the reasearch." He said that if you do the research first you'll be so bogged down in facts and figures and exactitudes that you'll never get around to writing the play. Write the play as a work of imagination and then do the research to get it right, if it has to be right. The job of the writer is to describe human beings.

I can imagine a small boy taking a crayon and a piece of paper and drawing a design or picture without ever having seen a design or picture before. In the wilds of Brazil, I can imagine someone whistling or singing. I can imagine someone sculpting an image or a statue. But I *cannot* imagine anyone ever writing a play who has never seen one. That passes my understanding. In order to write a play, you have to have seen or read a play; and then you think, "I can do a whole lot better than that," and you go ahead, and sometimes you do it. But playwriting is indeed one of the great creative marathons of all time, the torch being passed from one generation of playwrights to another to another to another, down through many, many ages and decades and as far into the future as our imagination can reach.

Q: What about the origin of *Born Yesterday*?

KANIN: I've often had the notion that a play is born not out of one idea, but of two (this is a little whimsical, but bear with me). You get an idea—call it the male idea—but there is another idea that serves as the female idea. When you get them together, a play can be born. I was once fussing around with the idea of a play about a girl who rents an apartment that is a little too expansive for her, and then she loses her job and has to sublet half of it. She rents it to a young man, and then he has a little trouble and sublets. . . . I monkeyed with this for a long time, but nothing came of it. Then when I was in the army and posted to Washington, I found myself in a city built to accommodate six hundred thousand people and with a wartime population of almost four million. It was not unusual to see people dining at 3:30 P.M., the only time they could get a table, or to see ten people in a taxi. It came to me that my idea for the girl in the apartment was exactly right for that situation, and so with a bright army buddy of mine, Robert Russell, we wrote it into a movie called *The More the Merrier* with Jean Arthur, Joel McCrea and Charles Coburn, and it was a success for everybody.

The *Born Yesterday* idea also came out of the wartime Washington setting, characters and experience, but it matched up with another idea—an experience I remembered from years ago—before it could finally take its present form as a play. There was a time in my life when I worked on Forty-second Street at the Eltinge burlesque theater as one of the comedians. We did five shows a day, and we had to be there almost all day. And there was this particularly audacious, vociferous stripper in the show named Belle. I liked her very much, and I would drop into her dressing room between shows to talk. One afternoon I found her reading *The Decline of the West*. She got me to read the works of Harold J. Laski. And in among all her dressing-room props, her stripper's paraphernalia, were works of Karl Marx, Engels, Dickens and some current literature. My memory of her and my Washington experience were the two ideas that combined to become the play *Born Yesterday*.

Q: Do you feel any influence from television?

KANIN: It's part of our life, like the telephone and the motorcar. There's no blinking at the fact that it's a tremendous force, and we have to pay attention to it. But as you consider the existence of television in our lives, I ask you to remember that the recorded theater is more than two thousand years old—and it isn't as though that two-thousand-year-old theater is only archaeological. I'm sure two or three of their plays are being performed somewhere in the world right now; they stand up very well. And they were *plays*, manuscripts set down by a playwright for actors to learn and eventually declaim in theater form to an audience, which sat and listened.

To me, one of the most exciting sights in all the world is to see the thousands of people, young and old, out-of-towners and native New Yorkers, streaming into the Broadway area before curtain time. They are going to the *theater* tonight, and there is excitement and anticipation in their faces. It's quite true that the batting average of the theater is low. But I've been reminded that Babe Ruth, perhaps the greatest slugging baseball player of all time, struck out three thousand times in his career. It should not be incumbent on any playwright to hit a home run or even get a hit every time he comes up to bat. But we have a tradition, a sense of continuity and deep, deep roots.

Television's instant replays are exciting and revealing, but it's not the same as being there at the game, is it? It's not the same as being part of that crowd. And movies certainly have wildly advantageous schemes of presenting spectacle and even stream of consciousness. But there is something about the empathy created in the two-thousand-year-old theater between living actors and living audience that is unique. The theater is a shoulder-to-shoulder experience sitting in an auditorium with hundreds of other people laughing at the same time, gasping at the same time, being still at the same time, learning somehow what we are meant to learn from the theater, namely, that we are all more alike than we are different.

TERRENCE McNALLY

Stage Struck

TERRENCE McNALLY: More than anything else, growing up in a town that didn't have television got me interested in playwriting—Corpus Christi, Texas, famous for being the biggest town in America without television. I used to listen to the radio and was probably the last person still listening to shows like *The Lone Ranger* and *Let's Pretend.* I remember seeing photographs of TV shows, and I made a puppet theater of *Kukla, Fran and Ollie* based on what they looked like in *Time* magazine, though I'd never seen them.

My parents were both from New York originally, and every couple of years they would visit New York and bring back theater programs and record albums. They were proud of having seen *South Pacific,* and the program was like an icon in the house. They also had the original cast album. All this made the theater seem very special to me.

Then we had something called the Corpus Christi Little Theater, which you went to see to watch your friends make fools of themselves. They loved to do plays with lots of children. They did *The Remarkable Mr. Pennypacker,* and it seemed everybody in town was in it, so it was great fun for the rest of us to go and laugh at them. I saw this amateur theater, and my parents made me aware of professional theater, but for me the best theater was the radio and in my mind, where I had to use my imagination.

I was brought to New York at five or six years old on a trip and saw Ethel Merman in *Annie Get Your Gun,* which made a lasting impression. When I saw the revival many years later, I remembered what she was going to do about thirty seconds before she did it, much more clearly than anything I've seen as an adult. When I was about twelve, I saw Gertrude Lawrence in *The King and I.* What I remember about these shows is the magic about these stars.

As the years went by, I outgrew the puppet theater and stopped listening to the radio—I was editing high school newspapers and sort of lost touch with it, I guess. I went to Columbia because I wanted to be a journalist and thought that after college I could go across the campus to the School of Journalism. But I started going to the theater every night, I'm not kidding, and that was my training. I cut out the coupons in the Sunday *Times* and sent in the checks for $2.90 for the last row in the balcony. I saw everything, I mean I saw *The Best House in Naples* by Eduardo de Filippo with Katy Jurado—no one saw that play but me and the few people in the world who were there for its three-performance run. I loved the theater, but I was still telling myself I was going to be a journalist. That's how people become playwrights, one day you wake up and realize you're a playwright. Children don't go around saying, "I'm going to be like Chekhov when I grow up." Chekhov just became Chekhov, he didn't decide to be Turgenev.

I had a full scholarship at Columbia, and I knew I could write, so senior year I thought it would be fun to write the varsity show (they had no one else to write it that year), and also it would be a way of saying thank you to the school for being so generous. I loved doing it. Then I graduated with a prize from the English Department and went off to Mexico to write the great American novel—and then I found myself writing a play, which I sent to Molly Kazan at the playwrights' unit at the Actors Studio. She said I showed talent but "I don't think you have ever been backstage or worked with real actors," because I had this wonderful scene ending where a man dumped a bucket of water over the heroine, who is sitting there in a new dress after a quick blackout. But Molly added, "I have a job open here as a stage manager, and I think you could learn a lot."

I spent two years stage managing there, but I was so in awe of the people I don't think I learned much. I looked at Marilyn Monroe a lot, saying to myself, "That's Marilyn Monroe!" There were a lot of celebrities like Geraldine Page and Kim Stanley in the classes. I was very nervous stage managing a play by Tennessee Williams with Geraldine Page, for instance, because if I did the lights wrong it would have been really terrible. So I didn't get the training I should have in that job. But I wrote a play there called *And Things That Go Bump in the Night*, and Alan Schneider directed an act of it at the Studio. He liked it and told the Rockefeller Foundation about it, and soon I was off to become a playwright-in-residence at the Guthrie Theater in Minneapolis, together with Arthur Kopit, who had written *Oh Dad, Poor Dad*.

I'd like to say that's where I started to learn about writing plays, but you can't learn when you are in a state of nervousness—even in a good sense—and excitement. It took me a long time to *listen* to plays of mine. I had a vision of my play in my head which bore no resemblance to what they were doing on the stage. I don't mean they were doing it badly, it was just different. I couldn't be in the same room with the actors. It's a terrible affliction, and I'm happy to know that other playwrights have gone through a period like this. What you wrote seems so vivid to you that the simplest "hello" you hear in your mind said one way, and even if you have Laurence Olivier in your cast, he says "hello" differently because he is Laurence Olivier. It makes you so nervous that you are not in the room with the actors—that's the only way I can put it. I couldn't *experience* my play. It wasn't like being petrified; it was like being rendered inactive because I wasn't really in an exchange with the actual experience of my own creation.

This went on through the whole production out there and even when the play was done on Broadway. But I was very lucky because my next play was directed by Elaine May. That's when I began learning about how to write and how to work with actors; learning that theater is moment-to-moment, that dialogue is like the tip of the iceberg, that plays are about what people *do*, not what they say. With that play, *Next*, I learned to accept that a play isn't something you write in your room and then rubber-stamp. You write *with* the actors, not against them, and you learn from them. Theater is a collaboration. You've got to get into the room with your creation and really look at it. With my first play, I could stand in the back of the theater and not really see it. Now I can look at one of my plays and think, "That's terrible, I have to fix that," as opposed to "It's the actors' fault" or "I hate this audience" or "They are out to get me."

I guess what I'm trying to say is, if you grew up in a town where you listened to the radio, and if you saw Ethel Merman and Gertrude Lawrence when you were very young, and if the rest of the time you were seeing your high school typing teacher playing Blanche DuBois and you're giggling when she's doing her tarantula speech, and if you went to Columbia as an English major, you weren't getting any practical training in theater. And sitting in the last row of all those theaters didn't train me to work with directors and actors. I was an audience, and it's very passive to be an audience.

Elaine May was very important for me—I could have stayed the other kind of playwright for a long time. I know people who've had several plays done and still don't think they can really *hear* them. They are still uncomfortable working in the theater. It's wonderful to write plays, but the magic really happens with that other part, the collaborative part. I'm glad I don't have that inhibition anymore, the fear that wouldn't let me rewrite or rethink or accept a perfectly valid way to say "hello," as though my plays existed only in my mind as a kind of Theater of the Head. If you're going to have your play done with actors and directors, you're going to have to learn to work with them— and I've learned that when you find the right actor, you go to the finish line with him. I was this person who sat in a corner in a rage because they weren't doing my play my way. My way? There's no such thing. You may have this tape recorder running in your head while you're writing, but then you have to let it go.

Sometimes I've written for specific performers. I wrote *Bad Habits* for Linda Lavin. I wrote *Next* for James Coco. He's someone whose voice hears the way I write, as much as my words hear the way he speaks. I've been blessed with certain actors for whom I can write well, because they hear me. They share my sensibility. When that hasn't happened, productions could be doomed. It can be no fun and very sad.

I saw an actor named Jason Alexander in *Merrily We Roll Along* and wrote his name down, and I asked him to come in and read for *The Rink*. He played eight different parts in that show, and he was superb. F. Murray Abraham appeared at a cold reading for *Where Has Tommy Flowers Gone?* He read the cab driver's speech, and he just *heard* the way it goes. James Coco was a friend of a friend of Robert Drivas, and when he said, "No one ever writes plays for fat character actors," I told him I'd do it. A weekend later I got the idea for *Next* while in a protest march down in Washington. It was very early in the war protest period, and people like my character Marion Cheever were standing at the curb shouting, "You're all Communists, get out of this country if you don't love it." I made the connection with a simple situation about the draft, which was on everyone's mind in those days. And I could just hear James Coco's voice.

Sometimes you've written a character and you can't find the right actor or actress, and you start changing the play to accommodate a performer. I've stopped doing that—I think it's better to part company or take your chances. At least you stick with the character instead of trying to rewrite it so the actor or actress will be better in it.

Casting is crucial, especially in a new play. You can compare Hamlets, but a new play is the first time the characters have seen the light of day, it's very important to present them to the audience. We took a long time with the five men in *The Rink*, and it paid off wonderfully—I'm very appreciative of the director A. J. Antoon's patience.

I've never had an awful experience like a producer asking me to make changes in order to make the show a hit. For example, *The Rink* had no chorus—it had a cast of two women and five men—and I can imagine some producers wanting a big ensemble number of an "up" number, because the second half of the show was dark. I would have said no, and I think my collaborators John Kander and Fred Ebb would have said no. I've never had that kind of an experience. I did rethink *Tommy Flowers* for a small cast in New York after we did it at Yale with a large cast, and it was compromised in the rewriting. And that was an example of a critic killing a show. Walter Kerr came to New Haven and reviewed it after we'd asked him not to. He hated it, and the New York producers vanished overnight. Fortunately, there was one left willing to do it, but in a scaled-down version. It was conceived as a kind of epic, with forty people onstage in the final tableau, and we tried to pretend that doing it with six actors wouldn't hurt it. I shouldn't have done it, but I wanted *Tommy Flowers* to be seen in New York. It's my favorite of all my work. I wanted to see it done in New York—with a cast of forty. It did shrink, no question.

I've done rewrites that made things worse—that can happen to any writer. You stay up all night working and feeling wonderful, you rush to rehearsal with the new scene, and they read it, and you can see their faces dropping. They say, "We'll stick with what we have," and you feel awful. Or sometimes the actors will say, "This is it, oh yeah!" and we wait a night or two until they know the new lines, and then it goes zloom. I think that with a play that's being performed on a nightly basis, it takes two or three performances for rewrites to begin to work. When you put in a new scene, it tends to nosedive, it is not precise, the actors are thrown by it.

The only foolproof law of the theater I know is that if the audience doesn't like your play, you certainly know it. You don't need any critic. That restlessness, that sighing, is a horrible sound.

Some actors want to be loved all the time, and it's a nightmare to work with them. They shouldn't be in my plays, because my characters tend not to be lovable all the time, and sometimes they are never lovable. Those people in *Bad Habits*—they were terrible people trying to change. You can't do that play unless you go with the playwright's vision of a very black comedy. In that sense, the playwright is final.

I hear the voices of the characters while I'm writing, but there are other playwrights who don't. If anyone watched me writing, I'd be embarrassed. I make faces and say the line. That's how I like to write. Other playwrights tell me, "It's all in the meaning of the sentence." But I absolutely hear voices.

My best writing comes usually when I feel like a stenographer typing as fast as I can to keep up with the characters I love. It's when I'm making them go word to word, line to line, that I get stuck, usually because they aren't *doing* enough, static in the worst sense that there is no real event in the scene. I teach at NYU, and I keep saying that playwriting is not people sitting in chairs talking, it's people *doing* something, and here I am after all these plays . . . sometimes you forget. You fall in love a little bit with the sound of your own voice, you think you have written a couple of great sentences. The theater can become literature, but when you are writing it's a very bad idea to sit there saying, "I am writing great literature." Try to write a good play that actors and audience will like, and if you are a good writer you will probably turn out something very like literature, but I wouldn't start out that way. I'd start out to make it practical, sturdy, something an actor can kick around a little bit. If your sentences are so fragile they can't take it, I doubt your play is going to last. The antiques I love best are those old tavern chairs you can still sit in. A play shouldn't be like those spindly French jobs.

All the great playwrights were practical people earning a living writing entertainment. Shakespeare's plays are filled with references to his competition, which was outgrossing him some weeks. Molière wasn't just a Frenchman in a wig writing couplets. These were practical men who dealt with critics, actors, sets that fell down, audiences that fell asleep. It's an incredibly *real* thing to be a playwright. Novelists with their floppy discs don't even have manuscripts anymore. Nobody comes up to a novelist, looks at his work and then comments, "I can't say this shit."

You've got to have a thick skin, but you can't be tough in an insensitive way. It's not the end of the world for a scene not to be right. That was hard for me to learn. I thought that I could be fallible in anything except a play—but the play had to be perfect. It was a big change to realize that a play could be fallible, it might need help but could be worked on, and I didn't have to do it all by myself, it's not me against them. It's nice to realize that. A playwright is not someone in an ivory tower; he has got to work with other people. You could say that's very simplistic, that's how you live life, relating to other people, but I didn't make that connection when I started writing plays. I thought a playwright was supposed to be some sort of god who controlled other people and got them to do exactly as he wanted.

Q: One of your characters, a playwright, is telling an actress friend he's done a lot of work off Broadway. She says, "That's not the theater, kid." She points to the Barrymore Theater and says, "That's the theater." Does part of you still feel that? Does part of you see the program of *South Pacific* and say, "That's where I want to be"?

MCNALLY: Probably. There are people who still have a certain nostalgia for Broadway the way it was. At the opening night of *Who's Afraid of Virginia Woolf?* I heard Abe Burrows say to Edward Albee, "Welcome to the theater." He meant it lovingly—but *The Zoo Story, The American Dream, The Death of Bessie Smith,* wasn't that "theater"? Broadway may have its financial troubles these days, but that is Broadway, that is not theater, although a lot of people confuse the two. I admit that I'm stage struck, maybe more so than most theater people. There is something *natural* about the theater. It fills some primitive need, and I don't worry about its future, even though audiences may be constantly changing.

When Birgit Nilsson made her comeback five years ago at the Met in *Electra,* I heard these two young people talking. One of them said, "I'm sort of disappointed." The other asked, "Why?" And the first one said, "She's louder on my record."

Disappointed in her live, but loved her record—audiences have changed, I swear it. This is the electronic age. If people growing up perceive theater as big musicals at a great distance, heavily amplified as they are in the Minskoff or the Gershwin Theaters, I can't imagine them falling in love with theater the way I did with Gertrude Lawrence. She wore that big skirt in *The King and I,* and there was a feeling of sashay, an English lady in white crinoline, so tactile, sensual on every level. And if you see a show at one of these modern playhouses, little specks come out. It's absurd. You look at your program and say, "That's supposed to be Carol Channing, and those loudspeakers sound like Carol Channing, so I guess that speck there is Carol Channing." But I can't imagine a young person always remembering Carol Channing in that show. We've lost that.

Playwrights were once asked to write short reminiscences of having their plays done at the Booth, the Broadhurst, the Brooks Atkinson for a little brochure put out by the League to Save the Theaters of New York. The playwrights mentioned very tangible things like the degree of smell, let alone sound and sight, that will be lost if these big new monstrosities keep going up. I don't want to pick on certain musicals that can be easily reproduced for ten companies on the road filling these 3,600-seat theaters, but if the voice cannot fill a theater, then clearly something is wrong with the size of the house.

Q: Are audiences more hostile now because they're paying more for theater tickets?

McNALLY: Probably. They're more cautious. People should go to the theater and judge for themselves, but at these prices you don't find many people experimenting. There is that second thought of "What did the critics say?"

I've just discovered a British playwright in Southern California, Steven Berkoff, who is, I think, sensational. He did a play in New York that got such bad reviews that when I got to Los Angeles, where he had a new play on, I said to myself, "That's the playwright who got such bad reviews, he must not be any good." Fortunately, someone made me go to see his play, and he's so terrific that I then flew to San Francisco just to see a new play of his. He's that good, he's worth a plane ride. But I was shocked to find myself playing the same game that Mr. and Mrs. Public play with the reviews. I was amazed that I had that capacity.

Q: Can good actors make a bad play good?

McNALLY: I don't think they can make it good, but they can fool you a little and make it less painful. Sometimes we go to the theater just to see a great clown, but I don't think an actor can make much out of a real turkey. An actor miscast can make a good play seem *less* than it is, especially if it is new. It is the first time you're going to meet the character—imagine if Willy Loman had been played by a bad actor. No doubt *Death of a Salesman* eventually would have found the production it deserved and become a classic anyway, but obviously when it was first done it had the performance it demanded.

Every so often a play is not well served by its first production. If it's a really good play, though, it will get done again—look at Eugene O'Neill's *A Moon for the Misbegotten.* It was once considered absolutely unproduceable. My first experience with it was the production Jose Quintero did with Colleen Dewhurst and Jason Robards, and I wondered how the world could not have known that this was a masterpiece. It's my favorite O'Neill play, but at one time it was scorned and dismissed. Such were the fortunes of Eugene O'Neill at that period of his life. As I was growing up he was a god, but when he died I read that he didn't have a play in print. I couldn't believe it. This amazing playwright had been allowed to be kicked around like that by the critics and the audience.

Q: Do you write with a scenario? Do you start with the idea, or the characters?

McNALLY: I try to think of a situation I'm going to enjoy spending a certain amount of time with. Usually the situation comes first and then the characters, as with *It's Only a Play*—I wanted to write about what it's like working on Broadway and going through opening a play there. Then I asked myself, "Who am I interested in, and how do they relate to this? Is it a producer, a director, a playwright?" And most of my plays have an end built in, one way or the other. The rink is either going to be torn down or not torn down. In *Next*, the character is either going to be drafted or not drafted. There are other kinds of playwriting, like Chekhov's "Maybe we'll go to Moscow, maybe we won't go to Moscow," but I have to write that last act.

Q: Can you describe the difference between writing a play and writing a book for a musical?

MCNALLY: I can think of a similarity: they're both hard.

Q: The book writer for a musical always seems to get nailed, doesn't he?

MCNALLY: Definitely. I knew that going in with *The Rink*. Everyone told me, "If you want to feel small, write a book for a musical." Well, I had collaborators and stars and a director who never made me feel anything but very, very big.

In a play, every word is yours; *The Rink* is by three of us. Sometimes John Kander and Fred Ebb would take three lines out of a scene I'd written and make them into a song. That never bothered me. I enjoyed it, and they were wonderful to work with. Perhaps when musicals were a little more tailored just for a star vehicle, a book writer may have felt badly, but I always felt I was working on a play with music, a show that had real integrity and was all of a piece, not three different things. It was organic, and I loved it very much. I never felt that we were compromised, or that I was writing to get from song to song.

Writing the book for a musical was fun—a lot of work, though, and a very different rhythm from playwriting. You wonder if you should spend your life trying to write a good play *or* a good libretto *or* a good half-hour TV comedy, which is very, very difficult because the pace is so fast in television. Plays are much more leisurely, and musicals are in between the two, in terms of how much time you have to develop a scene and give it some texture. Also, the rules change with every property you tackle. The rules that made one play work are going to disappear when you write the next play. It's a constant challenge and struggle. There's no formula for it, there's no way you could really write a book on how to write a play. You use common sense and work in the theater. That's the only way you're going to learn.

Q: How do you go about teaching it?

MCNALLY: I think it was Michelangelo who said that when he sculpted he was freeing figures already there in the stone. Teaching playwriting is freeing people to realize their potential as playwrights, if they have the gift, the real gift of writing dialogue in a situation. When I look back, I remember it was always such a struggle just to describe a room when I tried to write fiction, but I loved it when the characters were talking. My few attempts at fiction are ninety-eight percent dialogue, whereas other writers are concerned with the interior life of the characters, their emotions, their thoughts. Actors can be helpful to a writer, asking their questions like what is the subtext? what are the objectives? But you must have an ear for dialogue, a sense of rhythm. I mean, Proust is a very, very great writer, but I think anyone who urged Proust to write a play would have been an enemy of the world of literature. His gifts lie elsewhere.

Q: A lot of people are working part time in the theater but depending for their main income on outside activities. Can people really be professional if that is the case?

MCNALLY: Yes, being professional isn't just a matter of a salary. A lot of professionals work in the not-for-profit theater, developing work whose quality is very high. My play *Bad Habits* was first done on folding chairs with the same cast that eventually did it on Broadway. The actors believed in the play enough to work for six weeks free. We did *It's Only a Play* off off Broadway first, I think very successfully. We were twenty professionals, including the set designer and the director, working without the professional addition of salaries—but the work itself was very professional. Despite enormous odds, people are doing more theater today than they were when I was beginning. This seems to be against the tide of history, it shouldn't be happening, but it is. It proves that there's a reason why this form has lasted from the Greeks until today. There is something about it that people need. It's part of our food, and we are hungry without it.

MARC CONNELLY

80 Years a Playwright, and Proud of It

MARC CONNELLY: I started writing plays when I was eight years old, at about the same time Strindberg did. We both worked in the same category of subjects—social problems. He wrote *The Father*. I wrote about the escape of the Biddle boys from Western Penitentiary. He wrote *The Ghost Sonata*. I wrote a drama called *Saved by a Brave Sailor at Sea*.

We each had our own theater. He had the little Intima in Stockholm. I had the Marcus Connelly Opera House on the second floor of my father's hotel in McKeesport, Pennsylvania. Performances were given almost daily in my theater. I never really got the full schedule of Strindberg's. Prices varied, too. He charged krona. I don't know what I charged. I think if I got attention, that was considered pretty good reward.

Anyway, I was writing plays constantly. One day I heard my mother say to a neighbor, "I wish you could have seen the show Marcus wrote yesterday." This was pretty near an accolade to me, though, apparently, it was really a form of reproof. I didn't know that until later. What I had written, apparently, was something that had shocked my mother and everybody else.

I didn't write very much during school, but I guess the bug of writing never left me. When the panic of 1908 caused my widowed mother to lose the hotel she had just built and go into bankruptcy, I had to go to work. (I was the first of four or five generations not to go to Harvard.) Newspapers attracted me, and I went to work on a Pittsburgh paper—not as a reporter but as a collector of bills for classified ads. I walked all over town collecting two dollars here for this ad and one dollar there. I must have cleaned up doing that.

Eventually I did become a reporter, and after about my fourth or fifth year I wrote the lyrics for a musical comedy that was done by the Pittsburgh Athletic Association with enormous splash at one of the two big theaters in Pittsburgh. To everyone's delight, it did about $25,000 on the week, which was equivalent to about $100,000 today—not owing to my efforts, God knows, because I did nothing except write the words to some of the songs. But it occasioned a lovely Pittsburgher to commission the composer of that show and me to write an operetta, which we proceeded to do. I wrote the book and the lyrics. It came to New York for its triumphant production. A Broadway partner was taken on who looked at my script and probably detected slight flaws in it. It became one of the greatest meal tickets for every rewrite man around. By the time the show opened, I had the lyrics to one song left in it. It ran for two full weeks, and I didn't have enough money to get back to Pittsburgh. So I sponged on a friend, a former newspaperman who had an advertising job in New York, till I got a job on the old *Morning Telegraph*, which in those days was a newspaper that functioned as a sort of a sports and theatrical paper. It was known then as "the chorus girl's breakfast." While I was chasing Broadway news, I encountered a young man named George Kaufman who was doing the same sort of thing for the New York *Times*. Night after night we'd find our arms resting on the backs of the orchestra seats of the same theaters, and we became friends. We had a common intent to write plays. We decided to write a few together, and we did. The ball seemed to roll pretty well for us; we had four or five hits. Altogether we wrote about eight or ten plays and musical pieces, and we wrote skits for the *Ziegfeld Follies* and magazine articles and this and that.

I remember Fanny Brice bought a skit that George and I had written. George, I guess, was off on assignment, but I was in at the rehearsal at the old New Amsterdam one afternoon when Fanny leaned over the apron and said, "Are the authors here?" I said, "I'm here, Miss Brice." She said, "I'd like to have a joke right here." That was a rather peremptory request, I thought. So I said, "Well, what would you like? A wow, just a smirk, or would you like a giggle?" She said, "My God, they've got *degrees!?*"

Eventually, George and I decided to try to write plays alone, though George liked collaboration. But we kept up our friendship. I looked at almost everything he did. He looked at almost everything I did. We were about to write another musical play together when he had the illness that killed him.

☆

I don't know that the quality of the writing was any better back in the 1920s when we had something like 125 legitimate theaters constituting the Broadway group, but I do think there was greater concern for craftsmanship. If I seem to be leaning over Mt. Sinai here, forgive me, but I believe that, on the whole, there was more regard for structure—for architecture—than there is now. I think writers then had a greater sense of craft responsibility.

Right now we have a lot of talent that, to my mind, is handicapped by a desire to achieve a profitable entertainment rather than a good play. To my mind, right now we're going through an age of explosion. The hope for excitement seems to be behind the propulsions in today's playwright. It distresses me, because character is sacrificed, narrative is handicapped. A scene is built merely for the explosion in it.

The four principles of the Greeks are still present in a good play as they were two thousand years ago. There is first of all the protasis—the beginning. You and I sit in our theater seats, the curtain goes up. We see scenery. We start off with a very objective relationship with what's going on.

Next comes the epitasis, as the Greeks called it—the quickening. That's when the actors and the scenery disappear for us and we are with people in a place. We have gone through a process somewhat like that of falling asleep. Our minds continue to work, but they're working under a hypnoid condition. We are subject to perceptions rather than deliberation or any real cerebration.

I've used this example many times: On the way to the theater, you and I may have watched a quarrel between a man and a woman. If we paid any attention to it we might have thought that she was very much like someone we know and he was like someone we know. Well, up on stage, after we have solidified into an audience, the same quarrel may take place. But now we're omniscient. We know everything about them. We know more than the people in the quarrel know. It's odd how wise we have become. An audience, somehow or other, gets an incredible authority.

I remember a play called *Moon on the Yellow River*, a beautiful Irish play which deals with the arrival of heavy industry in a little Irish village. In the first scene, in the office of the English manager, a young fellow comes in with a rifle and a mask. He says, "Everyone in this room is under arrest!" He's wearing a pair of pants such as has never been seen by anyone in the audience before, incredible pants, the bottoms of them halfway between his knees and his ankles. Well, if the actor playing the part has authority, in about a minute and a half everybody in the audience knows that those are the only pants that that character could possibly be wearing. They're inevitable. Who gave us that authority? We *know*.

That omniscience goes on until we come to the third great movement, the catastasis, the crises, the climax. And the fourth is the catastrophe, the afterstroke, when the play resolves itself. At the conclusion of this, we are released from our hypnosis. The umbilical cord is cut, and we are returned to our original individualities.

A good playwright follows these principles instinctively. He doesn't have to know the Greek terms and definitions, but he senses the existence of these four movements. He has to feel them. A good carpenter doesn't have to know the scientific theories of displacement, but he does have to know how to hammer the nail. The practice of his craft teaches him that.

I wish the average young playwright today would be more concerned with the niceties of his craft. A beautiful play can be written by the most illiterate human being on earth and still be a great play. You can have a masterpiece written by a ditchdigger, as has been demonstrated, but you've got to have a concern about your work which is more than an enthusiasm for shock value. Don't ask, "Will this please an audience?" Ask, "Will this please me as a workman?"

☆

The theater is to me the greatest social instrument man ever invented. I have to tell you this as a confession of faith. The theater is my church.

The theater began, as you may recall, as a holy place. The first plays of which we have any record in the Western world were the satyr plays of ancient Greece, which were impromptu affairs set up on the roadside by worshippers of Dionysus on the way to a shrine. As they rested after a day's travel, they would have dances and put on amusing skits and have dialogues—anything that amused them which they thought might amuse the god. The idea behind the entertainment was to have the god Dionysus enter them. And that has been the basic idea of theater in its ancient classic sense. We have inherited that, and whether we know it or not, the theater today is still a holy place.

The ancient Greeks invariably would build beside their healing springs theaters that would seat between 15,000 and 25,000. And in those theaters, the clown was as much of a doctor as the physician a few yards away. Laughter has always been medicine.

The theater has been recognized from the beginning as a place where man has been able to examine his manners. It's been a place where bad habits have been corrected, in which morals and laws have been subtly changed, because the theater works by persuasion, not by argument, and persuasion invariably has twenty times the force of argument. That is why, as a weapon for good, the theater has twice the force of the biggest blasting powder that ever was made. That's why the theater, to me, is my church. It's my only church. And I believe in it.

The theater has given man so much more than man has ever been able to acknowledge. It is amazing to me that the theater can be regarded as lightly and flippantly as it sometimes is. I've heard playwrights talk about the theater dying. Well, you can't kill the theater, because it's not only part of man's birthright, it's part of man. It's part of man's genes. It survives as man survives. You can't kill it.

The playwright is just as important as any priest that ever was, because he *is* a priest. He's a very valuable element in any society. He has a right to be proud. I'm very proud. I hope I'm humble as a workman, but I'm proud to be a playwright.

Marc Connelly

Part Three
OUR PROFESSION

As former Dramatists Guild President Stephen Sondheim observed in his Part Two dissertation on musicals, writing is a lonely occupation—playwriting included—until the moment when a script is prepared for production. Even then, there is often only one author per show, so that opportunities for dramatists to get together and trade ideas and craft information are few in the normal course of their professional life. Under Mr. Sondheim's presidency and continuing under today's leadership, however, the Dramatists Guild (Peter Stone, president, Terrence McNally, vice president, Sheldon Harnick, secretary, Ruth Goetz, treasurer, David E. LeVine, executive director) has provided for a steadily increasing number of arranged discussions of all aspects of play and musical theater authorship, some of them formally staged in front of audiences, others taking place privately to encourage the most uninhibited exchange possible. All were recorded and many were published in the Dramatists Guild Quarterly to be shared by the whole Guild membership. Here is a selection of them.

BROADWAY PLAYWRITING: IMPOSSIBLE DREAM?

Frank D. Gilroy, Moderator
Jules Feiffer
William Gibson
Murray Schisgal
Lanford Wilson

FRANK D. GILROY: I don't think there's a sufficient audience to sustain a play on Broadway today, other than a musical or an out-and-out comedy. I want to emphasize that this is the case *regardless of reviews*.

I take that as a given, with rare exceptions. How do we deal with it?

WILLIAM GIBSON: I came here thinking that your proposition might be dubious. I'm not sure yet that it's self-evident.

JULES FEIFFER: How about British plays?

GILROY: They would be exceptions.

LANFORD WILSON: *Should* we be working for a Broadway situation? I don't, I found an institutional answer, I work at Circle Repertory. There was no one beating down my door asking me to do a play on Broadway, and when I finally did I had two flops in one season. I don't like to think that I reeled from that blow, but I did. I didn't work again for a whole year. To me, the Circle was a refuge. Just to start myself writing again, I went down there and mopped the floor, answered the phone, was around my friends again, and eventually it became logical for me to write something for them. I started doing little sketches, refocusing on the actual work rather than on the reception of the work.

FEIFFER: That's the unstated part of it that's so important: the ego damage done by the reception of your work on the part of the people who—logically, emotionally or intellectually—you don't care about. They can kill you if you take them seriously, and there's no way of *not* taking them seriously, whatever you may think about them.

WILSON: I was running away, trying to put a buffer between me and that situation, so that I could continue working. I've written a lot in the last five years, but in that short experience I had with Broadway I was under so much pressure that my focus was in the wrong place. I was trying to write a great play. God forbid we should try to write a great play.

FEIFFER: You brought *me* to the Circle. I went to the last performance of *The Hot l Baltimore* when Circle Rep was still uptown at Broadway and Eighty-third Street, and I saw that this was the kind of theater I wanted to write for. I was inspired by the production, by the play, by the sense of community on the stage.

There is something about finding a place where you can *do* your work, a theatrical home. It protects you. In your case, Lanford, you do a play down there first; if it moves and makes it, fine. If it moves and doesn't make it, that of course is disappointing for the short term, but it doesn't interfere with your work.

WILSON: You deliberately focus on the production at Circle. If it goes on, fine. If it doesn't, you've protected yourself because you can say to yourself, "I didn't *do* it for Broadway, I did it for the subscription audience down there, and we fulfilled that, and I can now do the next play I want to write." It's tricky—you're playing games with yourself. The focus really does have to be on just the work.

FEIFFER: You're playing games only in the sense of the logic of the commercial theater, which all of us have been brought up to think of as normal.

WILSON: Yes, it's difficult to get that long shot at midnight in the rain out of your head, the one where they open the papers, read the rave reviews and jump up and down.

GILROY: In our generation, in the back of the mind lingers what I always think of as the Moss Hart *Once in a Lifetime* syndrome. Your play opens on Broadway, and the next morning you grab some money out of the box office and take your family out of the tenement. That dream used to be a little bit possible, but it isn't possible, it doesn't exist any more. For years I paid lip service to this fact but I noticed when I came back with a new play I still had in the back of my mind that it could happen. What I feel now is, even if one were to *get* the reviews, the economics are such that the dream is not tenable. If I want to live as a playwright, I have to forget these six blocks. I have to have my plays done anywhere and get over the idea that, after Broadway, anywhere else is a bit demeaning.

WILSON: I was wonderfully prepared for knowing that Broadway is not what I want by *The Seesaw Log*. I read it and said to myself, "That has nothing whatever to do with the process as it should be, or as it could be—the dream." I saw that play and was knocked out; and then I read that book and said, "Oh, no!" And that was a *success* story.

GIBSON: Can you make a living that way today? I know I'm not making a living writing for Broadway.

GILROY: Who is? Lanford's the only one.

FEIFFER: Bill and Frank and Murray wrote plays that were received very well and had successful commercial runs. Do you think you'd find a Broadway producer and get them on today?

GILROY: I doubt it extremely. That's what I think has changed. But if you want to know what I'm maddest at myself about, that I feel like a dope about, it's that I put my head down on the block and gave away a large percentage of my subsidiary rights at twenty-one performances on Broadway. That's the part I resent. I could have these plays done all over the country and live on my subsidiary rights. I'd say to other playwrights: guard those rights.

GIBSON: For the sake of five more performances, maybe, you gave them away.

GILROY: I gave them away because of New York. But what I'm saying is, authors of other than musicals and out-and-out comedies now have to think about themselves and their work in a different fashion. As Lanford and others have done. For the play to have a life—numerous productions or a tour or whatever—treat New York as another stop somewhere down the line.

The audience that comes to see your play in New York is in no way superior to the audience that comes to see it in any other city. As a matter of fact, the Broadway audience is probably an inferior audience because of the price. They don't go to the theater regularly any more. They come to New York once a year and want to see *the* hit. They want to see the one that's won all the awards, that they're sure is going to be running so they can go back and brag to their friends. When you pay $45 to go to the theater, there's a whole different area of expectation.

GIBSON: I've retired from the theater three or four times—it's very easy to retire from but not too easy to stay out—and I live in Massachusetts. I don't think it's demeaning to work for other than Broadway audiences. I don't have that feeling. I got interested in Catholic theology a half dozen years ago, and I've written three church plays which I produced and directed for a congregation of worshippers. That's all they are, church plays, with a production budget of about five or six dollars. Norman Mailer came up to Stockbridge and dropped in to see one of them and found it ridiculous that so much energy was going into such a small project. But I don't have that value.

I've been to several theater conferences with important critics and producers, and everybody talks about money. I've never at any of these meetings heard any of these people talk about the theater in terms of that which I think has brought us all into it: namely, that we wish to use it as an expressive instrument. If there's a medium you can use as an expressive instrument, and you're able to work in it, you're in clover, whether you're making a living or not; in clover most people never find. And then if you can make money besides, that's marvelous. But it doesn't seem to me it should be in the grain of everyday expectations. Therefore I take it quite as much for granted that I can do a play with a church group of amateurs, and feel very happy if we raise two or three thousand dollars for the church on ticket sales, as doing a show like *Golda* where you're dealing with all that Broadway stuff.

I envy Lanford's solution. It's a solution that playwrights have always wished to come to. At one time I spent several years fooling around with the Berkshire Theater Festival, trying to make it a home for theater people in the summertime. Odets found such a home with the Group Theater. It was like all home life—blood flowed on the kitchen table every night—but still it was home.

WILSON: At Circle Rep we give up all that Broadway expectation and just concentrate on our little 160-seat theater. All of the Broadway stuff comes about incidentally.

GIBSON: In the natural flow of the business aspect of the culture.

WILSON: Exactly. When things were deemed commercial by a Broadway producer, they were moved. When they weren't—and of course it was always the better work that wasn't (*The Mound Builders* is still the best thing I've done, but no one would have been interested in it for a minute)—they weren't.

GIBSON: That's in the nature of the beast. If somebody can make a buck out of it, it will move into that arena where they can make the buck. And if they can't make the buck, then it stays on the level where you're just doing it expressively (and I agree with you, we're sort of playing games here).

MURRAY SCHISGAL: Perhaps the only way to address the question is subjectively and to work from one's own experience, one's own feelings in terms of the theater. That is precisely what Lanford and Bill have done. They're coming out of their own environment, Bill in Massachusetts and Lanford in the Village. For myself, I have to begin by saying that working in the theater has changed radically—for economic or other reasons, it doesn't matter for the moment—so that those of us who started as writers in the theater twenty or twenty-five years ago and enjoyed great opportunities both on and off Broadway find that we no longer fit in. We have not evolved associations with repertory companies so that we can work with them in a mutually advantageous way. We find ourselves in a bit of a bind.

Underlying that is a kind of sadness that the theater as we knew it, a theater which offered opportunities, a theater which rewarded good work, seems to us to be nonexistent. Suddenly it's a very strange animal out there that we're not very well acquainted with. Broadway is like a catbird, suddenly it's intimidating, suddenly it's doing all kinds of things and getting all kinds of notices that don't jibe with what we consider to be work that warrants this kind of attention. Off Broadway is nonexistent.

Now, I in my own mind, after I did the play *All Over Town* on Broadway, said to myself, well, maybe I should grow up. I have to make a living writing. That's how I earn my living. So I had to decide for myself: do you want to keep shooting craps with Broadway or can you perhaps turn to something else? So I decided to turn to something else. I wrote a novel and screenplays and what-not; also working, oddly enough, off off Broadway when I wanted to do something in the theater, expecting nothing and getting nothing other than the fun and excitement of doing it. But in terms of where I'm putting my energy as a writer, the bulk of my time is allotted to work on screen plays. I've done this because I had to come to the conclusion that in terms of paying the bills, the theater didn't seem to me a fair shake anymore.

But I want to say that we cannot disassociate ourselves from the knowledge that we have accumulated by working in the theater. I find it very tricky to talk about the theater without talking about Broadway, because if you're a major-league ball player you want to play in the major leagues. That's where the action is, that's where the attention is, and subsidiary rights are enhanced immeasurably by appearing on Broadway and getting that national focus. Therefore, giving away a percentage of your subsidiary rights may not be a bad idea in the long run if your play gets any kind of positive reception. How your play has or hasn't done in New York is very important in terms of getting regional theater and stock productions.

GIBSON: That is still true, but it's not as true as it once was.

SCHISGAL: I gather from what you've said so far that you've erased from your mind the notion of doing a play on Broadway. As for me, I may do it off off Broadway, but I always have the notion that if this happens and that happens, who knows? I don't know how one can separate the reality of the Broadway theater from working as a playwright in New York.

FEIFFER: I would face the prospect of another Broadway production with absolute horror. It would take an awful lot of convincing for me to go into one.

SCHISGAL: You're making a living as a writer in other ways. Therefore you can play this game with Broadway. But a guy who's concentrating on working in the theater, I don't know that he can.

FEIFFER: Playwrights, like many novelists and all poets, are going to have to stop thinking of themselves as making a living out of the work which they do because they love to do it. They have to find other ways of making that living. In most cases the life of a screenwriter is very, very frustrating; nonetheless, it's a living, and a very good living. Some writers earn their living through academics, others by other means. But whether this is a permanent situation or not, the Broadway theater doesn't exist any more as a commercial possibility for enough writers to make a serious difference. Because of a number of historic changes, commercial realities, cultural change, the disappearance of that audience that used to exist, Broadway is no longer able to satisfy the number of good writers that are around. They have to find other ways of expressing themselves; or, while expressing themselves, feeding themselves and their families.

SCHISGAL: Has your attitude toward working in the theater changed over the past ten or twenty years?

FEIFFER: It changes back and forth. I never saw myself as a potential success as a Broadway playwright. I always hoped, obviously, to strike it lucky and have a fluke.

GIBSON: Did you think of yourself as a committed playwright, or was playwriting one of several things you were doing?

FEIFFER: Once I began writing plays, I began thinking of myself as a playwright, as much as anything else, more than anything else. Theater became a kind of addiction which made commercial success or failure beside the point when one was in the middle of one's work. Obviously it becomes important when you're about to open.

I became well known as a cartoonist, and I was always a theater fan. Knowing the kind of play I was likely to write, I often said to myself and others that I wasn't going to get into playwriting because any play that I liked, that I thought was any good, invariably closed in seven days. Well, I wrote *Little Murders*, and it opened and closed in seven days. I was absolutely right about the business I was getting into, but by the time I'd written the play it no longer mattered. That's my point: the love for the work becomes the final proof of one's interest in continuing doing it. So I find now, having written one successful screen play and having gotten paid an awful lot of money for another screen play which may never be made, I'm dying to go back into the flop business. I'm dying to write some more plays that would have good productions, that would please me, that nobody would come to, but I'd be satisfied.

SCHISGAL: I disagree with you. For the great majority of writers it's a very real and immediate concern. How do I work as a playwright in the theater and hope to earn some kind of remuneration whereby I don't have to go on welfare? I don't think it's fair to suggest to those who have been working in the theater over a number of years that they write for love.

FEIFFER: I began by saying that most writers today *don't* make their living out of their writings.

GIBSON: They never did. When Faulkner was publishing his novels in the 1930s, they sold three thousand copies. Dos Passos novels sold three thousand copies throughout the nation. I'm talking about the bulwark of our culture in the novel. They did not make a living writing, and that was fifty years ago.

SCHISGAL: If I were a young playwright who said to you, "I have a part-time job clerking in a shoe store, can I hope one day to make a living in the theater? Is that a reasonable expectation, or should I forget any idea of earning a living at this craft?" how would you answer?

GIBSON: I would say it's not a reasonable expectation, but it's not a hopeless one. One out of a thousand might make it. I don't have to imagine such writers; I taught them at Brandeis. They have plays, no one is doing them, they're working behind counters.

FEIFFER: I'd say, "Shoe clerk, stick to your last."

GILROY: I look around the table at Dramatists Guild Council meetings, I see maybe one person who makes his living as a playwright.

WILSON: Before *Talley's Folly* opened on Broadway I was doing what everyone else was doing: a television play a year, a commission to do *Summer and Smoke* as an opera, and so forth.

GILROY: I know a successful professional writer about my own age who has always dreamed of having a play on Broadway. He has a play that people want to do in other places, but he can't bring himself to surrender it. I've explained to him that he's chasing a dream that doesn't exist anymore, and he says, "Don't tell me, you've tasted it, it's my dream and I want it." I hope through this discussion to reach some of the younger playwrights and tell them it's a very false goal. I realize how I've hurt myself by pursuing it.

WILSON: The energy you can put into that hope instead of into the work, the next play and the one after that . . .

GILROY: Exactly so.

WILSON: The road to Broadway, I swear, goes through off off Broadway, Louisville, Mark Taper Forum, Arena Stage. Where are your producers now? They're artistic directors of regional and other groups.

GILROY: Or they're dead.

WILSON: No one has come along to fill their shoes. There's not one exciting, innovative producer that I know of looking for scripts to do on Broadway today.

GILROY: You can't dismiss the ticket prices, which pretty much restrict the Broadway audience to the affluent and unadventurous. Instead of these new cavernous theaters that resemble converted garages and charge even more, we need intimate houses at modest scale. If that need is deemed unrealistic on economic grounds, we, to survive, must look elsewhere.

Sam Shepard has been the wisest guy in the world. He's never had anything to do with Broadway, but he's worked out a way of leading a very active life as a playwright. I could have done years ago what he did, except I have that damned Broadway glaze. Having tasted it a bit, I wanted more. I've now reached the point where I get just as much satisfaction out of knowing a play of mine is being performed for Chicago audiences as in New York.

GIBSON: I'm not sure we have a choice in this matter. I think you're wasting your energy berating yourself. Shepard's talent and personality (and I don't know very much about either) dictated the way he went.

I said that we use the theater as an expressive instrument; and when we do, we have in mind somebody who's hearing the sound we make. There's a kind of hypothecated audience out there for everybody who writes, different when you write a poem from when you write a play. Part of the "tragedy" of getting old in this business is that the audience dissolves out from under you, and then you no longer know whom you're addressing. For older playwrights, there's nobody out there to talk to.

Gilroy felt his audience was here, and Shepard felt his was elsewhere, and both worked accordingly. Arthur Miller said recently, "If it doesn't happen in

New York, it doesn't happen." By New York, he meant these blocks around here. It's still a fact that if a play is notorious on Broadway it gets done all over the world.

WILSON: If success on Broadway is now an impossible dream for a playwright just coming up, there are other encouraging signs: for example, Sam Shepard's *Buried Child* winning the Pulitzer Prize and being done all over the country, and deservedly so. It certainly didn't appear on Broadway; as a matter of fact, it closed off Broadway before it won the prize.

GILROY: I went to see it when it came back again at the Circle Rep, and I responded to it enormously.

GIBSON: There's a prior question here: are we losing our audience on account of, maybe, we're boring?

GILROY: I might have believed that at one point, but some plays have come along that even got good reviews. For example, a play at Circle in the Square called *Spokesong, or The Common Wheel,* one of the most delightful I've seen in the last couple of years, got wonderful notices, but lasted only seventy-seven performances.

GIBSON: Do you consider *A Lesson From Aloes* a serious play?

GILROY: Yes, and it closed. That's exactly my point.

GIBSON: All right, let's assume for the sake of argument that the audience no longer exists.

GILROY: It exists, but you don't get it in the proper concentration to make a profit on Broadway. You have to get at them in the way Lanford does.

WILSON: The Broadway audience didn't come to see my play. They came to see Judd Hirsch, the star of *Taxi* on TV. When we replaced Judd with an actor who also was very good indeed, the gross fell by two-thirds.

GIBSON: That's why we go out after stars when we're doing a Broadway show. So you corroborate what Frank was saying. But I don't know whether the audience ever *did* exist for the play. Robert Sherwood used to say that whenever he wrote a serious play he always got Lunt and Fontanne to be in it because that was the only way it could make a buck.

WILSON: Probably it's always been true.

GIBSON: That's my point.

GILROY: Bill, in the back of your mind you still cling to the idea—I can feel it—that you're doing this play, and if it's as good as you think it is it'll be just as successful as *Two for the Seesaw.*

GIBSON: No, I do a play, I give it to the agent, I try to forget about it and go on to something else, because I love writing for the theater but I hate working in the theater. I hate casting, I hate rehearsing, I hate directors. I especially hate costume people and set designers. To me, the whole production process is a great burden. I wish it didn't exist, because I'm a man of words, not a man of the theater.

I have a new play, by the way, a very severe play, one of the church plays, and finally a group down in Washington did it. It was pretty well received. The Washington *Post* said it had more dramatic meat in it than ten typical Broadway plays put together. I can't get a production in New York.

GILROY: So what's your next step?

GIBSON: I'm writing this other play, I'm absorbed in its tensions, I'm living in that other state of consciousness we feel when we're creating.

GILROY: When I was president of the Dramatists Guild I tried to set up a program marrying some of our members to the wonderful theaters in colleges and regional arts centers. I got in touch with a great many and tried to get them to take, not a retired playwright, but a working playwright who would profit by having such a theater at his disposal. The playwright would be in residence and would give seminars or whatever, but his first obligation would be to his own work. I spoke to academics and playwrights, and they thought it would be a great program; but when I finally tried to perform the marriage, I ran into difficulties on both sides. After two years, I managed to get one playwright to go to one university—and he left when he was offered a screen job. But this is one possible avenue; the playwright has first call on the college theater and would impart whatever knowledge he wanted to impart in whatever way he wanted to do it—but he wouldn't be obligated to anything except to use those facilities. It would be risky. Maybe if you planted twenty-five playwrights, only five would be productive. But let the colleges and regional theaters share some of the risk that we face every day of our lives.

FEIFFER: And now the bad news: that alternative is full of the same sort of pitfalls Broadway and off Broadway are full of—what some of them get you to sign, the rights that they ask for, are increasingly scandalous. They don't get away with it with established playwrights, but they get away with it with the younger ones. They get the right to be billed as an official producer of the play when it's put on anywhere else in a first-class production. They get a healthy slice of the writer's and the producer's royalties. They tie up rights so that if they're unable to do anything with the play themselves, you the writer are stuck with having them on your back while you're trying to get somebody else to do something.

WILSON: You're hobbled with an unacceptable previous contract.

FEIFFER: As a beginning playwright, you're so grateful for any kind of attention, you'll do anything to get the play on, not recognizing the fact that you're peddling away all kinds of possibilities.

GIBSON: On the other hand, just how many playwrights have been impeded in their future course by signing these contracts?

FEIFFER: We're talking about a field that is opening up more and more as a vital alternative. In my case, I see more and more of my work going toward these theaters. It's not going to be a problem for me, because I can end up getting the contract I want, but it can be a problem for writers who aren't established. It's important for us not to set precedents that might become injurious to the not-yet-established writers.

GIBSON: Regional theaters seem to me to be characterized by great ambition to do the premiere and no interest in the play otherwise.

FEIFFER: That always was the case.

WILSON: Premierism is a little less now than it was.

FEIFFER: It's the star system. The whole country—writers, universities, you name it—is interested in show biz. It's a peculiarly American problem. I don't think one finds it abroad.

WILSON: In Germany, plays are often done in five or six theaters within a week or a month.

GILROY: Why can't we do that here?

WILSON: I believe we can come to that, through one or another of the regional theater organizations.

GILROY: If I gave you the opportunity of opening a new play in six different places simultaneously across the country instead of in New York, would that not be an exciting alternative?

GIBSON: What happened to that American Playwrights Theater?

GILROY: It was ahead of its time, and it's now defunct. Each year I read all the plays I haven't seen that are nominated for the Hull-Warriner Award given by the Dramatists Guild Council. The ones this year were almost all from off Broadway. I was amazed—here was all this talent, one exciting script after another, none of it on Broadway, all of it coming to us from elsewhere.

SCHISGAL: Frank, the gist of your original question leads to this conclusion: it is wholly unreal for a playwright working in the theater today to think in terms of Broadway. Instead, he should consider the alternatives, concentrate on the work and proceed almost as if Broadway weren't there.

WILSON: Exactly.

GILROY: Let Broadway be a potential bonus somewhere down the line, the way Lanford is doing. You want your work to have a life. If a play comes to New York and gets good reviews but fails, the stock and amateur rights may be worth more because it's played New York; *but* if the play fails *and* gets bad reviews, the play is dead for years before you can do anything else with it, and you've given away forty percent of the rights besides. There is a healthier way of proceeding.

SCHISGAL: Almost no one presents a play to a producer nowadays with the expectation that it's going out of town and then coming in to New York. That doesn't exist any more.

GILROY: Brendan Behan used to say, "Any playwright who doesn't have a play on Broadway is in exile." I believed that, but I don't believe it any more. Take the late Preston Jones—he had these three plays, *The Texas Trilogy*, and they had a whole life until they came into New York. I have a feeling that the same thing is going to happen to Preston Jones as happened to Paul Osborn with *Morning's at Seven*—thirty or forty years from now someone will do his plays on Broadway again and they'll succeed.

If you get chopped enough, no matter how tough you are it has to affect you. We very seldom meet as we're meeting here to talk things over, so we all think of our problems as unique. I know very few playwrights in whom I don't detect an abiding bitterness, and we're not even aware of it—I include myself. Something gets corroded by this Broadway system that goes to the heart of your work. And it's unnecessary. When I go to the Broadway theater I look about and say, "Is this the audience I'm writing for?"

FEIFFER: We've been talking about the writer's problem, but I think there is also an audience's problem. It's not as if an audience didn't exist at one time. That audience has aged and has been winnowed out of the process, but it's not as if literacy won't sooner or later make a comeback.

GIBSON: "Literacy will make a comeback." I hope you're right.

SCHISGAL: We ought to get uniforms that say that.

FEIFFER: I don't think Broadway can go on forever as it is, in spite of the record-breaking grosses.

GILROY: Specious bookkeeping. A meal made up almost exclusively of dessert.

FEIFFER: What we may see eventually is a meeting of all the different interests in a kind of composite theater, with three five-hundred-seat houses in each single Broadway house, or the way the Guthrie is in Minneapolis, with one larger house and a couple of smaller houses. People can go in for a set admission charge and see one or two or three things. In an umbrella facility they'd be able to put on works of quality, works of commercial interest and works of obscure value, allowing the audience to choose which it wants to see.

Nothing is ever fixed in a culture. We have a tendency to think that the bad drives out the good, and maybe it does for a while, but the good always makes a comeback. It may be tentative and not very long lasting, but there continues to exist, quietly, not only a pursuit of craft but a pursuit of excellence. We need that—it may be just a minority need, but it's a need that has to be met.

WILSON: The schizophrenia of writing is so strange. When I'm writing—I'll say "I," but I have a suspicion that it's "we" and that Beckett feels the same way—I am concerned *only* with that piece, those characters, as much craft, truth and excellence as I can get into it. I'm trying to make the most wonderful piece I possibly can. We all are.

GIBSON: That's right.

WILSON: That's why it feels so exciting. But then when it's finished, schizophrenia time. I'm very proud of the piece, and I want the entire pie for it. I don't want a workshop in a two-hundred-seat house in Louisville if I can have the Booth.

I'm very different from Bill—I'm thrilled by the rehearsal process. I love the designers. They're all good buddies of mine down there at Circle Rep, and I like to be around them all the time. I'd go crazy in a studio by myself, I couldn't even write there. How do we keep our eyes off of that goal which has been the traditional American reward for playwriting excellence?—a three-year run at ten percent of the gross.

GILROY: In his life, a playwright may have, let's say, six Broadway productions. Four weeks' rehearsal each time means the playwright spends twenty-four weeks of his working life in the theater. It's no wonder he enjoys every last moment of it. I do love it.

GIBSON: I didn't say it wasn't fascinating, but so is a rattlesnake.

GILROY: There's a picture here at the Guild that represents to me what the Broadway theater was to older playwrights. It shows Howard Lindsay and Russel Crouse attending a rehearsal. One of them has his feet up. You can tell from their expressions the rehearsal is going well, and there's no place in the world they'd rather be. In those days a Broadway playwright knew he was at the center of the world. A pipe dream today that we can no longer afford to tolerate.

FEIFFER: That feeling can be translated into the theater of today. I once had a reading of my second play, a political play called *God Bless*, at Yale. The play was a failure, but the reading took place the day after the assassination of Martin Luther King. All the right forces were at work to bring out the political rage in the play itself. It went off like a piece of magic, it was one of the great theatrical experiences of my life. It didn't work ever again that way.

There were days when *Knock Knock* was in rehearsal, with Judd Hirsch figuring out how he would go at this part. His development was totally at variance with what I had seen in the script while writing it, and yet it was such an improvement that I felt a wonderful treasure was being presented to me. Other days I would feel like an intruder on somebody else's work in the rehearsal process. It sometimes made me wonder what the writer's job is here. I resent the fact that I don't have a real job in production except to be the cop, making sure they do all the things I want them to do.

SCHISGAL: If the director is any good, he'll always make you part of the rehearsal. He wants your ideas. It's the bad director who feels threatened by you, who makes you feel you have no place there.

GILROY: Either way, younger playwrights should avoid focusing their energy on the Broadway process. We all agree that if we have an idea for a play we sit down and write it. But I'll bet there are things that all of us have let go by, ideas that we could have spent time on, except that in the back of our minds we said, "Wait a minute, it's not the home run, it's not big enough, it might turn out to be only a one-acter." We keep looking for a home run, but in order to have a ball game you have to have singles and doubles too.

We don't realize how we betray ourselves in little ways. The Ensemble Studio Theater has a one-act play festival, and they asked me for something. I had nothing, but prompted by the invitation I wrote something which gave me satisfaction when it was done. It reminded me what I could have been doing all this time if I'd attached myself to a theater. But no, I wanted to own Forty-fifth Street again. Even when I was saying something else, that's what I was really aspiring to.

FEIFFER: I was brought up on the same movies you were, and on the basis of M-G-M and Warner Brothers I always wanted to see my name up in lights on Broadway. When I finally got a play on Broadway, the whole marquee system had changed. My name was up there in black and white, and it didn't have the same value.

WILSON: I was so disappointed in the Brooks Atkinson marquee, because you can't see it from Broadway. You can only see it from Eighth Avenue, and it's just not the same, somehow.

FEIFFER: Because of this traditional idea of the Broadway theater we think of writing in one form: a full evening. Why do we have to? Why not thirty-minute or forty-five-minute plays, or whatever? If enough people are turning out quality material, there will be a way of getting it on. First, the work has to exist; then, eventually, there will be a market for it.

GIBSON: You can say that to a poet or a novelist, but it's hard to say that to a playwright—production is part of the instrument. I taught a playwrights' seminar at Brandeis for a couple of years, and the question always arose either explicitly or implicitly whether their talent justified them in devoting their lives to playwriting. I never made any attempt to answer that question, except warning them that the theater is a horrible business and advising them that if they wanted to write plays they should try to hook up with a group somewhere, anywhere.

When I was growing up, to be a playwright meant to become Philip Barry, or Douglas Fairbanks Jr., in *Morning Glory*. That ideal existed, but what is the ideal the young playwrights in college have today? How do they picture themselves? Not as Philip Barry any longer, that world has gone, it is no longer a viable ambition. They model themselves after Lanford, they see themselves as in some way being productive and enjoying a position of respectability as authors.

FEIFFER: When I was teaching at Yale, an enormous influence on the young writers was Sam Shepard. They weren't looking toward commercial Broadway productions.

GILROY: I don't know whether or not Shepard was forced into his decisions, but they worked out fortunately for him. He's very wisely found an audience that sustains his work. What we're really talking about here is: how do you find your audience? You don't find it in these six blocks.

FEIFFER: First, how do you identify your own voice? Once you identify your voice, that voice is going to tell you who your audience is. Every time it seemed that I might have a big voice, when my plays were on Broadway and I heard that unintelligent mob laughter, it totally dislodged me from my own work. I started thinking in terms of gags. I had to get the sound of the audience out of my head before I could go back and do any legitimate work.

WILSON: I don't think about the audience at all when I'm working, but when I get the play on I'm awfully upset if I'm not grabbing them. Every once in a while you write a line and say to yourself, "That's an absolutely shameless line, but I'm not going to change it because it's going to bring down the house."

GIBSON: I think there's a preconscious vision of an audience. I don't think about an audience when I'm writing a play, but I'm in a different gear when I'm writing a poem. The difference in gear is that there is a preconscious anticipation of one kind of audience as compared with another kind. In that sense, the culture influences what we write.

GILROY: There isn't anybody in this room who hasn't given me pleasure, and we keep drifting back to what we all love: we all love the theater. What is stopping us? I think the rules have changed. And I think we must heed Shepard's example or abandon the game.

SCHISGAL: Everything you're saying is tied to the fact that if one doesn't hear it on television, then it seems not to have happened. People ask me, "What are you doing these days?" In the past year I've done four plays in four different productions: two off off Broadway, one at the Cincinnati Playhouse and one at the John Drew Theater. I also had a novel published. Yet I'll run into somebody who'll say, "You're not working?"

Not doing a play on Broadway doesn't mean I'm suddenly not working in the theater. The point is, it's obligatory to keep working where you *can* work.

GILROY: Would the idea of a university connection seem attractive to you?

SCHISGAL: No, because that's not the motivation for writing a play in the first place. If I have an idea, I'm going to write it; *then* I will try to think where I can have it done. The university idea doesn't help me any, because I don't need that place in order to work. All I need, frankly, is whatever my imagination can turn up. We cannot confuse ourselves as to what our work is: our work is writing plays as best we can. After our work is over we have every right to become frustrated, to indulge ourselves, but the main thing is *do* the work.

GIBSON: I've never trusted the theater. The first thing I do after finishing a play is begin writing something *not* for the theater.

FEIFFER: It's very important always to be involved in something else.

GIBSON: If we're assuming that Broadway is not a likely goal, and I certainly assume that . . .

GILROY: It's not a good primary target.

GIBSON: Where would you send young writers? These universities you speak of don't necessarily want young, unknown writers. They want writers who have had some plays on Broadway.

FEIFFER: What is the level of the work that comes to Circle Rep unsolicited?

WILSON: Two in a thousand we call up and say, "We're not interested in this play, but we're interested in your talent, would you like to join our work-shop?"

I got a letter recently from someone in a fairly good-sized town in South Carolina asking, "Should I come to New York? Should I give up my unfulfill-ing job? Should I send you a script for comment?" I advised him not to come to New York or send a script, but to stay where he was, find some actors and cre-ate his own theater. Believe me, if he can make it there, if it's any good, it'll spread on its own.

FEIFFER: Take those writers of an earlier generation who bought directly into that Broadway ethic—look what happened to them. William Inge, for ex-ample, had as much success on Broadway as any writer could dream of. When it all collapsed he had nowhere to go. He had no background which would allow him to continue to function.

I'm talking about a personal ethic that one buys into at a very early age: what is of value, what is important and what isn't. Just as it can build you into a star, it can just as easily—and almost invariably does—break you. Because that system no longer operates even at the level it once did, it's become more dangerous even than it was in the past; far too dangerous for writers who want to continue their lives beyond one or two plays.

WILSON: Knowing my own fragility, I have a great fear of the concept of writer as star, and of taking any of those rewards too seriously. The energy wasted in becoming a star is maybe one of the great tragedies of our time among writers for the theater.

GILROY: This is not a nourishing atmosphere. There's no continuity of atten-tion, no respect, nothing to sustain. So if you have a play, what are you going to do with it tomorrow morning?

FEIFFER: The first thing I do is figure out who I want to direct it. I find the director first. Once I do, I feel I've got a cushion, I'm not operating solo.

GILROY: Suppose he wants to go to Broadway?

FEIFFER: No director I would be interested in, with the single exception of Mike Nichols, would ever suggest Broadway as the first place for a play of mine.

GILROY: And if he did, would that be the end of the relationship?

FEIFFER: It wouldn't come to that. I'd disabuse him of the idea.

SCHISGAL: You mean to say, if you had a play that could be done on Broad-way, you would turn your back on it?

FEIFFER: I would never think of Broadway for the kind of plays I write now or have written in the past. In the case of *Little Murders,* I knew it was an off-Broadway play, but I thought it was important for it to be done in front of the audience it was about.

SCHISGAL: I would definitely go to Broadway. I would definitely try to get the kind of production that Broadway can provide.

FEIFFER: The production of *Knock Knock* was infinitely better downtown than it was uptown. I'm not sure this was caused by commercial pressures. Downtown the audience was like an adoring family. They welcomed the play, it absorbed them and they had a wonderful time. Uptown, the Broadway audience watching some verbal byplay and nonsense in the first act got no fun out of it. It was as if they were in a class in higher calculus, trying to figure out the symbols. They clearly hated the actors for giving them this problem. They hated the writer for presenting it. Just because for a moment they were being asked to accept something a little unfamiliar to them, they resented the hell out of it.

WILSON: I write for the Circle Rep actors. Half of my goal is to challenge them to do something they haven't done.

GIBSON: I would not want to go to Broadway. I've been through this six weeks on the road in which you decide the entire future life or death of the play, sick in hotel rooms, rewriting at three o'clock in the morning, popping antibiotics—not really the best circumstance under which to work. But if you go the Broadway route from the first, that's the only chance you have to look at the play on its feet in front of those paying customers in Boston or Baltimore. It seems to me a little wiser to get it done somewhere far away, look at it, think about it awhile.

SCHISGAL: So long as you make sure the people you are working with far away are giving you the kind of input of talent and imagination that more easily and frequently you will get on Broadway.

GIBSON: Frequently you don't get it on Broadway *either*.

SCHISGAL: If I want to work with a certain director, it's a pretty remote possibility that he'll go halfway across the country to do my play in a hundred-seat theater.

GILROY: Maybe he should.

GIBSON: I tried to get a couple of plays from one of our better-known colleagues for the Berkshire Theater Festival. He told me, "I can't let you have a play up there, because the theater is such a perilous enterprise nowadays it requires everything of the best to go into it." I don't feel that protective about what I write. Somebody's read a draft of a play I'm working on now and wants to do it up north this summer. If I had complete say-so I'd say, "Sure, go ahead and do it, I don't care what kind of actors you have, I'd just like to see it on the stage and see what it says to the audience." It would be directed by a college professor with Equity actors. The play isn't going to die forever if it dies up there. It's better than having it looked at with all your clothes off on Forty-fourth Street.

SCHISGAL: I truly want the best people I can get to work with. I think that's crucial. It's very damaging—and misleading—to work with people who aren't giving you what you need to do the play well.

GIBSON: I saw better performances by those ten people in that new play of mine down in Washington than in a whole cast on Broadway.

SCHISGAL: Fine. But if we're saying that there are alternatives to Broadway and that one should look to those alternatives, we must also say as playwrights that we must be protective of the work, we must ask for minimum standards from the people involved in the production. To have a production need not be beneficial per se. It can be destructive. The level of talent in alternative theaters is something you'd better check out before you make a commitment.

FEIFFER: Maybe this kind of theater doesn't exist any more, but I think it does: among the best performances I've ever seen were Dustin Hoffman's in *The Journey of the Fifth Horse* by Ronald Ribman at American Place or Al Pacino's in *The Indian Wants the Bronx* by Israel Horovitz or Jeffrey De Munn's in *Modigliani* by Dennis McIntyre. I don't see performances on Broadway that come near those.

GILROY: Sometimes you're forced to take an actor with a name instead of somebody you know would be wonderful, because of the economics.

GIBSON: Often you can get the theater only if you have the star.

FEIFFER: That's one of the drawbacks on Broadway. You may get the right star, and he or she may enhance the production. But in many cases you don't.

WILSON: It shouldn't surprise us that the plays produced in the commercial theater are commercial ventures. It shouldn't surprise us that people are trying to make money out of them.

SCHISGAL: As someone said before, we have lost a number of producers who were committed to doing plays and received personal joy and satisfaction out of doing good ones. That breed is gone. What you have now instead of producers are hucksters scrounging around the country looking for possibilities. The producer used to read a script and say, "I want to do it." Now they have to see it eighteen times and make eighteen changes, and it's a whole different ball game.

GIBSON: I agree with whoever said that neglect of one's work can be ruinous. Mailer once remarked on how souring—that was his word, souring—a lifetime of bad reviews can become. If we accept Broadway as a goal, we have to accept that squad of machine-gunners that go with it. By their own standards, they're doing a job telling people whether it's worth the price of a ticket to see a certain show. As a theatergoer, I take their advice too—they're not all that wrong. There's no way around them.

GILROY: Part of my given is that they've lost their leverage. Today, even if they like it, people don't go.

FEIFFER: I had generally wonderful reviews for both *Knock Knock* and *Hold Me* a season later. Both plays did well in their original runs at Circle Rep and American Place, but when *Knock Knock* moved to Broadway and when *Hold Me* moved to another off-Broadway house they drew nobody and failed despite the wonderful reviews. They couldn't have gotten bigger raves, and I couldn't have gotten more publicity. I found the experience so frustrating and embittering—not toward the critics but toward the audience—that it stopped me from writing for the theater for about two years. Usually you have critics to lash out at—"If I could only get through those critics and reach my audience"—but this time I didn't have that excuse. All I could do was retreat into anger, bitterness, self-pity and wait till that disappeared before I could get back to the craft I loved.

With *Hold Me*, it wasn't as if the audience in the theater hated it. They were clearly having a wonderful time. But in my case word of mouth worked in reverse. There were fewer and fewer people every night. I could never figure it out, and I never got a decent explanation.

GIBSON: I don't think literacy is going to make a comeback, but I don't think it's in a decline, either. What's happening is, the number of illiterates is mounting. As the society gets very large everything costs more and has to be geared to this rising number of illiterates—and neither publishers nor producers really know what makes a book or a play sell.

GILROY: I'm a gambler at heart, I love that throw of the dice for the whole stake on opening night. That's my nature, and I now have to resist it. How about you—deep down, do you like to gamble?

FEIFFER: A gambler I'm not.

WILSON: I'm your number-one chicken.

GILROY: But everybody in this room is a gambler in the deepest and best sense.

FEIFFER: I don't think of it as gambling. I know with a kind of inbuilt arrogance that it's going to work sooner or later—if not this play, then the next one, and that will reflect back on this, and this will have its day. There's not a doubt in my mind. When I was asked after the opening night of *Little Murders* about the adverse reviews, I said, "Well, I'm just going to keep bringing the play back until the critics get it right."

GIBSON: I admire you all for the faith you have in your objectivity about your own work. You don't believe critics when they say your work is sentimental, or this, or that. Whenever I run into those adjectives, I think they're seeing something I don't see. They have to be digested and transcended before being forgotten.

FEIFFER: One last thing on critics: a positive function as opposed to daily reviewing is spotting your writers, connecting them to the culture and publicizing them, finding social, cultural or political reasons to make a good writer fashionable and more accessible to the audience at large. An example would be the role a few critics played in developing the off-Broadway audience back in the 1950s.

GILROY: Any of you have any final thoughts to express?

WILSON: We've been assuming that twenty years ago a new, young, talented writer could get his play done by an intelligent producer and a good cast. Was it true?

GIBSON: Statistically there were more straight plays being produced, but it was never easy to get a play done. I wrote plays for twenty years before I was produced. It was never easy.

SCHISGAL: For myself and all of us, I want to thank Frank for getting us down here and opening up this topic. I feel nothing but admiration and gratitude for what he's done.

THE ANATOMY OF THE THEATER SONG

Richard Lewine, Moderator
Betty Comden
Sheldon Harnick
Stephen Sondheim
Jule Styne

RICHARD LEWINE: Welcome. I'd like to start by reading this quote: "I was becoming aware that pop music was of inferior quality and that musical comedy songs seemed to be made of better stuff. My thoughts turned more and more to show music." That was said sixty years ago by an eighteen-year-old George Gershwin. Theater songs have come a long way since then. Today, they're not just an extension of the book, they're part of it. Today, collaboration among the authors—the book writer, composer and lyricist—has never been so close. I think we can start with that premise.

STEPHEN SONDHEIM: On every show I've worked on, there have been weeks of discussion among the principal collaborators before a pencil was put to paper. When you have a so-called "creative" director with distinct ideas about what a show should be like, he then becomes a very valuable and stimulating part of the collaboration. Generally, however, the writers I've worked with have very distinct ideas of their own about the way things should be staged. I know when I write songs, I tend to put in a lot of stage directions which the director can follow or not.

That interesting Gershwin quote brings up the obvious divergence between popular music and show music today, as opposed to the time as late as the 1930s and 1940s, when shows—and movies—were very much the *source* of popular music. This split had started to occur by the time I was writing songs for the theater. Soon there were very, very few pop hits from shows—maybe one every two years. Now it's one every five years. I've written one hit song in my life, "Send in the Clowns," which became a hit three years after its show closed.

It's a shame that this divorce has occurred, not only because of what we theater writers miss in outside benefits, but also because it says something about what a theater audience receives from a show. At one time, the audience would go to a musical knowing that the songs would be the ones they'd be humming over the next months, or maybe even songs they were humming already. It has a different feeling. I remember going to *Hello, Dolly!* when the title song was already a hit. The feeling the audience had was of welcoming an old friend. That doesn't happen any more. Today, some of the biggest hit shows don't have any hit songs.

LEWINE: They used to have what they called "interpolations." They'd send over to Tin Pan Alley, and people would come over and play an assortment of hits. They'd pick one out for a spot in the show. One of the biggest hits Irving Berlin ever wrote, "Blue Skies," was interpolated into Rodgers and Hart's *Betsy.*

SHELDON HARNICK: I want to comment on the Gershwin quote, too. I don't think it's as true now as when he said it. There was a time when I was interested in "bop" because I found the music and the harmonies, the instrumental acrobatics, very exciting. But then I turned off pop music until about the time of the Beatles, when I found that I was listening again. I was hearing marvelous lyrics and unusual harmonies, which I didn't expect from a pop song.

On the way over today, I was thinking, "We're going to talk about the anatomy of the theater song," and I was trying to define to myself what a theater song is. Songs that I hear on certain pop albums don't sound as though they were written to be hit songs, but to say something the writers wanted to say. They don't seem to have been written as pop songs, either in terms of length or complexity. I asked myself: "If you put that on a stage, would that be a theater song?"

To round out a definition in my own mind, I finally arrived at this: "A theater song, as I'm talking about it, has to be part of a book, a song that comes out of a time, a place and a character all of which add to the weight and meaning of that song."

BETTY COMDEN: It's the origin that makes it a theater song, it comes out of character and situation. I gather that young people today are more interested in show music than they were six or seven years ago. Rock is still around, but it is no longer absorbing everything. There is an awakening to show music, an upswing, an enrichment of shows with more hit songs. There may be more shows done, with a comeback of show albums in a big way.

JULE STYNE: It isn't tough enough to write a show and get it on, you have a bigger problem. The composer and lyric writer are puppets in the hands of the disc jockeys. Except on special good-music stations, they do *not* play theater songs. In the case of Steve's "Send in the Clowns," Frank Sinatra happened to love the song, and after it was exposed by him others ran to it and people began to hear it. The problem is to be *heard.* You can walk into a recording company with the greatest song of Steve's or Betty's or Sheldon's and they wouldn't look at it because the top disc jockeys are beholden to a thing called the "Top Forty" and theater songs are not in that "Top Forty" list. It's like a plague.

At the time of *Gypsy* or *Bells Are Ringing* we could walk into a record company and say, "Here it is: So-and-so will record this number and so-and-so will do that one," and you had eight singles before the show opened. When the show played the theater out of town, the people knew the songs so well they applauded the overture. We don't have that any more. That wonderful culture of "standards"—the American musical comedy song—is having its problems. Nobody, including Hammerstein, including Berlin, including Gershwin, would have as many standards today—no way.

Sheldon was asking himself: "Would that marvelous Beatle song fit on the stage?" Yes, in a revue, possibly, because it has a record going for it. It's very tough for a songwriter to become known in theater nowadays unless he's writing for a recording star. The most important thing is to go along, and do our best, and *write*. Don't say to yourself, "I'm a musical comedy writer," get your song sung by some artist in a cafe. Somebody who records may hear it, some producer who hears it may say, "I want the fellow who wrote that song."

LEWINE: The musical theater will go on, with or without the opportunity for hit records. People who write shows can't let themselves be influenced by what they think will work commercially. You have to think of the show above everything else, especially today when it's tougher than ever to get an album or a hot record.

COMDEN: But isn't it getting better? I have a feeling that it is.

HARNICK: I think we've made the point that the theater is the wrong place for any writer who's looking for hit songs. Jule, Marvin Hamlisch described to me his experience with *A Chorus Line*, which was the exact opposite of what you were describing. He had never done a show, and he was working with the very gifted lyric writer and composer, Ed Kleban. They articulated the fact that they had a choice; they could have tried to write songs which might have had a chance in the commercial record market; or they could let Michael Bennett steer them in very specific directions towards songs which would probably be limited to their use in the show. They made the wise decision that they couldn't be in better hands than Michael's. They listened to him, and they wrote numbers which served the show exclusively. They made the decision right at the top not to worry about what songs might be recorded, but instead to ask themselves what is the situation? what would these characters say? what's going to be effective on the stage? how can we serve the *show*? Only the last song, "What I Did for Love," was an attempt to go for that hit. The show itself is an extraordinary knitting-together of all theater elements. I can't help feeling that Hamlisch and Kleban made absolutely the right decision.

SONDHEIM: That decision has been going on for the last twenty years.

HARNICK: With my first show in the mid-1950s, *The Body Beautiful*, my publisher told me, "I don't care what the show's about, you've got to give me a couple of songs." That's my background. I still approach every show with that voice ringing in the back of my head: "You've got to give me a couple of songs!"

That doesn't mean to sit down and write a hit song—I wouldn't know how to do that—but to see where the opportunities *are*, for songs you can just sit down at the piano and play.

There's a song in *She Loves Me* called "Ice Cream." During the run of the show, some of the cast, including Barbara Cook, were invited, with me, to lunch at the Dutch Treat Club. Barbara was going to sing "Ice Cream" and I was asked to introduce it. I started to describe to the audience what I thought they had to know in order to understand the song. I heard myself talking and talking and talking, saying she met this guy and this happened, and that happened, and I suddenly thought, "I ought to say to them if they don't understand the song, go see the show and it'll all be clear." That's a theater song. It occurred at a point in the show where everything that had preceded it was important at that moment to the song, and it works marvelously in the show. Outside the show, it works only for those people who know something about what the situation is.

I still look for situations where that *won't* be true; where a simple relationship between people can be expressed simply in a song that will serve the show but can also be extractable so that it can be recorded.

COMDEN: That reminds me of a story about Frank Loesser. When he first started to write for the theater he made the great discovery that you could express something simple in a theater song if the verse contained all the other material that Sheldon's talking about. For example, Loesser said, you have a verse that goes something like "Thanks for electing me governor, you'll all be paid back. I'll fulfill my promises to you, you really voted for the right man," and then the song goes "How'm I doin', hey, hey, twee-twee-twee-twa-twa."

My partner Adolph Green and I—and everybody else here, I suspect—have always approached shows looking for what is the right thing at the right time: whether the emotion is high enough to express musically. If it comes out as a simple song, so much the better. It's not a difficult decision when you're deciding to do what's right for the theater.

HARNICK: Given the choice of an extractable lyric or a lyric which is very book-oriented, I've usually tended to go towards the book. I fault myself for taking too often what I consider the easy way: grab something out of the book or the situation and weight the lyric line with it, even though it won't quite make absolute sense outside of the show. I think if I worked a bit harder I could find something that would be just as effective and still not have that burden placed on it.

LEWINE: That's right, the show should come first.

SONDHEIM: That's the Rodgers and Hammerstein revolution. They taught us all to believe that the show comes before the songs. They had this marvelous knack of writing songs that worked in the show perfectly—although their big song in *Oklahoma!* was cut out of town. They had a song which they plugged in the overture, in the entr'acte, they sang it twice during the first act and repeated it in the second act—it was called "Boys and Girls Like You and Me," and it was going to make their fortune. "People Will Say" was this charming little throwaway. The ruthlessness with which they cut "Boys and Girls" in Boston obviously helped the show. That's what they taught us all: sure, it's wonderful when you get both at once, but the show comes before the song.

I disagree with Sheldon on one thing—I heard Barbara Cook do "Ice Cream" in a nightclub, with an audience of, say, a hundred people. It is conceivable that those hundred people had seen *She Loves Me,* but I don't think so. They understood everything. The test of a good song is that everything is implicit in it. In the case of "Ice Cream," you *don't* have to see the show and you *don't* have to know the situation to enjoy the song. Even if some of the audience didn't get the subtleties or the specifics of the incident in the restaurant, they got the notion of the song and were moved by it, tickled by it. The situation *is* all contained in the verse, as in Betty's reference to Frank Loesser. Generally, I think, good theater songs *do* stand up by themselves. They don't necessarily become hits, but they aren't baffling, even when they're embedded in the book.

HARNICK: I'd like to believe that's true, but I tend to be a little skeptical. Another point: when you bring up Rodgers and Hammerstein or Rodgers and Hart it reminds me of an insight I once had having to do with the show you choose to write. If you're Rodgers and Hart or Hammerstein, you don't *do* a show that doesn't allow you to write their kind of songs, of which many will both serve the show and work out of the show. That's an important criterion for them, whereas it hasn't been so much for me. If you like the subject matter, and it reflects something you feel strongly about, you do it, you write the songs and hope that maybe one or two will be recorded—especially if the show itself goes down the drain. But that's a choice you make right at the beginning: will this material lend itself to romantic songs and novelties, or does it make you say to yourself, "I've gotta write this and forget about hits"?

COMDEN: Yes, particularly nowadays when you don't know what's going to be recorded. I'm sure Steve was surprised that they picked "Send in the Clowns." You wouldn't say that point in the show was where he decided to write the popular song he hoped to get recorded.

LEWINE: As Harold Arlen once said, when you write a song you send it out into the world on its own, like a child leaving home. Sometimes it makes it, and sometimes it doesn't.

An important function of theater songs is exposition. Steve, I wish you'd comment on "Comedy Tonight," which seemed such an ideal opening number in *A Funny Thing Happened on the Way to the Forum.*

SONDHEIM: It was a late substitute for another number, "Love Is in the Air," which was very charming but left the audience with the wrong idea of what kind of a show it was going to be. When Jerome Robbins came down to Washington to help us out, he said the opening number ought to catalogue exactly what was going to take place so that the audience really would be oriented. So I wrote a list song, "Comedy Tonight," saying "This is what you're going to see."

One of the most successful of all opening numbers is Sheldon's "Tradition" in *Fiddler on the Roof.* It not only orients the audience to where they are, the community, it also tells them what the show's about so they can't miss it, introducing all the family characters, the fathers, mothers, sons, daughters. It's the *echt* compendium number.

COMDEN: It's such a big idea, encompassing all cultures, all religions.

HARNICK: That particular opening is a result of endless conversations instituted by Jerry Robbins. It was an object lesson to all of us, as he kept asking Joseph Stein, Jerry Bock and myself what the show was about . . .

SONDHEIM: A small corollary to that: he asked for exactly the same sort of number in *West Side Story* to explain his own ballets. He was afraid the audience wouldn't understand them without a song being sung in a disembodied voice telling everybody what the ballets were about.

HARNICK: I just finished reading a biography of Noel Coward by the man who was his secretary and general factotum for thirty years. When he mentioned *The Girl Who Came to Supper,* he praised the vaudeville numbers that Tessie O'Shea did. They had nothing to do with the rest of the show, but they stopped it cold, tore the roof off. It was a very costly diversion, because the show was dead from that moment on. There was no way to get back into it. I felt that the people around me didn't care any more what the show had been after that number. It was interesting to me that apparently both Noel Coward and his friend based their opinions of that song solely on its immediate effect, the amount of applause it got.

SONDHEIM: Directors tend to judge the effect of songs by the amount of applause they get. If they don't stop the show—out. Performers quite often do, too. If the song doesn't get a huge hand they worry that it's no good, never mind what it contributes to the texture of the whole evening.

When I mentioned Jerry and the ballets, I was pointing out that sometimes you can overexplain. I don't approve of songs explaining things that are better just sensed or felt. It removes some of the theatricality.

COMDEN: I think openings always give trouble—many shows have more than one opening number before the right one is arrived at. In *Wonderful Town* we also struggled: we first had a number about 3.2 beer which came in that year, then one about self-expression because the show took place in Greenwich Village, then finally a much more literal one called "Christopher Street." This turned out to be the right one because in its own small way—*Wonderful Town* is not the big canvas of *Fiddler*—it set the background of what the Village was like and what the people who lived there were all about. Naturally, that also came from talking to Jerome Robbins.

Another specific kind of song is the one that describes character, like "Some

People" in *Gypsy*. It certainly establishes that lady in the most thorough and artful way.

LEWINE: In *South Pacific*, the "Cockeyed Optimist" number tells volumes about the Nellie Forbush character, very attractively and very quickly.

SONDHEIM: That's another Rodgers and Hammerstein tradition, the "I Am" song, usually the second one in the show.

COMDEN: I think in Jule's song the character is in the music as well as in the lyrics—the drive of "Some People." And for Judy Holliday in *Bells Are Ringing*, Jule was aware in all of his songs that this was a girl with a kind of small-town feeling, simple, warm, neighborly, wanting to live in a great big city as though she knew everybody on the block. The music is rather old-fashioned, simple, and that I think is the composer as dramatist. The composer is as much a dramatist in the theater as the people who write the words.

LEWINE: That may be the most important thing that's been said here.

STYNE: I agree with you that the show is the prime consideration, especially nowadays when records are nil. A show tune is a very special thing, an identification, a little above the Tin Pan Alley song—though there were some great Tin Pan Alley songs. Now when someone says, "I like that tune," I'm tempted to take it right out of the show.

Q: You said, "Get your song heard." How do you bring your material to the attention of cabaret performers?

SONDHEIM: Generally they find the material themselves. When we went to Boston with *Night Music*, Bobby Short came up to see it and stopped at the restaurant where we were having dinner and asked how he could get copies of some of the songs—so I sent them to him. They generally go out and find their own. I don't think anybody approaches them.

LEWINE: They're even harder to approach, probably, than a record company. But sometimes *they* find things that are ten, fifteen, twenty years old. "April in Paris" was ignored until a *bôite*-type singer recorded it five or ten years after its show, *Walk a Little Faster*, and it became an enormous standard. "I Can't Get Started" became a standard ten years after its show closed, because Bunny Berigan made a jazz record of it.

SONDHEIM: And "Bewitched, Bothered and Bewildered" . . .

COMDEN: And "Begin the Beguine," when Artie Shaw made a record long afterward . . .

LEWINE: And some very great songs were thrown out of shows, probably for very good reason. Gershwin's "I've Got a Crush on You" never got into a show, though it was tried in three of them—it was a great song that just didn't work dramatically.

Q: You indicated that 1950s audiences could be preconditioned to the music before they came to the theater. Without that kind of exposure, how do you deal with the fact that the audience, and particularly the critics, have one hearing only, and you have to persuade them on that basis?

SONDHEIM: It's horrifying.

LEWINE: There was a piece in the *Dramatists Guild Quarterly*—which I wrote—suggesting we should send the critics recordings in advance.

SONDHEIM: Remember first of all that most reviewers are ignorant musically, even those who pretend to have some education and mention F sharp in their reviews. They don't know the difference between arrangements and orchestrations, for example. There is no solution, because the more complex and subtle the music is, the more listening it requires. Generally, the critics tend to like anything that sounds familiar, which is also true of audiences.

Lyrics they think they can deal with because lyrics are language. Indeed, they know a little more, but not much more. I don't think there's a reviewer around who's any good on lyrics *at all.* Walter Kerr used to be, perhaps, a long time ago.

HARNICK: That's even more of a reason why we have to make sure the show works. If people like the show, they may be curious about the music and at least get the album.

Several years ago I had the opportunity to do the libretto for an opera. Along the way I began to realize that the composer's music was very difficult. I couldn't hear it until I'd listened to it two or three times, and then it began to open up to me.

One day we were talking, and he said, "I never get good reviews." He told me the best way to deal with this is to go to the library and get a book—I recommend it to all of you—*A Lexicon of Musical Invective* by Nicholas Slonimsky. It's a collection of reviews in major papers in Europe and America, from Beethoven's time to the 1930s. It's very comforting to read reviews of *Carmen* where the reviewers are saying, "What is one to make of this absolutely unmelodic trash?" They couldn't hear it.

So often the opera that makes a tremendous musical smash and reaches the audience its first night is dead a couple of years later. It's already in the audience's ears—they've heard it before, and that's why they respond to it.

SONDHEIM: In fairness to the reviewers, seeing a musical for the first time is an awful lot to take in. You have story, character, scenery, costumes, orchestrations, not to mention lyrics and music, all coming at you at once. It's very difficult to take it all in, particularly knowing that in an hour or two you're going to have to write articulately about it. I don't know that there's any solution, and I'm not sure that sending them the songs would help. First, I'm not sure they'd be willing to expend the energy to listen carefully. Second, it might take some of the freshness out, spoil the lyric jokes and surprises.

As I said, I'm not sure there's *any* solution. I consider that I have a very sophisticated ear, but I wouldn't want to write a review of a musical on one sitting. That's really a lot to ask. So generally, what's mediocre becomes easier to write about.

I'm impressed by Andrew Porter, who writes music reviews for *The New*

Yorker. He obviously studies the scores a number of times and goes to rehearsals of new pieces that are difficult or complex or very rich. But this takes time, and I'm not sure that reviewers who have to see three or four plays a week would have the time, not to mention the interest, to do it.

Q: Couldn't there be two reviewers, one of whom would specialize in reviewing the score?

SONDHEIM: Yes, we've talked about it at the Guild and made overtures to the New York *Times* about possible coverage by separate people. They almost never do this—the last time was Leonard Bernstein's *Mass.* I guess they just don't consider the musical theater important enough.

LEWINE: Douglas Watt of the New York *Daily News* became quite an expert on records of show music. It was wonderfully refreshing. And I remember that when *Oklahoma* opened, a New York critic said it had a very promising score, especially one song that he thought would go to the top of the charts, "Out of My Dreams." Out of seven standards, he managed to pick the one that just barely made it.

Q: Could pop hit tunes be interpolated into a show, or would they just overweight the score?

SONDHEIM: They tried it with *Sergeant Pepper's Lonely Hearts Club Band,* and it didn't work. I think the chances of making shows out of hit records are really very small. It's a very, very, very exceptional piece that'll adapt itself to the stage.

HARNICK: Ed Kleban and I were talking about how difficult and expensive it is to get a show on, and we began to wonder whether there would be a market for LP records which were, in effect, shows, with some kind of simple story line that would knit together all of the numbers. In that context, one could use more contemporary styles of music.

Q: When you reach for a hit tune, do you look for one that people can whistle going out, or one more complex?

HARNICK: It would depend on the texture of the show. If the show is anything like a traditional musical comedy, you'd want something as catchy as possible—something that would make toes tap. It's easier to affect people rhythmically, you don't then have to worry about the melody in order to leave everybody exhilarated, if that's what you want. But you may choose to leave them on a different note altogether—that's a choice you make.

SONDHEIM: I don't know how you draw the line where something's going to be simple and attractive. As soon as you use the word "hummable," you're in a lot of trouble, because what one person wants to hum another doesn't.

Q: How do you find a book writer?

SONDHEIM: They generally come from the ranks of the playwrights, and they have to have a feeling for music—not just an understanding, a *feeling.* When you find someone who understands what a play is about and feels what music is about, you have a book writer.

COMDEN: Adolph and I once had the experience of working with a book writer who, when a song was finished and we wanted to reprise a little bit to effect a carryover into the next scene, would say, "No, no! You've had your number, now the book takes over!"

HARNICK: When you look for a book writer, look for a very generous person, because he's going to get robbed right and left by the lyricist.

Q: Mr. Sondheim, were you deliberately trying for a hit song when you wrote "Send in the Clowns"?

SONDHEIM: It was a song that I wrote under protest for a scene in the second act which I thought belonged to the man. Hal Prince felt that it was the woman's scene, and that she should have a song. While I was writing it, I figured it would be the man's song because the impulse for the scene, the impulse for singing, was the man's as far as I was concerned. But Hal directed the scene in such a way that the impulse became the woman's. When I read the scene I still think it's his, but somehow on the stage it was hers.

Q: Between the book and the score, is there one that comes first, and if so, which is it?

SONDHEIM: The book.

COMDEN: It all grows out of the book.

LEWINE: You cannot survive a bad book.

COMDEN: When you're writing the book you're very much in control of the situation. It's a very secure feeling. Even if you fall in love with a scene and then realize that you have to throw it out because it would be better expressed in song, you know that nothing will be there unless the basic book is there.

HARNICK: The book is the matrix for the whole show.

SONDHEIM: Right, it's not just the verbal side.

Q: In regard to liftable songs, is it possible to retrain the audience's ears to something besides AABA?

SONDHEIM: It's changing slowly.

LEWINE: Theater writers are the people who've changed it. They started doing it with Jerome Kern, who's considered the father of present-day theater music. It was Kern who said, "Go on being uncommercial. There's a lot of money in it."

Q: Are you initiating your own projects?

LEWINE: Yes, I've just finished working on something.

COMDEN: I'm working on something Adolph and I initiated.

HARNICK: I'm working on something of my own.

SONDHEIM: I am too.

LEWINE: A lot of the time, theater writers start their own projects. Generally, it doesn't happen that a producer calls up a writer one morning to say, "I have something for you." On the other hand, a lot of writers start projects, optioning stories and books.

Q: How do you feel about the future of the musical theater under the present economic conditions?

HARNICK: Well, I keep reminding myself that production values, the expensive sets and costumes and so forth, are just icing on the cake. I keep remembering that fine old definition of theater: "Two planks and a passion." I keep thinking that whatever happens that still holds true, and then I notice the price of lumber.

THE VALUE OF CRITICISM

Robert Anderson
A. R. Gurney Jr.
James Kirkwood
Marsha Norman
Peter Stone

The American Theater Critics Association invited the five dramatists named above to state their views on "The Value of Criticism" to an audience of forty theater critics from across the United States. The moderator, Otis L. Guernsey Jr., editor of the Dramatists Guild Quarterly, *noted at the outset that this was not set up as a two-sided debate or discussion, but rather as a rare opportunity for reviewers, at their request, to hear from the reviewed in a press conference format. Each of the panelists made an opening statement, after which they answered questions from the audience.*

JAMES KIRKWOOD: When I was asked to be on a panel in front of an audience of drama critics, various wildly conflicting emotions tripped through my brain—whole words and phrases like "murderers," "sadists," "assassins," "no-win situation." When I took a young lady to the theater the other night and told her what I was going to be doing today, she said, "Oh God, Jimmy, mind your mouth."

Well, if I minded my mouth, I might as well stay home. I thought of sending a telegram saying, "Sorry, can't be with you this afternoon, have total laryngitis. Be assured I *would* be there if I had the plague."

It's odd how an event like this brings out parts of our personalities that we usually attempt to keep under wraps, like the child in us—that part of the child who's been punished in public and remembers the hurt. The scold in us, that part that wants to get back at those who have slighted and sometimes humiliated us. Then again, that other child in us that says, "Like me, love me," and wants to say, "Here, would you like a candy bar or a drink? Let's be friends." It's confusing.

Most writers feel about critics the same way a bull feels about being in the ring with the matador. Somebody's not going to make it out in one piece, and it's usually the bull. And there's an implicit warning signal attached to the critic when he enters the theater that says, "Oh, oh—something's wrong here." Or else why would he be there with his pad and pencil? Not just to doodle.

I think it's a shame that we have to be adversaries. We are, after all, in the same business—the theater—and when we're stroked (that's the exception, of course) we love it. As Noel Coward once said, "I love criticism as long as it's unqualified praise."

But most of the time we're hurt, and the hurt can be very dispiriting, especially when the critic is getting off a few witty one-liners in one day about a work which has taken us a year or two or three to write. Nobody sets out to write a bad play, although sometimes we're treated as though that were the intention. It takes as much time and effort to write a bad play as it does to write a good one. It's the *tone* of the criticism that is dispiriting, as much as the content.

We have no recourse, we can't answer the critics. There should be some forum, but there isn't, outside of a few crank letters, printed where no one reads them. So the tragedy of intentionally cruel and destructive criticism is this: it drives talented writers away from ever again writing for the theater. In a way, the critics themselves are killing off their own jobs by diminishing the ranks of playwrights, who simply can't afford to spend a whole year writing a play, knowing it might well be shot down in one night. Writing a novel at least produces a tangible book you can hold in your hand. It's there forever, there's a paperback life, maybe a film sale. Even writing for film, demeaning as that may be . . . a film often finds its audience despite a preponderance of bad reviews. And then there's television, in which the writer is paid a set fee and will get that fee despite the reviews or the ratings.

If you think my tone is antipathetic to critics, you're partially correct. Like Pavlov's dog, we get kicked, we bite back. There's even a difference in the artistic community in regard to maligning each other, you see. The critics go on with their jobs no matter what we say about them earning their salaries, fairly secure in their profession. But when they malign us, our plays are closed, our livelihoods are threatened, our source of income is cut off, to say nothing of our feelings.

I wish we could find a way of being more like collaborators than adversaries in the theater, to which we're mutually devoted. We shouldn't be the cobra and the mongoose, and I'd like to play even a small part in helping to change that.

ROBERT ANDERSON: My first wife used to say to me as I came grumbling out of the theater, "Thank God you're not the critic on the New York *Times*." I was a critic at one time, I used to review books for the *Atlantic Monthly*, and also was the critic on the Harvard literary magazine. In the beginning, before I became a playwright, I wanted to be a critic.

In my opinion, criticism is enormously valuable—criticism of other people's plays, that is. I can't get much out of a critic's review of my own play because I'm too raw, it means too much to me at that moment. I brought myself up on criticism in orienting myself to the theater and learning to write plays. George Jean Nathan . . . Brooks Atkinson's *Broadway Scrapbook* was my bedside reading for years . . . Stark Young . . . I love dramatic criticism. When I pick up a newspaper or a magazine, the first thing I go to are reviews of books and plays and movies. Whenever I would teach playwriting, I would always direct my students to read Walter Kerr's books, or John Gassner's. In that sense, the critic of somebody else's work is very important to me.

As far as my reviews of my own plays are concerned, appreciation is always welcome, and understanding of what I tried to put into them. What bothers me is somebody reviewing a play that isn't there, that I never wrote, with an attitude that from the very first line is antagonistic. For example, I had a new play at the Long Wharf Theater last spring, and the opening line of one of the reviews said, "Robert Anderson's most famous play was *Tea and Sympathy,* which we now know to be a totally dishonest play." That's how he started the review of the *new* play, *Free and Clear.*

Sometimes, criticism can be more interesting than the play. There was something in a review I read the other day that reaffirmed my feelings about what playwriting is: "The play is cluttered with a certain amount of interesting material, but it stops the tidal *move.*" That's a very important thought for young playwrights to keep in mind, about the general *moves* of a play. To that extent, reviews are helpful. But reviews of my own plays . . . they can scold me, tell me what I should have done . . . Benedict Nightingale can write articles about what we all should write about . . . it doesn't mean a thing to any of us, because we're all going to write about what we want to write about.

A. R. GURNEY JR.: I speak as one who has suffered the slings and arrows of adverse criticism a number of times in my life. I'd come down from Boston to have a play done, and when I'd slink back home my children would cower because I was so unhappy and disagreeable. Their mother would say, "Don't worry. It's the critics who did that to your father. He'll be all right."

But when I imagine a world *without* drama critics, without intelligent drama criticism, I think it would be far worse. It's like Winston Churchill's statement that democracy is the worst form of government except for all the other forms. A world without drama criticism would be a tennis match between Connors and McEnroe without the referee. Somebody has to call the shots. So while I suffer inwardly and outwardly when bad things happen, I must say that the thought of a world in which self-advertisement, the advertising budget, would determine what is good or bad is far, far worse.

If you look at drama criticism as opposed to standard literary criticism, there's a strange difference in tone which has always fascinated me. Most literary criticism, whether in a journal or in a book, tends to confront the material with a pleasant and benign tone. There's often a kind of easy acceptance of a book that doesn't seem to happen as much in drama criticism. Even Aristotle, the progenitor of all criticism, when he turns to plays displays a particular kind of commitment and emotion. He talks about Homer in a benign way that doesn't occur when he moves on to Euripides.

Why is that true, I wonder, and is it good or bad? It seems to me that drama requires on all of our parts a commitment, a submission to the material, a willful suspension of disbelief. Not so with literature. We *give* ourselves to drama, we get into it. Therefore when it doesn't deliver we feel radically disappointed. So maybe the tone I'm talking about is the tone of disappointment, which can sometimes turn the critic angry, sour and bitter, which you on your side might like to try very hard to avoid, because it can lead to tremendous pain and agony on our side.

MARSHA NORMAN: Criticism of our own plays isn't really for *us*. How we deal with it, who bandages us or goes out and celebrates with us is all very private.

But I have a real concern about the audience of young playwrights. Ideally, one should be able to learn to write a play by reading criticism as one is growing up. Kids ought to be able to read what intelligent people say about work other people have devoted their lives to and determine how it's done, what's interesting about it, what works and what doesn't, and learn from it what great rivers run through the world of the theater and who sits on what bank. Please remember that audience, those people who are learning to write plays by reading what *you* write.

Most of those people cannot afford to come see what we do, they have to wait until they can get it in the library. We as living playwrights are not within the reach of most student writers because our plays cost incredible amounts of money to go see. So you are the people who are teaching them about the theater. Ideally, someone living in a city and reading a critic consistently should learn how to go to the theater and make judgments of his own.

There are a number of things we need that are seldom found in criticism. We need a real distinction between the play and the production. We need to teach people how to tell who did what. It's tough to do—a lot of time you can't tell whether a piece of staging was in the stage directions, or was the director's idea, or the actor's idea, but it is absolutely something that needs to be done. The audience needs to understand that when they come to the theater, they're coming to a place of tradition. It's not a television moment that was pasted together by an agent. The theater is a place where people *do* have specific roles, where great fan clubs can exist. Where tradition is concerned, it's your work to carry it on. We can't do that, we just write the plays. When you say, "This play connects to that and that and this," the audience gets a little smarter about how to get to the theater. People don't have to be smart to be entertained by a lot of other forms, but in theater, education does help and even adds to enjoyment.

I'm very sad that we have somehow lost the glamor of the theater. Where are the fans, those people who will come to see Hume Cronyn, say, wherever he is and no matter what he does?—who will come to see whatever Jimmy Kirkwood writes? Writing *about* the theater is where that kind of work is done, that kind of interest is aroused, and we can't do that, we are dependent on critics for that, and it is much more critical than anything that is said about any single piece of work we do. It needs to be understood that the theater's fruit grows out of a long line of tradition. It needs to be explored and talked about, so that people reading criticism don't feel that the answer is simply yes or no, which cheats critics as well as us.

PETER STONE: I've been writing for the theater long enough to have developed a hard shell: and that, I suppose, is a comment in itself. In the very beginning, when I went out of town with a show and started listening to members of the audience I learned that every single individual member of the audience is wrong, but collectively they're always right. Shortly thereafter, by simple association I discovered that critics are members of the audience and, individually, are almost always wrong, but collectively they have something to tell you.

There is an adversarial relationship which exists for various reasons, the fact that critics have the last word being one of them. My first musical book was an adaptation of Jean-Paul Sartre, and the review in the New York Herald *Tribune* pointed out that among my sins I had created a line that would have made Sartre roll over in his grave. The fact that he was alive at the time seemed to make no difference. Incensed and young—two qualities I can no longer afford—I sent an angry letter saying that the line was, in fact, *verbatim* from Sartre, feeling very secure that this was, indeed, the final word. But an answer was printed in the *Tribune* underneath my own letter: "That may be true, but the play stinks anyway." A very important lesson was learned: don't mess around with anybody with a forum. I could reach eleven people, and they could reach everybody. You can't indulge in public debate with critics, you're dealing with people who have the last word.

I think our relationship *is* like a tennis match between McEnroe and Connors, and there *is* no referee—that's part of our problem. There are things built in to what critics do that don't seem fair to us. We notice, for instance, that critics have ambitions, as we certainly do, and one of the ways for them to move forward is to be quoted. I don't remember in a lifetime of reading criticism a single *favorable* one-liner about a play. All the clever lines in the anthologies—"ran the gamut from A to B" and so forth, we all know them—are unfavorable. A clever line is almost always negative; and we sometimes feel the critic is seeking the clever line and not the fair one.

We also feel that sometimes critics come to plays unprepared for them. We find that in the other literary forms success creates reputation, and reputation creates loyalty. If Michener's or Updike's new book comes out, there is a guaranteed sale based on the track record. One looks around at the great playwrights of America: Arthur Miller's last three plays, Tennessee Williams's last five plays, Neil Simon with the greatest record in the American theater having a play close after only a few nights on Broadway—this is a shocking testament. I saw Edward Albee savaged by the press without a shred of respect. Whatever happened to respect for proven ability? I see respect in literary criticism, even in film criticism, but I don't see it in theater criticism. I don't see the critic taking that step back and saying, "This is a man of talent, who has, in the past, performed not just well, but brilliantly."

In negotiation with the producers over a new contract, they questioned adamantly why a man or woman who has written a first play should receive what an experienced, famous, successful playwright gets. We pointed out that an experienced, famous, successful playwright receives no better reception from the critics and, therefore, the audience, than does a new playwright, not one iota better. In this business, it's the *play* that counts, and not the playwright.

And then, it offends us personally that most of us write so much better than most of you. But there's not much we can do about that. Writing isn't entirely the business you're in; your judgment is involved as well as your literary ability. It is upsetting to see as much grammatical abuse and sloppy writing as we do in criticism which is criticizing our writing. That is not to say that I do not have enormous admiration for good critics—enormous admiration for good anything. I know very few of you, but I'm sure many of you are good critics and I would appreciate your work.

Speaking a litle more parochially just for a moment, I'm in the musical theater, basically, as a "librettist"—a word I don't like. I don't think it describes what's being done in the musical theater since the 1930s and early 1940s, with the book becoming a musical play and not just connective tissue between songs. I prefer to call it the "book" or the "play" and there's a dwindling group of not more than seven or eight of us who are continually at this and keep coming back to the trough. We are a miserable lot in terms of facing critics. We firmly believe you don't know, really, what a musical book is. Most people think the book is just the dialogue, but that's nonsense; everybody knows the actors make that up as they go along. The structure of the musical, the libretto part (though I hate the word), is least understood. I've written eight or ten musicals, six or seven of which have been successful, and I've received generally good reviews for only one of these, which happened to be all book. Among the rest of the reviews, from the biggest paper to the smallest, not one of them touches on what a book really *is*. That's upsetting to the dwindling group of us (diminishing partly because it's so thankless). Critics can love every aspect of a musical and still knock the book. It's a common critical practice, and the musicals themselves don't seem to suffer much from it, though we book writers suffer intensely among ourselves.

I don't know why you should be good at criticizing musicals, it would be unusual to find a critic trained and knowledgeable in all of the many different elements—music, dance, play and so forth. It is the play critic who covers musicals, however, and he or she tends to treat them as plays without fully realizing the special properties of this form.

Q: Jimmy Kirkwood, if we're all going to be friends, we must find things that are in our interest and in your interest. One that occurs to me is writing about the play in such a way that we convey to our readers a true sense of what happens on the stage. Whether we say it stinks or not is secondary *if* we do that first job properly. Can the panel suggest other matters of common interest?

ANDERSON: I've read very negative reviews that made me want to go see the play because the critic *did* recreate the spirit of the show. Walter Kerr, for example, has a great gift of recreating performances. Even though he may end up not liking the play, he makes me want to go see that performance.

Q: Sometimes our description of a play may distort what you intended, but we can't help it because we're honestly trying to tell our readers what we saw happening on that stage.

ANDERSON: Everybody sees a different play, there's no question about it.

KIRKWOOD: The hurtful part is when you get a review of a play you really haven't written. I wrote a play called *P.S. Your Cat Is Dead* as an entertainment. I wasn't politicking for anything at all, certainly nothing in a sexual area. This play came out in 1975, about two months before *A Chorus Line*, and you would have thought I'd defecated on the American flag in the middle of Times Square. Clive Barnes gave it a review that I appreciated, because he said, "It's an entertainment, don't take your grandmother," but most of the other critics savaged me. I couldn't get over it. I was astounded. On the subway going to the Public Theater for rehearsal, I read Martin Gottfried's review and started to cry. It was embarrassing. I got to the Public Theater, found out Gottfried's phone number and called him up. "This is James Kirkwood," I said. "Oh, yes," he said. I said, "I just wanted to ask you how it feels to make a grown man cry. Your review was so off-base." It was also the review that closed the play. The producers were so dispirited by that review that they decided to close the show. It ran for three weeks in New York and never lost a penny, but everyone was so discouraged by the savagery, the anger of the reviews, that they said, "Close it, kill it."

Q: Did Martin misrepresent what happened on that stage?

KIRKWOOD: Yes, he did, and so did John Simon.

STONE: The most upsetting review is the one that says, "What you should have done was . . ." You must understand that the play that's there is the play we wanted to do. Telling us what we should have written is not helpful. Nor relevant.

Q: Isn't it the playwright's and producer's responsibility to present that material in such a way that it won't be misunderstood?

STONE: We cannot defend against misinterpretation.

Q: Don't you think that the critics brought their own emotional feelings about the characters to Jimmy's play? They didn't see the play he wrote. He's right, they savaged it.

KIRKWOOD: It came back off Broadway in a different production and ran for about ten months. I've seen productions of it all over the world—South Africa and Argentina—and audiences just have a good time, which is what I meant for them to do.

Q: When the curtain went up on your play, could there have been something that *didn't* happen onstage that caused Martin Gottfried to misinterpret your play? When you pull the curtain up on a play with a man with his pants down tied over a table, you're asking for it.

STONE: That's a very interesting statement. What you're saying is, don't start a play that way. I'll be *damned* if I won't start a play that way!

Q: If you start a play that way, doesn't the audience have to be prepared to say, "This is a very amusing way to start a play?"

KIRKWOOD: Well, actually the play doesn't start that way.

Q: I think critics are shameless in one respect: we have taught an entire generation of new critics that we are willing to overpraise, underevaluate, pander to, coddle young playwrights. I can't speak for everybody in this room, but I've been watching criticism closely for fifteen years, and I think that of all the crimes you're laying at our feet, you're not even approaching the big one. I'm assuming our motives are generous—we want to be responsible for keeping the theater alive by encouraging the young playwrights, by taking care not to nip anyone in the bud.

You've been speaking of pain—we know that you don't very often get the chance to talk to a whole room full of critics—of course, you're getting your rocks off. We understand that. But you're not contributing as much to this discussion as you could if, please, you'd address this one question: Do you really feel that critics have helped the young playwrights by not mentioning their rotten structure, their inability to shape a scene?

GURNEY: I do think it might be a problem in American criticism, in the nature of American life, that a young playwright can get there too fast, too soon. In the machinery of publicity that surrounds us, a young writer can be over-praised and find himself or herself with an image that is created not by their work but by the press around them. The history of American letters is full of people who have written themselves out because of this.

On the other hand, I wouldn't say that you're creating monsters. The theater is a beleaguered profession, a craft in a world of machine-made things. It's a craft, and therefore some coddling needs to occur. In my own experience, I wasn't lucky enough to be told at the age of twenty-seven or twenty-eight that a play I wrote was terrific. But over the years, occasional encouragement from certain critics—"You're not bad, stay with it"—was what kept me going. Yes, you can overdo, but I wouldn't say that's the main problem.

STONE: To paraphrase Thornton Wilder, good criticism is like manure, it should be spread around to encourage young playwrights to grow. And I think that it does. You were talking about praise that wounds future work . . . in my opinion, what one takes away from good criticism is, simply, the warmth of good criticism. I don't think playwrights continue to perform badly because they weren't brought up short early in their careers over things they performed badly. I understand what you're saying, and I don't disagree with it entirely. I only disagree with the sin of it.

Q: Isn't it possible that what you have called "savagery" in criticism wouldn't seem as savage if some of that negative quality had been applied earlier on? Doesn't the overkill occasionally arise because a playwright is going along without anyone ever having knocked him, and suddenly it happens?

STONE: It well might be, but you're speaking of savagery as though it were acceptable. Why is savagery acceptable at all as part of your craft? What do we do that requires a *savage* response? People in the arts get reviewed for everything they do—how would other professionals, doctors, lawyers, businessmen, like to live with the idea of picking up dozens upon dozens of unfriendly comments on *their* work the next day? It's a precarious existence.

ANDERSON: Arthur Miller said a while back that after Harold Clurman's death he had no critical base. In the thirty or forty years I've been writing for the theater, I've never had, except for John Gassner, a critical base of somebody who genuinely approved of the fact that I was writing plays, whether from time to time I came up with a bad play or a good play.

A long while ago I delivered to the New York *Times* in person an article they'd asked me to write, and I happened to notice that they were working on a story about Tennessee Williams's twenty-fifth anniversary in the theater. I told the editor, "That's great, you should run that kind of thing more often." He wondered what was so great about it, and I told him, "You treat us all like milliners—if we come in with a hat that's not in fashion this year, forget it. But we are writing a body of continuous work." Every time we come up, it's as though they'd never heard of us before. One of the plays I wrote got terrible reviews from the then *Times* critic, and I must say the paper published some of the letters telling them, "You treated him as though he were a stranger who came in and spit on the floor." Why shouldn't we ask for respect? We've been working at this profession for years, we've given our lives to it. You can hate our plays, but we should be treated as though we were trying to do something, even though we may have failed this time.

Q: I agree that critics should look at a writer's work in continuity. What bothers me as a reader of all kinds of journalism is that the major literary and other critics don't see playwrights as part of the mainstream of American literature. It would never occur to Updike in writing about Anne Tyler, for example, to talk about Anne Tyler in terms of Marsha Norman or Raymond Carver in terms of Sam Shepard. How did this happen? It wasn't always true.

ANDERSON: It was true in the nineteenth century, when the theater was looked upon with contempt. Even today, my novelist friends ask me, "And what are *you* doing?" with a kind of contempt.

STONE: I don't think literary critics are much interested in the theater. I don't think they go much.

Q: You'd think the top literary critics would cover the theater as part of the literary beat. You'd think they'd cover a promising playwright critically, in the same way they'd cover a promising novelist. There was a time when they'd talk about O'Neill in the context of American writing of that time. But you could read the *New York Review of Books* for years and never find a piece of criticism about a living playwright.

NORMAN: People don't have a concept that there's a difference between a play and a production. Most reviews you read don't give any indication that a play is a production of a *written* thing. One of the things that so annoys me is how often you get this single statement at the end of a review, "Admirably directed by so-and-so," referring to the person who has been basically in charge of the production of this written thing and is often the true author of the production. Can't we please sell copies of the play in the theater lobby? They do this in other civilized countries, they do this out in some of the regional theaters, let's do it here in New York. Even in the bookstores, the theater book section is usually back underneath the radiators. I think this is a crashing problem.

Q: Some people writing about the theater are not qualified and probably shouldn't be doing it, but on the same basis a lot of the plays that are produced should never be produced. I'm not talking about the plays of these panel members—there are thousands more authors whose plays we have to go see all the time. In a sense, some of those plays savage the audience. Just because a play is produced, should we respect it and think about all the work that went into it?

STONE: You say to yourself, "How can such a play get produced?" You've got to remember that a play is finished *upon* production, and doesn't look quite like a play until it *has* been put on the stage. Many, many a play that looks very promising just doesn't work when the skin is put over the bones and all the elements added. A play is a tricky combination of many collaborative efforts. While the script is unquestionably the core of the enterprise and all the rest is dressing, it's very, very hard to see a finished play on the page. Authors are probably not much better at it than producers. Everybody gets surprised by it. That's the nature of the process.

ANDERSON: I have to agree, there is a disgraceful number of poor plays done.

Q: What comes out over the footlights is a combination of all those efforts, so is it necessarily desirable for the critic to separate the play from the production? Sometimes bad direction, bad dialogue or one of the other elements stands out, but ideally it shouldn't, should it?

NORMAN: It's critical to separate the play from the production in a review. When that terrible notice comes and that play closes, the playwright is the only person who can't go get work tomorrow. Actors and directors move on, but the playwright is staring at a great empty space. In cases where the production is not successful, the play is not finished. When somebody says that in print, the playwright is then allowed another production somewhere.

The danger is, you can lose a play simply because of the production. I lost a play when all the critics in the world saw the production and Mel Gussow, bless his heart, was the kindest of all and called it "disappointing." No other theater in the world will do it now, so it went into the drawer, and it was two years before I had more or less recovered and went on to write again. That's why this subject is so important to me. The playwright must be allowed an opportunity to fix whatever is wrong in the play, if it is fixable.

Q: Obviously, we need to be very fair—not kind, but fair—and as explicit as possible. Why can't you all take the failure of a play as just that, and not the damning of a human being?

STONE: Because *we're* the human beings involved.

Q: It seems to be that playwrights are sometimes savaged by their directors in the production process. Why can't the playwright stand up for himself or herself at that point?

STONE: By contract, the director can cut nothing, change nothing, without the permission of the author.

KIRKWOOD: But you can be blackmailed. An actor, an actress or a director can say to you, "I like your play, but I will not do it unless you change the end of the first act." Then you have to make a choice. Sometimes you make bad compromises.

Q: We frequently see plays going in two directions, the director pulling one way and the playwright another way.

STONE: Mismatches do take place within a production. It's like a marriage when you start putting together the collaborative process. You often find out you've married yourself to the wrong mate, your relationship isn't functioning, you're working on different plays. Suddenly, you're caught: you're in production, economic forces are at work, and you find yourself locked in. But that's our problem. All we ask of you is that you understand that it's one of the situations that can arise during a production.

How much should a critic know about a show, anyway, as he or she goes into the theater? In many cases they've read the columns and heard all the gossip. I just did a musical that had a lot of trouble in Boston, but out of it all came a successful show. I say this categorically: I did not read *one single review* out of a hundred and some odd that did not talk about the trouble in Boston. Frankly, that's none of your business. That is the business of Page Six, it is *not* the business of criticism. Trouble in Boston wasn't visible on the stage when you saw the show—there wasn't a song called "Trouble in Boston." There was nothing in the program saying, "Remember the trouble in Boston." What on earth did the gossip have to do with *anything* that took place onstage?

I know it's hard *not* to pay attention to gossip—it's news, and you are not just critics, you work for the news media. It's hard to keep the two elements from slopping over one into the other. But I think the effort should be made.

Q: Why would Miss Norman want to have her script sold in the lobby, when what she's showing is the play—which is not a script, but a totality, a production of a script? The script is, after all, only a blueprint. As the author of the script, you have helped to create the production, along with other people who also had a hand in it. Why would you want to say, "Hey, if you didn't like what you saw onstage, here's the real goods"?

NORMAN: It's important for people to know that there is a piece of literature from which this production has come, that will continue to exist. You can put it in your coat pocket and take it home, read it later and pass it on to other people. We *are* all writers. We don't work in holograms.

STONE: You've seen the production, and when you read the play you'll have that production in your head.

KIRKWOOD: Part of the joy of reading *The Glass Menagerie* is that you imbue it with the production you found the most stimulating. I would much rather see copies of plays being sold in lobbies than T-shirts.

ANDERSON: Many people don't know there's such a thing as a playwright. I had a play called *Silent Night, Lonely Night* with Henry Fonda, and I heard one member of the audience say to another, "Hank Fonda always says such amusing things."

Q: I'm glad *The Glass Menagerie* was mentioned, because that's a very famous and prominent example of a critic, Claudia Cassidy, saving the life of that play in Chicago and probably the life and career of a very well-known playwright. It's been curious to hear so many references to us as adversaries. Obviously, you're speaking of real agony, and I'd like to talk to you about the agony of the critic. We see innumerable bad plays, plays that debase taste and values, and we feel it's our function to criticize them. Every once in a while we see something that knocks us out, and then the struggle is a very private one to find the words to communicate to a large audience how beautiful this work is. I guess I'm just a little bit disappointed that you don't realize that we're performing virtuous acts occasionally. Each person in this room could give you instances of his or her own writing of criticism prolonging the life of a play. I think you should see us as partners.

GURNEY: I don't see you quite as adversaries. I do think we have to have those referees, and you critics tend to perform that function. But it seems to me critics have to enter the economic arena in some way. In restaurant criticism, for example, they'll say, "It was a terrific hamburger for four dollars, but if you had to pay twenty dollars it might not be worth it." You might say of a play, "Fine, but not at that admission price."

I know we're all in this thing together, but another thing that concerns me about criticism . . . I know sometimes when I go to a play I'm just not up for it, something else is on my mind, I cannot give that play my attention the way I should. I come out snarling at it; I haven't concentrated, I haven't focussed. I can't imagine that doesn't happen to all of you in this room. What do you do when you're on the line, you're there on opening night and you've got a deadline, but you know that you haven't willfully given yourself over to the play the way you should?

Q: If the play is good enough, it will take us out of any mood we're in when we enter the theater.

ANDERSON: Not me.

KIRKWOOD: I saw *The Glass Menagerie* last night, and I was thinking of Claudia Cassidy. But the way the critics treated Tennessee Williams in his last few years I thought was deplorable. Not that the plays he was writing should have been heralded or that they were the equal of his greatest work, but so many critics said he was finished, through, washed up. Now, this man got up every morning and hit the typewriter. It was heartbreaking to see him trying to get to that typewriter after reading reviews of plays that were then being done in Miami, or Atlanta, or wherever. The critics were saying, "He's finished," but he wasn't finished until he died.

STONE: The irony is, in many papers across the country his obituary was turned over to the drama critic, and to a man or woman they deified him: "This was America's premier playwright, maybe ranking above O'Neill, America's poet playwright of our century if not of all time." I didn't see that in the review of his last play. I didn't see in that review that they were talking about a man they considered to be America's premier playwright. I'm not saying they *should* have said it, but it was very obvious that they didn't *feel* it. It was not behind the words of the reviews.

ANDERSON: We all know, as John Kennedy said, that life is unfair, and we know that it's a roll of the dice, but sometimes it's bewildering. For example, some time ago a new critic on the *Times* reviewed a play of mine, and he was the one critic who wrote a loathsome review. Two weeks later, the former critic, whom he had replaced, saw the play and told me, "If I'd reviewed it, it would have been a rave."

We all live by that toss of the coin. We go to see a play and come out disagreeing about it with the person with us. There's no such thing as objective criticism—it's all subjective. We are asking you to engage in a love affair, and you know what happens to a love affair that doesn't work. You are irritated, left on edge, and that is why you respond the way you do. You don't sit back and check off points, you're being sucked into this play. And then if we don't pay you off, naturally you're mad, and that's why you write with more intensity than the critic of a novel. We ask more of you.

The French have a phrase, *"assister au théâtre."* Every member of the audience is "assisting" at the theater. If we ask you to assist and then drop you, you get mad. And because we ask for a subjective response, if we touch something that's hurtful to you, the only way you can defend yourself is to attack. I've done it myself, I've seen my friends do it. My own father, going to an affectionate Andy Hardy movie at the same time as he was having a fight with my mother, would go "Phooey, phooey," whereas the happy couple in the row ahead of me would hold hands and say, "You see, dear?" I happen to write the kind of play in which I expose myself and which asks you to expose yourself. If you don't, your only defense is to attack me. And I can recognize the attack, because as you all know the critic exposes himself every time he reviews a play.

STONE: Our consenting to be here today shows our obvious respect for your profession. We didn't waste any of this short time telling you how terrific we think you are and how terrific you think we are. We've all had, pent up in us, complaints—personal and general. We are exchanging some of them with you because we think, in the time allotted, it might do us all some good. We think critics are necessary; it's the way the system moves. We are glad when we get very good reviews, and we try to be understanding when we get thoughtfully bad reviews. We are upset when we get what we think is savagery or reviews that are not really about our play. That's what's been going on here, so please don't think that any of us has anything but respect for the profession of criticism and most of the people practicing it.

AUTHOR AND DIRECTOR: PLAYS

Marshall W. Mason
Lanford Wilson

LANFORD WILSON: We met at Caffe Cino, of course. Didn't we?

MARSHALL W. MASON: Didn't everyone?

WILSON: I had a play that was called *Balm in Gilead.* It had fifty-six char-racters. I had been writing these two-character plays for the Caffe Cino, and it was an attempt to escape two-character plays. I really overdid it. *Balm in Gil-ead* was a play that could not possibly be done at the Caffe Cino, and of course Joe Cino said, "Do it here."

MASON: I read about your first play in the *Village Voice.* Michael Smith wrote a review of *So Long at the Fair,* and I caught the closing performance of it. That wasn't when we met, though. I had been working at the Cino, too, and, around your third or fourth production, Joe Cino finally introduced us. It was at the second production of *Home Free.* You were so happy about the work you'd done, and you came over to the table and Joe introduced us. You knew who I was, and I knew who you were, but we hadn't been introduced. And you said, "Isn't my work on *Home Free* so much better than it was before!" And I said, "No, I really don't think so. I liked the first version much better." Which, of course, is exactly what you wanted to hear. So we started off on a real good note.

I was wandering around the Village one night about a month or two after that, and Lanford was also wandering around the Village. We ran into each other somewhere around Sixth Avenue and Eighth Street, and it was cold enough that we went into Whelan's for a cup of hot chocolate. And you started telling me about this fifty-six-character play you had written. You said, "Would you like to come over and read it now?" I had insomnia anyway, so I said O.K.

So we went back to the Broadway Central, where Lanford was living (and out of which, undoubtedly, later came *The Hot l Baltimore*), and I went up to his room and sat on this awful little daybed and read the play from beginning to end. I finished it and handed it back to him and said, "It's really very cine-matic. You must have a brilliant director for this. It must be brilliantly directed or it won't work." And Lanford sort of said, "Thanks. Good night."

Subsequently, a mutual friend of ours came to me and said, "Why don't you

345

like *Balm in Gilead*? I think it's such a brilliant play." And I said, "What are you talking about? I love it. I think it's a wonderful play." And he said, "Well, Lance said you hate it." You have to understand something about Lance: If you don't simply faint and fall into a puddle at his feet, he thinks you hate it. If you say, "I really think it's very nice," he'll say, "You hate it."

WILSON: True.

MASON: So I told this friend of ours, "Please tell Lance I don't see how he could possibly think I didn't like it. I told him he needed a brilliant director. Didn't he understand I was volunteering?" So our mutual friend worked it out between us, and Lance asked if I would be interested in directing it.

By then, Lance had developed a rather bad reputation at the Caffe Cino for lording it over directors and making them do what he wanted them to do. Interfering in rehearsal.

WILSON: Well, I kept having directors who did the *damnedest* things with the plays. I mean, very strange things. Like, "I don't want the girl to appear. I want that whole character on tape." So, I kept saying no a lot.

MASON: When he asked me to do *Balm in Gilead,* he kind of interviewed me. "What have you done?" That sort of thing. In view of his reputation, I kind of lambasted him at that first meeting. I said, "You will not speak to the actors. Only *I* will speak to the actors." And so on. I laid down a bunch of rules. And he said, "O.K., O.K."

WILSON: But the good thing was, he also told me what *Balm in Gilead* was about. I was astonished. I was just knocked on my butt, because he had gotten every single thing I had tried to put in there. It was alarming.

Then, when we cast, I knew we were on the right track. We had this long, long casting process which, thank God, having a company at Circle, we don't have to go through anymore. Not like that, anyway. On first rehearsal, we had all the actors together. We were sitting in this huge room with this enormous cast, and I thought to myself, "Oh, my God, what are we in for?" Marshall said, "I work in beats. I want to divide the play now into the beats we'll be working in. The beats fall naturally in this script." So everyone opened his script and we started dividing. And there was not a single instance where Marshall had divided it differently from the way I would have if someone had asked me to. Sometimes it was in the middle of a speech, where one acting beat ended and another began! And we hadn't talked about this at all! So I thought to myself, "We're going to be all right."

MASON: He later accused me of directing with a wand. It was a very happy process. Right away it became evident that we had a similar sensibility about the theater, about acting . . .

WILSON: *Very* similar sensibility about acting. He knows how to get exactly what I want. I don't know how to do what he does. It's astonishing.

MASON: The first play of Lance's we did at Circle Rep was *Sextet: Yes.* A tiny little thing we did in our second season. That went well. So, the next year he wrote us another little one-act play, which we did with two other one-acts that Lanford had written, and they were very successful. By now, he was really beginning to get into the rhythm of writing for a specific company. Trish Hawkins and Conchata Ferrell did a play of Lanford's he had done much earlier called *Ludlow Fair.* Lanford was absolutely enraptured by the performances of these two actresses, so he began to write *Hot l Baltimore* specifically with those two people in mind. And then, as long as he was writing for them, he thought, "Who else is there around that I can use?" Well, there was Zane Lasky—this seventeen-year-old kid who had wandered in off the street and seemed to have some talent. And so he wrote the role of Jamie for Zane. And what with one thing and another, the first thing you knew, we had a whole play with a whole cast.

WILSON: Some things that weren't right had us both going "Aaargh!" In *The Mound Builders* we changed a scene just before the critics were coming in— the afternoon of the *day* the critics were coming in.

MASON: We held the press out in the lobby while we moved a scene from the second act into the first act. We had been through six previews, we knew we had a problem but we didn't know how to solve it. Then I had this bright idea: "Wait a minute! There's important information in that scene that we need in the first act." And so I asked Lance, "Can we move it?" And Lance said, "Do you think technically it can be done?" And I said, "We'll try." The scene was complicated technically. It involved slide projections and lights and sound cues.

WILSON: Our company stood there, half an hour before the New York *Times* was coming in, as Marshall said, "We're going to move this. We want to do this as economically as possible." And the company *took* it!

MASON: You couldn't have done that without a company, I assure you. It was really a big change. It wasn't the whole solution to the play's problems, but it made the play *play* better.

WILSON: I recently worked somewhere else with a company of stunning professionals. And I would say, "You know, I've never liked that line. Let's cut it." And they were so bollixed by having to lose a line or getting a new word a week before opening! I thought, "We're really more versatile and accepting of change than is normal."

MASON: Lance and I have never had a deadlock because, as we've said, there's a similar sensibility. We share the same goals. I'm not trying to do something that I have in my mind that is in some way separate from what Lance is trying to achieve. We've done twenty-five plays together. It's always been smooth. The longevity isn't the point. It was smooth from *Balm in Gilead* on because our goals have always been the same—to create a living play. For me, interpretation is making the play live in terms of your own experience.

WILSON: Marshall is very strange in the way he works with actors. I know because a while ago I acted in the e.e. cummings play *him.* There was this one speech I was having problems with, and he kept saying, "Lance, you're trying to *interpret* that speech. If you would just relax and look at Trish and say the words without trying to make us know what they mean." And boy is that difficult! If any of you have ever acted, you know. You feel so naked without your performance and your *interpretation*. But one night I did it, and I realized, "I'm just saying the words, and the audience is on the edge of their chairs—the first time they haven't fidgeted when I've done this speech."

Anyway, to get all this into a nice aphorism, Marshall later said, "Interpretation is what happens that night. You should not bring interpretation to it."

MASON: The audience takes interpretation away with it.

WILSON: So, that's the sort of thing we're after. I am trying to write vital, interesting characters and exciting situations, and Marshall is trying to make that live.

MASON: Sometimes playwrights—not Lanford, but other playwrights I've worked with—do have interpretations about what their work means. That can be problematic. I directed a play by a very excellent writer named David Starkweather called *The Love Pickle* which involved a woman being worshipped by a man. It took place in a men's room. I won't go into how. It's a funny play. It's a comedy. Anyway, this man falls down to the woman's feet and begins groaning, or some such. David had an interpretation for this. He believed that it meant that he worshipped Woman. I said that, given the context of the play, it was going to come out as a foot fetish. "I can't make it mean what you want it to mean. I can only *do* it. And those who think it's worship will think it's worship, and those who think it's foot fetish will think it's foot fetish."

I do not share the widely held view that playwrights should never direct their own plays. I think that sometimes, given the directors one might have to work with, it's the only sane thing to do. Some playwrights, in fact, are very good directors. I think, for instance, Lanford is a very good director. He's directed some of Robert Patrick's plays, and he directed a play called *Not to Worry* at the Circle Rep. He's also directed some of his own plays; he did the original productions of *The Rimers of Eldritch* and *This Is the Rill Speaking*. I think he does his own work very well. I couldn't have done better than some of the productions I've seen of his.

On the other hand, if you can find a relationship that really works for you as a writer, there is something very valuable about an outside eye, somebody else who filters through his or her own experience and brings another dimension to the work. If you find a director whose vision of what you're after is there, then I think you can really make use of that other experience, that other eye.

This would, I think, also apply to acting in your own play. I don't think there are any absolute rules, "You must never do this." But I do think other people's experiences are valuable.

Theater is a collaborative art. We are dealing with different people's visions of life coming together into a creation which is then going to be shared with an audience, which is made up of individuals who each have their own bundles of experience. These different bundles of experience are very useful—the way in which they interact and make the play something different than what it is on the page. I would tend to think that if the same person were the writer, lead actor and director, that would tend to limit the variety of experience which could be applied to a production. . . .

Edward J. Moore wrote a beautiful play called *The Sea Horse* for himself to act in. We worked very well together because, from the moment we went into rehearsal, Ed was the actor. The script was in fine shape from the beginning of rehearsal. The difficulty comes, I think, if there's still writing work to be done. Then I pity the poor actor-writer, because writing and acting are two different processes, and they don't occur simultaneously. I don't know how you would act and rewrite at the same time. . . .

Q: How do you decide if someone is the right director for you? What questions do you ask?

WILSON: I've said, "Tell me about my play. How do you see it? What do you see?" Once when I had written a play called *The Gingham Dog* and had a meeting with the director who was supposed to do it, he said, "All I know is I see Gloria at the end of the play hunched forward with her thighs out like this, hunger in her face, glaring out at the audience." What I had *written* for that moment was something like, "She moves over to the window. She has a cigarette, and she stares out the window, musing at the dawn. Nothing moves for about a minute except the smoke from her cigarette." Well, I didn't go with that director. His idea was so far from what I thought the play was about. I couldn't find a way to say, "I don't think we have anything to talk about." I just said, "Oh, yes. That's . . . marvelous." And I clutched the script and took it home.

I think if a director describes to you the play you think you've written, you're in fairly good shape. And if the director describes something else, you're in fairly hot water.

I haven't written a stage direction in I-don't-know-how-long, because I found that Marshall does better stage directions than I do. When a play is published, I find it very difficult to go back and add stage directions that will help someone read the script.

MASON: But Lance is very fair about it. When he does go back and write those stage directions, he really limits it. He puts down the things that are germane to the play but doesn't rip off the director's work. There are some writers, on the other hand, who mark down every cross and every piece of business. I recently talked to a young director who was about to do a project in some college somewhere of a play I had directed. I told him, "The first thing you must do is cross out all the stage directions." In that case, the playwright had written down everything I had told the actors. Every piece of business had been written down and put into the published script. I felt that if that young director were to have followed them, he would have been very limited by them. All those directions are really limiting on the imaginations of the other artists who do subsequent productions of the play.

WILSON: Of course, if it's germane to the action of the play—like *"He falls dead"*—you put it in. But I'll only put in an interpretive stage direction like *"Smiling"* to aid the actor if the line it refers to could be interpreted in two different ways; if the line sounds harsh and I really mean it ironically, for instance. I only put in stage directions where it's absolutely necessary to make something clear.

Writing for a company doesn't make it any easier to write a play, but it does make it—for me—so much more exciting. Usually, as you all know, you have in mind a character, but you have no specific actor in mind. You know generally what that character sounds and looks like, though, and the process of casting then becomes one of finding a decent compromise.

It's different writing *for* people. When you're writing for Conchata Ferrell, say, you know that you're writing for that deep voice and that incredible laugh and those gorgeous eyes and a woman who refuses to lie onstage. And the first reading, instead of having a compromise where you're getting 40 percent of it, you've got it all. You have 100 percent of what you'd imagined, plus all of the new things she'll find. It's thrilling to me to have the words said by the voice that was there in my head. I mean, there is that private performance in your head onstage, so everyone can see what you had in mind.

MASON: And sometimes the actors can come back with so much more than you thought they could do.

WILSON: Yes! You write for actors, and you think you know what they can do, and then they take that and just spin it on its tail sometimes. Boy, that's thrilling!

I don't attend the first rehearsals. Marshall has the actors improvise in their characters during the first four or five rehearsals, and I cannot stand to see the characters in other situations making up their own words. So I don't go to any of those improvisational rehearsals. Until they're saying my words, I just can't take it.

MASON: And then, you don't come to *every* rehearsal.

WILSON: Not to every rehearsal, no.

MASON: I really miss him a lot when he doesn't come, because he actively participates in the rehearsals when he's there. That rule I talked about the first time we worked together immediately dissolved into a collaboration, so we don't have a "You don't talk to the actors" kind of thing. If I spot an actor feeling uncomfortable or getting confused by what Lanford is telling him, I will take over. But that doesn't happen often.

I feel very strongly that a rehearsal is not the place for rewrites. A rehearsal is the place for the actors to investigate the material you've brought in. If a producer and director go into rehearsal unwilling that the script that they begin with appear onstage, they shouldn't be doing it. If you get into a situation where the writer is doing wholesale rewrites during rehearsal, the actors have no time to do their work.

I did a play with Irene Worth once where we worked on the play the entire time. It was necessary, because the play really needed the work. The play finally got there. I mean, it was a better script than we started out with. But Irene was really annoyed with me, and rightly so. She said, "You haven't given me any time. It's all been going to the script." And it was true.

Sometimes it is necessary to rewrite in rehearsal, but, as much as possible, try to get the rewrites done before the rehearsal process begins.

WILSON: What frequently happens in rehearsal is that someone will say, "Oh, we don't need those three lines," and everyone else will immediately say, "Of course we don't." Or sometimes in rehearsal we'll cut for time or clarity.

MASON: I came to the theater from a very different perspective than Lanford. My background is a classical background. The second production I directed was *The Trojan Women*, and early on I did *Cyrano* and *Mary Stuart*. Lanford wasn't the first living playwright I'd encountered by any means, but he was the first one who was a really ardent advocate of new plays as opposed to classics. So we really kind of met head-on in that sense. I would rhapsodize about Chekhov and the structure of Ibsen, and he would say, "Yeah, but that's all yesterday's news. The live sensibility is what's important." He had a very strong sense of the theater as a kind of circus. That's an early image he used to invoke. He wanted the theater to be as lively as it was in the Elizabethan era when you had the groundlings jostling each other and buying orange juice, and the play had to be really *good* and reach out and grab an audience to hold. To him, there was something so safe about the classics.

Our different points of view, I think, did intermix in a good way. Actually, we've almost switched places. He's read a lot of classics in the last ten years, and I've done a lot of new plays.

WILSON: I look back at all of those ideas I was spouting and say, "I'm not *grabbing* the audience with my plays." My work now sort of wafts across the night air and the audience catches what it can. What I do now is so different from, say, *Balm in Gilead*, which screams and yells and kicks and has outrageous theatrics and ridiculous things. I look at that and say, "How did I ever do that? I wish I could do that now." I start writing a play thinking that it's going to be open and free, and instead the characters sit there and talk all night, and it's another damn Lanford Wilson play.

MASON: Personality-wise, we're not too different.

WILSON: No, not much different.

MASON: I think the most serious problem, maybe, that we've ever had has been over the question of whether to go back to do productions of plays that I've already done . . . We've had numerous discussions on *The Mound Build-*

ers. The play was not finished when we went into rehearsal. When Lanford first told me about it, he said, "I'm writing this play, and the only thing I know about it is there are scary sounds in the night in the middle of the country. I don't know what it's going to be about, but there's something mysterious going on. There will be city people who don't belong there. Maybe a husband and wife, and the husband will be doing exercises, like sit-ups or something." Images of that sort.

Little by little, the play began to come together until we had something like a first act. Since he was writing for the company, we knew who the actors were. So we set a performance date. About a week before we went into rehearsal, he discovered they were archaeologists. But he didn't know the story. He didn't know how it ended. He didn't know anything about what was happening in the second act. Nevertheless, we went into the rehearsal process with a first act, and a second act still to come.

WILSON: That phrase, "to come," brings it all back, because in that script, during rehearsal, the actors would hit little markings that said "line to come" or "bridge to come." All the way through the first act. They threatened to call the play *Bridge to Come.*

MASON: Fortunately, as Lanford said earlier, I do have the actors research their characters through improvisation and discussion and what-have-you for a week. And so, during that first week, we were doing our research, finding out what an archaeologist is and what archaeology is about. During that week, Lanford was writing the second act. So, by the end of the improvisation period, we did have a second act, and we knew where we were going. Then we had that last-minute switch of scenes we told you about earlier.

The play was confusing to many. Other people say it's Lanford's best work to date. It's probably his most respected work, and he personally feels it's his best work.

Subsequently, we did it for public television. Lanford didn't want to be involved in the script for that. So, since I was directing it, and since television, like film, is a director's medium, I took the script and did my version of it. We had a wonderful experience. At least I did. Doing it on television clarified a lot of the problems in the script.

I think Lance got a new sense of the play in reaction to what I did with it. "What you did with it is not what I wanted to do with it. I wanted to do something else." So he *did* do something else. What he did appeared as the published version, which is quite different from either what I directed onstage or what was seen on television. It's a very different play. That version of the script has been directed a number of times, but I have not yet done it. I would like to do it.

What I started out to say was that the closest we ever came to a real problem was when I suddenly got an inspiration of how I wanted to do the play. It had to do with a change in the set, making the set more realistic. There was going to be a scrim wall, and this one character would be able to walk through the scrim and move into the present, and so forth.

Anyway, I described it all for Lance, and he said, "No, that's not what I want." Well, I had been so excited and so turned on, and then . . . Well, you know, if someone kind of slams a door in your face when you're in that mood, you'll want just to say, "Forget it then!" I kind of had that reaction at that moment. Subsequently, we've figured out that there are ways to get what we're both after.

WILSON: My saying no like that blocked Marshall. I understand that. Once I came to him and told him, "I'm working on a play about these two couples who are each going through a crisis in a different way. The men are very close and . . ." I was talking about what I eventually wrote as *Serenading Louie.* It's the most depressing, tragic play I've ever written. But his reaction to that description was, *"A Period of Adjustment."* Slam, right in my face. I didn't work on it for about a year.

MASON: Descriptions can be very superficial. I think the same thing happened with my production concept of *Mound Builders.* Had he seen it, he probably would have said, "Oh yes, this is exactly what I wanted."

WILSON: It's great fun to miss a couple of days of rehearsal, come in and be surprised with the new staging and say, "Terrific!"—which fortunately it almost always has been. Marshall isn't rigid, though. He doesn't fall absolutely in love with something he's done to the point where I can't say, "No, that line is not supposed to go like that. Right now, it sounds like she's knuckling under, but it's really supposed to be the climax of her argument." He'll say, "Oh, of course." And then he'll try to correct it.

I've seen some bad productions of my work elsewhere. That's painful, but it's not as if there was anything much I could do about it. Maybe I should have attended the rehearsals and tried to help. But my feeling is that if the people doing it are proud of their work, there's no point in hurting them. If the audience seems to be liking the show, in spite of how badly I think it's being done, I sort of say, "Well, who am I to disagree? Fine." I certainly don't say, "You're doing it all wrong." I may say to the director, "I do wish they'd stick to the script. I don't like improvisation with the lines onstage." I've said things like that. But I haven't yet had the experience of getting livid and saying, "You cannot do my play. This is absolutely wrong."

MASON: As a director, I really identify with what Lanford is talking about. I don't have the tolerance that he has at all. I find it just barely possible to smile and say, "Very interesting."

One thing authors must all work to try to acquire is the understanding that a play is meant to be done by different people in different ways over (let us hope) hundreds of years. And it will often be done without the author's having any control. If the actors, the director and the audience are having a good experience, then they're getting something out of the play.

WILSON: It may not be what *I* saw in it, but it's *some*thing. Also, there's a laziness in it. If I didn't go there to help them in the rehearsal process to make it right, then who am I to come in after they've been playing it for, say, three weeks and say, "That's all wrong." With a little more effort, I could have gone there—they usually are glad to have me—and helped them on it and at least snowed myself into thinking they were doing a good job; gotten so involved in the production that I couldn't tell whether it's any good or not.

MASON: Lee Strasberg said something once about actors to the effect that, generally speaking, if the actors aren't giving you what you want, it most likely is because they don't know how to. Usually they aren't willfully trying to do your play wrong, they just don't know how to do it right. Keeping that in mind brings about a certain amount of tolerance.

On the one hand, I think the author must be happy with the people who are going to work on the play. On the other hand, I do believe that if the director is well chosen, the actors become the director's tools. That is, it is through them that the director is going to create this work, just as the author works primarily with words and actions. So, if the director feels, "Oh, I can get this performance from that actor," and the author has confidence in the director, then that struggle shouldn't be too hard. Authors most often will accept an actor's audition piece, saying, "Oh, that surface thing I see is what I want in my play." Sometimes, if you cast on the basis of that surface thing, that's all you'll get. The director, with perhaps a more perceptive eye as to the actor's process, can sometimes see a hidden, inner quality that is much more impor-tant to the part and that can enhance the play in a way that the author might not have recognized. So if you don't have much confidence in your director, by all means sit in on the casting. Actually, you should sit in on the casting in any case.

WILSON: Oh yes, you must.

AUTHOR AND DIRECTOR: MUSICALS

Harold Prince
Stephen Sondheim

Q: Mr. Sondheim, you wrote in the *Dramatists Guild Quarterly* that you have a "secret metaphor" in mind for every show. What is the secret metaphor in *Sweeney Todd, the Demon Barber of Fleet Street?*

STEPHEN SONDHEIM: I suspect that Hal Prince and I have different metaphors for all the shows we do. For me, what the show is really about is obsession. I was using that story as a metaphor for any kind of obsession.

HAROLD PRINCE: I suppose people who are collaborating should be after the same thing, but Steve and I were obviously not with respect to *Sweeney Todd.* I think it's about impotence, and that's quite a different matter. The reason that the ensemble is used the way it is, the unifying emotion for the entire company, is shared impotence. Now, obviously Sweeney's is the most dramatic, to justify all those murders. Obviously all those other people who don't see the sky except through filthy soot-covered glass would not justify mass murder, but in fact they all suffer from the same kind of impotence, which then creates rage, and rage is what is expressed most by Sweeney's behavior.

SONDHEIM: When I talked about secret metaphors, I said that with all the shows that Hal and I have done, we'd probably sum up each with a different sentence, and yet we were writing the same show. Whatever way you relate personally to a show is what counts. Of course shows are about more than one thing. In connection with impotence, Hal just mentioned the set that Eugene Lee came up with. In case some of you may not have noticed, you never see any sky whatsoever. There's a big outdoor drop at the back. It's a hundred feet wide, and there is not one ounce of sky in it; and so, of course, the show is also about that hemmed-in feeling, that rage.

In his version of *Sweeney Todd,* Christopher Bond emphasized the whole class structure and how Sweeney came out of that, which of course was never in any of the other versions. So Hal and I are not contradicting each other as much as it may seem. Shows *are* about different things. I think that in *Company* and *Follies* we did hit on a common metaphor.

Q: How did you two meet?

PRINCE: We disagree on that, too, and it sort of speaks ill of the impression I made on him and quite well of the impression he made on me. It was the opening night of *South Pacific*—believe me, this is the truth. I went with the Rodgerses and Steve went with the Hammersteins. At the end of the show we were introduced in the aisle, at which time I made no impression whatsoever. He will tell you when he thinks we met, which is clearly the *next* time we met.

SONDHEIM: I thought we met a couple of years later, through Mary Rodgers, when Hal was stage-managing *Wonderful Town.* His version is certainly possible, but I don't remember it.

Q: How do you work through conflicts?

PRINCE: I don't think they happen, and I'll tell you why. When Steve writes a piece of material, if I think it's wrong for some reason or another I will say so. If he accepts that (accepting doesn't mean go along with it necessarily) and takes it home and worries about it and talks back to it, then something serious is happening—we are both involved in the decision-making process. If on the other hand I tell him I don't understand something and he says no, this is right, then I back away—because I trust him that much, and I am sure he's right. I suspect the same is true in reverse.

It amuses me the number of people who tell us that the set for *Sweeney Todd* is large, as though we hadn't noticed! Then the people who point out that the show neglects the industrial revolution in its text. We discussed all of that and agreed that it should.

SONDHEIM: In fact, if I may interpolate, when Hal first started to shape the show in his head that way, and we started to talk about that whole aspect of the piece, I was most concerned that we not soap-box it. He was too, because we both like didactic theater but don't like soap-boxing. I try to do it by just inserting here and there throughout the lyrics words like "engine," basic images, not just inserting the words but using them as little motivating forces to make a slightly wispy connection with the industrial revolution. I was afraid if we made too much of a connection it would put too heavy a weight on the image or on the metaphor. I don't think it did.

You asked about conflicts. There are collaborations, surely, which grow out of contention. There are human beings who love incessantly to fight.

PRINCE: Gilbert and Sullivan.

SONDHEIM: We don't like fighting, and we have done whole shows without ever fighting.

PRINCE: As a matter of fact, I can document the only arguments that we have had, when we get silly and really upset. They have had to do with one of us thinking that a performance was good and the other one thinking it wasn't. I'd be so relieved, because I'd think we made a breakthrough and were finding some plateau, and he'd say "Jesus, that was a real bummer." But we don't fight and I couldn't stand it. I don't like fighting.

SONDHEIM: I think generally we see the large things exactly alike, and the tiny things exactly alike, and it's only in the middle ground that we have disagreements—which is where, to use a favorite word of Hal's, the abrasion comes in and where new creative ferment starts.

PRINCE: This is one of the best things about any collaboration. One artist provides something unanticipated and larger and more exalting than anything that the other artist in the collaboration could conceive of in a given time. Every piece of material Steve writes, if it's good, is a surprise to me. I mean, he will say to me, "This is why I am going to write a song here," but when it's prime Sondheim it's something that I couldn't expect at all, much richer for the actor or the play, much more exciting for the scene. Designers do that, too. It's thrilling. The worst thing in the world is to not be a songwriter or set designer or director and ask for something and then get back exactly what you asked for.

Q: Whose decision was it to cut the Judge's song from the show, and why, and whose decision was it to put it back into the album?

SONDHEIM: Hal's always very patient about certain things, and he will often have a sense, particularly during the early stages of a rehearsal, of songs that are eventually going to be cut. But he always gives them a chance, which is one of the reasons I admire him.

We were aware that the first act of *Sweeney Todd* seemed too long, but we didn't want to make any decisions until it was playing right and until it was set right on the stage. It's very important always to let the actors play it in for a few performances. Of course, it's going to be clumsy in the beginning, every number is clumsy at the beginning. We had one of those agonizing reappraisals at the end of the first week when the show was playing fine and all that was required, we thought, was some careful manicuring and some careful changing.

The first item was, how do we cut ten minutes of the first act? About 80 percent of the first act is sung, so it's unlikely that the cut is going to come from the dialogue. The dialogue is as tight as we and Hugh could make it, and so it would have to come from one of two songs. Hal was leaning a little heavily on taking a big bite out of the Pirelli scene, but that would have meant that we would have to have played it in dialogue. The other place was the Judge's song, which is a song that Hal had sensed from the beginning wasn't going to belong in the show; and indeed, the Judge's song is one of two songs in the first act that isn't in the straight line of the story. The other is Mrs. Lovett's song, "Wait," in the middle of the act, but if she didn't have that it would be a great musical gap for her—and I am not talking about Angela Lansbury, I am talking about the character, Mrs. Lovett. Also, it sets up Sweeney's hesitation in killing the Judge.

We found we were able to tell what was necessary about the Judge in a couple of lines of dialogue spread throughout the rest of the act. I miss the song, however. I do not think we made a wrong decision, because the act played at the comfortable length—and I mean comfortable, you can feel it. It just felt like "Yes, that's a full and satisfying act, it's not too much and it's not too little, and the story seems to be told straight."

I sympathized with Ed Lyndeck, who played the Judge and sang the number so well, and I think it's an important color to the character—I don't think Hal will disagree with me. There was a chance to put it on the recording to show what had been there. It's not the first time that people have included songs that have been cut out of shows. I thought it enriched the character and would be fun to hear and also would please Ed. And I also restored two little bits of the Pirelli sequence on the record that are not in the show, again that were cut for length but that I am fond of, and I thought, "Why not?"

Q: We all know the show you end up with is always different from the show you start out with. How does that apply to *Sweeney Todd?*

SONDHEIM: I'll let Hal speak to that, but I want to point out one thing which I am very proud of: I think this may be the first musical ever that never had an orchestra call between the first preview and the opening night. We never have had to have a meeting with the orchestra or an orchestra rehearsal, because we never had enough new material going into the piece to warrant any changes that we weren't able to dictate. I don't think that's ever happened in a musical. What that means is that the show—in spite of its being overlong and in spite of some clumsinesses that we wanted to fix up—was the show that we were going to open with, so it opened in excellent shape, with less change, musically, than any other show. I think that's a record.

PRINCE: So much of the time on a show is taken up with finding out what the style of the show is to be, *how* you are going to tell a story. Once you really know how all of you are going to tell that story, then it takes about a year to create a show.

Sweeney Todd was four years between "Let's do it" and being seen. The first three years were about *how* in the hell do you tell that story and how large do you want it to be? I worried to death for the longest time that, first of all, I was the wrong director for it, inasmuch as I couldn't see beyond Sherlock Holmes. I saw structure, real bricks and some turntables, and that's it. I kept protesting—not out of modesty, I assure you, but out of my real sense that I didn't feel comfortable here. Finally we were able to determine what the show was going to be, what its "motor" was going to be. That's how I always think of it, as the motor—it has a lot to do with the way the scenery is going to look, and how the people are going to move around in the telling of the story. That's quite a different responsibility from Steve's. On the other hand, of course, it affects him a lot.

The point I'm making is, I don't think most of our shows have been intrinsically any different once they opened from where we wanted them to be on that first day of rehearsal. Change isn't necessary. *Sweeney Todd* had only four and a half weeks of rehearsals and two and a half weeks of previews before it opened. We didn't go on the road. This new way of doing things was introduced to me by working in opera, where they just don't have all that time. I dearly believe in Parkinson's Law. I think the more time we give ourselves, the more time we waste.

It was a lot easier to take the Judge's song out after two performances than it would have been if we had let it go two weeks—and we *would* have let it go two weeks if we had gone to Boston. It gets harder on the actor and harder on us. Jerry Robbins once said to me, "For God's sake, remind me that I don't think that this set is dressed well, otherwise I am going to go on to other things, forget, and get *used* to this empty room with all the wrong props in it."

Curiously, after *Sweeney Todd* had opened and seemed to be in one piece, people kept coming up to us and saying, "I saw the first preview, or the second preview, and I went home and thought, oh, God, it's so full of wonderful stuff but oh, how are they going to cope with these problems, the tangles?" Well, the truth is there weren't any problems to cope with. We were on a schedule. Every day we continued to go where we were going, aiming toward the opening night. We got just as much done by the first preview as we could conceivably do in four and a half weeks, and the next night we did some more, and the next day we did some more, but there was no point where we went home and said, "Oh, my God, how are we going to solve this problem?"

SONDHEIM: We always read through and play through the show a number of times before we go into rehearsal. That's crucial. Starting in March that year, when I had exactly five songs and Hugh Wheeler had a first draft, we got actors together and we read it. There was already a feeling of how the story was being told and what we required.

PRINCE: It was a very serious, heavy, relentless, misanthropic business with *no* humor, none anywhere. That was the first reading.

SONDHEIM: Then I wrote some comedy numbers. But in fact, the first five songs, the first few songs with the exception of Angela's song, are indeed very grim. The reading was a signpost to warn us to watch out for lack of variety, to watch out for a show that was only relentless. And so, by the time the beginning of summer rolled around, I had Pirelli's stuff and had started to gear to changes of texture and changes of mood. We were both encouraged: "Yes, yes, we can go along, it will flow." By fall, we had our third reading. With these pre-rehearsal tryouts, by the time we went into rehearsal the show was in much better shape than most shows are because they don't take the trouble in advance to read the script aloud. Sometimes Hal reads it alone and I play the songs. Sometimes we have actors do it. By hearing it over and over again you are forced to look at what is wrong. It's so easy to avoid what's wrong until suddenly you are in rehearsal, you've got a hundred other things wrong that you have got to get around to taking care of. That's why the shows we have done, whether they were successful or not, have had a minimal amount of changes between opening out of town and opening in New York.

PRINCE: The first reading of *A Little Night Music* had either no music or one number, and so in fact it was a play. It sounded sensational, and Steve and I thought there was absolutely no need for music in the piece.

SONDHEIM: And at the second reading the songs were so dark—because I was really writing to Ingmar Bergman rather than to Hugh Wheeler—that we could see it going right off the track. If we hadn't had that reading we wouldn't have seen it. I threw out practically all the songs I had written and started over again, because the book and the score were starting to diverge. Well, if you don't take care of that in the beginning, you end up in the third week of rehearsal having your first run-through and seeing that the book is here and the score is there and it's too late to rewrite the entire score.

Q: Your collaboration starts from the beginning of the project, doesn't it?

SONDHEIM: On each show there has been a slightly different genitive process. In the case of *Company*, I gave Hal some one-act plays because a playwright friend of mine, George Furth, didn't know what to do with them. Hal, to my great surprise, said, "Let's make a musical." He had a notion, he had a vision, and I followed him to his vision. With *Follies* it went through two processes. First, I went to James Goldman and said, "I want to write a musical with you." He said O.K., he had the idea. When many years later we brought it to Hal, Hal had a vision of it that was entirely different than ours, and we entered his vision again.

It's a matter of one person having a vision and convincing his collaborators to enter that vision. When Hal first presented *Pacific Overtures* to me, it was a full-blown idea complete with John Weidman's play and Hal's notion about the whole Kabuki aspect. I was very uninterested in Oriental theater and Oriental music, but I did it out of a sense of "Well, if he's that enthusiastic maybe I ought to try it." In one month I was in love with it. I entered the vision—but if in one month I hadn't the vision I would have gone to him and said, "I can't see what you're doing." What counts is that somebody's vision is so strong it makes his collaborators come with him.

Q: Have you completely abandoned the AABA form of song lyric?

SONDHEIM: No, but I seldom use it except when I am doing pastiche. Not very many composers use it any more. I think those rules were broken about fifteen years ago. The AABA form is much more common in pop music now than it is in theater music. Content dictates form, and it's what you have to say that motivates the form of the song. You decide as you go along. If you go down the list of shows on Broadway, even some of the more conventional ones, you will find very free use of song form. AABA is no longer standard.

Q: Should a librettist look for a director-choreographer at the beginning of trying to conceive a project, or should he wait until it's finished?

PRINCE: Let me say first that it's very nice that we have had such successful director-choreographers, but I think the musical theater is going to suffer plenty if it continues to proliferate in that direction. The emphasis on the part of director-choreographer *must* be towards dance movement, and dance movement isn't sufficient to accommodate ideas. That doesn't mean that there aren't plenty of terrific ideas in some of the dance shows, but I don't like the definition of director-choreographer. There are directors who choreograph, which is fine.

Now to get back to your question, it seems to me that the ideal situation is when someone hands you something like the seven plays, four of which comprise the basis of *Company,* but it just doesn't happen that often. More often than not, we have had to find a librettist and ask, "Will you do this show with us?" In the case, certainly, of *Pacific Overtures,* John Weidman brought me a very realistic play, so there was a body of work. It was completed. Now then, it ended up somewhere else entirely, and one was forced to say to him, "Listen, see what's happening. You've got a play that takes place all in one set, and it is a valid and valuable play, but what we are talking about is something else entirely. Are you willing?" "Yes." He proceeded with enthusiasm.

With *Company,* the birthday parties weren't there, and no character named Bobby, but there certainly were all those small plays which comprised the libretto. I don't think there are any rules about it, but I don't think that a librettist should go out looking for a director at that stage of things at all. I think that he should first serve the initial impulse to write something. Once he does find that director, he ought to be open to another assessment of what the piece is going to be in musical terms.

SONDHEIM: It is often useful and helpful to have a director in the beginning, but what really counts is getting the composer and lyricist and librettist together.

PRINCE: Sometimes librettos get written without signing composers and lyricists, and I think that's dangerous.

Q: At what point did Hugh Wheeler enter the picture in *Sweeney Todd?*

SONDHEIM: I first started *Sweeney Todd* as an out-and-out opera. I started to set Bond's text, and it's a compact play. It's short, but it is so jammed with material that I realized if I were to sing the whole it would turn out to be a nine-and-a-half-hour Ring cycle, and it didn't seem worth that kind of time or attention. So, I thought, I will do a little cutting and snipping—but it is plotted so well and so intricately that I got frightened. I bogged down, and at that point Hal came to my rescue. He suggested that it would help move it along if Hugh would be willing to do it. Hugh is British, he used to write murder mysteries, I had two enjoyable collaborations with him, he loves to write musicals and he loves to work with Hal. Hugh was an ideal choice. I was only worried that he might not want to take a piece that was so, in my opinion, well formed and needing so little changing. But in fact as we got to work on it, much of the second half of the piece started to change in shape and in tone and in style. That was the result of the three of us sitting in a room and pounding away at what it should and shouldn't be. It didn't change my approach to the way I wrote the songs.

PRINCE: One thing you just said, sitting in a room—it's accurate to report that at the core of so many creations of musicals, people do *not* sit in a room together. They do not talk, they operate independently and bring each other finished work. It's incredible that there's so little amount of time given to simply talking, exchanging ideas.

Steve sits there with a yellow legal pad, and you see him scribbling, and you think, "What did someone just say that was worth writing down?" In the same way, things are being absorbed by the other collaborators. But so many musicals are done in that strange sort of separate way—the book writers somewhere and the composers and lyricists somewhere else. There's kind of implied acceptance of the work when it comes in. "This is the song. Oh, all right. I'll fix that word." It's never engaging enough.

Q: How do you handle backers' auditions?

SONDHEIM: I hadn't done any backers' auditions since *Anyone Can Whistle*. At that time I sang about two-thirds of the score. With *Sweeney Todd* I had seven absolutely exemplary songs which covered all colors of the show, except that I didn't have any choral piece. That's all that was necessary. I think I have said it often before, I don't think a backers' audition should go beyond forty-five minutes, and I think there should be talk between songs so people can get a chance to absorb them. When you write long songs, as I do, seven is plenty, they have had it.

Q: Does it help for the librettist and composer to sit together?

SONDHEIM: Why, sure.

Q: How do you compare your experience in writing a total score yourself with your experience in collaboration with other people?

SONDHEIM: I don't particularly want to work alone, so I don't think I will ever do a book, music and lyrics. When I work on a score by myself, it is Hal and the librettist who supply the stimulation and encouragement, which are for me absolutely necessary, as well as the criticism. The obvious advantage of doing your own music with your own lyrics is that you don't have anyone to answer to—except I always have, as in this case with Hugh and Hal, collaborators to answer to. If they don't understand a line, if they find something clumsy they will tell me. Hal never says, "That isn't pretty." He always asks, "Is that pretty?" I will answer him truthfully. Sometimes I say no, and sometimes I say yes. I don't think I could *not* talk to people about my work. I need too much encouragement.

PRINCE: We all are such lazy people, but we are driven and work very hard sporadically. We are procrastinators, and I suspect that's why we enjoy collaborating. If you don't want to collaborate, really, honest to God, you don't belong in musical theater! Think of all the playwrights who left the theater to write novels because they simply couldn't stomach the interference of actors and directors and set designers. I totally accept that, only it's unrealistic to think you can work in the theater and not collaborate. And if you *need* collaboration to be excited, to stay awake, to create something, then you really are on the right track.

SONDHEIM: Yeah, it's nice to have somebody you have to be answerable to, at least it is for me.

Q: What part does the orchestrator play in the collaboration?

SONDHEIM: It's always the same, Jonathan Tunick and I get together right at the beginning, at about the same time that Hal gets together with the set designer. Just as Hal and the set designer will talk ideas—not specifics but whether the set should be big or small, just generalizing, just trying to zero in on what the show should be visually—I talk ideas like that with Jonathan. Without a note of music, I say, "The idea of this score is . . ." I remember saying in the case of *Night Music* that it should feel like perfume. I have no hesitation of using generalized images, because he doesn't want to be told, "I want six cellos and four violins." That's what *he* will decide, and he knows more about it than I.

In *Sweeney Todd* I said, "First of all we have to have an orchestra that can scare people." I wanted him to use an electronic instrument, and I wanted him to use an organ, because for me the loud crashing organ sound is as scary as anything and also has a wonderful Gothic feeling. And electronic sounds can unsettle you, too. I kept saying, "I want it to be unsettling, and I want it to be scary, and above all I want it to be very romantic, because it is a very romantic show."

Then, after I write maybe four or five songs, I'll ask Jonathan to come down and hear them. Then I play him every two or three songs as I do them, or sometimes every song. He comes to all those readings that I spoke about before, and he gets to know the show almost as thoroughly as we do. One of the reasons that Jonathan's orchestrations are in my opinion the best there are is, he comes to rehearsals and hangs around looking and listening and not making any specific comment for the first week but letting it soak in further, so that by the time he starts orchestrating we usually start giving numbers to the orchestra. By the end of the first week he has it thoroughly. Now, of course, before that he has picked the orchestra, because you have to contract for the men in advance, but he comes in on the project, sniffs around and gets into it. Most orchestrators just treat it as a job.

Q: Mr. Prince, do you ever find promising material in work submitted by unknowns?

PRINCE: Sure, I just did the other day. A young man came into the office with perhaps three finished songs, fragments of another eight or ten, an idea for a show that interested me a lot. Sure, I think you can tell. You know, it was self-evident that Steve Sondheim was incredibly gifted before any of his work was seen by anybody but some friends around a piano. I had the good fortune to have a career as a producer at a very young age. It wasn't giving me all that much pleasure, because it wasn't what I wanted to do at all, but still, I did have that. I am older than Steve by a couple of years, and we had done a considerable amount of talking as very young men about what we wanted from the theater and what we wanted to do to it. Nice daydreaming stuff. Arrogant, but we did feel it and we did verbalize it. I was fortunate to get an earlier foothold in the theater, and I remember vividly saying, "You know, Steve, you can't *not* happen." That's very small comfort to somebody when it's not happening, you know. On the other hand, I was right.

Now I want to say something sad. That was twenty years ago, twenty-five years ago, and I think now it can *not* happen, and that's really sad. There are just too few things getting done. Not-for-profit theater has done a great deal to encourage nonmusical playwriting and a great deal to raise the level of acting and scenic design, but it's done almost nothing to encourage the musical theater. And in the commercial theater, you can't ask people to finance a multi-million-dollar musical for a very possibly inspired but totally unknown group of collaborators. At the moment, I'm afraid, there are some good composers who aren't being heard. And because the problem is largely economic, it has very much affected the quality of people who are producing. You see, the ability to raise money doesn't necessarily connect up with the ability to have taste.

Q: What about pressure on established writers when the price tag is so high?

PRINCE: They are enormous, of course, on everybody. We lost a lot of money on the Broadway production of *Pacific Overtures*, parenthetically causing me to think "I can't produce for a while, because I don't enjoy looking for money." It used to be a lot of fun. It was like a game. It's no longer a game. I would like it on record that the individual entrepreneur *should* be a collaborator. Too often, recently, they are not collaborators. They are simply people who sign checks.

Q: Mr. Sondheim, you said content dictates form. Did it dictate the musical form of *Sweeney Todd* as a whole?

SONDHEIM: When I saw *Sweeney Todd* in London, it sang to me. That's the only time this has ever happened to me. I thought, "That would be fun to sing. It lays itself out. Oh, my goodness, an opera," as I realized it was composed of solos, duets, trios, etc. in terms of the structure of the piece. And so in that sense content dictated form. You have the material, you know what it's about, and now comes what is called style, the elusive style of the evening. That's the area where Hal and Hugh and I spent a lot of time talking. What we're really asking here is, how do content and form relate? I think we found the right form for the George Furth plays, for example. There may be another form for them, they could be done hundreds of ways and the writing be just as good. I think we found the right form for them in *Company*. . . .

Obviously, there are so many ways of treating anything and there is no way to test each one. I would love to test *Follies* in different ways. There are so many ways that show could have been done. There are many ways to do *Pa-

cific Overtures. There isn't necessarily only one solution, but one solution *feels* right and locks in. It has that inevitability of good art.

The end of *Sweeney Todd* is something we argued out for quite a while. It had to do very much with tone. Once the tone was decided on, there was a whole last-minute rescue, a humorous moment for Anthony and Johanna, that we wrote and that we actually put on the stage. It didn't quite work. But the planning that all the themes, the musical themes, would collide in the end was always there. I determined that it would be fun for *Sweeney Todd* to start each character with a specific musical theme and develop all that character's music out of that theme, so that each song would depend in the true sense of the word on the last one. Sweeney's opening scene dictates his next song, and so on. It's a handy compositional principle, and it seemed to me that it would pay off very nicely at the end.

Hal has always been very fond of a technique that I think works very well. We discussed it last summer in Majorca when I went there to work with him and Hugh. It actually started in *Night Music*. Hal wanted to have in *Night Music* a series of reprises of all the songs at the end. We didn't get in more than five songs, but it was very effective. Then when Hal worked on *Evita* he was impressed by the use of certain leitmotifs, and by the audience's recognition of them whenever they would occur. It's the movie music technique, you know, utilizing few themes but utilizing them many times so the same emotional underpinning occurs. Hugh said he thought that would be very useful at the end of *Sweeney Todd.* I not only agreed, but it was something that I had been working towards with these little modules. And so I wrote the last twenty minutes of *Sweeney Todd* while we were in rehearsal. Even Hal wasn't upset that I lacked the last twenty minutes because it seemed inevitable, all the homework and all the groundwork had been done. In fact, I had the best time writing the last twenty minutes of *Sweeney Todd* of anything I've done since the background music of *Stavisky.* It was just a matter of "O.K., let's scare them here." It was all just kids putting on a show, very easy.

Q: How much do you know about the way a song is going to be staged before you start writing it?

SONDHEIM: I don't, but I usually have specific ideas. What happens is, the collaborators sit down and discuss—I like everyone to mention every possible idea for a song that they can think of, so that I have pages of song ideas and don't run dry. Maybe I end up with three ideas on each page of the script because, you know, you can sing about anything, and then I start planning each one very specifically. But the point is, if you make a libretto then the choreographer and the director can make a libretto. That is to say, they can take what you have done and throw it all out, but there is a basis of structure. Many times Hal will do something completely different from what I had intended, but he *knows* what my intention was.

Q: Mr. Sondheim, has anyone ever taken a concept of yours and ruined it?

SONDHEIM: I don't think that's ever happened. I don't think there has been anything in any show I have ever done, not just the ones with Hal, where I would say that what I had written was totally distorted. I have certain disagreements on details, a few with Hal, a couple without Hal, but not an awful lot. Sometimes I deplore what an actor does, but that is quite a different thing. I don't think I have had that experience.

PRINCE: I have to think there are some.

SONDHEIM: No, I would still be angry about it.

PRINCE: I was very frightened of *Sweeney Todd,* I will have to tell you. I think that's a good sign now, a kind of key word. I shouldn't give this away, but whenever I say to myself, "Oh, God, is this pretentious," I am usually on pretty good ground. It's when I am not frightened that I have to watch out, because maybe it's too easy.

Q: How much did the Christopher Bond play contribute to your libretto?

SONDHEIM: In my opinion, our *Sweeney Todd* is very close to the spirit of the Bond play. Hal might disagree with me.

PRINCE: I confess I did not understand the Bond play until we were within a week of previewing. I read it years earlier, and except for Steve's assurances about the way it played, it seemed too terse. I couldn't fill out any of it. I couldn't imagine how those scenes were played. Then we got a libretto and went to work, and occasionally went back to Bond, and he was very helpful. But originally I did not understand that play.

Q: How do you pick a set designer for a particular project?

PRINCE: You cast a set designer just as you cast any other creative person. Certain set designers have a gift for the primitive abrasive . . . those are complimentary words. That's the stuff I like, just in case anybody is misunderstanding me. Other designers have an incredible gift for props; others, enormous structural facility and no patience whatsoever with props. You just have to pick the right person for the material. What is *nice* to report, in large part thanks to the regional theater, there are many good set designers around. It's thrilling. There didn't used to be. There used to be only a handful of people and they did everything.

Q: Do the actors take part in the collaborative process?

PRINCE: If they are good, they add plenty, they are collaborators. In the larger sense, a good actor is a contributor, depending on where his head is— whether he's there to serve the project or simply to serve or protect himself. A very talented actor who's only interested in serving himself presents more difficulty than he's worth. *Sweeney Todd* was the perfect experience from both our points of view. You couldn't ask for more creative actors—and that extends to the ensemble. Those people are extraordinary. It's not a large cast, only thirty-two or thirty-three people, and I fully expect a dozen of them are going to be principal players in musicals and nonmusicals.

SONDHEIM: The best kind of actor is the silent kind, whose presence and approach to the performance is what sparks you. I am talking from the writing point of view. *Sweeney Todd* was easy to write the minute we had cast Angela Lansbury—it wasn't a matter of writing for Angela Lansbury, it was a matter of writing for Angela Lansbury as Mrs. Lovett. Len Cariou was cast very early, and again it was a matter of writing for Len as Sweeney, not just Sweeney and not just Len. That's the best kind of collaboration. Shakespeare had the great advantage of writing for a company of actors whose capabilities he knew.

PRINCE: Actors can leave their mark on the show, and when they are replaced or you do another company, they have left something there that you don't want to throw away. Now, if you want to go through the process of amending again and restaging a scene with a new actor, you can do it and maybe discover some swell new things, but we tend to be lazy.

Q: Were there any projects that you started and dropped?

SONDHEIM: Oh, we had a terrific idea once when we were about four years old, an idea that I would still like to work on one day. It's the life of a particular man who interests me. He actually lived around the turn of the century. I am being coy about it.

PRINCE: I think of three or four aborted projects. Steve has written some terrific material. He sits down and plays the piano and says, "That's from *that* show that never happened, and that's from *that* show that never happened."

Q: Is temperament a factor in your collaboration?

SONDHEIM: I think our temperaments mesh very well. One of the reasons is, I never think beyond my nose and Hal *always* has some kind of plan for the next two years. He is active and I am passive. I wait for the phone to ring and for Hal to say, "Let's do a . . ." or "Have you read . . ." or "I have something that you should read . . ." or "I have a playwright I want you to meet . . ." or whatever.

Any story that interests me, I am perfectly willing to tell. I don't think in terms of breaking new ground, and I doubt if Hal does either. It's "That story would be fun to tell, and let's tell it this way." I might do a very conventional show, conventional in the sense of traditional. There's nothing wrong with that. *Night Music* was an attempt, if you look at it that way, though it was not a conscious attempt on our part. Our original intention was a much more elaborate, quite experimental memory piece, and it turned out that its best form was its simplest and most traditional. What we tried to do was infuse some rejuvenating life into the operetta form, because that is what the material seems to call for. Hal kept saying, "Let's not resist it just because it's called operetta. Nobody has done it in twenty-five years, but maybe it isn't old hat." Well, I think it's always a mistake to think about what you are doing. Just tell it. Agree, disagree?

PRINCE: Agree, yes. I put great faith in instinct, the subconscious, something that moves you in some direction. On the other hand, here's a contradiction: I *do* think about the direction that things are going. Today there is no idea that is not feasible, as far as I can see, for a musical.

SONDHEIM: I just want to say that I am not likely to be interested in something that doesn't try something new, because it is fun to explore unexplored territory and boring to go some place you've been. If somebody suggested, "Hey, let's do a backstage story about a show-business mother and tell about her relationship with her daughter over a period of ten years," it is unlikely that I would be interested in doing it.

PRINCE: You do, thank God, develop your craft, and you begin to know, *finally* you begin to know there are some things you can do, some effects you can create, that will grab an audience, manipulate an audience if you will. Well, while you are very glad to know that you can do this because you can't be inspired every damn day (whoever thought you could?), it also makes you very suspicious of this equipment. I mean, sometimes you just do something out of a lot of knowledge, a lot of earlier stretching, and a scene will play. Nevertheless I tend to walk away thinking that it came from the wrong place, which is why I said before that naked fear at the point right before you finally take the plunge and go into rehearsal is probably mandatory. If it isn't there, it makes me very uneasy.

SONDHEIM: Yes, comfortable work is usually dull work.

Q: Why has there been less dancing in your later work?

PRINCE: Personally, I've had enough of dancing musicals. It's hard to dance in depth what's going on with characters. In a conventional sense, the old musicals used to dance in depth, and it was as embarrassing as hell—rolling around in torment, or all those happy things on the green. I may get untired of dancing musicals one of these days, but right now I gravitate toward projects which diminish the possibility of dancing. There's something else called choreographed movement—the Pirelli number in *Sweeney Todd*, for example. Larry Fuller's work.

SONDHEIM: Absolutely, done by a choreographer.

Q: Does having outside producers as in the case of *Sweeney Todd* affect your collaboration?

PRINCE: The truth is, not all that much. They have been supportive and, you know, it hasn't been a big deal at all.

SONDHEIM: When I ride in a car and I am not driving the car, I am always slightly tense even if the driver is very good. I would imagine that Hal has just that feeling of being not exactly in the driver's seat. He is not making *all* the decisions, when he is used to making all the decisions. It doesn't affect me at all.

Q: Is the book musical dead?

PRINCE: No, to ask that comes from the same onerous desire to pigeonhole. Calling things operas, calling things musicals. Nothing is dead. Nothing is *not* dead. Book musical is a label that has no meaning whatsoever.

More to the point, in the theater we are competing with other media in a way that we never did before. That's reflected in the rejection of certain kinds of musical theater, that you can get at home by turning a dial. There's an invitation in the theater to explore what you can *only* get in the theater, what you can *only* get in that relationship between the audience and the live actor; larger-than-life excitement like *Sweeney Todd*. Talk about a lot of plot, that musical is about as linear as you can get. More than that, it's large. The emotions, the style of the acting would have been considered embarrassingly large and Victorian twenty years ago . . . screaming like that and chewing scenery that way. Well, I maintain that it's thrilling because they are doing it within the confines of the period, the characters they are playing and the style of the piece. It becomes new—again.

SONDHEIM: In fact, what is new and different in the theater is that there are so many forms that it can take. That's what's wonderful about it. I mean that's what's really *vibrant.*

Q: Why do there seem to be so many breakdowns of the collaborative effort, with more and more people coming in to make last-minute changes?

SONDHEIM: It generally means that the original collaboration wasn't kosher. They weren't doing the same show. When you read about all this changing partners, you know there's some lack of very basic rapport going on there, otherwise the show would have jelled. Not necessarily been successful, that's not what I mean, but everybody would have decided, "That's the show I want. Gee, why don't they like it?" and gotten to work on it.

PRINCE: The collaborative chemistry should include people who are not your contemporaries and are also new to the theater scene. It keeps things boiling. I'll give you a reverse example: In 1948 there was a show called *Miss Liberty* which had Moss Hart as the director, a book by Robert Sherwood, music by Irving Berlin and choreography by Jerome Robbins. Well, let me tell you, all you had to do was sit in the theater and look at the stage to know that everybody was being just too goddamn polite to everybody else. I am not talking about the need for fighting and being mean-minded, I am talking about being honest. Apparently it was very difficult to turn to somebody on *Miss Liberty* and say, "Is that really a good song? I don't like that song." I do believe that all those people were caught in a sort of respectful gavotte.

SONDHEIM: And the trouble is if you don't do that in the beginning, then you do it during rehearsals. "I never liked that song"—that's one of the worst sentences I ever heard in my life. Also, it is very important in a musical that there be somebody in charge. There has to be a boss. In today's theater it is usually the director, but in the old days it was the producer. That is one of the things Hal is deploring in these shows with a constant change of personality . . . there's no boss, and that's what's wrong.

Q: Does that apply to the writing as well as the production?

SONDHEIM: A writer's collaboration is a perfectly legitimate collaboration. *West Side Story* was a writers' collaboration. We wrote the show and then brought it to a producer. Of course, it's hard to have a boss in the writing process. But you need one later on when everything starts to fall apart, and the pressure is on.

Q: Do you have any special way of deciding what you're going to do next?

PRINCE: It could be a set of characters or a milieu . . . even the size and feel of a project. Talk about amorphous—but you say to yourself, "That's what I would like to do next." I don't know what the next step will be. It would be a lot easier if somebody would bring us a play that has characters and size ready-made. But you see, I don't think there are any rules about anything. You feel like moving to something else, not necessarily ahead, just somewhere else.

HUMOR

Russell Baker
Jules Feiffer
Herb Gardner
Terrence McNally
Joseph Stein

TERRENCE MCNALLY: I love low humor.

JULES FEIFFER: There're periods when people take only sophisticated humor seriously, as in Noel Coward, and then you'll find periods of reversion, with so-called lowbrow humor being considered highbrow. At the time the Marx Brothers were on Broadway they weren't considered highbrow humorists, but now they're taken very much that way.

RUSSELL BAKER: There's nothing which *everyone* perceives as funny, and forty to sixty percent of the population doesn't see *anything* as funny. But the suggestion that they don't have a sense of humor makes them nervous, so they laugh.

JOSEPH STEIN: Where'd you get that statistic?

BAKER: I'm very good at statistics.

STEIN: I would have said fifty-four percent.

BAKER: Either way you have to depend on the hype. Somebody has to say, "Funniest damn evening I've spent in the theater in years," and then these people will buy tickets and go, and they'll laugh.

HERB GARDNER: All of us here have some sense of absurdness. We have no way of writing a scene in which there won't be something funny. We hear life like that—with things missing. What would our version of *Death of a Salesman* be like? I don't know.

We have a useful schizophrenia, we've found a way to take what might have appeared to be imbalance if we hadn't become writers and make it work for us in some creative jiu-jitsu fashion. What was painful becomes funny, and what we'd like to go and see in the theater is what we write.

BAKER: What's funny usually results from disappointed expectations. An old woman walking down the street slips on a banana peel and falls—that's not funny. A man in a top hat slips and falls—that's funny because people in top hats aren't supposed to be able to fall. There's a sudden upsetting of your expectations.

FEIFFER: When I was a kid, I began to recognize humor as a finite thing when I began to read Robert Benchley. I never thought of humor as *humor* before that. Benchley somehow connected with my own inner life as a twelve-year-old in the Bronx. It was, curiously, my autobiography, although he was writing as an urbane Harvard graduate. He had nothing to do with my life, but he connected with all my doubts and insecurities—when to call out your floor to the elevator operator, how to order in a luncheonette, all that stuff that seemed too petty to think about but riddled me with anxiety. He taught me how to see all the petty hang-ups as funny rather than aggravating. It was an amazing breakthrough for me.

STEIN: When I became involved with Sid Caesar on *Your Show of Shows* it was a leap forward for me, because Sid wasn't doing the kind of things that were being done then in radio and television. He was doing character comedy—but very controlled and imaginative.

MCNALLY: Where I grew up in Corpus Christi, Texas, funny was *Catcher in the Rye,* but that was a kind of secret because it was a "dirty book." When I begin to think of legitimate stage comedy I keep coming back to A *Funny Thing Happened on the Way to the Forum.* It's such a sophisticated use of an old form of comedy.

GARDNER: For me, it was Henry Morgan. He had a fifteen-minute show from 6:15 to 6:30, and I used to feel that they made this man up, with this attitude and his tone of voice, and put him on the radio so that only I could hear him. You remember how personally you felt about your radio—I had this little yellow radio, and I knew he was going to be there at 6:15 and say these impossible things.

FEIFFER: I felt the same way about Morgan and some years later about Jean Shepherd like a kind of conspiracy. . . .

GARDNER: Humor and companionship. He'd come on at 6:15 and in about ten seconds set up an incredible premise you felt only you could understand. This attitude then becomes more and more plausible as he goes on. It's all connected with how I feel about humor. There has to be an attitude set without which no individual moment means anything. For some of us it was Benchley, for me it was Henry Morgan, the voice on the radio—you were alone with him, fighting against impossible odds.

BAKER: There're people I *didn't* think were funny when I was a kid that I now break up over—specifically, Laurel and Hardy. They used to bore me stiff, but now I can't see enough of them. They strike me as supreme artists. I grew up marinated in the radio of the 1930s, and the funniest guy who ever lived remains Fred Allen. Fifteen years later, Sid Caesar was sometimes doing on television what Allen did in radio, but Allen himself could never make the transfer.

STEIN: I don't think Caesar did the satirical, kind of biting thing that Allen did.

BAKER: No, but the spirit was the same.

MCNALLY: If I were making a list of things that aren't funny I'd start out with Aristophanes.

FEIFFER: Molière is terribly funny.

BAKER: Molière *reads* funny.

MCNALLY: Played passionately, Molière is funny. He writes about very bold subjects.

BAKER: You can read him and laugh right off the page.

FEIFFER: Yes, you understand the truth of Molière in a literary sense more than you do on the stage. There's no time when Molière's going to be mediocre.

FEIFFER: It's weird about comedy—you can go back and forth in a way you can't do with what is thought of as "more serious" literature. Some serious plays one loved in one's youth seem like kid stuff when you go back and see them years later.

BAKER: *The Petrified Forest.*

FEIFFER: Yes. Plays that once were enormous parts of my life but now seem like chestnuts. Go back to a comedy you once loved, and you find that much more of it still works, much more of it still seems fresh and enjoyable.

MCNALLY: I wouldn't mind a melodrama like *The Petrified Forest* not working, but I'd hate not to love *Catcher in the Rye.*

GARDNER: What about your own scripts?

FEIFFER: It's amazing, they all still work.

BAKER: I remember I spent a lot of time laughing at a man called Parkyacarkus.

FEIFFER: Yes, and a lot of material from those days is still very funny. I wrote a screenplay for *Popeye*, which drove me to go back and research the original *Popeye* cartoons done in the 1930s by E. C. Segar for King Features Syndicate. To my surprise, delight and amazement, it turned out to be a work of genius. Looking at the microfilms, I cracked up laughing at stuff that I know damn well I wouldn't have been sophisticated enough—or my family wouldn't have been sophisticated enough—to find really funny when it first came out. Things like: Popeye saves a girl's life, and she turns out to be the daughter of a millionaire. The millionaire wants to give him a reward and offers him a bag of gold with a dollar sign on it. Popeye says, "No, I don't accept rewards." The rich man says, "Look, I'm rich, I've got plenty of money, you've got to take this reward." Popeye says no. The rich man says, "I got rich because I always get my way. You have to take my reward." Popeye says, "I can't, it's against my moraliky." The guy says, "I'll give you ten thousand dollars if you take my reward," and he goes up to a million dollars trying to persuade Popeye to accept this one bag of gold. I was holding my breath as I followed Segar along this track, because I couldn't believe anything this marvelous, this brilliant. Who out there really understood how wonderful this was at the time it was going on?

BAKER: Noel Coward suddenly had this funny idea: a divorced couple, both remarried, meet on adjoining balconies. That's all he had to start with in *Private Lives*.

MCNALLY: By idea you also mean situation. Those adjoining balconies strike me as a funny idea, a way a play about marriage can begin.

STEIN: You have to start with a great deal more than that—who those four people are, the relationships, the conflicts, what you want to say with the play.

FEIFFER: If everyone here were given the adjoining balconies to do a play about, the plays would all be very different, because we all bring different attitudes and different biographies to it. One of the most interesting things about humor on or off the stage is the matter of disguise—how one is terribly evasive and elliptical about the truth of one's own life as translated into humor. Often the author himself or herself is unaware of what's going into it.

BAKER: Writing a column is often a process of exploring yourself. You don't know where you're going to come out when you go in. You get an opening line, and then the length is so short it's like swimming under water.

FEIFFER: Herb, a couple of years ago when I asked how something you were writing was going, you said, "I feel like a war correspondent going to my own life as though it were the front."

GARDNER: I think all of us float around in general distress until we hit upon the one way to get all the distress in one place. Terrence was saying, what's wrong with starting with a funny idea? I think he means what I mean: find that one channel for all those ideas you were floating around with that year, or ten years ago, and suddenly there's your scattered miscellaneous file all fitting into one place. You think of a mouthpiece, a character in the best sense of the word, or a situation that seems to have some distance to it. You've all had that moment, walking down the street or something, when you come up with a fifteen-rounder.

BAKER: Do you find that your best moments, the things you think are funniest if they work out, are spontaneous? You may know very well where you're going to come out once you go in, but you find that the stuff that is really the best is stuff that happens to you in the writing. It's not planned.

FEIFFER: I wouldn't think it was spontaneous, so much as unpremeditated. It doesn't happen out of thin air, but it's as if you can predict that unpredictable things are going to happen, once you get started.

BAKER: As if it's in the material. Michelangelo gets out the statue that's in the stone.

FEIFFER: You discover it's organic after you've done it. You didn't know that at the time.

MCNALLY: There are things that can't wait. You're going to write a play about these two people in this situation, and something is going to happen maybe an hour into the play that you can't wait to begin writing. There's a getting-up to that scene that you know has to be in it.

FEIFFER: Often I end up throwing out the scene that I was working toward all the time.

STEIN: Characters take on a life of their own and go in directions you hadn't anticipated. If you follow them you can find new exciting, unexpected areas.

FEIFFER: *Knock Knock* radically altered my way of writing. Up till then in my plays and in the movie *Carnal Knowledge* I had written what I thought of as illustrated essays. I knew the point I wanted to make, and I discovered a means of illustrating it theatrically, trying for characters who would have as much reality and connection to each other as possible. I knew where I was going, and if I took a detour I could usually find my way back to the point I wanted to make. With *Knock Knock* I simply wanted to give myself a good time. When I sat down I had no idea what I was getting into. I just put these two guys in the house and had them start talking. I didn't know where they were going, but I got interested in what they were saying, and out of that it seemed natural for Joan of Arc to come into the house. It wasn't until I'd finished the first act that I got the idea I was also writing a play *about* something. I guess I assumed that it would end up being about something, because any stream of consciousness is about yourself and your thoughts. Somewhere there lurks an idea, and if you're going to end up with a decent piece of work in any art form, that idea will eventually come to the surface.

McNALLY: Jules, when you started your play you didn't know Joan of Arc was going to be in it?

FEIFFER: No, I didn't.

BAKER: You were noodling.

FEIFFER: Exactly.

McNALLY: When I started *The Ritz*, Rita Moreno's part wasn't in it. Now it seems impossible that the play could ever *not* have her, just as you obviously wanted to write a play about Joan of Arc and thought of these two men after a while.

FEIFFER: I now love to do what I used to think real writers did, start off with people in a situation and then go back and trace the idea. I used to lay it out ahead of time. Now I try to start with no model at all. I feel free to let it follow its own trail, always assuming that it's going to lead where it's supposed to.

McNALLY: I start with some sensual image that I can see or hear or smell in my imagination. The play I'm working on now is based on hearing piano music through a door. That's the image of the play, like being at a big party, but you're in a little room, and every time somebody comes in or out you hear the voices and the music.

FEIFFER: It's weird for a cartoonist to say this, but I've never thought of a play in terms of images. I think of how I'm getting along with you and how you're getting along with me. Basically, it all begins with an attitude toward a relationship.

GARDNER: You no longer try to figure out in advance where the whole thing will be a third of the way through?

FEIFFER: No, but a third of the way through I'm curious, and so I *have* begun to figure out what's already happened within the work.

BAKER: What's the difference between writing funny for the page and the stage? One for the eye and the other for the ear, or both eye and ear?

FEIFFER: Gentleness. There's a theatrical tone you automatically take when writing for the theater that you don't fall into in fiction and other forms, where you're allowed to be more intricate. Obviously there's nuance and subtlety in theater, but it's basically unfriendly to very fine degrees of nuance. You seldom find even in the most brilliant and serious of plays the intricate levels of characterization that you find in a novel of the same substance. It can almost never be done. The only time I've seen it done is by Strindberg.

BAKER: When I do a column I visualize the characters in highly caricatured form, in a fictional context. But it's not like a scene in the theater, which is there only because it leads to the *next* scene.

FEIFFER: You're kind of cursed with total freedom. You can work in any form you want, all the way from straight opinion to out-and-out satire.

BAKER: That's very important for a newspaper column. People get tired of newspaper columns very quickly, they get fed up with somebody talking three times a week for ten years. Most columnists always come on the same, in the same form year after year—you read the first line and know just what the rest is going to be. I work on the principle that if you keep changing you'll hold back the audience's boredom a few more years. I'm always struggling to stop the audience from thinking "Why doesn't that Baker just go and jump off a cliff?"

MCNALLY: We're cursed with the same freedom—haven't we all written a straight opinion play? We know there'll come a day when people will get sick of us and no longer consider us funny.

BAKER: This may be a twentieth-century neurosis of all writers. It never occurred to Dickens that his audience was going to get sick of him. From *The Pickwick Papers* to *Our Mutual Friend,* he was perfectly self-confident.

STEIN: Jokes as such don't mean anything in the theater. They don't work. Relationships and characters are what count. If you have the right relationships and characters as a springboard, you'll find the humor. And much of the humor comes as a surprise—it's not carefully planned, as a joke would be. And sometimes you build a whole scene for humor because the characters are kind of pushing you in that direction.

BAKER: Are you making a distinction between humor and comedy?

STEIN: No, I think they're substantially interchangeable.

FEIFFER: Except that we mean different things when we call one person a comedian and another a humorist.

MCNALLY: If someone asked me to write a joke I'm sure I couldn't do it.

BAKER: I can't even *tell* a joke.

MCNALLY: But I wish I could. I feel like a classical singer who can't trill. I'm a comedy writer, and I should be able to write a joke.

GARDNER: I sometimes wish I could. I admire jokes.

MCNALLY: Have you ever been able to make up a joke and then go to a party and tell it and make people laugh? I haven't.

FEIFFER: I hear a lot of jokes, but I can never remember them.

BAKER: *Knock Knock* is full of jokes.

FEIFFER: It's full of old radio and vaudeville routines out of the garbage bin in my head.

BAKER: What's funny about a lot of those *Knock Knock* jokes is what lousy jokes they are.

FEIFFER: Exactly, exactly. Fibber McGee's closet. "I'll give you the answer, you give me the question." Everything I've ever listened to, dating way back to childhood.

GARDNER: Those wonderful dumb jokes being said . . .

FEIFFER: The thing is, they all come out of the situation and characters. They couldn't just be thrown into the play, they had a reason for being there.

MCNALLY: I have a list of about twenty-five play titles I hope to use some day. One of them was *Knock Knock*, but I'll forgive you.

BAKER: In lecturing you find that laughter begets laughter. A small audience in a big house sits apart from one another, and it's deadly. It's as though people were insulated from each other. Put that same audience into a small house where they're packed together, and when one guy laughs it's infectious—everybody laughs.

STEIN: It's very dangerous to depend on hired or canned laughter. And when I hear laugh tracks on TV it always comes into my mind that those are dead people laughing.

GARDNER: When they were doing a lot of live television comedy in New York there used to be a little four-hundred-seat theater called Television Preview Theater where, I was told, a lot of today's laugh tracks were originally recorded. Recently I was helping a friend with something he was doing on TV, and we were using this old track labeled "Television Preview Theater 1949–50." The man operating the machine has got it down to where he can supply ribald laughter, followed by an echo, followed by this one distinctive laugh, one little voice going "ah ha!" in Television Preview Theater in 1949, laughing at *Rhoda* tomorrow night. It's eerie.

BAKER: It's the basis for a poignant story. This guy has nothing to remember of his father, except he continues to exist as a laugh on a sound track. . .

GARDNER: These poor spirits will be forever laughing at next year's television shows. They're immortal.

FEIFFER: Worse than hired laughter is hit laughter. During the first six or eight weeks of the show the audience comes in knowing they're going to see *the* comic writer of the century, because isn't that what the critics said that morning?

STEIN: They laugh at the curtain.

FEIFFER: Yes. There's a relentlessness about the laughter that denies the show. The actors know within thirty seconds that they don't even have to *be* there. They get terribly depressed, so invariably you see a rotten performance. Their energy is being drained by the audience. They're being manipulated and destroyed by the audience.

MCNALLY: Conspiracy to have a good time. The night I saw *Dracula*, the sound of a wolf howling got a huge laugh even before the curtain went up. They all want to laugh at that old melodrama.

FEIFFER: Some things become so predictable that if you do them you feel yourself in disgrace—so you have to *not* do them. There's nothing wrong with having a limited audience. Attempting to broaden or deepen it artificially is a mistake that would seriously undermine one's gifts in the long run. You've got what you've got, you work with it the best way you know how. Whoever is there is going to be there.

MCNALLY: I think you'd have to agree that those of us sitting here tend to write funny things. We have to decide when we want our first laugh. It's how you get your first laugh that sets the entire tone of the play. If you begin with a joke, you're going to get a "heh-heh-heh." In some of my plays I've waited very long for that first laugh, but when it finally comes the audience really knows it's meant to be funny. In my first comedy, *Next*, they laughed when the character entered the room. There hadn't been one line of dialogue, but there was this huge laugh because it was a three-hundred-pound woman in a sergeant's outfit. In *The Ritz* I wanted to set up another mood, and they didn't laugh for a very long time. That first laugh is the crucial one. If you're just being funny with words you'll never get the kind of laugh that comes from the audience caring about your people.

FEIFFER: Every audience will react the same way once the play's set. There's a shakedown period during the first half-dozen previews or so when it all seems unsettled, then suddenly it'll settle down as if the same audience were coming back night after night. The laughter becomes more solidified and after a while it becomes almost like clockwork. In *Knock Knock* we could tell which way the evening was going to go by the frog story—if it didn't get a round of applause we were in trouble. In lecturing, too, you can tell by that first laugh how the rest of it will go, including the world-shaking stuff that's without humor. You can tell how the audience will follow you down any road.

GARDNER: If the jokes didn't need the play the audience wouldn't laugh as much.

STEIN: That's certainly true in musicals. Today's musical is written substantially as a play—the music, the humor are all integrated, part of the developing action, part of the script itself. It comes out of the characters and relationships of the play. The same is true of the lyrics, but very few can write a lyric that isn't *just* funny but also becomes part of the show's structure, like Frank Loesser's comedy numbers in *Guys and Dolls*. Songs like that set the tone for the whole show.

MCNALLY: Surely Cole Porter . . .

STEIN: Yes.

FEIFFER: Would you include Larry Hart?

STEIN: Larry Hart wrote funny lyrics, but not the kind used today which become part of the story.

FEIFFER: Very few songs make you hysterical with laughter when taken out of the context of the show.

STEIN: That's right. Take "Politics and Poker" in *Fiorello*—if you just sing it it's kind of bewildering, but within the show it's marvelous.

MCNALLY: Once in an audition I heard a score whose every number was hilarious even though you didn't know exactly what was taking place. But later, in the theater, it wasn't funny.

STEIN: Just one of those mysterious combinations of things that sometimes takes place. A song in a living room has a different impact from a song in a theater. If the audience doesn't go with the characters, or the performers, or the situation, the song will suffer. That's one of the reasons for the out-of-town rewrites.

FEIFFER: Sometimes the atmosphere is so good-humored, the song itself is so good-humored, that it's taken to be funny, like "I'm Just a Gal Who Cain't Say No" in *Oklahoma!*

BAKER: You set up a series of expectations with this wholesome, turn-of-the-century, family musical, and suddenly this character Ado Annie is singing in an entirely different way, "I'm Just a Gal Who Cain't Say No." It *is* funny.

STEIN: The biggest laughs in the shows I've done were like Tevye coming upstage in *Fiddler on the Roof* and saying, "What am I going to tell Golde? Another dream?" That's not in and of itself funny, but it relates to the whole situation in which he had previously made up an involved dream as an explanation to his wife.

FEIFFER: Which goes back to radio comedy. Jack Benny's biggest laughs had to do with previously known situations. His voice echoing and the sound of his footsteps going down into that dungeon put the audience into hysterics.

STEIN: The single biggest laugh Jack Benny ever got was being held up: "Your money or your life!"

BAKER: A long pause.

FEIFFER: Yes.

STEIN: Just the pause.

MCNALLY: There's something about Beatrice Arthur. They ask her a question, and she gets not one but two laughs—first her reaction, then her answer. "How old are you, Maude?" The audience howls. Then her answer. The audience howls again.

BAKER: In a way, that's the kind of laugh you're saying you don't want to get. That's the cheap laugh. You know you can get it anytime you want.

MCNALLY: No, that's in character. In a play, you don't get that kind of laugh until the second act.

FEIFFER: It's there, and the art is in not abusing it, not taking advantage of it.

If you're using it in a half-hour sitcom, that's one thing. If you're using it in a play you do so very judiciously—you know when and when not to use it. The rules are different.

STEIN: In a sitcom you're not writing for the laughs, you're writing for the situation. The laughs should build into the next situation.

FEIFFER: I find sitcoms very hard to watch—like *Rhoda*. While they begin with characters, they degenerate into wisecracks and jokes, so that my original affection for the character makes me offended at how that character is used.

GARDNER: You sometimes feel that the people who are writing the sitcoms have stopped having a real life of any kind. They're now basing the characters on other characters in other situation comedies. No one has a history. No one has a life around the story. We are all somehow in the past business, and we put ourselves in danger of literally running out of our past by going to write in Hollywood. In a couple of years your past ends, and all you can do is write a play about your agent. Things stop happening to you. Your day is made up of what "works" or "doesn't work," or whatever those expressions are. You stop having a history.

I once saw the Crazy Gang in a place called the Comedy Theater in London in a play called *The Bed-Sitting Room*. The premise of the play was that because of some nuclear holocaust a man is mutated into a one-room apartment. The curtain goes up, and a narrator's voice says, "As a result of our last war, I am a one-room apartment."

FEIFFER: Great!

GARDNER: A sort of play began after that, but it wasn't the same any of the three times I saw it. The ending was always the same, though, making use in some way of the fact that the audience always stands when "God Save the Queen" is played. The first night I saw it, Spike Mulligan came out wearing a diver's outfit and a huge diving helmet. He took out a comb and some tissue paper, opened the helmet, put in the comb and tissue paper and then closed it. From inside the helmet you heard "God Save the Queen" . . . and everyone stood up. When everyone was standing, he lifted the little lid in front of the helmet and said, "If you'll stand for that, you'll stand for anything." He didn't use the diving helmet again, but every night I saw the show he would come out with some outrageous way of playing "God Save the Queen." I don't know where you'd place this sort of comedy. It was undefinable—and mad.

BAKER: Writing for the theater, you leave a lot out, don't you?

FEIFFER: We were talking about this the other day, and Herb said when you first get an idea in mind you've got it one hundred percent. As you're walking home to write it down, it dribbles out, ten percent, twenty percent, fifty percent. . . .

GARDNER: Between my head and the paper, translating it into English from whatever colored images I started with, I end up with about twenty-two or twenty-five percent. And there are certain actors who bring back the seventy-five percent you lost on the way to the desk.

BAKER: Do you write with that in mind, that the actor will have to see to this?

STEIN: No. The theater is collaborative, and you depend a great deal on your actor, your director, even your set designer, but hopefully you visualize while putting the idea on paper that it's going to be done absolutely perfectly.

McNALLY: If I have an actor in the world it's Jimmy Coco. I can't *be* funny, and I envy him his ability to be funny onstage. To me, the words "comic" and "comedian" have always applied to performers. "Humorist," even—it means Will Rogers. I'm just a writer who likes writing for someone like Jimmy. I would have loved to have written for Zero Mostel.

STEIN: Zero, like a lot of performers who are marvelously funny onstage, sometimes had no idea what was funny. When I gave him that exit line I quoted earlier—"What am I going to tell Golde? Another dream?"—he said, "I can't walk out in silence." I assured him the audience would laugh, and he finally did it with great reluctance.

GARDNER: Joe, you were writing for Henry Morgan and Sid Caesar while we were being influenced by them.

STEIN: I was very lucky, I fell in with two very exciting performers and shows. It was a great training ground. When I was young I loved the Marx Brothers. I guess I still find them very funny, though I'm sometimes just a little disappointed when I see their work now. Nobody ever watches Chaplin any more, but I still think he was very funny. I loved those two-reelers.

GARDNER: The acid test is those nostalgia albums of old radio shows. I got one about a year ago and put off listening to it for days, because I didn't know what was going to happen. Finally I listened to it and I was happy to find that it was not only very funny, there were two Fred Allen sequences where he was making fun of all straight men with the most obscure, crazy connections.

FEIFFER: I loved Bob Hope when I was a kid. He may not seem as funny as he once did, but to be funny for twenty or thirty years is truly remarkable. In the late 1950s I was beginning to do cartoons and feeling that there was no one else out there. I turned on *Omnibus* on TV, and there was a couple named Mike Nichols and Elaine May nobody had ever heard of. It was a breathtaking experience.

BAKER: Richard Nixon.

McNALLY: You're not going to get a laugh out of him.

FEIFFER: No, the only way you'll get a laugh out of such people is intimidation, and then you haven't made a point anyway.

McNALLY: It's easier to be satirical. You're writing about people you don't like, and the audience agrees with you or they wouldn't be there. We all went through the period of writing our Vietnam plays, played to an adoring audience.

FEIFFER: That's not my definition of satire at all.

BAKER: Satire is political.

FEIFFER: One of the rules for me is to work from inside the characters, never from outside, whatever the comments are, whatever the political or sociological points you're making; to do it with an understanding of the logic that propels the characters you have no sympathy for to perform the actions they do, so that it's understandable to the audience. It's never about "those guys"—it's always about "us" watching.

MCNALLY: I agree, collaborating with the audience is a part of satire.

FEIFFER: From my knowledge of your work, I've never seen you be cruel about "them."

BAKER: Isn't wit un-American?

FEIFFER: Humor is basically un-American, and wit is the most un-American form of humor.

GARDNER: I assume that in the time of Oscar Wilde "wit" meant the individual statement, plays of a style where you could haul off and say, "Women of today are:" and make a statement. It was perfectly acceptable to have epigrammatical characters who spoke like that.

STEIN: Right, in *The Importance of Being Earnest* you don't care at all about who gets who, the play is all in the lines.

FEIFFER: Like the book of an old musical.

STEIN: In a kind of a way. Wit tries to make a statement about morals and mores. In Wilde's case he had a technical trick, he surprises you at the end of every line—like somebody saying, "I was sorry for myself because I had no shoes until I met a man who had no car."

FEIFFER: It's much simpler. Wit has an English accent.

BAKER: Restoration comedy. One right after another. Wit comes out of the classical tradition, the eighteenth century, and Americans are not a very eighteenth-century people. What makes us laugh is broad.

STEIN: Mark Twain.

BAKER: The tall tale, the extravagant story, the big gesture, and wit is the opposite of all that.

GARDNER: Those early things we all read and listened to were witty, but not in the same way; the same graceful use of language, but crazier, madder.

STEIN: Much broader.

BAKER: Groucho Marx came closer to wit than anybody else I can think of.

FEIFFER: Mark Twain had a kind of sly wit, country wit, a cross between wit and humor. Wit has a lot to do with the establishing of credentials. Right now, basically, we're talking about English wit, but there's a way blacks use mother wit, a way rural Southerners use sly and witty coded language is that available to the cognoscenti but not to the outsider.

BAKER: There was a Speaker of the House of Representatives who said of a member of the House he couldn't stand, "He never opens his mouth without subtracting from the sum of human knowledge." That's wit.

FEIFFER: Wit requires a certain degree of snobbery, often duplicitous snobbery. It's "I understand and you don't."

BAKER: Arrogance informed by intellectualism, always involving elegant wordplay.

McNALLY: I reread Wilde's four plays this summer on the beach, and they made me laugh out loud. The reality of those plays is very strong. I'd dispute Joe's statement that you don't care in Wilde who marries whom. With *Salome* I don't care about the ending so much, but with the others I do. Nobody even attempts to write in that style of wit anymore.

BAKER: What about Groucho saying to Chico, "Why don't you bore a hole in yourself and let the sap run out?"

STEIN: The other day I was standing next to two guys and overheard one of them say, "You could cover a monkey with shit and it'd still be a monkey." And the other one said, "Yeah, but it'd be a pretty damn unhappy monkey." I don't know whether that's wit or not . . . more like the broad Mark Twain kind of humor.

McNALLY: That's a wit talking to a realist. Wit is the man in the top hat. We want to throw the snowball. But do you think we're also antihumor?

BAKER: Forty to sixty percent.

FEIFFER: We Americans like to laugh, but the idea that we have a sense of humor about ourselves is a myth. We want to laugh at things that don't touch us personally. We're basically a very serious, straitlaced people—with occasional wonderful displays of refreshing exceptions to this.

GARDNER: We have larger visions of ourselves.

THE LIBRETTO

Arthur Laurents, Moderator
James Kirkwood
Alan Jay Lerner
Joseph Stein
Michael Stewart

ARTHUR LAURENTS: It was very hard to get a panel for this discussion, the reason being that there are very few people who write musical comedy librettos. One reason why few writers write musicals is ego—I don't mean egomania, I mean the need for recognition that everyone has. The librettist of a musical usually gets recognition only when the musical fails. He is credited with that. On the other hand, when a musical succeeds and time has passed, it is known as belonging to the composer and the lyricist. And the way musicals are written, I don't think this is fair or justified; at any rate, it is no satisfaction to be ignored. Even in the theater, very few people know who wrote the book of a musical, even while it's running.

There is another kind of ego, however, and that is the ego the writer must sacrifice when he is writing a musical, because everything, I think, should be done to support, to reinforce, to build to the music, to the musical moments. In a play you write climactic scenes, but the climactic moments really should be musical in a musical. You have to forget your own ego and serve the score.

Another reason there are very few librettists is that the technique of writing a musical is really very difficult. People go to see musicals and think, "I can do better than that." Try it. It requires, among other things, enormous economy. Not a line must be wasted. And the characters have to be larger than life, because they are going to sing and dance, yet they should not be cartoons.

A third reason is, it requires a faculty I'm not sure you can teach, or even learn. That's a kind of intuitive sense of what makes a character sing; when there should be music, and how you express it; how you *feel* what makes a musical moment.

I don't know whether it's a trend or not, but recently there have been musicals which are all singing or all dancing. In my opinion, even these have librettos. Those forms go back to the classics, in one case opera, in the other ballet—story ballet. *Giselle* has a very strong libretto. So does *Swan Lake*. So does *La Bohème.* So does *Tosca.* I can think of some musicals that would have benefited, even though they are mostly sung, if they had had librettists working with them.

I would like to begin by asking Michael Stewart, do you think there is a trend toward the banishment of the book from musicals?

MICHAEL STEWART: No, I don't think so. Maybe you're considering *Sweeney Todd,* where the book certainly is . . . I think if he'd gone any further, he would have made it the opera he had intended it to be in the first place. I don't see the book diminishing in importance. I think, on the contrary, it's grown in strength.

We book writers have never gotten to a position of respectability and probably never will. When you leave a musical, it's the score, it's the lyrics and the music you retain for the most part. We only lead up to the musical moment. So you're absolutely right when you say it's Jerry Herman's *Hello, Dolly!* It never was mine. I'm not blaming anyone for this, I could name a dozen musicals and you won't know their book writers either. But I think the book, on the contrary, has become most important, and we are little by little getting a bit more respectability. People are realizing what a contribution we make.

ALAN JAY LERNER: I think there is a trend, and I think it has started primarily because of the tremendous influence of the choreographic director. This is in no way meant to denigrate the role of the librettist, but I think there is a trend in the musical theater now toward style over content. I don't believe that a musical can realize itself unless it has a very pronounced style, as in the case of *Sweeney Todd,* as in the case of the things that Bob Fosse has done; a style that identifies, that keeps the unity of that piece. There is *Annie,* which is another style of musical. There are all kinds of musicals on Broadway, but if one looks to the leaders, such as Steve Sondheim, to see where things are going, I think you would have to say it is style that is beginning to assert itself over anything else.

LAURENTS: Don't you think, Alan, that content should determine style?

LERNER: Well, yes, except you could have told the story of *Sweeney Todd* a million ways. But the style was determined for *Sweeney Todd.* It was to be told almost in opera bouffe, practically all music with moments of dialogue, and the whole thing was a stylized piece in a sense.

STEWART: Do you think that was the authors' first choice? I would guess that they worked the other way, worked from content and found style.

LAURENTS: It seems to me that the style of that production was at odds with the material. The score is absolutely extraordinary. I think the score is black comedy. But you walked into the theater and the first thing you saw was this absolutely overwhelming set which screamed "This is important, this is socially significant." That's not what the piece is about. The piece really comes together with the song "A Little Priest," which is black comedy.

STEWART: You're talking about the set.

LAURENTS: No, I'm talking about the production, because the actors didn't all play in the same style either. But, apropos of what Alan brought up about style, does anybody think that the form of musical theater is being pushed too far?

LERNER: Oh, no, I think the musical theater has limitless horizons. Maybe because I also write lyrics, I don't feel an ego problem. First of all, the musical is the purest American venture we have made in the arts, and I don't think we have even scratched the surface of its potential. We need other people to fall in love with it and commit themselves to it.

There was a line that was broken back in the 1960s when we were all tossed away as part of the Establishment. I remember when I grew up my heroes were Rodgers and Hart and Cole Porter and George Gershwin. But I can assure you, in the 1960s I was nobody's hero, not even my own children's. Now there is suddenly a growing interest in the musical theater again. There is more demand for musical theater than there is supply, and I think as a result you're seeing an enormous number of revivals. There will be more revivals until eventually people will come along to catch up with this audience that is waiting there to enjoy musical theater.

LAURENTS: Do you think any of that has to do with the fact that producers do not want to risk money on serious plays?

LERNER: No. I can't believe that. The American theater is in a very strange position because we as Americans are in a very strange position. I don't think we know who we are or what we are. It isn't like England, where everybody in the theater is acutely aware of Britain's fall from grace, and they are either writing black comedies or bitter comedies or comedies about the middle class which are all underlined with the sadness of their plight. Over here, every serious play either has to do with leukemia or cancer or somebody in a straitjacket or somebody who is deformed. I'm not mocking that for a moment. But there are no plays that I've seen that have to do with "Who are we? Where do we belong? How are we connected to this society in which we live?" And I'm not sure that anybody really knows.

LAURENTS: Do you think—well, obviously you must—that that's the province of musicals as well?

LERNER: It *is*.

LAURENTS: But do you see any musicals today that are related to contemporary life?

LERNER: No, I don't. I'm not sure that the greatest contribution that the musical could make today wouldn't be to make you walk out of the theater feeling a little better than when you walked in. But that's very hard to do, too.

LAURENTS: What makes for a subject for a musical? Any limitations?

JOSEPH STEIN: There are no limitations to the subject for a musical, as there are no limitations to the subject for a play or novel. The only limitation that I can see is that it has to have an honesty about the relationship of people to each other. I think the musical can have a broad range—from farce to tragedy. It has very successfully been done as farce *and* tragedy. So I don't think there are any limits to the form or to the style.

To add to what Alan said, I think style is vital for the musical, but it has to be related to content. And sometimes a musical goes awry because it has one style, as Arthur suggested, which doesn't seeem to fit the content. But in terms of subject matter, I don't think there's any limit. Also, I don't feel that it necessarily has to have a relationship to our contemporary social state. Those musicals that have something to say about America today are very valuable, but that's not the essential in a subject. What *is* essential is that it has to be honest in terms of the relationship of the people to each other, and also it has to have the quality of larger-than-life characters in a larger-than-life situation. Because otherwise, what are you going to sing about?

JAMES KIRKWOOD: I feel like a neophyte here, because I'm mainly a novelist and have only been involved with one musical.

LAURENTS: No disclaimers.

KIRKWOOD: It's true—but I feel the same way about musical theater as I do about novels or films. I think you must engage the audience and make them care about two or three or four of the principals and make them feel empathy for whatever their plight is, whatever the story is. And I think the danger in some of the musicals in the past few years has been a fear of getting too sentimental, so that some of them have been coming out too cold. I think they have confused the audience. One of my favorite musicals in the past ten years is *Company.* I love the score and everything, but I think it's a very cold musical. I happen to have a friend who went into that as a replacement, and I noticed, having seen that musical eight or ten times, that once the bridge and tunnel crowd started coming into that theater, they were very confused. They didn't know what to make of that show. I think it was mainly because they didn't understand the leading character of Bobby. He was kind of a cypher, and whether that was the point of the authors or not, it confused the audience, and they didn't know what to make of him.

STEWART: Surely there must be a place for that sort of musical as well as for the more sentimental musical. You know, we're an odd panel. Except for Jimmy, we are very Establishment. We've all written what we would call the traditional American musical.

LAURENTS: Nonsense! I wrote a very untraditional musical.

STEWART: Classic examples of it: *Fiddler on the Roof, My Fair Lady,* my own *Hello, Dolly!* And Jimmy is the only one who has done a style that has been fairly alien to the rest of us with *A Chorus Line.*

LAURENTS: What about *Anyone Can Whistle?*

STEWART: I didn't see it. If *Anyone Can Whistle* was not a traditional musical, then you join Jimmy. But the two gentlemen on that side, Alan and Joe, and myself have come a cropper recently, maybe because we're writing the traditional American musical. Is there a demand for it any more? I have a flop with my co-librettist, Mark Bramble, with *The Grand Tour*, and these two gentlemen had equal lack of success with *Carmelina*. Are we barking up the wrong tree? Is that 1960s or 1950s musical dead, or is the audience demanding something different? Did we get the message? The musical theater is having one failure after another. Maybe they're telling us something.

KIRKWOOD: All of these musicals you're talking about came in the traditional way. That is, they rehearsed for four or five weeks and then went right into their theaters, whether on the coast or out of town, and then came right in to Broadway. One reason for the success of *A Chorus Line* was a very, very long time in rehearsal and workshop, so that we were allowed to make all of the terrible mistakes that anyone makes putting any show together with all of those egos and different personalities. I remember we had a first run-through of *A Chorus Line* in a rehearsal hall down on Nineteenth Street and, without an intermission, it was something like four hours and twenty minutes. We said, "We've wrought *War and Peace* as a musical!" and we were all depressed. But the fact is, we didn't have to raise a curtain that evening in front of a paying audience. Consequently, we could perform major surgery instead of doing patchwork. We didn't have to please an audience, we only had to please ourselves. We had such a long time in which to do it.

Also, when you work with a cast in rehearsal for three months, it's very difficult to write something that they can't say, because you get to know them well.

STEWART: But do you think those months at Joe Papp's down there would have helped my show—a traditional musical—or *Carmelina*? I think we could have worked for the next six *years*. . .

KIRKWOOD: Weren't there times when all of you had changes to make in the show when there just wasn't time to make them?

LAURENTS: I didn't see *Carmelina*. I think there is one innovative thing about *Chorus Line*, which is, it doesn't have a central character. Otherwise, I think it is a perfectly conventional musical. I did see *The Grand Tour*. Frankly, I think, if you'd had more time, it could have been a good show. I think the fault there was in not developing the characters. In the theater, the characters are the most important element. If you have a strong character, the show has an enormous chance of working. When characters are slighted, then the play or musical begins to fall. As I said, I didn't see *Carmelina*, but I know the story, and I don't know what you did about it. I read about it—story of a woman who, in one month, dallies with three different gentlemen, and then, for seventeen years, doesn't dally. I say, "What kind of woman is that?" How did you answer?

LERNER: First of all, let me say that I spent a good deal of time in little Italian villages when I was a child. The most respected woman in the community was always the widow, and they stayed widows. Of course, you find out rather quickly in *Carmelina* why this woman did. It was a true story—I read it in the

London *Times*. I didn't even know a film had been made of it. When I read the story, it didn't seem at all surprising to me.

But to get back to what Jimmy was saying a moment ago, I think one of the paradoxes of the musical theater is that in order to experiment you must be perfect. Everything must work beautifully in an experimental show.

LAURENTS: Certainly the standards are higher.

LERNER: If you slip one inch, you're in real trouble. What Michael Bennett and Jimmy did was invaluable. I must say that I don't think it would have made any difference to Mike Stewart or to Joe or to me if we were doing another kind of musical, stemming back to the days when you went out of town, you stayed for four or five weeks, you did what you had to do, then came in and opened.

LAURENTS: In the case of the most experimental musical I did, *Anyone Can Whistle*, with Steve Sondheim, we had ten days out of town, and we had thirty-two weeks of auditions when we should have been working.

STEWART: Was it thematically innovative?

LAURENTS: Every way you can think of.

STEWART: Was it a traditional musical libretto in terms of scenes? Because that's what I'm talking about.

LAURENTS: No. It was in three acts. The last half of the first act—about twenty-five minutes—was an amalgam of dialogue, song and dance. I've never seen that.

KIRKWOOD: I didn't see the show, but everyone has always said that it was way ahead of its time. Do you feel that if it were done now it would have a different reception?

LAURENTS: I would hope. But the trouble was, we knew it had faults and there was no time, because the dollars were ticking away.

KIRKWOOD: But that's what I was talking about. Suppose you had done that in a workshop situation?

LAURENTS: I think it might have worked, yes.

LERNER: But Arthur, is there room for the avant garde musical?

LAURENTS: Commercially? Yes. But when you venture to do more, you are judged more severely. On the other hand, you ask more from the audience, and I don't think most audiences want to be asked very much by musicals.

KIRKWOOD: Oh, I hope that's not true.

LAURENTS: I hope it's not true, but I think it is.

KIRKWOOD: I loved *Sweeney Todd*. I thought it was a beautiful show, if a bit overproduced. But I think if the whole style of that show had been taken from Angela Lansbury's performance, it would be much more popular.

LAURENTS: She's English, and she knows how to walk that terribly fine line. To go back to what Mike said, do you think the conventional musical is finished?

STEWART: That's an interesting question, and I'm a little worried. To be perfectly frank, it's the only kind I know how to write.

LAURENTS: What do you consider to be conventional?

STEWART: *Gypsy* to me is the perfect conventional American musical.

LAURENTS: The first scene of *Gypsy* has no real musical number.

STEWART: That is a fine point.

LAURENTS: No, it isn't. It's a question of the form.

STEWART: The form of *Gypsy* would be considered a good example of the American musical that had reached in 1959 a certain high point before it all began slightly to disintegrate.

LAURENTS: The leading character was a monster.

STEWART: That's another point. Can you write a musical about a monster? I'd say yes.

LAURENTS: Oh, absolutely.

STEWART: Is that form that we've been brought up on dead? Is the American public telling us it is dead? Are the critics who hit us on the head telling us it is dead? Should our fellow members of the Guild who are writing librettos consider seriously that the traditional form is finding less acceptance among critics, producers and the public? I'm asking, I'm not saying.

LAURENTS: What about *Annie*?

STEWART: That would be a perfect example to show that I'm wrong. At the same time, there has been only one *Annie*.

LERNER: A major change has occurred in the musical theater in the last fifteen years; it's the first time in anyone's memory that the music that's played in the theater is very different from the music played outside the theater. That makes a world of difference. Some people have tried to bridge that difference. Write melodic music, and if you have the right story there will be a way of bridging that enormous gap. Others like Steve have said, "The hell with what's going on out there. I'll just do what I want to do." And there's a tremendous amount to be said for that.

You also have to note the division between the audience and the critics. I think there is a wide divergence between what the critics seem to want and what the audiences are content with.

STEWART: *The Grand Tour* got mixed reviews, as *Carmelina* did, and we were not able to live. There was no way in the world for us to find our audience. We couldn't run any longer than three weeks on the chance that that sort of old-fashioned musical—which it certainly was—would find an audience . . .

LAURENTS: Going back to what Alan brought up, disco or soft rock or whatever being played outside the theater: you're talking about the sound. I'm talking about the content. When I go to a musical and they start a song, and I know in the first eight bars where they're going in the lyric, my mind wanders. That's where tradition has frozen certain people. I happen to love theater music, but what you're saying in a song has to advance a character.

STEIN: I don't quite know what you mean by a traditional musical. I would guess that if *My Fair Lady* opened next week it would be an enormous hit.

LERNER: I don't think so—but the point is, I wouldn't write *My Fair Lady* today. I don't feel *My Fair Lady* today.

KIRKWOOD: Could we address ourselves for a minute to the difference between a well-made traditional musical that is an original story and one that is based on material in a different form? I remember at the time I saw *On a Clear Day You Can See Forever*, I had recently seen four musicals based on books or plays or other things, and I remember in the intermission feeling so happy that I didn't know how *On a Clear Day* was going to end.

LERNER: I didn't either. That was the trouble.

KIRKWOOD: But I remember feeling a great buoyancy because it was a story I was involved with, and I didn't know how it was going to end. There aren't that many original musicals done, based on original material.

LERNER: The trouble is, you get no A for effort. There is no special commendation that is held out to you if you do attempt to write an original musical. I tried. When I was working with Frederick Loewe, we wrote five musicals in a row, all originals. One was successful. I finally thought, "Oh, the hell with it. I'll do an adaptation." I picked *Pygmalion,* and I received much more credit for that than I did with *Brigadoon.* . . .

Q: What's the difference between writing a book and writing a book and lyrics?

LERNER: Enormous. First of all, it takes twice as long.

STEWART: I only did the lyrics once. You do have the enormous pleasure of not passing the ball to that other person who suddenly comes in when you've done all the work and built up to it; and he takes a piece of it and does his little sixteen lines. You hear that applause, and you know it's not for the language used just before the song. It's wonderful to be able to have that moment for yourself.

LERNER: There is one undeniable fact about the musical theater. Good lyrics can make a play work, but it is the music that makes it endure. And no matter how much ego satisfaction there may be in writing the lyrics, I never forget for one moment that it is the music that, if the play is good, will place it on the shelf of things that will be done and done again.

Q: Any comment on the rise in importance of the director in musical theater?

LERNER: I believe that if we ever have a director's theater, and not a writer's theater, we're doomed. It's the writer who creates. The minute you play a musical for the backers and they say, "Fine, but who's going to direct?" then, boy, you are in trouble.

STEWART: Beware of the director becoming involved very early, before the work is sufficiently polished, because otherwise it's one more person in the room with the lyricist, composer and book writer. That's a lot of people. The hardest part of putting together a musical comedy is collaboration. It's very difficult for me to write sentences that will lead up to material written by a totally different person or persons. And they have to pick up without a seam.

LAURENTS: Everything begins with a book. The songs must grow out of it.

LERNER: Absolutely.

LAURENTS: The book writer and the lyricist and the composer work together. And then you bring in the director, and he says, "It's not my vision."

The way I do it, I write sort of an outline, and I always write ahead of the composer and lyricist. When I worked with Steve, he did what he called raiding the dialogue. He would begin the songs with something in the dialogue. In *Gypsy*, the song "Have an eggroll, Mr. Goldstone" happened to start with a line I wrote for the scene. It was infinitely more effective than if it had been spoken. But if you are doing your job as a librettist, you are preparing the way for the song. Part of the librettist's function is to indicate what the song should be about.

STEWART: I think it was Frank Loesser who said that when a scene reaches a pitch that is too strong to be spoken, whatever the emotion, then it must be sung.

STEIN: Sometimes you hit a happy accident. In *Fiddler* for example, I was writing about two elderly people. The parents. They were kind of barking at each other all the way through the show. I wanted at some point to show they had a very deep affection for each other. I wrote a scene in which, after one of the daughters runs off, Tevye says, "It's a new style—love." And then he says to Golda, "Do you love me?" And so I wrote the scene. When we were out of town, we found that we were short musically in the second act, and we needed some musical moment somewhere around that period. Sheldon and Jerry musicalized that scene. I think it's one of the loveliest moments in the play. But the reason for the scene was to help solidify the relationship between those characters.

LAURENTS: I'll give you another example. As a writer, I'm always more interested in what the characters don't say than what they *do* say. And that's where music comes in. At the end of the first act in *Gypsy*, I was also interested in doing the unexpected. What you have is this woman suddenly going absolutely bananas and saying to this ugly duckling, "I'm gonna make you a star." Then she sings a song called "Everything's Coming Up Roses," which, if you haven't seen the show, you'd think is hallelujah time and everything's just great. Actually, it's a woman going mad.

I think Mike's quote from Frank Loesser is terrific. It really is. Because you couldn't *say* all that, but it's an explosion musically. To me, what's interesting is that it's an explosion in the form of a perfectly conventional traditional Broadway musical comedy number, except that the character singing it is out of her head.

Now, I mentioned "Mr. Goldstone." That's not a very good song.

KIRKWOOD: Oh, I disagree.

LAURENTS: I'll tell you why. This is a fault I find with most songs in musicals. That song goes nowhere. It says, "Have an eggroll, Mr. Goldstone," *period*, and it drove Steve mad writing it. It goes no place. I think any lyric should be a one-act play.

KIRKWOOD: But it's a con job. She's conning him.

LAURENTS: She's done it already. At that point she's already done it. Where she does a *real* con job is on "Small World." People who don't listen to lyrics think that's a conventional love song. Instead, this woman is saying the most absurd things. "You're a man who likes children. I have children. Aren't we made for each other!" It's ridiculous, but she gets him that way. Through the music.

LERNER: As Irving Berlin said, "If you write lyrics for Ethel Merman, they better be good, because everybody is going to hear them."

KIRKWOOD: One of the moments I remember very well in the musical theater that did not burst into song was the end of the first act of *Camelot* when Richard Burton had just found out he had been cuckolded. He walked down to the center of the proscenium and said, "I will not have it!" followed by that marvelous speech. I thought it was one of the most touching moments, and it didn't burst into song. But it was a set speech, wasn't it?

LERNER: Well, to say that in words and music would have been Wagnerian. So I decided that what counted was to get the force of this feeling through to the audience. Burton is a marvelous actor and has this extraordinary voice, so why not do it in soliloquy form? But what very few people realize is, it's scored. He did not just stand there and say it. There is music underscoring every single line of that soliloquy. It rose and came to a climax just at the point of the climax of the soliloquy. That's an example of a dramatic composer, and there are damn few of those around.

Q: What with the amount of time the music, lyrics and dancing take up, the book is only about an hour long. How do you telescope all that action?

LAURENTS: You have to make every single line count. You have to be very good with a red pencil. You have to do it fast. In musicals, there really isn't time for chitchat.

STEIN: And it has to feel that it is not fast. It has to feel absolutely comfortable, but there has to be an extreme economy.

LAURENTS: But also, you know, an audience gets used to a style. They accept the wildest behavior in opera, for example. In musicals, if done well, they accept this swiftness. They really do—if again, and I keep coming back to it, if the character is large and clear enough.

Q: Do you think that maybe the times have grown more cynical, and that's the reason why the musical, which traditionally has not been cynical, has been having a hard time?

LERNER: I don't think you can change your personality to suit the times. You write what touches and amuses you. I am not cynical, and I'll never be able to write anything cynical no matter how hard I try.

STEWART: Optimism is not in favor, but I think if you're optimistic, as I am, you just have to go ahead.

Q: How do you feel about the director-choreographer?

STEWART: To me it's a terrific advance. It's one less person. It's like having a book writer who's also a lyricist. It means that two phases of the production are being done by one mind that has a single point of view.

LERNER: I sent Bob Fosse a telegram on the opening night of *Dancin'*. I said, "You finally did it. You got rid of the author."

Q: Didn't *A Chorus Line* begin as a series of taped interviews done by Michael Bennett?

KIRKWOOD: There has always been a controversy about those tapes. Ed Kleban, who was in on the project before I was, knows that I never heard those tapes. Michael played me about five minutes of them one time just to get the sound of all those people talking. I defy you to get twenty-some dancers in a room and have them all talk together and get a lot from them. I mean, I did get a transcript of it, but what you get from that is some characters, and you get a diversity of personalities to pick up on, but then the writer has to put that together.

Q: Don't you have a special feeling that each show you do is going to be a big success?

STEIN: On the contrary. We were astounded at the success of *Fiddler, which had a very strange history. We had very great difficulty getting it produced. The original producer who was toying with it said, "I kind of like the material, but what'll we do when we run out of the Hadassah benefits?"*

We wrote Fiddler because we felt it was a strong story we wanted to tell. We hoped it would be produced, and we had our fingers crossed.

LERNER: All the gentlemen sitting up here—and I will include myself if I may—are professional writers. I know damn well that nobody here is going to write badly. All that may happen is, they may not write a very good play or musical, but nobody here can write badly. We can't help being prepared for the fact that we're liable to be K.O.'d in the first round. But every time one of these gentlemen comes into the ring, I know there will be something that I want to see.

LAURENTS: I remember when we did *West Side Story*, it was turned down by virtually every producer on Broadway, including the one who finally did it. I myself thought we would be lucky if we got three months out of it.

Q: What do you think of integrating more of today's sound into musicals?

LAURENTS: I find the lyrics to rock songs so banal, so simplistic, that I do not think they work in the theater.

LERNER: If you hear a rock song, I defy you to tell me what the lyrics are.

Q: You said you would like to see form pushed further. What did you have in mind?

LAURENTS: I would like to see musicals more fragmented. I would like to see time fooled around with. I don't think we need linear stories that much. I would like to see more adaptation of film techniques. Let me say very clearly that I believed first in characters, second in story. I think you can throw it all up in the air and let all the pieces come down, but you have to have what I consider a very strong clothesline to hang all the pieces on. Why do you have to tell something in the traditional straightforward way? You don't have to. That's one thing that the advances in theater have given us. We don't have to tell it A-B-C-D-E.

The most important thing is to know where you are going to end. When I did *Gypsy*, I began with a very practical fact that the story concerning the girl who was going to become the striptease queen of America totally disinterested me. That would have to be a musical number, but the main character had to be the mother. Well, the mother had to do something to top the strip. So I began with what became "Rose's Turn," and the whole thing became rather easy. I worked back from there.

Q: I don't know if it's true for people on your level, but someone on my level has to prepare a tape of the score when submitting a musical to a producer. In the tapes, should you tell them about the book, or just present the music?

LERNER: First of all, don't make a tape. Fight to do it in person. Sing it to them in person. Even read it to them in person.

Q: Who do you think should be in charge of a musical, if anyone?

STEIN: Well, at some point it has to be the director. Until you get into production and rehearsal, of course, it's the writers. But once the show is in rehearsal, essentially the director has to be the one in overall control. It's still a collaborative process, but the director has to be related to all the departments.

LAURENTS: I think that is sort of true, but I think that in the best situations, everybody really works together. One thing I think the writers must do is not let the director divide and conquer, which is something they work very hard at. I'm a director. I *know*.

KIRKWOOD: I started with a director on a musical which I withdrew from before it even got its pants on. It was going to be about a drag show—like the *Jewel Box Revue*—closing. If such a show closes, what do all these people do? They are not the kind of people who can go and audition for *Carmelina* or any other regular musical.

Well, it was my idea to make it a club that had been in existence for thirty-five years, and the club was going to close, and what were those people going to do? I started out with Ron Field, who was going to direct it. It was his idea to do a show about these people to begin with. He called me, and I got to thinking: "What an odd bunch of people to deal with, what a strange profession they're in, and yet they're all really entertainers. What they want to do is entertain, no matter how they're doing it." I thought it could be a really very touching show and kind of moving, the last night of this club. What are these people going to do?

Ron and I went to San Francisco, talked to the female impersonators, went to the clubs. And suddenly Ron got a different attitude toward the characters. In a way, he wanted to wipe them out. I wanted people to empathize with their plight, and suddenly we were at totally different poles. Ron felt very strongly that they should not be allowed to go on in this very tacky old profession that had fallen into disrepair. I thought that certainly some character in the show can have that idea and that approach; but, as the creators, if we're going to put twenty-five or thirty people on the stage we want to wipe out, how we are going to make the audience care about them? I woke up one morning and thought, "No, I can't go on with this. If we're at such disparate poles right now, if we feel so differently about the chemistry of this material, then I'd better withdraw." So I called Ron and told him that I thought I shouldn't do the show, that I thought it was still a good idea, but I thought he was going to be in trouble if he held that view about these characters.

LAURENTS: For two years I was on the judging board of a university that wanted to give a prize for the best original musical by somebody who was totally unknown. They would give them a production on the campus. They sent each year, I think, four or five entries. They were all extraordinarily bad. I could trace every single one of them to some Broadway musical that had been a hit. There was no attempt at doing what, I suppose, is the object of anything, musical theater or plays: that is, really expressing yourself in your own way.

COMPOSER AND LYRICIST

Lee Adams
Charles Strouse

LEE ADAMS: We are talking about the art of composer-lyricist collaboration. Charles Strouse and I have been together for a long stretch—twenty-eight years—but I still wonder if we know a lot about it. I mean, do married people always know a lot about marriage?

The Oxford dictionary says "collaborate" means "to cooperate, especially in literary, artistic or scientific works." Webster says it means "to work together." It is work, and it is "co," and there is no easy way to do it any more than it's easy to find the right marriage partner for a number of years.

If you cannot cooperate, you cannot collaborate. It's not so much a merging of egos as a respect for each other's work and egos. It's *very* hard work, I don't know why, but if it works, it works, it's always exciting when it's finished, and it's not quite so lonesome as working alone.

CHARLES STROUSE: I am a composer with somewhat of a literary background. I've always been responsive to words, and in my earliest training I was very aware of the correct setting of the sort of words that are stressed naturally. I'm also very aware of the singer's voice.

As a composer I've been trained to work alone, but collaboration is a significant process in my life because a good collaborator like Lee helps to free my unconscious. There are other forces at work besides merely connecting notes. That is, I get certain words and I must set them.

A complex thing happens when Lee is willing to modify words and I, in the same spirit, can modify the music so, for instance, a phrase like "open the door" can become in collaboration a most graceful musical, lyrical expression. Because I have a certain rhythmic motor in mind, he might be willing to change "door" to "aperture." I am just improvising here, but I mean that Lee would be able to modify a phrase to the extent he can, and I can fuse a simple phrase into a musical statement.

That is, I think, the success of collaboration: the fact that two people can for a moment take the plainest or most heartfelt phrase, musically or lyrically, and blend it into something which suddenly you know is a fusion. That's what I've found with Lee. That's what I always aim for, and I think he aims for it with me.

ADAMS: I came to New York in 1949 to go to graduate school. I thought I was a lyricist because I'd written a show at Ohio State, *Howdy Stranger*, set in the Yukon. I had this book of five songs from the show—I thought they were probably not better than Cole Porter, but at least as good. A mutual friend thought that Charles, as a composer, should get to know me as a possible lyricist, so I went up to his apartment on the Upper West Side clutching the book of five songs. When he asked me if I'd brought anything, I put them proudly on the piano and thought, "Boy, now he's going to see something." Charles began to play the songs and sing them, which impressed me because I'd never before seen anyone who could sight-read. I sat back and waited for the adulation, but he ended up by pulling the songs apart and demolishing most of them. I very politely said, "Thank you a lot, goodbye, we'll be in touch," and took off, very, very hurt.

In the middle of the night I got up and looked through those lyrics and thought, "He's right, this is a cliché, this is trite. This is a non-rhyme and doesn't read right. The prosody is wrong here." The next day I called Charles because I realized that anybody who is that honest, who gives you an honest answer without trying to spare your feelings, is worth knowing. That's how we began working together.

When I come in with a lyric and we go over it, and he criticizes it or suggests changes, I don't think he's criticizing *me*. He's only criticizing this particular piece of work. It's like raising a child. When a child does something bad, you don't criticize him, you criticize what he did, right? One of the essences of composer-lyricist collaboration is intellectual, artistic and creative honesty. This has nothing to do with the underlying relationship, but it's hard on many people's egos. It's hard not to think you're being personally attacked, but it's something you have to learn to live through, and I think we both did.

STROUSE: I think I speak for Lee too when I say that we've also been fascinated with collaborating with the playwright. It's hard to define why music within the context of the spoken word on a stage brings a measure of joy or reassurance or sadness or whatever to people, because it is not real, not even using theatrical reality in the case of many plays and musicals. The extent to which the composer and lyricist can use their instincts to bend a theatrical moment to make a musical and lyrical fusion fascinates both of us. We've done that with many fine playwrights, like William Gibson and Clifford Odets and Mel Brooks. It's terribly interesting to me to see how reality will or will not bend to an audience.

Q: The obvious question: Which comes first with you two, the music or the lyrics?

ADAMS: Richard Rodgers is quoted as answering that question with, "What comes first is the check." With us, it works both ways. Lately, it seems, we've been more often sitting in a room together doing it word by word and note by note.

We also like to work from a scene in the show. We chew it over together—what's the musical pulse, what in the scene should be sung? Maybe we get an idea for a song out of the scene itself.

Q: Does a playwright suggest to you first?

ADAMS: Often.

STROUSE: Sometimes we pay attention, and often we don't.

ADAMS: We get perhaps a title, perhaps just a feeling. Sometimes I go off and write a lyric.

STROUSE: My feeling about this is, the playwright's instincts are too correct. I've always believed that a song should have a quality of surprise, whereas the playwright might feel that he had expressed himself eloquently a moment before and therefore the song should follow. But it's that eloquence which most likely would seize my imagination. If you know that he loves her, it's obvious that he's going to sing "I love you." But it's the moment *before* when he is tying his shoe and feels the crick in his back that interests me because the audience wouldn't expect a song about it.

This is where the collaboration comes in. Lee sees right away that the playwright's best line for a song title would be "Oh, My Back" and not "Oh, I Love You." We know it would make a funny song, and that the audience would be bored with the "I Love You" song.

ADAMS: Rephrasing what Charles has just said, we like to come obliquely on something. You don't need an "I Love You" song when the scene says "I Love You." It's boring. You have either to cut the scene or the song.

When we wrote *Bye Bye Birdie*, our first success, the actor playing the Elvis Presley type sang a number called "Honestly Sincere." We felt that was kind of an oblique approach to what was then rock 'n' roll, instead of having him sing an "I Love You, Baby" number, though it would probably be more correct for a rock singer at that time. We thought if we sang about his sincerity with great insincerity it would be funny—that's what I mean by an oblique approach.

In a sense, a musical is a very unnatural form. In a straight play, the conceit is that people are in a room talking, but in a musical they also stop and sing and dance. That's an extra handicap to reality, so we like to come in obliquely, which perhaps helps us to get inside a character's head a little bit. Maybe the character would sing what he's feeling rather than what's on the surface.

Quite often Charles will have a lovely tune that he has been saving for fifteen years. (A composer saves every scrap, right?) He says, "Maybe this will fit," and then I write a lyric or get an idea from it, and then we go over it together. At the last, we polish it together, together, together.

Q: Does the playwright come to you with an idea for a book, or do you bring it to the playwright?

STROUSE: It has come both ways.

ADAMS: Every way and from a producer, too, who'd like to feature a star or who has an idea for a property. David Merrick brought us an idea for a musical about the reign of Queen Victoria. We played it in London, briefly, but he ended up not producing it.

STROUSE: A producer came to us with the idea of making *All About Eve* into a musical. It became *Applause*. By coincidence, we had that same idea years before.

ADAMS: And couldn't interest anybody.

Q: Can you comment on working on speculation?

STROUSE: When I started out, I did a lot of it but didn't think of it as working on spec. Nobody was calling me, but I wrote a lot of material with Lee. A strong precedent has now grown that one shouldn't toil in the creative vineyards of producers, networks or movie companies without being paid for the effort. If somebody says, "I've got an idea for a pilot, or a musical," writers owe it to themselves and to the nature of the process to make sure everybody knows they will not work for naught.

ADAMS: There's no way not to work on spec if you have an idea you don't want to share with anybody else.

STROUSE: The way we've always worked, we've been co-authors of the book in a very real sense, but don't take credit for it, in the same way that book writers are co-authors of the songs in a sense. We are certainly co-directors too, we like to be in on every aspect of a show.

ADAMS: We like to jump in as early as possible and shape it as one piece. The shows we've been most successful with have been as seamless as possible. We don't sit down to write a bunch of pop songs and drop them in a show. We try to write for that theater piece, find out the motivation of the characters and place ourselves in the play as much as possible.

STROUSE: The kind of playwright or property may cause us to veer toward adding songs to the basic material rather than trying to shape it more to our needs. *Golden Boy* was a very different experience from *Bye Bye Birdie*. Clifford Odets tried his damnedest to shape many of the scenes to what we all thought were musical ideas.

ADAMS: You haven't got much elbow room to develop characters in musicals, remember. Half the running time is music and dance.

STROUSE: The fifty-minute book.

ADAMS: Oscar Hammerstein once said that seventy-five pages was a good length for a musical comedy book. It's got to be tight. It's very hard on playwrights and us too, because the more the characters are developed, the more you want to hear them sing, and the better the songs are.

Q: Is there a main person, a final arbiter in your collaboration?

STROUSE: No. It's as Lee said, similar to a marriage. Someone tends to dominate a certain moment, but if you're sensitive to one another, even in those moments one would tend to understand the dominance. You give, you bend, and when you don't bend you have to understand your own subjectivity, and the other person's subjective needs, and the object of the song. It's very complicated, but *we* recognize when the fusion takes place. I can't review the process any more than I can remember how I learned to walk. I can't say at this moment, "This note was carved because of my dominance," or "That word is there because of Lee." It's just that we're on the same wave length.

ADAMS: Further down the line when a show is written, in the first or second draft the final arbiter in some cases might be a strong director who says, "I cannot stage this" . . .

STROUSE: . . . or a star who says, "I cannot sing this."

ADAMS: That's not arbitration, that's coercion . . .

STROUSE: . . . which is a whole other subject.

Q: How do you write for a star, and to what degree do you respect collaboration from a star performer?

STROUSE: Stars have a good deal of turf to defend. In the case of Lauren Bacall, she was firm, but she yielded to good artistic reasons. With Bacall, it was a collaboration. She listened to everything we offered, and when she turned us down we felt it was for valid reasons, not ego reasons.

With Sammy Davis those principles were generally operative, but he was more of a superstar, and we really had to cater more to the Sammy Davis image. He's very thoughtful, but there's a kind of superstar behavior. We met him naked, literally, in the steam room of the Sands Hotel to discuss a scene—he said it was the only time he had, and there we were, naked, explaining the scenes of a musical.

ADAMS: Sammy is not just a superstar, he's a truly complex and sensitive man—infuriating at times, very emotional, extremely creative. We learned a lot about musical theater timing from him. He has an ear you wouldn't believe. He's an incredible performer, with an extra sense of audience. He can sense what is happening in every part of the house at any moment and adjust to it.

STROUSE: Anyway, you *do* have to collaborate with a star, and you learn from it. One of my biggest shocks was the first time a director said to me, "Look, the star is offstage too long here, she needs a song." To me, it seemed the most crass kind of pandering.

What sometimes transcends what the musical is about is the actual affection and interest an audience feels for an actor as a *person*. They like the right actor or actress so much, they want to take them home to lunch. I've learned to respect that feeling. It's very important to make that performer really score. Dick Van Dyke, for instance, wasn't a star in the beginning of our relationship, yet we sensed a quality about him and worked and worked until his every facet was revealed to the audience. When you are working with a performer, you try to make him or her into a star. When you are working with a star who is trying to collaborate with you and at the same time keep his or her stardom, you sometimes give in.

Q: Are there special dangers involved with the lyricist also writing the book?

ADAMS: It's terrific if the lyricist can write the book. I've always collaborated more or less with book writers, as has Charles, but I've never tried to write book and lyrics solely by myself. Probably it's just fear, it's hard enough for me to do the one thing.

Q: Why do adaptations seem to be more frequent in modern musicals than original works?

ADAMS: It makes it a little easier if you have a scaffolding to build on, created characters and a structure that works. A *Chorus Line* proves magnificently that an original is terrific if it's done right. We've done both adaptations and originals, and it's no special kick either way.

STROUSE: I disagree, I think an original is more of an open invitation to a composer. In one original we were working on, we discovered that a guy just walking across the stage cleaning up suddenly became a major character because we wrote a good song for him. You can't do that if you're adapting *All About Eve*.

ADAMS: I'm a constructionist by nature. I like to see the structure laid out, I like to know where the beginning is, and where we are going, and how it's going to end. I like to see that scaffolding. I feel that I can work better within a structure. Charles is just the reverse, and that's one of the reasons why this collaboration works. He often says to me, "Forget the construction," and he frees it up.

STROUSE: I feel that if we can bring the characters to life it's going to work out even though we destroy the structure. I feel suffocated writing toward a situation or ending where a guy has to walk through a door at the end of the scene.

Q: Both of you have collaborated with other people. Are they any different?

STROUSE: Sheldon Harnick tells me that Jerry Bock puts down a whole bunch of tunes on a tape, and Sheldon listens to them and gets an idea for one or another of them. That's the way they write songs. I don't say they never get together, but that's the first impulse, and then they develop from it. Martin Charnin likes me to write a tune first, and then he sets the lyric.

ADAMS: It's as different as individual people are different. There are no rules about it at all.

Q: Do you anticipate any new formulas of musical theater developing?

ADAMS: Each work takes its own shape. I don't think Michael Bennett and his *A Chorus Line* collaborators said to themselves, "We're going to start a whole new trend of musical theater." They just solved that particular problem in that particular way.

STROUSE: I do think movies have had a profound effect on musicals. We use film cuts in a way that would never have occurred to Victor Herbert. Things stop and start in a more restless, plastic way. Directors use the stage in sweeps of color and rhythm, and choreographers have people dancing whole scenes. But "trends" in the musical theater are things that Sunday article writers—

who have nothing else to write about—want to organize into something that seems cohesive for a reader. If an author sits down saying to himself, "I am going to do it new," he is going to write something phony. To the extent that you are sophisticated, you've got to be aware of what Michael Bennett and Jerome Robbins and Elliott Carter and perhaps Frank Loesser have done, but if you use your own feelings, depending on the kind of person you are it's going to come out new.

ADAMS: Economics has a lot to do with trends. We are seeing fewer musicals with seventy people onstage. We are seeing lighting used in place of cumbersome sets.

STROUSE: There's no Broadway show that doesn't use electronic instruments.

Q: Mr. Adams, I'm surprised that you are inclined to writing lyrics but not to writing books.

ADAMS: I probably will try it. I've always collaborated on the book—and I wish Arthur Laurents, a terrific book writer, would try to write lyrics. Lyrics is a special craft. You are writing on the head of a pin, your whole job is condensation. It's a miniaturist versus a landscape painter.

Q: Does a percentage of the songs have to be rousers like the Act One ending of *A Chorus Line*?

ADAMS: No, there's no formula for it. It wouldn't be wise to have too many songs that are introspective and possibly slow. We like to have no more than a minute and a half or two minutes between songs, because we feel that's what the audience wants. They don't want to hear all this talk about what my mother did to me, they want to hear songs.

Nevertheless there's a long scene in *1776*—I remember discussing it with Stuart Ostrow—in Peter Stone's book when nothing went on except they talked about the Declaration of Independence for what seemed like thirty-five minutes. Well, they were right, it worked, it held.

STROUSE: You can't make rules.

ADAMS: The audience shapes you. As smart as you think you are, the audience will accept certain things.

STROUSE: And the work shapes you. You don't have to start with a big opening number, and you don't have to end the first act with a big closing number. When you start thinking of formulas you are thinking of short cuts. You're thinking of what should be done rather than what you have just done.

Q: How do you handle out-of-town pressure?

ADAMS: A musical that is coming toward New York is a juggernaut that is rolling along, but we work well under that excruciating pressure. We do a lot of our best work out of town and always add material.

STROUSE: We like it, because we feel we know the characters much better than we did on the printed page.

Q: What happens to the songs you cut?

STROUSE: We're seldom able to use them in another show.

ADAMS: We try to tie them to story and character, and we almost never get a retread. We've tried it a couple of times with a complete rewrite, but we might as well have written a new song anyway.

STROUSE: It seems to me that we have our greatest success when we trap a moment that comes from our hearts. You don't set out or expect to write a beautiful phrase—you're thinking about something else, and suddenly this beautiful phrase comes to mind. It happens to composers all the time, and the best of them learn to trap it. For that reason I believe that openness should be a general rule of writing for the theater, and I like writing for the theater very much.

ADAMS: Some structure can be a help, but not to the point of becoming claustrophobic and limiting your creativity. I'm not sure I can tell exactly how the creation of a musical takes place. It evolves as you work, and work, and do it.

STROUSE: That's the beauty of it. It's like a dream—a dream reflecting your own sense of self.

SHORT PLAYS, SMALL MUSICALS

Eve Merriam, Moderator
Terrence McNally
David Mamet
Albert Innaurato

EVE MERRIAM: I'll ask each of you to give us a quick idea of what you think a short form *is*, so that we all know we are talking about the same thing. If it's just a one-act, then it could be *A Chorus Line* or *1776*, which are hardly short forms.

TERRENCE MCNALLY: In the form we call one-act, as differentiated from the short play, action starts at the very top, and you want to see it to its conclusion as quickly as possible. You don't want an intermission or a change of scene; it's like a train speeding along. It's a strong action that begins with the first beat of the play. My play *Next*, for example, begins with a man saying: "You have made a mistake. I've got to get out of here." You wouldn't want a break after that. It's a one-act premise. In the one-act form, the play doesn't change where it's going in the course of its action. You're driving a pretty straight road.

DAVID MAMET: A play in its short form is a continuous action toward the solution of a problem which is presented at the outset of the play. In the short form, the evolution of a character from problem and pain to perception is not going to outdistance the problem which brings him into the play at the outset. In the beginning of my play *Reunion*, for example, two people say, "Here's my father, I haven't seen him in twenty years, how am I going to get next to him?" and, "Here's my daughter, I haven't seen her in twenty years, how am I going to get next to her?" The play is a quest toward answering that question; whereas in a full-length play (although in one act) like *Oedipus*, the character starts out asking, "How am I going to find out what is causing the difficulties in Thebes?" and ends up discovering that he killed his father.

ALBERT INNAURATO: I resent it when people look down on one-acts. A one-act can provide a powerful, memorable experience, whereas the spinning out of endless complications doesn't offer any artistic value per se. The length of a play is conditioned by the material you choose to work with. You start with the idea, and it may generate complexities and complications two hours' worth or twenty-five minutes' worth. No one should sit down and say to himself, "I'm going to write a nineteen-hour trilogy because that's artistically important, and the New York *Times* is going to like it." The idea conditions the length of the play.

MERRIAM: Terrence, what is the impulse that makes you come up with a short form rather than something long? Does it happen at the beginning, or does it come gradually?

MCNALLY: It's very much an impulse; it either feels like a one-act or a full-length. I agree with Albert about people who look down on one-acts. It's ridiculous, the one-act play is a marvelous form, and I'm frustrated when people feel there's something suspect about it.

As to length, I just sort of know how long a play is going to be before I begin. Usually I've thought about my characters a long while and tried to find the right situation to put them in. If the story you want to tell about these people needs several situations, the play gets bigger—by "bigger" I just mean "longer," although David did very well with a set of different scenes in one-act form in *Sexual Perversity in Chicago*. Albert's *The Transfiguration of Benno Blimpie* also used different scenes but never changed the subject from its beginning theme: "I am bent on eating myself to death." The few one-act plays in which I tried to use different scenes I found very hard to control. In *Tour* I tried to show the disintegration of an American couple touring Vietnam in the back of a cab in twelve short scenes. Every time the lights went down I felt I lost the audience.

MERRIAM: Have you ever taken a short play and made it longer, or vice versa?

MCNALLY: No, but sometimes I think one of the reasons my play *Broadway, Broadway* didn't succeed and closed out of town was that maybe it was a one-act play and I didn't know it. No matter what I did, the first twenty minutes of Act II remained the emotional and comic climax of the play, and there was nowhere to go after that. No matter how much rewriting I did, no matter how late I stayed up trying to improve it, nothing seemed to help. The play seemed to be over, and there were still forty-five minutes to go. Of course, I was riveted by those forty-five minutes, otherwise I never would have written them. It was just the critics and audiences who didn't cotton to them.

MERRIAM: David, do you know instinctively as you start a play that it's going to be short form or long?

MAMET: Yes. And when I find that I'm wrong about the short one, when I think it's going to be short and it becomes longer, I usually just go ahead and write it. If I'm wrong the other way around, if I think it's going to be in long form but doesn't want to be, I usually throw it out. Somebody once said, "A good writer is somebody with a full wastebasket." I sometimes start out by filling up my wastebasket.

MERRIAM: I must say, I am awed by all this. Albert, are you sure about form from the beginning?

INNAURATO: I'd say yes, on the whole, but it's only comparatively recently that I began thinking in terms like that. My earlier plays like *Wisdom Amok* and *Earthworms* tend to be rather long, but I wouldn't call them multi-act plays. *Wisdom Amok* is about a colony of mad nuns called "Our Lady of Eternal Clarity Convent," who devour mad priests. It's a very long play but essentially in one act; there is not an action that can be subdivided. It provides a full evening, but it's really a one-act.

The same holds true for *Benno Blimpie*, which lasts about an hour and ten minutes if it is done well, providing a very strong experience. *Gemini* is a much more realistic and structured play, and it seemed to me that it needed to be in two acts.

We have inherited attitudes toward play construction from a time when there was no television, no movies. In a well-made play, the first act dealt with exposition, two maids with dusters talking, and then the mistress of the house comes in. You get an idea of who everybody is, a problem is posed, and then in your second act there is a working out of that problem to a crisis point. In the third act you have a resolution. It is rather neatly laid out in the plays of Scribe and Sardou and other works which adhere to that form. In Ibsen and Shaw there's a lot of sleight-of-hand and cleverness in masking exposition, masking propositions of the question, but it's essentially the same play skeleton.

Today, when we have a camera conditioning a scene, those skeletal bones are less important to us. You see, a camera can tell you everything in one shot, you don't need a ten-minute speech or even a scene. And the television form, which I think unconsciously influences us all now, has tended to push us toward a short, short form, toward a tendency to condense exposition and the proposition of the question. That is really what we are dealing with when we ask, "What's a one-act?" Our contemporary sensibility has to do with camera and the way camera structures time and experience, very different from the way things happen in the theater, a real change in style. Somehow I don't think we will write well-made plays any longer.

MAMET: You hear a lot of people leaving theaters saying, "It was too long," but you never hear people saying, "It was too short." You hear people say, "I didn't have a good time," but you never hear them say, "That wasn't a well-made play." So these ideas are foisted off on us by those who are out of touch with our emotions and needs, presented as challenges by those who'd rather not talk about the real issues but mention the well-made play as if, having said that, one need go no further, but won't consider whether it's a *good* play.

For a few years I wrote plays so conditioned by television that they all ran fifty-six minutes and had seven-minute scenes.

INNAURATO: That's life today in the theater. We've all been influenced by our sources—not that I grew up glued to television, or loved television, but it's automatic. We're used to seeing a dramatic event structured as an hour program with little breaks. *Gemini* brought in a television audience. You watch this audience, and it's like clockwork. Every seven minutes they have to go to the bathroom. They turn around and talk. They go out to get something to eat. When this first started happening, I thought, "They hate my play," but then I realized their behavior had nothing to do with that. They loved the play, but they could not deal with sitting there paying attention for a sustained span. They need that sixty-second break every seven minutes. We may say to ourselves, "We are not of that world," nevertheless it does affect how we structure our plays.

MAMET: I think I agree with you.

McNALLY: I know I agree with you, and I only wonder why there aren't more plays like *Plaza Suite* and *California Suite*. I would think revues would be more popular now, too.

MAMET: Don't agents always say, "Don't write one-act plays"?

McNALLY: If you tell your agent you're writing one, he groans.

MAMET: They will say, "If you write two one-act plays they'll put them both in the same evening, and if one of them fails, that's what the people are going to remember."

McNALLY: I don't think you can deduce anything from the commercial theater anymore. Nothing works, you know, the things that succeed are so strange. I mean, some plays *do* work, but none of them adhere. Looking back on the past five seasons, it's impossible to make a generalization about the plays that have succeeded. They are totally different kinds of experiences. Look at the musical theater. A single season encompassed *Sweeney Todd* and *They're Playing Our Song*, both enormous successes, totally opposite experiences, and neither really your typical musical.

MERRIAM: Is this inferiority complex about one-acts strictly commercial, or is there also a put-down in the area of quality?

MAMET: Producers don't advertise *Plaza Suite* or *You Know I Can't Hear You When the Water's Running* as a program of one-act plays, even when they are successful. Producers are scared of one-acts.

I never heard of a one-act play until *The Zoo Story* and *Krapp's Last Tape* came along. Seeing that evening was partly the reason I write plays. I thought, "God, what you can do in under an hour and forty minutes!" Ironically from the producers' standpoint, that program was one of the greatest successes ever and ran for about five years.

McNALLY: One of the longest-running plays I've ever had was the one-act *Adaptation* on a double bill downtown with Elaine May's *Next*. You could say that the two scripts had nothing to do with one another; certainly they did not share a cast or a set. Obviously you can't categorically state that an evening of one-act plays won't do well, even when they are two quite dissimilar plays by different authors. But as I said, what do I know?

MAMET: If the likes and dislikes of producers are going to influence what you write for any reason, you are in trouble. That is just a way of talking yourself out of impulses. Sit down and write the play, let it be however long it is. This is what you have to say, rather than what someone else is going to accept.

INNAURATO: If someone has a terrific one-act play idea, there's no reason to discourage him because you fear one-act plays. You fear everything.

McNALLY: Even with a full-length play you are going to have trouble getting it on, so what difference does length make?

MAMET: Chance and accident have always been important in the theater. That was as true with Chekhov and Ibsen as it is today.

INNAURATO: What you had in 1890, 1920 and even in 1950, it seems to me, was a large public that wanted to go to the theater, and this audience cut across all kinds of lives. I've met people in their seventies and eighties who went to the American theater as a means of learning to speak good English. Middle-class people went to the theater, society people went to the theater, to have a good time, to be educated, to have an experience. They were excited by the notion of live theater.

If you look back at the pre-1940s seasons, you'll find a lot of things that would not stand up if done today, but you also had real public support for an Ibsen play or a Chekhov play or an interesting new Hellman play. You were not dependent on the whims of reviewers who, whether or not they are intelligent or sincere or supportive of the theater, nonetheless are labelers, people under pressure to describe something in a few paragraphs overnight, making or breaking a play you may have worked on for three years. Unless you have a public that is spontaneously drawn to the theatrical experience, you must rely on the critics, you must rely on artificially formulated producing organizations who are only producing to keep *themselves* alive. You are dealing throughout this country with producers whose primary interest is themselves and their careers. Their audiences do not pressure them, the audiences don't care. They are content to be led by people who jump on the newest bandwagon created by the New York *Times*.

I feel bitter about this in a way, because I've experienced tremendous frustrations and difficulties in getting my plays on. Every time you write a play, no matter how much success you think you may have had, you always deal with this incredible frustration—people who do not care about American writers but just want the things that get the reviews, because that's how they get their gross and their movie sale. They may do a one-act next year and have a big success with it, but that doesn't mean anything for the future.

MAMET: The question is, if you want to write this one-act and no one wants to produce it, would you rather not write the one-act? If the answer is, "No, of course not," then write the one-act anyway. If they say, "I'm sorry, you are going to have to write a two-person sex comedy or we just can't talk to you," is that going to make it worthwhile to write a two-person sex comedy if you don't want to?

INNAURATO: All I know is, it seems to me there has been a shrinking.

MCNALLY: Sometimes when a play or musical is in trouble, the magic solution is to turn it into a one-act. I think this is a terrible solution. The psychology of an intermission is terribly important in modern play construction. I'm always suspicious at a preview when that sign in the lobby reads "At this performance *Sing, Sing, Sing* will be performed without intermission."

MAMET: My play *Reunion* has two characters, fourteen scenes and runs an hour. Robert Brustein wanted to produce it at Yale, so he said, "You have to write something to go with it." I said okay and mucked around on the train on the way to rehearsal and wrote the first draft of a play which eventually became seven minutes long, not the perfect play to accompany a play that is an hour long. But Mr. Brustein and I decided, what the hell, that was what I wanted to do, so that was the evening: seven minutes, then a two-minute break, then an hour-long play. We all looked at each other and said, "It's really a full evening, it's emotionally expressive, it completes a statement," and we all nodded.

Then Marshall Mason wanted to do this program, so I said, "Here it is, Marshall, don't tell me it is too short." The first week he said, "No, I'm not going to tell you it's too short." By the second week I was saying, "It's too short, isn't it?" The third week I said, "It's too short," so I wrote this other play to round out the evening. I felt really sissy about it, I said to myself, "Goddammit, if you write these two plays, and they are long enough to say everything you wanted to say, why don't you leave it like that?" But I started rehearsing, and I was very apprehensive until the last couple of days, when I finally realized that in *this* particular instance those plays were just too short. That's my story.

Q: I still don't think we have much of a definition of a one-act play. Are many scenes really acceptable in a one-act play?

MAMET: It's a very difficult form in which to have a multiple-scene play, but it can very well manage two scenes.

Q: *Sexual Perversity* has many scenes, doesn't it?

MAMET: Yes, twenty-seven scenes in an hour and ten minutes.

Q: Isn't that very long for a one-act play?

MAMET: It may or may not be, but I think the play is definitely a one-act. I think we all know what a one-act play is, except we can't say it. It's very difficult to write a full-length play, incredibly difficult, and for me it gets harder the older I get. If one happens to have the talent for writing a one-act play, then writing a one-act play is easier than writing a full-length play (but this is not to denigrate that talent). Some have a talent for writing a full-length play—Philip Barry, for example, thought in that scope. Maybe it would have been difficult for him to write a one-act play.

Q: Exactly what is the talent for writing a one-act play, is it precision?

MAMET: It's the way one thinks, the scope of one's thoughts. It's like an actor who may be comfortable expressing a certain impulse in a certain way but goes on trying to give himself more fully: "Yes, yes, I feel this impulse, but what do I do next, what does this *lead* me to?" That's a more difficult way to act because it forces you to examine fully not only your feelings but also your intentions; not only the immediate ramifications but also the real consequences. That's what I think a full-length play is: taking the action beyond the immediate consequences of the beginning. It's much more difficult to write.

Q: Isn't it dangerous to let your one-acter be produced together with a one-acter by another author quite different in style, tone, etc., or a lot worse than you think yours is?

McNALLY: To give your one-act play to a producer and say "Put it on a program with anything" would be insanity, it could destroy everything you were trying to accomplish. When Israel Horovitz, Leonard Melfi and I did the program *Morning, Noon and Night,* we didn't collaborate in the sense of asking each other, "Do you like mine?" but we agreed on certain demands. No one was going to come up with a two-hour play that would pressure the others to cut. We'd share a cast and unit set and director. More importantly, I like their work. There was no way we could be *that* uncomfortable. It definitely matters who you're paired with.

Q: There must be at least fifty variations of the one-act form, and theoretical definition is hard, but there *is* a difference between one-acts and full-lengths, isn't there? Short is not long.

McNALLY: Do you want to write your father a long letter today, or do you just want to send him a postcard? Sometimes a writer has something very short to say and just says it, and sometimes you can say a lot in a very short time. One of my favorites among my own plays is *Botticelli,* which I think says a lot in eleven minutes and would be terrible as a thirty-minute play.

Q: Are there many places for short plays to be done outside of New York?

MAMET: As the regional theaters got more and more of the scent of megabucks in their nostrils, as their first-stage theaters have gotten a lot more staid and Broadway-minded, appealing to a mass audience, they began to spawn second-stage theaters doing more creative work; and a lot of these second-stage theaters spawned cabarets. These places are actively looking for short plays to try out, to reinvent the American theater at a level which hasn't been tainted. The Actors Theater of Louisville has one, the Goodman has one, Yale has one, and there are many more. This phenomenon is in the air. The necessity for them is in the air.

INNAURATO: My very first play was a three-act, then I went through a lot of one-acts and learned a lot. It seemed to me that they still, finally, had the same structure as the five-act classic form now reduced to three acts. You still have to have your exposition and development, and you can learn about construction without having to worry about second-act and third-act problems, which are hard to deal with when you are very green. I went back and started to work with the one-act form and kept expanding—not that the one-act form is something you grow out of, I don't mean to imply that. But I would recommend the kind of one-act opportunities David is talking about to young playwrights.

Q: *Benno Blimpie* is stream-of-consciousness, while *Gemini* is a much more structured two-act play. If you want to be absurdist with a bare stage and no craft, is that what ends up being a one-act play?

INNAURATO: The problem with *Benno Blimpie* is reconciling an hour of time in which the character of Benno speaks to the audience, while a little girl comes out and has speeches which don't make any sense, and there are mimetic scenes in which definite actions are acted out by the characters, all crammed together without any sort of continuity in a very discontinuous play. You know, if you set up a convention in which one character is going to break the proscenium and talk to the audience in the present, and then you suddenly wrench away to a scene that has happened in the past and is being acted as though there were a wall there, the audience is unable to make the adjustment, and consequently the play doesn't have the effect it ought to have. The reason *Benno Blimpie* is in that form is because the emotion of the fantasy is so powerful it demands a short impact. You can't sustain it over a long period of time, it's an erupted thing. *Gemini*, on the other hand, is laid out according to a kind of naturalistic convention.

There is something in the theater called an Action—one of those awful words Aristotle used—the motor of the play, that quest or conflict that moves the play inexorably from one moment to the next and provides the illusion of inevitability. That Action is found and beats in every second of a play; and what my plays tend to lack (and a lot of contemporary plays lack) is a strong Action. What interested me in *Gemini* was bringing together a bunch of people and exploring their reactions as they come together, like a combustion. The boy's sexual crisis is an excuse for that, but it's only an excuse, not an Action. The entire play could have been focussed on the question, "Is this character homosexual, and why doesn't he commit suicide at the end of the play?" It would have had to be a very strong play, but I dispensed with that. In *Gemini*, each of the subsidiary themes could be a play on its own: the father's relationship to his son, the neighbor woman's search for a man, Herschel's search for a friend.

So I would say that perhaps a one-act play is one in which there is a clearly defined simple Action that can be contained in a short span.

MAMET: And you can't get out of the Action or off the subject.

INNAURATO: Obviously, the Action in *The Zoo Story* is different from the Action in *Who's Afraid of Virginia Woolf?* The Action in *The Zoo Story* is "kill or be killed," while the Action in *Virginia Woolf* is a process of discovering or revealing something.

MAMET: Right, George does not recognize the Action of the play when he enters it, but halfway through the second act he realizes what he must do. That is too long for a short form.

INNAURATO: And those characters with their dense and complex levels demand a longer playing-out.

MCNALLY: When Elaine May directed *Next*, all she rehearsed were the first five minutes. I kept reminding her, "You've never rehearsed the big scene," and she told me, "If the first five minutes are right in a one-act, two-character, single-situation play, nothing can go wrong, but the first five minutes must be perfect." I think that says something about the form. If the rocket is fired correctly, the trajectory cannot fail.

INNAURATO: There may have been some shift in the form. I haven't seen *Reunion*, but it sounds like a series of scenes, which seems more cinematic in technique. We perceive a television play in exactly that term. We perceive it as a single quest for a single object, even if that wasn't intended by the author.

Q: Do you think the one-act play makes an easy transition to television?

INNAURATO: Television in the hour or half-hour format is a one-act play format, so that the conventionally conceived one-act is very appropriate to television. The action is condensed; you get right to the problem and it is solved. TV isn't a medium for ambiguities, because the camera goes right in—it's there or it's not. Proficiency in writing one-act plays is a very useful and practical gift to have if one wants to write for television.

Richard Maltby Jr., Moderator
Howard Ashman
Word Baker
Christopher Durang
Nancy Ford
Stephen Schwartz

RICHARD MALTBY JR.: I have a resistance to this panel's subject, "Small Musicals." After you have said that a big musical has more music, more scenery, more costumes, a bigger orchestra, then you have said just about everything you can say. And what does any of that have to do with writing? *They're Playing Our Song* is a big musical, and it is small, with only two characters. What can we say about it? Yet it does seem undeniably true that when you choose one scale for a show as opposed to another, your writing standards may vary in some way. So perhaps this discussion can be useful.

Small, it seems to me, is something that is defined not by writers but by audiences and sometimes by critics. Would they pay to see this show? Sometimes they get a full evening with only two people on the stage, or an empty evening with more scenery than you could fit in the city of New York. I want to ask Stephen Schwartz about a show I admired a lot: did you have a sense of production scale while you were writing *Working?*

STEPHEN SCHWARTZ: Yes, absolutely. What's surprising about it is that the show, which did not succeed on a Broadway scale, is succeeding enormously on a different and I think proper scale. One must be careful to recognize proper scale. There's a tendency to take something that's doing well with a little audience of 200 and try to work it up for an audience of 20,000.

With *Working*, there was enormous pressure from the producers to have a great big production. The content is important enough to require little more than a basic setting with a scaffold and some levels, but we had to have scenery with moving trucks and flashing lights. I found out that once producers have spent a million dollars building scenery they are very loath to take it down. Also, the authors can get used to it, and things happen which change the focus of the production. In the case of *Working* on Broadway, there was so much time expended trying to get the production into the theater, let alone on the stage, that there was little time left for attention to things like cutting it down from its eight-hour length. I have done shows, *Pippin* notably, where the amount of time spent on technical considerations was merited, but *Working* didn't need the technical advantages, and in fact they got in the way.

I happen actually to think that *Working* is a large musical, not a small musical, because I have a different way of defining it. The theme of *Working* is enormous, just as *A Chorus Line* is a very large musical—no scenery, one set of costumes, not a lot of people on the stage, but it has this huge *feel. The Baker's Wife*, on the other hand, was a genuinely small musical, a tiny little story that you have to be right on top of. *She Loves Me*, a show I like a lot, is a genuine small musical, and they can't seem to make it work in a large theater, it's too fragile. We tend to think of "small" as how many people in the cast and how much scenery, but I don't think that's necessarily the case. It has more to do with the content and feel of the show—its fragility, its power. This is important to consider, because it affects your choice of theaters, the size of the orchestra and a lot of other things that may swamp you in the end if you're not careful.

Q: Are the economics of today's musical theater forcing it in the direction of small shows?

MALTBY: That depends on whether the basic impulse comes from the producer or from the writer.

SCHWARTZ: Most of us generate our own shows, and the producers' impulses have come later.

NANCY FORD: Gretchen Cryer and I have never started writing a musical with the thought in mind that it was going to be physically big or small. Our thought is to realize a particular idea or concept. With our first show, we found we had written a musical with a big cast but it was basically small, so we cut the cast down to fit the size of the material and did it, appropriately, in an off-Broadway theater. In Chicago, we recently moved a show from a 299-seat theater to a 1,100-seat theater. Then they took out 200 seats to make a stage for us, leaving 900 seats. It has worked very well.

You can't always tell where a show is going to fit. Our *Shelter* was a very small musical, and we tried to do a production that was too big, with thirty-two rear-screen projectors. I still think if we'd done it off Broadway it would have fared better. We're now turning that show into a one-act musical and putting it on a program with *The Last Sweet Days of Isaac*. We're trying to make it work as a small show.

Q: Are the characterizations, the focus, the motion different? Why would that story work better in a smaller place?

FORD: I think the bigger theater required a lot too much production. But if you've written a show and a producer wants to do it on Broadway instead of off Broadway, it's kind of hard to say no. Who doesn't want to have a Broadway musical, after all?

WORD BAKER: There never was much difference until somebody drew the line between a 299-seat theater and a larger theater. In the 1920s, *The Little Shows* were so golden nobody ever decided whether they were big musicals or small. They didn't seem much different from those with choruses of eighty-five.

Q: If you were told you could take *The Fantasticks* to a big Broadway production, would you feel you could do it?

BAKER: Absolutely not. It isn't meant for that. As originally written and conceived, *The Fantasticks* was enormous, with a cast of forty-five. We had the chance to do it in one act with nine people, and we did it. Then we put it in the Sullivan Street Playhouse because that was the only theater we could get. It can't move because it was remade to go in that shape, but it started out as something else. It's past commenting on whether you could now re-tailor it to another size, putting back the aunts, cousins, cowboys and other characters.

MALTBY: Every show has a scale, though the conception may be very elusive. I felt on the third day of rehearsals that *Ain't Misbehavin'* was going to be an enormous show, because of the personality of Fats Waller. We were working toward having the whole show personify that man. His sense of humor was so great, his sense of life was so great that it was spilling out of the music, I felt there was no limit to the size of the theater it could fill. This proved to be true when it moved. It only fails when a performer makes the mistake of trying to sing "big." When they perform more simply, truer, the emotion is big enough to fill any theater.

Q: Is there a reason why some shows are called a "play with music" instead of a "musical," even when there's more music than text?

CHRISTOPHER DURANG: My play *A History of the American Film* was called a "play with music" both on and off Broadway, not because of anything like union regulations, but for audience expectation. *Strider,* advertised as a "play with music," is not the same thing as *Ain't Misbehavin'* or the traditional book with songs in it like *On the Twentieth Century.*

Each of the theaters in New York is classified by the musicians' union, and you have a certain number of positions that must be covered if a show is a musical. *American Film* went into a theater which in retrospect was like an amphitheater and eventually proved too large for us. It has a union requirement of twenty-five musicians, so even if you use only five you have to pay the other twenty. My composer, Mel Marvin, suggested that we should try to keep the sound of a small musical; but since we were paying them all, we might as well have them all in the theater. One song would need a clarinet, another would need a saxophone, and so forth.

I thought that would be great, but at the first preview it sounded enormous—I don't know enough about music to know why. Apparently there were only four instruments, but it sounded like the whole twenty-five to me. We were trying to keep the show small, but we didn't manage to. In one number the leading lady sat on a piano and sang with full orchestration, but the song didn't work. When we took everything out except the piano, then the song worked. Whatever it was in the Broadway version, the scale just wasn't right.

SCHWARTZ: I saw *A History of the American Film* in Washington. I thought it was sensational, an absolutely huge show in terms of theme, a very broad canvas. But one of the things that worked for it at the Arena Stage—I don't mean this in a pejorative sense—was a certain sloppiness. (*Godspell* is another example of a show that has to be a bit raggle taggle.) During the musical numbers the Washington production of *American Film* was very unslick, they weren't really singers, they were obviously having a wonderful time. The choreography was sort of slung together, and it had an extremely endearing quality.

This was also true of *Magic to Do,* a revue of my songs done in Cincinnati. It was sort of raggle taggle and thrown together, the set was junky looking, and it was extremely successful—it gave you a very good feeling. Then they took it to Washington, and suddenly the set was beautiful wood and chrome, the costumes were just so, the choreography was lovely and the whole show went out the window. Smallness, I think, implies a lack of pretentiousness and a casualness that is important to consider.

American Film is a large show but demands a certain off-the-cuff-ness. It's written tongue-in-cheek and off-the-cuff, and if you do it neatly, and the choreography is just so with everybody lifting his or her leg the same distance, it's not going to work. Such matters are easy to lose sight of when you're doing a show. When you finally write a good, solid show, it's a shame to have it loused up because of incorrect production choices of which you yourself can be a part—so you have to watch it.

HOWARD ASHMAN: I think that's a very good point, but I am thinking of a small show—*Tintypes*—which couldn't be less casual or off-the-cuff. There is a precision about the performance that works exquisitely.

MALTBY: What we're talking about is being in full control of the eloquence of all the evening's elements. Scenery, orchestrations, lighting—these are dialogue elements in a musical. These things are speaking; and sometimes they speak to the audience in very profound ways that you may not want. If you speak to the audience with a big overture that arouses a certain expectation, they will think the rest of the show you wrote is wrong if you don't proceed to go down that road. You have to be aware that everything in a musical speaks to the audience, feeds into the evening.

BAKER: What is the advisability of the writer or conceiver directing as well, to control all those elements?

MALTBY: Ideas come to me in a full stage way, and writing is what I do after that in order to make the ideas happen. So I don't feel that I direct my own work. I write because that's the only way the show I'm directing in my head can exist.

SCHWARTZ: One of the reasons I directed *Working* was that I wasn't writing the whole score; I don't think I would have directed if I'd been doing all the writing. It's extremely important, especially in the early stages of a show, not to be so involved that you can't have a certain kind of objectivity. Also, you badly need collaborators.

ASHMAN: There are some writers who are not directors and some directors who are not writers. I don't think that a writer should direct his own work unless he has the ability that Richard just called seeing things "in a full stage way."

Q: I would like to ask Nancy Ford, when you found yourself faced with the two-character *The Last Sweet Days of Isaac*, after the work you'd previously done was a big musical, was your approach to the writing of the music any different?

NANCY: Yes, the approach was very different. Most of the songs were inside the character's head, things that he was thinking and fantasizing. None of it was sung dialogue. It was written to be played by a small group, essentially a rock group, though it wasn't rock music.

Q: An audience experience at the Sullivan Street Theater has to be different from an audience experience in the last row of the Majestic. Isn't that a factor in determining why some shows work better small and others work better large?

BAKER: I think the question is being posed backward. Ideally, you try to find an idea that sings to *you*, so that you say to yourself, "Everybody else may think I'm crazy, but I hear music in that." Then you write it so that it works for you, and then you ask, "Is this a big show or a small show, Sullivan Street or Majestic?" Size of cast and emotion, breadth or small details—all these things must be taken into consideration, but I don't think one sets out at the beginning to write a big or a small show.

ASHMAN: If it's easier to get a small musical produced, then it's probably not a bad idea to look for source material suited to the form. If I took a Kurt Vonnegut book that appealed to me and did the work of musicalization honestly, it would have to result in a small musical, because it was a small-scale, intimate idea to begin with.

Q: *The Baker's Wife* was a tiny, fragile idea. How did the musical version grow so big?

SCHWARTZ: We all went down the garden path together on that show, an example of material that should have been recognized as extremely fragile and intimate. The whole show is subtext, with everybody saying one thing and meaning something else. It examines the inner workings of two people, and how they affect one another. We should have seen that it was tiny. We wound up at the Dorothy Chandler Pavilion; we must have been out of our minds.

Q: Is there a difference in the relationship between the writer and composer in a small-level musical as compared with a large-level musical?

FORD: I don't know. I've never done a really large-level musical.

SCHWARTZ: I've never found any.

Q: How about the relationship of the writers to the producer?

SCHWARTZ: In the case of *Pippin*, and I would imagine in a show like *On the Twentieth Century* or *Annie*, the production elements get to be enormously important, and rightfully so. You have more collaborators.

Q: Is there a point at which the writer says to himself, "I am writing a big show"?

ASHMAN: Well, I think Jerry Herman must have known when he was writing "Put on Your Sunday Clothes" that he was going for a costume parade. The number builds through four choruses, with one group after another bringing on a collection of glorious clothes. It's a number specifically built for the entrance of a series of costumes, and it's gigantic. I doubt he would have constructed the number that way had he believed himself to be writing an intimate show.

MALTBY: I think a good large musical can start small and then get bigger and bigger and bigger—*Ain't Misbehavin'* is a good example of that. It's not a danger to a musical to start small. But it's an enormous danger for a small musical to get too big, because you can lose the point of a small musical in a big production.

Q: When you moved *The Baker's Wife* from California to Cincinnati, did you rewrite to make it more intimate?

SCHWARTZ: No, there was an enormous amount of rewriting done, but it had nothing to do with scale.

Q: After you selected the Fats Waller songs, how much of the structure of *Ain't Misbehavin'* was worked out in the actual doing of it?

MALTBY: I went into rehearsal with certain long lines, structural ideas of where we were going, but no clear decisions about how we were going to get there. To me, it's a very deeply structured show working on a lot of levels all the time, always making sure that the first level, the entertainment level, is intact.

One idea was: the cast was going to personify the humor in Fats Waller's fingers when he played the piano. Waller is the wittiest pianist I've ever heard—he teases the audience. He plays with them all the time. It's joyous. Our actors were going to do that.

Another idea: we were going to conjure Waller up like a mosaic. We were going to present little pieces of him in different numbers and characters, and somewhere in the course of the evening—I couldn't quite define where—I hoped the audience would have the feeling that we were in Waller's presence. People have told me that this happens; all I did was release it to happen. I trust that it does, but if for some people it doesn't, that's fine, because they can still have a good time on the surface level, listening to the songs.

Q: Why is it that when there was a cast change in that show, the show itself didn't reshape to the new personality?

MALTBY: Every person cast in the show was required to do it exactly the same as everyone else, not vary a finger or a note. We went into rehearsal with a different group of people from different backgrounds, with different gifts and experiences, and suddenly they put on their wigs and dresses and out came the same show. This did not kill the performers' personalities—curiously, it worked exactly the opposite: only by duplicating the show exactly did the performers' unique qualities show through.

Q: How is it that *Godspell* never changed with the increasing size of its productions from La Mama onward?

SCHWARTZ: I've always thought of *Godspell* as a big show, which is why I barely mentioned it in talking about small musicals. It worked best in a 199-seat house because of the relationship between cast and audience. But I've seen it in huge theaters, and the impact was much the same, because it deals with "the greatest story ever told."

Q: Possibly it's less the size of the theater that's important than the way the collaborative staff—the writers, director and producer—are looking at the musical in terms of size. When *Ain't Misbehavin'* moved from off-Broadway cabaret to Broadway, it stayed with one piano. You retained the certain quality you wanted it to have.

MALTBY: We needed to add a little bit of magic, so we made the piano move. We had limited stage tricks, about twenty-five, but we gave them to you one at a time so it seemed we could go on forever. Actually, we ran out after the third number in the second act. We had the option to add dancers, and one element I think the show could have used was a little more tap dancing. The impulse to add more dancing was tremendous, but we couldn't do it without adding more people, so we didn't.

Q: I saw *A History of the American Film* here in New York with someone who kept saying, "They made it too big." Was that your original concept?

DURANG: When I wrote it I wasn't very practical-minded, and I wasn't thinking whether it should be small or large. When it began in Washington at a five-hundred-seat house, there were very large moments, but also some of the acting was intricate and delicate—Swoosie Kurtz was fascinating in her role. In the big New York theater, this weird schizophrenic thing happened: some excellent actors were doing tiny work miles away, while others with Broadway musical experience were whacking it to the back of the house. It may have been better for the house, but it wasn't good for what was happening on the stage. Maybe I wouldn't say they made it too big, because I think it can be done large; but whatever it was, it was just the wrong size.

FORD: Maybe we could make one generalization: If you have a wonderful small musical it may have a chance in the larger theaters if you keep it the way it was. Once you perfect in a small space, you can put it in a larger space if you don't try to beef it up and make it something it wasn't to start with.

MALTBY: A show has to be bigger than the space it's in. The triumph of *Sweeney Todd* was that Hal Prince defeated the Uris Theater. *Porgy and Bess* looked like a tiny show in that theater, but Hal virtually rebuilt the theater so that two people on stage filled it.

Q: Was it the writers Hugh Wheeler and Stephen Sondheim whose talent made *Sweeney Todd* so big that it filled the theater, or was it the director Hal Prince, the producers, the collaborative process itself?

SCHWARTZ: Wheeler wrote big-scale people, and Prince knew that these people needed a universe to exist in, and Sondheim wrote an enormous score.

FORD: In musicals as well as in straight plays there is this tug-of-war in which writers are sometimes accused of writing and directing at the same time. Writers will be told they are writing out of their province: "Don't write that. Let the director stage it." I say, write everything and work it out later with the director. As for size, probably a lot of us are going to have to write for smaller rooms. But I think we should just sit down and write whatever it is we want to write and then try to find the right production afterward.

THE ART OF ADAPTATION

Eve Merriam, Moderator
Jay Presson Allen
Donald Driver
Ruth Goetz
Frances Goodrich
Albert Hackett
Sheldon Harnick
Thomas Meehan
Stephen Schwartz
Michael Stewart
Keith Szarabajka

EVE MERRIAM: I read in the double introduction to *Dodsworth* that the novelist Sinclair Lewis would say to the adaptor Sidney Howard so often that it became a slogan, "How did this lousy line get into this play?" And Howard would reply, "It came out of the book." And Lewis would say, "It's got no place in the play, take it out." Howard said that by the time he'd finished there was practically no line left of the original book.

I'd like to ask Jay if she worked directly with Muriel Spark on *The Prime of Miss Jean Brodie.*

JAY PRESSON ALLEN: Oh, no. I had a very hard time with that novel. I decided it was totally remarkable. I bought it for myself, and having got the damned thing I couldn't work on it. I thought the dialogue in the book was absolutely brilliant, and at first I couldn't simulate it. Do you really want to know how I finally did it?

MERRIAM: Yes!

ALLEN: I asked my doctor to recommend a hypnotist. I told him my problem, and he gave me six sessions in which he taught me to hypnotize myself. At the end of six weeks he said, "Now you can do it." I felt better, I really felt well, but I knew I *couldn't* do it because I hadn't dreamed the way he told me to. He had told me at every session to dream about the project, and I hadn't.

But I was determined that I would sit at the typewriter for eight hours a day for the four weeks I had left of the option. I did my little exercise when I went to bed the night before, and then I went to sleep. I got up the next morning, did my little exercise, sat at the typewriter and wrote the only thing I knew how to write—"Act One, Scene One" (I still hadn't reread the book since a year before). Eighteen hours later I came to and found I'd written more than a third of the script. I wrote it all in three and a half days. Obviously I'd been thinking about it all the time, unconsciously, on a level I wasn't aware of. What appeared on the stage was pretty much what I wrote then, with some refining.

That was the last block I ever had, though. It came from being frightened of the process of rape and dismemberment, which is what adaptation always is. You have to violate the original property.

MERRIAM: Donald, how did you have the daring and intelligence to pick Shakespeare as a collaborator on *Your Own Thing* and *Oh, Brother*?

DONALD DRIVER: Hal Hester and Danny Apolinar came to me in the 1960s with the terrific basic idea of adapting *Twelfth Night*, the Viola-and-Sebastian comedy, where you can't tell the boys from the girls. They had a script outline, I think the title was *The London Look*, having to do with Carnaby Street and all that sort of thing. I told them, "Well, that will only last until the fashions go, but I will do it if I can do a free adaptation."

I went home with *Twelfth Night* and within two weeks had a script by simply imposing the Sixties on the play, not necessarily using Shakespeare or trying to be true to his form. I threw out Andrew Aguecheek and all the subsidiary characters and just kept Orson, Olivia, Sebastian and Viola—just those four. Everybody else was just voices of people like Shirley Temple, John Wayne, Humphrey Bogart and so forth, but they were commenting on the stage action exactly as Aguecheek and everybody else did, so in a way the script was keeping Shakespeare's structure.

With *Oh, Brother* I followed *The Comedy of Errors* right straight through. The only superimposition was to set it in Egypt, where East meets West and you can create a lot of fun. There was no rape or violation of the material, we stayed within its structure. But when you can't be sued by the original author, you can really go ahead and do what you want.

ALLEN: But you feel the danger of violation if the original is something you admire.

DRIVER: Oh, yes.

ALLEN: So that no matter whether or not you have to cope with a living author, just the admiration can inhibit you.

DRIVER: One thing I would not do with Shakespeare—unless for an absolutely necessary comedic or other purpose—is use his lines. Everything else is a paraphrase or not used at all. You can say to yourself, "I'll take his plot, he stole it, why can't I steal it?" But I would never use his lines because I don't write that well.

MERRIAM: I looked up the word "adaptation," and one dictionary definition is "to make suitable or more suitable, especially by changing." Another is "to change (oneself) so that one's behavior, attitudes, etc., will conform to new or changed circumstances." Sheldon, what about the change that comes about in adaptation? What happens to your own personality? Do you consider yourself primarily an adaptable person?

SHELDON HARNICK: I'm not as adaptable as I once thought I was. At one time I thought if a project interested me I would be able to write lyrics for every character in that project—but I find that's not completely true. I am most comfortable, and I think most successful, when I'm writing for characters I really empathize and identify with. Then I can call on myself to feel the way the character might feel in a given situation, and supply appropriate words.

But there are other characters I have great difficulty writing for. In 1976 I did a musical called *Rex*, and on the road I discovered how much I really disliked Henry VIII.

MERRIAM: Was that based on another property or just the character of Henry VIII?

HARNICK: It was based on history and on Henry. Sherman Yellen did an original book based on his research. I found I couldn't identify with Henry, so it was extremely difficult to write convincing lyrics for him or for the other English aristocrat characters. The longer I write the more important I feel it is for me to choose projects that I really do identify with; otherwise not only am I not good at it, I cease having fun at it.

MERRIAM: Did you feel a lot of empathy with the Sholom Aleichem material in *Fiddler on the Roof*?

HARNICK: Absolutely, and I felt great identification with everybody, including the villain, in *She Loves Me*. I felt akin to their hopes, their ambitions, their vulnerabilities.

MERRIAM: What about *The Umbrellas of Cherbourg*?

HARNICK: That wasn't so much an adaptation as simply a translation. It was decided at the very beginning of the project not to change it, but simply to translate the film score for the stage. My job was to find singable, flowing language for what Jacques Demy had written in the French text. It also happens that I loved all those characters.

MERRIAM: Frances Goodrich and Albert Hackett did the adaptation of *The Diary of Anne Frank* and walked away with every prize it's possible to get. How did you make that enormous leap from the very private material of a diary to the public form of drama?

FRANCES GOODRICH: From one point of view, the fact of the child talking helped.

ALBERT HACKETT: She was a wonderful reporter.

MERRIAM: But a reporter is not the same thing as a character in a drama. Did you start with Anne as a narrator?

HACKETT: She had to read that diary—it was part of what we knew we had to do.

GOODRICH: The voice reading the diary bridged time and all the events that were important and that turned into drama.

MERRIAM: You knew from the beginning that was going to be your device?

HACKETT: We knew the girl's fun and humor was the only thing that would make the play possible. We didn't think anybody would sit through a play of this sort if there were a lot of breast-beating. We felt if we could capture what she had, her spirit, it would really make the play go.

GOODRICH: I remember Kermit Bloomgarden telling us, "Let it flow, let it flow."

MERRIAM: Did you know the beginning and ending before you began writing the play?

HACKETT: We knew from the diary what the end was, and we went over to Europe and talked to Mr. Frank about the beginning.

GOODRICH: Mr. Frank had to approve the script.

MERRIAM: Wasn't it difficult to feel he was breathing down your neck?

GOODRICH: No, he was wonderful.

MERRIAM: Ruth, in adapting works like Gide's *The Immoralist* and Henry James's *Washington Square*, which became *The Heiress*, did the fact that you were collaborating make it easier to do an adaptation or harder than working alone?

RUTH GOETZ: Collaborating was one of the joys of my life because it was done with a very gifted man, my husband Augustus Goetz. We went to see André Gide together and told him that we were interested in making a play of *The Immoralist*. Gide said, "Impossible. You can't." I said, "I think we can. We like the fatality in it—the unstoppable quality of the problem between the two people." I said it first in English because I was looking at my husband. Gide said "What?" and I repeated it in French. "Unstoppable" was the right word, and Gide agreed we could make a play of it.

MERRIAM: Did the original impetus to say "We can make a play of this" come from you or your husband?

GOETZ: I read it first. It was a completely forgotten novel which had failed in this country as well as in France. The problem of homosexuality was very much a problem in the life of one of the brilliant and talented people who worked with us on the production of *The Heiress* in London. I was touched by the horrors he had lived through, and I said to my husband, "I think we can do something on this subject. I think we can handle this material where no one else can." Then Gus read *The Immoralist* and liked it, and I wrote to Gide asking to come to Paris to see him.

MERRIAM: Had you known Gide before?

GOETZ: No.

MERRIAM: After you wrote the script, did you show it to him?

GOETZ: Yes. He gave us all the world rights except France, because he said he would like to be the translator of the script back into French. He died before he could do it. He was a most extraordinary man—very timid and very brave.

MERRIAM: In the case of *The Heiress*, did you also read the novel long before you decided to adapt it?

GOETZ: Yes, but one night I reread it, and it seemed to me Henry James left out the most important scene. I gave it to Gus the next day, and after he read it he said, "There's a missing scene." I told him what I thought the missing scene was, and he said "Yes," and then helped me to write it.

MERRIAM: So you were reading the novel as a dramatist.

GOETZ: Yes, we all do. You make it come alive, you make the mood yourself as you read.

MERRIAM: How did you go about obtaining the rights?

GOETZ: We found that there was a lawyer taking care of the affairs of James's great nephew, I think it was, and the family had no interest in the novel.

MERRIAM: You obtained the rights before you went to work.

GOETZ: Oh, yes. You must *always* do that. You must always search out who is responsible. That is absolutely necessary. You *must* protect yourself that way.

MERRIAM: Between *The Heiress* and *The Immoralist*, which was the harder to adapt?

GOETZ: *The Immoralist*—it was a devil, unspeakable. There had never been a play about homosexuality in the American theater. Every single producer turned it down. Paul Osborn read the play, loved it and told us, "You're not doing the right thing with this. You need a gambler like Billy Rose." I took it to Billy, who kept it two nights: first he read it, then he gave it to his friend Ben Hecht to read. Ben said, "Do it," and Billy said, "Absolutely, let's do it."

We had trouble with the casting, too. We sent it to some very good leading men who wouldn't touch it because they were afraid it might ruin their careers. We sent it to Louis Jourdan, who was enlightened and so good about it that he said, "It's not good for me, but I have no career in the theater here anyway. I don't care." He did it, and he did it beautifully—probably the best thing he ever did in his life. And Geraldine Page was a great defender of the play. She loved the play and helped us even in the casting. She and Herman Shumlin were the only two people I knew who had ever seen James Dean, and when Shumlin suggested that Dean come up and read, Geraldine said, "Yes, absolutely." And he did. So we had the best.

I disagree with Sheldon, though. I love bad characters who are monstrous to everybody. I love people that I don't like.

HARNICK: I don't disagree at all. But some of those people I can write for, others I can't. My point was, at one time I thought I could write for anybody, but I can't.

MERRIAM: Michael, did you have any notion when you were adapting *The*

Matchmaker that *Hello, Dolly!* was going to be the interplanetary success that it was?

MICHAEL STEWART: No, I didn't. I loved the play when I saw it with Ruth Gordon, and when David Merrick—who is a very great man in the theater—asked me if I'd like to do a musical adaptation of it, I said, "Of course I would," but I didn't realize until I saw a touring company of *Hello, Dolly!* eighteen years after the original production that I had written a musical comedy classic. This, despite the fact that the original reviews were far from complimentary about my adaptation.

MERRIAM: You don't remember the good reviews?

STEWART: Alas, on *Dolly* there were none. Not for my libretto, in any case. Anyhow, it's good to remember the negative reviews, it keeps you on your toes. Finally, the work *has* survived and all subsequent reviews have paid tribute to the book—so much for the original notices.

Back to adaptations—for me, there are three categories. *Dolly* is an example of the first. I took a script that a superb playwright had written and made of it a new piece of work, one that had an entity all its own and still did not betray the author's intent. The author in this case is Thornton Wilder, and I don't think you can point to anything in my adaptation that does not follow a course set by Mr. Wilder in *The Matchmaker*. Wilder died some years ago, and although we never met, he did tell Carol Channing on more than one occasion that he was more than satisfied with the musical version and thought it was very true to his play. What he said in *The Matchmaker* I said in *Hello, Dolly!* Nothing that was strongly thematic did I throw out. At the same time, I wrote something that has a very distinct life of its own.

MERRIAM: You mentioned three categories of adaptations.

STEWART: A second way is to take off and use the original work only as a springboard. You can do that with a play you have no great respect for. *I Love My Wife* is an example of this. I thought it was an amusing play, nothing more. I used it as a jumping-off place and built my own completely new work on top of it.

The third category is one in which you respect the original work, use it as an inspiration, digest it thoroughly, then create an entirely new work that is often light years from the original play or novel. *Gypsy*—in my opinion the best musical ever written—is an example of this.

To sum things up, I consider adaptation close to collaboration. The quality of the collaborator, though he might be present only in the pages of a book or film or play, is what determines how heavily you depend on him. In the case of Thornton Wilder, my dependence was enormous; in some other adaptations I have done, less so. But the end result must be a new work that takes on a life of its own, otherwise there's no reason to collaborate—or adapt—in the first place.

MERRIAM: Tom, I remember running into you in New York and hearing you tell me, "I don't know anything about the theater but I have somehow gotten involved in this project." I remember saying, "Once the theater gets its hooks into you, you will understand every addict in the world—there is no way you will leave it." And you looked at me skeptically and said, "I don't think this thing is going to get any place." There did seem to be difficulty while you were at the Goodspeed. The word was out—trouble, a lot of trouble. Why did you persevere with *Annie*?

THOMAS MEEHAN: I had never been in the theater, and the years were passing by. I've been stage struck since I was a small boy and came to New York with my parents to see plays. In 1972 Martin Charnin phoned to tell me he had this wonderful idea for a Broadway musical: "I can't even tell it to you over the telephone." A few days later, in his office, he said, "Here it is: 'Little Orphan Annie.' " I said, "Yuck." I considered it to be a terrible idea—I just don't like the two-dimensional—but we started to talk about it, and it seemed as if there might be something interesting in the kid and this enormously wealthy man.

Harold Gray, who had died, began the strip in 1924, so there was no period per se. It was my idea to place it in the Depression in New York. I think of *Annie* at some level as a political play, and in 1972 the Vietnam War was continuing.

MERRIAM: Warbucks is certainly a political name.

MEEHAN: We had to fight that to make him sympathetic. In the comic strip he was originally a munitions man, but not in the show—we sort of ignored that his name means "war bucks."

There was a recession in 1972, with feelings of pessimism and downness. The Depression quickly came to mind as an analogous time, with the country very down. The idea was to do something kind of up, optimistic, fighting cynicism and pessimism. In Act Two, as far as I'm concerned, Annie becomes a metaphor figure, appearing in the White House, standing on the desk and singing "Tomorrow." She stops being real and becomes totally a metaphor for the spirit of how to survive and get out of bad times, how to endure, how to keep on keeping on. That's what it's about.

Looking through fifty years of the endless, boring adventures of this dirty child, I found nothing I could use except the child. The character of Annie, I thought, was terrific in a kind of stalwart way, gallantly fighting against adversity, always keeping going. Just the idea that Warbucks had endless amounts of money was interesting, and then there was the dog. You had to have the dog. So really, the whole adaptation was constructed from characters, not incidents. The story is basically sort of Cinderella.

MERRIAM: Were there any restrictions from the Harold Gray estate?

MEEHAN: Not at all. We got the rights from the Chicago *Tribune–Daily News* Syndicate, and they never even saw it until it opened in New York. We were free to write anything we wanted to, we never had the kind of problem others might have had with Mr. Frank or André Gide.

Some people were offended by our making Warbucks more of a friend of Roosevelt. Harold Gray was an extraordinarily right-wing person, and in the 1950s there's a sequence in "Little Orphan Annie" where Warbucks gets his own private air force and atom-bombs China. That character didn't fit our view. We wanted him to be the rugged kind of American individualist, a self-made millionaire, a nineteenth-century sort of figure, a little ruthless but with a heart of gold, a friend of Roosevelt and part of the New Deal.

MERRIAM: Did you find the theater a great change from the writing you had been doing before?

MEEHAN: Yes, I certainly relied a lot on my collaborators. It appeals to me that what we were doing is called a musical, and the music comes first. I felt myself writing scenes that might become songs. I wrote too long—everything I write always comes out about four hundred pages; in fiction and stories the problem of terrific condensation doesn't come in. A full-length, two-and-a-half-hour play like *The Matchmaker*, a play that I loved too, has to be condensed into less than an hour for the book of a musical. That's where I think Michael did such a terrific job.

MERRIAM: Did you find *I Remember Mama* easier because it was more definitely shaped than a comic strip?

MEEHAN: That was a whole different experience. I agreed to do it just on the memory of what I'd seen on the screen and in stock, and because Richard Rodgers was doing the music. Was I going to say no to Richard Rodgers? When I then read the play I was taken aback, I thought it was really very shallow and thin. It didn't have any of the scenes a musical needed, but I was locked in and did a number of drafts. I battled with it, but it never worked. I did violate it, I changed it and turned it all around, inside out, and added a lot of new scenes to give it what I thought was the structure of a musical.

MERRIAM: Keith, did the whole Organic Theater company work on the adaptation of *Huckleberry Finn*,* or did you do it by yourself?

KEITH SZARABAJKA: From the first day of rehearsal we worked completely collectively.

MERRIAM: It seems to me you followed the Mark Twain book very closely.

SZARABAJKA: Exactly. Stuart Gordon, the artistic director of the Organic Theater in Chicago, directed us in adapting it in much the same way he would direct us as actors acting it. The first day of rehearsal we read the book straight through, out loud. By the end of the week—basically in a process of editing—we had our playscript, though the first act was three hours long. Ultimately it was about an hour and forty-five minutes long.

MERRIAM: As you read it, were you getting up to act things out?

SZARABAJKA: No, we sat in a circle. And we kept reading it again and again.

ALLEN: Did you assign different scenes to different people?

---

* Not to be confused with a later musical adaptation of *Huckleberry Finn* entitled *Big River*.

SZARABAJKA: No, we just . . . whoever was in the scene sort of did the adaptation. We had a green crayola for Huck's narration, an orange crayola for stage directions—which were parts of the narrative we cut out—and a yellow crayola for dialogue which everybody would be saying together. . .

DRIVER: Are you saying that all the actors are writers in this case?

SZARABAJKA: Yes, and we all wrote *Bleacher Bums,* too. We are an ensemble, and we did everything—built the sets, hung the lights.

DRIVER: At what point do you stop writing and somebody says, "O.K., this is what we are going to do"—and who is that person?

SZARABAJKA: Stuart was the artistic director, so if you had something to change you came back to him on it. We all own a piece of it.

DRIVER: But ultimately it's all funneled through him?

SZARABAJKA: Well, he's . . . you have to have somebody who is going to function as editor, you know. . . We all recognize that. There are only two speeches in our adaptation of *Huckleberry Finn* that are not actually on the printed page, either as Twain's dialogue or first person narrative.

MERRIAM: These are certainly polarized viewpoints. Steve, are you polarized?

STEPHEN SCHWARTZ: I'm polarized on both sides. I have a slightly different point of view because, being a composer-lyricist, one is *always* doing an adaptation. You have a script, and you ask yourself, "What part of this script or story am I going to turn into a song?" So whether it's the book writer's original play, or whatever, one is always adapting.

In the case of *Godspell,* the show was conceived by John-Michael Tebelak while he was still at Carnegie Tech. He'd done a version of it at Cafe La Mama, with songs that didn't really function as musical numbers so much as they gave little respites. Thinking of moving it to off Broadway, people called me and asked me to provide the score. I worked very closely with John-Michael on that. The notion was to stay very close to the words of St. Matthew, or in some cases Episcopal hymns which were interpolated—but to say those words from a different point of view, to make a point in the way it was staged and presented.

The actual story was all in subtext. The actors were saying lines and telling parables that were presumably familiar to the audience, underneath which was the developing relationship among them. One contribution I think I made to the point of view (and I think maybe it is a useful rule generally) was this: although we were doing "the greatest story ever told," and everyone knew it, we should pretend that no one had ever heard it before. No one was coming into the theater feeling anything about it, and therefore if we wanted to have a relationship between Jesus and Judas we had better get the audience to care about that relationship. That is what led to a number like "All for the Best," which was just as you would do it in any musical comedy. We have these two characters, and we want them to be friends and care about each other, so we have them do a number together.

In the case of *Working*, where I was billed as the adaptor of the book, there was a situation very similar to the one Keith described. The value there was that the characters' words were true. I read a description of the Studs Terkel book and immediately thought, "I've got to get that book, it's something for me to do." I ran out and bought it, read it and then called Mr. Terkel.

ALLEN: I use that book as a reference book.

SCHWARTZ: What I think was telling about what Mrs. Allen said earlier is that one goes through a process of assimilating the work and in a sense regurgitating it in your own form. That can be a hurdle: you must at some point face the fact that the material has got to come out again in a different way. But after all, why choose to adapt something unless you feel that there is something you can do with it that hasn't been done before? It would be boring to do in another medium what the author has already done. I don't think any of us does that.

SZARABAJKA: I take exception to that—I believe the whole point of adaptation is to take what you believe is wonderful in one medium and transpose it to another. Otherwise, why don't you just write a new play?

DRIVER: But you *are* adding something, you're adding *you* to it.

SZARABAJKA: And there's another exception I have to take. You referred to adaptation as "rape and violation." I refer to it as making love to what the author's work was.

MERRIAM: In translating poetry, I found I had to stop myself from doing an adaptation instead of translation, making it more like my own style. Is there a love-hate experience of being drawn to the material and then having to give up some of your own personality to the personality of the original author?

ALLEN: It's different every time. I've done a lot of movie adaptations, and you can make a good movie out of very raw material—you need a strong narrative, but you can take it from there. On the other hand, you sometimes get your hands on something absolutely dazzling and want to put everything you see in it on the screen. We've all seen *Brideshead Revisited*. That novel has been put on to the screen—I've never seen anything as faithful to the original as that.

SCHWARTZ: It's interesting you should mention that, because I had always heard about it being the most Catholic novel and had not read it. And suddenly there was the most explicit gay relationship I had ever seen on television. I couldn't believe that was really in the book.

ALLEN: Whenever you *see* something it is much more explicit than when you *read* it. If you have two guys exchanging looks on the printed page, the reader can make the choice of glossing over it or reading something into it. On the screen, the director makes the choice.

SCHWARTZ: Exactly. It transfers to another medium.

SZARABAJKA: This goes back to what Donald said—Shakespeare stole all his plots, and he didn't give credit. When you adapt someone else's work for the stage, changing it completely, you are writing a new piece. It's not the same as adapting.

DRIVER: I'm inclined to say that's what I've done in the past. I wasn't trying to be faithful, to put Shakespeare into another form. I was taking what I wanted and spewing it out some other way. If I were to take a novel or a play and try to be faithful to it in adapting it to another medium, I don't think it would set me on fire. But I would do it for money, make no mistake.

SZARABAJKA: We're all doing this for money in the end, but I think an adaptation should be a matter of love. Why do someone's novel in another medium unless you thought it was really wonderful? I understand we've got to pay the rent, but it bothers me a little bit.

SCHWARTZ: There has to be an intrinsic love for the material, in some cases just for the idea.

SZARABAJKA: And ultimately, respect.

SCHWARTZ: With *Working,* we tried *so* hard to stick to what the character said, even in the lyrics. And yet the fact that I respected the material so much caused me to take much longer to get it right. First, I had to come to the realization that there was no way I was going to get that whole book onto the stage. I was going to have to choose some aspects and go for those. Second, it wasn't until after the New York production that I was able to get enough distance from the book to say, "All right, forget about the book, what in the show works and what doesn't work?" and make it live as a stage piece.

It was shown on Public Service television, and we had to rethink it specifically for that medium. Studs comes in and introduces it, and we tried to make it look like a standard documentary that, almost without your knowing it, was turning into a musical.

SCHWARTZ: What we're saying is, we don't want to violate the thing that made us care about the material in the first place—the essence.

ALLEN: That's really what it is all about.

SZARABAJKA: Exactly.

SCHWARTZ: It is taking the heart of the matter from one medium and translating it as well as possible into another medium. That is what adaptation is about. Otherwise, you are just writing a new play.

MERRIAM: Given your choice and all things being equal—money, space, hypnotism—and provided you are crazy about the material, would you prefer working on an adaptation to doing an original, or is it somewhat hampering?

SCHWARTZ: I always prefer to do an original because you have more freedom. For example, right now I'm talking about doing something from a nonfiction story. We finally decided we'd have to make up our own story, because we were hampered by the truth—that is, we were hampered by the *facts* as opposed to what we perceived to be the truth.

DRIVER: I'd prefer doing an original. The only thing is, an adaptation gets more attention in the commercial market from the people who raise the money. Producers are more interested because they have a frame of reference. They get a different sense of your worth.

SZARABAJKA: If someone comes to you and says, "I'd like you to adapt this piece," it's marketing, is what it is. It is easier to sell Dickens or Twain or Vonnegut than to sell Keith Szarabajka. But there is a happy medium somewhere between mercenary instinct and love of art. The question is, "How can I use my love of this material to make me some money?"

Q: I'd like to ask Sheldon Harnick, how did you do a new version of *A Christmas Carol* and not be inhibited because it had already been done in so many versions?

HARNICK: I wasn't inhibited, because I hadn't seen them. That adaptation was the first time I've done both book and lyrics from the beginning. I began with others the book of *The Apple Tree,* but this one was my own. I was first assigned to do it as a television show, and I did, but for various reasons it never got on. Then two very active producers wanted me to do a stage version to tour at Christmas time. I did it in about three weeks, but they weren't able to get it on until the following year, with Richard Kiley as an absolutely wonderful Scrooge. But I think, initially, I made two basic mistakes with the adaptation. One was, I stayed entirely too close to Dickens. I stuck to his dialogue, and I discovered that what works on the printed page does not always work on the stage coming out of the mouths of characters.

Another mistake: I wrote it for television, which is very intimate, and after adapting it for the stage I found it was still too intimate. We rehearsed in a relatively small space, so we were fooled by the fact that it communicated, it was moving. At our first tryout town, Elmira, on a huge stage, there weren't seventeen-inch faces right in front of you, they were a long distance away and their emotions as I had written them were not projected. And some of the Dickens dialogue was still very stilted, although by that time I had changed a lot of it.

Also, I had allowed myself to write long dialogue scenes, and the balance between book and music was dreadful. It seemed to take forever to get to a musical number. In Wilmington and Baltimore I cut a lot of the dialogue so everything skipped along. Everything had to be done in broader, bolder strokes. I began to invent dialogue which, to my delight, surprise and relief, worked. By the time we got to St. Petersburg, for the first time we got three excellent notices. Up to then everything had been mixed, or lethal.

Q: Lately we have been seeing so-called "adaptations" of such classics as *Hedda Gabler* and *The Cherry Orchard.* At what point does a translation become an adaptation?

GOETZ: One of our great playwrights did a version of *An Enemy of the People* some years back, and they billed it "reconceived by," or something like that. I think that's an impertinence. I can understand making new translations—I recently saw a new translation of *Peer Gynt* at the Classic Stage Company, a fascinating and wonderful production. But I don't think it's fair to put another name on Chekhov or Ibsen, under the guise of something or other.

MERRIAM: I would think that the question of when does something become something else, when does it tip over, is probably a matter of how much you depart from the text. It could be as simple as that. If you are going to change the characters, if you are going to change the ending, if you are going to change the relationships, then I would think you are doing an adaptation and not a translation.

As they say, "Poetry is what gets lost in the translation." You have to have a tremendous empathy for the work. We are all good and evil, all these things in ourselves, but some kind of identification is the impetus of the work—and then there's that tricky thing of how selfless you are going to be.

Q: What is your reason for doing an adaptation? What do you think the stage version offers that cannot be found in the original?

GOODRICH: If you can make visual something that was speeches or prose, if you can make it move, for me it is the greatest thrill in life—making visual what is as ephemeral and ungraspable as an idea, making people see a relationship that is almost unnameable. That's heaven.

HACKETT: Being able to hear people talk and play scenes is part of how I feel. If you read something and can see scenes, make it play; if not, drop it.

Q: What do you do about those second-act characters introduced late in the original work?

GOETZ: Stay away from them; they may be of some importance but they never work for you. A play must place its organic main characters within the first consciousness of the audience. Absolutely.

Q: In an adaptation of a musical, does the composer and/or lyricist have as much responsibility as the adaptor, and just how much input does the composer and/or lyricist have?

SCHWARTZ: You have just as much responsibility but different areas of expertise. What I like to do in *any* musical, adaptation or not, is first let the book writer write a play. In fact, I don't like them to leave me space for songs. Sometimes that gets me into trouble; sometimes they write so well that you have to tell them, "Gee, this scene is very good but we have to fix it because there has to be a song sooner or later, and we might as well do one here"—and so we have to fracture the scene.

In general, though, I feel that first a playwright should structure a play. I usually have many meetings with the writer in advance to discuss what is going to happen. Some writers like to have an extremely accurate outline, others just talk and talk and talk and then say, "O.K., goodbye, I'll see you."

My responsibility after that is to pick the right places to musicalize—the most important decision on a musical, even more so perhaps than the song itself: where do they sing, and why, and what are they singing about? And a musical these days has so much music in it that in the end you have an awful lot of control over the "feel." Any time someone sings about something it takes on enormous importance. I find this terribly exciting, and the book writers usually find it terribly exciting, too, that in this play someone stopped and sang this emotion and the whole thing has twisted a little bit. They often have to go back and restructure a scene after that. So in answer to that question, I feel it is very much a shared responsibility, with different roles to be played.

DRIVER: When somebody sings, it had better be an important moment. You don't say "I love you" in a scene and then turn around and sing a song "I love you," because it is already done. All you'd have is a stage wait. What I do is write a play, take a big hunk out that is an important dramatic moment and turn it into a song.

ALLEN: That's the most important thing, the music has got to be the highest point. Your best scenes are those where the music is.

DRIVER: Right.

SCHWARTZ: Exactly.

ALLEN: And you are going to remove those scenes from the book to make a place for the music, so the book really exists to support the music. I mean, that's what it's there for.

Q: The way you are talking about your work, there seems to be love in everything. What I get from all of you is, you fell in love with the original works.

ALLEN: Of course. You do what you want to do.

STEWART: You fall in love sooner or later.

MEEHAN: I fell in love later, and I learned the hard way that you should have a lot of affection for the original work. There's also a kind of wild, strange, weird, ugly challenge: "Maybe I, Thomas Meehan, can do better than the original author did." That has to be taken into account. In the back of your mean little head is the idea, "I'll do it better."

STEWART: I agree, I've felt that. It was wrong, but I felt it.

MEEHAN: We're all playwrights—I didn't say book writers, I said playwrights. To do that properly is the hardest part of all. It's a tough, tough job, adaptation. Once you decide *why* you want to do it, it's a great deal easier. Do you want to do "better than"? Do you want to give the original author another form of life? Or do you want to take off and do something completely on your own?

MERRIAM: I'd like to wind up by reminding you that one of the greatest adaptations is still read—and still even acted—by a great many people: the dramatization of a portion of Belleforest's *Histoires Tragiques* made by William Shakespeare and called *Hamlet*.

INDEX

NAME INDEX

TITLE INDEX